HISTORICAL DICTIONARIES OF EUROPE
Jon Woronoff, Series Editor

27. *Gypsies (Romanies)*, by Donald Kenrick. 1998. *Out of print.*
28. *Belarus*, by Jan Zaprudnik. 1998.
29. *Federal Republic of Yugoslavia*, by Zeljan Suster. 1999.
30. *France*, by Gino Raymond. 1998. *Out of print. See no. 64.*
31. *Slovakia*, by Stanislav J. Kirschbaum. 1998. *Out of print. See no. 47.*
32. *Netherlands*, by Arend H. Huussen Jr. 1998. *Out of print. See no. 55.*
33. *Denmark*, by Alastair H. Thomas and Stewart P. Oakley. 1998. *Out of print. See no. 63.*
34. *Modern Italy*, by Mark F. Gilbert and K. Robert Nilsson. 1998. *Out of print. See no. 58.*
35. *Belgium*, by Robert Stallaerts. 1999.
36. *Austria*, by Paula Sutter Fichtner. 1999. *Out of print. See no. 70.*
37. *Republic of Moldova*, by Andrei Brezianu. 2000. *Out of print. See no. 52.*
38. *Turkey, 2nd edition*, by Metin Heper. 2002. *Out of print. See no. 67.*
39. *Republic of Croatia, 2nd edition*, by Robert Stallaerts. 2003. *Out of print. See no. 74*
40. *Portugal, 2nd edition*, by Douglas L. Wheeler. 2002. *Out of print. See no. 73.*
41. *Poland, 2nd edition*, by George Sanford. 2003.
42. *Albania, New edition*, by Robert Elsie. 2004. *Out of print. See no. 75.*
43. *Estonia*, by Toivo Miljan. 2004.
44. *Kosova*, by Robert Elsie. 2004.
45. *Ukraine*, by Zenon E. Kohut, Bohdan Y. Nebesio, and Myroslav Yurkevich. 2005.
46. *Bulgaria, 2nd edition*, by Raymond Detrez. 2006.
47. *Slovakia, 2nd edition*, by Stanislav J. Kirschbaum. 2006.
48. *Sweden, 2nd edition*, by Irene Scobbie. 2006.
49. *Finland, 2nd edition*, by George Maude. 2007.
50. *Georgia*, by Alexander Mikaberidze. 2007.
51. *Belgium, 2nd edition*, by Robert Stallaerts. 2007.
52. *Moldova, 2nd edition*, by Andrei Brezianu and Vlad Spânu. 2007.
53. *Switzerland*, by Leo Schelbert. 2007.
54. *Contemporary Germany*, by Derek Lewis with Ulrike Zitzlsperger. 2007.

Historical Dictionary of the Russian Federation

Robert A. Saunders
Vlad Strukov

Historical Dictionaries of Europe, No. 78

The Scarecrow Press, Inc.
Lanham • Toronto • Plymouth, UK
2010

Published by Scarecrow Press, Inc.
A wholly owned subsidiary of The Rowman & Littlefield Publishing Group, Inc.
4501 Forbes Boulevard, Suite 200, Lanham, Maryland 20706
http://www.scarecrowpress.com

Estover Road, Plymouth PL6 7PY, United Kingdom

British Library Cataloguing in Publication Information Available

Library of Congress Cataloging-in-Publication Data
Saunders, Robert A., 1973–
  Historical dictionary of the Russian Federation / Robert A. Saunders, Vlad
Strukov.
    p. cm. — (Historical dictionaries of Europe ; no. 78)
  Includes bibliographical references.
  ISBN 978-0-8108-5475-8 (cloth : alk. paper) — ISBN 978-0-8108-7460-2
(ebook)
  1. Russia (Federation)—History—Dictionaries. 2. Soviet Union—History—
Dictionaries. 3. Russia—History—Dictionaries. I. Strukov, Vlad, 1973– II. Title.
  DK36.S285 2010
  947.003—dc22   2009047935

Printed in the United States of America

Contents

Editor's Foreword

On closer scrutiny, no country is easy to understand. But probably no other country is quite as complex as what is now known as the Russian Federation. In less than a century, it has undergone not one but two massive revolutions: First, the Bolshevik Revolution, which turned one of the most conservative monarchies into purportedly the most advanced, and at any rate, furthest left of regimes under the Communist Party. Then, in recent years, a less bloody and less dramatic revolution (more like an accident actually) that turned Russia back into a much freer but harder to define entity. Its economy is again supposedly a market economy, but not quite. It boasts a degree of democracy that could not even be dreamed of in the past and yet is not the real thing. And, in the place of conformity and unity—imposed from the top—there is now a state of interminable flux. Obviously, most of the satellites of Soviet times have gone their own way, while some remain relatively faithful out of self-interest. But that is only part of the story, for within Russia itself there is an incredible maze of smaller units, each trying to shape its relations with the center. Within every one of these subsets, and the country as a whole, there are political, ethnic, and religious groups staunchly defending their own interests, and on occasion willing to die, or at least kill, in order to achieve their goals. Yet something new and hopefully better is emerging, although no one knows just what it will be.

Amid all this uncertainty and confusion, it is extremely useful to have a reference work that looks at the situation from many different angles, providing succinct information on the numerous state bodies, political parties, ethnic groups, and religions, among other things. Given the role played by specific persons, such entries are equally important, including earlier Communist leaders, those of the transition period, and today's policymakers, plus a bevy of oligarchs and some dissidents. And this in turn is put in the global context through entries on different aspects of Russian policy and Russia's relations with former satellites and Cold War foes. That is what can be found in this amazingly broad and penetrating *Historical Dictionary of the Russian Federation*, which fortunately embeds the "new" Russia, that of the past two decades, in the older Russia from which it has sprung. Along with literally hundreds of entries in the dictionary section, there is a useful chronology that traces the path year by year and month by month as well as an introduction that helps put it all in context. This is certainly a good starting point for readers interested in present-day Russia, but hardly enough for those who have special concerns, and fortunately they can find access to considerable further reading through the ample bibliography.

This book was written by Robert A. Saunders and Vlad Strukov. Dr. Saunders is presently an assistant professor in the Department of History, Economics and Politics at the State University of New York, Farmingdale. There he teaches mainly on Russian politics, Central Asia, and global history. He has written extensively on the "new" Russia, including numerous articles and two books. Vlad Strukov is presently an assistant professor in the Department of Russian and Slavonic Studies (as well as at the Centre for World Cinemas) of the University of Leeds. He has also written extensively on the "new" Russia, including a coauthored book called *Celebrity and Glamour in Contemporary Russian Culture*. Drs. Saunders and Strukov are founding editors of the journal *Digital Icons: Studies in Russian, Eurasian, and Central European New Media* (formerly known as *The Russian Cyberspace Journal*). Between them, from different angles and in different ways, they have drawn an amazingly broad, varied, and informative portrait of what remains one of the most important and powerful—if often confusing— places on earth.

Jon Woronoff
Series Editor

Reader's Note

Russian is written in the Cyrillic script. In this volume, Cyrillic lettering is transcribed into the Roman alphabet. Two forms of transliteration have been employed. In the first case, transliterations of Russian words and concepts that appear in italics (typically either before or after their English translations) employ the Romanization system adopted by the United States Library of Congress as displayed below:

Cyrillic letter	Roman transcription	Pronunciation
а	a	"f*a*r"
б	b	b
в	v	v
г	g	"*go*"
д	d	d
е	e	"*yes*"
ё	io	"*yo*lk"
ж	zh	"trea*s*ure"
з	z	z
и	i	"s*ee*"
й	i (after vowels)	"bo*y*"
к	k	k
л	l	l
м	m	m
н	n	n
о	o	"b*o*ught"
п	p	p
р	r	r (rolled)
с	s	s
т	t	t
у	u	"r*u*le"

ф	f	f
х	kh	"lo*ch*" (hard 'h')
ц	ts	ts
ч	ch	"*ch*urch"
ш	sh	sh
щ	shch	"Chris*t*ian"
ъ	" (indicates there is a voiceless glottal stop)	—
ы	y	"*i*ll"
ь	' (indicates that the preceding consonant is palatalized)	—
э	e	"*e*gg"
ю	iu	"*u*se"
я	ia	"*ya*rd"

In the second case, we use a simplified form of Romanization that eschews diacritics and avoids the sometimes confusing "Ia," "Ie," and "Iu" transliterations. This system is employed for Russian words and concepts that have entered the English language (e.g., perestroika, krai, raion, and demokratizatsiya), as well as the names of Russian people, publications, and places (e.g., Yegor Gaydar, *Izvestiya*, and Kareliya). These transliterations do not appear in italics (unless they are publications, films, etc., which would normally be italicized in the English language).

When a term has an entry of its own in the Dictionary, that term appears in **bold** upon its first appearance in a given entry. Other forms of cross-referencing are *See* and *See also*.

Acronyms and Abbreviations

9/11	Attacks of 11 September 2001
ALROSA	Diamonds of Russia-Sakha
AO	Autonomous oblast
AOk	Autonomous okrug
APEC	Asia-Pacific Economic Cooperation organization
APR	Agrarian Party of Russia
ASEAN	Association of Southeast Asian Nations
ASSR	Autonomous Soviet Socialist Republic
Black PR	"Black" public relations
BRIC	Brazil, Russia, India, and China
BSEC	Black Sea Economic Cooperation Organization
Cheka	Extraordinary Commission to Combat Counterrevolution and Sabotage
CIA	Central Intelligence Agency
CIS	Commonwealth of Independent States
CNG	Compressed natural gas
COMECON	Council for Mutual Economic Assistance
CPSU	Communist Party of the Soviet Union
CST	Collective Security Treaty
CSTO	Collective Security Treaty Organization
DPRK	Democratic People's Republic of Korea (North Korea)
EAEC	Eurasian Economic Community
EMERCOM	Ministry for Emergency Situations
EU	European Union
EurAsEC	Eurasian Economic Community
FBI	Federal Bureau of Investigation
FNPR	Federation of Independent Trade Unions of Russia
FSA	Federal Space Agency

FSB	Federal Security Service
FSK	Federal Counterintelligence Service
G7	Group of Seven
G8	Group of Eight
GCTC	Yury A. Gagarin State Science Research Cosmonauts Training Centre
GDP	Gross domestic product
GKChP	State Committee of the State of Emergency
Glavlit	Central Publishing Agency
GUAM	GUAM Organization for Democracy and Economic Development
Gulag	Chief Administration of Corrective Labor Camps and Colonies
ICBM	Intercontinental ballistic missile
IGO	Intergovernmental organization
IMEMO	Institute for World Economy and International Relations
IRP	Islamic Renaissance Party
ITAR	Information Telegraph Agency of Russia
KBR	Kabardino-Balkariya
KFOR	Kosovo Force
KGB	Committee for State Security
KGNK	Confederation of Mountain Peoples of the Caucasus
KKV	Kuban Cossack Host
Komsomol	Communist Union of Youth
KPRF	Communist Party of the Russian Federation
LDPR	Liberal Democratic Party of Russia
LGBT	Lesbian, gay, bisexual, and transgender
MGIMO	Moscow State Institute of International Relations
MIRV	Multiple independently targetable reentry vehicle
MSU	Moscow State University
MVD	Ministry of Internal Affairs
NatBols	National Bolshevik Party
NATO	North Atlantic Treaty Organization
NBP	National Bolshevik Party
NDR	Our Home—Russia
NGO	Nongovernmental organization
NIS	Newly Independent States

NPSRF	National-Patriotic Forces of the Russian Federation
NPT	Nuclear Non-Proliferation Treaty
OCAC	Organization of Central Asian Cooperation
OPEC	Organization of the Petroleum Exporting Countries
OSCE	Organization for Security and Co-operation in Europe
OSI	Open Society Institute
PDPA	People's Democratic Party of Afghanistan
PfP	Partnership for Peace
PRC	People's Republic of China
REP	Russian Ecological Party
RIA Novosti	Russian Information Agency Novosti
RNU	Russian National Unity
ROC	Russian Orthodox Church
ROCOR	Russian Orthodox Church Outside of Russia
ROK	Republic of Korea (South Korea)
Roscosmos	Russian Federal Space Agency
RPP	Russian Pensioners' Party
RSFSR	Russian Soviet Federative Socialist Republic
RT	Russia Today
Runet	Russian Internet
SCO	Shanghai Cooperation Organization
SDPR	Social Democratic Party of Russia
SPS	Union of Right Forces
SSR	Soviet Socialist Republic
START	Strategic Arms Reduction Treaty
SVR	Foreign Intelligence Service
TASS	Telegraph Agency of the Soviet Union
TSR-TKR	Trans-Siberian Railroad–Trans-Korean Railroad
UES	Unified Energy System
UK	United Kingdom
UN	United Nations
UNESCO	United Nations Educational, Scientific and Cultural Organization
UOC	Ukrainian Orthodox Church
UOC-KP	Ukrainian Orthodox Church—Kiev Patriarchate
U.S.	United States
USSR	Union of Soviet Socialist Republics
UTO	United Tajik Opposition

VAT	Value-added tax
VKPB	All-Russian Communist Party of the Future
VTOTS	All-Tatar Public Center
VVS	Russian Air Force
WMDs	Weapons of mass destruction
WTO	Warsaw Treaty Organization
WTO	World Trade Organization
Zhensovet	Constituent Assembly of Soviet Women

○ Federal City of Moscow (Capital)

1 - Novgorod	7 - Ivanovo	13 - Tambov	19 - Samara	25 - Kabardino-Balkariya
2 - Kaluga	8 - Kostroma	14 - Penza	20 - Bashkortostan	26 - North Ossetiya
3 - Moscow Oblast	9 - Nizhny Novgorod	15 - Ulyanovsk	21 - Udmurtiya	27 - Ingushetiya
4 - Yaroslavl	10 - Mordoviya	16 - Chuvashiya	22 - Stavropol Krai	28 - Chechnya
5 - Ryazan	11 - Oryol	17 - Mari El	23 - Adygeya	29 - Kemerovo
6 - Vladimir	12 - Lipetsk	18 - Tatarstan	24 - Karachayevo-Cherkessiya	30 - Khakasiya

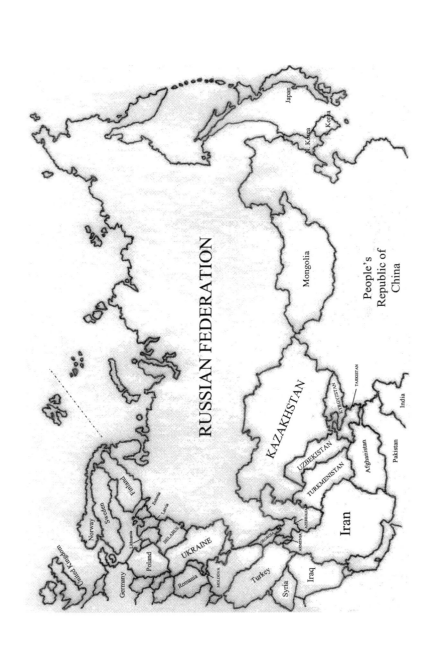

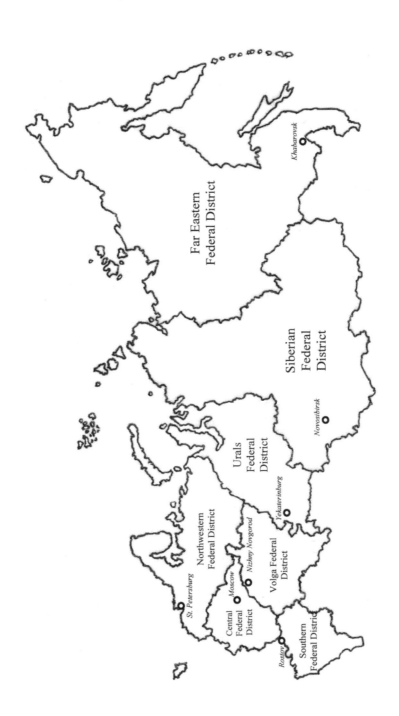

Far Eastern
Federal District

Khabarovsk

Siberian
Federal
District

Novosibirsk

Urals
Federal
District

Yekaterinburg

Northwestern
Federal District

Nizhny Novgorod

St. Petersburg

Moscow

Volga Federal
District

Central
Federal
District

Rostov

Southern
Federal District

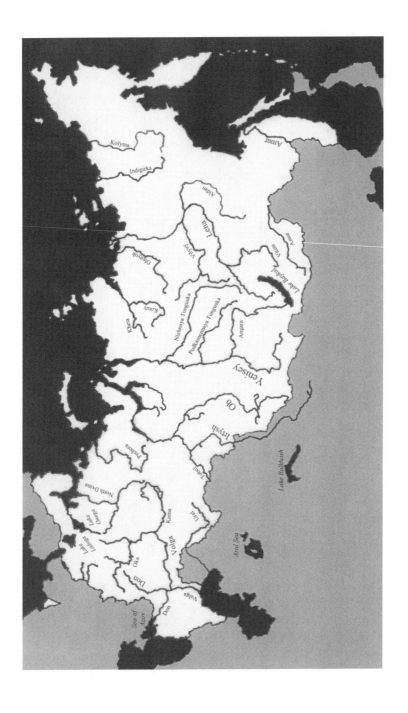

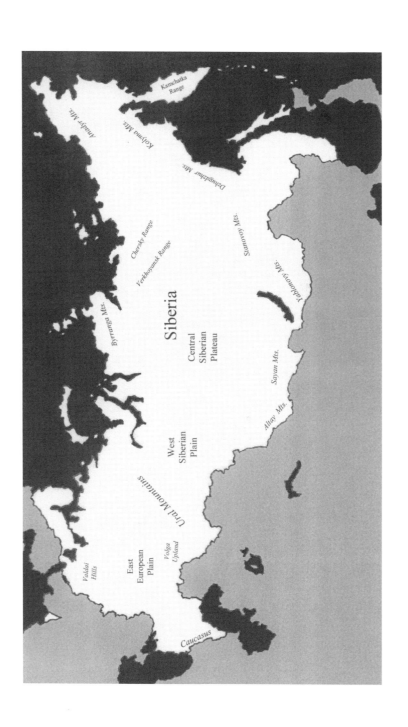

Chronology

SOVIET ERA (1917–1985)

1917 **February:** Bread riots in Petrograd ("February Revolution"). **March:** Abdication of Nicholas II; establishment of the Provisional Government and election of the Soviet of Workers' Deputies. **16 April:** Vladimir Lenin returns from exile. **7 November:** Soviet power is established ("October Revolution"). **6 December:** Finland declares its independence from Russia. **15 December:** Armistice with Germany is signed. **20 December:** The Extraordinary Commission to Combat Counterrevolution and Sabotage (Cheka) is established.

1918 **January:** Constituent Assembly is dissolved, ending democracy in Soviet Russia. **February:** Russia adopts the Gregorian calendar; Lithuania and Estonia declare independence from Russia. **10 July:** Constitution of the Russian Soviet Federative Socialist Republic (RSFSR) is ratified. **17 July:** Execution of Nicholas Romanov and his family at Yekaterinburg.

1922 **April:** Joseph Stalin becomes general secretary of the Communist Party. **25 October:** Soviets occupy Vladivostok, ending the civil war. **30 December:** Establishment of the Union of Soviet Socialist Republics (USSR); inaugural members include the Russian and Transcaucasian SFSRs and the Soviet Socialist Republics (SSRs) of Ukraine and Belarus.

1924 **21 January:** Death of Lenin. **31 January:** The Constitution of the USSR is ratified. **27 October:** Delimitation of Central Asia creates new republics of Turkmenistan, Uzbekistan, and Tajikistan.

1928 First Five-Year Plan is introduced.

1936 Initiation of the Great Purges, which last for nearly three years; political persecution continues until Stalin's death in 1953. **5 December:** The culmination of the national delimitation process produces the final borders of the Central Asian union republics.

1939 **24 August:** The USSR and Nazi Germany sign the Molotov-Ribbentrop Pact, secretly dividing Eastern Europe.

1940 Soviet annexation of Estonia, Latvia, and Lithuania, as well as portions of Romanian territory that will become part of Moldova.

1941 **22 June:** Germany invades the Soviet Union, bringing the country into World War II on the side of the Allies. **28 August:** Ethnic Germans are deported from European Russia to Siberia and Central Asia; seven other nations, including the Chechens, will suffer the same fate in the coming years.

1945 **8 May:** The USSR, United States, and Great Britain accept the unconditional surrender of Germany, ending the war in Europe. **9 August:** The USSR invades Manchuria, joining the U.S. in the war against Japan; the Soviet Union will subsequently annex parts of Sakhalin Island and the Kuril Islands.

1947 Events in Czechoslovakia trigger the beginning of the Cold War between the United States and the USSR.

1949 **5–8 January:** COMECON is established as an economic union among the states of the Eastern Bloc. **29 August:** The first atomic test is performed by the Soviet Union.

1953 **5 March:** Joseph Stalin dies. **14 March:** A struggle for power begins between Lavrenty Beria and Nikita Khrushchev.

1954 Establishment of the KGB.

1955 **14 May:** The Warsaw Pact is established in response to West Germany's admission to the North Atlantic Treaty Organization (NATO).

1956 **25 February:** Khrushchev's "secret speech" condemning Stalinism. **6 July:** Karelo-Finnish SSR merged into the RSFSR.

1957 **4 October:** Launch of the artificial satellite *Sputnik* initiates the space race.

1964 **13 October:** Khrushchev is removed from power and replaced by Leonid Brezhnev.

1968 **21 August:** Warsaw Pact troops invade Czechoslovakia, putting down the "Prague Spring" experiment in "socialism with a human face."

1978 **December:** Afghanistan signs an agreement with the USSR that provides for military assistance.

1979 **14 April:** Afghan government requests the use of Soviet helicopters. **3 July:** U.S. government begins covert aid to the Afghan mujahideen. **24 December:** Soviet troops invade Afghanistan.

1982 **10 November:** Brezhnev dies and is succeeded by Yury Andropov.

1984 **9 February:** Andropov dies and is succeeded by Konstantin Chernenko.

GORBACHEV ERA (1985–1991)

1985 **11 March:** Chernenko dies; Mikhail Gorbachev becomes the general secretary of the Communist Party of the Soviet Union (CPSU). **April:** Eduard Shevardnadze replaces Andrey Gromyko as foreign minister. **May:** Gorbachev introduces aspects of his reform agenda and announces the anti-alcoholism campaign. **July:** Unilateral moratorium on nuclear weapons testing. **November:** First summit between Gorbachev and U.S. President Ronald Reagan. **December:** Boris Yeltsin assumes control of the Moscow Communist Party.

1986 **25 January:** Gorbachev proposes decommissioning all nuclear warheads by the end of the century. **11 February:** Jewish dissident Natan Sharansky is released from prison and emigrates; other Jewish "refuseniks" will follow. **19 February:** The *Mir* space station is launched. **25 February:** Beginning of the 27th Congress of the CPSU; Gorbachev begins the implementation of perestroika in an attempt to counter economic stagnation; he uses the term *glasnost*, arguing for transparency in this process. **26 April:** The Chernobyl nuclear power plant in Ukraine explodes, sending radiological pollution across the USSR and northern Europe. **July:** Withdrawal of Soviet troops from Afghanistan is announced, as are plans for improving relations with the People's Republic of China. **7 July:** Gorbachev opens the door to possible reunification of Germany in a meeting with the West German president. **October 11:** Gorbachev meets Ronald Reagan in Iceland to discuss nuclear missile reductions. **December:** The Jeltoqsan riots occur in Kazakhstan, protesting the appointment of a non-Russian as the head of the republic; the dissident Andrey Sakharov is allowed to return to Moscow from internal exile.

1987   27 January: Gorbachev calls for democratization at the Central Committee of the CPSU plenum. **12 February:** 140 dissidents are pardoned or rehabilitated. **22 July:** Gorbachev unexpectedly agrees to discuss the elimination of intermediate-range nuclear missiles without conditions. **July:** In Moscow, Crimean Tatars protest against their continuing exile in Central Asia. **August:** Demonstrations against the 1940 annexations occur in the Baltic States. **October:** Yeltsin is removed from power in a dispute over the speed of reforms. **8 December:** Intermediate Nuclear Forces Treaty is signed in Washington, D.C.

1988   February: More than two dozen Armenians are killed in the Sumgait pogrom in Azerbaijan. **18 February:** Gorbachev declares that all socialist countries have the right to choose their own systems, presaging an end to the so-called Brezhnev Doctrine. **14 April:** USSR agrees to evacuate all its troops from Afghanistan by early 1989. **May:** The Law on the Cooperatives introduces the first genuine free-market reforms in the USSR since the 1920s. **7 May:** The Democratic Union is founded, the first new political party since 1918. **31 May:** Ronald Reagan addresses students at Moscow State University during his first visit to the USSR. **28 June:** At the 19th All-Union Party Congress, Gorbachev expands his call for democratization of the political system of the USSR, including a new approach to federalism; glasnost is adopted as an official policy; the 1,000th anniversary of the Russian Orthodox Church is celebrated. **13 June:** Talks with the Vatican are opened. **September:** Attacks on Azeris in Armenia and Nagorno-Karabakh result in mass migrations. **October:** Spitak earthquake rocks Armenia, leaving more than 25,000 people dead. **November:** *Little Vera* opens in Moscow, breaking the Soviet taboo on sex scenes in film, while portraying the extreme pessimism of the country's youth. **16 November:** The Estonian Supreme Soviet declares the republic's sovereignty, though not its independence. **December:** Estonian is adopted as the official language of the Estonian SSR, beginning a series of similar "language revolutions" throughout 1989.

1989   January: Soviet authorities institute direct rule over Nagorno-Karabakh to stop Armenian-Azeri violence. **10 January:** Gorbachev orders an end to single-candidate elections, telling the Central Committee that they must earn the "right to rule." **18 January:** Gorbachev slashes the Soviet Union's military budget; Poland's Communist Party votes to legalize Solidarity. **February:** Soviet troops begin to leave Hungary. **15 February:** The last Soviet soldier departs Afghanistan, ending the Soviet-Afghan War. **26 March:** After being purged from power, Yeltsin returns to public life as a Moscow delegate in the Congress of People's Deputies. **7 April:** The K-278 *Komsomolets* sinks in the Barents Sea, killing 41 submariners. **9 April:** Soviet crackdown on demonstrators in Tbilisi leaves 20 dead. **17 April:** Solidarity is granted the right to participate in Poland's upcoming elections, signaling the end of the one-party system in the Eastern Bloc. **25 April:** Andrey Gromyko and other antireformers are purged from the Central Committee. **May:** Interethnic violence between Abkhaz and Georgians begins; the Uzbek pogrom against the Meskhetian Turks triggers their evacuation to Russia; Mikhail Khodorkovsky registers Menatep Bank, which will become the core of his economic empire. **2 May:** Hungary opens a 240-kilometer stretch of its border with Austria, effectively ending the Iron Curtain (all border restrictions will end in August). **8 May:** Restoration of the Republic of Estonia. **14 May:** Gorbachev visits the People's Republic of China, the first state visit since the 1960s. **June:** Tiananmen Square protests in China are crushed. **2 June:** Mintimer Shaymiyev becomes the head of Tatarstan. **July:** Coal miners begin strikes across the country; Gazprom is founded. **6 July:** Gorbachev makes his "Common European Home" speech in Bonn, West Germany. **23 August:** Citizens of the Baltic republics commemorate victims of the 50th anniversary of the Molotov-Ribbentrop Pact in a 600-kilometer human chain known as the "Baltic Way." **23 September:** Azerbaijan declares its sovereignty. **20 October:** Multiparty elections set in Hungary. **25 October:** Foreign Ministry spokesman Gennady Gerasimov announces the existence of the "Sinatra Doctrine" on *Good Morning America*, signaling the unequivocal end of the Brezhnev Doctrine of Soviet interference in the internal affairs of its Warsaw Pact allies. **7 November:** East Germany's Communist government resigns. **9 November:** The fall of the Berlin Wall. **10 November:** Bulgaria's leader Todor Zhivkov steps down, ending the Communist dictatorship; South Ossetia declares its intent to merge with North Ossetiya, following interethnic violence with the local Georgian population. **17 November:** The "Velvet Revolution" begins in Czechoslovakia; the Communist Party renounces its monopoly on power 11 days later. **December:** Vladimir Zhirinovsky establishes the Liberal Democratic Party of the Soviet Union, which will later be renamed the Liberal Democratic Party of Russia. **3 December:** At a summit with George H. W. Bush in Malta, Gorbachev declares: "The Cold War has ended." **10 December:** Mongolia abandons Communism. **22 December:** Nicolae Ceauşescu flees the Romanian capital as Ion Iliescu assumes power; Ceauşescu and his wife are captured and executed on Christmas Day. **29 December:** Former dissident Václav Havel is elected president of Czechoslovakia; the U.S., Great Britain, France, and the USSR meet to discuss the future of divided Berlin.

1990   January: Soviet troops kill 130 in Baku during protests over the situation in Nagorno-Karabakh; *Time* magazine names Gorbachev "Man of the Year." **31 January:** The first McDonald's opens in Moscow. **February:** Riots in Dushanbe over the prospect of relocation of ethnic Armenians result in Tajikistan declaring a state of emergency. **7 February:** The USSR adopts a presidential system, thus ending CPSU's monopoly on power in the country. **28 February:** Law on Peasant Farms passed, allowing individual property ownership. **9 March:** Georgia declares its sovereignty. **11 March:** Lithuania's independence is declared. **12 March:** Estonia calls on the United Nations (UN) to restore the country's recognition as an independent state. **14 March:** Gorbachev becomes president of the Soviet Union. **31 March:** Soviet troops seize Lithuanian printing presses in order to stifle pro-independence newspapers. **13 April:** The Soviet Union issues an apology for the Katyń Massacre of Polish officers during World War II. **24 April:** At Moscow's behest, Aeroflot begins service to Saudi Arabia to allow Russian Muslims to conduct the hajj. **4 May:** Latvia declares its independence. **16 May:** Congress of People's Deputies is formed, giving rise to a genuine parliamentary system. **29 May:** Yeltsin is elected president of the Russian Soviet Federated Socialist Republic; he declares that Russian laws trump Soviet laws. **1 June:** U.S.-USSR treaty on the destruction of chemical weapons is signed. **2 June:** Anti-Uzbek riots break out in Kyrgyzstan. **10 June:** Alexius II is enthroned as the Patriarch of Moscow and All Rus. **11 June:** Russia declares its sovereignty and right to determine its economic future. **20 June:** Uzbekistan declares its sovereignty. **23 June:** Moldova declares its sovereignty. **July:** Gorbachev drops his objections to a unified Germany's membership in NATO. **12 July:** Yeltsin resigns from the Communist Party. **16 July:** Ukraine declares its sovereignty. **27 July:** Belarus declares its sovereignty. **31 July:** Gorbachev and Bush sign the START I agreement. **5 August:** Yeltsin makes a speech in Kazan urging Russia's republican leaders to "take all the sovereignty they can swallow." **22 August:** Turkmenistan declares its sovereignty. **23 August:** Armenia declares its independence. **25 August:** Tajikistan declares its sovereignty. **30 August:** Tatarstan declares its state sovereignty. **September:** The 500 Days Program of economic reform is announced. **October:** Andrey Kozyrev becomes Russian foreign minister. **3 October:** Reunification of Germany. **8 October:** Buryatiya declares its state sovereignty. **13 October:** First Russian Orthodox ceremony held in St. Basil's Cathedral in Red Square in 70 years. **15 October:** Gorbachev is awarded the Nobel Peace Prize for his role in ending the Cold War. **16 October:** The radical Russian National Unity Party is founded. **25 October:** Kazakhstan declares its sovereignty. **23 November:** "The Patriotic Song" is adopted as the new Russian national anthem. **27 November:** Checheno-Ingush Autonomous Soviet Socialist Republic (ASSR) declares its state sovereignty. **December:** Gorbachev slows the course of reforms, appointing conservatives Boris Pugo and Valentin Pavlov to top posts; Shevardnadze resigns as foreign minister. **12 December**: Kyrgyzstan declares its sovereignty; Georgia revokes the autonomy of South Ossetia. **20 December:** The Central Bank of Russia is founded from the assets of the former State Bank of the USSR.

1991 **13 January:** Soviet troops besiege the Vilnius TV tower, killing 14 Lithuanian civilians. **February:** Members of the Warsaw Pact announce their intent to disband the organization. **19 February:** Yeltsin calls for Gorbachev's resignation. **22 February:** Some 400,000 march on Moscow in support of Yeltsin. **8 March:** Plans for the New Union

Treaty are made public. **17 March:** The All-Union Referendum is held to determine the future of Soviet federalism; 76.4 percent of Soviet voters seek to preserve the union, though Georgia, Armenia, Moldova, Lithuania, Latvia, and Estonia boycott the poll. **20 March:** NATO declares it will not expand into Eastern Europe for fear of alienating the USSR. **April:** General strike in Belarus in favor of independence. **23 April:** Novo-Ogarevo Pact (9+1 Agreement) is signed, moving forward the new union negotiations. **4 May:** The Don Bass coal miners end their strike. **6 May:** Russia creates its own state security apparatus. **16 May:** Sino-Russian Border Agreement signed. **12 June:** Yeltsin wins the Russian presidency with 57 percent of the vote. **28 June:** COMECON is abolished. **July:** Eduard Shevardnadze establishes the Movement for Democratic Reforms. **1 July:** Warsaw Pact is disbanded. **3 July:** Adygeya becomes a republic of Russia. **12 July:** The final version of the New Union Treaty is drafted by the Russian Supreme Soviet. **20 July:** Yeltsin bans CPSU activities in the workplace. **19 August:** The hard-line coup against Gorbachev is initiated; the State Committee on the State of Emergency is established. **20 August:** Estonia declares independence. **21 August:** Latvia repeats its declaration of independence. **23 August:** In the face of popular opposition led by Yeltsin, the coup collapses. **24 August:** Gorbachev resigns as general secretary of the CPSU; Ukraine declares its independence. **25 August:** Belarus declares its independence. **27 August:** Moldova declares its independence. **29 August:** The USSR Supreme Soviet bans all activities of the CPSU. **31 August:** Uzbekistan and Kyrgyzstan declare independence from the USSR. **6 September:** The USSR recognizes the independence of the Baltic States of Lithuania, Latvia, and Estonia. **9 September:** Tajikistan declares its independence from the USSR. **17 September:** The Baltic States are admitted to the UN. **October 27:** Declaration of Turkmenistan's independence; Jokhar Dudayev wins the presidency in Chechnya. **1 November:** Chechen declaration of independence. **6 November:** Yeltsin outlaws the CPSU. **8 December:** The leaders of the Russian, Ukrainian, and Belarusian republics sign the Belavezha Accords, declaring the Soviet Union dissolved in favor of the Commonwealth of Independent States (CIS). **10 December:** Russian, Ukrainian, and Belarusian parliaments back the formation of the CIS. **24 December:** Official dissolution of the USSR and creation of the Commonwealth of Independent States (Russian Federation, Ukraine,

Belarus, Moldova, Armenia, Kazakhstan, Uzbekistan, Turkmenistan, Kyrgyzstan, and Tajikistan); Yeltsin informs the UN that the Russian Federation will assume the USSR's permanent seat on the Security Council. **25 December:** Gorbachev resigns as president of the USSR. **26 December:** USSR Supreme Soviet dissolves itself. **31 December:** Russian tricolor replaces the Soviet flag over the Kremlin.

YELTSIN ERA (1991–1999)

1992 2 January: Price controls lifted on many goods. **26 January:** Yeltsin announces that Russia's nuclear weapons will no longer be targeted at the United States. **February:** Aleksandr Rutskoy calls Yeltsin's plans for the country "economic genocide"; fighting in South Ossetia intensifies. **25 February:** The Khojaly Massacre claims the lives of more than 600; Armenian forces, aided by the Russian military, are blamed. **2 March:** Armenia, Azerbaijan, Kazakhstan, Kyrgyzstan, Moldova, Tajikistan, Turkmenistan, and Uzbekistan become members of the UN. **31 March:** Federation Treaty establishes power-sharing agreements between the central government and the republics and other administrative units. **6 April:** Nuclear explosion at the Tomsk-7 Reprocessing Complex. **May:** Tajik Civil War begins. **5 May:** Crimea declares its secession from Ukraine; the declaration is rescinded five days later. **7 May:** Russian Ministry of Defense is established. **19 May:** First Worldwide Congress of Tatars is held in Kazan. **25 May:** Russia-Kazakhstan Treaty of Friendship, Cooperation, and Mutual Assistance is signed. **June:** Yegor Gaydar is appointed acting prime minister. **1 June:** Russia is granted full membership in the International Monetary Fund (IMF). **6 June:** Yury Luzhkov is appointed mayor of Moscow. **17 June:** START II negotiations begin between Bush and Yeltsin. **20 June:** Estonia replaces the ruble with the kroon. **July:** Ethnic Russians in Estonia protest against new citizenship laws; cease-fire is brokered between Moldova and Transnistria; Yeltsin attends the Group of Seven (G7) Summit. **14 July:** Russian peacekeeping operation in South Ossetia begins. **23 July:** Abkhazia declares its independence from Georgia. **25 July:** The Games of the XXV Olympiad begin in Barcelona; Russia competes as part of the Unified Team, which includes all the former Soviet republics except the Baltic States. **31 July:** Georgia is admitted to the UN. **15 August:** Unified Energy System is founded. **27 September:** Sukhumi falls to Abkhaz rebels, reputedly backed by Russian advisors. **15 October:** Serial killer Andrey Chikatilo, the "Red Ripper," is convicted of 52 murders. **November:** Russian troops are deployed to prevent further Ossetian-Ingush violence. **6 November:** Tatarstan's constitution is passed, rejecting the Federation Treaty with Moscow. **9 December:** Russia's parliament refuses to confirm Yegor Gaydar as prime minister; the following day Yeltsin condemns the Congress of People's Deputies as a "fortress of conservative and reactionary forces." **12 December:** A date in April 1993 is set for a referendum on the new constitution. **14 December:** Viktor Chernomyrdin is confirmed as prime minister.

1993   1 January: The independent television station TV-6 begins broadcasting. **3 January:** START II, banning the use of multiple independently targetable reentry vehicle (MIRV) warheads, is signed by Bush and Yeltsin in Moscow. **February:** Russia's Ministry of Defense declares it has strategic interests along Georgia's Black Sea coast; terrorist attack in Kislovodsk kills 10. **10 March:** The Congress of People's Deputies opens its session with scathing attacks on Yeltsin, threatening impeachment. **20 March:** Yeltsin goes on national television to declare his institution of a "special regime," significantly expanding presidential power. **April:** Russia crafts its new "Foreign Policy Concept," calling for better relations with East Asian countries and a primary focus on diplomacy with the CIS states; a Russo-Kyrgyz military agreement is signed; the Gore-Chernomyrdin Commission is established to expand bilateral cooperation between the U.S. and the Russian Federation. **15 April:** Yukos is created through the merger of several Samara-based oil companies. **25 April:** Referendum on presidential power in the Russian Federation; the poll shows support for Yeltsin continuing his reform agenda. **May:** First attempts at creating a common economic space among the CIS states; Ukraine and the United States begin developing military and economic ties; Treaty of Friendship between Russia and Tajikistan. **July:** G7 announces $43 billion aid package to Russia. **16 June:** The Working Party on the accession of the Russian Federation is established. **31 August:** Last Russian troops leave Lithuania. **September:** Plans for the joint U.S.-Russian International Space Station are announced. **1 September:** Yeltsin attempts to suspend Vice President Aleksandr Rutskoy; the matter is referred to the Constitutional Court two days later. **21 September:** Yeltsin dissolves the Supreme Soviet and the Congress of People's Deputies in violation of the constitution. **23 September:** Congress of People's Deputies impeaches Yeltsin; a standoff ensues with the parliamentarians holing up in the White House. **24 September:** Kirsan Ilyumzhinov wins the governorship of Kalmykiya. **4 October:** Pro-Yeltsin military units storm parliament and arrest the opposition members. **10 October:** Vladimir Gusinsky launches NTV. **November:** The Yabloko political bloc is established. **12 December:** The Constitution of the Russian Federation is adopted; nationalists and Communist parties win the lion's share of seats in the newly formed State Duma.

1994   January: U.S. President Bill Clinton declares eastward expansion of NATO is inevitable; Trilateral Agreement on Ukraine's nuclear disarmament is signed. **18 January:** Kozyrev signals a shift in foreign policy toward more Russian involvement in the "near abroad" based on fear of threats emanating from the region. **5 January:** Lithuania becomes the first post-Soviet republic to apply for NATO membership, angering Moscow. **February:** Agrarian Party of Russia and the Communist Party of the Russian Federation (KPRF) are founded; striking communications workers pull the plug on television stations across half of the country; Russia gains the right to station troops along Georgia's border with Turkey. **15 February:** Tatarstan and Moscow delimit their political and economic relations, bringing an end to fears of secession. **21 February:** CIA officer Aldrich Ames is arrested for providing classified information to the Russian security service. **March:** Kazakh-Russian ties are deepened; agreement on Baikonur Cosmodrome is reached; the last Russian long-range bombers leave the country. **April:** Ethnic Russians accuse Estonian government of ethnic cleansing. **May:** Russian peacekeepers are deployed along the Abkhazia-Georgia border; an MVD report states that organized crime controls a significant number of Russian companies. **5 May:** Bishkek Protocol is signed, producing a cease-fire in the Nagorno-Karabakh War. **27 May:** Exiled author Aleksandr Solzhenitsyn returns to Russia. **June:** U.S. and Russia agree to end plutonium production for nuclear weapons; the European Union (EU) concludes the Partnership and Cooperation Agreement with

Russia. **July:** Voucher privatization process comes to an end. **20 July:** Alexander Lukashenko takes over as president of Belarus. **August:** Inflation reaches 50 percent per month; bilateral treaty signed between Russia and Bashkortostan. **31 August:** Russia completes its military withdrawal from Estonia and Latvia. **September:** Azerbaijan signs the "deal of the century" with Western oil companies to exploit the Caspian Sea, displeasing Moscow. **3 September:** Russia and China agree to end targeting of nuclear weapons at each other. **October:** Russian commitment to leave Transnistria is announced; Elizabeth II, Queen of England, visits Russia. **November:** Kozyrev declares Russia's intention to counterbalance American dominance in the Middle East at a meeting with Syrian President Hafez al-Assad. **30 November:** Abkhazia's new constitution declares its independence from Georgia. **December:** Russia joins the Group of Seven, making it the G8. **11 December:** Russian troops enter Chechnya, initiating the first Chechen War.

1995   January: Russia expands its relationships with Kazakhstan and Belarus; Russo-Turkish protocol on combating terrorism is signed. **8 January:** Zarubezhatomenergostroy, a Russian company, signs a deal to restart Iran's nuclear reactor project at Bushehr. **9 January:** Cosmonaut Valery Polyakov completes 366 days aboard the *Mir* space station, breaking a duration record for space travel. **February:** Russian troops take control of Grozny; border controls between Russia and Belarus are abolished; a majority of Russians polled believe the country is sliding into chaos. **10 February:** "Memorandum on Maintaining Peace and Stability in the Commonwealth of Independent States" is signed by all 12 CIS members. **15 February:** Yeltsin initiates a new anticorruption program. **March:** Gazprom is privatized; Ukrainian government moves against Russian nationalists in the Crimea; North Ossetiya signs a power-sharing agreement with the Kremlin; support for continuing reforms reaches a nadir. **27 March:** Nikita Mikhalkov's *Burnt by the Sun* wins the Academy Award for Best Foreign Language Film. **1 April:** Ukraine takes direct control of Crimea; U.S. and Russia sign a new $20 million deal on protecting nuclear weapons sites. **3 April:** The Federal Security Service (FSB) is created. **21 April:** Kozyrev reiterates Russia's right to use military forces to protect ethnic Russians in the near abroad. **May:** Chernomyrdin announces his new political party named "Our Home—Russia." **31 May:** Russia joins NATO's Partnership for Peace. **June:** Russia and Ukraine split the Soviet Black Sea Fleet. **14 June:** Hostage crisis in Budyonnovsk, Stavropol Krai, begins; 166 hostages are killed when Russian troops storm the hospital several days later. **14 September:** Communists in the State Duma attempt to impeach Yeltsin over his handling of the crisis in the former Yugoslavia. **25 October:** Estonia and Russia make progress on lingering border disputes. **December:** Foreign Minister Andrey Kozyrev is replaced by Yevgeny Primakov. **17 December:** Communists emerge as leading political party after State Duma elections.

1996   January: Chechen gunmen take 2,000 hostages in Kizlyar, Dagestan; dozens die in subsequent fighting with Russian troops. **22 January:** Russia is admitted to the Council of Europe. **February:** Yeltsin announces plans to run for the presidency despite low approval ratings; massive strike hobbles the mining industry. **2 April:** Commonwealth of Russia and Belarus is initiated. **14 April:** Yeltsin and Communist presidential candidate Gennady Zyuganov attend Easter mass at the rebuilt Cathedral of Christ the Savior in Moscow. **26 April:** The Shanghai Five is created with the signing of the Treaty on Deepening Military Trust in Border Regions between Russia, China, Kazakhstan, Kyrgyzstan, and Tajikistan. **30 April:** Yeltsin warns his compatriots that if Zyuganov wins the presidency, a new "iron curtain" will fall over the country. **May:** IMF announces $10 billion in aid to Russia. **9 May:** Uzbek President Islam Karimov rejects further economic and political integration of the CIS. **16 May:** Yeltsin introduces a moratorium on the death penalty in Russia. **17 May:** CIS Summit results in universal support for Yeltsin's reelection. **30 May:** Yeltsin condemns eastward expansion of NATO and calls for a reform of the military. **June:** Yeltsin articulates the future of Russian national identity as "multiethnic"; the nonethnic term *rossiiskii* is used instead of *russkii* to refer to citizens of the Russian Federation. **11 June:** Four are killed by a bomb in the Tulskaya metro station in Moscow. **16 June:** First round of presidential elections; Yeltsin wins 35 percent of the vote and Zyuganov captures 32 percent. **18 June:** General Aleksandr Lebed is appointed as secretary of the Security Council of the Russian Federation. **26 June:** Russian-brokered peace agreement ends the Tajik Civil War. **July:** The Russian Federation team participates for the first time in Olympic competition at the Atlanta Games. **3 July:** Runoff of presidential election results in a Yeltsin victory. **9 August:** Yeltsin is inaugurated. **22 August:** Cease-fire in Chechnya is agreed. **31 August:** Khasav-Yurt Accord effectively ends the first Chechen War. **5 November:** Chernomyrdin briefly assumes the role of head of state while Yeltsin undergoes heart surgery. **November:** Agreement on Russian withdrawal of troops from Chechnya is signed; Estonia abandons its claims to all Russian territory, ending a border dispute; Russia regains formal access to international capital markets. **9 November:** Undersea gas line from southern Russia to Turkey is announced. **19 November:** Major reduction of troop levels on the Sino-Russian border is announced. **December:** Russo-Iranian relations enter a new era with Primakov's visit to Tehran; the Kremlin drops its opposition to the construction of a pipeline connecting the Caspian nations to Western Europe.

1997 1 January: Aslan Maskhadov is elected president of Chechnya. **22 January:** Hearings on Yeltsin's poor health are called in the State Duma. **February:** Yasser Arafat visits Russia on his first stop as the elected president of the Palestinian Authority. **17 February:** Russia asserts that it has the right to threaten the use of nuclear strikes under certain circumstances. **March:** Clinton-Yeltsin summit in Helsinki; U.S. promises not to include post-Soviet states in NATO and Yeltsin admits legality of a U.S. missile defense shield. **27 March:** Limited nationwide strike over unpaid wages. **April:** Sino-Russian declaration on multipolarity in international politics. **2 April:** Union of Russia and Belarus is established. **May:** Yeltsin visits Kiev; Russia-Ukraine border issues are formally settled; Russia-NATO Founding Act is signed in Paris. **12 May:** Treaty of Peace and Principles of Relations is signed between Moscow and Chechnya. **17 June:** Radiation leak at a nuclear research institute near Nizhny Novgorod. **20 June:** New port facilities in the Gulf of Finland are announced, allowing Russia to avoid transit of oil and natural gas through the Baltic States. **8 July:** Violating the terms of an earlier understanding, NATO invites former Warsaw Pact members Czech Republic, Poland, and Hungary to join the alliance in 1999. **23 July:** Yeltsin vetoes a controversial law that would provide extensive rights to the Russian Orthodox Church at the expense of other faiths and denominations. **9 August:** In order to cope with hyperinflation, the Central Bank announces it will remove three zeros from the ruble moving forward. **10 October:** GUAM Consultative Forum is established to counter Russian military dominance of the CIS. **6 November:** Yeltsin ratifies an international convention barring chemical weapons, and pledges to destroy existing stockpiles by 2007. **23 November:** Russia joins the Asia-Pacific Economic Cooperation (APEC) organization. **15 December:** Yeltsin is hospitalized with a "brain spasm." **30 December:** Russian-Chinese nuclear deal worth $3 billion is signed.

1998   January: U.S-Baltic Charter establishes a pathway for the former Soviet states to join NATO. **2 January:** New ruble note is introduced. **30 January:** Yeltsin rules out running for another term in 2000. **23 March:** Sergey Kiriyenko, an economic reformer, is appointed prime minister; Yeltsin begins positioning the outgoing Chernomyrdin for a run for the presidency in 2000. **April:** Shamil Basayev temporarily assumes control of Chechnya while Maskhadov takes the hajj in Saudi Arabia; new laws banning narcotics and psychotropic drugs are introduced. **May:** Yeltsin's representative in Chechnya, Valentin Vlasov, is kidnapped and held hostage for six months. **9 May:** Constitutional Court rules that Yeltsin is eligible to run for president in 2000. **13 May:** A bomb rips through Moscow's Lubavitch synagogue. **June:** Russia signs a deal to support the development of nuclear reactors in India, despite a G8-imposed ban and Moscow's condemnation of Indian nuclear tests earlier in the year. **29 June:** Yeltsin publicly denies the existence of an economic crisis in the country. **17 July:** The remains of the last Romanov tsar and his family are buried in St. Petersburg. **25 July:** Vladimir Putin is appointed head of the FSB. **12 August:** Russian stock market dips to its lowest level in two years. **17 August:** The Russian financial crisis begins; the ruble will lose 70 percent of its value in the coming weeks. **23 August:** Yeltsin dismisses his government including Prime Minister Kiriyenko, replacing him with the veteran Chernomyrdin. **31 August:** Chernomyrdin declares the country is on the verge of economic and political collapse; U.S. President Clinton publicly urges Yeltsin to continue with reforms. **September:** Russian regions assume more control of their local economies following the federal government's inaction. **11 September:** Stymied by the Duma over Chernomyrdin's appointment, Yeltsin puts forth Yevgeny Primakov as prime minister; he is enthusiastically confirmed by the Duma. **30 October:** Russia turns to the U.S. for food aid after the season's exceptionally poor harvest. **16 November:** German Chancellor Gerhard

Schröder makes his first visit to Russia. **20 November:** Democratic activist and prominent politician Galina Starovoytova is gunned down. **25 November:** Lukoil and Gazprom establish a major strategic alliance. **December:** Belarus and Russia announce plans to develop common economic and military policy; Russia withdraws its ambassadors from Washington and London in protest over air strikes against Iraq. **9 December:** A Communist parliamentarian blames Jews in Yeltsin's cabinet for conducting "genocide against the Russian people."

1999   January: Azerbaijan invites the U.S. to establish a military base on its territory. **17 February:** Federation Council ratifies the Treaty for Friendship, Cooperation, and Partnership between Russia and Ukraine; Chechnya begins a phased introduction of Islamic law. **March:** Russia angrily condemns NATO military strikes on Serbia. **7 March:** Plans for an invasion of Chechnya are announced, but not executed. **12 March:** The Czech Republic, Hungary, and Poland join NATO. **20 March:** More than 60 are killed in a bomb blast in Vladikavkaz. **29 March:** Putin becomes secretary of the Security Council of the Russian Federation. **1 April:** Russia announces plans to send a warship to the Mediterranean to monitor the situation in Kosovo. **16 April:** The Duma recommends that Yugoslavia be admitted to the Union of Belarus and Russia. **12 May:** Sergey Stepashin replaces Primakov as prime minister; the appointment is seen as temporary. **11 June:** Russian troops occupy Pristina, the capital of Kosovo, despite promises not to enter the country before NATO troops. **7 August:** Shamil Basayev and Ibn al-Khattab launch an armed incursion into Dagestan. **8 August:** Yury Luzhkov's "Fatherland" party announces its union with the "All Russia" bloc in advance of parliamentary elections. **9 August:** Vladimir Putin becomes Russia's acting prime minister; Yeltsin backs Putin to assume the presidency. **16 August:** Putin is confirmed as the head of government. **26 August:** The Russian military acknowledges it has begun an aerial bombing campaign in Chechnya. **27 August:** Putin visits Dagestan, where he orders attacks on Wahhabist villages. **September:** Apartment bombings in Moscow and other cities kill 300 and are ultimately attributed to Ibn al-Khattab; "Unity" party is created to support Vladimir Putin's candidacy for president. **1 October:** Putin declares the Maskhadov government in Chechnya to be illegitimate. **5 October:** Upward of 30,000 Russian troops begin moving into northern Chechnya.

12 October: Assault on Grozny begins. **19 October:** Putin promises the G7 that he will take a strong stand against international money laundering. **8 December:** Treaty on the Creation of a Union State of Russia and Belarus is signed. **11 December:** EU threatens Russia with sanctions over its actions in Chechnya. **19 December:** Legislative elections are dominated by the Communists and the pro-Putin Unity. **22 December:** Tatarstan's powerful governor Mintimer Shaymiyev switches his support to Putin, along with that of his All Russia bloc. **31 December:** Yeltsin unexpectedly announces his resignation; he appoints Prime Minister Putin as acting president and moves the presidential elections forward to March 2000.

PUTIN ERA (2000–2008)

2000   January: Poland expels nine Russian diplomats for spying; the Kremlin announces a 50 percent rise in defense procurement. **February:** Russian troops assume control of Grozny. **12 February:** Putin signs a federal law granting Yeltsin and his family immunity from prosecution. **March:** Putin visits Chechnya and orders a reduction in combat troops. **26 March:** Putin wins the presidential election with 53 percent of the vote. **May:** Presidential decree creates seven federal districts; World Bank report decries the "feminization of poverty" in Russia. **7 May:** Putin is inaugurated as the second president of the Russian Federation; he appoints Mikhail Kasyanov as prime minister. **25 May:** Russia announces it has plans ready for air strikes against the Taliban in Afghanistan. **June:** Media mogul Vladimir Gusinsky is jailed shortly after reporting that Putin was ready to bring cases against certain regional leaders, signaling the beginning of Putin's campaign against the oligarchs; Putin and U.S. President Clinton meet in Moscow. **July:** Fifty-four people are killed in a suicide bombing at a police station in Chechnya; Putin appoints former anti-Russian mufti Akhmad Kadyrov as head of the regional administration. **19 July:** President gains the right to dismiss regional governors. **28 July:** Putin meets with 21 of Russia's leading oligarchs and instructs them that their hold over the Kremlin has come to an end. **31 July:** A new foreign policy doctrine is announced, with reintegrating protection of ethnic Russians as a top priority. **12 August:** The *Kursk* submarine sinks in the Barents Sea, losing all hands on board. **14 August:** Tsar Nicholas II is canonized. **28 September:** New restrictions on guest workers from the CIS are imposed; customs and tariff agreement is signed by Iran, India, and Russia. **30 October:** Successful EU-Russia Summit makes way for improved relations with Brussels; Organization for Economic Cooperation and Development (OECD) backs Putin's agenda for economic reforms. **December:** Ukrainian-Russian gas dispute is prompted by Ukrainian President Leonid Kuchma's admission that the theft of gas was state sanctioned; Cuban-Russian relations are reinvigorated after Putin meets Fidel Castro. **20 December:** Major trade deal with Canada is signed. **21 December:** Duma approves the import of nuclear waste for storage. **27 December:** The new "National Anthem of Russia" is adopted; it reprises the post-1944 Soviet anthem's music.

2001 5 February: A bomb blast in Moscow's Belorusskaya metro station kills eight. **18 February:** American FBI agent Robert Hanssen is arrested for spying for Russia. **March:** Nigerian President Olusegun Obasanjo's visit to Russia marks a new era of relations; Russian economy returns to pre-1994 levels. **23 March:** The *Mir* space station enters the earth's atmosphere and crashes into the Pacific Ocean. **April:** Gazprom takes over control of NTV; *Segodnya*, a daily newspaper critical of the Kremlin, is shut down. **10 April:** New "pragmatic" alliance between Russia and Germany is announced. **15 June:** The Shanghai Cooperation Organization is declared, recognizing the admission of Uzbekistan into the Shanghai Five. **16 June:** Putin meets the new U.S. president, George W. Bush, in Slovenia. **11 July:** New federal law places certain limits and restrictions on the formation of political parties. **16 July:** China and Russia sign the Treaty of Good-Neighborliness and Friendly Cooperation. **18 July:** Putin declares that NATO has no reason to exist. **11 September:** Putin becomes the first world leader to speak with American President Bush after the 9/11 attacks. **24 September:** Putin publicly endorses the presence of U.S. troops in Central Asia as part of the campaign against the Taliban, and puts forth a new counterterrorism doctrine for Russia. **27 September:** Putin calls on NATO to admit Russia. **October:** Putin gives a well-received speech to Germany's Bundestag in German; Russia conducts a series of raids against Chechen rebels in Georgia's Pankisi Gorge. **November:**

Bush and Putin meet in Crawford, Texas. **22 November:** Putin changes course, stating that Russia has no interest in NATO membership. **27 December:** Moldova-Russia Treaty of Friendship is ratified. **29 December:** Russia agrees to an Organization of the Petroleum Exporting Countries (OPEC) request to cut oil production for the first six months of 2002, sending prices higher.

2002   January: Russia announces a deal to build advanced warships for China; Putin visits Poland, the first visit of a Russian president since 1993; Azeri President Heydar Aliyev declares a marked improvement in relations with Russia, calling Moscow a "strategic partner." **22 January:** TV-6, the last nationally broadcast independent channel, ceases operations. **February:** Putin proposes an OPEC-like cartel for natural gas producers. **20 March:** Terrorist Ibn al-Khattab dies of poisoning. **28 April:** Aleksandr Lebed dies in a helicopter crash. **9 May:** Bomb attack at Victory Day celebrations in the Dagestani city of Kaspiisk kills 42. **June:** Meskhetian Turks protest ethnic discrimination in Krasnodar with a hunger strike; deadly floods occur in southern Russia. **26 June:** Law is passed allowing private farmland. **27 June:** Russia gains full membership in the G8. **August:** Russian plans for new energy export routes in the Baltic and Barents seas worry neighbors; Moscow conducts military strikes in Georgia's Pankisi Gorge and its largest joint operation to date in the Caspian Sea. **26 September:** Chechen rebels make an incursion into Ingushetiya; Stalin-era mass grave is found near St. Petersburg. **October:** The Russian Federation's first census is conducted; EU-Russian row over Kaliningrad. **7 October:** The Collective Security Treaty Organization (CSTO) is founded. **26 October:** Nord-Ost theater siege leaves 130 hostages and 42 Chechen terrorists dead. **30 November:** Reduction in gas supplies to Belarus, following a dispute between Alexander Lukashenko and Putin over the Union of Belarus and Russia; Putin cancels a trip to Denmark in protest of Copenhagen's harboring of Chechens. **31 October:** Arrest warrant is issued for Boris Berezovsky. **13 November:** Duma restricts media freedoms related to the coverage of terrorism. **21 November:** The Baltic States are invited to join NATO. **December:** Organization for Security and Co-operation in Europe (OSCE) mission in Chechnya is closed by Russian authorities. **22 December:** Moscow criticizes U.S. plans for an invasion of Iraq. **27 December:** Suicide bombing in Grozny destroys a four-story building and kills 72.

2003 January: Russia ends its participation in the United States Peace Corps program. **February:** France, Germany, and Russia jointly condemn the Anglo-American push for war with Iraq. **5 March:** Fiftieth anniversary of Stalin's death demonstrates his growing popularity in Russia. **10 March:** Russia announces it will veto any UN resolution on using force against Iraq. **23 March:** Referendum in Chechnya backs new constitution. **12 May:** Suicide bombing in northern Chechnya kills dozens. **28 May:** Beijing and Moscow announce their intent to double foreign trade between the two countries. **3 June:** Russia temporarily halts export of nuclear technologies to Iran, though Moscow declares cooperation will continue. **9 June:** More than 100 suspected Islamist militants are arrested in Moscow. **2 July:** Russian troops, operating under the Kosovo Force (KFOR) command, withdraw from Kosovo after four years. **6 July:** "Black Widow" bomb attacks on a Moscow rock concert by female suicide bombers kills 15. **16 July:** Federal raid on Yukos offices. **12 September:** Britain refuses to extradite Boris Berezovsky. **17 September:** Putin announces that companies gained through illegal privatization will be dealt with in the courts. **1 October:** Earthquake in Siberia leaves 1,800 homeless. **5 October:** Akhmad Kadyrov is elected president of Chechnya. **August:** A suicide bomber driving a truck filled with explosives kills more than 50 people in an Ossetian hospital. **25 October:** Mikhail Khodorkovsky is arrested on fraud and tax evasion charges, triggering a drop in the stock market over economic fears. **23 October:** Vladimir Putin opens the Kant Air Base in Kyrgyzstan, Russia's first new foreign military installation since the end of the Cold War. **2 November:** Parliamentary elections in Georgia set off Rose Revolution that will bring Mikheil Saakashvili to power. **3 November:** Khodorkovsky resigns as head of Yukos, hoping to save the company. **December:** A female suicide bomber kills five outside the National Hotel in Moscow. **7 December:** Parliamentary elections are held, giving Putin backers control of the Duma; OSCE criticism of the elections follows. **29 December:** Boris Gryzlov becomes the new chair of the State Duma; authorities seize thousands of copies of books that suggest the FSB conducted the 1999 apartment bombings. **30 December:** Yukos is ordered to pay $3.5 billion in back taxes.

2004 February: A bomb in the Moscow metro near the Avtozavodskaya station leaves 41 dead; assassination of Chechen leader in

Qatar leads to a diplomatic standoff between Moscow and Doha. **24 February:** Viktor Khristenko becomes acting prime minister in the wake of Mikhail Kasyanov's dismissal. **5 March:** Mikhail Fradkov is appointed prime minister. **9 March:** Sergey Lavrov becomes the new foreign minister. **14 March:** Putin easily wins the presidential election. **29 March:** Estonia, Latvia, and Lithuania join NATO, along with several other former members of the Warsaw Pact, prompting a warning from Moscow not to build up troops on its borders. **1 April:** New bill restricts the location of political rallies outside government buildings and other sites. **1 May:** Estonia, Latvia, and Lithuania join the European Union. **9 May:** Chechen President Kadyrov dies after a bomb blast at a stadium in Grozny. **June:** Chechen insurgents seize control of Nazran, Ingushetiya, for two days. **16 June:** Mikhail Khodorkovsky's trial begins; Uzbekistan signs a strategic partnership with Russia, bringing the country back into Moscow's sphere of influence. **July:** The motion picture *Night Watch* becomes the first Russian-made blockbuster since 1991. **9 July:** Russian-American journalist Paul Klebnikov is gunned down in Moscow. **August:** Bombs on two domestic flights claim 89 lives; a suicide bomber kills 10 and injures 30 at Moscow's Rizhskaya metro station. **September:** Ukrainian presidential candidate Viktor Yushchenko suffers from dioxin poisoning; he later implicates the Russian security service. **1 September:** Beslan hostage crisis at School Number One begins, ultimately resulting in the deaths of 344 civilians. **13 September:** Putin calls for major restructuring of the country's federal structure in order to combat terrorism. **24 September:** Russia presses the UN to adopt a stronger policy against international terrorism. **30 September:** The Duma begins the implementation of electoral reforms allowing the president to appoint regional governors. **November:** Russia ratifies the Kyoto Protocol, bringing it into force. **21 November:** Runoff in the Ukrainian presidential election triggers the Orange Revolution and the reduction of Russian influence in the country. **15 December:** Yukos files for bankruptcy; its assets will ultimately fall to Rosneft. **17 December:** Parliament raises the minimum wage to 1,100 rubles per month. **21 December:** The international monitoring organization Freedom House downgrades Russia's status to "Not Free." **24 December:** Japan demands the return of the disputed Kuril Islands. **30 December:** Turkmenistan cuts gas supplies to Russia.

2005   January: The MVD creates new units to combat the flow of trafficked persons across Russian territory. **23 February:** Bush-Putin summit in Bratislava signals an end to their previously warm relationship. **March:** Tulip Revolution in Kyrgyzstan; ousted President Askar Akayev ultimately flees to Moscow. **8 March:** Aslan Maskhadov dies during an FSB-led operation to capture him. **16 March:** At the behest of Putin, the Duma approves the creation of the Public Chamber to oversee the regions. **31 March:** The Kremlin recognizes the depth of the HIV/AIDS crisis in Russia. **April:** Agreement is reached on an undersea pipeline connecting Russia to Germany. **15 April:** Nashi youth movement is founded to prevent a "color revolution" in Russia. **May:** New benefits for mothers announced in order to increase Russia's birth rate; row over the 50th anniversary of the Soviet liberation of the Baltics during World War II creates international controversy. **13 May:** Andijan massacre in Uzbekistan; Western condemnation of the crackdown will result in Uzbekistan forcing U.S. troops out of the country. **25 May:** Inauguration of the Baku-Tbilisi-Ceyhan pipeline; major power outages grip Moscow. **31 May:** Mikhail Khodorkovsky is sentenced to nine years for fraud and tax evasion. **24 June:** New mosque is opened in Kazan to mark the city's millennium. **29 June:** Russia cancels $2.2 billion in African debt. **June:** Renewed conflict with Estonia over border issues. **30 June:** Russia gains observer status with the Organization of the Islamic Conference (OIC). **18 August:** Joint Russian-Chinese military exercises begin on the Shandong Peninsula. **21 September:** The new president of Kyrgyzstan declares a new era of strategic partnership with Russia. **29 September:** The long-running and controversial "loans for shares" program is officially terminated. **October:** Attacks on government buildings in Nalchik, Kabardino-Balkariya result in nearly 100 deaths. **14 November:** Treaty of Allied Relations is signed with Uzbekistan; Dmitry Medvyedev becomes deputy prime minister. **December:** Broadcasts of the international English-language channel Russia Today begin. **19 December:** Negotiations over Russia's admission to the World Trade Organization (WTO) fall through again.

2006   January: Russia forgives Afghanistan's Soviet-era debt; significant espionage row erupts between Britain and Russia; a new law is passed giving the government oversight of nongovernmental organizations. **1 January:** Russia cuts gas exports to Ukraine; supply is restored three days later. **February:** Increased use of the term "sovereign democracy" demonstrates Putin's resistance to Western-style political reform. **21 February:** Russia stops issuing entry visas to Georgian citizens. **March:** Russia bans the import of Georgian wine; attacks on ethnic minorities increase dramatically. **18 March:** Environmentalists protest pipelines to be built near Lake Baykal. **10 May:** Putin lashes out at the United States, calling the country "wolflike" in an address to the nation. **19 March:** Alexander Lukashenko retains his post, surviving the failed "Jeans Revolution" that followed disputed presidential elections in Belarus. **29 June:** Russia announces a new Arabic-language station to be launched by the end of the year; the Kremlin hires the multinational public relations agency Ketchum to improve its image worldwide. **July:** The Duma grants Putin the right to hunt down terrorists anywhere in the world. **1 July:** Currency controls are lifted to provide impetus to foreign investment in the country. **10 July:** Shamil Basayev is reported to have been killed in Ingushetiya. **15 July:** G8 summit begins in St. Petersburg. **August:** Three Japanese fishermen are detained near the Kuril Islands. **September:** Putin is awarded France's highest military decoration for promoting friendship between the two countries. **26 September:** Russian-Georgian tensions deepen over a spy scandal. **28 September:** Transnistria votes for union with Russia in a nonbinding referendum. **7 October:** Liberal activist Anna Politkovskaya is gunned down. **28 October:** The Fair Russia political party is established. **16 November:** Russia and Pakistan expand their relationship, agreeing on a number of areas of cooperation. **23 November:** Aleksandr Litvinenko dies in a London hospital from polonium poisoning; the fallout will bring Russian-British relations to their lowest point since the Cold War. **December:** Belarus-Russian gas dispute interrupts flow to the European Union. **21 December:** New poll shows nostalgia for the USSR continues to rise 15 years after its dissolution; the longtime leader of Turkmenistan dies, putting in question the country's relationship with Russia and gas deals.

2007   8 January: Russia cuts flow of oil across Belarus in a spat over illegal siphoning, harming relations with Germany. **February:** Russia condemns U.S. policies on Israel-Palestine. **15 February:** Ramzan Kadyrov is installed as Chechnya's president. **23 April:** Boris Yeltsin dies. **27 April:** Beginning of cyberattacks on Estonia in the wake of the "Bronze Soldier" controversy. **May:** The U.S. acknowledges Russia's return to superpower status. **12 May:** Major Russian-Turkmen gas deal is signed. **29 May:** Russia test fires new intercontinental ballistic missile. **June:** Garry Kasparov begins campaign against Putin. **7 June:** Putin invites the U.S. to establish missile defense in Azerbaijan. **2 July:** Bush hosts Putin at his family estate in Kennebunkport, Maine, in an attempt to repair frayed relations between the two countries. **14 July:** Russia withdraws from the Treaty on Conventional Armed Forces in Europe. **26 July:** Massive security operation begins in Ingushetiya following insurgent attacks. **August:** Russia makes an undersea territorial claim to the North Pole. **7 August:** Shanghai Cooperation Organization military exercises take place in Chelyabinsk. **17 August:** Putin announces plans to resume long-range strategic bomber flights. **14 September:** Viktor Zubkov becomes prime minister after Mikhail Fradkov's resignation two days earlier. **1 October:** Putin signals plans to become prime minister in 2008. **24 November:** Beginning of the Dissenters' Marches in St. Petersburg. **29 November:** Russian court finds Boris Berezovsky guilty of massive embezzlement in absentia. **December:** Russia closes regional offices of the British Council, triggering a further dip in bilateral relations. **2 December:** Legislative elections produce another resounding victory for the pro-Putin United Russia party. **10 December:** Putin backs Dmitry Medvyedev for president. **17 December:** United Russia picks Medvyedev as the party's candidate for the upcoming presidential elections. **21 December:** Poland and the Baltic States gain admission to the Schengen visa-free zone, directly impacting trade along the countries' Russian borders. **31 December:** *Time* magazine names Putin "Person of the Year" for 2007.

2008   January: Dmitry Rogozin's appointment as Russia's representative to NATO signals a hard turn away from cooperation; Russia and Serbia sign a new deal on energy cooperation. **22 January:** Russia's largest post-Soviet naval operations take place off the coast of France. **17 February:** Kosovo declares its independence, which is recognized by a number of European and North American states on the following day; the move is subsequently condemned by Russia, which blocks UN recognition. **March:** Moves by Georgia and Ukraine to join NATO are roundly condemned in Moscow. **2 March:** Medvyedev is elected the third president of the Russian Federation, winning 70 per-

cent of the vote. **3 March:** Gazprom cuts gas supplies to Ukraine for two days. **April:** Russia solidifies its relations with Abkhazia and South Ossetia, angering the Georgian leadership.

MEDVYEDEV ERA (2008–PRESENT)

2008   7 May: Medvyedev is sworn in as the third president of the Russian Federation. **8 May:** Putin becomes prime minister for the second time. **7 August:** The South Ossetian War begins with Georgian attacks on Tskhinvali; Russian troops cross the border the following day. **12 August:** A six-point peace plan is agreed, signaling the end of the Russo-Georgian conflict. **20 August:** U.S.-Poland deal on missile defense results in threats of military force by Russia. **26 August:** Medvyedev recognizes the independence of South Ossetia and Abkhazia. **3 September:** Archeologists locate ancient Khazar capital in southern Russia. **17 September:** Medvyedev promises Abkhazia and South Ossetia military support against third parties. **November:** Russia expands its military presence in Central Asia. **5 November:** Russia announces it will deploy a new missile system and radar-jamming facilities in Kaliningrad in response to the U.S. missile defense shield in Central Europe. **December:** Frayed Russia-NATO relations begin to improve six months after the South Ossetian War. **5 December:** Patriarch Alexius II dies. **14 December:** Russian competitor wins Miss World 2008 title. **22 December:** Moscow police are flown to Vladivostok to squelch popular protests over tariffs on imported cars. **31 December:** Changes to the Russian Constitution come into force, lengthening the term of the Russian presidency and the term of office of Duma deputies.

2009   2 January: Countries in the Balkans report shortages of gas supplies as a row between Ukraine and Gazprom interrupts supplies. **1 February:** Patriarch Kirill I of Moscow is enthroned as the Patriarch of the Russian Orthodox Church. **March:** Moscow issues a global call for ethnic Russians to return to the country. **10 March:** Medvyedev inaugurates a multiyear reform of the civil service. **28 March:** New military forces are announced to police the Arctic Ocean. **April:** Uprising in Moldova pushes the country closer to the European Union and away from Russia. **1 April:** Medvyedev meets U.S. President Barack Obama in London in advance of the G8 summit. **15 April:** Medvyedev makes a speech supporting the growth of civil society in Russia, signaling his first major departure from Putin. **June:** Russia rejects full membership in OPEC. **1 June:** Russia closes all casinos in the country, except for those in four regions: Altay, Kaliningrad, the Black Sea coast, and Primorsky Krai. **7 July:** Obama meets Putin for the first time. **9 July:** Russia asks Kyrgyzstan for permission to build a new base after failing to oust the Americans from the country. **14 July:** Plans for an upgraded Black Sea naval base to replace Sevastopol are announced. **August:** Russian submarines ply the waters off the U.S. east coast in a bid to promote arms sales to India. **17 August:** An industrial accident at the Sayano-Shushenskaya hydroelectric plant in Khakasiya leaves 74 dead. **29 August:** Venezuela recognizes South Ossetia and Abkhazia, the third UN member to do so. **September:** A row erupts between Poland and Russia over Moscow's release of documents suggesting a pre–World War II German-Polish plan to destroy the USSR. **20 September:** U.S. President Obama scraps plans to deploy a missile defense shield in Poland and the Czech Republic, reducing tensions with Moscow over the issue. **30 September:** An EU report finds that Georgia precipitated the 2008 South Ossetian War while condemning Russia for expanding the conflict to Abkhazia and allowing the ethnic cleansing of Georgian villages in South Ossetia.

Introduction

All countries are unique, but Russia—particularly contemporary Russia—is undoubtedly *sui generis*. Underscoring this point, British Prime Minister Winston Churchill once described the country as "a riddle wrapped in a mystery inside an enigma." Putting aside such biased declarations, this text aims to explore contemporary Russia in all its forms. In the past three decades, Russia has seen some of the most dramatic political, social, and economic changes in world history. In 1985, Russia constituted the core of the Union of Soviet Socialist Republics, one of only two superpowers in the world. By the mid-1990s, Russia had become a weak, some would argue failing, state with an economy smaller than that of South Korea. However, the new millennium has been kind, restoring Russia to the status of world power, filling the state coffers with petrodollars, and reversing a slide into anarchy.

This transformation has been costly, both in economic and psychological terms. While Russia remains the world's largest state in terms of geography, the "loss" of the union republics that accompanied the dissolution of the Soviet Union proved to be a powerful blow to the psyche of the Russian nation. In 2005, Vladimir Putin—the second president of the Russian Federation—described the collapse of the Soviet empire as "the greatest geopolitical catastrophe of the century," referring simultaneously to territorial losses and the socioeconomic suffering wrought by the demise of the Soviet Union. In addition to the loss of roughly one-quarter of Soviet lands and one-third of the country's population, the new Russian Federation had to grapple with 25 million ethnic Russians who were stranded in sometimes hostile states in the "near abroad," that is, the non-Russian post-Soviet republics.

Despite possessing the world's largest nuclear arsenal, the Russian military languished in the new era, unable to adjust to the demands of a post–Cold War world and plagued by lack of funds. Most

1

embarrassingly, Russia's new armed forces proved unable to decisively win a war with the small breakaway republic of Chechnya. Following the first Chechen War (1994–1996), Russia's international status plummeted as evidence of mass atrocities and rampant corruption in the military surfaced.

With much of the world community coming to view Russia as an oversized banana republic, it was not surprising that the United States, the European Union (EU), Turkey, China, and Iran expanded their influence into areas historically associated with Moscow. Recognizing the weakness of the central government, Russia's regions, especially the ethnic republics, wrested increasing authority from the Kremlin. Some, such as Tatarstan, even went as far as issuing their own passports and conducting relations with foreign governments.

Economically, the situation was no better. Beginning with the last Soviet Premier Mikhail Gorbachev's economic restructuring (*perestroika*), Russia saw a drop in living standards in the late 1980s. Conditions continued to worsen in the 1990s under the first democratically elected president of the Russian Federation, Boris Yeltsin. Privatization was conducted in a murky environment dictated by extended networks of economic elites and the old Soviet *nomenklatura*. While consumer goods lined the once-barren shelves of Russia's shops, the average Russian fell victim to the excruciating effects of "shock therapy." Personal savings evaporated overnight, entire industries disappeared, and large numbers of the population were in danger of losing their homes and livelihoods. Within the space of a few years, one of the most egalitarian societies on the face of the planet was afflicted with a massive wealth gap. Women in particular suffered during the first decade after independence, as unemployment, alcoholism, HIV/AIDS, and crime rates soared. Popular resentment of Western-style reforms quickly translated into a conservative revival of Russian Orthodoxy, Soviet nostalgia, and ultranationalism.

Vladimir Putin's rapid ascent to power quickly reversed a number of Yeltsin-era trends. While economic recovery was already under way when the former KGB agent took the reins in early 2000, he was able to steer the country away from financial collapse. His "strong hand," particularly in the early stages of the second Chechen War, won him the respect of older Russians, as well as the new elite who were confounded by the country's sociopolitical chaos. Under Putin, state coffers brimmed over with oil and natural gas profits, the middle class began to grow, improvements were made in the health-care and education systems, and Russia resumed its position as a major player in international affairs.

There was a price to pay, however, for this "New Russia." Terrorism, virtually unknown in the late Soviet era, became commonplace by the end of Putin's first year in office, and by 2005, Russia became one of the most terror-prone countries on earth. With the backing of the masses, Putin muzzled the press, arrested business tycoons, hobbled the country's nascent civil society, and suffocated the political party system. Despite the election of a new president, Dmitry Medvyedev, in 2008, Putin's shadow still looms large, as do those of the so-called *siloviki*, that is, members of the secret police, armed forces, and other "power ministries."

As Russia grapples with the effects of the most recent global recession, it is clear that the boom period of the early and mid-2000s is now a memory, but even with recent contractions in the economy, the country's largest corporations are now household names around the world. Investments in the health-care and social security systems are producing dividends, and a sizable middle class is finally being established. As Russians look forward to the third decade of post-Soviet independence, there are other reasons for optimism. With a new military footprint that includes dominance in the Arctic Ocean, Central Asia, and the Caucasus, Russia's status as a world power is once again unquestioned. Russia's quick victory against Georgia in the 2008 South Ossetian War boldly underscored this point.

LAND AND PEOPLE

Dominating the Eurasian supercontinent, the Russian Federation (*Rossiiskaia federatsiia*) is the world's largest country, occupying 13 percent of the earth's surface. Nearly twice the size of the United States, Russia's land mass is 16,377,742 square kilometers, and its water area is 720,500 square kilometers. It is situated between the Arctic Ocean, the northern Pacific Ocean, inner Eurasia, and Central Europe. Russia's continental land mass lies between the latitudes 77°44' N and 41°11'N and the longitudes 27°20' E and 169°38' W. Russia is over 8,000 kilometers wide, and from the northern reaches of Franz Josef Land to the country's southern border it is more than 3,500 kilometers long.

The country sits astride the Ural Mountains, the historic divide between the European and Asian continents. The range is equally important in Russian geography, dividing European Russia, Russia's most populous and industrialized region, from Siberia. In the southern reaches of European Russia, the North Caucasus represents a separate historical and geographic zone. Siberia, in turn, gives way to the Russian Far East, a region with an entirely different climate from the harsh continental clime of Russia's vast interior. The country's last geographic area, the Far North, stretches from Lapland to Alaska.

Not surprising given its size, Russia possesses more international borders than any other country, more than 20,000 kilometers in total. Moving counterclockwise from the northeast of the country, they are as follows: Norway (196 kilometers); Finland (1,313 kilometers); Estonia (290 kilometers); Latvia (292 kilometers); Lithuania (227 kilometers); Poland (432 kilometers); Belarus (959 kilometers); Ukraine (1,576 kilometers); Georgia (723 kilometers); Azerbaijan (284 kilometers); Kazakhstan (6,846 kilometers); China (3,645 kilometers); Mongolia (3,441 kilometers); and North Korea (17 kilometers). There is also a maritime border with the United States between the Bering and Chukchi seas.

With 37,653 kilometers of coastline, the country is washed by a number of the world's most important bodies of water. Clockwise from the northeast, these include the White Sea, the Barents Sea, the Kara Sea, the Arctic Ocean, the Laptev Sea, the East Siberian Sea, the Chukchi Sea, the Bering Sea, the Pacific Ocean, the Sea of Okhotsk, the Sea of Japan (East Sea), the Caspian Sea, the Black Sea, and the Baltic Sea. Lake Baykal, the world's largest freshwater lake, is located in Russia. The country's major rivers include the Volga, Don, Ob, Irtysh, Yenisey, Lena, and Amur. Russia's major islands and island chains include Franz Josef Land, Novaya Zemlya, Severnaya Zemlya, the New Siberian Islands, Wrangel Island, the Kuril Islands, and Sakhalin. Important peninsulas include the Kola, Taymyr, Yamal, Kamchatka, and Chukchi.

Russia's climatic zones include tundra, found mostly north of the Arctic Circle; taiga, stretching across northern European Russia, Siberia, and the Russian Far East; temperate broadleaf forests and steppe-forests, found mostly in European Russia and along the southern rim of Asiatic Russia; semiarid steppe, which dominates extreme southern

European Russia; and mountainous biomes, which characterize the Caucasus, Urals, Altay, Sayan, and other ranges. The highest point is Mount Elbrus (5,633 m), while the lowest is the Caspian Sea (–28 m).

Russia's climate, though largely continental in nature, is character- ized by extremes. The country has hot summers with long, snowy winters. Autumn and spring are rather brief with dramatic bouts of rain. Temperatures range from 35°C to –60°C, with Moscow having an average annual temperature of 5.4°C. Average annual rainfall differs based on region: the East European Plain sees 500 millimeters per year, while the arid southern zones and the tundra get less than 20 millimeters annually; the Russian Far East receives significant precipitation and is part of the world's monsoon belt. The inhospitable climate makes provision of energy and foodstuffs difficult in the Far North and much of Siberia.

Despite being a major agricultural producer, less than 10 percent of Russia's land is arable (neither the taiga nor the tundra is amenable to crops). In southern European Russia, chernozem and other fertile soils are common. Combined with ample sunshine, this allows for the cul- tivation of grains, potatoes, legumes, and vegetables. Russia's citrus, tobacco, and other warm-weather crops are produced in a relatively compact area in and around the North Caucasus. Animal husbandry, particularly reindeer herding, remains a traditional occupation in the boreal zones of the country. Birch, oak, and aspen are the most common trees in the north, while pine, spruce, fir, and cedar exist farther south. The steppe is dominated by vast tracts of grass, punctuated by copses of birch trees near water sources.

Owing to its vast geography and low population density (particularly east of the Urals), the country's fauna is extremely diverse. In the Far North, a wide variety of Arctic animals and cold-water fish can be found. In the taiga and broad-leafed forests, reindeer, elk, lynx, sable, boars, deer, and mink exist in sizable numbers, as do various species of birds. Both Lake Baykal and the Caspian are home to several unique species, including the Nerpa freshwater seal and the Beluga sturgeon, respectively. Russia's access to seas, lakes, and large rivers affords it one of the world's largest fishing industries.

Russia commands the largest share of the world's natural resources, including valuable commodities such as oil, natural gas, uranium, iron ore, aluminum, gold, silver, diamonds, and other precious metals. On the other hand, due to Soviet-era industrialization, strip mining, and depredatory land use policies, Russia is one of the world's most polluted countries. Major issues include air pollution from heavy industry, power generation, and transportation; agricultural pollution and soil erosion; deforestation; radioactive contamination; and toxic waste.

Moscow and St. Petersburg dominate Russia's economic geography, while there are dozens of other large cities across the country, including Voronezh, Krasnodar, Rostov-on-Don, Volgograd, Saratov, Nizhny Novgorod, Kazan, Ufa, Yekaterinburg, Chelyabinsk, Omsk, Novosibirsk, and Vladivostok. Most of the population is concentrated in the European core, particularly the so-called chernozem zone, where agriculture and industry meet. There are also population centers along the 9,200-kilometer Trans-Siberian Railway, which stretches from Moscow to the Korean Peninsula. The vast majority of Russia, however, has a population density of less than one person/per square kilometer, and migration patterns suggest that this statistic will only decrease in the coming decades. Severe poverty afflicts certain areas of the North Caucasus, the Far North, and much of the Russian Far East.

Russia consists of 83 administrative units (known as federal subjects); most of these are remnants of the Soviet administrative structure. Each subject of the federation belongs to one of the following categories: ethnic republic, oblast, krai, autonomous oblast, autonomous okrug, or federal city. While these entities possess equal representation in the upper house of the Russian parliament, they differ in the amount of autonomy they possess. Ethnic republics enjoy the highest level of autonomy, followed by autonomous okrugs. Krais and oblasts (the latter being the most common type of subject) have roughly the same level of autonomy, and are differentiated primarily by historical factors.

Ethnic republics are nominally autonomous, with a constitution, president, and parliament. Each serves as an ethnic homeland for at least one ethnic population (e.g., Tatars are in the titular nation of Tatarstan). The republics of the Russian Federation—listed in order of population from largest to smallest—are as follows: Bashkortostan, Tatarstan, Dagestan, Udmurtiya, Chuvashiya, Chechnya, Komi, Buryatiya, Sakha (Yakutiya), Kabardino-Balkariya, Mordoviya, Mari El, Kareliya, North Ossetiya-Alaniya, Khakasiya, Ingushetiya, Adygeya, Karachay-Cherkessiya, Tuva (Tyva), Kalmykiya, and Altay (Gorno-Altay). The autonomous okrugs are Chukotka, Khantiya-Mansiya, Nenetsiya, and Yamaliya. As is the case with the aforementioned republics, autonomous okrugs serve as ethnic homelands for a national minority.

There are 46 oblasts (regions): Amur, Arkhangelsk, Astrakhan, Belgorod, Bryansk, Chelyabinsk, Irkutsk, Ivanovo, Kaliningrad, Kaluga, Kemerovo, Kirov, Kostroma, Kurgan, Kursk, Leningrad, Lipetsk, Magadan, Moscow, Murmansk, Nizhny Novgorod, Novgorod, Novosibirsk, Omsk, Orenburg, Oryol, Penza, Pskov, Rostov, Ryazan, Sakhalin, Samara, Saratov, Smolensk, Sverdlovsk, Tambov, Tomsk, Tula, Tver, Tyumen, Ulyanovsk, Vladimir, Volgograd, Vologda, Voronezh, and Yaroslavl. With a few exceptions, these take the name of the largest city in the oblast. Russia has nine krais (provinces): Altay, Kamchatka, Khabarovsk, Krasnodar, Krasnoyarsk, Perm, Primorsky, Stavropol, and Zabaykalsky (formerly Chita Oblast). There is one autonomous oblast: the Jewish Autonomous Oblast (also known as Birobijan). Last, there are two federal cities that function as separate regions: Moscow and St. Petersburg.

According to a 2009 estimate, the population of Russia is 140,041,247, making it the ninth most populous country in the world. The population growth rate is one of the worst in the world at –0.46 percent, with only 11.1 births and 16.1 deaths per 1,000 residents. The median age is 38.4, and the country is aging rapidly. Since 1991, the country has seen its population drop by 5 million. Demographic challenges related to low levels of fertility (1.4 children born per woman) and shrinking life spans (59 years for males and 73 years for females) suggest that the Russian population will shrink to 100 million in the coming decades.

However, Russia is one the world's most popular destinations for migrants (second only to the United States). More than 8 percent of the national population is foreign born, and Russia—as a receiving country—accounts for 6.5 percent of the world's immigrant population. If current levels of immigration are maintained, this will somewhat offset the decline in the country's total population. Emigration, a major issue after the dissolution of the Soviet Union, has stabilized, and no longer poses a major threat to the country's demography.

Like other European countries, Russia is highly urbanized, with three-quarters of the population living in cities. Despite this, Russia has one of the world's lowest population densities at 8.3 persons/per square kilometer. The country's sparsely peopled provinces, however, contrast sharply with the situation around the densely populated cities of

Moscow and St. Petersburg. Literacy is nearly universal (99.6 percent), and Russians have a school life expectancy of 14 years; both figures are comparable to statistics in northern Europe, despite dramatically lower spending on education in Russia.

In terms of the country's ethnic makeup, Russians are a clear majority at 80 percent, though this number is decreasing over time due to lower fertility rates among ethnic Russians when compared to the country's 175 ethnic and national minorities. The second-largest group is the Tatars, who make up nearly 4 percent of the population, followed by Ukrainians (2.04 percent), Bashkirs (1.16 percent), Chuvash (1.14 percent), Chechens (0.94 percent), Armenians (0.78 percent), and Mordvins (0.58 percent). The other major nationalities—listed in decreasing order of population—include Avars, Belarusians, Kazakhs, Udmurts, Azeris, Mari, ethnic Germans, Kabardins, Ossetians, Dargins, Buryats, Sakha, Kumyks, Ingush, Lezgins, Komi, Tuvans, Jews, Georgians, Karachay, Gypsies, Kalmyks, Moldovans, Laks, Koreans, Adyghe, Komi, Tabasarans, Uzbeks, Tajiks, Balkars, Greeks, Karelians, Turks, Nogays, Khakas, Poles, Altays, Lithuanians, Nenets, Evenks, Chinese, Finns, Turkmens, Bulgarians, Kyrgyz, Rutuls, Khanty, Latvians, Aguls, Estonians, Vietnamese, Kurds, Evens, Mansi, and Chukchi.

While the Russian language is the dominant medium of communication in education, media, literature, public life, and the economy of the Russian Federation (97 percent of all Russian citizens are fluent in Russian), the country is home to millions of speakers of Tatar, Chechen, and Bashkir, as well as dozens of languages spoken nowhere else in the world. In the ethnic republics and autonomous okrugs, local languages enjoy government support. Linguistic diversity is particularly high in the Volga-Ural region, the Far North, and the North Caucasus. The languages of Russia can be grouped into the following five categories: Slavic (Russian, Ukrainian, Belarusian, and Polish); Finno-Ugric (Karelian, Mari, Udmurt, Erzya, Moksha, Nenets, Komi, Khanty, and Mansi); Turkic (Tatar, Bashkir, Karachay-Balkar, Nogay, Altay, Sakha, Tuvan, Khakas, and Chuvash); Mongolic (Kalmyk and Buryat); and Caucasian (Adyghe, Kabardian, Chechen, Ingush, and the languages of Dagestan). Other languages include Ossetic, Yiddish, Romany, Mandarin Chinese, Korean, and Armenian.

Since the collapse of Communism and the end of restrictions on religious practice, identification with the country's four principal faiths—

Orthodox Christianity, Islam, Judaism, and Buddhism—has increased sharply. Animism and shamanism have also seen a revival, particularly among the indigenous peoples of the Far North and the Russian Far East. Other forms of religion have also flourished, particularly neo-Paganism and certain denominations of Protestantism. However, due to the Soviet legacy of state-sponsored atheism, Russia continues to have one of the world's lowest levels of religious identification and extremely low attendance rates at houses of worship.

Religious affiliation is typically determined by ethnicity. Slavs (Russians, Ukrainians, and Belarusians)—as well as Ossetians, Armenians, and Georgians—are predominantly affiliated with the Russian Orthodox Church or other Eastern Orthodox churches. Tatars, Bashkirs, and the various peoples of the North Caucasus are traditionally Muslims, though a certain percentage of these populations has embraced Christianity. Jews, who are considered an ethnic population in Russia, have returned to their ancestral faith in large numbers since 1991 (though many of the most religious have quit the country for Israel and the United States). Last, the Kalmyks and Buryats, along with other small ethnic groups in the Russian Far East, practice Buddhism, though often in a syncretic manner, mixing the faith with other systems of belief.

HISTORY

Tsarist and Soviet Periods (before 1985)

While this volume does not attempt to cover Russian history prior to the late Soviet period in detail, a few words on Russia before the introduction of perestroika are in order. Varangians from Scandinavia established the first Russian state, Kievan Rus, in the 9th century around the modern-day capital of Ukraine. The Viking rulers later intermarried with their Slav subjects, and adopted Orthodox Christianity. Kievan Rus fell to the Mongol conquerors in the 1200s. A new vassal state, the Grand Duchy of Muscovy, formed in the 14th century, ultimately threw off the so-called Tatar Yoke. Ivan IV, known as "the Terrible" in Western accounts, assumed the title of "Tsar of All the Russias" in 1547 as he built Muscovy into a major regional power.

Over the next hundred years, bands of Cossacks loyal to the tsar would lay claim to a huge swath of territory stretching from the Don River to the Pacific Ocean. In the early 1600s, the Romanov family assumed the throne of Russia, which was turned into an empire under Peter the Great (1682–1725). In the ensuing centuries, Russian expansion knew no limits as Poland, western Ukraine, the Caucasus, Kazakhstan, Central Asia, and new Pacific territories were added, including Alaska. Once a rather compact and homogenous state, by the mid-19th century Russia had become a far-flung multinational empire peopled by a panoply of ethnic groups, speaking hundreds of languages and confessing dozens of faiths.

While Western European states embraced the Enlightenment and instituted economic and social reforms in the 19th century, tsarist Russia emerged as the model of autocracy, liberating its serfs only in 1861. Economic and social reform at the end of the 19th century could not satisfy demand for political change. From 1905 to 1917, Russia experienced three revolutions. While the first failed, the February Revolution of 1917 forced the abdication of the last tsar, Nicholas II, and saw attempts at the introduction of liberal democracy. The Provisional Government, however, decided to continue the country's participation as belligerent in World War I (1914–1918), thus sealing its fate. In the autumn of 1917, Vladimir Lenin led a second uprising, and instituted rule by the local soviets or "councils."

Within a year, Lenin's new government had swept away any semblance of democracy and replaced it with a dictatorship of the proletariat administered by the Bolshevik Party. For more than four years, a civil war raged across the country, pitting the Bolsheviks ("Reds") against their foes, collectively called the "Whites," and foreign armies that had invaded the country to put down the socialist revolution. In 1922, the Bolsheviks emerged victorious and christened their state the Union of Soviet Socialist Republics (USSR).

In the wake of Lenin's death in 1924, a grand struggle for control of the Communist Party of the Soviet Union broke out. Joseph Stalin, initially a minor figure in the party, ultimately consolidated power and forced his primary opponent, Leon Trotsky, into exile. During his reign, which lasted until 1953, Stalin industrialized the Soviet Union, executed hundreds of thousands, purged millions from their jobs and positions of power, and created a cult of personality without compare.

The Soviet victory over Nazi Germany in World War II (1939–1945) and the country's detonation of an atomic bomb in 1949 solidified Stalin's position as equal—and arguably superior—to that of Lenin in the minds of many Soviet citizens. After Stalin's death in 1953, Nikita Khrushchev attempted to attenuate the evils of Stalinism at home, while expanding the Cold War with the United States abroad. In 1964, he was succeeded by Leonid Brezhnev, who led the USSR at the height of its power. Buoyed by high oil prices, the Kremlin saw its influence abroad swell, while at home corruption, stagnation, and apathy eroded the foundation of the entire Soviet system. Following Brezhnev's death, leadership passed to Yury Andropov (1982–1984) and then Konstantin Chernenko (1984–1985); neither premier made a major impact on the direction of Soviet history.

The Gorbachev Era (1985–1991)

On 11 March 1985, Mikhail Gorbachev became the general secretary of the Communist Party of the Soviet Union (CPSU). At 54, he was significantly younger than his predecessor, Chernenko, who had come to power while in his eighties. From the onset, Gorbachev embraced acceleration of the sluggish Soviet economy. In order to wrench the system out of self-perpetuating stagnation, he pursued a policy of restructuring combined with transparency. The twin policies of perestroika and glasnost became the hallmarks of his six-year reign as head of the Communist Party.

Within a year of taking office, Gorbachev ran into serious difficulties. His antialcoholism campaign, though well intentioned, drained state coffers and triggered a rise in alcohol-related deaths from homemade spirits (*samogon*). The continuing decline in world oil prices (down 70 percent since 1980) and the strain placed on the Soviet economy by the Soviet-Afghan War exacerbated an already difficult situation. Furthermore, American President Ronald Reagan's aggressive spending on defense was putting pressure on the Soviet military to follow suit.

The political fallout from the 1986 nuclear power plant explosion at Chernobyl triggered a crisis between the "old thinkers" within the party, who were set on preserving the status quo, and Gorbachev and his allies. Gorbachev ultimately prevailed and pushed forward on further reforms. However, the growing black market—a response to the shortage of goods—and spiraling inflation prevented the USSR from achieving its goals in the short term. In 1987, Gorbachev began a campaign to win over the Soviet people.

His support for limited democratization within the Communist Party earned him enemies on the right, as well as criticism from those who felt he was moving too slow (including the future President Boris Yeltsin). By 1988, Gorbachev was able to introduce private ownership of small firms, creating the basis for an embryonic market economy. In order to protect the progress made up to this point, Gorbachev began to strip the Communist Party of its exclusive control of the political system.

During the same period, Gorbachev reoriented Soviet foreign policy. Assisted by his Foreign Minister Eduard Shevardnadze (1985–1990), a staunch reformer, Gorbachev redefined the Soviet Union's relations with its historic enemies—particularly the North Atlantic Treaty Organization (NATO) countries of Europe and the United States—while reducing the Kremlin's control of the Eastern Bloc. His new orientation promoted respect for human and minority rights, as well as the creation of a "common European home" that included the USSR.

Through a series of groundbreaking initiatives, the USSR also agreed to reduce its nuclear arsenal and conventional weapons, though Gorbachev's goal of a nuclear weapons–free world has not yet been attained. Recognizing the futility of continuing the war in Afghanistan, Moscow also began withdrawing troops, with the last soldier leaving the country in 1989. That same year saw the radical transformation of politics across Poland, East Germany, Czechoslovakia, Hungary, and other Soviet satellites. True to his word, Gorbachev allowed events to play out across the region, with local Communist parties being ousted from power one by one.

At home, the policy of glasnost was reaping unintended consequences. Freer flows of information and the publication of long-suppressed material, previously only available in *samizdat* (self-published) form, shed light on a host of issues, including the gulag system, the Great Purges (1936–1938), Stalin's pact with Adolf Hitler, and the deportation of whole nations during World War II. The media also turned its focus on contemporary problems, including alcoholism, drug abuse, environmental degradation, and corruption. In such an environment, the entire system began to buckle under the pressure.

Chronic shortages of goods and growing discontent created a volatile political situation in Russia proper, while minority nationalism in the non-Russian republics was pulling at the country's seams. The situation was especially acute in the Baltic States, where the new liberalism had resulted in the rise of stridently anti-Russian elites within the political system; glasnost's uncovering of Stalin's crimes against the Baltic peoples only fueled the fire. Pro-independence movements were gaining ground elsewhere as well, including Georgia, Armenia, and Ukraine.

In the southern Caucasus, ethnic violence erupted between Armenians and Azeris over the contested region of Nagorno-Karabakh. In Uzbekistan, a pogrom of Meskhetian Turks forced their evacuation, further suggesting that the Kremlin's hold on power in the regions was disintegrating. In early 1990, Moldova saw the trends of ethnic strife and the struggle for independence merge, as the republic's titular majority embraced unification with neighboring Romania while its Slavic population established their own republic to escape the danger of "Romanianization."

After briefly tacking back on his reform agenda, Gorbachev surged forward once again and assumed a title: president of the Soviet Union. Reflecting this shift, the Communist Party formally renounced its monopoly on power on 7 February 1990. However, Gorbachev quickly found himself outflanked by the former Communist Boris Yeltsin, who became chair of the Russian Supreme Soviet in May 1990. While Gorbachev struggled to keep a lid on the independence movements, Yeltsin mastered the winds of nationalism and populism. Unable to mollify Lithuanian nationalists, Gorbachev used force against the tiny Baltic republic in January 1991. The subsequent bloodshed brought on international condemnation and weakened Gorbachev's position vis-à-vis Yeltsin. The crisis in Vilnius did little to discourage independence movements elsewhere, serving rather to enflame tensions.

Hoping to preserve the Soviet Union, Gorbachev introduced plans for a new union of socialist republics. On 17 March 1991, Soviet citizens strongly backed preservation of the union in a modified form (although the Baltic States, Armenia, Georgia, and Moldova boycotted the referendum). In June, Boris Yeltsin won Russia's first genuine democratic election, becoming president of the Russian Soviet Federative Socialist Republic; he handily defeated the Gorbachev-backed Communist Party candidate Nikolay Ryzhkov.

As summer set in, plans for the new entity moved at a rapid pace. However, the signing of the new union treaty never occurred. On the day before it was to be made law, Communist Party hard-liners and members of the KGB attempted to take control of the government. Gorbachev, vacationing at his dacha in Crimea, was held hostage during the crisis. Out of sight, he was quickly upstaged by Yeltsin, who turned the situation to his advantage and rallied the masses against the putsch-ists. Ironically, the attempted coup produced exactly what it intended to avoid, the breakup of the USSR.

In the following months, Gorbachev was eclipsed by Yeltsin. Dem-onstrating his independent power base, Yeltsin recognized the indepen-dence of the Baltic States, thus beginning the dissolution of the USSR. In early December, the leaders of Russia, Ukraine, and Belarus met outside Minsk where they signed the Belavezha Accords, effectively seceding from the Soviet Union and establishing the Commonwealth of Independent States (CIS). Over the next two weeks, the remaining republics abandoned the Soviet Union in favor of independence and membership in the CIS. Gorbachev, recognizing the end of his tenure, resigned as president on 24 December 1991. The following day, the Soviet Union passed out of existence.

The Yeltsin Era (1992–1999)

Russia entered 1992 as an independent state, while the USSR failed to survive long enough to witness its 70th anniversary. As president of the newly independent Russian Federation, Boris Yeltsin saw economic reform as his first priority, widening and deepening the experiment begun under Gorbachev. Under the influence of Western economists, Yeltsin and his team of young reformers pursued a "shock therapy" model for the Russian economy.

With Prime Minister Yegor Gaydar at the helm, Russia introduced neoliberal reforms, slashed price subsidies, stripped down the welfare and health-care systems, and allowed the ruble to float. In order to promote the emergence of a market economy, the Yeltsin administra-tion aggressively pursued privatization. In its first stage, this process employed a scheme whereby vouchers were issued to Russian citizens. The goal was to transfer the state's wealth to the people, but the actual result was the consolidation of ownership by existing managers, former

Soviet *nomenklatura*, and well-connected entrepreneurs with access to capital. During this period, Russian organized crime infiltrated the economy and industry, even at the highest levels. Liberalization of the economy brought hardship to most Russians as inflation skyrocketed and factories closed; the precipitous drop in defense spending hit the workforce particularly hard.

Backed by growing discontent among certain segments of the populace, conservative parliamentarians moved against Yeltsin in 1993. The dispute, commonly referred to as the Constitutional Crisis, escalated quickly when members of the Congress of People's Deputies recognized Yeltsin's Vice President Aleksandr Rutskoy as the country's executive. After a tense standoff, Yeltsin ordered military action against the opposition members. The army shelled parliament, where the opposition was holed up, before storming the building and arresting the ringleaders. The two branches of parliament, the Supreme Soviet and the Congress of People's Deputies, were subsequently abolished. Shortly thereafter, the new constitution was passed. The legislature was also reconstituted as the Federal Assembly of Russia, divided between the upper house, known as the Federation Council, and the lower house, or State Duma. The radical Liberal Democratic Party of Russia (LDPR), led by the colorful Vladimir Zhirinovsky, and Gennady Zyuganov's newly formed Communist Party of the Russian Federation (KPRF) dominated the Duma when the new parliament was seated. From 1994 onward, Yeltsin grappled with the forces of Soviet nostalgia and ultranationalism, both of which were growing as the pain of transition became more apparent.

After independence, Russia faced numerous challenges as it crafted an entirely new foreign policy. As the largest and most populous post-Soviet state, Russia naturally assumed the USSR's permanent seat on the United Nations (UN) Security Council. With the assistance of the United States, all nuclear weapons on former Soviet soil were transferred to Russia as well. With the Cold War over, Russia expanded its relations with historic enemies such as Turkey, Japan, and South Korea. Under the influence of Foreign Minister Andrey Kozyrev (1990–1996), Moscow pursued an Atlanticist foreign policy, hoping to bind Russia to Western Europe and North America. During the first years of independence, Russia increased cooperation with the EU and NATO in its bid to become a "normal European country."

Embracing the former Soviet republics as equals proved more difficult. Conversely, economic domination and geopolitical manipulation often defined Russia's relations with the Newly Independent States. A flurry of separatist conflicts (Nagorno-Karabakh, Transnistria, South Ossetia, and Abkhazia), as well as civil wars in Georgia and Tajikistan, allowed Russia to deploy peacekeepers from 1991 onward; these troops proved to be a handy mechanism for exerting influence over the Commonwealth of Independent States. The Kremlin also used the presence of 25 million ethnic Russians in the post-Soviet republics as a lever of power, particularly in the Baltic States. Subsidized oil and natural gas, as well as a suite of CIS-related initiatives, allowed the Kremlin to wield extensive political control over the post-Soviet region, despite American, Chinese, and European attempts to displace the Russians.

Besides the economy and foreign affairs, Yeltsin also had to deal with the prickly question of federalism. On 31 March 1993, the Kremlin adopted a series of agreements to address the concerns of regional elites and the country's national minorities. The new dynamic weakened the power of the federal government and provided significant economic, cultural, and legislative autonomy to Russia's administrative units. Moscow retained control of currency, finance and banking, communications, justice, and space exploration, while sharing responsibility for the environment, historic preservation, education, and key areas of the national economy. The ethnic republics, in particular, gained substantive control of their own affairs, while the oblasts received less independence, thus creating a system of asymmetrical federalism. Despite such dramatic devolution of power to the periphery, Tatarstan and the self-declared Chechen Republic of Ichkeriya refused to sign the new agreement, precipitating friction between Moscow and both regions.

As he moved toward his reelection campaign, Yeltsin's advisors prompted the president to launch a war in Chechnya to reincorporate the breakaway republic into the federation. Despite promises from top military brass, the first Chechen War proved to be neither short nor popular, and dragged the economy down further. It also exposed Russia—particularly the North Caucasus and surrounding hinterlands—to terrorist attacks, hostage taking, radical Islam, and arms trafficking. The Budyonnovsk hospital crisis of June 1995 epitomized the widening effects of the conflict, as Shamil Basayev and his fellow Chechen rebels took more than 1,500 civilians hostage, resulting in the deaths of 129 people.

Desperate for cash as the result of military spending and economic mismanagement, the government auctioned off shares of major state enterprises such as Sibneft, Yukos, and Norilsk Nickel for loans, redistributing much of the country's mineral wealth and industry into the hands of the so-called oligarchs (Boris Berezovsky, Mikhail Khodorkovsky, and Roman Abramovich, among others). As these tycoons amassed their fortunes, they expanded their political power.

Going into the 1996 presidential election, Yeltsin suffered from abysmal popularity ratings. He was forced to forge an array of alliances with these oligarchs to gain access to enough capital and influence to mount a viable campaign against the Communist Party candidate Zyuganov. The skillful use of political technologies, Western-style media framing, and popular fear that the KPRF would lead the country toward civil unrest and into a new Cold War allowed Yeltsin to scrape by in the first round. After co-opting the popular military figure Aleksandr Lebed, Yeltsin decisively defeated his opponent Zyuganov in the second poll.

In the wake of the presidential elections, the Russian and Chechen leadership agreed to the Khasav-Yurt Accord, bringing an end to the war in the North Caucasus. However, Yeltsin's second term was soon marred by the 1998 ruble crisis, which wiped out many Russians' savings and savaged the already flagging economy. Additionally, the Russian stock market plummeted and unemployment jumped. Yeltsin, whose victory in the elections had not signaled renewed popularity, capitulated to the forces of nationalism and anti-globalization to stave off impeachment.

After failing to get his chosen appointee into the job, Yeltsin picked Yevgeny Primakov as his prime minister. Primakov, who had been foreign minister from 1996 until 1998, had already steered the country away from its pro-European stance toward closer ties with Muslim and Asian countries, particularly Iran and the People's Republic of China (PRC). As head of the government, he stridently opposed NATO action in the former Yugoslavia and expansion of the organization into the Baltic region. Recognizing Yeltsin's weakness, Primakov positioned himself as the president's successor despite poor personal relations between the two politicians.

Plagued by low popularity ratings, poor health, and the looming threat of impeachment, Yeltsin began paving the way for his successor in 1999. He plucked Vladimir Putin, a former KGB agent, from obscurity and then placed him in one important post after another before appointing him prime minister. Growing violence in the North Caucasus, particularly Shamil Basayev's invasion of oil-rich Dagestan, and a spate of apartment bombings in Moscow and other cities, allowed the positioning of Putin as a law-and-order politico. By launching the popular second Chechen War in October, Putin guaranteed his political future. On 31 December 1999, Yeltsin unexpectedly stepped down and appointed Putin as the acting president of the Russian Federation.

The Putin Era and Beyond (2000–Present)

Vladimir Putin assumed the presidency in debt to his patron Yeltsin. As a quid pro quo, Putin issued a decree protecting the former president and his family from corruption charges. Three months later on 26 March 2000, Putin won the presidential poll with 53 percent of the vote, becoming the second popularly elected president of the Russian Federation. For the outside world—as well as for many Russians—Putin represented a conundrum: little was known about him other than his KGB background. Most Russians greeted with enthusiasm the teetotaling judo enthusiast after years of rule by the chronically ill and infamously drunken Yeltsin. Putin promised to end Russia's slide toward chaos (*bespredel*) and immediately moved to construct what he referred to as a "vertical of power." The first step was to dismantle the federation's convoluted system of asymmetrical federalism. The president quickly gained the right to dismiss the heads of the country's federal subjects and began the process of bringing regional law into harmony with federal laws.

Putin then moved against the oligarchs, demanding they avoid direct involvement in Russian politics in return for the safety of their vast fortunes. Over the next several years, a number of oligarchs would lose their fortunes or be forced into exile, including Vladimir Gusinsky, Boris Berezovsky, and Mikhail Khodorkovsky. In order to further weaken the Yeltsin-era tycoons, Putin aided the rise of a competitive clique of pro-Kremlin magnates with close ties to the "power ministries" (the

Federal Security Service [FSB], the military, and the Ministry of Internal Affairs [MVD]).

After an initial honeymoon period, Putin faced his first and only public relations nightmare: the *Kursk* submarine disaster of 2000. However, he quickly recovered from the mishandled crisis, focusing the country on its "war against terror." Spillover from the Chechen conflict continued to translate into bombings, kidnappings, and hostage taking across the country. Putin's tough talk and liberal use of force, however, met with wide approval, as did his muzzling of the media after the Nort-Ost theater siege in 2002. In the wake of the 9/11 attacks on the United States, he was also able to persuade Western governments to view Chechnya as an important node in the global Islamist terror network. This diplomatic coup followed the expansion of the Shanghai Cooperation Organization's efforts to combat extremism in Central Asia.

In the wake of the Beslan hostage crisis, Putin enacted his sweeping 2004–2005 electoral reforms, which gave the president the right to appoint regional governors and consolidated the political party system in the Duma. Collectively, these reforms strengthened Russia's executive branch and expanded Putin's personal power. While major combat operations in Chechnya wound down after the first year of fighting, the counterterrorism campaign continued. The FSB, the KGB's successor, conducted a number of covert actions against Chechen militants, including the killings of the Saudi-born terrorist Ibn al-Khattab (2002), former President Aslan Maskhadov (2004), and Shamil Basayev (2006). Extrajudicial killings in Qatar and elsewhere, however, harmed Russian relations with certain foreign countries.

With anti-Americanism rising on the global stage in the wake of the Iraq War (2003–present), Putin expanded ties with the French and German governments, while criticizing the unipolarity of international politics. Russia's ratification of the Kyoto Protocol won him more kudos from Berlin and Paris. As U.S. President George W. Bush drew the ire of the world community for his unilateral actions and failure to locate the "promised" weapons of mass destruction in Iraq, Putin saw his own position buttressed.

Through a combination of economic power and geopolitics, Putin expanded Russian influence over the near abroad, especially during his second term when Uzbekistan—long suspicious of Moscow—returned to the fold following its bloody crackdown against Islamists. However, Russia experienced a weakening of its influence in portions of the post-Soviet world, particularly in Georgia and Ukraine, after their "color revolutions" in 2003 and 2004, respectively; however, Moscow maintained some level of control through natural gas exports. Reacting to what the Kremlin perceived as "Western meddling," Russia successfully shored up the dictatorial regime in its union partner Belarus to prevent a similar outcome.

At home, Putin's approval ratings as president rarely dropped below 65 percent and often ran as high as 85 percent. Playing to Soviet nostalgia and the "brown" fringe of society, he touted nationalism at home and began a modest rehabilitation of Joseph Stalin. A soft cult of personality, which positioned the new president as a post-Soviet celebrity, also swept the country, with Putin-themed products and songs, as well as emulations of his active, abstemious lifestyle. Putin's "strong hand," when combined with high oil and natural gas prices, proved irresistible to the electorate, especially given his favorable coverage in the now-pliant press.

During his second administration, Putin became more strident in his defense of "sovereign democracy," both in Russia and the increasingly authoritarian states of Central Asia. Russia's weak civil society withered further, particularly after the Kremlin began funding its own youth movements and pseudo-nongovernmental organizations (NGOs), while simultaneously disrupting the activities of foreign-backed NGOs. The arrest of oligarch and philanthropist Mikhail Khodorkovsky in October 2004 debilitated local sources of support for grassroots organizations. Physical intimidation, increasingly restrictive regulations, the use of selective tax evasion prosecution, and a number of unsolved murders of journalists hobbled the once-free press in Russia, further weakening the social fabric of the country.

Despite the withering of civil society and the suffocation of liberal pluralism, the people of Russia continued to support the direction in which their country was headed. This was due in no small part to the booming economy. Russia's gross domestic product doubled during the Putin years. Industry—particularly arms manufacturing, mining, and energy—grew as did salaries, while unemployment noticeably decreased. A new middle class developed, though the wealth gap remained a problem and inflation remained a perennial issue. Furthermore, Russia's so-called national champions (large enterprises such as Gazprom, Lukoil, and Norilsk Nickel) became major players in the global economy.

In the late Putin era, Russia resumed the role of global superpower through a number of new initiatives: expansion of arms exports and diplomatic support to a number of unpopular regimes including Venezuela, Syria, and Iran; resumption of long-range bomber missions; military expansion in the Arctic Ocean in order to lay claim to valuable shipping routes and energy resources in coming decades; and joint military exercises with the PRC and other allies. The choice of Sochi as the site of the 2014 Olympic Winter Games also reinforced Russia's return to international respectability.

On 7 May 2008, Dmitry Medvyedev, Putin's heir apparent, became the Russian Federation's third popularly elected president. The following day, he appointed Putin as prime minister. Unlike Putin, who had enjoyed the benefits of high oil prices, Medvyedev was almost instantly hobbled by the global economic recession. The 2008 South Ossetian War, while popular at home, harmed the economy and sent Russian relations with the West into a deep freeze. While the economy is on the mend, as are ties to Europe and the United States, the country's future remains uncertain, particularly given the ambiguity associated with the Medvyedev-Putin diarchy, wryly referred to in Russian political circles as the "ruling tandem."

Since taking office, Medvyedev has generally avoided direct confrontation with his mentor, Putin. However, the current president has strongly condemned Russia's economic dependence on the very hydrocarbons that salvaged the country's international standing after the debilitating 1998 ruble crisis. This position contrasts strongly with the prevailing notion under Putin that Russian power comes from its oil and natural gas.

The most dramatic departure came when Medvyedev decried the anemic state of Russian civil society. In his criticism, he obliquely attributed the state of affairs to his predecessor's crackdown on domestic NGOs and international agencies like the British Council and George Soros's Open Society Institute. Medvyedev has also been more realistic about the human rights situation in his country, calling it "less than perfect." While these comments may seem to be minor deviations from the status quo, such sentiments do signal a decision to at least slow Russia's return to authoritarianism in the new millennium and promote a more economically advanced society in the coming decades. It is likely that Medvyedev is also seeking to build a separate power base by putting together a coalition of commercial elites who realize that good relations with the EU, Japan, and the United States are good for business.

Medvyedev's reforms remain in the developmental stage; however, it is clear that he is moving ahead with his program to improve the country's judicial and legal system, with the aim of improving tax collection, promoting increased foreign investment, and making government officials more accountable for their actions. In his speeches, Medvyedev consistently links together the economy, the demographic situation, and democratization. He hopes to improve all three simultaneously, while also addressing instability in the North Caucasus.

Such an agenda may prove unpalatable to Russia's new oligarchs, that is, those members of the security services and other "power" agencies who have amassed their fortunes under Putin. If this happens, Medvyedev will certainly fail in any bid for reelection, particularly if he has to run against his old patron. Yet, Medvyedev may not disappear from the political scene entirely after the next round of presidential elections. His youthfulness, optimism, corporatist bearing, and Internet savvy provide him with a strong suite of attributes that symbolize the "new Russia," a confident country that is sloughing off the mental shackles of a moribund ideology and moving beyond the historical wreckage of the 20th century.

The Dictionary

500 DAYS PROGRAM. The 500 Days Program (*programma "500 dnei"*) was the colloquial name for the partially implemented economic reform plan intended to transition the Soviet **economy** from a command-and-control system to a more market-based economy. Published in the late summer of 1991, the original report upon which the program was based was known as "Transition to the Market," which envisaged a 400-day timetable for implementation. The plan's main architects were **Grigory Yavlinsky**, who went on to become a major voice for economic liberalization in post-Soviet Russia, and the free-market advocate Stanislav Shatalin. Modeled on **Poland**'s "**shock therapy**" model of rapid transition, the program called for huge budget cuts for the **KGB** and **military**, mass **privatization**, an end to price-fixing by the state, and integration into the world economic system. While the program received strong backing from Russian leader **Boris Yeltsin**, **Mikhail Gorbachev** was less enthusiastic. Owing to harsh criticism of the plan by conservative Prime Minister Nikolay Ryzhkov and delays in the **Supreme Soviet**, the 500 Days Program was watered down and a timetable for implementation was abandoned.

1996 PRESIDENTIAL ELECTION. As **Boris Yeltsin** had been elected president of the **Russian Soviet Federative Socialist Republic** on 12 June 1991, the 1996 presidential poll represented the first postindependence opportunity for the Russian people to select their executive. Following the difficult transition to a market **economy**, Russia's weakened international position, and the disastrous effects of the first **Chechen War**, Yeltsin entered the campaign with abysmally low popularity ratings. Conversely, the well-organized **Communist Party of the Russian Federation**'s (KPRF) candidate

Gennady Zyuganov enjoyed significant support, particularly among the **military**, former members of the **security services**, and disaffected quarters of the population such as the elderly and rural poor. The radical nationalist **Vladimir Zhirinovsky** was also popular in early polls.

Certain elements within Yeltsin's inner circle urged the president to cancel the elections and govern the country as dictator. However, Yeltsin rejected this approach, opting instead to delegate power to his daughter **Tatyana Dyachenko** and the head of the **privatization** campaign, **Anatoly Chubais**. By instituting the **loans for shares program**, Chubais was able to win over the support of a significant portion of the country's entrepreneurs and managers, who benefited from the accelerated program of privatization of enterprises in the lead-up to the poll.

Through their control of the **media** and flush with cash, Yeltsin's key allies painted Zhirinovsky as a buffoon and Zyuganov as a bloodthirsty warmonger. Recognizing discontent with his policies, Yeltsin promised to end the war in **Chechnya**, increase spending on social welfare, and abandon his most controversial economic reforms. In the provinces, Yeltsin bought off local administrators to win votes. Meanwhile, Dyachenko worked closely with three American political consultants (George Gorton, Dick Dresner, and Joe Shumate) to develop a Western-style campaign based on political advertising, replete with "truth squads," focus groups, public relations appearances on television, and message framing. After refusing to engage in so-called black PR, Yeltsin, who suffered a heart attack in early June, ultimately consented to running a negative campaign against the Communists in the last months before the first round of the elections.

Fearful that the KPRF would plunge the country back into a cold war with the West by trying to recapture the **near abroad** and/or provoke a civil war by renationalizing the country's industries and jailing its entrepreneurs, many voters shifted to Yeltsin at the last moment, despite their obvious displeasure with his first administration. In the first round of voting on 16 June 1996, which saw a turnout of more than two-thirds of the electorate, Yeltsin claimed a narrow plurality (35 percent) over Zyuganov (32 percent), thus forcing a runoff. Yeltsin moved quickly to consolidate his position by appointing the third-place finisher, the populist former general **Aleksandr Lebed**, to the position of national security advisor. With Lebed's forces in tow and the support of liberals who had previously voted for **Grigory Yavlinsky**, Yeltsin won a majority (53.8 percent) of the vote in the 3 July runoff election, though Zyuganov won a commanding share of the vote in Russia's agroindustrial **Red Belt**.

1998 ECONOMIC CRISIS. *See* RUBLE CRISIS.

2004–2005 ELECTORAL REFORMS. *See* ELECTORAL RE-FORMS OF 2004–2005.

– A –

ABKHAZIA. An autonomous republic of **Georgia**. During the Soviet era, Abkhazia existed as an **Autonomous Soviet Socialist Republic** (ASSR) within the Georgian Soviet Socialist Republic. Due to its geographic location on the **Black Sea** coast and warm **climate**, the region functioned as the "Soviet Riviera" during the second half of the 20th century. During 1989, tension over educational policy in the region between **Orthodox** Georgians and the Abkhaz—a **Muslim** Caucasian people closely related to the **Cherkess**—sparked **ethnic violence**, resulting in more than a dozen deaths. Georgia's boycott of the March 1991 **all-Union referendum** and overwhelming Abkhazian support for remaining within the Union of Soviet Socialist Republics (USSR) further enflamed tensions as the Soviet Union collapsed.

In 1992, Georgia's restoration of its pre-Soviet 1921 constitution triggered fears among the Abkhaz that their region's autonomous status was in jeopardy. Abkhazia's Supreme Soviet then declared the republic's independence from Georgia, prompting an invasion by the Georgian military. After an initial Georgian victory, volunteers from the **Confederation of Mountain Peoples of the Caucasus** rallied to the Abkhaz cause. The **separatists** also received tacit support and covert **military** aid from Russia. A year later, separatists retook the Abkhazian capital Sukhumi in a bloody battle that nearly took the life of then-Georgian President **Eduard Shevardnadze**. Ethnic cleansing of Georgians followed the Abkhazian victory, with nearly the entire Georgian and Mingrelian population fleeing the republic.

The 1994 Agreement on the Ceasefire and Disengagement of Forces turned Abkhazia into a state within a state, allowing the region de facto sovereignty. On 30 November 1994, Abkhazia's new constitution declared its independence from Georgia. Sanctions imposed by the **Commonwealth of Independent States** (CIS) in 1994 hobbled the economy during the mid-1990s. However, Russia's informal opening of trade in 1997 funneled money and tourists into the region. **Moscow** exercised increasing influence over the region during the administration of **Vladimir Putin**, granting Russian Federation citizenship to nearly 90 percent of the republic's population and expanding trade and transportation links. The presence of CIS **peacekeeping** troops in the region, principally comprised of Russian soldiers, also served to place Abkhazia in Russia's sphere of influence within the **Caucasus**.

Mikheil Saakashvili, who came to power after the 2003 Rose Revolution, made Tbilisi's reassertion of authority in the breakaway republics of Abkhazia, **South Ossetia**, and **Ajaria** a central plank of his presidential administration. However, his condemnation of Moscow's meddling in Georgia's internal affairs, combined with the country's push to join the **North Atlantic Treaty Organization** (NATO), resulted in Russia's expansion of its backing of both the Abkhazian and South Ossetian regimes (Saakashvili reestablished control over Ajaria in 2004 and oversaw the departure of Russian troops in 2007). Tensions between Moscow and Tbilisi were further strained in 2006 by Georgia's move into the Kodori Gorge, in violation of the 1994 cease-fire agreement.

After the 2008 **South Ossetian War** between Russia and Georgia, Russian President **Dmitry Medvyedev** formally announced his country's recognition of Abkhazia as an independent state. While the decision to recognize Abkhazia's statehood was condemned in many Western capitals, the move was backed by **Belarus** and other Russian allies. To date, Guatemala and **Venezuela** are the only other **United Nations** members to formally recognize Abkhazian statehood. In mid-September 2008, Russia further solidified its relationship with the breakaway republic by signing a military agreement to guard the republic's borders and making plans to build a military base in the region. *See also* COLOR REVOLUTIONS; ETHNIC VIOLENCE.

ABRAMOVICH, ROMAN ARKADYEVICH (1966–). Oligarch. Born into a **Jewish** family in the provincial capital of **Saratov**, Abramovich was orphaned as a young child. As a result, he lived with his relatives in various parts of the Union of Soviet Socialist Republics (USSR), including **Komi** in the Russian **Far North**. He left university studies before obtaining a degree, though he later earned a correspondence degree from Moscow State Law Academy. In the late 1980s, when **Mikhail Gorbachev's perestroika** reforms permitted private enterprises, Abramovich began his business career specializing in black market goods before moving into the **oil** trade.

In 1995, together with **Boris Berezovsky**, he acquired a controlling interest in the Sibneft oil company through the controversial **loans for shares** program. Through Berezovsky, he also developed a relationship with **Boris Yeltsin's** inner circle, known as "the Family," and was particularly close to **Tatyana Dyachenko**. Abramovich and Berezovsky later fell out over business dealings. Eventually, Abramovich's business empire grew to include **Aeroflot** airlines, aluminum plants, automobile manufacturers, a television station, food processing companies, real estate firms, and other concerns.

Indicted in several trials and fraud investigations, Abramovich has always managed to avoid conviction. In 2002, he acquired immunity from persecution by becoming an elected governor of **Chukotka**. During his tenure as governor (2000–2008), he invested over a billion dollars into the region, boosting local incomes and curbing **unemployment**. In 2005, he sold a lump share of Sibneft to the state-owned **Gazprom**. That year, he was reappointed as Chukotka's governor by President **Vladimir Putin**, with whom he reportedly had a close working relationship. Abramovich resigned his governorship immediately after **Dmitry Medvyedev** was inaugurated in 2008.

Ranked as one of the world's richest figures according to *Forbes* magazine, Abramovich owns property in Russia and Europe, and mainly resides in **Great Britain**, where he is considered to be the second-richest person. He owns Millhouse Capital, a British-registered investment fund that manages his vast holdings. He also owns Chelsea Football Club, an English premiership football team, which accounts for his global fame. He frequently appears in the British and Russian tabloid press in relation to his extensive personal security detail, taste for fine art, and massive expenditures on cars, homes, and yachts.

ADOPTIONS. *See* INTERNATIONAL ADOPTION.

ADYGEYA, REPUBLIC OF. An **ethnic republic** of the Russian Federation. An autonomous **oblast** under the Soviet Union, Adygeya was elevated to the status of republic of the Russian Federation on 3 July 1991. The first president of the republic was Aslan Jarimov. Adygeya is part of the Southern **Federal District** and the North Caucasus **Economic Region**. An enclave within the **Krasnodar Krai** in the northern foothills of the **North Caucasus**, Adygeya is a heavily forested area of 7,600 square kilometers. The republic, though one of Russia's poorest regions in terms of gross regional product per capita, is rich in **oil** and **natural gas**. The republic's **economy** is primarily based on **agriculture**, with wheat, sugar beets, tobacco, rice, and fruits being the major crops. Animal husbandry, including horse breeding, is also important. In the industrial sector, furniture manufacture and metalworking are the leading sectors. The capital city, Maykop (pop. 157,000), was founded as a Russian outpost in 1857.

The titular nationality of the republic is the **Adyghe**, an indigenous Caucasian people sometimes called **Circassians** (a loose categorization that also includes the **Cherkess** and **Kabardins**). Of the republic's 447,000 inhabitants, only 24 percent are Adyghe; **ethnic Russians** represent a majority of the population (65 percent). The republic is strongly committed to preserving the cultural traditions of the Circassian peoples though museums, festivals, and theater. Over the past several years, the Union of Slavs, a nongovernmental organization supporting the interests of Russians and **Ukrainians** in Adygeya, has been actively campaigning for the republic to be fully integrated into the Krasnodar Krai, a proposal opposed by the titular minority that has controlled the local government apparatus since Russia's independence. The move for unification has not been met with support in **Moscow**, though the Head of the Southern Federal District, Dmitry Kozak, strongly favored the plan.

The former president, Khazret Sovmen, stepped down in 2006 in the midst of a fierce political battle over the status of the republic. Sovmen, a university professor and gold miner, was an enigmatic figure, in part due to the fact that he was one of Russia's richest men governing one of its poorest regions. He reputedly was engaged in informal negotiations to merge the republic with Krasnodar when in Moscow, while vociferously denouncing the idea when at home. The current president, Aslan Tkhakushinov, a political appointee of **Vladimir Putin** who has been in office since 2007, strongly opposes the change in designation.

ADYGHE. Ethnic group. The Adyghe, or Adygs, are a nationality of the northwest **Caucasus** region living principally in the **Republic of Adygeya**, where they represent 24 percent of the population, **Kabardino-Balkariya**, where they represent 55 percent of the population, and the **Karachay-Cherkess Republic**, where they represent 11 percent of the population. Worldwide, the Adyghe community—including the diaspora—is estimated at 2.9 million, with the largest community, known as the *Muhajirs* (Arabic: "refugees" or "emigrants"), living in **Turkey**.

Sometimes called **Circassians** or Cherkessians, Adyghe are traditionally a warlike people whose values of bravery, dignity, and honor are affirmed through an orally transmitted code of rigid and complex customs and social norms called *Adyghe Xabza*. Adyghe are Sunni **Muslims**, but elements of pre-Islamic paganism persist among many communities. Adyghe speak **languages** from the Northwest Caucasian family, which includes Adyghe, Kabardian, Abkhaz, Abaza, and the recently extinct Ubykh.

The republican social movement Adyghe Khase, established under **glasnost**, represents the premier nongovernmental organization intended to advance the interests of the Adyghe in the Russian Federation. While it promoted independence in the past, its current mission is to facilitate the "integration of the peoples of the **North Caucasus**, protection of their cultural-ethnic and socioeconomic rights and interests, and preservation of originality of the North Caucasian people." However, recent studies show that support for **separatism** among Adyghe remains close to 50 percent.

AEROFLOT—RUSSIAN AIRLINES. One of the oldest airlines in the world, Aeroflot was established by the Soviet regime in 1923 and remains Russia's de facto national carrier. The airline is based at **Moscow**'s Sheremetyevo International Airport and operates in nearly 50 countries; it remains an important carrier for connecting Moscow to the cities of the **Commonwealth of Independent States**. While under state control, the airline was the world's largest. However, the firm was semiprivatized after the **dissolution of the Soviet Union**, and today ranks as one of the most profitable carriers in operation. During the 1980s, President **Ronald Reagan** banned Aeroflot from operating in the **United States** in retaliation for the Soviet **air force**'s downing of Korean Air Flight 007 in 1983; service resumed in 1990. Despite a rebranding campaign, the carrier retained its iconic hammer-and-sickle logo, reminiscent of Aeroflot's Soviet origins. *See also* ABRAMOVICH, ROMAN; BEREZOVSKY, BORIS.

AFGHANISTAN (RELATIONS WITH). Russian involvement in Afghanistan dates to the 19th-century geopolitical struggle for Eurasian dominance with **Great Britain**, known as the "Tournament of Shadows" or "Great Game." With the incorporation of **Central Asia** into the tsarist empire (1860–1885), Russia sought to exert control over the ethnically and politically fractured country. In the wake of the Bolshevik Revolution, Moscow supplied the Afghans with **arms** and money, hoping to undermine Britain's influence. During the 1950s, cooperation between the Soviet and Afghan regimes expanded greatly.

In 1978, the People's Democratic Party of Afghanistan (PDPA) staged a coup and instituted a series of radical reforms; the PDPA also signed a treaty of friendship with Moscow. Under the auspices of the new relationship, the Union of Soviet Socialist Republics (USSR) committed troops to the country in late 1979 to secure the unpopular PDPA regime under threat of an overthrow by **Islamist** guerillas, known as mujahideen, initiating the **Soviet-Afghan War**. Within a year, the Soviets were drawn into a full-fledged occupation of the country that would last until 1989. During the 1980s, Afghanistan's foreign policy mirrored that of the USSR, and the country was a reliable member of the **Eastern Bloc** of nations. Upon his ascendency, **Mikhail Gorbachev** began a withdrawal of troops from the country and directed the Afghan leadership to pursue a policy of national reconciliation.

After withdrawal, Moscow continued to support the regime of Muhammad Najibullah, including the provision of **military** aid transferred from vacated sites in Eastern Europe. As the country descended into a civil war that lasted from 1992 until 1996, Russia maintained contacts with a number of contenders for power. When the Pakistani-backed Islamists known as the Taliban emerged victorious, **Boris Yeltsin** threw his support behind the Northern Alliance, led by the anti-Soviet mujahideen leader Ahmad Shah Masood, in an attempt to protect Russia's interests in Central Asia.

Beginning in the mid-1990s, Russian military personnel and border guards in **Tajikistan** were drawn into skirmishes with Taliban forces. Yeltsin feared a spillover of radical Islamism from Afghanistan into Russia's neighbors, which share historical and ethnic ties with the country. Additionally, the Kremlin resented the Taliban's support of **Chechen separatists**. In the wake of the **September 11** attacks, **Vladimir Putin** signaled his approval of the **United States'** late 2001 invasion of the country, as well as Washington's plans to build air bases in **Uzbekistan** and **Kyrgyzstan**. After the conclusion of major military operations in the country, Russia sought to rebuild its long-standing partnership with Kabul.

The country's first postwar president, Hamid Karzai, expanded links with Russian businesses and the government, while suggesting that Moscow should help rebuild the country in reparation for the damage inflicted during the Soviet-Afghan War. Russia did commit to humanitarian aid and reconstruction costs in the wake of the U.S.-led invasion. Upon assuming the presidency, **Dmitry Medvyedev** has highlighted the deteriorating situation in Afghanistan, urging his fellow member states of the **Shanghai Cooperation Organization** to take collective action to shore up the country's security and ability to combat **narcotics** trafficking.

AFGHAN WAR (1979–1989). *See* SOVIET-AFGHAN WAR (1979–1989).

AGA-BURYATIYA. *See* ZABAYKALSKY KRAI.

AGRARIAN PARTY OF RUSSIA (APR). Political party. Known in Russian as the *Agrarnaia partiia Rossii* (APR), the Agrarian Party was a leftist political party dedicated to the interests of Russia's farmers and rural residents. It was one of the few parties in the Russian Federation that catered to a specific socioeconomic or interest group. Mikhail Lapshin founded the party in February 1993, and guided the APR to a respectable showing and 53 seats in the **State Duma**. Lapshin, also president of the **Altay Republic** (2002–2006), would be the party's guiding force until he stepped down in 2004.

The party originated at the behest of the All-Russian Council on Collective Farms and other stakeholders in the newly independent Russian Federation's agroindustrial complex. The party platform included the protection of farmers' rights, support for **agriculture**, and advocacy of Russia's rural residents. It sought to exercise influence on the federal government's agrarian policies and renew the centrality of the countryside in Russian society. The party possessed a strong socialist leaning, and worked to improve the status of the poor and place quotas on food imports, while supporting perpetuation of collective farming. Patriotism and pride in the motherland were also tenets of party ideology.

Not surprisingly, the APR often allied itself with the **Communist Party of the Russian Federation** (KPRF); in the mid-1990s, the two parties collectively controlled 25 percent of the Duma. The APR's popularity was halved (from 8 percent to 4 percent) in the 1995 Duma elections, bleeding support mostly to the better-organized KPRF. The party's poor showings continued into the new millennium, though the party's candidate, Nikolay Kharitonov, placed second in the 2004 presidential election, winning 13.7 percent of the vote. In 2007, the Agrarian Party failed to win any seats in the Duma and merged with the pro-government **United Russia** the following year. *See also* RURAL LIFE.

AGRICULTURE. Due to its **geography** and **climate**, agriculture in Russia is limited to approximately 7 percent of the country's territory or 1.2 million square kilometers. Despite this limitation, Russia is one of the world's largest producers of foodstuffs. The Russian Federation ranks fourth in arable land and is a major producer of the world's grain (wheat, corn, oats, and barley), sugar beets, sunflower seeds, vegetables, potatoes, fruits, beef, and milk. It is the fourth-largest international producer of wheat. The areas of the country most associated with farming include the **Chernozem** or "Black Earth" region, the **Krasnodar Krai**, the **Volga** basin, and extreme southern **Siberia**. While most of Russia's crop yield comes from products that tolerate extreme cold, tropical fruits are grown in the **Caucasus** and around the **Black Sea**.

The country's history is closely linked to agricultural policy, beginning with the long period of serfdom that ended in the mid-19th century. Under the Soviets, agricultural lands were nationalized to form state farms (*sovkhozy*) or collectivized to form collective farms (*kolkhozy*). The post–World War II period was characterized by a high degree of bureaucratization, which created massive inefficiencies, resulting in agricultural outputs that were dwarfed by per capita yields in Western Europe and North America. In the 1970s, over-reliance on mineral fertilizers and pesticides together with irrational irrigation schemes caused significant damage to the **environment** and, in some cases, rendered certain areas barren.

During the 1980s, low-level **privatization** resulted in significant improvements in production. Despite **Mikhail Gorbachev**'s reforms such as the Law on Peasant Farms in 1990, the country—long the breadbasket of Europe—became a net food importer. **Boris Yeltsin** sought to introduce market-based reforms into the agricultural sector, providing mechanisms for the creation of private farms. However, fear of economic uncertainty resulted in a slow progression toward the privatization of agriculture in the 1990s. Government subsidies continued, and the cause of the farmer became a major political issue for parties such as the **Communist Party of the Russian Federation** and the **Agrarian Party of Russia**.

During the mid-1990s, crop yields plummeted and livestock herds shrank as Russia suffered from the effects of **shock therapy**. Many Russians took to cultivating household plots to combat rising prices during the country's economic transition. As the Russian **economy** recovered under **Vladimir Putin**, the country was forced to import increasing amounts of food, particularly meat, to keep pace with demand; in 2008, Russia imported 40 percent of its food. The general failure of land reform, combined with competition resulting from *globalization*, continues to plague the sector. First, as president,

Putin's emphasis on "food security," including state intervention in pricing and continued subsidies of poorly performing farms, created problems with Russia's bid to join the World Trade Organization (WTO). Later, as prime minister, Putin has emphasized technological advancement as the key to increasing agricultural yields in the near term. *See also* FOREIGN TRADE; RURAL LIFE.

AIR FORCE. The Russian air force (*Voienno-vozdushnyie sily Rossii* or VVS), formed out of the Soviet air force, is the division of the **military** dedicated to the airborne defense of the Russian Federation. Aleksandr Zelin is the current commander of the air force's 200,000 personnel. Under **Boris Yeltsin**, the VVS was streamlined, particularly after the consolidation of the once-separate Air Defense Force. In terms of aircraft, the Sukhoi Su-27 forms the backbone of the force's fighter aircraft and also serves in reconnaissance. The Mikoyan MiG-31 is the principal interceptor. The Sukhoi Su-24 is the primary bomber. The VVS also has a large number of attack helicopters, which were used in the **Soviet-Afghan War** and the two **Chechen Wars**.

With nearly 3,000 aircraft, it is the second-largest air force in the world, behind only that of the **United States**; however, a significant percentage of these aircraft, particularly the MiG-29s, are in poor condition. In the last years of **Vladimir Putin**'s presidency, the Russian air force resumed long-range bomber missions over the **Arctic Ocean**, as well as portions of the Pacific and Atlantic oceans, prompting fears in the West of a renewed **Cold War**. During the same period, Russian military aircraft violated the air space of a number of its neighbors, including **Finland**, **Georgia**, and the **Baltic States**.

The VVS maintains a military presence at bases in Kant, **Kyrgyzstan**, and Gyumri, **Armenia**. In 2009, **Venezuela** reportedly extended an offer to establish a Russian air base on its territory, though Moscow declined. After the **South Ossetian War** in 2008, the VVS expressed interest in acquiring a new base in **Tajikistan**.

AJARIA. An autonomous republic of **Georgia**. During the Soviet era, Ajaria was an **Autonomous Soviet Socialist Republic** (ASSR) within the Georgian Soviet Socialist Republic. The region is dominated by ethnic Georgians known as Ajars, many of whom profess **Islam**. In postindependence Georgia, Ajaria was granted extensive autonomy by Tbilisi.

Under the leadership of the local strongman Aslan Abashidze, Ajaria enjoyed economic success, but also became a site of organized **crime** and **corruption**. President **Eduard Shevardnadze**, fearful of pushing Ajaria toward open revolt, did little to reestablish Georgian sovereignty over the region after establishing a *modus vivendi* with Abashidze. While Ajaria did not claim de facto statehood like Georgia's other autonomous republics, **South Ossetia** and **Abkhazia**, Abashidze did enjoy increasing Russian protection against Georgian efforts to reassert authority. In the wake of the 2003 **Rose Revolution** that swept Shevardnadze from office, Abashidze declared a state of emergency in the region, prompting suspicion that he might try to make a bid for outright independence. Facing protests at home and threats from the Georgian central government, Abashidze flew to **Moscow** to seek support from his Russian sponsors. The Russian Foreign Ministry backed Abashidze, characterizing his critics and pro-Georgian protestors as "extremists."

Despite Moscow's posturing, Georgia's new president, **Mikheil Saakashvili**, put intense pressure on the Ajarian leadership to reintegrate into Georgia's political fabric, ultimately triggering a crisis in the spring of 2004. In May, Secretary of the Russian Security Council **Igor Ivanov** visited the region in the midst of extensive protests. Within one day, Abashidze stepped down and flew to Moscow, where he remains. Shortly thereafter, the Georgian Constitution was amended to reflect greater central control over Ajaria. In 2007, Abashidze was convicted in absentia for misuse of office and embezzlement of state funds. *See also* FOREIGN RELATIONS.

ALAKBAROV, VAHID (1950–). Oligarch. Also spelled Vagit Alekperov, the **oil** magnate was born in Baku, **Azerbaijan**, to an oil worker in one of the world's oldest centers of petroleum production. After beginning a career in the petroleum industry at 18, he took a number of positions across the Union of Soviet Socialist Republics (USSR) before being appointed as the country's youngest-ever minister of oil and gas in 1990. With Russia's independence, he oversaw the creation of **Lukoil**, ultimately becoming the company's president in 1993. While retaining his position at the world's second-largest oil company where he is known as "the General," Alakbarov has also expanded his holdings in other areas, and controls interests in **banking** and **media** companies, including *Izvestiya*.

ALCOHOLISM. Alcoholism remains one of Russia's main social problems, often bemoaned as "Russia's curse." The habitual consumption of large quantities of spirits impedes economic growth and cultural development, as well as having an especially pernicious impact on the nation's demography. It is estimated that the economic damage caused by alcoholism is about $750 million per year. Alcohol-related problems annually account for between 500,000 and 900,000 deaths in Russia; it is estimated that alcohol is a factor in nearly half of all deaths of men between the ages of 25 and 54.

In the 1980s, **Mikhail Gorbachev** launched a war against alcoholism, including banning advertising of alcohol and promoting an alcohol-free lifestyle. As with many of his reforms, aspects of the alcohol-free campaign verged on the absurd; for example, many valuable vineyards in **Crimea**, **Armenia**, and **Georgia** were destroyed. While alcohol sales dipped (with an accompanying loss of tax revenues), the production of *samogon* (homemade alcohol) skyrocketed, resulting in many deaths from poisoning.

In contrast, during the 1990s, **Boris Yeltsin**'s government was generally indifferent to the alcoholism problem, enjoying high taxes from alcohol sales. Yeltsin's well-documented alcoholism resulted in a number of scandals, negatively impacting his political career. Under **Vladimir Putin**, a teetotaler, the government tried to address the issues of alcoholism by raising penalties for improper consumption of alcoholic drinks, shifting the blame for alcohol-dependent children onto their parents, and raising the population's awareness of the severity of the problem.

Though consuming alcohol—especially vodka and beer—is a traditional pastime in Russia, the problem of alcoholism had been exacerbated by the economic downturn of the 1980s and the chaos and crisis of the 1990s, causing many underprivileged Russian citizens to turn to drink. The most vulnerable members of society have been worst afflicted by the phenomenon. While support exists in the form of clinical, social, and cultural associations and awareness of the problem of addiction is on the rise, Russian society's historical tolerance to excessive alcohol consumption typically undermines the effects of antialcoholism campaigns. However, in the new millennium, there have been considerable attempts to change the image of drinking, by stressing the dangers of alcohol addiction and advocating a glamorous alcohol-free or alcohol-moderate lifestyle. Despite such efforts, alcohol consumption continues to rise. Today, Russians consume 15 liters of hard liquor per year, which is slightly below the European average and nearly twice as much as the average American. *See also* DEMOGRAPHIC CHALLENGES.

ALEXIUS II, PATRIARCH (1929–2008). Religious leader. Alexius II, also known as Aleksey II, was the 15th Patriarch of Moscow and All Rus and the Metropolitan of Tallinn, making him the effective leader of the **Russian Orthodox Church**. Elected Patriarch of Moscow in 1990, he became the first Russian patriarch of the post-Soviet period.

Born Aleksey Mikhailovich Ridiger, Alexius II was a descendant of a Baltic **German** family, with his ancestors adopting **Orthodoxy** during the reign of Catherine the Great. Aleksey's father became a refugee after the October Revolution of 1917 and settled his family in **Estonia**, where he became a priest in 1940. During the late **Stalin** era, Aleksey entered theological education; he was subsequently ordained a deacon. After serving as the highest-ranking member of the Orthodox Church in Estonia, he became the Metropolitan of Leningrad in 1986. In 1990, he was the first Patriarch in Soviet history to be chosen without government pressure. Upon his election, Alexius became a vocal advocate of the rights of the Orthodox Church, addressing to **Mikhail Gorbachev** a letter proposing reforms to state-church relations. In 1989, he was elected a people's deputy of the Union of Soviet Socialist Republics (USSR), and was involved in a number of cases undermining the role of the **Communist Party of the Soviet Union**.

During his administration, **Boris Yeltsin** developed a working relationship with the religious leader to buttress his own popularity. Under Alexius's leadership, a large number of martyrs and confessors who suffered under Communism were glorified, including Tsar Nicholas II and his family. In 2005, Alexius became the first laureate of the State Prize of the Russian Federation for humanitarian work. His work was highly praised by Russian presidents, particularly **Vladimir Putin**. President **Dmitry Medvyedev** capitalized on the patriarch's death by turning his burial into a mass spectacle, aimed at instilling a sense of national unity. Alexius II had difficult relationships with the Roman Catholic Church, particularly over property rights in **Ukraine**, which resulted from the abrupt **dissolution of the Soviet Union**. Other major controversies included his alleged links to the **KGB**, his reception of Hamas leaders from the Gaza Strip in 2006, and his strong opposition to **homosexuality** and nontraditional relations and **gender** identities in Russia. After his death on 5 December 2008, he was succeeded by **Patriarch Kirill I**. *See also* ROMANOVS.

ALL-TATAR PUBLIC CENTER. *See* TATARS.

ALL-UNION REFERENDUM (1991). In late 1990, **Mikhail Gorbachev** proposed a referendum to the Congress of People's Deputies that would determine the future of the Soviet state. Held on 17 March 1991, the poll asked the following question: "Do you consider it necessary to preserve the Union of Soviet Socialist Republics (USSR) as a renewed federation of equal sovereign republics in which **human rights** and freedoms of any nationality will be fully guaranteed?" While the **Baltic States**, **Moldova**, **Armenia**, and **Georgia** did not participate, the overall turnout was 80 percent (**Lithuania** and Georgia took the opportunity to poll their citizens on the declaration of independence from the USSR instead). More than three-quarters of all voters supported the preservation of the union. In the **Russian Soviet Federative Socialist Republic**, an additional question was added that resulted in nearly 70 percent of the electorate supporting the introduction of a directly elected president.

ALMA-ATA PROTOCOL. *See* DISSOLUTION OF THE SOVIET UNION.

ALROSA. ZAO ALROSA is Russia's diamond monopoly; the original name of the corporation is Almazi Rossii-Sakha (Diamonds of Russia-Sakha). The company is jointly headquartered in the **Sakha** town of Mirny and **Moscow**. It accounts for nearly half of Sakha's budget revenues. ALROSA mines annually produce about one-quarter of the world's diamonds. During the 1990s, ALROSA sold most of its rough diamonds through the South Africa–based De Beers diamond concern; however, a ruling by the European Commission forced the relationship to cease by 2009. ALROSA has since expanded its own marketing efforts. *See also* ARCHANGEL OBLAST.

ALTAY KRAI. An administrative province of the Russian Federation. Part of the Siberian **Federal District** and the West Siberian **Economic Region**, Altay Krai—sometimes called the "Pearl of **Siberia**"—shares a border with **Kazakhstan**, **Novosibirsk**, **Kemerovo**, and the **Altay Republic**. It has a population of 2.7 million and covers 169,000 square kilometers of foothills, mountains, and grasslands.

Established by the wealthy Demidov family in the 18th century, Barnaul (pop. 650,000) is the regional capital. The province has both heavy and light **industry** (power generation, engineering, petrochemicals, building materials, and textiles), although its **economy** has contracted significantly since 1991. Altay Krai is a major producer of **agricultural** products for Siberia, being the only Russian region in the area to grow crops such as sunflowers, soybeans, sugar beets, and certain kinds of fruit. The area's mineral-rich mountains include deposits of lead and iron ores, manganese, tungsten, bauxite, gold, and other rare elements. Forests cover much of the large territory, providing the region with rich timber reserves.

The ethnic makeup of the population is dominated by **ethnic Russians** (92 percent); however, there is a sizable community of **Germans** (4 percent), many of whom descend from Mennonites who settled in the region in the early 1900s. Descendents of early communities of **Old Believers** and **Cossacks** are also prevalent.

A former prosecutor, Aleksandr Karlin, is currently the governor of the Altay Krai administration. During his term of office, he has developed strong trade links with **Belarus**. Karlin was appointed by **Vladimir Putin** to replace Mikhail Yevdokimov, who died in a car crash in 2005.

Yevdokimov was a popular singer and stand-up comedian before assuming the governorship; he was one of only a few governors to win office against a Putin-backed competitor—the incumbent Aleksandr

Surikov—in the last years of popular elections. Yevdokimov was under pressure to resign when he was killed; his death came shortly after he suffered a no-confidence vote, which passed by a vote of 46 to 5.

While his death was not suspicious in nature, it did cause a national outcry when the driver of the other car, Oleg Shcherbinsky, was sentenced to four years of imprisonment (the decision was later overturned). The case highlighted the problem of irresponsible driving on the part of state officials, which often puts average citizens in danger; Yevdokimov's car had been traveling at a rate of more than 120 kilometers per hour. *See also* RELIGION.

ALTAY REPUBLIC. An **ethnic republic** of the Russian Federation. Known as the Gorno-Altay Autonomous **Oblast** (1948–1991) and then as the Gorno-Altay **Autonomous Soviet Socialist Republic** (1991–1992), the region was given its current name in 1992. It is part of the Siberian **Federal District** and the West Siberian **Economic Region**. The republic is situated in the center of the Asian continent between the **Siberian** taiga, the steppes of **Kazakhstan**, and **Mongolia**'s deserts. The republic also shares a short border with the Xinjiang Uyghur Autonomous Region of **China**. Internally, the republic is bordered by the **Altay Krai, Kemerovo, Khakasiya**, and **Tuva**.

Often referred to as "Russia's Tibet," Altay lays claim to Siberia's highest peak, Mount Belukha (4,506 m). Covering part of the Ob River basin, the republic is also home to the Russian portion of the Altay Mountains, the original homeland of the Turkic peoples. Its geographic area is 92,600 square kilometers. **Agriculture**, animal husbandry, **tourism**, and mineral resources form the bulk of the region's **economy**. With extensive fast-flowing rivers, the republic also has significant hydroelectric capacity. The capital, Gorno-Altaysk (pop. 53,000), is built on the site of the 19th-century village Ulala.

Altays are the titular minority, forming 31 percent of the republic's total population of 203,000 inhabitants; **ethnic Russians** account for 57 percent and **Kazakhs** represent 6 percent. The State Assembly (El Kurulrai) is the highest legislative body in the republic. Until 2001, local law stipulated that the chair of the republican government and parliamentary chairperson must be of different ethnic groups, effectively legislating that one of the two must be an ethnic Altay.

In the late 1990s, the head of the government was Semyon Zubakin; he received a vote of no confidence in 1999 for his mishandling of the region's finances. Despite a modest improvement in recent years, approximately 85 percent of the regional budget still comes from federal subsidies. Altay was one of the worst-hit regions by the 1998 **ruble crisis**; after **Chukotka** and **Koryakiya**, it suffered from the highest wage arrears in the federation. The current president is Aleksandr Berdnikov, an ethnic Russian who was appointed by **Vladimir Putin** according to Russia's new electoral laws. He replaced Mikhail Lapshin, the former leader of the **Agrarian Party of Russia** (Lapshin went on to become a member of the **Federation Council** from **Omsk**).

In 2006, the residents of the republic, led by the cultural group Ene Til (Altay: "Mother Tongue"), demonstrated against the possibility of a merger with the Altay Krai; subsequently, Berdnikov has declared that the republic will remain a distinct political unit in the future. A number of major development projects, including gas pipelines, have been proposed for the area but remain controversial due to indigenous opposition to any major alteration to the region's ecosystem.

On 1 July 2009, the Altay Republic became one of only four locales in Russia where casinos are legal (the others being the Azov region, **Kaliningrad**, and **Primorsky**).

ALTAYS. Ethnic group. The Altays, or Altaians, are a Mongol-Turkic people who principally reside in the **Altay Republic**, **Altay Krai**, **Tuva**, and **Mongolia**. In the Russian Federation, there are approximately 67,000 Altays. They were known by the ethnonym "Oyrat," until it was declared counterrevolutionary under **Joseph Stalin**, causing the usage of the term "Altay" to become standard. Until the mid-20th century, Altay **national identity** as such did not exist; instead, the various indigenous peoples of the region described themselves as Tubalars, Chelkans, Kumandins, Teleuts, Telengits, and Altai Kizhis.

Their traditional **language**, Altay, is a member of the Kyrgyz-Kypchak subgroup of Turkic languages; while native language use continues among the ethnic Altay, the majority are fluent in the **Russian language**. Altays are predominantly **shamanistic**, although a minority practice **Orthodox Christianity** or **Buddhism**. Burkhanism or *Ak Jang* (Altay: "White Faith"), a millenarian, anti-Russian faith from the early 20th century, is also seeing a revival as a political vehicle for national unification; other forms of syncretic, ecologically oriented shamanism such as Ak Suus and Ak Sanaa have also been growing in popularity, even in urban areas of the Altay.

The discovery of a 2,500-year-old Scythian mummy, later named the Ukok Maiden, in the Altay in the mid-1990s also played an important role in energizing national consciousness among ethnic Altays. A group of Altay shamans blamed the federal government for a series of earthquakes in the wake of the mummy's removal to **Moscow** and demanded the remains be returned to the Altay Republic and reburied.

Economic mismanagement and **corruption** in the Altay Republic have led to an increase in support for secession from the Russian Federation at a time when such desires are in decline in other **ethnic republics**.

AMUR OBLAST. An administrative region of the Russian Federation. Part of the Far Eastern **Federal District** and **Economic Region**, Amur borders **Zabaykalsky**, **Sakha**, **Khabarovsk**, the **Jewish Autonomous Oblast**, and **China**. It has a population of 887,600 and covers 363,700 square kilometers. The region is heavily forested and is dominated by the Amur and Zeya rivers and the Stanovoy Range. Blagoveshchensk (pop. 219,000) is the regional capital, making the region one of the few **oblasts** that does not share its name with the administrative center.

Amur's historic association with the Qing Empire until the mid-19th century and recent increases in illegal **Chinese** migration have made the region a sensitive issue in Sino-Russian relations; the prosperous Chinese city of Heihe lies just across the border. The region maintains strong trade and transportation links with China; however, cross-border trade has contributed to an increase in the sale and use of psychotropic drugs in the region. **Ethnic Russians** are the largest ethnic group (92 percent); **Ukrainians**, **Tatars**, and other ethnicities are also represented.

The region depends on **agriculture**, timber, and mineral extraction. Amur houses a heavy-bomber **air force** base and a stockpile of **nuclear weapons**. It is also the site of the Svobodny Cosmodrome.

In July 1993, the region declared itself a republic, a move not recognized by Moscow and which resulted in the dismissal of the regional executive. The current governor is Nikolay Kolesov, who was nominated after **Vladimir Putin** dismissed his predecessor, the Communist-leaning Leonid Korotkov, both for exceeding his powers and for embezzlement related to the regional football club (Aleksandr Nesterenko served as interim governor until Kolesov took office). Kolesov, a native of Kazan, has announced plans to build a new civilian spaceport in the region.

ANDROPOV, YURY VLADIMIROVICH (1914–1984). Politician. Born to a father of a Don **Cossack** noble family and a mother of ethnic **German** origin, Yury Andropov was orphaned in his teens. He joined the **Komsomol** youth organization and became a member of the **Communist Party of the Soviet Union** (CPSU) in 1939. He fought as a partisan during World War II and then climbed the party ranks in **Kareliya** before moving to **Moscow**. He was ambassador to Hungary during the 1956 revolution and played a key role in its suppression. After returning to Moscow, he was elected to the CPSU Central Committee and then assumed the directorship of the **KGB**.

Fearing a repeat of the Hungarian Revolution, Andropov took a hard line against the developments in Czechoslovakia, resulting in the draconian suppression of the "Prague Spring" of 1968. At home, he was at the forefront of the suppression of the burgeoning **dissident** movement in the Union of Soviet Socialist Republics (USSR). As a full member of the Politburo, he was a key supporter of the decision to initiate the **Soviet-Afghan War** in 1979. Upon the death of **Leonid Brezhnev**, he became general secretary of the CPSU on 12 November 1982. During his 15 months in office, he attempted to implement systemic reform through economic "acceleration" (*uskoreniie*). His administration saw a shakeup of the *nomenklatura*, with significant dismissals and personnel changes, particularly directed at **corruption**. Relations with the **United States** further deteriorated over arms control and the downing of Korean Air Flight 007 in 1983.

His health quickly deteriorated, and, before passing, he recommended that **Mikhail Gorbachev** assume control of the Politburo, effectively designating the young Communist as his heir apparent. Despite his wishes, **Konstantin Chernenko** became the next premier. Andropov died due to complications from renal failure on 9 February 1984.

ANTIGLOBALISM. *See* GLOBALIZATION.

ANTI-SEMITISM. The roots of anti-Semitism in Russia are deep. In 1791, Catherine the Great instituted the Pale of Settlement, which restricted **Jewish** residents in the lands of the former Polish-Lithuanian Commonwealth from settling in other parts of Russia. The territorial confinement served to prevent the burgeoning Jewish middle class from dominating Russia's economic life.

During the 19th century, successive tsars placed new restrictions on Jews, expelled many from Russian cities, and encouraged populist acts of religious violence, including pogroms. It was also during this period that the infamous *Protocols of the Elders of Zion* was fabricated and distributed, ostensibly by a member of the Russian secret police, as "proof" of a worldwide Jewish conspiracy. Many Jews chose to emigrate to the **United States** or Palestine, while others gravitated to revolutionary movements such as the Bund and Bolshevik Party. Among Russia's peasantry, popular resentment of the **Communist Party of the Soviet Union** and anti-Semitism were often intertwined, especially during the early period of Soviet rule and the Russian Civil War when the Whites described the Bolsheviks as a "gang of marauding Jews."

Later, under **Joseph Stalin**, many Jewish Bolsheviks were purged and a vigorous anti-Zionism campaign created new problems for the country's Jewish population. The continued conceptualization of Jews as an **ethnic minority** and not a religious population ensured that Jews, despite their high level of assimilation to Russian culture, would continue to be viewed as non-Russians. The Soviet Union's difficult relations with **Israel** further complicated the situation of Russian Jews, particularly during the Arab-Israeli wars of the second half of the 20th century.

In the late Soviet period, many Jews, colloquially known as refuseniks, attempted to emigrate to Israel but were barred by bureaucratic hurdles that were internationally condemned. With the **dissolution of the Soviet Union** in 1991, a virulent form of popular anti-Semitism found fertile ground in a society wracked by the hardships of transition to a market **economy**. **Political parties** such as the **Liberal Democratic Party of Russia** and the **Communist Party of the Russian Federation** made attacks on the mostly Jewish **oligarchs** a basic component of their populist message. **Neofascist** and neo-Nazi youth groups also fed the fire of resentment against Jews. In the past decade, attacks against synagogues and hate crimes against Jews have been on the rise (doubling in 2005), despite new legislation targeting ethnically or religiously motivated **crimes**. *See also* ZHIRINOVSKY, VLADIMIR.

APARTMENT BOMBINGS OF SEPTEMBER 1999. A series of explosions ripped through apartment blocks in the cities of **Moscow**, Buynaksk in **Dagestan**, and Volgodonsk in the **Rostov Oblast** between 4 and 16 September 1999. The death toll of the combined bombings approached 300. Occurring around the same time as **Shamil Basayev**'s incursion into Dagestan, the bombings were a key factor in Moscow's decision to embark on a second **Chechen War** later that year. According to a 2002 federal investigation, the bombings were organized by Achemez Gochiyayev, an ethnic **Karachay**, and ordered by the Arab-**Circassian Ibn al-Khattab**. A number of figures in and outside of Russia, most notably **Boris Berezovsky**, have asserted that the bombings were a false flag operation by the **FSB** to bring **Vladimir Putin** to power, though little evidence has ever been brought to light that would support such a theory.

APPARATCHIKS. The noun *apparatchik* derives from the Russian word *apparat* ("apparatus"), designating an agent or employee of one of the many organs of the Soviet state. The term defines a loyal member of the ruling elite, particularly a functionary of the **Communist Party of the Soviet Union**, and is also used in a derogatory manner to refer to a member of Soviet bureaucracy. Apparatchiks were characterized by their cronyism and social distance from the Soviet masses. They are the embodiment of Marxist theoretician Milovan Djilas's "new class" enabled by the imposition of state socialism. The term fell into disuse in the postindependence period with the emergence of new types of social and political classes, such as the **oligarchs** and the *siloviki*.

ARBATOVA, MARIYA (1957–). Feminist. Born Maria Gavrilina in 1957, Mariya Arbatova earned her name thanks to her intellectual salon in her room in the communal flat in the Arbat district of **Moscow**. Often referred to as "Russia's chief feminist," Arbatova has campaigned against sexual harassment, domestic violence, and workplace discrimination of **women**.

Arbatova was educated at the Department of Philosophy of the **Moscow State University** as well as in the arts department of the Gorky Literary Institute; she was also trained in psychoanalysis. She has authored 14 plays that have been staged in Russia and abroad, 20 books, and numerous articles in newspapers and periodicals. Since 1991 she has been involved in the Harmony Club, an association of Russian feminists who provide assistance and psychological rehabilitation for Russian women. Since 1996 she has been engaged in campaigning for a fairer representation of women in Russian **politics**. In 1999, as a member of the **Union of Right Forces**, she made an unsuccessful attempt to win election to the **State Duma** from the University District of Moscow. In 2000, she worked as a consultant for Ella Pamfilova, the first woman to be nominated for the post of the president of the Russian Federation.

Arbatova is especially famous because of her media appearances. For five years she co-hosted the popular **television** show *I, Myself* on the TV-6 channel and aired a **human rights**–related program, *The Right to Be Yourself*, on Radio Maiak. Arbatova is also known for her controversial views. In 2008 she created a scandal by publicly voicing her belief that a jailed pregnant woman should not seek amnesty. *See also* GENDER.

ARCTIC OCEAN. The Arctic Ocean is the northernmost of the world's oceans, and is almost completely surrounded by the **Eurasian** and North American landmasses. It is covered by ice most of the year; however, in recent years, global warming has resulted in less ice than in centuries past. The basin is roughly circular, and covers an area of 14,000,000 square kilometers. Russia's is the longest national coastline, comprising about half of the Arctic's total of 45,390 kilometers. Other countries with Arctic coastlines include **Canada**, the **United States**, **Norway**, and Denmark (via Greenland). A number of Russian islands are located in the Arctic Ocean, including **Novaya Zemlya**, Franz Josef Land, Severnaya Zemlya, Wrangel Island, and the New Siberian Islands.

Under **Vladimir Putin**, Russia began to aggressively defend its status as an Arctic power. A submarine mission planted a Russian **flag** on the seabed at the North Pole, and new geological expeditions have been undertaken to prove that the Lomonsonov Ridge is part of Russia's Eurasian shelf, thus expanding the country's territorial waters. Canada and Denmark both reacted harshly to the new posture. At stake are both revenues from increased transit via the ice-free portions of the ocean during the summer, and rights to future **oil** and **natural gas** exploration.

In 2009, the Kremlin announced plans to create a new **military** force dedicated to defending Russia's national interests in its northern waters. Moscow views the Arctic as potentially its top strategic resource base in future decades. Canada, the country with the second-largest Arctic coastline, and the United States have responded by beefing up their own military presence in the Arctic Circle.

ARKHANGELSK OBLAST/ARCHANGEL. An administrative region of the Russian Federation. Part of the Northwestern **Federal District** and the Northern **Economic Region**, Archangel shares a border with **Kareliya**, **Vologda**, **Kirov**, **Komi**, and **Yamaliya**; it administers **Nenetsiya** (which it also borders), as well as the Arctic islands of Franz Josef Land and **Novaya Zemlya**. The region, originally named Dvina Land, lies on the White, **Barents**, and Kara seas. It has a population of 1.3 million and covers 587,400 square kilometers.

The regional capital Arkhangelsk (Archangel) served as Russia's principal seaport until the country gained access to the **Baltic Sea**. Archangel was also the site of the Anglo-American invasion of Soviet Russia during the Russian Civil War. Once icebound during the winter, ice-breakers now enable year-round shipping and **fishing** from the port. The oblast's geography is divided between **taiga** and forests of pine, fir, larch, aspen, and birch. The regional **economy** is focused on **agriculture**, timber, and mineral extraction (diamonds, bauxite, **oil**, and **natural gas**); upward of 50 percent of the industrial **labor force** is engaged in the forestry sector. The region includes a number of important **naval** installations and is also the site of the Plesetsk Cosmodrome. The oblast is also an important site of Russia's **military-industrial** complex.

Ethnic Russians make up 94 percent of the population, with Belarusians and **Nenets** being the next largest groups, respectively. The current governor is Ilya Mikhalchuk, appointed by **Vladimir Putin** on 11 April 2008. Mikhalchuk, a member of the **United Russia** party, was previously the mayor of the **Russian Far East** city of Yakutsk, and is known for his confrontations with the governor of **Sakha**. His administration's stated goals include stamping out illegal logging and improving the region's relationship with **Gazprom**. He replaced the last popularly elected governor, Nikolay Kiselyov, the former director of a dairy plant. Kiselyov, who was elected governor in 2004, failed to secure Putin's support for another term and became one of the first governors to suffer from the **2004–2005 electoral reforms**. Prior to Kiselyov, the region was run by two-term governor Anatoly Yefremov. During his tenure, Yefremov took over direct rule of the Solovetsky Island during a period of economic crisis in 1999 and began construction of a new **nuclear energy** plant on Novaya Zemlya.

On 1 January 2008, Archangel assumed greater control of the Nenets **Autonomous Okrug** (AOk), including unification of taxation, though Nenetsiya remains a **federal subject** of the Russian Federation. Agreements on **taxation** and power sharing have proved controversial, with officials in Nenetsiya being reluctant to abandon control of lucrative natural resources in the polar region. A merger of the two units remains a distinct possibility; consolidation is strongly backed by federal authorities, who are seeking to streamline center-periphery relations, and **Lukoil**, which has had stormy relations with the leadership of the Nenets AOk.

ARMENIA (RELATIONS WITH). Armenia, formerly the Armenian Soviet Socialist Republic from 1936 until its independence from the

Soviet Union in 1991, was incorporated into the Russian empire in the early 19th century. Armenia is a small, transcontinental country in the southern **Caucasus**; it borders **Turkey**, **Georgia**, **Iran**, and **Azerbaijan**. With no contiguous border with the Russian Federation, a shared faith in Eastern **Orthodoxy**, and only a nominal **ethnic Russian** population, Armenia has been called "Russia's only ally in the south" by Foreign Minister **Igor Ivanov**.

Both Russia and Armenia are founding members of the Russian-backed **Collective Security Treaty Organization**. Russia's 102nd Military Base is located in Gyumri, Armenia, and Armenia forms part of the air defense perimeter of the **Commonwealth of Independent States** (CIS). Armenian border guards work in conjunction with the Federal Security Service (**FSB**) and regular Russian **military** personnel guard the CIS borders with Turkey and Iran. Russia has long supported the **Armenian** people against their historical enemy, the Turks.

During World War I, Ottoman Armenian support for the **Romanov** Empire was a catalyst for the Armenian Genocide of 1915; as the ethnic cleansing turned violent, tsarist Russia functioned as a refuge for tens of thousands of ethnic Armenians. Moscow's support for a nominally independent Armenian republic within the Union of Soviet Socialist Republics (USSR) in the 1930s was welcomed by the worldwide Armenian diaspora, despite totalitarian controls on the economy and society.

In the waning days of the Soviet Union, **Moscow** further ingratiated itself with the Armenian authorities and the community abroad by backing the Communist government and later independent Armenia against neighboring Azerbaijan in the Nagorno-Karabakh War (1988–1994). During the conflict, ethnic Armenian forces in the self-declared **Nagorno-Karabakh** Republic, aided by the Armenian government and Russian mercenaries, were able to wrest control of the region away from Azerbaijan and establish the Lachin Corridor to connect the region to Armenia proper. In 1994, the Russians brokered an end to formal hostilities. In the years after the conflict was frozen, Russia secretly provided **arms** and other **military** supplies to Armenia. In 1997, **Boris Yeltsin** and Levon Ter-Petrosyan signed a comprehensive "Treaty on Friendship, Cooperation, and Mutual Assistance," deepening the country's dependence on Russia.

From the mid-1990s onward, Armenia faced a crippling Azeri-Turkish blockade on its eastern and western borders. As a consequence, Armenia's economy, and particularly its energy sector, is dominated by transnational Russian interests, and in particular, **Gazprom**. Russia also controls the telecommunications and railway sectors. Remittances from the large number of Armenian guest workers in Russia are also a vital part of the country's economy.

During the second administration of **Vladimir Putin**, Russia undertook a modest realignment in the southern Caucasus, placing a greater emphasis on Azerbaijan, much to the dismay of Armenian policymakers. In this new environment, Putin put pressure on Armenian president Robert Kocharyan and Azerbaijan's head of state, Ilham Aliyev, to resolve the crisis; however, no final solution was agreed. Moscow's rapprochement with Baku brought other changes in the region as well. Yerevan is particularly distressed over the construction of the Olya-Astara-Qazvin rail line connecting Russia to Iran via Azerbaijan, thus bypassing Armenia altogether.

Armenia has compensated by expanding its diplomatic and trade links with the **United States** and Iran. Despite such efforts, Russian-Armenian relations were reaffirmed by the current president Serzh Sargsyan, who quickly shored up his relationship with Moscow in the wake of the disputed 2008 Armenian presidential elections and their violent aftermath. However, the 2008 **South Ossetian War** has severely complicated Armenia's diplomatic position, since it is so closely tied to Russia, but dependent on neighboring Georgia for international trade, as nearly three-quarters of its imports and exports pass through the **Black Sea** country.

ARMENIANS. Ethnic group. Officially numbering over 1 million, Armenians are Russia's seventh-largest nationality. Some estimates, however, suggest that upward of 2.9 million, many being unregistered guest workers, reside in the federation.

Armenians are an Indo-European people from the Southern **Caucasus**; most are Christians, adhering to the Armenian Apostolic Church founded in the 4th century, though some confess Armenian Catholicism. Worldwide, there are more than 8 million Armenians; 3.2 million reside in the Republic of **Armenia**. Armenians have been settling across the Russian lands since the late medieval period, typically occupying positions as merchants and artisans. Armenians are particularly numerous in **Moscow** and the southern regions of the federation. In **Stavropol Krai** and **Krasnodar Krai**, they account for more than 5 percent of the local population; in some areas, entire villages are ethnically Armenian.

Since 1991, Armenians, who are often of dark complexion, have been targeted for **ethnic violence** by **neo-Nazis** and ultranationalists. Punitive legal actions have also been taken against "non-Russian" merchants in recent years, which have disproportionately impacted urban Armenian communities. In a 2008 visit to the Armenian expatriate community in Moscow, Armenia's President Serzh Sargsyan advocated a policy of assimilation for his co-nationals in an effort to combat xenophobia, stating: "Being a good Armenian means being a good Russian."

There are also important divisions within Russia's Armenian community, particularly between "old" (pre-1985) Armenian settlers and newer, post-Soviet immigrants who fled the war in **Nagorno-Karabakh**. The Union of Armenians in Russia is the primary social organization catering to the diaspora. Since the mid-1990s, Russia has been granting citizenship to ethnic Armenians in the Javakheti region of **Georgia**, an action that has been criticized by Tbilisi as undermining the Caucasian state's sovereignty.

Andranik Migranyan, a key foreign policy advisor in the **Yeltsin** administration and author of the so-called **Monroeski doctrine**, is an ethnic Armenian. *See also* CHRISTIANITY; ECONOMY.

ARMS EXPORTS. The Russian Federation is the world's second-largest exporter of arms, selling to nearly 100 countries worldwide. In 2009, the country sold approximately $8 billion in **military** hardware and other weapons. Combat aircraft account for one-half of all sales. In recent years, sales to the **Middle East** and Latin America have grown rapidly. Arms sales to Syria and **Iran** have often created problems in Russia-**United States** relations. Russia has developed a special relationship with **China** and **India** for arms development. Established by Russian Presidential Decree No. 1834 on 4 November 2000, the national arms export agency is Rosoboronexport State Corporation; Russia's arms export monopoly was formerly known as Rosvooruzheniye. The AK-47, manufactured at the Izhevsk

Mechanical Works in **Udmurtiya**, remains one of the most popular assault rifles in the world. *See also* FOREIGN TRADE.

ARMY. Officially known as the Russian Ground Forces (*sukhoputnyie voiska Rossiiskoi federatsii*), the army in its current form dates to 1992 when a plan to maintain a joint military among the various members of the **Commonwealth of Independent States** broke down; however, the Russian army has a long historical tradition associated with both its Soviet and tsarist heritage. The Ground Forces are currently commanded by General of the Army Vladimir Boldyrev, who replaced Alexey Maslov in 2008.

The primary responsibility of the army is to defend the Russian Federation from aggressors as well as retain occupied territory. The major units include motorized rifle troops, tank troops, rocket forces and artillery, and special units. The Ground Forces were formed during a chaotic period shaped by the large-scale withdrawal of military units from the former **Warsaw Pact** members (1989–1991) and **Newly Independent States** (1991–1993) that formerly comprised the Union of Soviet Socialist Republics (USSR). The Russian army, however, still maintains a **peacekeeping** presence in a number of former Soviet states, including **Tajikistan**, **Moldova**, and the breakaway republics of **Abkhazia** and **South Ossetia**. Since 1991, it has served in small numbers in Croatia, Bosnia, Lebanon, and sub-Saharan Africa.

Immediate post-Soviet plans for reform were complicated by conflicting opinions among the leadership over the role and purpose of the army in a post–**Cold War** environment. The **constitutional crisis of 1993** did little to improve the image of the new force as it was drawn into a political dispute between **Boris Yeltsin** and members of the Congress of People's Deputies. Shortly thereafter, Yeltsin initiated the disastrous first **Chechen War**. The army's performance in the conflict was universally lambasted. The Ground Forces' difficulty in taking the capital Grozny, abuses of civilian populations, **criminal** behavior including selling weapons to insurgents, and numerous desertions of soldiers diminished the army's reputation in the country at large.

A series of reforms instituted in 1997 did little to improve the situation as resources were siphoned away from the basic needs of the army (most notably, the abolition of the Ground Forces Head-quarters) in favor of special units and detachments. Under **Vladimir Putin**, the headquarters was reinstituted and **military** spending increased for the first time in years; however, the army continues to suffer from significant social and financial issues. As a result of positive changes, the army performed comparatively well during its 2008 deployment in the **South Ossetian War** with **Georgia**. Due to its legacy as a conscript army serving the interests of a quasi-totalitarian society, the culture of leadership leaves much to be desired. Economic demands placed on young officers, who are poorly paid, exacerbates this situation.

Hazing of younger recruits, known in Russian as *dedovshchina*, is rampant and results in significant numbers of injuries and suicides on an annual basis. Currently, about one-half of the army's 400,000 personnel are conscripts, each serving a one-year term. Most conscripts come from the provinces or from underprivileged families, as wealthier Russians normally avoid conscription through university deferments, spurious medical documents, or other means. The laws and conscription practices have been tightened under **Dmitry Medvyedev**, with many young men who fail to report for conscription facing imprisonment.

Women, who are not conscripted, make up about 10 percent of the army. The poorly paid contract soldiers, known as *kontraktniki*, tend to be of low quality, often joining the army as a last resort when they have failed at other careers. Despite the current situation, Russia's military planners hope to raise the number of volunteer soldiers to 70 percent in the near future. *See also* AIR FORCE; COMMITTEE OF SOLDIERS' MOTHERS OF RUSSIA; NAVY.

ART. *See* VISUAL ARTS.

ARYANISM. Social movement. Russian Aryanism, though influenced by the Nazi variant of the 1930s, represents a distinct social movement with its origins in the late Soviet period. The term Aryan refers to descendents of the proto-Indo-Europeans, a prehistoric ethno-linguistic group that migrated to and then came to dominate southern Asia and the European continent. Proponents of the ideology contend that the Slavs (sometimes called the Aryan-Veneds) represent the oldest, and thus purest, descendents of the proto-Indo-Europeans, who originated either in the southern Russian **steppe** or, less likely, in Arctic **Eurasia**. The ideology is closely linked with **neo-paganism** and has served as a tool for the far right in postindependence Russia, being embraced by **neofascist** and other extremist ethnonational organizations and skinhead movements. The connection to ultranationalism is further buttressed by the fact that the Nazi regime in interwar **Germany** expropriated the term to support its racist and **anti-Semitic** ideology. *See also* EURASIANISM.

ASTRAKHAN OBLAST. An administrative region of the Russian Federation. Part of the Southern **Federal District** and Volga **Economic Region**, Astrakhan lies on the **Caspian Sea** and is adjacent to **Kalmykiya, Volgograd**, and western **Kazakhstan**.

With slightly over a million inhabitants, the region covers an area of 44,100 square kilometers, much of which is semidesert lowlands except around the Volga-Akhtuba deltas, where the region's **agricultural** base is located. Chief industries include meat and salt production, as well as transport of oil from **Azerbaijan** and shipping traffic to and from **Iran**. The region is a transit zone for illicit **narcotics** and has the second-highest number of drug-trafficking arrests in the country. The region also possesses substantial natural resources such as **natural gas**, **oil**, and sulphur.

The administrative center is Astrakhan (pop. 502,000), formerly known as Khaji-Tarkhan; the city lies 22 meters below sea level. **Ethnic Russians** account for 70 percent of the population; the remainder are mostly **Muslim** peoples, including **Kazakhs** (14 percent) and **Tatars** (7 percent). Recent in-migration of Tajiks and people from the **North Caucasus** has increased the ratio of **Muslims** to non-Muslims in the region and triggered a popular backlash against migrants.

The regional governor is Aleksandr Zhilkin, who has made expansion of trade and transport with **Turkmenistan** a central part of his administration. He assumed the office when his predecessor, Anatoly Guzhvin, died of a heart attack while on vacation in 2004. Zhilkin was popularly elected to the post later that year.

ASYMMETRICAL FEDERALISM. Growing out of the so-called parade of sovereignties of the last years of **Mikhail Gorbachev**'s rule, the push for local control of resources and policies among Russia's various regional divisions reached fever pitch in the midst of the **dissolution of the Soviet Union**. Hoping to win allies among the regional *nomenklatura*, Russian president **Boris Yeltsin** famously urged republican leaders to "take all the sovereignty you can swallow" in Kazan on 5 August 1990. Reflecting this approach, the Russian Federation subsequently embraced a system of asymmetrical federalism that granted differing amounts of autonomy to its various **federal subjects**. In the case of the **ethnic republics**, local authorities enjoyed immense freedom from central control, including control over **tax** revenues, the right to implement constitutions, and the ability to designate official **languages** in addition to **Russian**; less autonomy was granted to the **krais** and **oblasts**. **Tatarstan**, which issued its own passports and attempted to conduct independent **foreign relations**, represented the extreme example of this system of governance. Upon coming to power, **Vladimir Putin** publicly declared his intention to reduce the level of asymmetry in the federation, reduce the power of the republican leadership, and harmonize laws across the country. Putin used the tragic events surrounding **Beslan** to push through reforms that partially accomplished these goals. *See also* ELECTORAL REFORMS OF 2004–2005; FEDERATION TREATY OF 1992.

ATHEISM. Under the Soviets, and particularly the failed seminarian **Joseph Stalin**, Russia was transformed from a deeply religious and superstitious country into a model of state atheism with enforced secularism, restriction of religious practices, and eradication of the clergy.

During the 1920s, the **Communist Party of the Soviet Union** (CPSU) supported the work of the Union of Godless Zealots, who actively campaigned against the practice of Russia's principal faiths: Eastern **Orthodoxy**, **Islam**, **Judaism**, and **Buddhism**. By the late 1970s, most Soviet citizens gave little thought to organized religion, though many continued to practice their faith at the risk of political persecution. Strict atheism was an absolute prerequisite for admission to the **apparatchik** class and the CPSU; however, some secretly practiced their faith. Under **perestroika**, however, a religious revival began, resulting in the widespread embrace of religiosity in the post-Soviet period.

Many politicians gravitated toward the **Russian Orthodox Church** in the 1990s, including **Boris Yeltsin**, **Vladimir Putin**, and **Yury Luzhkov**, while **Muslim** and **Jewish** groups blossomed. The rehabilitation of faith, however, has not eradicated atheism in contemporary Russia. According to recent estimates, less than one-quarter of the population consider themselves to be practicing Christians, while only 7 percent of Russians are observant Muslims. Less than half of all Russian citizens "believe in God," compared to 79 percent of Americans.

Lack of **religion** does not, however, preclude spirituality (*dukhovnost'* in contemporary Russia, and many people embrace various aspects of nonscientific beliefs such as faith healing, **neo-paganism**, and so forth. Identification with a particular religious community has emerged as an important part of **economic** life in post-Soviet Russia, particularly as a tool for forging alliances and developing social networks. Since 1991, there have been some minor attempts, such as those by the Moscow Society of Atheists, to revive organized or "scientific" atheism in the country; however, the strong protections afforded by the **Constitution of the Russian Federation** to religious freedom (or freedom to have no religion) dampen the need for such groups, although the recent creep of pro-Orthodox sentiment into the **education** system is of concern to some nonbelievers. *See also* HOLIDAYS.

ATLANTICISM. Sociopolitical ideology; also called Euro-Atlanticism. The Atlanticist orientation of the late Soviet and early postindependence period of Russia can be traced back to the reforms of Peter the Great (1682–1725). Often called the Westernizing tsar, Peter attempted to embed Russia in the West, and Europeanize its people and customs. Since the 18th century, a series of **Westernizers** (*zapadniki*) have sought to continue this trend, often competing with **Eurasianists** who argue for the "uniqueness" (*samobytnost'*) of Russia as neither fully Western nor Eastern.

This political debate came to the fore as **glasnost** allowed greater levels of integration between Eastern and Western Europe. The origins of contemporary Atlanticism can be dated with **Mikhail Gorbachev**'s seminal 1987 speech in Czechoslovakia in which he declared an "All-European House" of which Soviet Russia was a part. With Gorbachev's June 1989 joint declaration with West German Chancellor Helmut Kohl supporting national self-determination, mutual reduction in nuclear and conventional forces, and a "Common European Home" in which **Canada** and the **United States** have a role, the shift toward integration in the Euro-Atlantic community began in earnest. With the **dissolution of the Soviet Union** and a definitive end to the **Cold War**, the door to a transatlantic partnership including Russia, Western Europe, and North America became feasible.

Under the direction of **Boris Yeltsin**'s team of reformers, including Foreign Minister **Andrey Kozyrev** (1990–1996), an attempt was made to transform Russia into a model Western European–style democracy, economically linked to the West rather than the USSR's old allies and client states. While the elites in Russia embraced the Euro-Atlantic shift, the **Communist Party** and nationalists rejected cooperation with the country's erstwhile enemies, often with popular support from rural and lower-class Russians. Over the course of Boris Yeltsin's first administration, enthusiasm for the West began to wane, especially after the **North Atlantic Treaty Organization** (NATO) expansion in the former **Eastern Bloc**, the **Clinton** administration's failure to meet its economic commitments to a democratic Russia, and the Bosnian War.

The ascension of **Yevgeny Primakov** as foreign minister in 1996 signaled a shift away from Atlanticism toward **Eurasianism** in Russia's **foreign relations**. Russia's exposure to global economic markets, the devaluation of the **ruble**, and the Russian **financial crisis of 1998** further soured the Russian masses on the merits of Euro-Atlanticism, critically weakening those voices that encouraged greater integration with Europe. Although the **September 11 attacks** brought Russian and American interests into closer alignment (at least until the U.S. invasion of Iraq in 2003), there has been little interest among Russian foreign policy elites in returning the country to a pro-Atlantic footing.

AUGUST COUP (1991). Also known as the August Putsch. Organized by hard-liners within the **Communist Party of the Soviet Union** (CPSU) with support of certain members of the **military** and the **KGB**, the coup was a last-ditch effort to reverse the reforms of **Mikhail Gorbachev**.

Since 1990, Gorbachev had been forced to grant increasing control to the republican leaders, including **Boris Yeltsin**, while simultaneously curtailing the influence of the CPSU. The steady erosion of the Soviet state generated intense animosity among the older generation of Soviet leaders who saw Gorbachev as nothing more than a funeral director of the **Marxist-Leninist** experiment. The immediate catalyst for the putsch was the impending **New Union Treaty**, which would have significantly restructured the relationship between the various republics of the Union of Soviet Socialist Republics (USSR).

With Gorbachev on vacation at his **dacha** in **Crimea** and Yeltsin in **Kazakhstan** for consultations with President Nursultan Nazarbayev, the putschists, led by Vice President of the Soviet Union Gennady Yanayev, Prime Minister Valentin Pavlov, and Minister of Interior Affairs Boris Pugo, established the State Committee of the State of Emergency (*Gosudarstvennyi komitet po chrezvychainomu polozheniiu* or GKChP) to deal with challenges to their authority. They also ordered hundreds of thousands of handcuffs and arrest papers for the coming unrest. The GKChP soon declared Gorbachev to be "ill," and chose Yanayev to replace him.

Beginning on 19 August, they took control of mainstream **media** outlets and ordered troops into **Moscow**. However, the failure of the coup plotters to detain Yeltsin upon his return from Kazakhstan undermined their effectiveness. The Russian president rallied popular sentiment against the coup, resulting in large-scale demonstrations against the actions of the GKChP, and gained the support of certain military figures. Lacking unity and facing a popular backlash, the putschists ultimately ordered the troops out of the capital and agreed to consultations with Gorbachev. On 22 August, most of the plotters were arrested; Pugo committed suicide shortly thereafter. Two days later, Gorbachev resigned as general secretary of the CPSU amid widespread attacks on the authority and symbols of the party's control of the Soviet state.

The failure of the coup dramatically increased support for independence among those **union republics** that had previously favored the creation of a new union and depleted lingering support for the Communists among most ordinary Russians. Within a few months,

Yeltsin outlawed the CPSU in Russia, before presiding over the **dissolution of the Soviet Union** in December. *See also* ALL-UNION REFERENDUM.

AUTONOMOUS OBLAST (AO). *See* OBLAST.

AUTONOMOUS OKRUG (AOk). Political subdivision of the Russian Federation. Known as national okrugs until 1977, the Autonomous Okrugs are **federal subjects** of the Russian Federation that are, in most cases, simultaneously subordinated to another federal subject. In each case, the AOk possesses at least one non-Russian titular population; however, these units possess less sovereignty than **ethnic republics**. Today, only four AOks remain: **Nenetsiya, Yamaliya, Khantiya-Mansiya**, and **Chukotka**. The current AOks are all located in Russia's **Far North**. Since 1990, the number of AOks within Russia has been substantially reduced, particularly under the presidency of **Vladimir Putin**, who publicly declared his intention to streamline the federal system upon entering office. In recent years, the lesser **Buryat** homelands of Aga-Buryatiya and Ust Orda were respectively incorporated into **Zabaykalsky Krai** and **Irkutsk Oblast**; **Evenkiya** and **Taymyriya** became districts of **Krasnoyarsk Krai**; Komi-Permyakiya was subsumed within **Perm Krai**; and **Koryakiya** was demoted to a district of **Kamchatka Krai**. *See also* BURYATIYA.

AUTONOMOUS SOVIET SOCIALIST REPUBLIC (ASSR). Political subdivision of the Soviet Union. During the Soviet era, the Autonomous Soviet Socialist Republic (ASSR) was the second-most sovereign political subdivision within the Union of Soviet Socialist Republics (USSR), subjugated only to the **union republics** or Soviet Socialist Republics (SSRs). Most ASSRs were subnational entities within the **Russian Soviet Federative Socialist Republic** (RSFSR), with the important exceptions of **Moldova, Abkhazia** (which was part of the Georgian SSR), and Karakalpakistan within the Uzbek SSR. Unlike the union republics, the ASSRs lacked the nominal right to secede from the union. Under **Joseph Stalin**, the process of national delimitation (1922–1936), which established the Soviet Union's internal borders, saw a small number of ASSRs elevated to the status of union republic, for example, the Kazakh ASSR, while others, like the Mountainous ASSR, were broken into smaller units based on ethnic divisions, for example, **Chechnya** and **North Ossetiya**. During World War II, the Crimean and Volga German ASSRs were abolished when their titular populations were deported to **Siberia** and **Central Asia**; during the same period, **Kareliya**, in a gambit to annex portions of **Finland**, was raised to the status of a union republic, and then returned to an ASSR in 1956. In the waning days of **perestroika**, several ASSRs unsuccessfully sought to elevate their status to SSRs, including Chechnya. Other lesser political units, such as **Adygeya** and the **Altay Republic**, successfully joined the ranks of the ASSRs prior to the **dissolution of the Soviet Union**. Prior to Russia's independence, most ASSRs declared their sovereignty and renamed themselves as **ethnic republics** of the Russian Federation. *See also* ETHNIC GERMANS.

AVARS. Ethnic group. The Avars are a **Muslim** people populating the **North Caucasus**, principally the Republic of **Dagestan** where they are the largest ethnic group (758,000). Sizable communities are also resident in **Chechnya**, **Georgia**, and **Azerbaijan**. The Avar **language** is a member of the Northeast Caucasian (Nakh-Dagestanian) language family. Originally inhabiting mountainous zones adjacent to Chechnya, Avars have increasingly settled in lowland areas of the **Caspian** basin since the mid-20th century. The Avar ethnonym is used as a collective term by a host of linguistic groups, including Andis, Botlikhs, Karatins, Akhvakhs, Bagulals, Tindins, Chamadins, Godaberins, Tsezs or Didoys, Hvarshins, Genukhs, Bezhtins or Kaputchins, Gunzibs, and Archins. During the Soviet period, the Avars dominated the political apparatus of Dagestan, but were slowly marginalized under the rule of Magomedali Magomedov, an ethnic Dargin, during the 1990s and first half of the 2000s. In 2006, **Vladimir Putin** appointed an ethnic Avar, Mukhu Aliyev, as the head of Dagestan.

AZERBAIJAN (RELATIONS WITH). Azerbaijan, a Caspian country in the southern **Caucasus**, was incorporated into the Russian Empire during the early 1820s through the Treaties of Gulistan and Turkmenchay with Persia. The discovery of petroleum in the

1870s resulted in an expansion of Russian interests in the region, particularly around the capital Baku. In the aftermath of World War I (1914–1918) and the Bolshevik Revolution, Azerbaijan was incorporated into the Transcaucasian Socialist Federative Soviet Republic, before becoming a Soviet Socialist Republic in 1936.

In the late 1980s, ethnic relations between the republic's titular Turkic **Muslim** majority (Azeris) and minority **Christian Armenians** soured over the disputed **Nagorno-Karabakh** region, an **Autonomous Soviet Socialist Republic** within Azerbaijan. Violent pogroms against Armenian residents in Baku triggered an invasion of federal troops in 1990, during which more than 100 Azeri civilians lost their lives. As Azerbaijan transitioned to independence, the Nagorno-Karabakh War (1988–1994) with its neighbor **Armenia** grew in intensity. Baku's relationship with Moscow worsened during the early 1990s as many in Azerbaijan saw Russia as a backer of Armenian aggression. Russia's purported support of **Orthodox** Armenia against Shi'a Azerbaijan was viewed in certain quarters as an early instance of the coming "clash of civilizations."

Resentful of Russia's meddling in the conflict, Azerbaijan steadily gravitated toward **Turkey** and the **United States**, after its initially warm relations with **Iran** chilled in the wake of President Abulfaz Elchibey's endorsement of autonomy for Iranian Azerbaijanis in the early 1990s. Azerbaijan, a major oil producer, soon became the site of fierce international competition among transnational energy companies including British Petroleum, Amoco, and **Lukoil**. Soviet-era infrastructure directed oil exports toward two cities on the **Black Sea** coast, the Russian city of Novorossiysk and the Georgian city of Supsa.

In an attempt to more safely reach energy-hungry markets in Western Europe, Azerbaijan agreed to develop the Baku-Tbilisi-Ceyhan (BTC) pipeline in 1998. The BTC, the world's second-longest pipeline, delivers oil from the Azeri-Chirag-Guneshli oil field in the **Caspian Sea** to the Mediterranean Sea via **Georgia** and Turkey, much to the chagrin of Russia. The route avoids the need to transport petroleum through the environmentally sensitive Bosporus and circumvents regional trouble spots in Georgia. The more southerly route through Georgia proved valid in 2008 when the Baku-Supsa pipeline was closed due to the **South Ossetian War**. A shorter route via Armenia was rejected by Azerbaijan due to the conflict over Nagorno-Karabakh and by Turkey due to lingering issues related to the Armenian massacres of 1915. Azerbaijan's plan to sell transit capacity to other Caspian nations, including **Uzbekistan**, **Turkmenistan**, and **Kazakhstan**, also figured highly in the decision to develop a Mediterranean-oriented rather than Russia-oriented **oil** and **natural gas** export infrastructure, though such a strategy places Baku in direct competition with Moscow as an energy provider to the West.

In recent years, Russian corporations have trebled the price of natural gas exports to Azerbaijan. In response, the Caspian country rapidly modernized its infrastructure and exploited the newly discovered Shah Deniz field in the Caspian Sea; Azerbaijan is now an exporter of natural gas. The Russian energy giant **Gazprom** offered to sign a long-term deal to buy Azerbaijani gas at market prices, but fears that this was simply an attempt to divert gas from the European market and expand Moscow's leverage over the southern Caucasus led Baku to reject the deal. Azerbaijan ships much of its natural gas to Georgia and Turkey via the Southern Caucasus pipeline, which parallels the BTC.

Vladimir Putin's rise to power triggered a new era in Russia-Azerbaijan relations. After his official visit to Baku in 2001 and President Heydar Aliyev's reciprocal trip to Moscow the following year, economic and political ties were expanded. Despite the rapprochement, Azerbaijan has continued to embrace a multivector foreign policy. In 2001, the state became a founding member of the **GUAM Organization for Democracy and Economic Development**. The organization brings together the more anti-Russian members of the **Commonwealth of Independent States** (CIS). Furthermore, it is backed by the United States and includes Turkey as an observer—and it is seen as a tool for balancing Russia's dominance of the CIS. Aliyev's son and successor upon his death in 2003, Ilham Aliyev, further irritated Moscow with a visit to Brussels in 2006 to sign a **European Union** (EU) Neighborhood Policy Action Plan; later that year, a Memorandum of Understanding on a strategic partnership between the EU and Azerbaijan in the field of energy was also finalized.

In addition to uneasy energy and strategic relations, there are other complications as well. Two Azeri villages—Xraxoba (Khrakhoba) and Uryanoba—transferred to Russia's **Dagestan** region decades ago were due to be returned to Azerbaijani control in 2004, but Russia has failed to do so, impeding a final delimitation of the two countries' shared border. With more than 600,000 Azeris living in the Russian Federation, the Kremlin's crackdown on illegal **immigration** and frequent instances of **ethnic violence** against people from the Caucasus and Muslims have negatively colored relations between Moscow and Baku.

The most important issue, however, remains the status of the self-declared republic of Nagorno-Karabakh. Armenia's occupation of 16 percent of Azerbaijan and the failure of the **Organization for Security and Co-operation in Europe**'s Minsk Group, co-chaired by Russia, to settle the dispute has led to reports of a massive weapons buildup in Azerbaijan. Despite the tense situation in the southern Caucasus, **Dmitry Medvyedev** has made efforts to further improve relations by declaring Baku to be a "strategic partner," and focusing on the issues of cross-border trade, which currently stands at $1.5 billion. The completion of the Olya-Astara-Qazvin rail line connecting Russia to Iran via Azerbaijan in the coming years is expected to increase this to $2 billion. *See also* FOREIGN TRADE.

– B –

BABURIN, SERGEY NIKOLAYEVICH (1959–). Politician. Born in Semipalatinsk, **Kazakhstan**, Sergey Baburin holds a PhD in law from Leningrad State University. While serving in the Supreme Soviet of the **Russian Soviet Federative Socialist Republic**, he was one of the few high-ranking officials who voted against the **dissolution of the Soviet Union**. He achieved national prominence during the **constitutional crisis of 1993** for his strident anti-**Yeltsin** position, accusing the president, as well as **Mikhail Gorbachev** and other prominent politicians, of being a disloyal "fifth column" of the West. Baburin established the *Narodnaia Volia* (People's Will) movement, which ultimately became the **People's Union** (now the Russian All-People's Union). His political views are nationalistic and **Eurasianist**. He is vice chairman of the **State Duma**.

BALKARS. Ethnic group. The Balkars are a Turkic ethnic group of some 108,000 inhabiting the **North Caucasus**. They are sometimes referred to as Malkars, though many self-identify as *Taulu* ("mountaineers" in Karachay-Balkar). They are one of two titular peoples of the Republic of **Kabardino-Balkariya** (KBR), which they share with the much larger, indigenous Caucasian ethnic group, the **Kabardins**.

Balkars are closely related to the **Karachays**; both groups speak dialects of the same **language** (Karachay-Balkar), which is part of the Kypchak branch of the Turkic language family. They are thought to be descendents of the ancient Bulgars who migrated to Europe from Asia beginning in the 2nd century. The Balkars adopted Sunni **Islam** comparatively late, being animists until the 18th century. However, their attachment to Islam has proved greater than that of their Kabardin neighbors who originally proselytized the new faith to them.

Under **Joseph Stalin**, along with their Karachay cousins and several other North Caucasian nationalities, the Balkars were subject to forced deportations to **Siberia** and Soviet **Central Asia** during World War II. Of the 37,000 originally deported, more than a quarter died in the first year. After their return from Central Asian exile, their numbers were greatly reduced. In 1991, the Balkar National Congress campaigned unsuccessfully for the creation of an autonomous Balkariya within the **Russian Soviet Federative Socialist Republic**. However, the imposition of consociational, that is, ethnicity-based, representation, which guaranteed high-level Balkar representation in the republican government, effectively assuaged the desire to quit the KBR during the 1990s, though calls for an independent Balkariya were raised again in November 1996.

Today, the potency of Balkar **national identity** is on the rise, but since the Balkars represent a mere 9 percent of the population in Kabardino-Balkariya, they have few political outlets for their national renaissance. Some intellectuals have instead embraced **pan-Turkism**. The Balkars are part of the Assembly of Turkic peoples, alongside the Azerbaijanis, Kumyks, and Nogays.

In 2005, approximately 1,000 Balkars protested in the regional capital Nalchik against the designation of two Balkar-dominated villages, Khasanya and Belaya Rechka, as suburbs of the capital. The move—accompanied by the murder of the Balkar mayor of one of the villages—was seen as evidence of the Kabardins' creeping monopoly on power in the republic. **Chechen separatists** have frequently lent their support to the Balkar national cause, though within the framework of a larger (non-Russian) Caucasian federation or caliphate. Some disaffected Balkars have gravitated toward violent and nonviolent **Islamism** in recent years.

BALTIC SEA. The Baltic Sea is a brackish inland sea in northern Europe bounded by the Scandinavian Peninsula, **Finland**, Russia, the **Baltic States**, **Poland**, **Germany**, and Denmark. Its surface area is 377,000 square kilometers, with a maximum depth of 459 meters.

Russia gained access to the sea during the reign of Peter the Great, who, in 1703, founded **St. Petersburg** on the Baltic coast as Russia's "window to the west." During the 18th and 19th centuries, **Romanov** Russia expanded its access through the acquisition of Finland, **Estonia**, **Latvia**, **Lithuania**, and parts of Poland. Much of this territory was lost after World War I, though Soviet Russia maintained territory around Leningrad (now St. Petersburg). After World War II, the annexation of East Prussia (**Kaliningrad Oblast**) and the Baltic States reverted much of the Baltic coastline to Moscow's control. With access to the North Sea controlled by the **North Atlantic Treaty Organization** (NATO) member Denmark, Soviet **naval** traffic in and out of the body of water was carefully monitored by the **United States** and its allies during the **Cold War**. Tensions with Sweden also flared due to violations of the neutral state's waters by both NATO and **Warsaw Pact** navies.

With the **dissolution of the Soviet Union** in 1991, the military situation in the sea became relatively calm, accompanied by a comparatively amiable delineation of new maritime boundaries. Economic activity in the region is extremely robust. With the exception of Kaliningrad and the environs around St. Petersburg, the basin countries all currently belong to the **European Union**. Baltic cruises that dock in St. Petersburg, Helsinki, Tallinn, and Riga are now popular with **tourists**.

In recent years, a Russo-German plan to develop the Nord Stream **natural gas** pipeline under the Baltic has angered the Baltic States and Poland, which fear they will be politically and economically sidelined by the project, viewing it as removing them from the political calculus of European energy security. **Environmentalists** also reject the proposed project, favoring overland alternatives. *See also* ESPIONAGE; GAZPROM; SCHRÖDER, GERHARD; ST. PETERSBURG; TRANSPORTATION.

BALTIC STATES. The Baltic States, in the context of post-Soviet Russia, traditionally refers to the former Soviet republics of **Estonia**, **Latvia**, and **Lithuania** (though less often, the term is used to describe all countries washed by the **Baltic Sea**, including **Finland**, **Poland**, Sweden, Denmark, **Germany**, and Russia itself).

The post-Soviet Baltic States, including **Kaliningrad Oblast**, were annexed by the Union of Soviet Socialist Republics (USSR) during World War II. Estonia, Latvia, and Lithuania had all been part of the **Romanov** Empire, but—along with Finland—these states gained their independence with the collapse of the *ancien régime*. The **United States** and most of its **Cold War** allies refused to recognize these states' admission to the USSR as **union republics** in the 1940s, allowing the Baltic States' pre–World War II leadership to maintain diplomatic missions in exile in many Western countries. During **perestroika**, national revival movements exploded in the three republics, often coordinating with one another on linguistic, cultural, and economic policy. Led by Lithuania, the region's struggle for independence and the Kremlin's sometimes-violent suppression of the nationalist movement hurt **Mikhail Gorbachev**'s international standing in the late Soviet period. In 1991, the three republics voted to cut ties to Moscow, initiating the **dissolution of the Soviet Union**.

In the post-Soviet period, these states have had a particularly complicated relationship with the Russian Federation, evidenced by their resolute refusal to join the **Commonwealth of Independent States** or any other Russia-dominated political or economic bloc. Additional problems stemmed from the three countries' move to join the **North Atlantic Treaty Organization** (NATO), economic disputes related to **oil** and **natural gas** pipelines, and the discrimination of **ethnic Russians** in the newly independent republics. The Baltic States, along with Poland, have sought to use their membership in the **European Union** and NATO to constrain Russian actions, which they view as neo-imperial violations of their national sovereignty. *See also* ESTONIAN CYBERWAR; FOREIGN RELATIONS; NEAR ABROAD; RUSSIAN LANGUAGE.

BALLET. Russia's contribution to ballet, which dates to the 18th century, remains important, though ideological pressure and high-profile defections by a number of dancers during the Soviet period somewhat tarnished the image of the **art** in the country. The term "Russian ballet" refers to a school of dance that has specific characteristics. The most common method of training and performing is the Vaganova method. In the Soviet Union, ballet was one of the main arts and it carried a strong ideological message. Ballet schools and theaters were established in all major cities; however, **St. Petersburg** (the Mariinsky Theater) and **Moscow** (the Bolshoy Theater) were the main centers. After **perestroika**, ballet was de-ideologized but its cultural and social significance decreased. Since the 1980s, the number of independent ballet companies has increased dramatically owing to a decrease in state funds for cultural projects. The style of performing also became more diverse and now includes elements of contemporary dance.

BANKING. Under **Mikhail Gorbachev**, the banking system, previously dominated by Gosbank (State Bank), was diversified to create new lending agencies. Despite the reforms, the Russian Federation inherited a system that consisted of a small number of large, state-owned banks, including **Sberbank**, Vnesheconombank, and Bank VTB (formerly known as Vneshtorgbank). The Central Bank of the Russian Federation, established in 1990, is charged with setting monetary policy and maintaining the stability of the **ruble**, the country's national currency. It replaced Gosbank in 1991. From 1991 to 1995, Russia saw the establishment of nearly 3,000 commercial banks (that number has shrunk to 1,000 since the late 1990s).

A large number of corporate banks, beholden to the interests of large firms such as **Lukoil**, were also founded, as well as institutions that were used by the **oligarchs** to protect and expand their personal fortunes, often at the expense of account holders. The **mafia**'s use of and influence over Russia's system of banking and finance during this period is well documented. The proliferation of "new" banks was also important to the federal and regional governments, which sought loans from these institutions during the 1990s. During the 1998 **ruble crisis**, a number of banks' assets were frozen, and account holders were directed to transfer their holdings to Sberbank at a fixed rate.

The use of personal checks remained tepid in the postindependence period due to a slow clearance process, resulting in a predominantly cash-based **economy**. Credit and bank cards, rare in Russia during the 1990s, have exploded, with approximately 120 million in circulation by 2009.

BANYA. With deep cultural associations that date to pagan times, the steam bath or *banya* was once an integral part of Russian **rural life**; however, with increased urbanization, banya has become a rarity. Today, its primary function has changed from an essential tool of personal hygiene to a social institution that aims to provide entertainment and opportunities for social interaction. Traditional Russian banyas had an accompanying set of particular practices including the *shapka* or felt hat, *venik* (birch, oak, or eucalyptus branches used to increase blood circulation), and aromatherapy. Taking the steam was seen as a social activity, a cure for common ailments, and a form of personal hygiene. In the Soviet Union, banyas ceased being private spaces and became a common area where individuals had an opportunity to engage in conversation, drink tea, and even conduct business transactions. In post-Soviet Russia, it became common for the **mafia** to use banyas as meeting places so as to avoid police or **FSB** surveillance. After 2000, many banyas in Russian cities either closed or became health spas and beauty centers. The Sandunovskie banyas in **Moscow** are an example of a traditional establishment that now also includes swimming pools, superb restaurants, and luxurious spa treatments.

BARENTS SEA. The Barents Sea is part of the **Arctic Ocean**, roughly bounded by Franz Josef Land, Novaya Zemlya, **Nenetsiya**, **Murmansk**, Svalbard, and northeastern **Norway**. It has a surface area of 1,400,000 square kilometers. As a border zone between the Soviet Union and the **North Atlantic Treaty Organization** (NATO) member Norway, the sea was strategically sensitive during the **Cold War**. Russia's Northern Fleet is located at the southern rim, at Polyarny. There are significant deposits of **oil** and **natural gas** under the seafloor, the largest of which is the Shtokman field in Russian waters. Boundary disputes over territorial waters and pollution from Russian naval reactors plague relations between Moscow and Oslo. The sea is an area of intense commercial **fishing** activity and enjoys a wide diversity of animal and plant life. On 12 August 2000, the nuclear cruise missile submarine *Kursk* sank with all hands lost in the Barents Sea.

BARKASHOV, ALEKSANDR PETROVICH (1953–). Politician. Born on 6 October 1953 to working-class parents in **Moscow**, Aleksandr Barkashov graduated from secondary school in 1971. He then did his **military** service, later taking up his father's trade as an electrician. After becoming interested in world history and martial arts, Barkashov joined the ultranationalist, **anti-Semitic Pamyat political party** in 1985, ultimately becoming second-in-command under Dmitry Vasilyev. On 16 October 1990, he and a group of other radical Pamyat members formed what would become the **Russian National Unity** (RNU) party. During the **constitutional crisis of 1993**, he led a group of fighters in defense of the White House against **Boris Yeltsin**'s forces. After the situation was defused, Barkashov was sought by the authorities for nearly three months before being arrested and charged with arms possession and inciting mass disorder, though he was granted amnesty by the newly elected **State Duma** in 1994. Later that year, he published *The ABCs of a Russian Nationalist*, which became the manifesto of the RNU. In 1999, the RNU was banned in **Moscow**, and Barkashov lost control of the organization a year later. He was arrested again in 2005 for assaulting a police officer.

BASAYEV, SHAMIL SALMANOVICH (1965–2006). Guerilla commander and **terrorist**. Born in a village in southeastern **Chechnya**, Basayev was named after the famed 19th-century military commander Imam Shamil. He was born to parents who, like all other contemporary Chechens, had been deported to **Central Asia** during World War II; they returned to Chechnya in the late 1950s. After a stint in the **army** as a firefighter, he spent several years in **Moscow**, studying and working as a salesman.

In 1991, Basayev reportedly participated in demonstrations against the plotters of the **August Coup**. Later that year, he hijacked a Turkish-bound **Aeroflot** plane to publicize the situation in Chechnya, returning to his homeland after the event. From there, he became a full-time insurgent leader, participating in the **Georgian Civil War** on the side of **Abkhazia** as a prominent member of the **Confederation of Mountain Peoples of the Caucasus**. When the first **Chechen War** broke out, he quickly emerged as one of the country's fiercest warlords, commanding significant numbers of fighters. In 1995, he led a raid on a hospital in Budyonnovsk, **Stavropol Krai**, that resulted in the deaths of 129 people. The Kremlin's agreement to cease-fire talks in the negotiations was seen as turning point in the war over Chechnya.

Following the Russian withdrawal in 1996, Basayev stood for president of the self-declared republic, finishing second after the more moderate **Aslan Maskhadov**. In the late 1990s, he gravitated toward radical **Islamism** and joined forces with the Arab-**Circassian** terrorist **Ibn al-Khattab**. Hoping to create a caliphate across the **North Caucasus**, the two led a raid into neighboring **Dagestan** in 1999, which along with a series of **apartment bombings** across Russia, precipitated the second Chechen War. For the next five years, Basayev planned and directed a series of terrorist attacks that made him the most feared man in Russia. He claimed to be behind the **Nord-Ost theater siege** in 2002 and the 2004 assassination of **Akhmad Kadyrov**, the sitting president of Chechnya. He also took responsibility for the planning of the **Beslan crisis** in 2004 and a raid on Nalchik, **Kabardino-Balkariya**, in 2005.

Russian and Chechen authorities ultimately initiated a massive manhunt for Basayev. On 10 July 2006, he was killed in **Ingushetiya**; Russian officials claimed his death was the result of an **FSB** special operation. His remains were positively identified by forensic experts in December 2009. *See also* SOVIET-AFGHAN WAR.

BASHKIRS. Ethnic group. Russia's fifth largest nationality, Bashkirs are a Turkic people who form the titular minority in **Bashkortostan**. Sizable communities also live in the **Chelyabinsk**, **Orenburg**, **Perm**, **Sverdlovsk**, **Kurgan**, and **Tyumen oblasts** of the Russian Federation. In total, there are more than 1.6 million Bashkirs in the Russian Federation.

The Bashkir **language** is closely related to **Tatar** and is part of the Kypchak subgroup of Turkic languages. Only two-thirds of Bashkirs claim knowledge of their mother tongue, while **Russian language** fluency is near universal. During the first half of the 20th century, many Bashkirs adopted the Tatar language, especially in northwestern Bashkortostan. However, there has been a relative decline in the numbers of Bashkirs who speak Tatar as their first language over the past 50 years, especially since 1989, when language reforms increased the use of Bashkir in the public sphere.

Bashkirs are predominantly Sunni **Muslims** of the moderate Hanafi school of jurisprudence, though a small percentage practice Russian **Orthodoxy**. Culturally speaking, the Bashkirs are closely linked to the Tatars and intermarriage rates run high, though resentment exists, especially regarding what is seen as Tatar "cultural imperialism" in Bashkortostan. This was most evident in the early 1990s when the radical Bashkir National Party declared that only ethnic Bashkirs should have the right to determine the form of the republic. More radical Bashkir nationalists advocate the creation of a "Greater Bashkortostan," which would include all or part of Orenburg and thus create an international border with **Kazakhstan**. Such a territorial change is seen as the first step in establishing conditions for a completely independent nation-state or federation of Volga peoples similar to the short-lived Idel-Ural Republic, which existed from 1917 until 1921.

BASHKORTOSTAN, REPUBLIC OF. An **ethnic republic** of the Russian Federation. Historically known as Bashkiriya, this ethnic republic was an **Autonomous Soviet Socialist Republic** (ASSR) within the **Russian Soviet Federative Socialist Republic** during the Soviet era. In 1990, the ASSR's Supreme Soviet declared the state sovereignty of the Bashkir Soviet Socialist Republic (SSR); however, unlike preexisting SSRs, Bashkiriya did not gain independence with the **dissolution of the Soviet Union** in December 1991, though it did declare itself to be independent.

In 1992, the delineation of authority and power was established between Bashkiriya and **Moscow**, creating the current Republic of Bashkortostan. It is part of the Volga **Federal District** and the Urals **Economic Region**. Along with **Tuva**, **Tatarstan**, **Sakha**, and **Buryatiya**, the republic declared in 1993 that its laws superseded those of the Russian Federation. It possessed the highest level of autonomy within Russia's **asymmetrical federal** system. This relationship was formalized in 1994 with the signing of a power-sharing agreement between the government bodies of the Russian Federation and the republic. Bashkortostan maintains **foreign trade** relations with nearly 100 countries around the world; particularly strong are those with European countries and the **Commonwealth of Independent States**.

The republic contains part of the south **Ural Mountains** and adjacent steppes, covering an area of more than 143,000 square kilometers, and contains a large number of rivers, which form part of European Russia's **transportation** network. Bashkortostan's **economy** is driven by its petroleum exports, and it is one of the richest territories of Russia in terms of mineral resources. The region possesses substantial **industrial** and scientific capacity, stemming from the World War II–era relocation of factories from European Russia.

The titular minority, the **Bashkirs**, account for 30 percent of the total population of over 4 million; **ethnic Russians** are the largest group at 36 percent, while **Tatars** account for 24 percent of the population. In terms of **language**, **Russian** is spoken by the entire population, with Tatar (34 percent) and Bashkir (26 percent) ranking second and third. Historically, Bashkortostan has close ties with Tatarstan and is central to any future Volga-Ural state, the goal of Tatar nationalists and supporters of **pan-Turkism**. In recent polls, more than half the titular population supports independence from Russia.

The republic's administrative capital is Ufa, which has a population in excess of 1 million. The president, in office since 1993, is Murtaza Rakhimov. Rakhimov, whose third-term election victory was marred by rigged voting, came under intense pressure to step down in 2005 but weathered the crisis; he secured the Kremlin's backing in 2006 for his fourth term, which, under the new **electoral reforms**, was a fait accompli. Under **Vladimir Putin**, the Kremlin has sought to wrest away much of the republic's authority and apply federal laws within Bashkortostan. Such actions have stirred discontent among the republic's various ethnic organizations and **political parties**.

BELARUS (RELATIONS WITH). The region of contemporary Belarus was annexed by the **Romanov** Empire during the partitions of the Polish-Lithuanian Commonwealth in the late 18th century. Like **ethnic Russians** and **Ukrainians**, Belarusians are an East Slavic people confessing **Orthodox Christianity**. After a short-lived period of independence during the Russian Civil War, Belarus was renamed as the Belarusian Soviet Socialist Republic in 1919 and became a founding republic of the Union of Soviet Socialist Republics (USSR) in 1922. With the territorial redistribution that followed World War II, Belarusian territory was expanded to the west at the expense of lands held by interwar **Poland**. The Belarusian republic held a seat at the **United Nations** from 1945 onward.

Heavily Russified and dependent on Soviet-style subsidies, Belarus's first generation of postindependence leaders, including President Stanislau Shushkevich, sought accommodation with the Russian Federation, but blocked the market reforms that characterized **Boris Yeltsin**'s first administration and remained suspicious of the country's shift toward democratization. Under the presidency of Aleksandr Lukashenko, who has ruled the country since 1994, Belarus has pursued the most pro-Russian foreign policy among the former Soviet republics. As the Belarusian economy faltered and Yeltsin's embrace of pluralism lessened, Lukashenko made integration with his eastern neighbor the central guiding principle of the mid-1990s.

In 1997, Lukashenko's desire for economic as well as political integration with his country's eastern neighbor culminated in the establishment of the **Union of Russia and Belarus**. The supranational entity promised common citizenship, a common currency, and joint armed forces for the two states, governed by a Supreme Soviet comprised of leaders from both countries. While all these benefits have yet to be fully realized, the new relationship effectively slowed Belarus's transition to a market-style economy and its integration with Europe by tying the country closely to Moscow and the **Commonwealth of Independent States**. The treaty was opposed by the left in Russia as detrimental to the country's economic situation and own reform process; however, many Russian nationalists, including then-Foreign Minister **Yevgeny Primakov**, strongly endorsed the scheme as a step toward Russia's return to great power status in **Eurasia** and a stopgap measure against **North Atlantic Treaty Organization** (NATO) expansion.

Still ravaged by the effects of the **Chernobyl** nuclear disaster, Belarus sought to leverage the renewed relationship with Moscow to protect its public sector from challenges posed by **globalization** and as a political shield against Western condemnation of Lukashenko's authoritarian rule. However, during the administration of **Vladimir**

Putin, the Kremlin became much more critical of Belarusian politics, and many of the economic benefits of a close alliance began to wane.

President Lukashenko depends on the continued subsidization of Russian-produced **natural gas** and **oil** to maintain his popularity. However, in the winter of 2006, **Gazprom** subjected Minsk to the same "marketization" of energy prices that had been deemed political "punishment" for the pro-Western states of **Georgia** and **Ukraine** in the previous 12 months. Belarus occupies the intermediary position between Russia's hydrocarbon fields and lucrative European markets; as a result, Russia's increasing control of Belarus's transit infrastructure has emerged as a major political issue between the two governments.

Despite the appearance of fraternal relations, Lukashenko's regime has fallen afoul of Russia's commercial elites, due to protectionist policies and failure to assist Moscow in improving trade links between **Kaliningrad** and the rest of the country. While the economic relationship between the two states remains dynamic, Moscow continues to support Lukashenko's authoritarian rule, fearful that a "color revolution" might produce an anti-Russian regime similar to that in Georgia.

During the lead-up to the failed "Jeans Revolution" of 2006, the Kremlin, under the banner of "East Slavic brotherhood," loudly backed the sitting president and condemned the opposition as stooges of Poland, the **European Union**, and the **United States**. While Polish, Lithuanian, and Ukrainian nongovernmental organizations have supported the development of youth-oriented **civil society** in Belarus, their efforts are consistently countered by Moscow's political and economic influence in the country. All three countries have also become home to political dissenters and journalists fleeing the Lukashenko regime. Poland's decision to host the European Interceptor Site (EIS), an American antimissile system that Moscow believes is aimed at encircling Russia, has further worsened relations between Belarus and the rest of Europe after the announcement that Moscow may place missiles in the republic.

Minsk offered diplomatic support to Russia in the wake of the 2008 **South Ossetian War**, with Lukashenko backing (though not formally recognizing) the independence of **South Ossetia** and **Ab-**

khazia. In mid-2008, a spokesperson for the Belarusian-Russian Union State invited three Russian-backed breakaway republics— **Transnistria**, Abkhazia, and South Ossetia—to join the union. *See also* FOREIGN RELATIONS; RUSSIFICATION.

BELAVEZHA ACCORDS. Sometimes referred to as the Minsk Agreement, the Belavezha Accords were signed by **Boris Yeltsin**, Stanislau Shushkevich, and Leonid Kravchuk on 8 December 1991 at a state **dacha** in Belovezhkaya Pushcha in **Belarus**. Representing the original core of the Soviet Union, that is Russia, Belarus, and **Ukraine**, the three republican presidents effectively abrogated the treaty that bound together the **union republics** and replaced it with the **Commonwealth of Independent States**. On 12 December, the Supreme Soviet of the **Russian Soviet Federative Socialist Republic** ratified the agreement, legally terminating the 1922 treaty that formed the Union of Soviet Socialist Republics (USSR). The events surrounding the meeting at Belavezha laid the groundwork for the 21 December 1991 Alma-Ata Protocol, the agreement that ultimately completed the **dissolution of the Soviet Union**. *See also* AUGUST COUP.

BELGOROD OBLAST. An administrative region of the Russian Federation. Part of the Southern **Federal District** and the Central Black Earth **Economic Region**, Belgorod borders **Voronezh**, **Kursk**, and northeastern **Ukraine**. It has a population of 1.5 million and an area of 27,100 square kilometers covering part of the Central Russian Highlands.

During the 1990s, the region was a reliable part of Russia's **Red Belt**, with strong support for the **Communist Party** as well as the **Liberal Democratic Party** of **Vladimir Zhirinovsky**. As a "Black Earth" (**chernozem**) region, **agriculture** is highly developed, with grains, sugar beets, and sunflowers being the leading crops. **Mining** is a key part of the **economy**, and the region has huge iron-ore deposits, forming part of the Kursk Magnetic Anomaly.

In office since 1993, Yevgeny Savchenko is the region's governor; he is a member of the **Agrarian Party** and a strong supporter of **Vladimir Putin**. He easily defeated his Communist challenger, Vasily Altukhov, in 2003, receiving 61 percent of the vote. Savchenko has led a campaign against delinquency, forbidding swearing in public, imposing a 10:00 p.m. curfew for minors, and limiting the capacity of nightclubs to two persons per square meter. In recent years, he has become embroiled in a conflict over land **privatization** with the agroconglomerate Inteko. The region's compact size, fertile soil, well-developed roads, and stable village populations have attracted significant investment from large agrobusinesses.

BEREZOVSKY, BORIS ABRAMOVICH (1946–). Oligarch. Also known as Platon Elenin, Boris Berezovsky was born in **Moscow** to a **Jewish** family; his father worked in construction and his mother was a nurse. His early career exemplifies the life of the Soviet Union's midlevel professional **intelligentsia** (he studied forestry and applied mathematics, receiving his doctorate in 1983) and ever-growing research bureaucracy (from 1969 to 1987, he was a research assistant at the USSR Academy of Sciences). He began his business career in 1989 under the economic chaos of **perestroika**. Initially, he capitalized on the collapse of the Soviet distribution system, buying and reselling cars from the state manufacturer AutoVAZ. He eventually began trading Mercedes-Benzes and in 1992 created the new company LogoVAZ, an exclusive consignment dealer of AutoVAZ. Berezovsky excelled in trading state-owned assets and products, so it is not surprising that his own company became Russia's largest private enterprise in 1995 while AutoVAZ was struggling to survive.

During the mid-1990s, Berezovsky used his connections to gain access to "the Family," that is, President **Boris Yeltsin**'s inner circle; he developed particularly close relationships with Yeltsin's daughter **Tatyana Dyachenko** and the president's longtime chief of staff. As a result, Berezovsky acquired special access to state companies that were undergoing **privatization** such as **Aeroflot**, the **oil** company Sibneft, and those in the aluminum industry. To serve his growing commercial empire, Berezovsky established a **bank** and purchased several news **media** holdings, including the **television** channels ORT and TV-6 and the **newspapers** *Nezavisimaia Gazeta* and ***Kommersant***. He aggressively utilized his financial and media institutions to sway the **1996 presidential elections**, resulting in Yeltsin's reelection.

His controversial political career often overshadowed his financial success. Yeltsin appointed Berezovsky executive secretary of the

Organization for Coordinating the **Commonwealth of Independent States** and deputy secretary of the National Security Council. Berezovsky was also elected to the **State Duma**. Reportedly, Berezovsky was instrumental in the appointment **Vladimir Putin** as prime minister in 1999 as a quid pro quo for Putin's future loyalty to Yeltsin and Berezovsky himself. However, Berezovsky's opposition to the initiation of the second **Chechen War** and his media outlets' critical coverage of the *Kursk* **submarine disaster** quickly soured relations with Putin.

In response to an investigation into his business activities, Berezovsky fled to and then gained asylum in **Great Britain** in 2001. The Russian government subsequently charged Berezovsky with **corruption** related to his management of Aeroflot. In 2007, a Moscow court found him guilty of embezzlement and sentenced him to six years' imprisonment in absentia.

His purported links to the Russian **mafia** and **Chechen terrorists** is also an issue of concern to the Kremlin. In his capacity as the deputy secretary of the National Security Council, Berezovsky developed extensive contacts among the Chechen diaspora in Russia and abroad, and transferred large sums of money to **Shamil Basayev** to secure the release of Russian hostages during the incident at Budyonnovsk. In the mid-1990s, *Forbes* magazine accused him of being the head of organized crime in Russia, though the publication later issued a retraction. He has been accused of involvement in a number of recent scandals, including the 2006 assassination of Russian journalist **Anna Politkovskaya** and the poisoning of **Aleksandr Litvinenko**. Despite his long absence from Russia, he remains involved in its domestic **politics**, including launching the failed Liberal Russia party. In the late 2000s, he declared his aim is to bring down Putin "by force," if necessary.

Berezovsky's very career popularized the term "oligarch" and he was saddled with a host of controversial titles, among them a latter-day "Rasputin," "the Gray Cardinal," "the epitome of Russian robber capitalism," and "the godfather of the Kremlin." While he is loathed by many average Russians, Berezovsky's notorious business and political career has been memorialized in Russian **literature** and **film**. Pavel Lungin's 2002 film *Tycoon: A New Russian* traces the rise of the cynical Russian billionaire. In 2004, Berezovsky changed his first name to Platon, to adhere symbolically to the film's protagonist Platon Makhovsky, and his last name to Elenin, a coinage derived from his wife's name. The subject of several assassination attempts, he now resides in a virtual fortress in the suburbs of London, England, and maintains a security detail comprised of veterans of the French Foreign Legion.

BESLAN CRISIS. On 1 September 2004, the first day of the new school year, **Islamist terrorists** took control of School Number One in Beslan, **North Ossetiya**. More than 1,000 people, mostly children, were taken hostage for three days. The hostage takers, reputedly directed and funded by the **Chechen** guerilla leader **Shamil Basayev**, demanded an end to the second **Chechen War**. Ultimately, Russian security forces, which had initially stated that force would not be used, stormed the school, resulting in the deaths of more than 330 hostages, including 186 students. The assailants, 31 of whom were killed in the assault, were mostly of **Ingush** and Chechen backgrounds, though there were also a number of foreign fighters including two British citizens of Middle Eastern origin. The terrorist attack inflamed ethnic relations between the local **Ossetian** population and their **Muslim** Ingush neighbors, as well as sparking attacks on various individuals of **North Caucasian** appearance across other parts of Russia. **Vladimir Putin** used the postcrisis political environment to augment his promised **vertical of power**, most importantly by abolishing direct election of regional governors and instituting a proportional system for the **State Duma**. Both reforms served to expand his own influence and deter criticism of the Kremlin. *See also* ELECTORAL REFORMS OF 2004–2005; ETHNIC VIOLENCE; NORD-OST THEATER SIEGE.

BLACK EARTH. *See* CHERNOZEM.

BLACK SEA. The Black Sea is an inland sea that washes the Eastern Balkans, **Ukraine**, southern Russia, **Georgia**, and **Turkey**. The sea's outlet to the Mediterranean, and thus the Atlantic and Indian oceans, is via the Bosporus and Dardanelles straits, both of which are controlled by **North Atlantic Treaty Organization** (NATO) member Turkey. The surface area of the sea is 436,400 square kilometers, and its maximum depth is in excess of 2,000 meters. Due to its salubrious climate, there are a large number of holiday resorts and spas on the Black Sea coast.

During the **Cold War**, the Black Sea was an area of heightened tensions, particularly during conflicts in the **Middle East**. After the **dissolution of the Soviet Union**, Russia removed its **nuclear weapons** from its fleet. However, Russia continues to maintain a significant naval presence in the area, known as the Black Sea Fleet (*Chernomorskii flot*). Sevastopol, a city on the **Crimean** coast, has been a major sticking point in relations between Kiev and Moscow since 1991. The old Soviet navy was partitioned between Ukraine and Russia, with the latter maintaining a long-term lease on key facilities at Sevastopol. The Russian **navy** is also based in the **Sea of Azov** and at Novorossiysk, which is expected to become the headquarters of the fleet after 2017.

In recent years, Russo-Georgian tensions have resulted in minor skirmishes between the two navies, particularly over the status of the breakaway republic of **Abkhazia**. The Abkhazian port of Sukhumi is economically tied to Russia, and it is a popular **tourist** destination for many Russian citizens. In 2008, **Dmitry Medvyedev** recognized the independence of the republic; the Kremlin later announced that it would establish an air base and naval facilities in Abkhazia. Ukrainian-Russian relations have also been impacted by Kiev's demands that it be asked permission before military missions are launched from its territory. During the 2008 **South Ossetian War**, the presence of U.S. and other NATO warships in the Black Sea drew harsh criticism from Moscow.

There are a number of intergovernmental and nongovernmental organizations that unite the various countries of the Black Sea basin, including: the Organization of Black Sea Economic Cooperation (BSEC), **GUAM Organization for Democracy and Economic Development**, the Black Sea Forum for Partnership and Dialogue, and the International Black Sea Club.

BRAZIL, RUSSIA, INDIA, AND CHINA (BRIC). The acronym "BRIC" (Brazil, Russia, **India**, and **China**) is used in the international financial community to refer to the four largest emerging markets, that is, **economies** that lie outside the Group of Seven (G7).

The term was first used by international bankers at Goldman Sachs in 2001. None of these countries were part of the so-called First World, but due to the changing nature of international political economy in the post–1989 environment, all these states have emerged as vital components of global capitalism. In each case, these economies have transitioned from high levels of state control to market-based economies in the past two to three decades. Goldman Sachs argued that their combined economic power would eclipse that of the G7 by 2050. When the term was first used, these states did not act in any concerted way to achieve their economic goals; however, this changed by 2008 with the introduction of BRIC summits between the members. Former Russian President **Vladimir Putin** was the driving force behind the move toward some form of concerted action among the BRIC members. In the wake of the 2008–2009 **global financial crisis**, the ability of the four nations to achieve common goals has been thrown into doubt due to China's overreliance on American consumer spending, Russia's exposure to weakening **oil** and **natural gas** prices, and the shift to a G-20 model for economic cooperation since **Barack Obama** assumed the presidency of the **United States**. *See also* ECONOMY; GLOBALIZATION; MEDVYEDEV, DMITRY.

BREZHNEV, LEONID ILYICH (1906–1982). Politician. Born the son of a steelworker in Dniprodzerzhynsk, **Ukraine**, Leonid Brezhnev enjoyed the upward mobility provided to working-class youth in the early Soviet period. He began a career in metallurgy, and after nearly a decade in the **Komsomol** youth organization, he became a member of the **Communist Party of the Soviet Union** (CPSU) in 1931. He was a political commissar during his initial **military** service and was later elevated to party secretary of his hometown.

During World War II, he returned to the military, serving under **Nikita Khrushchev**, who would become his primary political patron in the coming decades. He ultimately attained the rank of major general, though he remained a political rather than combat officer. In the post–World War II period, he took over the administration of the newly annexed territories of Soviet **Moldova**. In 1952, he joined the Central Committee of the CPSU. Two years later, he assumed control of the Community Party in **Kazakhstan**. His alliance with Khrushchev paid dividends in the late 1950s, and Brezhnev emerged from the party's internal struggle as a full member of the Politburo.

In 1960, he became president of the Presidium of the Supreme Soviet, and thus the nominal head of state. Khrushchev, as general secretary of the CPSU, however, still wielded ultimate power. Brezhnev and a number of other conspirators removed Khrushchev from office in 1964, and after a period of power sharing with Aleksey Kosygin and Anastas Mikoyan, Brezhnev emerged as the undisputed leader of the Union of Soviet Socialist Republics (USSR). In **foreign relations**, Brezhnev ordered the military suppression of Czechoslovakia's experiment in "socialism with a human face" in 1968 via an invasion by **Warsaw Pact** nations; he also failed to prevent worsening relations with **China**. The Soviet Union reached its zenith as a world power under his rule.

In the 1970s, the **United States** and the USSR began a period of negotiations known as détente, which resulted in new arms control agreements. However, in the last years of his tenure, Brezhnev ordered the invasion of **Afghanistan**, initiating the disastrous **Soviet-Afghan War** that would plague his successors. On the home front, the USSR benefited from high petroleum prices in the wake of the 1973 **oil** embargo. Standard-of-living increases and political stability became the hallmarks of the Brezhnev era. However, mismanagement of the **economy**, overreliance on heavy **industry**, and a failure to adjust to changing market dynamics on the world stage resulted in stagnation.

This stagnation was defined by an ineffective command economy, commitment of resources to defense, high secrecy, inflation, and the rise of the black market. Concurrently, few scientific or economic innovations were implemented, and there was general resistance to new practices. During this period, Brezhnev enjoyed a cult of personality that bordered on the pathetic: he was awarded over 150 medals, and constantly hosted parades. The public reacted to Brezhnev and his rule with apathy and cynicism.

After developing a dangerous addiction to prescription **narcotics**, Brezhnev died of a heart attack on 10 November 1982. He was succeeded by **Yury Andropov**.

BRYANSK OBLAST. An administrative region of the Russian Federation. Part of the Central **Federal District** and the Central **Economic**

Region, Bryansk borders eastern **Belarus** and northern **Ukraine**, as well as the **oblasts** of **Smolensk**, **Kaluga**, Orel, and **Kursk**. Its area is 34,900 square kilometers, and it has a population of just fewer than 1.4 million. Its **geography** is defined by the Central Russian Highlands and the Desna River.

Bryansk administers the Russian exclave of Sankovo-Medvezhye, an area of some 4.5 square kilometers near the Belarusian city of Homel and the Russian border city of Dobrodyevka; the region is uninhabited and highly contaminated as a result of the **Chernobyl disaster**. Bryansk is a major industrial area of the Russian Federation specializing in building materials and metalworking, as well as a center of **agricultural** production. Due to its proximity to the fallout from Chernobyl, the region continues to grapple with high rates of thyroid and other types of cancer.

Part of the **Red Belt**, Bryansk's **Communist** governor Yury Lodkin, a former ITAR-TASS correspondent, was removed by **Boris Yeltsin** after the **constitutional crisis of 1993**. He returned to power in 1996, subsequently improving relations with **Moscow** and campaigning for **Vladimir Putin**; he was reelected in 2000, though with only a plurality (29 percent) of votes cast. The current president is agrobusinessman Nikolay Denin of the **United Russia** party; he won office in 2004 only after Lodkin's name was removed from the ballot days before the election. No longer backed by the Communists, Lodkin has declared himself an independent in the lead-up to the poll, but was barred by a court injunction from running due to the "use of administrative resources, bribing voters, and illegally running for a third term."

BUDDHISM. Buddhism is an indigenous **religion** of a number of Russia's ethnic groups and **national minorities**, including the **Kalmyks**, **Tuvans**, and **Buryats**. Nationwide, there are approximately 70,000 Buddhists in the Russian Federation. Nearly all of these follow the Lamaist school, which is associated with Tibetan Buddhism and part of the Mahayana branch of the religion, though immigrants from **China** and Vietnam practice Theravada Buddhism. A small number of **ethnic Russians** have also converted to Buddhism in recent years. There are Buddhist temples in **Moscow** and **St. Petersburg**, which serve various diasporic communities of Buddhists.

The history of the faith in Russia dates back at least four centuries to when imperial expansion began to include areas in southern **Siberia** and the **Russian Far East**. In the 17th century, the Mongolic Kalmyks migrated to the lower **Volga** region, establishing the only Buddhist community on the European continent. Tsarist authorities were relatively tolerant of Buddhist *inovertsy* (non-Orthodox subjects), while the Soviets attempted to mold the faith and its leaders to fit the ideological needs of the regime. In post-Soviet Russia, Lamaist Buddhism (along with **Orthodox Christianity, Islam**, and **Judaism**) is recognized by the 1993 **Constitution of the Russian Federation** as a "native" religion, and is thus free from the restrictions placed on nonindigenous faiths such as Protestantism and Scientology.

In the traditionally Buddhist regions of the Russian Federation, a spiritual revival has been under way since the late 1980s; this is particularly true in **Kalmykiya** where President **Kirsan Ilyumzhinov** has funded the building and renovation of temples. In Asiatic Russia, traditional forms of **shamanism** are often syncretisticly incorporated into the practice of Buddhism.

The spiritual leader of Tibetan Buddhism, the Dalai Lama, has twice visited the faithful in Russia, once in the early 1990s and again in 2004, sparking criticism from **China**. The Ivolga Datsan, a monastery located in **Buryatiya** near **Lake Baykal**, is the most important Buddhist site in the Russian Federation.

BURYATIYA, REPUBLIC OF. An **ethnic republic** of the Russian Federation. Modern Buryatiya once comprised part of the larger Buryat-Mongolian **Autonomous Soviet Socialist Republic**. In 1937, several districts were excluded from the region, and reformed as the Aga district in Chita (now **Zabaykalsky Krai**) and the Ust-Orda in **Irkutsk**; however, while these units were established as Buryat **autonomous okrugs**, they lacked contiguity with Buryatiya.

Contemporary Buryatiya covers 351,300 square kilometers of the part of southern **Siberia** known as Trans-Baykal (*Zabaikal'e*). It is part of the Siberian **Federal District** and the East Siberian **Economic Region**. Much of western Buryatiya sits on **Lake Baykal**. In addition to neighboring Irkutsk and Zabaykalsky, the republic shares a significant international border with **Mongolia**, as well as a short internal border with **Tuva**. Buryatiya's former territories of Ust-Orda and

Aga are encapsulated by its western and eastern neighbors, Irkutsk and Zabaykalsky Krai, respectively.

Along with a dozen other republics, Buryatiya declared its sovereignty in 1990, and has been granted high levels of autonomy in postindependence Russia. With a population of nearly 1 million, **ethnic Russians** represent a majority (68 percent) of the population. The titular minority, the **Buryats**, account for about 30 percent of the population; the remainder is comprised of nearly a hundred other nationalities. The main faiths of the republic are Russian **Orthodoxy**, **Buddhism**, and **shamanism**.

The region's **economy** is dependent on **agricultural** and commercial products including wheat, timber, furs, and textiles; **industrial** sectors include aircraft manufacture, shipbuilding, and machinery. The region possesses extensive, though underexploited, mineral reserves including half of Russia's lead-zinc ores. Baykal, the deepest freshwater lake in the world, is an important **tourism** destination. Sitting on the **Trans-Siberian** rail line, the capital, Ulan-Ude (pop. 360,000), is a historic trading center that has long connected Russia to Mongolia and **China**.

The National Khural of the Buryat Republic is the republic's representative and legislative body; the parliament has steadfastly resisted efforts by political elites to rescind the requirement that the republican president speak both Buryat and the **Russian language**. Leonid Potapov, an ethnic Russian and former railway engineer, and part of the late Soviet *nomenklatura*, has served as the president of the republic since 1994. Formerly the chairman of Buryatiya's Supreme Soviet, Potapov was popularly elected three times, commanding 68 percent of the vote in the most recent election in 2002.

During the 1998 election, he ordered troops to crush an uprising by Buddhist monks who were advocating greater influence of Buryat culture in the republic, a move that significantly diminished his popularity. He won the hotly contested election because his main competitor dropped out and endorsed him a few days before the election. Potapov abandoned the **Communist Party of the Russian Federation** in 2002, soon gaining the backing of the pro-Kremlin **United Russia**. Potapov has proposed the creation of a greater Baykal region that would include Buryatiya, Irkutsk, Zabaykalsky Krai, and the two formerly autonomous Buryat districts (Ust-Orda and Aga), effectively re-creating the old Buryat-Mongol Republic that was abolished by **Joseph Stalin** in an effort to weaken pan-Mongolism. During his tenure, Potapov has also worked to abolish tariffs on trade with Mongolia and **China**.

In 2007, **Vladimir Putin** nominated Vyacheslav Nagovitsyn, the former vice governor of Tomsk's regional administration, as the president of the republic. An ethnic Russian who had never been to the republic before taking it over, Nagovitsyn declared that knowledge of the Buryat language was a necessary qualification for the presidency and hired a Buryat tutor immediately after coming into office (the language requirement had been waived prior to his appointment).

BURYATS. Ethnic group. Buryats, or *Buryaad*, are the largest minority nationality in **Siberia**, numbering nearly 450,000. While the majority of Buryats reside in the **Republic of Buryatiya**, they also live in the **Irkutsk Oblast** and **Zabaykalsky Krai** (formerly known as the Chita Oblast), especially within the formerly autonomous Ust-Orda and Agin-Buryat **okrugs** of these two administrative units. Only in Aga Buryatiya do they form a majority (63 percent).

The Buryats are a mix of Mongol, Turkic, and Tungus peoples. Buryats are traditionally divided among the following subgroups: Khora, Bugalat, Ekhirit, Khongodor, and Tabunut. Culturally, they resemble Mongolians, possessing similar traditions of nomadic pastoralism and many customs (**sports**, oral history, etc.). Their **language**, Buryat, is a form of Mongolian that has used the Cyrillic alphabet since 1939 (a Latin alphabet was employed in the previous decade). In order to stanch pan-Mongolism in the 1930s, the dialect that least resembled standard Mongolian was chosen for the Buryats by the Kremlin.

The Tibetan form of **Buddhism** (Lamaism) is the dominant religion among Buryats, though many still practice **shamanism** and animism, often in conjunction with Buddhism. Many Buryats living in Irkutsk and other western areas of their traditional homeland have embraced Russian **Orthodoxy**. Founded in the 1990s, the All-Buryat Cultural Association and the Congress of the Buryat People seek to foster Buryat **national identity** in and outside of Buryatiya.

The world-famous model Irina Pantaeva is an ethnic Buryat and was born in Ulan-Ude; she chronicled her early life in Buryatiya in her 1999 autobiography *Siberian Dream.*

BUSH, GEORGE HERBERT WALKER (1924–). American politician. As the 41st president of the **United States** (1989–1993), George H. W. Bush oversaw dramatic changes in relations between Washington and Moscow. Having previously served as vice president (1981–1989) under **Ronald Reagan**, director of the Central Intelligence Agency (CIA), and U.S. ambassador to the **United Nations** (UN), Bush was well versed in foreign policy and had a deep understanding of Soviet affairs.

During the first six months of the Bush presidency, it became clear that the Union of Soviet Socialist Republics (USSR) had loosened its hold on the **Eastern Bloc**, a fact underscored by the destruction of the Berlin Wall in October. Shortly thereafter, Bush met with Soviet Premier **Mikhail Gorbachev** in Malta to discuss the future of American-Soviet **foreign relations**; the summit soon came to symbolize the beginning of the end of the **Cold War**. A careful diplomat, Bush later won support from Gorbachev for the U.S.-led Persian Gulf War (1990–1991) even while his administration openly condemned Moscow's actions against pro-independence forces in the **Baltic States**.

In 1991, the two met again in Moscow where they signed the Strategic Arms Reduction Treaty (START II), significantly reducing both countries' stockpile of **nuclear weapons**. During the **August Coup**, Bush provided public support to **Boris Yeltsin** against the **Communist** hard-liners, thus laying the groundwork for a positive relationship with the newly independent Russian Federation. Though the two signed a number of agreements solidifying the radically altered relationship, Bush did little to assist the new regime in efforts to democratize and institute free-market reforms during the campaign year of 1992. Bush, preoccupied and weakened by domestic issues, was defeated by **Bill Clinton** that November. Both he and Clinton attended Yeltsin's funeral in **Moscow** in 2007.

BUSH, GEORGE W. (1946–). American politician. The son of **George H. W. Bush**, George W. Bush became the 43rd president of the **United States** in early 2001. That summer, he met with **Vladimir**

Putin, who himself was relatively new to the post of Russian president. During the summit in the Slovene capital Ljubljana, Bush, who lacked his father's foreign policy experience, remarked glowingly of Putin, "I looked the man in the eye. I found him to be very straightforward and trustworthy. . . . I was able to get a sense of his soul."

The Bush-Putin relationship deepened shortly after the **September 11 attacks** on New York and Washington. Putin was the first world leader to offer his condolences to the American president and, against the wishes of many of his advisors and Russian public opinion, offered the U.S. substantial support in its "war on terror," including backing plans for American military bases in **Central Asia**. The Bush administration reciprocated by adding **Chechen** groups to its list of international **terrorist** organizations and refraining from harshly criticizing Putin's increasingly neo-authoritarian tendencies. Bush and Putin both spoke of a new "strategic partnership" that had replaced the mistrust and suspicion of the past. However, the warm relations were short-lived.

With a foreign policy team dominated by neo-conservatives, Bush was soon at loggerheads with Russia over how to handle Saddam Hussein, **Iran**'s nuclear program, democracy in the **near abroad**, and a host of other issues. Buoyed by rising **oil** and **natural gas** revenues, Putin took a harsh tone with Bush after the U.S. invasion of Iraq. Despite continued affirmations of a personal "friendship" between the two leaders, U.S.-Russian relations grew more complicated in Bush's second term. The issue of missile defense, which Bush had promised in his first election campaign, eventually sent Russo-American relations to their lowest point since Russian independence, with the Kremlin threatening **North Atlantic Treaty Organization** (NATO) members **Poland** and the Czech Republic with military action.

By 2008, it was clear that Bush had misjudged Putin's willingness to cooperate with the United States and that the American president no longer had any leverage over Putin, who was now prime minister. The **South Ossetian War** triggered accusations and counteraccusations between the Bush and **Medvyedev** administrations, further souring relations. In the first high-level meetings between the new presidential administration of **Barack Obama** and Foreign Minister **Sergey Lavrov**, Secretary of State Hillary Clinton declared Washington's intentions to "press the reset button" with Moscow, explicitly criticizing the poor state of relations wrought by the final years of Bush's presidency. *See also* FOREIGN RELATIONS.

– C –

CANADA (RELATIONS WITH). The Soviet Union established diplomatic relations with Canada in 1942 in the context of a joint military campaign against Nazi **Germany**. Historical ties between the countries were built on similar geography and sharing of **agricultural** knowledge related to their common **taiga** and **steppe**/prairie biomes.

During President **Boris Yeltsin**'s second presidential administration, commercial and diplomatic ties between Ottawa and Moscow were substantially expanded. Both countries are members of the **Group of Eight** (G8) and numerous other international governmental organizations. Bilateral trade was tepid during the 1990s, but a number of new joint ventures (particularly in the **mining** industry) and an expansion of commercial exchange followed the election of **Vladimir Putin**. In 2003, the two countries signed bilateral agreements on combating **terrorism**, organized **crime**, illegal **immigration**, and **narcotics** trafficking.

Diplomatic relations were challenged in 2001 when a Russian diplomat struck and killed a woman in Ottawa while driving under the influence of alcohol. The expulsion of a reputed spy, a Russian citizen operating under the fake name of Paul William Hampel, further dampened relations in 2006.

While Russia and Canada do not share a contiguous border, both countries are increasingly finding themselves in a competitive position in the **Arctic Ocean** as global warming opens the Northwest Passage. The potential for petroleum exploration in the Arctic in the coming decades, as well as lucrative benefits from Arctic shipping, has resulted increasingly in provocative actions by both sides. In 2001, Russia made a new claim to 740,000 square kilometers of the Arctic seabed. In 2007, a Russian submarine planted an underwater **flag** at the North Pole, and Russia began strategic bomber flights over the region.

In response, Canadian Prime Minister Stephen Harper unveiled plans for new naval patrols, 1,000 new Arctic Rangers, and a deep-water port to combat Russian expansion within the Arctic Circle. Under his principle of "use it or lose it," Harper announced in 2008 that Canada will expand its territorial waters by 500,000 square kilometers. While Denmark (via Greenland), **Norway**, and the **United States** all claim status as Arctic nations, Canada's and Russia's long Arctic coastlines make these countries the likeliest competitors for development of the Arctic shelf. *See also* FOREIGN RELATIONS.

CASPIAN SEA. The Caspian Sea is the world's largest enclosed body of water, technically categorizing it as a lake. The sea is intercontinental in nature, separating Europe from Asia, with a surface area of 371,000 square kilometers and a maximum depth of 1,025 meters. It is one-third as salty as ocean water and is home to a large sturgeon population, thus providing much of the world's caviar haul. The **Volga River** empties into the Caspian, consequently serving as a key connection to Russia's shipping and shipbuilding industries.

During much of the 20th century, the Union of Soviet Socialist Republics (USSR) controlled most of the coastline, with **Iran** being the only other country along the basin. However, with the **dissolution of the Soviet Union** in 1991, the newly independent states of **Kazakhstan**, **Azerbaijan**, and **Turkmenistan** became Caspian states, though the Russian Federation retains a significant portion of the coastline. The Russian regions washed by the sea include **Astrakhan**, **Kalmykiya**, and **Dagestan**, which taken together share a 685-kilometer coastline. The Caspian basin is rich in hydrocarbons, and one of the first major **oil** fields is near Baku.

In the post-Soviet period, Azerbaijan has sought to free itself from Russian domination of its export routes for Caspian oil, as well as **natural gas** from its newly tapped Shah Deniz field. The **United States**-backed Baku-Tbilisi-Ceyhan (BTC) pipeline, which transports Azeri oil to the Mediterranean, is the most obvious outgrowth of this strategy. The builders of the more recent Nabucco pipeline similarly seek to circumvent Russian control of transshipment routes.

Iranian-Soviet and post-Soviet agreements on the division of energy and **fishing** rights have complicated relations between the littoral states for decades. During the **Cold War**, Iran and the USSR divided the sea into two sectors and shared the fishing resources. After 1991, Azerbaijan, Kazakhstan, and Turkmenistan argued that they were not parties to the treaty and claimed rights over what they saw as their own territorial waters. Russia, the dominant power in the region, has pushed for a sectoral division of the seabed, with surface resources shared among the littoral states. While this is now the de facto scheme for division of the Caspian, some disputes—particularly between Baku and Tehran—linger.

A 2009 presidential summit between Iran and Kazakhstan underscored that, while some steps have been made toward a final solution, the status of territorial division is still ambiguous. In terms of energy exports, Russia—which commands older pipeline routes—has sought to block any new, westward-bound trans-Caspian pipeline on **environmental** grounds. Turkmenistan and Kazakhstan, however, are interested in diversifying their export routes and escaping Russia's current bottleneck on transshipment to the energy-hungry **European Union**. Kazakhstan has also backed the building of a canal linking the Caspian to the **Black Sea**, thus opening maritime routes for the **Central Asian** nation, as well as landlocked Azerbaijan and Turkmenistan.

With the dissolution of the Soviet Union, Russia became the dominant **military** power in the basin, keeping most of the assets for its own **navy**. Turkmenistan's plans to develop a major new metropolis at the port city of Türkmenbaşy is expected to increase that country's profile as a Caspian state. Kazakhstan's development of the Tengiz oil field on the northeastern shore of the Caspian, one of the largest discoveries in recent history, is also an important development for the future of the basin. *See also* FOREIGN RELATIONS; POLLUTION.

CAUCASUS MOUNTAINS. The Caucasus is a 1,000-kilometer-long mountain system between the **Black Sea** and **Caspian Sea**; its watershed serves as one of the divides between Europe and Asia. The chain is divided between the northerly Greater Caucasus Range and the parallel Lesser Caucasus Range, which lies approximately 100 kilometers to the south. Mount Elbrus (5,642 m) is the highest peak in the range, as well as Europe's tallest mountain.

The chain, which includes a number of stratovolcanoes, is prone to earthquakes, and in 1988 the Spitak earthquake killed more than 25,000 **Armenians**. There are extensive deposits of rare minerals in the range, as well as **oil** and **natural gas** fields. The mountains define two geopolitical regions: the **North Caucasus** (Ciscaucasia), which includes the Russian regions of **Krasnodar** and **Stavropol Krais**, **Adygeya**, **Karachay-Cherkessiya**, **Kabardino-Balkariya**, **North Ossetiya**, **Ingushetiya**, **Chechnya**, and **Dagestan**, and the South Caucasus (Transcaucasia), comprised of the newly independent republics of **Armenia**, **Azerbaijan**, and **Georgia**.

The terms "Caucasus" (*Kavkaz*) and "Caucasian" (*kavkazskii*) are often used in the Russian **language** to denote all indigenous peoples of the region, often with derogatory undertones. Many Russians associate the **Chechens**, Azeris, and Georgians with the **mafia** and/or **terrorism**.

Russian expansion into the region began with the Caucasian War (1817–1864), and continued with the incorporation of Ottoman territories in the southern zones during the second half of the 19th century. The region is historically part of the **Muslim** world and has been the scene of intense civilization conflict for nearly two centuries. Russian **literature** has long represented the region as a wild but noble environment. As the Russian Orient, the Caucasus was romanticized in the works of Aleksandr Pushkin, the Russian national poet, and later became a focus of many of the works of Leo Tolstoy. Seemingly unending conflict in the region is the key theme of contemporary Russian **cinema**.

The landscape is highly variable, consisting of glaciers, marshlands, **steppe**, and alpine meadows. Snowfall is particularly high in the northerly range. Geographic challenges presented by the steep topography make **transportation** and commercial activity quite difficult. The Caucasus is rather poor and underdeveloped in terms of **industry** when compared to other parts of the former Soviet Union. *See also* ETHNIC VIOLENCE; IMMIGRATION; ISLAM; ISLAMISM.

CENTRAL ASIA (RUSSIAN ROLE IN). The region of Central Asia is generally defined as the geopolitical space between Russia, Europe, **China**, and the Indian subcontinent. Since the **dissolution**

of the Soviet Union, the term generally refers to the five republics of **Kazakhstan, Uzbekistan, Turkmenistan, Kyrgyzstan**, and **Tajikistan; Afghanistan** is sometimes included as well. The region is alternatively called Middle Asia or Inner Eurasia, though these terms tend to be more inclusive and may include parts of **Iran** and China, as well as **Mongolia**.

Russia began to expand into the region more than 300 years ago, the result of treaties signed with the **Kazakhs**, who sought protection from marauding bands of Mongolic Dzungars. In the 19th and early 20th centuries, the **Romanovs** expanded southward, conquering the old Silk Road cities of Samarkand, Khiva, Bukhara, and Kokand. Fearful of Russian encroachment in South Asia, **Great Britain** expanded its presence in the region, triggering the century-long contest between the two empires known as the "Great Game" or "Tournament of Shadows." During the Russian Civil War, the Bolsheviks were able to subdue nationalist movements in Central Asia, though a decade-long **Islamist** insurgency known as the Basmachi Rebellion prevented Moscow from exerting complete sovereignty over the region.

During the Soviet period, Central Asia remained relatively unknown to the outside world, and transborder contacts with neighboring China and Afghanistan were significantly curtailed. Moscow subsidized the development of **industry, agriculture**, and **education** throughout the region, resulting in precipitous increases in the standard of living combined with the destruction of traditional **culture** and economic systems. Militarization of the region increased dramatically with the **Soviet-Afghan War**, particularly in Uzbekistan, which served as the staging ground for military activity against the **United States**–backed mujahideen.

With the dissolution of the Soviet Union in 1991, the **union republics** of Central Asia reluctantly embraced independence. Long dependent on subsidies from Moscow, the comparatively poor states remained economically tied to the new Russian Federation. However, over the next few years, exploitation of hydrocarbons and the development of new relations with Iran, the United States, and European nations fomented an increased self-sufficiency among the five republics. However, control of transshipment routes, the presence of millions of **ethnic Russians** in the republics, and the **Tajik**

Civil War allowed Russia to continue to exert a substantial influence over the region. To this day, Russian border control units continue to patrol Tajikistan's frontier with Afghanistan, interdicting **narcotics** and other contraband.

Boris Yeltsin and the five postindependence presidents found common cause in their opposition to Islamist movements, allowing for sustained political cooperation on a number of fronts including the establishment of the Shanghai Five (later the **Shanghai Cooperation Organization** or SCO). All the republics joined the **Commonwealth of Independent States**, though Uzbekistan, under Islam Karimov, generally resented what it saw as Russian neo-imperialism in the region, and went as far as to temporarily join the anti-Russian **GUAM Organization for Democracy and Economic Development**. Turkmenistan, which has a stated policy of neutrality, opted out of all security-related organizations, including the SCO and the **Collective Security Treaty Organization**.

The ascent of **Vladimir Putin** significantly changed the relationship between Russia and the Central Asian republics. Shortly after the **September 11 attacks**, Putin gave a green light to a U.S. military presence in the region, resulting in the establishment of bases in Uzbekistan and Kyrgyzstan. However, as the result of the U.S. invasion of Iraq, Putin's attitude toward the Americans soured, and after Washington's condemnation of events in Andijan, Uzbekistan, in 2005, the SCO moved that the United States set a timetable for removing all its troops from the region. The American base in Uzbekistan was closed within a matter of months, and, shortly after **Barack Obama** assumed the presidency, Kyrgyzstan demanded that the United States close its facilities at Manas, though a subsequent plan allowed Washington to maintain a lessened presence at the site. As a result, Russia has reassumed its position as the sole great power in the region. *See also* FOREIGN RELATIONS; NEAR ABROAD.

CHECHEN REPUBLIC OF ICHKERIYA. Also called the *Noxçiyn Respublika*, the Chechen Republic of Ichkeriya was a secessionist republic established by **Jokhar Dudayev** on 1 November 1991. The only country to recognize **Chechnya**'s independence as Ichkeriya was **Georgia**, under the leadership of Zviad Gamsakhurdia. After several years of Ichkeriya's de facto independence, **Boris Yeltsin**

ordered federal troops into the region, initiating the first **Chechen War**, effectively bringing the region back under Russian control. Ichkeriya is an old place name from the Turkic Kumyk language meaning "that place over there," and was adopted by Dudayev for its romantic connotations from Russian **literature** and its ease of pronunciation in foreign languages. The **Chechen** government in exile continues to use the appellation.

CHECHENS. Ethnic group. With a population of more than 1.3 million, the Chechens (or *Nokhchi*, as they call themselves) are the largest **national minority** in the **North Caucasus** and the sixth-largest ethnic group in the Russian Federation. Like the **Ingush**, they are Vainakh, a grouping of indigenous Caucasian mountaineers. Even in a region known for its martial traditions, the Chechens have long had a reputation as fierce warriors.

Their **language**, Chechen or Nokhchin, is a member of the Nakh subgroup of the Northeast Caucasian language family. While Chechens lack perceptible internal social stratifications within the nation, there is a regional divide between the "Russified" lowlanders in the north and the highlanders in the south, who have maintained more traditional Caucasian cultural practices. Chechen society is strongly influenced by clan (*teip*) affinity. Through the clan structure, enforcement of customary laws (*adat*) in daily life was resurrected after the end of Soviet rule.

Most Chechens observed a locally derived, Sufi-influenced brand of **Islam** prior to the 1990s, although, in the decade after Russia's independence, a significant number embraced the radical and ascetic **Wahhabist** tradition imported by foreign **Islamists**.

The Chechens are the titular majority of **Chechnya**; prior to 1991, they were one of two represented groups in the Checheno-Ingush **Autonomous Soviet Socialist Republic**. In 1944, **Joseph Stalin** ordered their forced removal from the Caucasus as Nazi collaborators. The entire nation was sent in cattle cars to **Siberia** and parts of **Central Asia**, suffering extremely high mortality rates in the process (nearly 80,000 died en route, with a quarter of the remaining population perishing in the first five years). This was the second large-scale deportation of Chechens; after the Great Caucasian War in the 19th century, a sizable portion of the population was exiled to the Ottoman

Empire, punishment for their central role in the 25-year resistance to Russian conquest. In 1957, the Chechens were rehabilitated and they returned to their ethnic homeland; however, unlike other **punished peoples**, the stigma of treason clung heavily to the nation. Suspicion ran so high that Moscow prevented a Chechen from holding the highest office in the republic until 1989.

Anticommunism, Russophobia, and ethnic nationalism were effectively used by **Jokhar Dudayev**'s administration in 1991 to advocate for absolute independence from Russia. Unlike other **ethnic republics** within the **Russian Soviet Federative Socialist Republic** that proclaimed their sovereignty in the final days of the **Soviet Union**, the Chechens attempted genuine secession from Russia. For several years after Russia's independence, Chechnya functioned as a de facto state until **Boris Yeltsin** ordered Russian troops into the country in 1994, triggering the first of two **Chechen Wars**. The chaos that ensued resulted in hundreds of thousands of Chechens fleeing their republic and living as refugees in neighboring **Ingushetiya** or other parts of the Russian Federation. Chechens are widely mistrusted throughout the Russian Federation, as they are commonly associated with the **mafia** and **terrorism**. *See also* ETHNIC VIOLENCE.

CHECHEN WARS (1994–1996 and 1999–2005). In the midst of the **dissolution of the Soviet Union**, the leadership of **Chechnya** declared their independence of Moscow. Rather than confronting **Jokhar Dudayev**'s secessionist regime directly, **Boris Yeltsin** generally ignored the problem after Russian troops were forced out of the area in late 1991, though Moscow supported anti-Dudayev militias with weapons and financing. In late 1994, however, Yeltsin, in an attempt to "restore constitutional order," sent federal troops back into the breakaway region, which now called itself **Chechen Republic of Ichkeriya**. Hopes of a rapid defeat of the rebels were quickly dashed as guerilla fighting and poor morale took their toll on the Russian **military**.

Tens of thousands of civilians were killed in aerial bombardments and urban warfare, and the Kremlin found itself condemned at home and abroad for its conduct of the war. While the Russian **army** was eventually able to take the regional capital Grozny, outright victory proved nearly impossible. **Separatist** warlords such as **Shamil**

Basayev soon took up **terrorist** tactics, such as hostage taking in neighboring regions such as **Stavropol**, **Ingushetiya**, and **Dagestan**. Chechnya's chief mufti, **Akhmad Kadyrov**, then declared the war against the Russians to be a jihad, thus implying that it was the duty of all **Muslims** to defend the breakaway republic. Upward of 5,000 foreign fighters flocked to the Chechen cause, while irregular bands of **Cossacks** lent their support to federal forces, creating an extremely volatile situation across the **North Caucasus**.

Yeltsin, who had hoped that a short and popular war with the separatists would buttress his authority, soon realized that the war was becoming unmanageable and that terrorist attacks were impacting national security. Despite the death of Dudayev on 21 April 1996, the worsening military situation and increasing accusations of routine violations of **human rights** severely hampered Yeltsin's popularity, nearly costing him the **1996 presidential election**. In August, renewed conflict in Grozny and the threat of the complete destruction of the city by military commanders precipitated the **Khasav-Yurt Accord**, which brought about a cease-fire, followed by the withdrawal of all federal troops from the republic in December 1996.

On 12 May 1997, Chechen President **Aslan Maskhadov** visited **Moscow** where he and Yeltsin signed a formal peace treaty and established economic relations between the republic and the rest of the federation. The war cost the lives of 3,800 federal troops, 3,000–4,000 separatists, and more than 100,000 residents of Chechnya, mostly civilians. The civilian casualties were dominated by ethnic **Chechens** but also included approximately 35,000 **ethnic Russians** who died during the initial taking of Grozny.

In the wake of the Khasav-Yurt agreement, a number of the more radical combatants gravitated toward **Islamism**, embracing a strict form of **Wahhabism** combined with a political ideology that advocated the creation of a caliphate in the North Caucasus. Basayev and the Arab-Circassian **Ibn al-Khattab** represented the most dangerous of these belligerents. In the late summer of 1999, the two launched an armed incursion into neighboring Dagestan that roughly coincided with a series of **apartment bombings** in Moscow and other Russian cities (also linked to Chechen rebels). The Kremlin responded by sending federal troops back into Chechnya, ending its de facto independence and triggering the Second Chechen War.

Rather than risk another poorly executed ground war, the Russian military initially favored aerial bombardments to target the Chechen militants. While the tactics were condemned abroad, the actions taken by president-in-waiting **Vladimir Putin** proved popular at home. From December 1999 until February 2000, Russian troops laid siege to Grozny, resulting in massive civilian casualties and the exodus of much of the city's population to neighboring Ingushetiya and elsewhere. With much loss of life, the city was ultimately placed under federal control. In May, Putin appointed Akhmad Kadyrov as president of the republic, reestablishing nominal authority and bringing an end to full-scale war in the region.

Anti-Russian forces continued a deadly guerilla campaign for several years, which led to harsh reprisals from Russian forces and allied militias. Disappearances and cases of torture became commonplace during the period from 2000 to 2005. Terror attacks, hostage taking, and assassinations plagued Chechnya for the next five years. Basayev and others orchestrated a series of terrorist attacks across Russia that claimed nearly 1,000 lives during the same time period. Kadyrov was killed on 9 May 2004 by a bomb blast during World War II memorial celebrations. His son **Ramzan Kadyrov**, a pro-Russian militia commander, ultimately succeeded him as president of the republic.

On 2 February 2005, the leading rebel commander, Maskhadov, declared a unilateral cease-fire, marking the end of major guerilla operations (Maskhadov was killed a month later). In 2006, Basayev was also killed, removing one of the major organizers of war-related terrorism. From 2006 to 2007, the situation in Chechnya greatly normalized; the period saw the return of many refugees and extensive building projects in Grozny. While the war has not been declared officially over, the Kremlin announced that major **counterterrorism** operations ended in April 2009.

The second Chechen War took the lives of upward of 10,000 federal soldiers and police. Roughly the same number of militants—many of them recruited from abroad—died in the fighting, and between 25,000 and 50,000 civilians perished in the fighting and subsequent chaos. Collectively, the two wars have rendered the region an **environmental** disaster zone, claimed nearly 200,000 lives, and created lasting resentment between the various ethnic and religious communities of the entire region. Veterans of the war suffer from intense social problems, and the conflict has had lasting negative impacts on the culture of the army and the police. The effects of the Chechen-led terror campaign have sparked endemic racism across Russia directed at those of "Caucasian" appearance, often resulting in **ethnic violence**.

CHECHNYA, REPUBLIC OF. An **ethnic republic** of the Russian Federation. The Chechen Republic covers an area of 15,300 square kilometers, and has an estimated population of 1.1 million. Of this population, 93 percent are **Chechens**; **ethnic Russians** are 4 percent of the population, and the remaining 3 percent are Kumyks, **Ingush**, and other ethnic groups.

Chechnya is part of the Southern **Federal District** and the North Caucasus **Economic Region**. Its capital is Grozny, a city of slightly more than 200,000 (down approximately half since the mid-1990s). Chechnya is bordered by **Dagestan, Stavropol, North Ossetiya-Alaniya**, and **Ingushetiya** and shares an international frontier with **Georgia**. Its border with Ingushetiya, to which it was bonded during the Soviet era, has yet to be delimited. In the north, the region is defined by fields and forests, while the south is extremely mountainous.

Ravaged by war and **terrorism**, the Chechen **economy** was nearly destroyed in the 1990s. Counterfeiting, **oil** siphoning, illicit trade in **arms** and **narcotics**, hostage-taking, and other **criminal** activities became a central part of the regional economy, alongside traditional occupations such as animal husbandry. The federal government began funneling massive amounts of aid into the region after 2000. Since 2005, stability has allowed for a spate of new building in the capital, creating an economic revival centered on the construction and **banking** industries. Plans for greater local control of the oil sector have also been raised as a way to help the republic wean itself off of federal subsidies.

Tsarist Russia violently incorporated the Chechen lands into the empire during the Great Caucasian War (1817–1864). The conquest was colored by forced conversions, eradication of whole villages, and a scorched-earth policy, which permanently strained relations between the conquering Russians and the subdued **Muslim** nations, particularly the Chechens, who put up the fiercest resistance. Once subdued, many Chechens were forcibly deported to **Turkey** and other parts of the **Middle East**. After a brief period of self-rule in the early days of the Bolshevik regime, the country was once again brought under tight control by **Moscow** and integrated into the Mountain People's Republic of Soviet Russia in 1920.

After the establishment of the Union of Soviet Socialist Republics (USSR), Chechnya became an autonomous oblast within Russia. In 1936, two years after its merger with the Ingush autonomous oblast, a Checheno-Ingush **Autonomous Soviet Socialist Republic** (ASSR) was established as a biethnic homeland for the two nationalities. The ASSR was abolished in 1944, and the Chechens—along with other **punished peoples**—were deported en masse to inner Asia, charged with Nazi collaboration. About a third of all Chechens died en route or as a result of poor conditions upon arrival. During the "thaw" that followed **Joseph Stalin**'s death, the Chechens were rehabilitated and allowed to return to their historical homeland. The displacement and debilitation of the nation, however, produced multiple generations of marginalized and discontented Chechens, resulting in their "criminalization," as many turned to black-market activities to sustain themselves in exile.

The twin policies of **glasnost** and **perestroika** provided an opportunity for Chechen elites to roll back the effects of Russian domination. Inspired by the devolution of power from Moscow to the **union republics** at the end of the 1980s, the Chechens unilaterally declared the creation of the Chechen-Ingush Republic in 1990. This was done in hopes of raising the country to a coequal status with **Lithuania**, **Estonia**, and the other Soviet Socialist Republics, which were beginning to move in the direction of independence from the **Soviet Union**.

In the autumn of 1991, the Supreme Soviet of Chechnya-Ingushetiya, at the direction of the Soviet **air force** general **Jokhar Dudayev**, voted itself out of existence. A **Chechen Republic of Ichkeriya** was declared, and a less-than-fair presidential election put Dudayev in power. With tacit approval, Ingushetiya broke off from the existing republic, allowing Chechnya to pursue its own plans for independence from Moscow. This move effectively paved the way for independence from Russia. The Kremlin—fearing a second round of decolonization which might rend **Tatarstan** and other integral parts of the newly formed Russian Federation from its control—balked at the move, rejecting the declaration of independence as illegal and the election of Dudayev as invalid.

After 1991, Chechnya held an ambiguous status: the country possessed de facto sovereignty without international or Russian recognition of its independence. In 1993, Chechnya did not participate in federal elections and rejected the country's new **constitution**. The diplomatic stalemate lasted until 1994 when **Boris Yeltsin** sent in troops to reintegrate the breakaway province, starting the first **Chechen War**. Yeltsin had been advised that the war would be short, decisive, and popular and would shore up his position going into the **1996 presidential elections**. However, the operation went badly, with atrocities and **human rights** violations regularly committed by both sides.

On 21 April 1996, President Dudayev was killed by laser-guided missiles, after the Russian **military** recognized his mobile phone signature. He was succeeded by his vice president, the Islamist Zelimkhan Yandarbiyev. At the end of the summer, Lieutenant-General **Aleksandr Lebed** and the future Chechen president **Aslan Maskhadov** negotiated the **Khasav-Yurt Accord**, effectively bringing an end to open conflict and delaying action on the status of the republic until 2001 (a formal peace treaty took effect a year later in 1997). During the troubled peace that followed the first Chechen War, the local leadership of the secessionist movement fractured. Once a clearly nationalist affair under Dudayev, by the end of the decade, the political landscape of Chechnya included revolutionary Islamists, the most notorious of whom were **Shamil Basayev** and **Ibn al-Khattab**. Through a nexus of radical imams, Arab influence, and veterans of the **Soviet-Afghan War**, the Chechen nationalist movement was transformed into a transnational Islamist struggle during the first Chechen War.

Following Dudayev's death at the end of the first war, Maskhadov, elected president in 1997, attempted to maintain a secular, nationalist façade in order to sustain support among Western advocates. However, Maskhadov steadily saw his authority sapped by Islamist paramilitaries like Basayev. The 1995 declaration of jihad by Chechnya's supreme mufti, **Akhmad Kadyrov**, attracted numerous Islamist combatants from across the Caucasus, as well as experienced "Afghan-Arab" mujahideen and would-be jihadis from around the Muslim world. The influx of foreign fighters, an expansion of terror attacks, and the limited application of Islamic law (including *shariah* court-ordered executions beginning in 1996) rapidly changed the nature of the conflict. Though Kadyrov would later publicly revoke the decree, ally himself with **Vladimir Putin**, and condemn the "Wahhabification" of his country, his call to jihad permanently reordered Chechen politics and linked the conflict to international terrorism.

From the end of the first Chechen War, the Islamists were no longer content with an independent Chechnya. Instead this increasingly prominent clique articulated its aim of creating a miniature caliphate in the Caucasus where *shariah*, rather than secular law, would prevail. After taking over Chechnya, the goal was to expand the boundaries of the theocratic state to include all the Muslim regions of southern Russia, parts of Georgia, and potentially even oil-rich **Azerbaijan**. Basayev's raid into neighboring Dagestan in August 1999 provided a threatening salvo in this new struggle for ideological supremacy in Chechen politics. Occurring the same month as the Dagestan incursion, the **apartment bombings** in Moscow stimulated renewed calls in Moscow to reign in the Chechens.

On 24 September 1999, then–Prime Minister Putin initiated the second Chechen War under the banner of the "reconquest" of Chechnya. The Russian invasion prompted Maskhadov to return to his earlier role as a guerilla leader (he would die violently in 2005). Federal forces took control of Grozny in 2000, and Putin initiated direct rule of the region from Moscow. His chief administrator was Kadyrov, who was appointed head of the republican administration until he was elected president of the republic in 2003. His rule saw devolution of power from Moscow to Grozny, though federal rule of the province remained partially in effect.

A 2003 referendum to implement a new constitution received strong support, though many Western governments and intergovernmental organizations (IGOs) questioned the viability of holding such a vote given the chaotic conditions in the republic. Kadyrov was assassinated in a Victory Day bombing in 2004. He was succeeded by Alu Alkhanov, who was later dismissed by Vladimir Putin. **Ramzan Kadyrov**, a militia leader and son of the late president, became president in 2007 after reaching the minimum age requirement; he had previously held the office of prime minister and had been functioning as the region's de facto leader for some time. His paramilitaries, dubbed *Kadyrovtsy*, have assumed a major role in security operations since 2005. In recent years, stability has returned to the regional capital, though guerilla and terrorist attacks are still somewhat common. Kadyrov and federal forces have yet to extinguish the shadow government of the Chechen Republic of Ichkeriya, which operates from mountain redoubts in the **North Caucasus** abroad and via its spokesman Akhmed Zakayev, who resides in **Great Britain**.

CHELYABINSK OBLAST. An administrative region of the Russian Federation. Part of the Ural **Federal District** and **Economic Region**, Chelyabinsk is situated in the southern **Urals**, predominantly within Asia. It borders **Kurgan, Sverdlovsk, Bashkortostan, Orenburg**, and northwestern **Kazakhstan**.

The region is highly urban (82 percent) and heavily populated (3.6 million), and covers an area of 87,900 square kilometers. **Ethnic Russians** form a clear majority (82 percent); however, more than 10 percent of the population is either **Tatar** or **Bashkir**.

As a major site for relocation of World War II–era factories, the region is one of Russia's most industrialized, focusing on metallurgy, petrochemicals, and tractor manufacture; as such, it suffers from one of the country's highest **pollution** rates. Due to the 1956 Kyshtym nuclear accident, certain areas of the region are still unsuitable for **agriculture** and water remains unsafe. The region houses a number of "closed cities," including plutonium processing and storage sites, as well as weapons manufacturing plants. The regional capital, Chelyabinsk (pop. 1 million), was, during the Soviet era, also a closed city, though it is now open to **tourists** and investors. The famed Soviet industrial city of **Magnitogorsk** is also located in the oblast.

First elected in 1996 on the ticket of the **Communist Party of the Russian Federation**, Pyotr Sumin is the regional governor of Chelyabinsk Oblast of Russia. He was reelected in 2000 and reappointed for a third term by Russian President **Vladimir Putin**. Once a laggard in terms of **foreign investment**, Chelyabinsk has signed a number of deals in recent years to attract capital from abroad, particularly from **Germany**. *See also* FOREIGN TRADE.

CHERKESS. Ethnic group. The Cherkess, or Cherkessians, are a subgroup of the **Adyghe**. They number approximately 60,000 and are one of two titular nationalities in the **Karachay-Cherkess Republic**, comprising 11 percent of the population. As one of the several **Circassian** peoples, they have cultural and linguistic connections with the **Kabardins** and Abazins, as well as Adyghe who reside in **Adygeya**. Their native **language**, Adyghe, is part of the Northwest Caucasian language family. Ethnic friction with their numerically dominant Turkic **Karachay** neighbors flared in the wake of the 1999 presidential election in their shared republic. *See also* ETHNIC VIOLENCE.

CHERNENKO, KONSTANTIN USTINOVICH (1911–1985). Politician. Born to a miner and a farmer in **Krasnoyarsk Krai**, Chernenko joined the **Komsomol** youth organization in the mid-1920s. After gaining membership in the **Communist Party of the Soviet Union** (CPSU), he took a number of positions in the area of propaganda, first on the Sino-Soviet border and then in **Moldova**. He soon became a protégé of **Leonid Brezhnev**, ultimately serving as his chief of staff after 1960.

Despite the recommendation of **Yury Andropov** that **Mikhail Gorbachev** succeed him as Soviet premier, Chernenko maneuvered himself into the top position upon Andropov's death in 1984. However, Chernenko was already quite ill by this point, and called upon Gorbachev to represent him at many Politburo meetings.

During his 13-month reign as general secretary of the CPSU, Chernenko accomplished little, though he effectively negated Andropov's attempts at economic acceleration (*uskoreniie*). On the international front, he made the decision to boycott the 1984 Olympiad in Los Angeles, in what most viewed as retaliation for the **United States**–led boycott of the 1980 Moscow games in protest of the initiation of the **Soviet-Afghan War**. By early 1985, Chernenko suffered from a variety of illnesses, including hepatitis. He died of heart failure on 10 March 1985; Gorbachev replaced him as premier within a day. *See also* FOREIGN RELATIONS; SPORT.

CHERNOBYL DISASTER. The Chernobyl nuclear reactor accident occurred on 26 April 1986 in Pripiat, **Ukraine**, then part of the Soviet Union. As a result of the explosion of reactor four of the nuclear power plant, a plume of highly radioactive fallout was sent into the atmosphere, covering an extensive geographical territory of the western Union of Soviet Socialist Republics (USSR), as well as other northern European countries. Large areas of Ukraine, **Belarus**, and Russia were contaminated, resulting in the evacuation and resettlement of over 300,000 people. The total cost of counteracting the results of the disaster exceeded $200 billion.

It is believed the nuclear accident occurred as a result of a badly planned and poorly managed scientific experiment that was aimed at testing the work of the reactor's cooling pump system in the possible event of a failure of the auxiliary electricity supply. The overheating reactor caused multiple explosions that blew off the reactor's roof. Because the reactor was not housed in a reinforced concrete shell, the building itself sustained severe damage and large amounts of radioactive pollutants escaped into the atmosphere. The administrators of the nuclear reactor ordered firefighters to climb onto the roof of the reactor and to fight the blaze; many of the personnel died on site or later because of exposure to radiation. The official statistics claimed that 30 people were killed in the explosion; a further 209 involved in the cleanup operation were treated for radiation poisoning. All exposed to radiation were transported to **Moscow** where they received treatment in specialized medical institutions. Within four months of the accident, 28 people died from radiation or thermal burns, and another 19 died later on. The evacuation of the civic population of Pripiat was ordered almost immediately; however, the real explanation for abandoning the city was not given until the information leaked to the press. If the government had not been secretive about the accident, there would have been fewer victims of the disaster in Pripiat and fewer people would have ultimately suffered from radiation poisoning.

Initially, manpower was used to contain the results of the explosion; however, it soon became necessary to use helicopters to drop sand and lead in an effort to prevent further radioactive contamination. Despite these efforts, the Chernobyl disaster released at least 100 times more radiation than the atom bombs dropped on the Japanese cities of Nagasaki and Hiroshima. The number of people who could eventually die as a result of the Chernobyl accident is highly controversial and is believed to be between 9,000 and 90,000. It is assumed that even more people will die of cancer-related problems, with thyroid cancer being the most common cause of death.

Because of the direction of the wind, traces of radioactive deposits were found in many countries in the northern hemisphere; however, Belarus, Russia, and the Scandinavian countries were most affected. Various types of decontamination, preservation, and decommissioning work, including the construction of a replacement shelter covering the reactor's remains, have been carried out. This work has been funded from national budgets—Ukrainian and Russian—as well as by foreign governments and international organizations.

The disaster initiated a major review of the Soviet nuclear program (reactors similar to the Chernobyl one are operating in various parts of the former Soviet Union such as the **Voronezh Oblast**). As part of this initiative, over 1,000 nuclear engineers from the former Soviet Union have visited Western nuclear power plants and there have been many reciprocal visits. The explosion marked a sad coda to the Soviet Union's decades-long campaign to achieve technological and scientific supremacy on the world stage. Arguably, the disaster occurred as the result of a flawed reactor design and because the reactor was operated by inadequately trained personnel and without proper regard for safety.

Mikhail Gorbachev's government initially concealed the news about the explosion from the public; however, the information eventually leaked into the press and caused a nationwide uproar. The government's failure to convey the truth to the citizens caused the government to adopt the principles of political transparency, later known as **glasnost**. The Chernobyl explosion became the first in a series of natural disasters and technological accidents that hit the USSR at the end of the 1980s and early 1990s.

The Chernobyl disaster was largely forgotten in the 1990s as other political, social, and economic issues dominated the **media** and popular imagination, especially with Ukraine becoming an independent state following the **dissolution of the Soviet Union** in 1991. However, the Russian press occasionally reports on the processes of decontamination and preservation being conducted in the 25-kilometer exclusion zone around Chernobyl. Officially, no one is allowed to live in this zone, but some people, especially the elderly who had lived in this area prior to the disaster, continue to do so. In recent years, the exclusion zone has become a source of various legends and conspiracy theories. The Chernobyl tragedy has been memorialized in a number of feature and documentary films. A number of **Internet** sites dedicated to the disaster feature materials related to the construction of the nuclear power station, the accident, and the legacy of the disaster; they serve as a virtual museum of the disaster. *See also* NUCLEAR ENERGY.

CHERNOMYRDIN, VIKTOR STEPANOVICH (1938–). Politician. A long-serving member of the **Communist Party of the Soviet Union**, Viktor Chernomyrdin became the chairman of **Gazprom** when the Union of Soviet Socialist Republics's Ministry of Oil and Gas was reorganized in 1989. Shortly after Russia's independence, **Boris Yeltsin** appointed him prime minister, a position he would hold until 1998.

Chernomyrdin gained an international profile in 1995 when he undertook direct negotiations with **Chechen terrorists** who were holding hostages at a hospital in Budyonnovsk, **Stavropol Krai**. The event was seen as the turning point in the first **Chechen War**. That same year, he established **Our Home—Russia**, a centrist political bloc that supported the president. Despite his reputation as a rather stolid politician, he was often touted as a possible replacement for Yeltsin, most notably by **United States** President **Bill Clinton**. Chernomyrdin had worked closely with Clinton's vice president, Al Gore, in 1994 to improve U.S.-Russian relations in a number of areas including the environment, technology, business development, energy, and defense conversion.

Yeltsin sacked Chernomyrdin on 23 March 1998, ostensibly for his slow progress in implementing economic reform, though Yeltsin tried to reinstate him after the **ruble crisis**. Chernomyrdin then assumed the position as a special envoy to the Balkans, dealing with **Serbia** during the height of the the **North Atlantic Treaty Organization** (NATO)–led assault. In 2001, **Vladimir Putin** appointed him as ambassador to **Ukraine**. His style and statements often grated on the Ukrainian foreign policy elite, and he was relieved by President **Dmitry Medvyedev** shortly after making dismissive comments about the government in Kiev. He was subsequently named a presidential advisor. Chernomyrdin is infamous for his poor command of the **Russian language** and frequent malapropisms.

CHERNOZEM. A darkly colored soil, chernozem or "black earth" contains high percentages of humus, phosphorus, and ammonia, thus making it one of the most fertile types of soil on Earth. There are two chernozem belts in the world; one is the Black Earth Region (*tsentral' no-chernozemnyi region*), which stretches from **Ukraine** to **Siberia**, and the other is found in the **Canadian** prairies. The Russian regions that span the **Eurasian** chernozem belt include **Voronezh**, **Lipetsk**, **Belgorod**, **Tambov**, **Oryol**, and **Kursk**. Historically, this region, along with parts of Ukraine, has served as the breadbasket of Russia, as well as providing grain exports to Europe and forming the **agricultural** core of the country. During the mid-19th century, tsarist authorities, hoping to better understand the ecology of the chernozem zone, established a large area that was to remain uncultivated and in its natural state; this area is today known as the Central Chernozem Biosphere Reserve. Due to the presence of iron ores associated with the Kursk Magnetic Anomaly, the Soviets also industrialized much of the area during the 1930s and beyond. In the post-Soviet period, the chernozem region formed the core of the **Red Belt**, and reliably supported the **Communist Party of the Russian Federation** during the 1990s. *See also* INDUSTRY.

CHINA, PEOPLE'S REPUBLIC OF (RELATIONS WITH). Chinese-Russian relations date to the tsarist conquest of the Russian Far East in the late 17th century. During the early Soviet period, Moscow supported the nationalist Guomintang Party before switching its backing to the Chinese Communist Party led by Mao Zedong. After the establishment of the People's Republic of China (PRC) in 1949, the Union of Soviet Socialist Republics (USSR) supplied weapons, advisors, and financial support to the Chinese Communist Party.

Fraternal relations broke down during the **Khrushchev** era over border disputes, doctrinal disagreements, and global competition for leadership of **Marxism-Leninism**. Relations between Moscow and Beijing reached rock bottom after the opening of relations between

China and the **United States** during the 1970s. Realignment of China's interests in the wake of Mao's death allowed for normalization of relations in the 1980s. With the **dissolution of the Soviet Union** in 1991, Russian-Chinese relations entered a new era based on shared political, security, and economic interests. The first step was to establish the 1991 Sino-Russian Border Agreement, which created mechanisms to solve the two countries' long-standing border disputes. In 2004, the last areas in contention were finally demarcated to the satisfaction of both sides, thus providing a clear Russo-Chinese border for the first time in history.

In 1997, **Boris Yeltsin** and Chinese President Jiang Zemin issued a joint declaration acknowledging a multipolar world and challenging American hegemony in international affairs. This reorientation in diplomacy reflected the ascendency of Foreign Minister **Yevgeny Primakov**, whose doctrine was built on the development of a Moscow-Beijing-New Delhi axis to counter American dominance of the post–**Cold War** world order. The summit of the two leaders marked the beginning of a strategic partnership between the East Asian neighbors. Unfortunately for Taiwan, this new vector undermined the substantive, but unofficial relationship it had developed with the Russian Federation from 1991 until the mid-1990s. Under **Vladimir Putin**, Russia affirmed that Taiwan is an "inalienable part of China" as part of the establishment of a 20-year treaty of friendship between Moscow and Beijing.

Foreign trade—the result of import of cheap Chinese goods and the long 4,300-kilometer-long common border—provided the basis for developing a comprehensive approach to trade and commerce. Annual Russian-Chinese trade, which reached $50 billion by the end of the Putin administration, is growing rapidly. Heilongjiang province, in particular, is engaged in substantial development projects in Asiatic Russia. **Military** hardware and hydrocarbons are key Russian exports. The allure of Russian markets and wide-open spaces has drawn approximately 1 million **Chinese** immigrants across the border, stimulating talk of a new "yellow peril" in Russia, particularly in **Siberia** and the **Russian Far East** where the population density is a fraction of that across the border in northeastern China.

Some friction also exists in the realm of petropolitics; in 2003, Putin scuttled a widely supported **Yukos** plan to develop an oil pipeline to China. Citing the need for market diversification in the western Pacific Rim, he instead opted for a Nakhodka route that confined the pipeline to Russian territory; the move infuriated Beijing and prompted a 2004 visit by Prime Minister Wen Jiabao, who attempted to preserve the Yukos plan. Later, however, Russia's pipeline monopoly **Transneft** began an auxiliary pipeline from Skovorodino in **Amur Oblast** to Daqing, China, which is to be completed in 2009.

The two countries—along with **Uzbekistan**, **Tajikistan**, **Kazakhstan**, and **Kyrgyzstan**—have found common cause against the threat of violent **Islamism**, resulting in the establishment of the **Shanghai Cooperation Organization** (SCO) in 2001. The intergovernmental mutual-security organization, established in 1996 as the Shanghai Five, is dedicated to intelligence and resource sharing to confront **separatism**, **terrorism**, and other forms of extremism within and across their borders.

While many analysts speculate that a new, three-way (Russia-China-U.S.) "Great Game" is now under way for dominance in the region, Chinese and Russian interests have effectively dovetailed in Central Asia, while Washington has been somewhat marginalized. This was particularly evident when China and Russia both backed Uzbekistan's 2005 request that the United States vacate its air base at Karshi-Khanabad.

Members of the SCO held war games in **Chelyabinsk** in 2007; this cooperation followed the Russian-Chinese amphibious exercises in the Yellow Sea known as Peace Mission 2005, which marked the first substantial military cooperation between China and Russia in decades. In the wake of the Treaty of Good-Neighborliness and Friendly Cooperation (2001), the two countries have laid down similar positions on **weapons of mass destruction** (WMDs), international conflict management, and the U.S.-led war in Iraq. Each has also supported the other's position on separatism in their most restive regions: Xinjiang and Tibet (China) and **Chechnya** (Russia).

Both states are key members of the Six-Party Talks on the nuclear disarmament of **North Korea**, a country with which both share an international border. Informally, China and Russia are able to exert significant influence on global markets through the Asia-Pacific Economic Cooperation (APEC) organization and as one-half of the **BRIC** economies, which also includes India and Brazil.

In 2008, **Dmitry Medvyedev** chose Beijing as his first stop outside the former Soviet Union after assuming the presidency, breaking with protocol, which had hitherto dictated that a European capital be the initial overseas destination of the Russian head of state. The itinerary provoked international speculation that Russia had shifted its primary focus to developing its relationship with the East over that with the West. On the visit, Medvyedev met with Chinese leader Hu Jintao and signed a $1 billion agreement on uranium enrichment. In the wake of the 2008–2009 **global financial crisis**, Russia and China drew closer together based on the former's need for access to loans, which were harder to obtain from Western sources. *See also* FOREIGN RELATIONS.

CHINESE, ETHNIC. Ethnic group. While the statistics are highly disputed, there are approximately 500,000 Chinese immigrants living within the Russian Federation, most of whom are in the country illegally. Chinese tend to reside in areas proximate to the Chinese border, namely, **Amur Oblast** and the **krais** of **Primorsky**, **Khabarovsk**, and **Zabaykalsky**. The presence of so many Chinese in areas with historic ties to China, when combined with a steady exodus of **ethnic Russians** from the region, has emerged as a national security issue in contemporary Russia. Most Chinese outside the **Russian Far East** engage in shuttle trade with **Moscow** and other parts of western Russia, often employing the **Trans-Siberian Railway** or other transcontinental routes to move cheap goods to European markets. *See also* FOREIGN TRADE.

CHITA OBLAST. *See* ZABAYKALSKY KRAI.

CHRISTIANITY. The history of Christianity in Russia dates back over a millennium to when Prince Vladimir I of Kiev officially adopted Christianity of the Byzantine rite. As a result of the Great Schism (1054), the eastern (Orthodox) and western (Catholic) branches of Christianity were permanently sundered. Within **Orthodoxy** itself, religious reforms continued throughout the centuries. One reform concerning liturgy principles caused a schism at the end of the 17th century between the so-called **Old Believers** and other members of the Orthodox faith.

With the exception of the Catholic Poles and Lithuanians, most Christian subjects of the **Romanov** Empire were Eastern **Orthodox**, with the vast majority being members of the **Russian Orthodox Church**. Under tsarist rule, Slavic Christians enjoyed the highest status, while non-Orthodox subjects (*inovertsy*), including **Muslims** and **Buddhists**, were often subjected to economic, spatial, and political restrictions. Under Soviet rule, the state vigorously promoted **atheism**, while effectively co-opting the leadership of the Moscow Patriarchy. During World War II, **Joseph Stalin** allowed a resurgence of religious life, particularly among Russian Christians, in an effort to increase patriotism and mollify his Western allies; the new openness toward **religion**, however, was short-lived and the old sanctions were soon reinstated.

Under **perestroika**, restrictions on religious practice were significantly lessened. Since the **dissolution of the Soviet Union**, Russia's identity as a Christian state has returned in force, with many politicians—including **Boris Yeltsin**, **Vladimir Putin**, and **Yury Luzhkov**—striving to demonstrate their religiosity. While a number of **Eurasianist** ideologues stress the positive aspects of Russia's confessional diversity, changes in state policy have led to an increasing Christianization of the **education** system, with Russian Orthodoxy being linked to patriotism.

In the wake of the passage of the 1993 **constitution**, the Russian government recognized four "native" religions: Eastern Orthodoxy (including its Russian, **Ukrainian**, Belarusian, **Armenian**, and Georgian variants); **Islam**; Buddhism; and **Judaism**. While there are still a good number of indigenous Catholics in the country, they, as well as members of other Christian sects, particularly Protestants, face regulation and, in some cases, have been arrested and/or deported. The high birth rate of Russian **Muslims**, when compared to the low fertility rate of the country's Christian population, has generated social issues similar to those found in various countries of the **European Union** that face similar demographic changes. *See also* ALEXIUS II; ISLAMISM.

CHUBAIS, ANATOLY BORISOVICH (1955–). Politician and **oligarch**. Born in the Belarusian Soviet Socialist Republic, Anatoly Chubais was the son of academics; his father was a university lecturer in scientific Communism and his mother was an economist. He continued the family tradition by graduating from the Leningrad Economic Engineering Institute as an economist, joining the **Communist Party of the Soviet Union**, and taking a teaching job at his alma mater. In the early 1980s, he became a leader of an informal market-oriented circle of economists where he met the future prime minister of Russia, **Yegor Gaydar**, and established a network of intellectuals who eventually became distinguished members of the Soviet government.

In the early 1990s, Chubais combined his research activities with a political career, following **Anatoly Sobchak**, who was elected as the chairman of the Leningrad Soviet, into **politics** as his deputy. They both advocated the idea of turning Leningrad into a special economic zone. In 1992, Chubais became a backer of economic **shock therapy**, meant to remedy the economic crisis of the **Gorbachev** years. However, the policy resulted in economic chaos and hyperinflation, as well as mass **unemployment** and poverty. Chubais was also responsible for the controversial voucher program initiated by Yeltsin. As a result, a small number of politically connected individuals, particularly the oligarchs, including Chubais himself, became fabulously wealthy while the rest of the nation was gripped by unprecedented poverty.

In the **1996 presidential elections**, Chubais proved instrumental in returning Yeltsin to office, and was made head of the presidential administration in return. In 1998, after transitioning through several top government posts, including head of the Federal Commission on Securities and Stock Market, he became the head of **Unified Energy System**, which controls the country's power grid. He remained in this role for 10 years until becoming the director of Russian Corporation of Nanotechnologies.

Chubais served as one of the co-leaders of a liberal **Union of Right Forces**. In 2003, the party failed to gain access to the **State Duma**; Chubais's unpopularity with average Russians harmed by the economic chaos of the 1990s was seen as a major reason for the **political party**'s weakness. *See also* ECONOMY.

CHUKCHI. Ethnic group. The Chukchi are the titular minority of the **Chukotka Autonomous Okrug**, but also reside in the **Sakha**,

Magadan, and **Kamchatka** regions of the **Russian Far East**. In total, there are only some 15,000 Chukchi, making them one of the smallest **national minorities** in the Russian Federation. Most Chukchi speak **Russian** as well as Chukchi, which is a member of the Chukotko-Kamchatkan (*Luorawetlan*) language family, and is related to Koryak and Itelman. Chukchi are divided between maritime (Chukchi: "Anqallyt") and reindeer herding (Chukchi: "Chauchu") groups. Chukchi are **shamanistic**; many still retain a belief system that all things—animate and inanimate—possess a spirit, or life force, which can be either beneficial or harmful. The Chukchi have engaged in a modest cultural revival since the initiation of **glasnost**. *See also* INDIGENOUS PEOPLES OF THE NORTH.

CHUKOTKA/CHUKOT AUTONOMOUS OKRUG. An administrative district of the Russian Federation. Located in Russia's extreme northeast, Chukotka shares land borders with **Kamchatka Krai**, **Magadan Oblast**, and **Sakha**. It is part of the Far Eastern **Federal District** and **Economic Region**. It sits on the Bering, Chukchi, and East Siberian seas; at the closest point, it is only 5 kilometers from the American state of Alaska, with which the region has been developing closer trade and **transportation** links since 1991. The region covers an area of 737,700 square kilometers, including Wrangel Island in the **Arctic Ocean**.

Chukotka has a population of just over 55,000, one half of what it was during Soviet times. The principal town and administrative center is Anadyr (pop. 11,000). Chukotka has large reserves of **oil**, **natural gas**, coal, gold, and other natural resources; much of the indigenous population remains linked to traditional occupations such as reindeer herding, hunting, and **fishing**. Once part of the Magadan Oblast, Chukotka declared its independence from the **oblast** in 1991, and officially became a **federal subject** of the Russian Federation in 1993, though it, like other **autonomous okrugs**, remains partially subordinate to another federal subject (in this case, Magadan). Recently, a proposal has been made to reverse this development.

The titular minority, the **Chukchi**, account for 24 percent of the population. **Ethnic Russians** form a majority (52 percent) in the province, with **Ukrainians** (9 percent), Yupik (3 percent), and Even (2.6 percent) rounding out the population.

Beginning in 2000, the billionaire **oligarch** and owner of the Chelsea Football Club, **Roman Abramovich**, served as governor of the region. He replaced the unpopular Aleksandr Nazarov. Abramovich has invested hundreds of millions of dollars in Chukotka and reportedly used the region as a **tax** haven for his company **Sibneft**, while the company made major investments in the local **economy**. Abramovich was reappointed, reportedly against his wishes, as governor in 2005 by **Vladimir Putin**. In 2008, Roman Kopin, a former aide to both Nazarov and Abramovich, took over the governorship.

CHUVASH. Ethnic group. At 1.6 million, the Chuvash are Russia's fourth-largest **ethnic minority**. Their origins can be dated to the establishment of the Volga-Bulgar state in the 10th century. Ethnically, the Chuvash are a mixture of Turkic Bulgars and Finno-Ugric **Maris**; however, their **language**, Chuvash, is the only surviving member of the Oghur subfamily of Turkic languages, which includes the dead languages of Khazar, Hunnic, and Bulgar.

Chuvash identity experienced a renaissance in the 1980s, centered on the Chuvash Public Cultural Center. This cultural revival gained political strength with the establishment of the National Rebirth Party (led by the philologist Atner Khuzangai, son of the preeminent Chuvash poet of the 20th century) and other nationalist organizations in 1991, and the increasing tendency of ethnic Chuvash to speak their mother tongue in public areas. Nationalism, which was quite tepid (described by some pundits as "ethnic nihilism") in the late 1980s, grew in strength by 1991 when some nationalist leaders, including the future president Nikolay Fyodorov, called for **Chuvashiya**'s elevation to the status of a **union republic**.

While the vast majority of Chuvash are nominally **Russian Orthodox** due to mass conversions in the 18th century under Russian rule, some retain **Islam** from the period when they were governed by the **Tatars**, while others have more recently converted due to proselytizing effort of **Muslims** from **Turkey** and **Central Asia**. Until the mid-20th century, **Christianity** as practiced by the Chuvash remained highly syncretic, continuing many animist folk practices. Since the **dissolution of the Soviet Union**, a number of Chuvash have embraced Sardash, a form of **neo-paganism** based on ancestral practices and purportedly influenced by Zoroastrianism. This belief system has been promoted by many Chuvash intellectuals as a national religion; it also has a strong ecological orientation, which has attracted **environmentally** minded Chuvash.

CHUVASHIYA/CHUVASH REPUBLIC. An **ethnic republic** of the Russian Federation. Chuvashiya is a densely populated republic covering 18,300 square kilometers of the heart of European Russia. It is part of the **Volga Federal District** and the Volga-Vyatka **Economic Region**. Encompassing part of the Volga valley, the Chuvash plateau is defined by wooded **steppe**, low hills, and ravines. The Chuvash Republic is crisscrossed by the Volga, Sura, and Tsivil rivers, while also possessing more than 400 lakes.

The region is both well situated and economically well developed, being a major center for electricity generation, **natural gas** refining, metalworking, and chemical manufacturing, as well as **agricultural** output, particularly hops production for the country's beer-making industry. It is bordered by the ethnic republics of **Tatarstan**, **Mari El**, and **Mordoviya**, as well as the **Nizhny Novgorod** and **Ulyanovsk** oblasts. The capital, Cheboksary (pop. 450,000), is situated in the extreme north of the republic, on the right bank of the Volga.

Chuvashiya has one of Russia's highest population densities, ranking fourth among the regions. Out of a population of approximately 1.3 million, the titular majority, the **Chuvash**, account for 68 percent, while **ethnic Russians** are about 27 percent of the population; **Tatars** are the third-largest ethnic group in the republic. Rare among titular nationalities, Chuvash are demographically dominant in nearly every part of their republic, the exceptions being the Alatyr and Porets districts.

Nikolay Fyodorov is the republic's president; he took office in 1994 and was reelected in 1997 and 2001. He has promoted market reforms and entrepreneurial activity, as well as encouraging **foreign trade**. The economic fortunes of the republic suffered greatly from the **dissolution of the Soviet Union**. Competition with foreign producers doomed the local tractor factory, and the region's cotton mills lay fallow without imports of Uzbek cotton. The Khimprom installation, which produced half of the Soviet Union's chemical weapons, was forced to retool for a post–**Cold War** world.

A lawyer by training and a former member of Russia's Ministry of Justice, Fyodorov left **Boris Yeltsin**'s administration in protest over the coming **constitutional crisis of 1993**. An ethnic Chuvash, the president has made ethnic harmony a keystone of his governance, while supporting a resurgence of the **Russian Orthodox Church**. He gained popularity among ethnic Russians in the region by promising not to pursue the "Tatarstan model" for the republic. While generally maintaining good relations with Moscow, the president clashed with Yeltsin in 1995 over the participation of Chuvash soldiers' service in **Chechnya** and served as spokesman for the six republican presidents who opposed the Kremlin's policy toward the breakaway region.

Despite such independent-mindedness, Fyodorov was clearly the establishment candidate in the 1997 elections; federal-level support for his reelection was given by **Yury Luzhkov** and **Aleksandr Lebed** among others, helping him beat back a wave of **Communist** and radical Chuvash nationalist antipathy. In recent years, Fyodorov has begun to tout his region's morality, spirituality, and healthy living as a solution to the social problems facing 21st-century Russia.

CINEMA. *See* FILM.

CIRCASSIANS. Ethnic group. A rather vague term, "Circassian" is used to refer to a number of ethnically related Northwestern Caucasian peoples including the **Adyghe**, **Kabardins**, **Cherkess**, and, to a lesser extent, Abkhaz, the titular population of the breakaway Georgian republic of **Abkhazia**. Once simply an exonym applied by the conquering Russians, it has become a self-identifying term for many non-Turkic, **Muslim** *muhajirs* (Arabic: "emigrants") who fled the North Caucasus during the 19th century.

CIVIL SOCIETY. Due to Russia's status as an autocratic state under the **Romanovs** and decades of totalitarianism under **Joseph Stalin**, the country did not develop the overlapping and interlinking networks of civic associations that characterized many countries in Europe and the Western Hemisphere during the 20th century. Even societal organizations that resembled Western-style civic groups, such as the Pioneers and **Komsomol** youth organizations and volunteerism initiatives such as the *subbotniki* (weekend labor programs), were controlled by the **Communist Party of the Soviet Union** and thus not autonomous from the state. At the same time, Soviet citizens engaged in a number of unofficial, underground networks that often resulted in political and/or criminal persecution. Furthermore, philanthropy in the Union of Soviet Socialist Republics (USSR) was anemic, thus explaining the historical weakness and small numbers of charitable and nonprofit organizations.

During the 1990s, the country entered a new era in which many hoped for the birth of a genuine civil society (*grazhdanskoie obshchestvo*). Such expectations stemmed from the proliferation of "informal," horizontal organizations under **Mikhail Gorbachev**'s **perestroika**. During this period, three principal categories of nongovernmental organizations (NGOs) flourished: cultural organizations dedicated to the revival and preservation of minority **languages**, **religions**, and identities; special-interest groups comprised of individuals with a common cause, such as **Pamyat**, the **Committee of Soldiers' Mothers of Russia**, the Association of Private Family Farmers and Agricultural Cooperative Enterprises of Russia (AKKOR), **Russian Orthodox** associations, and **women**'s groups; and ecological and **environmental** organizations, particularly in the wake of **Chernobyl**. Regarding the latter, Moscow's decision to abandon its plans to divert some **Siberian** rivers as part of **Central Asian** irrigation schemes is seen as the first great victory for a Soviet grassroots movement.

However, the social disruption caused by the **dissolution of the Soviet Union** wreaked havoc on many voluntary organizations, eliminated the need for some, and resulted in the co-optation of others by the state or **political parties**. During **Boris Yeltsin**'s administration, many new civic groups formed, but most were unable to sustain themselves in the chaotic economic and social environment due to a general lack of professionalization of their leadership and difficulty in securing funding. The latter problem was, to some extent, ameliorated by wealthy foreign donors such as the Ford Foundation and **George Soros** and financing by Western governments, particularly the **European Union**, **United States**, and **Great Britain**. Today, more than half of all Russian NGOs receive some foreign funding. However, lingering mistrust of organizations stemming from their compulsory nature under the Soviets, both among high-profile **dissidents** and the average citizen, has kept participation in civic organizations low.

The Soviet state's co-optation of **trade unions** and Russian society's comparative classlessness also hampered the post-Soviet development of its civil society, especially given that Russia's professional classes (doctors, academics, engineers, etc.) suffered most under **shock therapy**, thus limiting their ability to support the growth of citizen associations. During the late 1990s, a number of **oligarchs** began funding their own pet projects through philanthropy, which helped some hand-picked NGOs including **Jewish** groups, **educational** foundations, and charitable organizations.

With the rise of **Vladimir Putin**, the status of Russia's NGOs has become more uncertain. New legislation made the registration of civic organizations more difficult and expensive; critics suggest that corporate and government interests are colluding to prevent citizens' organizations from making their voices heard. The funding of government-organized civic organizations, particularly patriotic youth groups, served to undermine the allure of genuine grassroots organizations. Many civic organizations took the arrest of **Mikhail Khodorkovsky** as an ominous sign that anti-Kremlin activism was becoming increasingly dangerous. In recent years, attempts at strengthening Russia's "sovereign **democracy**" have led to the government shutting down or harassing **human rights** activists, Western-funded NGOs, and pro-democracy groups.

In recent years, migrant support groups as well as anti-**immigration** organizations have flourished in the Russian Federation. The taming of the Russian **media** under Putin has also negatively impacted the country's civic commitment, as **television** programming has turned from a focus on hard news and social problems toward "infotainment." At the same time, the rapid development of Russian cyberspace has supported the growth of virtual advocacy groups across the Russian Federation. In a number of cases, **Runet**-based activism has resulted in legislative reform and policy changes.

In 2009, President **Dmitry Medvyedev** called on Russians to join civic organizations, arguing that they were essential to the fabric of society. In part, he was responding to new demands placed on the government as a result of the 2008–2009 **global financial crisis**, suggesting that NGOs could shoulder some of the burdens on the country's educational and **health care** systems. In an implicit criticism of his predecessor's restrictions on NGOs, he condemned the attempt by those in power to maintain "total control." *Izvestiya* estimates that there are about 70,000 civic organizations operating in Russia at present.

CLIMATE. Due to its sheer size and bicontinental **geography**, Russia's climate runs to the extremes; however, it is largely continental in nature, with hot summers and long, snowy winters. Autumn and spring are rather brief, both featuring periods of *rasputitsa* (quagmire season), characterized by rapid rainfalls and melting of the ground snow, that make many roads impassable. Russia's harsh winter weather has historical relevance, stymieing invasions by both Napoleonic **France** and Nazi **Germany**. Summers in the European part of Russia are very warm and beautiful with plenty of sunshine and long balmy evenings. In the summer, many Russians move out to the countryside to enjoy the delights of rural and **dacha** life. There are numerous resorts, especially near rivers and lakes, where Russians spend their summer holidays.

The record low temperature is –71° Celsius, recorded in 1974 in the **Far North**; this is the lowest recorded temperature in any inhabited portion of the globe. In most of European Russia, the average yearly temperature is just below freezing, while in **Siberia**, the average is much lower. Russia's large mountain ranges, as well as the Himalayas, tend to block moderating climate patterns from the Indian and Pacific oceans. Unlike most of northern Europe, Russia is too far to the east to benefit from the warming influence of the North Atlantic Current. Unfortunately, the north-south axis of the **Ural Mountains** does little to protect the country from weather patterns originating in the **Arctic Ocean**. Exceptional climatic zones include the maritime climate of the Baltic exclave **Kaliningrad**, small subtropical areas around the **Black Sea**, the **tundra** in Russia's Far North, and the monsoonal climate of the **Russian Far East**.

During the winter, railways and other **transportation** routes in Siberia use frozen rivers and lakes, due to the dependability of the cold conditions. In the Far North, many edifices are built directly on the permafrost. At the northern latitudes, the lack of sunlight, long nights, and cold temperatures require increased demands for **health care** and energy; during the Soviet era, much of this was subsidized by the state, but since the **dissolution of the Soviet Union**, life in these regions has become more difficult and many Russians have quit the north, heading to **Moscow, St. Petersburg**, or southern Russia. The exception is regions where hydrocarbon and mineral exploitation allows for higher wages, such as **Khantiya-Mansiya** and **Sakha**. Precipitation in Russia is comparatively low; this is especially the case along the Arctic Ocean coastline and the semiarid **steppe** zones near the 6,500-kilometer-long **Kazakhstan** border.

The climate's influence on **agriculture** is profound; in much of the northern half of the country, the **taiga** dominates, preventing most forms of traditional agriculture. As a result, animal husbandry, particularly reindeer herding, remains a traditional occupation. In the southern reaches of Russia, **chernozem** and other fertile soils are common, which, combined with the region's ample summertime sunshine, produce grains, potatoes, and vegetables in large quantities. Russia's citrus and other warm-weather crops are produced in a relatively compact area in and around the **North Caucasus**. *See also* RURAL LIFE.

CLINTON, WILLIAM JEFFERSON ("BILL") (1946–). American politician. With little foreign policy experience, the former governor of Arkansas and 42nd president of the **United States** Bill Clinton tended to focus on his personal relationship with **Boris Yeltsin** in U.S.-Russia relations. Far from being a micromanager of **foreign relations**, Clinton delegated key policy decisions to subordinates, especially Deputy Secretary of State Strobe Talbott, who was known colloquially as the "Russian hand." Clinton often leveraged his strong personal bond with Yeltsin to encourage Yeltsin to accept American policies that were deeply unpopular in Russia.

On Clinton's watch, the United States strongly advocated **shock therapy** for the Russian **economy**, expanded the **North Atlantic Treaty Organization** (NATO) into the former **Eastern Bloc** and ultimately up to Russia's borders, and bombed **Serbia**, a traditional Russian ally and fellow **Orthodox** country in defense of **Muslim** Bosnians and Kosovars. Clinton, who was generally more focused on domestic economic concerns than foreign affairs, steadfastly backed Yeltsin during his darkest hours, including the violent **constitutional crisis of 1993**, the first **Chechen War**, and the president's frequent bouts of erratic behavior brought on by **alcoholism**.

In 1994, Clinton directed his vice president, Al Gore, to collaborate with Prime Minister **Viktor Chernomyrdin** on an expansive reworking of Russo-American ties, which established a working relationship on issues such as **environmentalism**, **foreign trade** and **investment**, energy, security, and promotion of **democracy**. The relationship between Clinton and Yeltsin became somewhat frayed in the last year of the 1990s as the **ruble crisis** forced Yeltsin to purge his cabinet of economic reformers and pro-Western **Atlanticists** and stack it with nationalists and strong statists like **Yevgeny Primakov**.

Disputes over the situation in **Kosovo** and the prospective admission of the **Baltic States** into NATO proved especially controversial in Russia. Clinton's own political weakness—both as a lame duck and the target of impeachment hearings over his sexual relationship with an intern—limited his ability to sway Russia on these issues. Following the precipitous departure of Yeltsin from national politics in 2000, Clinton had few levers of influence in Moscow. **Vladimir Putin**, realizing he had nothing to gain from embracing the disgraced Clinton, received him coldly and waited for his successor to be determined and then inaugurated.

Clinton, along with his predecessor **George H. W. Bush**, attended Yeltsin's funeral in 2007.

COLD WAR. The Cold War refers to the nearly half-century-long ideological, **military**, economic, and cultural struggle between the **United States** and the Soviet Union. In the wake of World War II, the erstwhile allies fell into repeated disputes over the postwar settlement in Europe, and in particular, how to deal with a defeated **Germany**. By 1948, the conflict had boiled over into the near East, with the U.S. backing anti-Soviet regimes in Greece, **Iran**, and **Turkey**. In Moscow, the American strategy of "containment" of Soviet expansion was viewed as a calculated policy of encirclement, and the Kremlin responded by providing economic and military support to national liberation struggles in the **Middle East**, Africa, Asia, and Latin America.

Three "proxy wars," involving substantive military support of allies, were fought between the two powers: the Korean War (1950–1953), the Vietnam War (1959–1975), and the **Soviet-Afghan War** (1979–1989). Full-scale conflict between the two powers was dutifully avoided due to each side's possession of large arsenals of **nuclear weapons**. The conflict was felt most keenly in Europe; the continent was divided along ideological lines, colloquially named the "Iron Curtain," a division that cut Germany and its largest city, Berlin, in half. In the **Eastern Bloc**, the Union of Soviet Socialist Republics (USSR) wielded extensive control over both the foreign and domestic policies of its allies through the **Warsaw Pact**, while in Western Europe, the U.S. acted as a political hegemon via the **North Atlantic Treaty Organization** (NATO) and a domineering partner through its domination of the neo-liberal economic system.

Punctuated by periods of crisis and détente, frictions were intense during the first years of **Ronald Reagan**'s presidency before abating under the new Soviet Premier **Mikhail Gorbachev**. The two leaders began negotiations on the reduction of their nuclear arsenals in the 1980s, which culminated in the Strategic Arms Reduction Treaty (START), and laid the groundwork for START II which was signed by **Boris Yeltsin** and **George H. W. Bush** in 1993. Gorbachev's internal reforms (particularly **perestroika** and **glasnost**) and his shift in policy toward the Soviet Union's Eastern European satellites significantly lessened hostilities between the superpowers.

From 1989 to 1991, the fall of the Berlin Wall, the abandonment of one-party totalitarianism in the Eastern Bloc, and the end of the **Communist Party**'s monopoly on power in the USSR led to an effective termination of the Cold War. The **dissolution of the Soviet Union** in December 1991 and new diplomatic relations between an independent Russian Federation in 1992 solidified this development.

In recent years, there has been talk of a "new" Cold War in political media circles, a reaction to Vladimir Putin's increasingly aggressive foreign policy and provocative actions, particularly against NATO aspirants **Georgia** and **Ukraine**. However, relations between Washington and Moscow remain relatively cordial compared to the period from 1948 to 1985. *See also* FOREIGN RELATIONS.

COLLECTIVE SECURITY TREATY ORGANIZATION (CSTO). Military alliance. Also referred to as the Tashkent Treaty, the Collective Security Treaty Organization is a military extension of the **Commonwealth of Independent States** politico-economic union intended to protect the territorial security of its members. The CTSO stipulates that an attack on one member of the group, which includes the Russian Federation, **Tajikistan**, **Armenia**, **Belarus**, **Kyrgyzstan**, **Kazakhstan**, and **Uzbekistan**, will be interpreted as an attack on all the members. Members also agree not to join other collective security arrangements such as the **North Atlantic Treaty Organization** (NATO), which is seen as the greatest threat to the military pact.

In 2008, the first major joint military exercises took place in Armenia under the banner of "Rubezh 2008." An as-yet-unproven rapid reaction force for dealing with threats in **Central Asia** is currently in development. The organization, originally comprised of only six members, was created on 7 October 2002; Uzbekistan formally joined in 2008. After 2006, the organization, which had seen tepid participation by its members, became more politically salient in the face of spreading **color revolutions** across post-Soviet space. An annual rotating presidency is employed among the member states.

The current secretary general is the Russian General Nikolay Bordyuzha. In 2007, he made headlines by implying that **Iran**, a state from outside the former Soviet Union, could potentially join the organization in order to help combat **narcotics** trafficking in **Central Asia**, a major concern of all members.

COLOR REVOLUTIONS. The term "color revolution" has been applied to a number of political upheavals across the former Soviet Union, beginning with the Rose Revolution in **Georgia** (2003), the Orange Revolution in **Ukraine** (2004–2005), and the Tulip Revolution in **Kyrgyzstan** (2005).

In Georgia and Kyrgyzstan, a sitting president was ousted by street protests that employed no or low levels of violence. In Ukraine, the results of a hotly contested election to replace the incumbent led to similar political action, resulting in the ultimate victory of Viktor Yushchenko over the pro-Russian candidate, Viktor Yanukovych. In the first two instances, the **United States** and other Western powers strongly backed the antiestablishment forces, whereas Washington had little public involvement in Kyrgyzstan events.

The antiauthoritarian bent of the protestors and Western backing (primarily through distribution of information, nongovernmental organizations, and **civil society**–building tools), combined with

Russia's loss of influence in Georgia, Ukraine, and—at least initially—Kyrgyzstan, resulted in **Vladimir Putin** taking a strident stand against further "color revolutions" in post-Soviet space. Consequently, Putin provided unflinching support to **Uzbekistan**'s president Islam Karimov when he violently crushed an uprising in the Andijan province in 2005. Putin gave substantial support to Aleksandr Lukashenko's regime in **Belarus** when it faced a popular election in 2006, thus averting the "Jeans Revolution" promised by the opposition.

At home, Putin consolidated the Kremlin's control of the mainstream **media** and formed pro-state youth groups such as **Nashi** to prevent similar uprisings against his increasingly neo-authoritarian rule. Fearful of Western-backed regime change via such uprisings, other members of the **Commonwealth of Independent States** (CIS), including **Kazakhstan** and **Armenia**, have made their opposition to such "revolutions" known. Moscow has used this fear to expand its own influence in the "managed democracies" of the CIS. *See also* FOREIGN RELATIONS.

COMMITTEE OF SOLDIERS' MOTHERS OF RUSSIA. Nongovernmental organization. As the **Soviet-Afghan War** drew to a close, the returning soldiers and officers began to tell their accounts of the disorder and brutality they had experienced in the Soviet army. Many of their stories leaked into the press and became one of the main concerns of the burgeoning **glasnost** and **perestroika** period. In 1988, the Soviet government changed the existing conscription law, keeping young men from postponing **military** service in order to complete their higher education. The alteration of the law caused an uproar in the nation and triggered a wave of protests across the country, led by the mothers of young conscripts. At the same time, Mariya Kirbasova, responding to the rise in political action among military families, founded the Committee of Soldiers' Mothers of Russia (later known as the Union of Committees of Soldiers' Mothers of Russia) in 1989. Its main objective was to protect **human rights** of soldiers serving in the Russian military. The members of the organization lobbied successfully to change the conscription law, bringing back a set of laws allowing student deferments.

Since then the committee has sought to end abuses in the **army**, especially the unofficially institutionalized bullying of junior conscripts (*dedovshchina*). Their campaigning resulted in a series of new laws and practices that were introduced by the Soviet and eventually Russian government. For example, in 1990, **Mikhail Gorbachev** established a special government committee to investigate deaths and trauma in the Soviet army. In 1991, for the first time, life and health insurance was provided to Russian service members. The same year, it was decided that voluntary consent rather than mandatory conscription was necessary for military service in the **Caucasus**. In the mid-1990s, many soldiers who had refused to serve in the army in **Chechnya** (and thus faced criminal prosecution) were released thanks to the efforts of the committee. Also in response to the organization's efforts, the government allocated funds in the army budget for the search and identification of deceased military personnel. Thus, the committee helped to shape a more humanistic environment in the Russian military; however, members of the committee recognize they are still far away from eradicating all atrocities. Therefore their strategic goal is promoting the transition from a conscript system to a volunteer military service.

While working with service members, the committee also provides legal and financial assistance to the families of dead soldiers. With its main task being to expose the violation of human rights in the army, the organization conducts research on service-related deaths and injuries in the military. The committee has been involved in educational projects to inform recruits, army soldiers, and their families of their rights. The members of the committee have also been involved in political activism; in 1995, they organized "The March of Compassion" that went from **Moscow** to the Chechen capital Grozny and drew support from **Chechen** mothers opposed to the first **Chechen War**.

The work of the committee has been recognized internationally; it was nominated for the Nobel Peace Prize in 1995.

COMMONWEALTH OF INDEPENDENT STATES (CIS). Intergovernmental organization. In the wake of the **August Coup** of 1991, the leaders of the **union republics**, excluding the **Baltic States** and **Georgia**, strove to preserve some aspects of the union that had bound their countries together since 1922. However, political expediency, domestic issues, and popular resentment at the now-defunct **Communist Party of the Soviet Union** (CPSU) made the conversion of the Union of Soviet Socialist Republics (USSR) into a proposed Union of Sovereign States a nonstarter during the **dissolution of the Soviet Union**. The **New Union Treaty** failed to be ratified, and in early December 1991, the leaders of Russia, **Belarus**, and **Ukraine** met outside Minsk to sign the **Belavezha Accords**. This meeting produced the Creation Agreement, which abolished the Soviet Union and established a loose confederation known as the Commonwealth of Independent States.

On 21 December, **Kazakhstan**, **Kyrgyzstan**, **Turkmenistan**, **Uzbekistan**, **Tajikistan**, **Moldova**, **Azerbaijan**, and **Armenia** joined, bringing the organization to 11 members. Georgia, in the midst of its own civil war, waited until 1993 to become part of the group. The Baltic States, which had been annexed during World War II, abstained from any post-Soviet alliances with Russia. Ukraine and Turkmenistan, though signatories to the CIS treaty, have never ratified the CIS charter, making the former a participating member and the latter an associate member. In the wake of the 2008 **South Ossetian War**, Georgia declared its intention to leave the CIS by the end of 2009.

The purpose of the CIS is to provide a regional framework for security, economic, political, and legal cooperation among its members. While the CIS meets regularly and engages in policy discussions, the organization has few powers, causing it to be often referred to as a "paper tiger." Substantive cooperation occurs in the CIS' affiliated organizations such as the **Collective Security Treaty Organization** and the **Eurasian Economic Community**. During the **Yeltsin** administration, the Russian Federation used the CIS as a mechanism for **peacekeeping** operations in **Central Asia**, the **Caucasus**, and other parts of the former Soviet Union.

The CIS was thus seen as a postimperial extension of the Kremlin's power, giving rise to the notion of a **Monroeski Doctrine**. Under **Vladimir Putin**, the organization has been reinvigorated, after almost passing out of existence in 1998–1999. Recently, it has been used as a tool to stanch the spread of so-called **color revolutions** across post-Soviet space. Since 2000, the CIS has also engaged in election monitoring in the region and backed the increased use of the **Russian language** in its member states. While the CIS has never evolved into a Eurasian counterpart to the **European Union**, it remains a forum for discussion and debate among the former Soviet republics. In 1992, the CIS sent a joint team to the Barcelona Olympic Games; such cooperation was not repeated in subsequent Olympiads. *See also* FOREIGN RELATIONS.

COMMUNIST PARTY OF THE RUSSIAN FEDERATION (KPRF). Political party. Known in Russian as the *Kommunisticheskaia partiia Rossiskoi federatsii*, the KPRF is the political successor to the banned **Communist Party of the Soviet Union**, also known as the Bolshevik Party. Out of the ashes of the banned Communist Party of the **Russian Soviet Federative Socialist Republic**, **Gennady Zyuganov** established the party in 1993, with the help of Soviet-era politicians **Yegor Ligachev** and **Anatoly Lukyanov**. Under the influence of Zyuganov, the party married **Marxism-Leninism** with nationalism, sometimes called popular patriotism. **Anti-Semitism**, neo-Slavophilism, and **Stalin** worship are also evident in the party platform, which shares certain attributes with other "great power" (Derzhava) political parties.

The ideologue **Aleksandr Dugin** exercised influence over the party during its early days, thus injecting a strain of **neo-Eurasianism** into the KPRF's approach to domestic **politics** and **foreign relations**. The Communist Party, like other ultranationalist parties, pays lip service to the restoration of Russia's historical boundaries, including reincorporation of the **near abroad** and abrogation of the **Belavezha Accords**. The KPRF is stridently anti–**North Atlantic Treaty Organization** (NATO) and is particularly suspicious of British and American foreign policy; anti-**globalization** is also part of the party platform. On the domestic front, the party supports free **education** and **health care**, an end to labor "parasitism," collective rights and security, and the ultimate realization of Communism as the future of mankind.

In order to obtain these goals, the KPRF advocates ending the **mafia**'s alleged control over the state and **economy**, terminating Russia's forced capitalization, and introducing state regulation of all major economic sectors. While the newly formed KPRF fared rather poorly against Russia's other political parties, particularly the **Liberal Democratic Party of Russia** (LDPR), in the 1993 **State Duma** elections, Zyuganov turned the Communists into the country's most popular party by 1995 when the KPRF outpaced its nearest rival by more than two-to-one, taking 157 of the Duma's 450 seats. The Communists were especially popular in the so-called **Red Belt**, a band of regions in southern European Russia that favored continued subsidies of health care, support for local **industry**, and restrictions on **foreign trade** and **investment**.

In the **1996 presidential election**, Zyuganov emerged as the early front-runner as **Boris Yeltsin** scrambled to regain his earlier popularity. The KPRF established the **Russian All-People's Union** as a leftist umbrella organization in order to increase Zyuganov's influence at the national level. Only after a hard-fought campaign, in which forces allied with the Kremlin—including the **oligarchs** and regional governors—branded the Communists as warmongers and *chekists* (secret police), and a second round of elections did Yeltsin emerge victorious over Zyuganov.

The KPRF continued its electoral success in the 1999 Duma poll, winning more than 24 percent of the vote, though the party obtained fewer seats than in 1995. With the ascent of **Vladimir Putin**, the Communists' popularity suffered, particularly in the 2003 parliamentary elections. Putin's use of Potemkin parties, a pliant **media**, and the **terrorist** threat allowed him to effectively sideline the KPRF. Recognizing the futility of running against the popular president, Zyuganov sat out the 2004 elections, throwing the KPRF's support behind the **Agrarian Party**'s Nikolay Kharitonov. The party also suffered from several high-profile defections and attempts to split its constituency, though the KPRF has remained the largest opposition party in the country through the first decade of the new millennium.

Zyuganov returned to presidential politics in 2008, running against **Dmitry Medvyedev**; he claimed a respectable 17.8 percent of the vote. Since the 2008–2009 **global financial crisis**, Zyuganov's popularity and influence are on the rise, and Prime Minister Putin has taken an increasingly conciliatory position toward the KPRF. Party membership exceeds 500,000, with nearly 20,000 new members joining annually. However, unlike the LDPR, the Communists tend to be older on average. The party has a well-developed media arm, including newspapers and radio.

COMMUNIST PARTY OF THE SOVIET UNION (CPSU). Political party. Known in Russian as *Kommunisticheskaia partiia*

Sovetskogo Soiuza, the CPSU was formed by the Bolshevik faction of the Russian Social Democratic Labor Party, which was established in 1898. Under the leadership of **Vladimir Lenin**, the Bolsheviks led the first successful socialist revolution, establishing Soviet Russia in 1917 and the Union of Soviet Socialist Republics (USSR) in 1922. The party platform embraced **Marxism-Leninism**, a revolutionary ideology based on the dictatorship of the proletariat, state control of **industry**, a centrally planned **economy**, and the creation of a classless society.

The CPSU, and its counterparts in the **union republics**, established a legal monopoly on political power and constitutionally guaranteed itself a "leading role" in Soviet society, effectively turning the USSR into a totalitarian state. The party dominated cultural, social, economic, and political life in the Soviet Union through its control of the **Komsomol** youth organization, the **media**, the **military**, the **KGB**, Congress of People's Deputies, Gosplan (State Planning Commission), the Writers' Union, and other administrative arms. Party members, colloquially known as the *nomenklatura*, rarely exceeded 10 percent of the population, and enjoyed multiple benefits including foreign travel, access to special shops, the best housing, and occupational mobility.

During the reign of **Joseph Stalin**, the general secretary of the CPSU became the highest political position within the Soviet Union. While collective leadership briefly reemerged in the early **Khrushchev** and **Brezhnev** eras, the general secretary remained the epicenter of power in the USSR. In the early 1980s, the leadership of the party was accurately described as a gerontocracy, while much of the party's work was done by slavish **apparatchiks**. This began to change with the appointment of **Mikhail Gorbachev** to the party's top post.

Gorbachev's policies of **perestroika** and **glasnost**, implemented to bring about economic acceleration (*uskoreniie*), set in motion a series of reforms that slowly chipped away at the CPSU's monopolization of power. By the end of the decade, numerous newly formed cultural and civic organizations had begun to function as de facto political parties, challenging the CPSU's privileged position, while the CPSU had decided to allow multicandidate elections at the local and regional levels. In 1990, the creation of the Soviet presidency formally distinguished the head of state from the leader of the party; Gorbachev held the position of president until the **dissolution of the Soviet Union** (he was succeeded as general secretary of the CPSU by Vladimir Ivashko).

In 1991, after giving up many of its other powers, the CPSU voted to end its monopoly on political action, opening the door to legal opposition parties like the **Liberal Democratic Party** and various national fronts in the non-Russian republics. In the last years of his administration, Gorbachev, finding it difficult to work with the often intransigent members of the party's hierarchy, often bypassed the CPSU altogether and used popular support to push through his agenda. Reacting to plans to reform the treaty of union between the Soviet republics, Communist hard-liners led the **August Coup** against Gorbachev. In the wake of the failed putsch, Russian President **Boris Yeltsin** banned the CPSU on 26 August 1991; the Supreme Soviet suspended party activity shortly thereafter.

Hoping to revive the party, a number of *nomenklatura* established the Communist Party of the **Russian Soviet Federative Socialist Republic**, though it remained a marginal player until **Gennady Zyuganov** restructured it in 1993 to form the **Communist Party of the Russian Federation**. *See also* CIVIL SOCIETY.

COMMUNITY OF DEMOCRATIC CHOICE (CDC). Intergovernmental organization. Established on 2 December 2005, the Community of Democratic Choice is comprised of nine post-totalitarian states, including **Ukraine**, **Estonia**, **Latvia**, **Lithuania**, Romania, **Moldova**, **Georgia**, Macedonia, and Slovenia. It aims to promote the rule of law, democracy, and **human rights** in the former **Eastern Bloc**, including the post-Soviet republics. The organization builds on foundations established by the **GUAM Organization for Democracy and Economic Development**, including counterbalancing Russian predominance in Eastern European affairs. The organization is also seen as a tool of cooperation for states with a decidedly pro-European orientation, particularly Ukraine and Georgia, which both wish to join the **North Atlantic Treaty Organization** (NATO) and the **European Union** (EU). The organization also has a youth forum intended to promote dialogue and cooperation among young people across Eastern Europe. *See also* FOREIGN RELATIONS.

CONFEDERATION OF MOUNTAIN PEOPLES OF THE CAU-CASUS (KGNK). Paramilitary organization. Sometimes known as the Confederation of the Peoples of the Caucasus (KNK), the Confederation of the Mountain Peoples of the Caucasus (*Konfederatsiia gorskikh narodov Kavkaza*) is a defunct paramilitary group comprised of volunteers from across the **North Caucasus**, particularly **Chechens**. The confederacy formed in the last days of **perestroika**, and took part in **Abkhazia**'s struggle for independence from **Georgia**. The organization was, in part, an attempt to reconstitute the unity of **Muslim** Caucasian peoples that existed in the early Soviet period, when the North Caucasus region was constituted as the Mountain **Autonomous Soviet Socialist Republic** (ASSR). Its leadership hoped to create a so-called Caucasian Switzerland with extensive cultural and political autonomy for the indigenous peoples of the region. The mountaineers have been accused of war crimes and **human rights** violations by the Georgians in relation to their activities in the 1993 siege of Sukhumi, during which many civilians and prisoners of war died. Under the direction of Musa Shanibov, the group took a stridently anti-Kremlin position during the first **Chechen War**, but political changes in **Kabardino-Balkariya** ultimately made the confederation's open opposition to the central government unpopular. In such an environment, Shanibov's anti-Moscow stance weakened the organization and undermined the organization's ability to influence policy in the region. The group has been inactive since the assassination of its second leader, the Chechen parliamentarian Yusup Soslambekov, in 2000. *See also* ISLAMISM; MAFIA.

CONGRESS OF PEOPLE'S DEPUTIES OF RUSSIA. Originally known as the Congress of People's Deputies of the **Russian Soviet Federative Socialist Republic**, the Congress of People's Deputies was the supreme governing body of Russia from 1990 until 1993 when it was abolished by **Boris Yeltsin** in the midst of the **constitutional crisis of 1993**. It was succeeded by the bicameral **Federal Assembly of Russia**. The Congress was responsible for electing the **Supreme Soviet of the Russian Federation**, a legislative body that governed the country between the congressional sessions.

CONSTITUTIONAL CRISIS OF 1993. As president of the **Russian Soviet Federative Socialist Republic** (RSFSR), **Boris Yeltsin** assumed the presidency of the Russian Federation upon its independence following the **dissolution of the Soviet Union** in 1991. However, the tenets of the 1977 Soviet-era RSFSR constitution remained in effect. In order to steer Russia toward economic and political reform, Yeltsin assumed increasing powers from 1991 onward. This led to a political standoff with the Russian parliament, which in 1993 was comprised of the **Congress of People's Deputies** and the **Supreme Soviet of Russia**.

Confident of popular support for his governmental restructuring, Yeltsin used the outcome of an April referendum on his job performance and a call for early parliamentary elections to dissolve the legislature on 21 September. Led by Chairman of the Supreme Soviet **Ruslan Khasbulatov**, parliament impeached Yeltsin, declared Vice President **Aleksandr Rutskoy** acting president, and barricaded themselves in the White House. Ten days of street fighting commenced between police, pro-parliamentary demonstrators, and groups loyal to the president. Eventually, the **army**, which had remained neutral in the early days of the crisis, obeyed Yeltsin's order to shell and then storm the White House on 4 October. The surviving leaders of the resistance were arrested, though many were later granted amnesty to assuage the strong nationalist sentiments they provoked among disaffected members of post-Soviet Russian society.

Government statistics state that 200 people died in the siege and street fighting, though other estimates put the number at 2,000. The crisis laid bare the growing divisions between a nostalgic, anti-Western electorate that would, in the future, gravitate toward the **Liberal Democratic Party of Russia** and the **Communist Party of the Russian Federation**, and more liberal, pro-reform constituencies. In the wake of the events, Yeltsin consolidated his position, expanded the powers of the executive, and pushed through the adoption of the 1993 **Constitution of the Russian Federation**. *See also* POLITICS.

CONSTITUTION OF THE RUSSIAN FEDERATION. Adopted by national referendum on 21 December 1993, the Russian Constitution officially replaced the 1977 Soviet-era Constitution of the **Russian Soviet Federative Socialist Republic** on 25 December 1993. A narrow majority of voters approved the new constitution in a poll that saw the turnout of 55 percent of the electorate. The preamble stresses the democratic and multinational character of the Russian Federation, as well as a strong sense of nationalism. The creation of a new constitution precipitated the constitutional crisis of 1993 in which President **Boris Yeltsin** used the **military** against the parliament, which opposed the strengthening of executive powers. The document, which was agreed to after the crisis, lays out the fundamentals of the constitutional system, the rights of the country's citizens, the principles of Russian federalism, and the powers of the presidency and the **Federal Assembly**, among other aspects of governance. Its chief architect was Oleg Rumyantsev, who spent months at the **United States** Library of Congress studying the drafting process of the country's 1787 constitution. The Russian Constitution has been criticized for granting too much power to the president, an inadequate separation of powers, and confusing language on center-periphery relations and the concept of "people's sovereignty," and for failing to focus heavily enough on rule of law. *See also* HOLIDAYS.

CORRUPTION. During the Soviet period, the accumulation of commodities rather than capital drove corruption. Through extended informal networks, Soviet citizens used *blat* (connections) to acquire everything from meat and fruits to apartments and refrigerators. The Soviet command-and-control form of state capitalism created a nexus binding together **Communist Party** officials, firm managers, and commodity-hungry citizens. With the introduction of **perestroika** and the small-scale market reforms under **Mikhail Gorbachev**, entrepreneurs were able to take advantage of the so-called shortage economy to provide high-quality and in-demand goods to consumers. This required a rapid expansion and careful management of their blat-based networks; the most successful of these proto-business-people would emerge as **oligarchs** in the new regime.

With the transition to a market-based system under **Boris Yeltsin** and his team of neo-liberal reformers, mass **privatization** and the capitalization of the post-Soviet **economy** occurred. Preexisting and new networks of budding capitalists and state officials transferred the Soviet state's massive holdings—which once belonged, at least in name, to the people—to a small number of individuals in an environment devoid of transparency, creating massive wealth for a few and impoverishing tens of millions. A shadow economy grew rapidly in this environment, abetted by poorly paid bureaucrats who regularly shook down small-business owners for every sort of bribe imaginable.

Large transnational companies hoping to invest in Russia's hydrocarbon and **mining** industries also felt the pinch. Full and honest reporting of profits in the 1990s would result in **taxation** rates that would destroy any business. Consequently, the keeping of two sets of books and bribing of government officials became common business practices in Yeltsin's Russia. Wage arrears, rampant inflation, evaporating savings, and low salaries promoted corruption in a number of professions beyond commerce, government, and **industry**. Police, particularly traffic cops, became infamous for their solicitation of bribes for the unlucky to avoid real and imagined offenses. In the field of **education**, it became commonplace for students to pay teachers for grades; a big bribe would result in a good grade, while a small one would produce a poorer mark. In the **health care** industry, doctors would see patients who bribed them before those who did not; access to certain treatments was also informally monetized.

As a result, corruption became a "normal" fact of life in post-Soviet Russia, with payments to corrupt state employees taking the place of paying taxes. Under **Vladimir Putin**, a vigorous anticorruption campaign was announced. While it is unclear if actual levels of corruption have dropped since 2000, public awareness of such practices has increased dramatically, partially as a result of enforcement and publicized court cases. In 2008 alone, 12,000 cases were filed against officials accused of corruption. Their collective take from such bribes was estimated to equal one-third of the state's budget. Corruption as an aspect of daily life has decreased since 2000, especially since a majority of employees now receive their wages through bank transfers. Furthermore, a new system of examination was introduced in Russian universities to prevent malfeasance. The availability of private health care has also made corruption less pervasive in the medical field. *See also* OIL; NATURAL GAS.

COSSACKS. Social group. The first Cossack (*Kazak*) hosts, or paramilitary bands also known as *voisko*, were formed in 14th-century

Ukraine. Over the next few centuries, other hosts formed in southern Russia, and ultimately allied themselves with the **Romanov** tsars, gaining special rights of autonomy for their service as the vanguard of colonial expansion, especially in **Siberia** where they established new hosts after subduing the local populations.

During the Russian Civil War, many Cossack hosts supported the anti-Bolshevik forces, and as a result, those who did not emigrate were subjected to intense repression for more than a decade, known as de-Cossackization (*raskazachivaniie*). The Don, Terek, and Kuban hosts were hit particularly hard.

Perestroika allowed for the reformation of hosts and the creation of new ones. Since the **dissolution of the Soviet Union**, Cossack movements have flourished, particularly in southern Russia and the **North Caucasus**, as well as Siberia and northern **Kazakhstan**.

The Russian Federation has granted the Cossacks special rights within the **military** and the ability to form police or paramilitary units in their traditional homelands, such as **Krasnodar Krai** (sometimes referred to as Kuban, a reflection of the importance of the Kuban Host in the region's history). Known for their self-sufficiency, law-abiding ways, social conservatism, and religiosity, the Cossacks are often idealized as the paragon of the new patriotic ideal in 21st-century Russia, though their vigilante activities, often against immigrants from the **Caucasus** and **Central Asia**, are worrying to many who fear Russia may become a quasi-fascist state. Cossack regiments and volunteer units participated in a number of conflicts in the **near abroad**, including in **Transnistria**, **Abkhazia**, **South Ossetia**, and the **Chechen Wars**; they have also been enlisted in Russia's **counterterrorism** efforts.

Until 2005, Moscow still refused to recognize the Cossacks as an **ethnic** or **national minority** and continues to categorize them as **ethnic Russians** in national censuses. The original Cossacks tended to be **Orthodox** Slavs; however, generations of intermarriage with Russia's various national minorities, including Greeks, **Armenians**, Turkic **Muslims**, and various Caucasian peoples, has created a unique—if predominantly Russophone—**national identity** among many contemporary Cossacks. However, when **Vladimir Putin** introduced successful legislation known as "On the State Service of the

Russian Cossacks," the Cossacks were for the first time recognized as a distinct ethnocultural entity indigenous to Russia.

COUNCIL OF EUROPE. Intergovernmental organization. Established in the wake of World War II, the Council of Europe was created to promote reconciliation between the various peoples of Europe and prevent the vicious nationalism that characterized earlier periods of history. Founded by Western European governments, most of which were **North Atlantic Treaty Organization** (NATO) members, the organization focused on **human rights**, democracy promotion, and the rule of law. As such, the council emerged as a keen critic of the actions of the Soviet Union and the various regimes of the **Eastern Bloc** during the **Cold War** for their treatment of **ethnic minorities** and religious groups. Such criticisms were integral to the Union of Soviet Socialist Republics (USSR) and its allies subscribing to the Helsinki Accords in 1975, which committed the regimes to respect of human rights and dignity.

Beginning in 1989, the council was reinvigorated by the political shift as the Iron Curtain fell across East-Central Europe. As part of their larger project of European integration, the post-totalitarian regimes of Eastern Europe and the former Soviet republics began to actively seek admission to the organization. With the spread of **ethnic violence** in the **Caucasus**, **Moldova**, and other parts of the former USSR, the council became an important player in publicizing minority issues and resolving conflicts. Russia joined the organization on 28 February 1996, after promising to end the death penalty (although a number of executions took place after that date). Russia's membership, however, has been criticized as diluting the overall mission of the council since the country, as a permanent member of the **United Nations** Security Council, is not beholden to any external political influences and frequently flouts Europeans norms, particularly in relation to its conduct in **Chechnya**.

COUNTERTERRORISM. Russia has a well-developed counterterrorism program, which grew out of late Soviet-era operations directed at minority nationalist and counterrevolutionary organizations. While terrorist attacks under the totalitarian regime were rare, the opening of Russia's borders, the spread of **ethnic violence**, the growth of transnational **crime** syndicates, and **narcotics** trafficking created an environment in the 1990s that made **terrorism** a tangible threat to the new Russian Federation. However, spillover from the first **Chechen War** proved the greatest catalyst for developing a robust antiterrorism program as **Islamist** militants and other groups targeted civilians in the **North Caucasus**, **Moscow**, and other parts of the country.

In 1998, the Federal Law on Combating Terrorism was passed to more effectively combat terrorist groups, and clearly delineated the role of the **FSB** and the Ministry of Internal Affairs (**MVD**) as the principal agencies charged with counterterrorism. However, the other agencies that assist in the effort include the Foreign Intelligence Service, Federal Protection Service, Defense Ministry, and Federal Border Service. With the **apartment bombings**, the beginning of the second Chechen War, and **Vladimir Putin**'s ascendance in 1999, counterterrorism policy shifted into high gear, with new powers accruing to the relevant agencies. After the **September 11 attacks**, the Kremlin began to cooperate more extensively with European, American, and Chinese counterterrorism agencies to address threats emanating from the **Middle East**, **Central Asia**, and elsewhere. Russia has also cooperated with **Kazakhstan**, **Afghanistan**, and **India** on international counterterrorism activities.

On the home front, **surveillance** expanded exponentially and the **media** were reined in, particularly after the **Nord-Ost theater siege** in 2002. In **Chechnya** and its surrounding republics, counterterror operations led to frequent accusations of extrajudicial killings, "disappearances," and torture. Some targeted assassinations, such as that of **Ibn al-Khattab** in 2002, were also made public as part of Russian strategy. In 2004, two Russian intelligence agents were convicted of killing the former Chechen president Zelimkhan Yandarbiyev in Qatar. In 2006, an updated Law on Counteraction to Terrorism stipulated that the Russian government could act beyond Russian soil to deal with terrorist threats, mirroring **United States** policy enacted under **George W. Bush**. Over time, Putin has used counterterrorism as a reason for expanding his **vertical of power**, particularly after the **Beslan crisis**, which led to the **electoral reforms of 2004–2005**.

COURTS. *See* JUDICIAL SYSTEM.

CRIME. Over the past 30 years, the very notion of crime has undergone significant revision in the Russian context. Crimes against the state such as counterrevolutionary activity, membership in banned organizations, and publication of **samizdat** materials were seen in the Union of Soviet Socialist Republics (USSR) as more perfidious than "common" criminal actions; however, the definitions changed rapidly as **Mikhail Gorbachev** abandoned totalitarianism, freeing **dissidents** and ending the **gulag** system.

The most pernicious crime in contemporary Russia is the result of the growth of the **mafia**, which has expanded greatly since 1990. Contract killings, extortion, racketeering, and other illicit activities connected to organized crime became frighteningly normal during the years of the **Yeltsin** administration. The spread of the **narcotics** trade, particularly the transshipment of opium and heroin from **Afghanistan** to Europe, has also made Russia much more crime-prone. In many cases, current or former government employees, especially ex-**KGB** agents, were complicit in these undertakings. As a result of conflicts in the neighboring republics and **corruption** in the police and **army**, large numbers of weapons made their way into the hands of civilians during the first decade of independence.

With the reduction of the police state, rising inequality, and the economic crisis of the early 1990s, petty crimes also skyrocketed in Russia. Money laundering and counterfeiting of foreign and domestic currencies also became rather commonplace. As the result of the country's poorly constructed **tax** code, the keeping of two sets of books and tax evasion became a requisite part of daily business. The worsening of alcoholism throughout the country, on the rise since the 1980s, also led to increasing occurrences of domestic violence, rape, and theft. At one point, Russia suffered from one of the highest homicide rates in the world. Trade in black market goods during the Soviet period laid the groundwork for the development of a robust market in pirated intellectual property, such as DVDs, computer software, and **music**. Russia also became a major destination for stolen cars, particularly from Europe. During this period, many young **women** also turned to prostitution, while others were virtually enslaved and trafficked abroad for sex work.

Under **Vladimir Putin**, significant improvements in the standard of living and targeted campaigns improved the overall situation significantly; officials are able to produce more reliable crime statistics than they did in the 1990s, thus making crime prevention efforts more effective. Petty crime and violent crime are on the decline; however, an explosion of **terrorism** from 1999 to 2005 made the situation worse as more of the police force was diverted to **counterterrorism** action. Ethnically motivated attacks, particularly on **immigrants** from the **Caucasus** and **Central Asia**, remain high; murders of Russian **journalists** shot up on Putin's watch. In 2009, a study showed that crime among Russian **military** officers reached a 10-year high.

CRIMEA. In geographic terms, Crimea is a peninsula located on the **Black Sea** and the **Sea of Azov**; it has a population of nearly 2 million and covers 26,200 square kilometers. It is connected to the European mainland by the Isthmus of Perekop and is less than 10 kilometers from the Russian-controlled Kerch Peninsula. Due to its moderate climate, the area is popular with **tourists** and has many spas and health resorts. The region was the site of the eponymous Crimean War (1853–1856) and the Yalta Conference during World War II. Politically speaking, the term "Crimea" refers to the Autonomous Republic of Crimea, an administrative unit of **Ukraine**, with its capital at Simferopol.

Rulers of the Crimean Peninsula have included the Greeks, Persians, Huns, Khazars, Mongols, Genoese, and others. The Crimean Khanate, which was a vassal state of the Ottoman Empire, was conquered by the **Romanov** Empire in the 18th century. During the Soviet period, **Nikita Khrushchev** transferred control of the region to Ukraine to mark the 300th anniversary of the union between Ukraine and Russia; the region was an **Autonomous Soviet Socialist Republic** (ASSR) of the **Russian Soviet Federative Socialist Republic** from 1921 until 1945. **Ethnic Russians** represent a majority of the population (58 percent); **Ukrainians** are the second-largest group (24 percent), while Crimean **Tatars** account for 12 percent of the republic's populace. The Crimean Tatars were one of the **punished peoples** of the Soviet Union and were expelled to **Central Asia** by **Joseph Stalin**. Since the **dissolution of the Soviet Union**, many have returned to their ancestral lands, though spatial and economic displacement has resulted in many Tatars turning to **crime**, creating social problems with other ethnic groups.

Ukrainian is the republic's official **language**, but only one-tenth of the population are native speakers. Spoken by more than three-quarters of the population, the **Russian language** has been granted special status as the language of interethnic communication. Crimean Tatar is a recognized regional language. During the 1990s, the status of Crimea severely complicated relations between Kiev and Moscow. The division of the Soviet Black Sea Fleet, which had been based in Sevastopol, between the two countries, proved especially problematic, as was Russia's continuing use of the city for its **naval** activities.

Nationalist politicians in the Russian Federation also used the status of ethnic Russians in Crimea as a populist tool, often inflaming anti-Ukrainian rhetoric. Tensions lessened somewhat during the second **Yeltsin** administration, following the signing of the 1997 Treaty of Friendship, Cooperation, and Partnership between Kiev and Moscow. Problems resurfaced in 2005 with disputes over certain properties in and around Sevastopol and Cape Sarych; the situation was not improved by the Kremlin's discomfort with the effect of Ukraine's **color revolution**. Responding to the expansion of Ukrainian-**United States** military cooperation under Viktor Yushchenko, anti–**North Atlantic Treaty Organization** (NATO) protests flared in 2006. Distribution of Russian passports to residents of Crimea has also soured relations. *See also* COSSACKS; NATIONAL IDENTITY; TURKEY.

CUBA (RELATIONS WITH). During the second half of the **Cold War**, Cuba enjoyed the status of *primus inter pares* among the Soviet Union's satellites. However, during the period of **glasnost**, the Caribbean nation became a principal target for domestic critics who resented the large subsidies that kept Fidel Castro's regime solvent. In 1991, Moscow began to divest from Cuba, canceling a number of joint projects. Two years later, the Russian Federation removed all its **military** personnel from the country, though an **espionage** station was maintained at Lourdes near Havana until 2002. Economic contacts during the early **Yeltsin** administration were dramatically reduced; however, the two countries did participate in a "sugar for **oil**" program. Under pressure from Washington, Foreign Minister **Andrey Kozyrev** oversaw Moscow's near-total delinking from Havana in the 1990s. Without its Cold War patron, the Castro government was forced to reform its inefficient economy and seek new allies, ultimately settling on **Venezuela** after the election of Hugo Chavez. With the new foreign policy vector under **Yevgeny Primakov**, Cuba resumed its strategic position as a counterweight to the **United States**, although the Russian **financial crisis of 1998** precluded substantive economic aid to the impoverished island. Upon becoming president, **Vladimir Putin** publicly criticized his predecessor's treatment of Cuba. Since 2000, relations have improved steadily. In 2008, **Dmitry Medvyedev** visited Cuba's new leader, Raul Castro, and declared the dawn of "intense" new contacts between the countries, including possible Caribbean oil exploration by Russian transnational corporations. *See also* FOREIGN RELATIONS.

– D –

DACHA. The term signifies a house on a plot of land located within reasonably easy reach of a city. It is intended for intermittent family residence, especially during the summer. People residing on their dachas are called *dachniks*, which is the linguistic form for a peculiar social identity based on the principles of living away from the city and enjoying the delights of the Russian summer, including the cultivation of flowers, herbs, berries, and even fruits and vegetables.

In the late 1980s, the **Gorbachev** administration provided large sections of the Soviet society with allotments, signifying the first step toward **privatization** of land in the Union of Soviet Socialist Republics (USSR). This wide availability of plots meant that dachas became a mass phenomenon, with virtually every family having at least a single plot of land. For working-class families, dachas provided a cheap alternative to summer holidays on the **Black Sea**. Massive construction projects were initiated at the end of the Soviet era, transforming the appearance of the Russian countryside and forcing an upgrade in the country's roads and **transportation** system. Furthermore, small and large businesses were established to cater for the growing needs of Russian dachniks.

In the 1990s, when the society lived through a series of economic crises, dachas became centers of **economic** activity and **agriculture**, with dachniks focusing their cultivation efforts on goods for sale rather than for personal consumption. This trend was reversed in the most recent decade as dachas again became centers of family summer recreation. For some Russians, having a dacha provides a symbolic link to the earth and nourishes their Slavic **rural** roots. For others, living at the dacha is a form of suburban life with regular, if not daily, commutes to the city and involves a bond with their local dachnik community.

A typical dacha involves a plot of land of normally about 100 square meters, a one- or two-story house with a veranda, a patio, and a barbeque area, and a small fruit and vegetable garden. Dacha settlements are normally found in picturesque settings by a river or on the edge of a forest. Since the time of Peter the Great, dachas have been a sign of social distinction. Under **Joseph Stalin**, dachas were the property of the state—the so-called *gosdacha* (state dacha); these were made available to individuals at no charge, and marked their contribution to the state. In post-Soviet Russia, dachas became emblematic of business and social success, with many dachas of the Russian political and economic elite as well as celebrities being equipped with the state-of-the-art **sporting** facilities and **surveillance** systems, turning the modest dacha into a country estate.

DAGESTAN, REPUBLIC OF. An **ethnic republic** of the Russian Federation. From 1920 until 1991, Dagestan (also Daghestan) was an **Autonomous Soviet Socialist Republic** of the **Russian Soviet Federative Socialist Republic**; in 1992, the republic acceded to the Russian Federation, declaring its sovereignty a year later. It is part of the Southern **Federal District** and the North Caucasus **Economic Region**.

Dagestan is unique among the Russian Federation's ethnic republics in that it lacks a titular majority/minority. The republic's name comes from the Turkish word for "mountain" (*dağ*) and the Persian suffix for "land" (*-stan*). Of its 2.5 million inhabitants, the largest ethnic group is the **Avars** (30 percent), followed by the Dargins (17 percent), Kumyks (14 percent), and **Lezgins** (13 percent). Other nationalities include **ethnic Russians**, Laks, Tabasarans, Azeris, **Chechens**, and Nogais. Overall, there are more than 30 local **languages** spoken in the republic, many of which are from the Northeast Caucasian (Nakh-Dagestanian) language family, though a few are

Turkic (Kumyk and Nogai) and Iranian (Tat) in origin. **Russian** is the lingua franca. Given such complex ethnic cleavages, the system in the republic is, at least nominally, a consociational democracy, which grants a majority of its 122 parliamentary seats to candidates of a given ethnicity.

Political identity is closely linked to familial, clan, and village bonds, which are nested identities within one's ethnic affiliation. Due to the tenuous situation between the republic's nationalities, support for **separatism** remains extremely low when compared to the Russian Federation's other ethnic republics. Ninety percent of the population is **Muslim**, while the remainder is **Orthodox**. More so than in other Muslim-majority areas of the Russian Federation, Dagestan has witnessed a growth in political **Islam**; the republic is also the most religious in terms of numbers of mosques, shrines, and active practitioners of the Muslim faith. A number of **Islamist** political parties are or were active in the 1990s, including the Islamic Renaissance Party (IRP), Jamaat-ul-Muslimin, and the Union of Russian Muslims.

The capital of the republic is Makhachkala (pop. 462,400); other major cities include Kaspiysk, Khasavyurt, and Derbent. Covering 50,300 square kilometers of territory, Dagestan is situated on the **Caspian Sea** and borders **Kalmykiya**, **Stavropol Krai**, and **Chechnya**, as well as **Georgia** and **Azerbaijan**. A mountainous region, much of Dagestan's population is engaged in animal husbandry, **agriculture**, caviar harvesting, and viniculture, while the main industries are **oil** and **natural gas** production, electricity generation, and metalworking. The republic's economic situation has been badly damaged by the **Chechen Wars**. High **unemployment**, low wages, and rampant **crime** remain a problem for the republic; unlike other ethnic republics, Dagestan attracts little **foreign investment**.

The region's proximity to Chechnya has resulted in extreme instability. In 1996, **Chechen** rebels, under the leadership of Salman Raduyev, took 2,000 hostages in the border town of Kizlyar, ultimately resulting in the deaths of 41 civilians. In the late 1990s, a group of Islamists, deemed Wahhabis by the federal authorities, established a small sharia state in the foothills centered on the villages of Chabanmakhi, Kadar, and Karamakhi, and expelled local police and republican authorities. The most serious incident occurred in August 1999, when 500 insurgents, led by **Shamil Basayev** and **Ibn**

al-Khattab, invaded Dagestan with the aim of uniting it with Chechnya and initiating a regional jihad across the **North Caucasus**. The incursion, along with the **apartment bombings** in September, was used by the Kremlin as the pretext for initiating the second Chechen War.

Since 2000, the republic has suffered from low-level guerilla warfare and several high-profile **terrorist** attacks, including a Victory Day bombing on 9 May 2002 that killed 42 and injured more than 130 people. Magomedali Magomedov was chairman of the State Council of the Republic of Dagestan from 1987 to 2006. He was a strong supporter of Russia's territorial integrity, and an ally of Moscow against the rising tide of Islamic extremism in the North Caucasus. According to Dagestan's 1994 constitution, he was required to step down in 1998, to be replaced by a successor from one of the republics' other 10 principal constituent nationalities, but was able to avoid removal from office through judicial legerdemain. He resigned on grounds of age in 2006 and was replaced by Mukhu Aliyev, who was appointed by **Vladimir Putin** to reverse the rise of Islamism in the republic. The Kremlin's choice of Aliyev, an ethnic Avar, has softened the discontent of the republic's largest ethnic group, who chafed under the leadership of Magomedov, an ethnic Dargin. *See also* WAHHABISM.

DARGINS. *See* DAGESTAN.

DEDOVSHCHINA. The name given to the informal system of subordination of junior conscripts, *dedovshchina* (regime of the grandfathers) is one of the most pernicious problems afflicting the Russian **military**. Going beyond simply hazing, the practice involves denial of food, rape, and intense physical and psychological abuse, often resulting in serious injuries and death. It also contributes to the extremely high rate of suicide among young soldiers. In recent years, the **Committee of Soldiers' Mothers of Russia** has actively campaigned against the practice, bringing the worst abuses to light. *See also* ARMY; HUMAN RIGHTS.

DEMOCRACY. The concept of democracy in Russia has evolved significantly since its use by the **Communist Party of the Soviet Union** to describe its totalitarian system, which was underpinned by regular elections consisting of a single candidate from the only legal **political party**. The process of **democratization** (*demokratizatsiia*) pursued under **Mikhail Gorbachev** led to the introduction of multicandidate and eventually multiparty elections in the Union of Soviet Socialist Republics (USSR).

Under **Boris Yeltsin**, popular elections became a mainstay of the country's system of governance, though Yeltsin's increasing power vis-à-vis the legislative branch, evidenced most dramatically by the **constitutional crisis of 1993**, and the control of the **media** by allies of those in power weakened Russia's claim as a genuine democracy. Free and fair elections in the country's **ethnic republics** during the 1990s became rarer and rarer as the incumbents used their control of the local **economy** to ensure loyalty.

Under **Vladimir Putin**, Russia began to develop its own form of "rule by the people," which has been categorized as a "Potemkin" or "managed democracy," though the Kremlin prefers the term "sovereign democracy." Both reflecting and influencing the form of republicanism common in **Central Asia**, the Russian system came to exhibit strong signs of neo-authoritarianism combined with a panoply of democratic trappings, including regular presidential elections, a bicameral parliament, and opposition parties. In reality, the presidential elections of 2004 and 2008 were a foregone conclusion, as the legislature is dominated by a "party of power" that is doggedly loyal to the executive, and the opposition political parties are either for show or prevented from gaining parliamentary representation by electoral hurdles imposed from above.

Putin has further undermined democracy by curtailing certain **journalistic** practices and closing critical media outlets, particularly after the **Nord-Ost theater siege** in 2002. Responding to international criticism, Putin steadfastly defended his country's right to pursue a unique form of democracy based on its history, geopolitical position, and economic situation. Since coming to office, President **Dmitry Medvyedev** has made clear his intention to improve the quality of Russia's democracy, particularly in relation to the growth of **civil society**. *See also* POLITICS.

DEMOCRATIC CHOICE OF RUSSIA. *See* UNION OF RIGHT FORCES.

DEMOCRATIC PEOPLE'S REPUBLIC OF KOREA (DPRK). *See* NORTH KOREA.

DEMOCRATIZATION/DEMOKRATIZATSIIA. The term "democratization" (*demokratizatsiia*) refers to a gradual introduction of democratic principles of governance into post-totalitarian societies. In the **Russian language**, the term implies a delay in the acceptance of **democracy** as the main structure of society. While **Mikhail Gorbachev** insisted on democratization, **Boris Yeltsin** banked on democracy, which resulted in the shift from the slow social reforms of the 1980s to the **shock therapy** of the 1990s. The term also has a negative connotation referring to American hegemony and enforced democratization of states around the globe with the purpose of even more aggressive exploitation of people and natural resources. *See also* UNITED STATES.

DEMOGRAPHIC CHALLENGES. Russia is facing a demographic crisis as the country's population is declining by at least 700,000 people per year. The phenomenon is particularly acute in the **Far North** and **Russian Far East**, but the emergence of "ghost towns" in European Russia is also becoming evident. Domestic and international observers predict a decline from the 2009 estimate of 140 million people to 80–100 million people by 2050. The complex network of demographic challenges includes low birth rate, high mortality rate, high migration rates, and an increasingly aged workforce.

The most difficult situation is in Russia's central and northwestern regions due to a high degree of urbanization, a dramatic fall in living standards (especially in the 1990s), and a greater number of retirees (many Russians who have worked in northern parts of Russia retire to the central and southern parts where the climate is very pleasant). The Pacific Rim and southern regions have enjoyed a more stable demographic situation, with young people outnumbering people of other age groups in the former, and the higher proportion of **ethnic minorities**, particularly of the **Muslim** faith, which have traditionally high birth rates, in the latter.

The current demographic crisis has many causes. Historical factors include those stemming from **Joseph Stalin**'s purges and losses from combat and invasion during World War II. Another major cause of the crisis is the country's rapid industrialization and urbanization, which resulted in a destruction of traditional lifestyles that privileged large families needed for **agricultural** work. Finally, the country's **health care** system, with its crumbling infrastructure, is unable to tackle the health issues of the population; the crisis is exacerbated by high levels of alcohol consumption—an estimated one-third of Russian men abuse alcohol—and smoking rates remain some of the highest in the world. More recent factors include the rapid spread of illicit **drug use**, drug-resistant tuberculosis (caused and spread though Russia's inadequate incarceration system), and **HIV/AIDS**, which remains a taboo issue, with heavy social stigma attached to victims of the illness. Environmental degradation and **pollution** are also increasing mortality rates: pollution in Russian urban centers has increased manifold since 2000 as the amount of traffic in cities has skyrocketed. Life expectancy for males is now at 58.4 years, the lowest in Europe.

As in Western countries, Russian **women** tend to have few children and delay pregnancy because of professional fulfillment: the fertility rate is 1.2 children per woman and the average age of maternity is 25 years. High abortion rates (currently 130 abortions per 100 births), partly the result of Russia's extremely conservative views regarding contraception, also contribute to low levels of fertility. As a result of the partial post-Soviet abandonment of state-sponsored **health care**, child mortality rates are also on the rise; current annual spending is a paltry $115 per capita. In 2009, the reputable British health journal *Lancet* blamed rapid **privatization** and economic **shock therapy** under **Boris Yeltsin** for the dramatic drop in life expectancy since Soviet times.

In 2007, **Vladimir Putin**, who in his first major address in office identified a shrinking population as the nation's greatest threat, introduced new measures aimed at improving the demographic situation in the country, including aggressive propaganda in favor of large families in mass **media** and monetary awards to women having two or more children. However, the government is reluctant to loosen laws regulating adoption and **immigration**. The government is concerned about an uncontrolled influx of immigrants, particularly from neighboring **China** and **North Korea**, as well as **Central Asia** and the **Caucasus**. However, in recent years, Moscow has improved its efforts to both stanch emigration and attract **ethnic Russians** from the **near abroad** and farther afield. In addition, Russian popular views toward adoption have begun to change from explicitly negative (an extension of the Bolshevik ideals of raising new Soviet citizens collectively) to moderately positive, with more well-off families adopting children from Russian orphanages. This and other improvements on the demographic front are a result of higher living standards and a massive public campaign that is run by the government on all levels. *See also* FAR NORTH; RURAL LIFE.

DERIPASKA, OLEG VLADIMIROVICH (1968–). Oligarch. Born in Dzerzhinsk, **Nizhny Novgorod**, Oleg Deripaska grew up in **Krasnodar Krai** and graduated from both **Moscow State University** and the Plekhanov Academy of Economics. Seeking to avoid poverty, he abandoned theoretical physics in favor of more practical studies, a decision that ultimately led him into metals trading. He later became the chief financial officer of Aluminprodukt, which allowed him to obtain a stake in a Siberian aluminum smelter. He survived and eventually excelled in the **mafia**-linked world of aluminum, ultimately allying with **Roman Abramovich** to create Russian Aluminum (RusAl). The company, currently the world's second-largest aluminum producer, has annual sales of $4 billion. Deripaska also has interests in the automobile, energy, and insurance industries. He is chief executive officer of Basic Element Company (BasEl), one of Russia's leading investment firms. *Forbes* magazine ranked him as Russia's richest man in the spring of 2008, though the periodical estimated that Deripaska lost more than three-quarters of his fortune during the subsequent 2008–2009 **global financial crisis**. Deripaska is on good terms with **Vladimir Putin** and enjoyed a close relationship with **Boris Yeltsin**'s inner circle. He has also gained some popular support through his funding of renovation projects for dilapidated **Russian Orthodox** churches.

DISSENTERS' MARCH. The "Dissenters' March" (*Marsh nesoglasnykh*) refers to a series of political protests that occurred during 2007 in the run-up to the 2008 presidential election that put **Dmitry Medvyedev** into office. The marches occurred in **Moscow**, **St. Petersburg**, Nizhny Novgorod, and other cities, ranging from several hundred protestors to thousands, depending on the venue. The protests brought together extreme right-wing organizations, like **Eduard Limonov**'s **National Bolshevik Party**, with liberal organizations, such as the United Civil Front headed by **Garry Kasparov**. **The Other Russia**, an umbrella organization of critics of the **Putin** administration, organized the marches. Russian **media** took a critical stance against the display of civic action, and police used harsh measures to control and then disperse the crowds. In each case, the organizers were denied permits to march, thus allowing the security forces to treat the activists as criminals; Kasparov was arrested during the 24 November 2007 march in Moscow and was jailed for five days.

DISSIDENT. In broad terms, a dissident is someone who actively challenges an established political regime, policy, or institution. In the Soviet Union, the notion was used during the **Brezhnev** era to refer to citizens who overtly or subtly criticized the authority of the **Communist Party of the Soviet Union**. They did so through protests and production and dissemination of **samizdat** literature. Dissidents would often find themselves demonized in the official **media** and unable to publish their works or seek official employment in the Soviet Union. Furthermore, they often suffered from harassment, persecution, and imprisonment by the **KGB**. Eventually, the term began to connote a nonconformist who attempted to inform the public, at home and abroad, of the violation of **human rights** in the Union of Soviet Socialist Republics (USSR).

Historically, there were a number of types of dissidents in the USSR: "true Communists," who maintained that Soviet ideology presented a case of perverted Marxism; "Western liberals," who believed that capitalism and political pluralism were the only acceptable systems; Russian nationalists, who supported the view that Russia had its own unique trajectory of development with emphasis on **Eurasianism** and Russian **Orthodoxy**; minority activists, who fought for the rights of **national minorities** and the titular populations of the **union republics**; **religious** activists, who demanded freedom to observe their faith without prejudice or hindrance; and artists and authors, like **Aleksandr Solzhenitsyn**, whose views were a combination of different strands of the dissident movement.

DISSOLUTION OF THE SOVIET UNION. Often described as the inevitable outcome of the combined effect of **Mikhail Gorbachev**'s policy triad of **perestroika, glasnost,** and **democratization,** the dissolution of the Soviet Union in 1991 was viewed by few in the Union of Soviet Socialist Republics (USSR) or the West as likely a few years prior to its occurrence. However, the increasing instances of **ethnic violence** in the **Caucasus,** when combined with internal social pressures stimulated by the end of the one-party totalitarian system in the **Eastern Bloc** in 1989, the aftereffects of the **Chernobyl disaster,** and dissemination of information on **Joseph Stalin**'s repressions, triggered a wave of centrifugal nationalism across the **union republics.**

Spearheaded by **Boris Yeltsin,** self-styled Russian nationalists lobbied for increasing powers within the **Russian Soviet Federative Socialist Republic,** creating centripetal pressures on the USSR. Gorbachev worked diligently to hold the union together from 1990 to 1991. However, nationalist agitation in the **Baltic States** and **Georgia,** combined with the rising tide of animosity toward the **Communist Party of the Soviet Union** (CPSU), made some reorganization of the union a political necessity. Ironically, the proposed renegotiation of the treaty of union, in effect since 1922, led to the failed **August Coup** of 1991.

In the wake of the crisis, the CPSU was outlawed, Russia recognized the independence of **Estonia, Latvia,** and **Lithuania,** and Gorbachev was marginalized. In early December, Yeltsin met with the heads of the Belarusian and Ukrainian Soviet Socialist Republics outside Minsk. There they signed the **Belavezha Accords,** effectively terminating the USSR and establishing the framework for the **Commonwealth of Independent States** (CIS). This occurred despite a national referendum that stipulated the majority of Soviet citizens' desire to preserve some form of genuine union. Later that month, the leaders of 11 of the union republics—Russia, **Ukraine, Belarus, Moldova, Armenia, Azerbaijan, Kazakhstan, Uzbekistan, Kyrgyzstan, Turkmenistan,** and **Tajikistan**—met in Alma-Ata (Almaty), Kazakhstan, where they declared their independence and formalized the creation of the CIS on 21 December 1991.

The so-called Alma-Ata Declaration finalized the dissolution of the Soviet Union. Georgia, while not represented at the meeting, ultimately acceded to the new commonwealth, though the Baltic States did not. Following the breakup of the USSR, the **Newly Independent States** sought to redefine their relations with one another, and particularly with Russia, the successor state to the now-defunct USSR. The end of the Soviet Union proved especially difficult for the 25 million **ethnic Russians** living outside the new Russian Federation but within the former Soviet Union (in the ensuing decade, nearly 10 million would quit the **near abroad** for Russia or Third World countries).

DRUG USE. Drug use is one of Russia's most serious social problems. Currently, it is estimated there are about 6 million people who use drugs, roughly 1 million of whom are aged 11–24. Every year, approximately 70,000 people die of drug-related causes. Russian official statistics indicate that a drug addict normally dies within four years after beginning drug use.

The ninefold increase in drug use since 1990 has been caused by a number of factors. First, the **political** and **economic** crises of the 1990s, and especially the failure of the state to control its new borders, resulted in greater availability of drugs (particularly **narcotics**), greater exposure of young people to the drug culture, and the rise of drug sales as a new form of economic activity. Second, drug use has enjoyed the connotations of the liberal appeal, freedom from societal pressures, and part of a new post-Soviet **glamour**-based lifestyle. At the same time, drugs became the only escape for many disenfranchised Russian individuals who did not manage to fit in the new system either socially or emotionally. Finally, the rise in drug use is accounted for by the collapse of late Soviet-era drug prevention systems and medical institutions.

The Russian Federation inherited the Soviet penalty system as regards drug abuse; the state penalizes drug users by forced registration with medical institutions, fines, and criminal conviction. These discriminating practices, as well as social stigma, discourage people from seeking support from the **health care** system, resulting in low rates of voluntary treatment for addiction. Many average Russians equate drug addiction with alcohol dependence and fail to report the problem at the right time. Many drug addicts live in abandoned industrial sites, or move out into the countryside where their activities often go unnoticed.

Since 2000, there has been a positive tendency as regards the role of the state in preventing drug abuse. It appears the state began to differentiate between victims of drug addiction and drug dealers. However, state support and fair **media** representations are rudimentary, with the exception of a few recent **films** that tackle the issue of drug use, such as Igor Voloshin's *Nirvana* (2008). *See also* ALCOHOLISM; CRIME.

DUDAYEV, JOKHAR MUSAYEVICH (1944–1996). Born during the forced deportation of the Chechen nation to Soviet **Central Asia**, Jokhar Dudayev returned to **Chechnya** in 1957. He defied the odds by rising to the rank of Major-General in the Soviet **air force**. After participating in the **Soviet-Afghan War**, he was stationed in **Estonia**, where he displayed empathy with local nationalists during the late 1980s. He returned to his homeland in 1990 and entered politics, supporting the campaign to elevate the Checheno-Ingush **Autonomous Soviet Socialist Republic** (ASSR) to the status of a **union republic**. In the wake of the **August Coup** of 1991, Jokhar Dudayev moved against his pro-Communist opponents and declared an independent **Chechen Republic of Ichkeriya**, with himself as its president. **Boris Yeltsin** ordered federal troops to move against the **separatist** regime but withdrew them after being confined to the airport by forces loyal to Dudayev. Ichkeriya was recognized by **Georgia**, then in the midst of its own civil war, but received little support from other quarters. Dudayev oversaw Chechnya's split from **Ingushetiya** in 1992, a development that buttressed his own authority in the region. He then instituted a number of reforms, including a series of disastrous economic policies and the abandonment of the **Russian language**, as well as the universal right to bear arms. His rule grew more authoritarian in 1994, allowing the Kremlin the opportunity to fund and arm opposition groups within Ichkeriya. Hoping to win a short and popular war in advance of his reelection campaign, Yeltsin initiated the first **Chechen War** in 1994. Dudayev was forced to quit the capital, Grozny, but promised to continue leading a guerilla war until the Russians relented. After more than a year in hiding, Dudayev was killed on 21 April 1996 by two laser-guided missiles that targeted the satellite phone he was using. He was succeeded by his vice president, Zelimkhan Yandarbiyev.

DUGIN, ALEKSANDR GELYEVICH (1962–). Political philosopher and geopolitician. Born into a **military** family on 7 January 1962, Dugin studied at the Moscow Aviation Institute before taking a job in the **KGB** archives. During the late Soviet period, he worked as a **journalist** and joined the **anti-Semitic** party **Pamyat**. In the first years of Russian independence, he served as an advisor to the **Communist Party of the Russian Federation** before becoming the chief ideologue for the **National Bolshevik Party**. He also served as the chief geopolitical advisor to Gennady Seleznev, the speaker of the **State Duma** at the turn of the millennium. By the end of the 1990s, he declared himself independent from political parties and offered his services as a one-man think tank for the authorities, though he later established the anti-**globalization**, radical centrist **Eurasia Party** in 2002. Dugin represents the premier intellectual force behind contemporary Russian **neo-Eurasianism** and is the leading theoretician of the Russian far right (though many in Russia view him as a dangerous eccentric). He advocates a "conservative revolution," intended to overturn post-Enlightenment ideals embedded in Russian politics and society. He sees no contradiction between Russian dominance and minority nationalism, and contends that only through a restoration of a liberal Russian empire in **Eurasia**, including the former **Eastern Bloc**, can world stability be achieved. Reminiscent of the writings of British geographer Halford Mackinder, who theorized the "heartland" theory of world politics, Dugin's geopolitical vision supports a Berlin-Moscow-Tehran-Tokyo axis in opposition to the **United States**, **China**, **Great Britain**, and **Turkey**. He has zealously supported the **Eurasian Economic Community** and other schemes to integrate Russia with the former Soviet republics. His main theoretical work is *The Fundamentals of Geopolitics* (Osnovy Geopolitiki), published in 2000.

DUMA. *See* STATE DUMA.

DYACHENKO, TATYANA BORISOVNA (1960–). The daughter of the late Russian president **Boris Yeltsin**, Tatyana Dyachenko rose to prominence during the **1996 presidential election** campaign. With a background in computer science and little experience in **politics**, she acted as an informal personal advisor to Yeltsin and coordinated key aspects of his **media** strategy. She also mitigated his growing neo-authoritarian tendencies and counterbalanced his advisors from the more aggressive "Party of War," which supported banning the **Communist Party of the Russian Federation**, canceling the elections, and dissolving parliament. As a principal member of "the Family," a group of close advisors to the president, she also acted as a critical go-between for certain **oligarchs**, such as **Boris Berezovsky**. While she was briefly retained as an advisor to **Vladimir Putin**, she was sacked in 2000 when her name was linked to **corruption** charges surrounding Swiss construction contracts. In 2001, she married Valentin Yumashev, father-in-law of the oligarch **Oleg Deripaska**.

– E –

EASTERN BLOC. Also known as the Soviet Bloc, the Eastern Bloc was the geopolitical region that included the Union of Soviet Socialist Republics (USSR) and its Eastern European satellites. At the end of World War II, the Red Army liberated much of Europe from fascist control, only to quickly assume the role of occupiers. As the result of tacit agreements with the **United States** and **Great Britain** on postwar spheres of influence, **Joseph Stalin** was able to achieve Communist control of a band of states from the **Baltic Sea** to the **Black Sea**. In some cases, the local Communist party achieved power through elections manipulated by Moscow, while in other countries power was achieved through coup d'état.

In 1946, Winston Churchill condemned the Soviet Union's increasingly imperial control over the region, stating, "From Stettin in the Baltic to Trieste in the Adriatic an iron curtain has descended across the Continent." By 1948, this group of states included East Germany, **Poland**, Czechoslovakia, Hungary, Romania, Bulgaria, and Albania; however, after the Sino-Soviet split, Tirana switched its allegiance to **China**. Yugoslavia was sometimes included as part of the Eastern Bloc due to its Communist system, but after 1948, Belgrade left the Soviet Union's orbit and embraced neutrality. In 1949, Moscow established the Council for Mutual Economic Assistance (COMECON) as an economic union of its client states; **Mongolia**, Vietnam, and **Cuba** later joined. In response to West Germany's accession to the **North Atlantic Treaty Organization** (NATO) in 1955, the Soviet Union established the **Warsaw Pact** as a collective security organization uniting its client states in the region.

The Soviet military intervened in the region on several occasions to prevent its allies from abandoning socialism, most dramatically in Hungary (1956) and Czechoslovakia (1968). The Soviet **military** maintained large garrisons across the region, and backed Eastern Communist leaders' policies of restricting emigration, crushing **dissident** movements, and censoring the **media**. By the end of the 1970s, political and economic changes in the Eastern Bloc were afoot that laid the groundwork for the dramatic events of 1989. Through Bonn's policy of *Ostpolitik*, East and West Germany initiated cultural and economic contacts after decades of being on a war footing. Fearful of Soviet intervention, the Polish government declared martial law on 13 December 1981 and crushed the labor movement Solidarity, which had hitherto threatened its control on society.

Hungary was benefiting from its pro-market reforms, colloquially referred to as "goulash Communism," which would serve as a model for the USSR's attempts at economic acceleration (*uskoreniie*). Romania, under Nicolae Ceauşescu, bucked Moscow's lead, pursuing an independent foreign policy while maintaining Stalinism at home. With the ascendency of **Mikhail Gorbachev**, Soviet policy toward its satellites in Eastern Europe changed rapidly. In 1987, the Soviet premier stressed his desire that the Eastern Bloc, including Russia, would soon find its place in the "common European home," suggesting an eventual end to ideological, military, and economic divisions of the past.

By the end of the decade, Gorbachev formally abandoned the Kremlin's stated policy of military intervention to prevent abandonment of socialism (a policy dubbed the **Brezhnev** Doctrine in the West). Instead, he instructed the Communist leaders of the bloc that they would be responsible for determining their own paths to political and economic development; Soviet Foreign Ministry spokesman Gennadi Gerasimov jokingly referred to this new approach as the **Sinatra Doctrine**. During the watershed year of 1989, the countries of the Eastern Bloc transitioned from one-party, socialist states to multiparty democracies with transitional market economies (Albania and Yugoslavia, members of the Eastern but not Soviet Bloc, experienced similar changes in the years to come). In most cases, these revolutions took place peacefully; however, in Romania, bloody street fighting and the televised execution of the Ceauşescus occurred on 25 December 1989.

Gorbachev, preoccupied with the worsening ethnic situation in the Caucasus and economic difficulties across the Soviet Union, did virtually nothing to stop the Soviet empire in Eastern Europe from disintegrating. By mid-1991, the various states of the Eastern Bloc had formally ended their participation in the Warsaw Pact, COMECON, and many other treaties binding them to the USSR. After the **dissolution of the Soviet Union**, **Boris Yeltsin** strove to establish new, fraternal relationships with the countries of the former Soviet Bloc, though Russophobia in Poland and some other states made normal relations difficult. By the mid 1990s, most of the USSR's former client states had applied for admission to NATO and begun the accession process with the **European Union**, effectively ending Russian dominance in the region. *See also* COLD WAR; FOREIGN RELATIONS.

ECOLOGY. *See* POLLUTION.

ECONOMIC REGIONS. Established in accordance with the 1993 **Constitution of the Russian Federation**, the country's 12 Economic Regions are as follows: Central; Central Black Earth; East Siberian; Far Eastern; Northern; North Caucasus; Northwestern; Volga; Urals; Volga-Vyatka; West Siberian; and Kaliningrad, the only region to include only a single **oblast**. Ostensibly, the regions were formed on the basis of common historical, economic, ecological, geological, and social characteristics; however, in Asiatic Russia, there are vast internal differences within the three easternmost regions. *See also* FEDERAL DISTRICTS.

ECONOMY. With the exception of a brief period of entrepreneurial experimentation under **Vladimir Lenin**'s "New Economic Policy" (NEP) from 1921 to 1928, the Soviet economy was historically dominated by the state. **Joseph Stalin**'s centrally planned economic policies, as well as the collectivization of **agriculture**, ensured that the **Communist Party of the Soviet Union** exercised almost total authority over farming, manufacturing, **foreign trade**, and natural resource exploitation. The production, pricing, distribution, and availability of nearly all goods and services were thus within the dominion of the state.

During the **Brezhnev** era, the high price of hydrocarbons buoyed the Soviet economy; however, the 1980s saw a dramatic downturn in the country's fortune as **oil** prices plummeted. This was exacerbated by expenses incurred during the **Soviet-Afghan War** and the arms race with the **United States**. By this point, preference for spending on the **military** and heavy **industry** over light industry and consumer goods had produced a "shortage economy" in the Union of Soviet Socialist Republics (USSR), contrasting sharply with the consumer- and information-based economies of **Japan**, Western Europe, and North America.

Hoping to bring about economic "acceleration" (*uskoreniie*), the new premier **Mikhail Gorbachev** instituted a "restructuring" (**perestroika**) of the economy in the mid-1980s, focusing on technological advancement and liberalization of the centrally planned economy in an effort to "keep up" with the West. The new environment allowed for the proliferation of new cooperatives and the marketization of certain firms, which could produce badly needed goods and engage in profit taking (colloquially referred to as "self-financing"), something that had been anathema to the system for generations. Entrepreneurial individuals with well-developed networks (*blat*), particularly among the *nomenklatura*, were able to increase their fortunes quickly.

However, reduced tax income due to Gorbachev's anti-**alcoholism** campaign, increasing **unemployment**, food rationing, and the lessening of subsidies on necessary goods produced a combined effect that lowered standards of living. Hoping to lessen the pain of transition by speeding up the shift to a market economy, the most liberal members of the government advocated a **500 Days Program** to overhaul the economy, attract foreign investment, and establish a functioning **banking** system. However, this was watered down and produced few results before the **dissolution of the Soviet Union** in late 1991.

After the dissolution of the Soviet Union, **Boris Yeltsin** undertook serious reforms, including the marketization of prices and the opening of the country to **foreign investment**. Banking and commercial regulation, however, were only half-heartedly implemented during his first administration. The failure of the rule of law to take root during these years allowed the **mafia** to exert substantial control over the economy, a fact that was admitted by the president himself on more than one occasion. During the transitional period, the need for state protection of these budding commercial ventures produced an environment conducive to clientelism and widespread **corruption**.

During the 1990s, these relationships led to the "insider **privatization**" of many formerly state-owned enterprises to joint-stock companies, thus transferring massive amounts of property from the "people" to a small number of **oligarchs**. This process was abetted by the distribution in 1992 of state-issued privatization vouchers worth 10,000 rubles toward the purchase of state assets; wealthy speculators purchased and consolidated these transferable vouchers to acquire **mining**, oil, steel, and other companies. Concurrently, the end of the **Cold War** and the opening of Russia to economic **globalization** resulted in the closure of a significant percentage of the country's factories, throwing many out of work. Wage arrears also emerged as a major issue for many regional and federal government employees. Transfer of wealth from the periphery to the country's two principal cities—**Moscow** and **St. Petersburg**—also accompanied the transition process, and certain **federal subjects** (e.g., **Khantiya-Mansiya**, **Tatarstan**, and **Tyumen**) enjoyed the benefits of economic liberalization while others (**Kalmykiya** and portions of the **Far North** and the **North Caucasus**, in particular) saw their regional economies ruined.

Application of **shock therapy** to the Russian economy ultimately produced mixed results: while production was rationalized, inflation was rampant during the early 1990s as the amount of currency in circulation was doubled several times. Many Russians moved into the "shadow economy" during this time, engaging in nontaxable forms of work. During Yeltsin's second term, the Asian economic "flu" spread to Russia, resulting in the 1998 **ruble crisis** that destroyed much of the population's savings. However, Yeltsin's resolve not to return to state control of the economy won him support outside Russia, ultimately resulting in a spot for the country within the **Group of Eight** (G8) advanced economies.

Under **Vladimir Putin**, Russia's economic fortunes improved greatly, due mostly to a rise in oil and **natural gas** prices. However, growth in **arms exports**, manufacturing, foreign trade, agricultural output, the financial industry, and the services sector (particularly outsourcing) also occurred during the Putin era. The national gross domestic product increased sixfold on his watch, though inflation is a perennial problem in Russia. The 2008–2009 **global economic crisis** severely affected the Russian economy. Adding to the problem, capital flight—a major issue during the 1990s—reemerged in the wake of the 2008 **South Ossetian War** as skittish investors and wealthy individuals quit Russia for more stable countries. However, the country's stabilization fund, implemented to mitigate the effects of a drop in hydrocarbon prices, allowed the Kremlin to partially stabilize the situation, while buying up a number of former state assets that had fallen into the hands of the oligarchs during the Yeltsin era. Regardless, the Russian economy plummeted by more than 10 percent in the first half of 2009, the first drop since the early 1990s.

EDUCATION. As was the case under the Soviet regime, education in Russia is predominantly provided by the state and is regulated by the Federal Ministry of Education through a nationwide curriculum and examinations. Several education reforms have occurred since 1991, resulting in a partial **privatization** of the educational sector. While in the 1990s education reform was a result of the need to depoliticize and to de-ideologize education, Russia's main challenge after the year 2000 was the need to compete on the world stage and to integrate into the global education system by adopting rules and practices established in other countries, especially those of the **European Union**.

While the early Bolshevik government set a series of inspirational and truly democratic principles and practices—it was the first government in Russian history to establish free education for all citizens—under **Joseph Stalin**, Soviet education became a major political battleground, with the subjugation of knowledge for the sake of ideology and the dismissal of teachers and professors becoming a regular occurrence. Consequently, the purpose of the education reform introduced by **Mikhail Gorbachev** in the 1980s as part of

the **perestroika** and *uskoreniie* (acceleration) processes was to improve the education system by removing excessive politicization and
ideologization. Gorbachev also attempted to lessen the power of the
entrenched *nomenklatura*, who had long wielded total control over
the curriculum, as well as **sports**, culture, and recreation centers.
Gorbachev's education reform was well publicized and hotly debated
in the **media**. One of the immediate outcomes of perestroika was the
1990 law "On Freedom of **Religion**," which meant that by permitting
religious education, the state gave educational institutions greater
freedom to develop their own curriculum and teaching practices.

The main outcomes of the extensive and heated discussions of the
previous decade found their way into the Russian Federation's 1992
law "On Education," which authorized three curriculum components
for state schools: federal, regional, and local. The first component is
compulsory, and successful completion is required to receive a nationally recognized certificate of secondary education. The remainder
of the curriculum content is delegated to local authorities. For the first
time in the history of Russian/Soviet education, priority was given to
effective pedagogy and the personal development of the student, with
a secondary focus being placed on the needs of society and state. By
delegating some of the power to regional and republican authorities,
the Russian state also recognized the equality and independence of
all titular and nontitular peoples and their right to further their own
cultural, historical, and ethnic traditions. In addition to regulation of
the curriculum, the law regulated the financial and practical side of
the educational policies: local governments were now responsible
for fixing the local budgets, for constructing and maintaining school
buildings, and for supplying equipment to schools. At the same time,
the federal government reserved the right to monitor the level of
academic achievement through examinations and the provision of
professional training by means of a state certification agency that was
independent of the school administration.

Russia's contemporary educational system includes a series of
components: preschool education (nurseries and kindergartens);
primary and secondary education (elementary, middle, and senior);
higher education (four- to five-year degree courses at universities or
vocation, technology, or specialized "institutes" and "academies").
Postgraduate education in Russia involves a three- to five-year

program resulting in a degree of *kandidat*, similar to the Anglo-American PhD.

In the Union of Soviet Socialist Republics (USSR), a large number of vocational and technical schools were supported by their respective industries, and a career path was almost guaranteed for the graduates of these establishments. Since 1991, the links between **industry** and education have been severed due to the collapse of Soviet heavy industry and lack of funds that could be used for training purposes. Working under new market conditions, technical colleges have to compete for applicants, and it has become increasingly difficult to attract Russian youth to certain professions, resulting in the lack of a qualified workforce in certain industries, which are filled with **immigrant** workers from other former Soviet republics.

At present, by law, all certificates of secondary education (*attestat zrelosti*, literally meaning "proof of maturity"), irrespective of the school, region, or program of training, conform to the same standard and are considered to be fully equivalent. The state ensures the quality of education and fairness of grading by holding unified state examinations (*edinyi gosudarstvennyi ekzamen*). The first such nationwide exams took place in 2007; the purpose of the introduction of these exams was to provide students with a common curriculum, to enable students to use their grades to apply for studies in any Russian university or universities abroad, and to combat **corruption** in the educational system. Previously each institution of higher education would run its own entry examinations, testing the knowledge of the applicants in specific subjects, resulting in poor quality of the student body, low standards, and widespread bribery.

Nowadays, students may obtain a degree of higher education in a number of ways. They can apply to state-funded universities and get their education for free (in fact, in addition to free tuition, they will get a small stipend from the state to help them with their living costs), or they can enroll in the same universities, but as fee-paying students (for fee-paying students admission requirements are lower, and they do not receive any financial support from the state). Alternatively, students can choose to study at fully private universities, where fees are paradoxically lower than tuition fees at state-funded universities because they are new institutions only establishing their reputation.

The program of education at the university level normally lasts five years and culminates in a degree of higher education (*spetsialist*).

Following the Bologna process, which is aimed at reorganizing and streamlining the system of higher education in Europe, Russia has introduced its own bachelor's and master's degrees. At the moment, the bachelor and *spetsialist* tracks are available to all students; however, it is expected that in 2010 all *spetsialist* programs will be discontinued. The changes in the curriculum brought about by the Bologna process will not affect funding or management of the university educational system, as these are provided by the state. Coinciding with the start of the Bologna process, the Federal Ministry of Education established federal centers of excellence in teaching and research. Three centers in the north, south, and east of the country have been established so far (**Moscow State University** did not take part in the program because this university enjoys a special status as it is funded directly from the state budget). Their purpose is to test the transition from the Soviet to European model of teaching and to consolidate the number of discrete educational institutions.

The outcome of this reform is still not clear; Russian **journalists** often complain about the destruction of the Soviet educational system, which previously provided training to all citizens, resulting in almost universal literacy (according to the 2002 census, the literacy rate in Russia was 99.4 percent); however, the old system failed to compete on the global educational market. In 2004 in Russia, state spending for education was 3.6 percent of GDP. Private institutions accounted for 1 percent of preschool education, 0.5 percent of primary and secondary education, and 17 percent of university education. In Russia, **women** have higher rates of education than men, including university education.

ELECTORAL REFORMS OF 2004–2005. Upon entering office as president, **Vladimir Putin** declared his intention to increase the **vertical of power** associated with the executive branch of government. During his first term in office, he marginalized the political power of the **oligarchs** and constrained the **media**. He was, however, unable to implement his most dramatic reforms until the **Beslan crisis** in 2004. Framed against the threat of continuing **terrorism** and promising an end to the instability of the country, he proposed sweeping changes to the legislative system and federal system of power sharing. With almost universal support from the masses and political elites, he was able to abolish popular elections in Russia's **federal subjects** and institute a proportional system for the **State Duma**. As a result, he—as president of the Russian Federation—gained the ability to recommend gubernatorial candidates in the regions, to then be approved by the local legislature, thus making them beholden to the center. His reforms within the **Federal Assembly** guaranteed his control of parliament through a system that advantaged pro-Kremlin parties and marginalized liberal and other opposition **political parties**, which had been able to gain seats through the election of deputies without large party memberships.

ENVIRONMENTAL DEGRADATION. *See* POLLUTION.

ENVIRONMENTALISM. In a country where almost no **civil society** developed outside the purview of the **Communist Party of the Soviet Union**, the environmental cause defied the odds to become one of the first major popular causes in the 1980s. Due to a Leninist approach to the environment, the Union of Soviet Socialist Republics (USSR) suffered from widespread environmental degradation resulting from wasteful irrigation schemes, aluminum smelting, overuse of fertilizers and pesticides, **nuclear weapons** testing, and chemical spills. An excessive emphasis on heavy **industry** contributed to massive emissions of carbon, as well as other dangerous industrial pollutants.

The catalyst for the environmental movement, however, was the meltdown of the **Chernobyl** nuclear power plant in **Ukraine**. Intellectuals, public activists, and indigenous **ethnic minorities**, under the comparative protections of **glasnost**, mobilized in the wake of the event, helping to expose other major ecological tragedies in the Aral and **Caspian** seas, northeastern **Kazakhstan**, and **Lake Baykal**. In 1987, a new state agency, the USSR State Committee for Environmental Protection, was established to oversee the Soviet Union's ecology.

In 1992, **Boris Yeltsin** received a country devastated by decades of hazardous environmental exploitation, radioactivity, and rampant air and water **pollution**. However, the difficulties associated with the country's transition to a market **economy**, combined with the relative weakness of civic organizations, precluded the development of a mass environmental movement. A number of **political parties**, including the **Russian Ecological Party** and the **Agrarian Party of Russia**, sought to improve ecological conditions, as did the **indigenous peoples of the north** and other ethnic and cultural organizations. Neighboring countries—**Norway**, in particular—have also sought to promote a more effective environmental protection regime in the Russian Federation.

Unfortunately, a powerful array of interests, including **oligarchs**, transnational corporations, and the **military** and **security services**, stonewalled any meaningful action, despite the existence of relevant laws meant to safeguard the environment and **wildlife**. In recent years, Russian corporations have demonstrated more concern for their impact on the environment, and, after some prevarication, **Vladimir Putin** signed the country to the **Kyoto Protocol**. However, environmentalism in Russia remains anemic when compared to other northern European countries.

ERZYANS. *See* MORDVINS.

ESPIONAGE. During the Soviet era, the Kremlin developed a global espionage network, using agents of the **KGB**, the **military**'s secret service apparatus, and **Communist** sympathizers in Third World countries. The main target of such activities was the **United States**, but other **North Atlantic Treaty Organization** (NATO) members, particularly **Great Britain** and West **Germany**, were also targeted, as well as neighboring countries such as **Turkey** and **Japan**.

During the 1980s, the Union of Soviet Socialist Republics (USSR) began to develop spy rings that were disconnected from the embassy system and which used corporate rather than diplomatic covers; these individuals are referred to as "NOCs" (nonofficial cover). **Aeroflot**, **Gazprom**, and **Lukoil**—among other Russian firms—have been implicated in such activities. While the transition to democracy reduced the need for a large internal security force, the Russian Federation maintained much of the USSR's foreign espionage network through its military wing, the Main Intelligence Directorate or GRU, and the **FSB**.

During the post-Soviet period, a number of Americans have been convicted of spying for Moscow, including Aldrich Ames in 1994 and Robert Hanssen in 2001. After a relative decrease in activity in the late **Yeltsin** administration, **Vladimir Putin**, a former foreign intelligence operative, beefed up the FSB's Foreign Intelligence Service (known as the SVR, or *Sluzhba vneshnei razvedki*). While the focus of espionage has shifted toward industrial espionage (particularly in the computer and software sector and dual-use technologies like lasers), military readiness is still an area of intense interest. In 2009, two Russian diplomats were ejected from NATO headquarters in Brussels for engaging in espionage. Energy issues top the list of espionage-related activities in the **European Union**. Russia also has a prodigious network of spies across the **near abroad**, particularly in more hostile countries such as **Azerbaijan**, **Georgia**, and the **Baltic States**.

In terms of counterintelligence, Russia moved against agents working for Turkey, Pakistan, Iraq, and Saudi Arabia in 2001, and stepped up its defense against the spy services of **China**, **Israel**, and **Iran**. While the same diligence was applied to the United States, the **security services** simultaneously shared intelligence on **Islamist** extremists with Washington after the **September 11 attacks**. In the last years of the Putin administration, accusations flew between Moscow and the UK, with both claiming **Cold War** levels of spy activity in their respective countries; a number of diplomatic expulsions led to a further chilling of relations. Moscow's decision in 2008 to redefine espionage as including the delivery of sensitive information to foreign nongovernmental organizations—an outgrowth of the dispute with the British Council over its activities in Russia—drew condemnation from the international community. *See also* FRADKOV, MIKHAIL; LITVINENKO, ALEKSANDR.

ESTONIA (RELATIONS WITH). Estonia passed from Swedish to Russian rule during the early 18th century with the Treaty of Nystad. Despite two centuries of Russian rule, the region maintained much of its Lutheran and Teutonic heritage. With the early abolition of serfdom and commercial connections to other **Baltic** countries, Estonia earned a reputation as one of tsarist Russia's most economically liberal regions.

A national awakening began in the 20th century, culminating in a push for independence from Russia during World War I (1914–1918). After the **Bolshevik Revolution**, Estonia was occupied by **German** troops before taking up a war of independence with Soviet Russia, which recognized the sovereignty of the state in 1920 under the terms of the Treaty of Tartu. During the interwar period, Estonia functioned as part of the *cordon sanitaire* of newly independent Eastern European states hostile to the Soviet Union. Under the secret protocols of the 1939 Molotov-Ribbentrop Pact, the Union of Soviet Socialist Republics (USSR) invaded the country and declared Estonia a Soviet Socialist Republic in the summer of 1940 after a pro-Communist coup d'état. Despite Nazi occupation of the region during World War II, **Moscow** reimposed its annexation of Estonia in the waning days of the conflict; a small portion of eastern Estonia was then transferred to the **Russian Soviet Federative Socialist Republic**.

The **United States**, **Great Britain**, and a host of Western countries never formally recognized the incorporation of Estonia and the other **Baltic States** into the USSR. During the Soviet era, the republic suffered from the deportation of a significant portion of its **intelligentsia** and political elites. Policies of Russification and settlement of **ethnic Russians** (particularly **military** personnel) in the region further led to a dilution of Estonian culture. However, in the post-**Stalinist** era, Estonia benefited from a comparatively liberal economic and media regime, including the ability to receive television broadcasts from and travel to neighboring **Finland**. Under **perestroika**, Estonian nationalists, economic liberals, and the Greens sidelined the **Communist Party**, which was increasingly viewed as a tool of foreign (Russian) domination and imperialism. Tallinn, along with Vilnius and Riga, emerged as a hotbed of anti-Soviet activity from 1988 until the **dissolution of the Soviet Union**.

Estonia regained its independence by the end of the summer of 1991 as the USSR's Supreme Soviet recognized the republic, followed by the reestablishment of formal relations with Washington. As an independent state, Estonia moved quickly to develop its relations with the Nordic countries and Western Europe, particularly Germany. Estonia, like its Baltic neighbors **Latvia** and **Lithuania**, refused to countenance inclusion into Russia's **near abroad**, despite nearly five decades of Soviet rule, and eschewed membership in any post-Soviet organization, including the **Commonwealth of Independent States**. Its geopolitical situation, however, was complicated by the presence of Russian troops (the last of whom left the country in 1994) and a sizable Russian minority.

Tallinn's 1992 decision not to grant its ethnic Russians (and other non-Estonians) citizenship unless they or their ancestors were citizens of the republic prior to the 1940 annexation created lasting problems in Estonian-Russian relations. While Estonian citizenship could be obtained through **language** proficiency and swearing an oath of loyalty, approximately a quarter of the country's population was effectively rendered noncitizens (*negrazhdane*). The problem was especially acute in the area around the eastern city of Narva, which is predominantly Russian. Many in Russia felt that Brussels and Washington were turning a blind eye to the poor treatment of its "countrymen" in Estonia, despite the **European Union** (EU) and America's regular urging of Estonia to treat its **national minorities** with respect. This situation, along with Estonian overtures to the United States, transformed Tallinn into an easy target of Russian ultranationalists during the **Yeltsin** administration.

Washington's 1997 decision to invite the **Baltic States** to join its mutual defense treaty, the **North Atlantic Treaty Organization** (NATO), further chilled the relationship between Tallinn and Moscow during the latter years of the Yeltsin administration. Economic relations between the two states also deteriorated during this time, with spats over customs duties and transit of **oil** and **natural gas** and threats of sanctions. Relations were also complicated by Tallinn's insistence on the return of territory annexed to Russia in 1945; disputes over the border delimitation continue to this day. Estonia joined NATO on 29 March 2004 and became a member of the EU on 1 May 2004. Membership in the unions added heft to tiny Estonia's position in its negotiations with Moscow but also precipitated a worsening of bilateral relations with its large eastern neighbor.

Vladimir Putin's more aggressive foreign policy resulted in Estonia being branded a threat to Russian interests. Frequent accusations of Estonians as "fascists" began to pepper the Russian **media** during the first decade of the new millennium, reaching a fever pitch in 2005 as Russia prepared to celebrate the 60th anniversary of the end of World War II. In 2007, a poll found that Russians considered

Estonia to be the most unfriendly regime in the world. The relationship between the two countries reached its nadir in 2007. Prompted by the controversy surrounding the relocation of the Bronze Soldier of Tallinn, the **Estonian Cyberwar** was launched by pro-Russian hackers. The attacks, which targeted Estonian government websites, triggered an investigation by NATO and plunged Estonia, a global leader in e-governance, into chaos. In the wake of the 2008 **South Ossetian War**, Estonian fears of Moscow's potential "liberation" of Russian citizens living in Narva was pushed to the forefront of international diplomacy. *See also* FOREIGN RELATIONS.

ESTONIAN CYBERWAR (2007). Also known as the 2007 Cyber-Attacks on **Estonia**, the events involved a massive, multipronged denial of service (DoS) attack and more sophisticated forms of cyber-warfare directed at Estonian government servers, as well as various websites associated with Estonia. The attacks crippled the country's e-government system, which is seen as one of the most advanced in the world. Estonia's foreign minister accused the Kremlin of having a hand in the attacks. While direct Russian involvement was never proved, the attacks were clearly a response to a decision by the Estonian parliament (*Riigikogu*) to relocate the "Bronze Soldier," a Soviet-era war memorial commemorating those who died liberating Estonia from Nazi control, to the outskirts of Tallinn. The statue has particular significance to the **ethnic Russian** community in the Baltic republic, and its removal was taken as a further instance of ethnic prejudice on the part of the Estonian government toward its Russian population. Many of the attacks were directed from the breakaway republic of **Transnistria**. A member of the pro-Kremlin *Nashi* youth group later admitted organizing the attacks, though many observers claimed the scale and scope of the attacks suggested support from the Russian **security services** and/or major corporate/**mafia** interests. The crisis forced the **North Atlantic Treaty Organization** (NATO) to begin to develop plans for responding to and defending its members against cyberspace-based attacks. *See also* FOREIGN RELATIONS.

ETHNIC MINORITIES. Generally speaking, the term "ethnic minorities" can refer to any of the Russian Federation's non-**ethnic Russian** peoples including those historically classified as **national**

minorities (i.e., ethnic groups whose ancestral homelands lie within the current boundaries of Russia, e.g., the **Tatars**, **Bashkirs**, **Chechens**, **Sakha**, **Udmurts**, and **Chuvash**), as well as ethnic or cultural groups from beyond Russia's contemporary borders (including recent **immigrants**). The latter group is best defined by ethnic **Ukrainians**, **Armenians**, **Roma** (Gypsies), and **Chinese**, as well as the peoples of **Central Asia**. Due to their historical classification as an ethnic group (as opposed to a religious group), Russian **Jews** are sometimes listed as ethnic minorities, while the country's **Muslims** and **Buddhists** are categorized based on their culturolinguistic affiliation. *See also* LANGUAGE.

ETHNIC REPUBLICS. Among Russia's 83 **federal subjects**, the 21 ethnic republics represent those constituent units that possess the highest level of sovereignty, including—in most cases—a president, constitution, parliament, **flag**, anthem, control of their own borders, and an official **language** other than **Russian**.

The republics can be grouped into four geographic areas: the **North Caucasian** republics (**Adygeya**, **Karachay-Cherkessiya**, **Kabardino-Balkariya**, **North Ossetiya**, **Ingushetiya**, **Chechnya**, **Dagestan**, and **Kalmykiya**); the Volga-Ural republics (**Mordoviya**, **Chuvashiya**, **Mari El**, **Udmurtiya**, **Tatarstan**, and **Bashkortostan**); southeastern **Siberian** republics (**Altay**, **Khakasiya**, **Tuva**, and **Buryatiya**); and the northern republics (**Kareliya**, **Komi**, and the **Sakha Republic**). During the Soviet period, nearly all these units were designated as **Autonomous Soviet Socialist Republics** (ASSRs) within the **Russian Soviet Federative Socialist Republic** (RSFSR). Kareliya formerly enjoyed status as a **union republic** of the Union of Soviet Socialist Republics (USSR) from 1940 until 1956, while Tuva was an independent country from 1911 to 1944. In most cases, each republic is structured as the ethnic homeland of a particular nationality, though in some cases (specifically, Karachay-Cherkessiya, Kabardino-Balkariya, and Dagestan), the republic is shared among two or more groups.

The demographic status of the titular nationality ranges from a high of 93.5 percent (Chechnya) to a low of 9.2 percent (Kareliya). In nine republics (Adygeya, Altay, Bashkortostan, Buryatiya, Kareliya, Mari El, Mordoviya, Udmurtiya, and Khakasiya), **ethnic Russians** enjoy majority or plurality status at the expense of the titular group; titular nationalities command a statistical majority in only seven republics (Ingushetiya, Kalmykiya, North Ossetiya, Tatarstan, Tuva, Chechnya, and Chuvashiya). In the waning days of **Mikhail Gorbachev**'s **perestroika**, a number of ASSRs declared their sovereignty within the RSFSR, often accompanied by a name change that abandoned the Soviet-era nomenclature. In some cases, including Chechnya and Tatarstan, the republics unilaterally declared themselves to be union republics with the right to ultimately secede from the Soviet Union; such declarations were rejected by Moscow.

In the post-Soviet period, **Boris Yeltsin** urged the leaders of the republics to take "all the sovereignty they could swallow." The ensuing policy of **asymmetrical federalism** allowed for the development of strong presidential systems in many republics, as well as systems of political patronage based on loyalty to the "Little Fathers," that is, the long-serving heads of state. After **Vladimir Putin**'s 2005 gubernatorial reforms, which required nomination of regional leaders by Russia's president, the power of the republican leaders has diminished, though many still command enormous influence on the regional and even federal levels. During his tenure, Putin also outlawed linguistic reforms in Tatarstan, which had instituted a shift to the Latin alphabet, and forced the republics to bring their constitutions into line with the federal **constitution**, signifying a reimposition of federal control over the non-Russian republics. Chechnya has been largely exempted from restoration of central control in an effort to preserve the comparative peace that has reigned in the troubled republic since 2005.

ETHNIC RUSSIANS. Ethnic group. One principal use of this term refers to Russia's titular majority, which accounts for approximately 80 percent of the population, that is, residents of Russia who are defined by their ethnic belonging and/or cultural association, including **language**, **religion**, and traditions (called *russkie* in the **Russian language**). They are thus differentiated from the Russian Federation's 175 **ethnic minorities** (**Tatars**, **Chuvash**, **Udmurts**, etc.); the latter are referred to in Russian as *rossiiane*, a word that stems from the word *Rossiia*, which linguistically designates Russia as a multicultural, multiconfessional association of different peoples.

Alternatively, the term refers to those Russians—or people who view Russianness as their primary cultural identity—living outside the borders of the Russian Federation. From the point of view of their ethnic background, they are not always Russian; however, they have strong links with the Russian Federation and thus define themselves as Russian.

There are currently some 19 million ethnic Russians residing in the so-called **near abroad** (down from 25 million in 1991). Large numbers of diasporic Russians can also be found in **Germany**, the **United States**, **Canada**, and elsewhere. Many are descendents of Russian Civil War–era émigrés and Soviet **dissidents**, as well as post-1991 economic **immigrants**. The Russian Foreign Ministry estimates the total number of Russians living outside the Russian Federation at 30 million people worldwide. During the first administration of President **Boris Yeltsin**, the cause of Russia's "countrymen," i.e., ethnic Russians living in the **Newly Independent States**, became a political tool for ultranationalists as well as the **Communist Party of the Russian Federation**. In particular, Russian relations with **Estonia** and **Latvia** were compromised by those countries' treatment of ethnic Russians, particularly after legal changes transformed many "Baltic Russians" into noncitizens in the early 1990s.

ETHNIC VIOLENCE. Beginning in the late 1980s, ethnic violence emerged as a significant problem within the Soviet Union. The comparatively open environment enabled by **glasnost** forced many of **Joseph Stalin**'s crimes against the country's non-Russian populations, particularly the **punished peoples** and **Ukrainians**, into the open. With ethnic nationalism on the rise, Stalin's delimitation of borders based on the principle of "divide and rule" came under question, as did the situation of "relocated" Soviet citizens, either as internal deportees or "colonizers." Resentment of **ethnic Russians** in the **Baltic States** (and **Kazakhstan**) and **Meskhetian Turks** in Uzbekistan led to street clashes and urban rioting with ethnic overtones.

In **Moldova** and the **Caucasus**, the situation degenerated into outright conflict. Slavs and Russophones, fearful of "Romanianization," mobilized against ethnic Moldovans and created the **Transnistrian** enclave; **Armenians** and Azeris conducted a series of pogroms against one another that led to a war over **Nagorno-Karabakh**;

Ingush and **Ossetians** clashed over property disputes linked to the former's deportation to **Central Asia** during World War II; and, in **Georgia**, there were bloody episodes between ethnic Georgians and minority Abkhazians and Ossetians. These disputes played a high-profile role in the **dissolution of the Soviet Union** in 1991. The newly independent Russian Federation continued to suffer from ethnic conflict in the **North Caucasus**, where **Muslim**/Christian, Turkic/**Circassian**, and Slav/non-Slav determiners frequently led to ethnically charged violence.

Since the mid-1990s, the number of xenophobic attacks on non-Russians has skyrocketed. In recent years, **neofascist** and neo-Nazi youths have targeted **immigrants** from Central Asia and other parts of the former Soviet Union, including the beheading of a Tajik man in 2007, an attack broadcasted on the **Internet**. Attacks on **Jews** and synagogues have also increased in recent years. There have even been attacks on **national minorities** from within Russia, such as the murder of a **Sakha** (Yakut) in 2007. Violence directed at ethnic Georgians within Russia also flared around the time of the **South Ossetian War**. Clashes between non-Slavic **ethnic minorities** are also on the rise. The majority of such attacks among ethnic groups are rooted in commercial and/or political disputes. *See also* LIBERAL DEMOCRATIC PARTY OF RUSSIA.

EURASIA. Eurasia is a large landmass covering about 53,990,000 square kilometers, or 10 percent of the Earth's surface and more than one-third of its land area. The population of Eurasia is 4.8 billion, or more than 70 percent of the world's population. Eurasia is comprised of both Europe and Asia but is recognized by some geographers to constitute a single continent, as the traditional continental divides—the **Ural Mountains**, the Ural River, the **Caspian Sea**, the **Caucasus**, and the waters connecting the **Black Sea** to the Mediterranean—do not present significant barriers to the movement of human beings, fauna, or flora.

The historical division of Europe from Asia results from ancient Greek geographers' fallacious conviction that the two spaces were separated by large bodies of water; however, during the 18th century, Russia's rise as a European power forced a reconceptualization of the borders of the European continent. The word itself is a portmanteau of "Europe" and "Asia," names of female characters in Greek mythology.

In terms of geopolitics, the word "Eurasia" (*Evraziia*) is uniquely associated with the former Soviet Union and is somewhat controversial. The **Baltic States** and, to a lesser extent, **Ukraine** reject categorization as Eurasian states, though Russia, the Transcaucasian republics, and Central Asian countries embrace the term. **Kazakhstan**, in particular, promotes itself as a Eurasian nation, both territorially (like **Turkey** and the Russian Federation, Kazakhstan has both European and Asian portions) and ethnically (a slight majority of Kazakhstanis are Asiatic, with the rest being mostly European in terms of their ancestry).

With the **dissolution of the Soviet Union**, Russian politicians briefly considered renaming the **Russian Soviet Federative Socialist Republic** "Eurasia" before settling on "Russian Federation." The move had support from **neo-Eurasianist** political elites, who stress the multicultural and multiconfessional nature of the various peoples of contemporary Russia, which include Finnic, Ugric, Caucasian, Turkic, Mongolic, and Tungusic nations alongside the numerically dominant Slavs, as well as practitioners of **Orthodox Christianity**, **Islam**, **Buddhism**, **Judaism**, and **shamanism**. The Russian Federation covers about one-third of the Eurasian supercontinent, though it contains less than 3 percent of its human population. *See also* EURASIA PARTY.

EURASIA PARTY. Political party. A socially oriented, étatist political party, the Eurasia Party was founded in 2002 by the right-wing ideologue **Aleksandr Dugin**. The Eurasia Party rejects **Atlanticism** and Western-style values for Russia and supports Russia's centrality in **Eurasian** affairs. Historically, it has fielded few candidates, opting instead to support the ruling elite (principally **Vladimir Putin** and his successor, **Dmitry Medvyedev**) with which it has close connections. Rather than being a party of pure Russian **nationalism**, the party advocates in the name of all constituent peoples of the **Russian Federation**, including **Tatars**, **Kalmyks**, and **Chechens**, among others, as well as supporting the traditional interpretations of the four principal Russian faiths: Russian **Orthodoxy**, **Judaism**, **Islam**, and **Buddhism**. The party has a membership of over 2,000 and has 50 provincial branches across Russia.

EURASIAN ECONOMIC COMMUNITY (EAEC or EurAsEC).
The Eurasian Economic Community began as a custom union established in 1996 among the **Commonwealth of Independent States'** members of Russia, **Belarus**, and **Kazakhstan**. The current entity was agreed on 10 October 2000, and added **Kyrgyzstan** and **Tajikistan** to the group. In 2006, **Uzbekistan** formally joined the Eurasian Economic Community, thus alleviating the need for a separate Organization of Central Asian Cooperation, which was folded into the EAEC. The members hope to establish a single economic space by 2010; Kazakhstan's president, Nursultan Nazarbayev, has called for the implementation of a single currency for the group, tentatively titled the *yevraz*. Freedom of movement has ostensibly been established between the nations, though border controls remain in place in many areas.

EURASIANISM. Sociopolitical ideology. Often contrasted with **Atlanticism**, contemporary Eurasianism or neo-Eurasianism is a revival of an earlier stream of thought that Russia should embrace its unique role as both a European and Asiatic country, free of the spiritual, intellectual, and cultural domination of Romano-Germanic civilization. Nikolay Danilevsky first defined **Eurasia** as a distinct geopolitical entity during the 19th century, beginning the Russian fascination with its predominance in the "new" world region. While older forms of Eurasianism argued for a grand cultural alliance of the Slavs and Turanians (Finno-Ugric and Turkic peoples), neo-Eurasianists typically embrace the wider **Muslim** world, principally **Iran** and anti-Western Arab regimes (**India** and **China** are sometimes part of this political calculus as well). The ideology is strongly anti-Zionist, anti-Western, and anti-American, with overtones of **anti-Semitism** in certain quarters. Its proponents suggest that it is the only viable alternative to the paradigm of "techno-economic **globalization**" that currently dominates the world system and reinforces American hegemony.

In its intellectual form, neo-Eurasianism is most closely associated with the works of geopolitician **Aleksandr Dugin**; in the realm of **politics**, former Foreign Minister and Prime Minister **Yevgeny Primakov** presents the strongest advocate for adopting a pan-Asiatic orientation in opposition to integration with the West. **Vladimir**

Putin's conduct of **foreign relations** is recognized as having a strong Eurasianist bent, but treads carefully so as not to totally reject the influence of the West on Russia's sociopolitical development. Neo-Eurasianism both shares aspects of and is seen as the replacement for the older ideology of **pan-Slavism**. *See also* MONROESKI DOCTRINE; NEAR ABROAD; UNITED STATES.

EURO-ATLANTICISM. *See* ATLANTICISM.

EUROPEAN UNION (RELATIONS WITH). In the early days of the **Cold War**, the **United States** encouraged its allies on the Continent to enter into an economic cooperation regime in an effort to prevent a future Franco-German war; Washington used its Marshall Plan funds and created the **North Atlantic Treaty Organization** (NATO) to provide both capital and security for the new arrangement. The original coal and steel customs union, established in the early 1950s, soon blossomed into the more robust European Economic Community (EEC) four years later.

In its first decade, the EEC had almost no formal contact with the Union of Soviet Socialist Republics (USSR) or its Communist allies in the **Eastern Bloc**. However, with the return of Charles de Gaulle to **France**'s presidency, U.S. influence over the grouping weakened, and new ties with Moscow were established. In the wake of the 1973 oil crisis, European dependency on Soviet **oil** and **natural gas** precipitated even closer cooperation. In the 1980s, **Mikhail Gorbachev**'s "New Thinking" in the USSR's **foreign relations** and his advocacy of Eastern Europe and the Soviet Union in a "common European home," in conjunction with a closer East-West cooperation among the European states, particularly the two **Germanys**, broadened EEC-Soviet cooperation.

In the early 1990s, the **dissolution of the Soviet Union** and the end of the Cold War made it politically feasible for the previously neutral states of **Finland**, Austria, and Sweden to join the newly formed European Union (EU). The **Baltic States** and most of the former Eastern Bloc nations began the accession process as well. Under **Boris Yeltsin**, the relationship between the EU and the Russian Federation was, in large part, determined by forces from across the Atlantic. American policymakers did not wish to see Russia included in either NATO or the EU, while the Kremlin refused to become part of the second-tier European Neighborhood Policy, which Russian elites saw as subordinating the country's national interest to Brussels without the benefits of full membership in the EU.

Vladimir Putin provided a solution to the impasse between 2003 and 2005 by expanding previous partnership agreements between Moscow and Brussels, stressing that the EU was Russia's natural and "most important" partner. The result was the EU-Russia Common Spaces program, which focuses on the establishment of a common economic space; a common space of freedom, security, and justice; a space of cooperation in the field of external security; and a space of research, education, and cultural exchange. In essence, Russia, ever protective of its domestic sovereignty, observes some—but not all—of the burdensome *acquis communautaire* the EU requires for its prospective members. Trade with EU countries accounts for about one-half of all of Russia's **foreign trade**. The EU purchases half of Russia's oil exports and more than 60 percent of its natural gas, which represent 20 percent and 40 percent of the EU's overall purchases, respectively.

The new era of cooperation was underpinned by events abroad, including the **September 11 attacks** on the United States, which stimulated joint **counterterrorism** projects, and Russia's common cause with France and Germany against the Anglo-American invasion of Iraq in 2003. The influence of American neo-conservatives in **George W. Bush**'s administration shaped the dynamics of EU-Russian relations as a wedge was driven between "old" Europe (France, Germany, and Belgium) and "new" Europe (the former Soviet satellites and republics—particularly **Poland** and the Baltic republics). The latter have attempted to use their position in the EU to prevent Russian bullying. At the same time, Russia has sought to press the EU on the protection of more than 1 million **ethnic Russians** in the newly admitted states.

Russian-EU relations remain closely tied to energy issues, and the recent disputes between **Gazprom** and **Ukraine** have presented acute problems; likewise, the planned undersea Baltic gas pipeline has resulted in internal EU frictions as the Baltic States and Poland have condemned Germany's eagerness to accommodate Russian demands on energy provision. The EU condemnation of Russian

military action in **Georgia** during the 2008 **South Ossetian War** prompted retaliatory rhetoric from the Kremlin. Issues surrounding visas for Russian citizens traveling to the **Kaliningrad** exclave—now separated from Russia proper by the EU's Schengen zone of visa-free travel—also proved problematic for the two entities. The EU's move to create a security apparatus separate from NATO has also been of concern to the Kremlin; however, the first military-to-military contacts between Brussels and Moscow were established in 2002.

Despite cooperation on the **Moldova-Transnistria** issue, Brussels and the Kremlin have failed to solve a problem that both parties recognize as vital to their respective interests. In May 2009, the EU announced a new plan called the Eastern Partnership, which is intended to shore up the stability of Ukraine, Georgia, **Azerbaijan**, Moldova, **Belarus**, and **Armenia** while simultaneously preventing them from "backsliding" into alignment with Russia. Russian Foreign Minister **Sergey Lavrov** expressed concern at the new initiative, suggesting it subverts Russia's special relationship with its neighbors in the **near abroad**.

EVENKIYA/EVENKIYSKY MUNICIPAL DISTRICT. An administrative district of **Krasnoyarsk Krai**. Formerly a **federal subject** of the Russian Federation known as the Evenk Autonomous Okrug, the region (along with the Taymyr Autonomous Okrug) was merged with Krasnoyarsk Krai on 1 January 2007, following a 2005 referendum. In the poll, 79 percent of registered voters gave their support for the merger, while 20 percent voted against consolidation. The last governor of the region was Boris Zolotaryov. The region's titular minority is the **Evenk** people, who account for 21 percent of the region's population of some 18,000; **ethnic Russians** form a majority at 62 percent. *See also* TAYMYRIYA.

EVENKS/EVENKI. Ethnic group. Formerly known as the Tungus, the Evenks are an indigenous Paleo-Siberian population of approximately 35,000, widely scattered across some 2.5 million square kilometers. They are classified as one of the **indigenous peoples of the north**. The Evenki **language** is a member of the northern branch of the Manchu-Tungus family, distantly related to Manchu. The Evenks reside in a huge swath of **Siberian taiga** from the Ob River in the west to the Sea of Okhotsk in the east, and from the **Arctic Ocean** in the north to Manchuria in the south. While they form the titular minority of **Krasnoyarsk Krai's Evenkiysky Municipal District**, where they make up 21 percent of the population, they are also located in the Russian regions of **Tyumen, Tomsk, Irkutsk, Zabaykalsky, Amur, Buryatiya, Sakha, Khabarovsk, Sakhalin**, and other parts of Krasnoyarsk, as well as **Mongolia** and **China**. Evenks are nominally **Russian Orthodox** but maintain many of their traditional **shamanistic** beliefs. *See also* EVENS.

EVENS. Ethnic group. The Evens or Eveny, an **indigenous people of the north**, were formerly known as *Lamuts* (Even: "Sea People"). They number fewer than 20,000, and are found mostly in **Magadan** and **Kamchatka**. Evens are ethnically and culturally related to the **Evenks**; about one-third of the population speaks Even, a Tungusic language related to the Evenk language. While most confess Russian **Orthodoxy**, **shamanistic** practices remain strong among the Even. Traditionally working as reindeer herders, most Evens were forcibly settled during the Soviet era and now live on collective farms (*kolkhozy*).

– F –

FAIR RUSSIA. Political party. Known in Russian as *Spravedlivaia Rossiia: Rodina/Pensionery/Zhizn'*, the party's name is sometimes translated as "Just Russia." The party was formed on 28 October 2006 through a merger of **Rodina**, the Russian Party of Life (*Zhizn'*), and the **Russian Pensioners' Party**. In 2007, the People's Party also merged with Fair Russia. **Sergey Mironov**, the former head of the Zhizn' party and a close ally of **Vladimir Putin**, is the party's chairman. In 2007, Mironov's proposal to merge Fair Russia with the **Communist Party of the Russian Federation** (KPRF) was rejected by the KPRF leader, **Gennady Zyuganov**. While Fair Russia claims to be a genuine left-wing party, its strong support of the Kremlin places it squarely within Russia's political center. In 2008, the party backed the candidacy of Putin's handpicked heir, **Dmitry**

Medvyedev. Despite the fealty of Fair Russia toward the country's leaders, its aim is to provide a counterweight to **United Russia**, and establish a genuine two-party political system in Russia built on the notion of loyal opposition. Due to its left-of-center economic orientation combined with nationalistic and sometimes **anti-Semitic** tendencies, the party has steadily been increasing its popularity at the expense of the **Liberal Democratic Party of Russia**. In the 2007 **State Duma** elections, the party placed fourth, winning 38 seats and capturing 7.7 percent of the vote. Hoping to wither the KPRF's position, the Kremlin gave Fair Russia significant support prior to the elections in an effort to put it over the newly initiated 7 percent threshold for gaining seats in the Duma.

FAR NORTH. The Russian Far North (*Dal' nii Sever*) or Extreme North (*Krainii Sever*) is the area of Russia that lies in the northern periphery of the **Eurasian** landmass. Located mostly above the Arctic Circle, the Far North includes the **federal subjects** of **Murmansk**, **Nenetsiya**, **Yamaliya**, **Taymyriya**, northern **Sakha**, and **Chukotka**, as well as the **Arctic Ocean** islands of **Novaya Zemlya**, Franz Josef Land, Severnaya Zemlya, the New Siberian Islands, and Wrangel Island. Informally, the northerly portions of **Archangel**, **Komi**, **Evenkiya**, **Magadan**, **Koryakiya**, and **Kamchatka** are sometimes included as well.

The region is defined by **tundra** and harsh **climate**, and, as a result, lacks major population centers. During the Soviet era, many of the country's **gulags** were located in the region; this preserved secrecy but also allowed forced labor in the harsh conditions. The Soviets paid very high wages (the "northern bonus") to those willing to locate voluntarily to the region for employment, resulting in a **demographic** revolution in the region. Since the institution of **perestroika**, native peoples have become increasingly active in their attempts to protect the region's **environment** and traditional cultural and economic practices.

Today, laborers continue to be entitled to higher levels of compensation due to the harsh, even dangerous working conditions. However, the cold temperatures and high prices associated with consumer goods make life very difficult for the local population. Life expectancy, particularly among the **indigenous peoples of the**

north, is dramatically lower than in the rest of the Russian Federation. As a result, emigration is reducing the region's population in the post-Soviet period. **Oil** and **natural gas** extraction and **mining** are the primary **industrial** occupations, while indigenous peoples tend to engage in traditional forms of labor including reindeer herding, fur farming, **fishing**, and seal and whale hunting. The region's fragile ecosystem has been negatively impacted by industrial **pollution**, particularly from aluminum smelting. As part of the Arctic Ocean basin, the region has received renewed geopolitical interest in the past decade as **Vladimir Putin** has sought to strengthen Russia's position as an Arctic power. *See also* NORILSK NICKEL.

FATHERLAND—ALL RUSSIA (OVR). Political bloc. Known in Russian as *Otechestvo—Vsia Rossiia*, the OVR was a short-lived alliance of **Yevgeny Primakov**, **Yury Luzhkov**, and former **St. Petersburg** mayor Vladimir Yakovlelv in order to field a political bloc in the 1999 **State Duma** elections. Rather than representing a constituency, the bloc was based on the interests of its elites, who were generally nationalistic and opposed the policies of then-president **Boris Yeltsin**. Its primary competition came from **Unity**, with which it later merged, to form Russia's dominant political party, **United Russia**. The bloc enjoyed support from many regional governors, which attenuated provincial opposition to Moscow and the federal government. Despite this, the group placed a disappointing third in the poll, with 13.3 percent of the vote, placing it behind the **Communist Party of the Russian Federation** and Unity. *See also* POLITICAL PARTIES.

FEDERAL ASSEMBLY OF RUSSIA. Created by the 1993 **Constitution of the Russian Federation**, the Federal Assembly is the Russian Federation's bicameral legislative body and is divided between a lower house, the **State Duma**, and an upper house, the **Federation Council**. It was preceded by the Congress of People's Deputies of the Russian Federation. All bills must first be passed by the lower house, and then approved—without changes—by the upper house.

FEDERAL DISTRICTS. The Russian Federation consists of seven Federal Districts: Central, Southern, Northwestern, Far Eastern, Siberian, Urals, and Volga (each of which contains between 6 and 18 federal subjects). These coincide with the Interior Ministry's preexisting military regions. This system was created in 2000 by the newly elected president, **Vladimir Putin**, to provide greater oversight of the regions by the federal government and harmonize laws across the federation. Each has a plenipotentiary representative who reports to the president.

FEDERAL SUBJECTS. Russia is a federation that consists of 83 subjects, down from 89 subjects during the 1990s. These entities possess equal federal rights within the **Federation Council** (upper house of the Russian parliament), having two seats each. However, they differ in the degree of autonomy they command. The highest level of autonomy is possessed by the republics, followed by **autonomous okrugs**, which, while federal subjects in their own right, are at the same time considered to be administrative divisions of other federal subjects (excepting the **Chukotka Autonomous Okrug**). Each subject of the federation belongs to one of the following categories: **ethnic republic**, **oblast**, **krai**, autonomous oblast, autonomous okrug, or federal city. The convoluted system is both a legacy of the Soviet Union's nationalities policy, which stressed the maintenance of ethnic homelands for its various nationalities, as well as the weakness of the **Yeltsin** administration in dealing with challenges from the periphery.

Ethnic republics are nominally autonomous, with a constitution, president (or chairman), and parliament. While the federal government officially represents these states in international affairs, many conduct economic and commercial relations directly with foreign countries. The republics are, in most cases, eponymously named after their titular majority (or minority), for whom the republic exists as an ethnic homeland. The republics of the Russian Federation—listed in order of population from largest to smallest—are as follows: **Bashkortostan**; **Tatarstan**; **Dagestan**; **Udmurtiya**; **Chuvashiya**; **Chechnya**; **Komi**; **Buryatiya**; **Sakha** (Yakutiya); **Kabardino-Balkariya**; **Mordoviya**; **Mari El**; **Kareliya**; **North Ossetiya-Alaniya**; **Khakasiya**; **Ingushetiya**; **Adygeya**; **Karachay-Cherkessiya**; **Tuva** (Tyva); **Kalmykiya**; and **Altay** (Gorno-Altay).

Being the most common administrative category, there are 46 oblasts (regions), with federally appointed governors and locally elected legislatures; they do not possess a (non-Russian) titular majority. These take the name of the largest city in the oblast and its administrative center (with the exceptions of the Leningrad Oblast, which maintains the Soviet name for St. Petersburg, and Sverdlovsk, which has seen its capital's name revert to Yekaterinburg). The oblasts are: **Amur**; **Arkhangelsk**; **Astrakhan**; **Belgorod**; **Bryansk**; **Chelyabinsk**; **Irkutsk**; **Ivanovo**; **Kaliningrad**; **Kaluga**; **Kemerovo**; **Kirov**; **Kostroma**; **Kurgan**; **Kursk**; **Leningrad**; **Lipetsk**; **Magadan**; **Moscow**; **Murmansk**; **Nizhny Novgorod**; **Novgorod**; **Novosibirsk**; **Omsk**; **Orenburg**; **Oryol**; **Penza**; **Pskov**; **Rostov**; **Ryazan**; **Sakhalin**; **Samara**; **Saratov**; **Smolensk**; **Sverdlovsk**; **Tambov**; **Tomsk**; **Tula**; **Tver**; **Tyumen**; **Ulyanovsk**; **Vladimir**; **Volgograd**; **Vologda**; **Voronezh**; and **Yaroslavl**.

Russia has nine krais (provinces), differentiated from oblasts in that they were once considered frontier zones; they are as follows: **Altay**; **Kamchatka**; **Khabarovsk**; **Krasnodar**; **Krasnoyarsk**; **Perm**; **Primorsky**; **Stavropol**; and **Zabaykalsky** (formerly Chita Oblast). There is one autonomous oblast: the **Jewish Autonomous Oblast** (also known as Birobijan). There are four autonomous okrugs, each with a predominant **ethnic minority**. Autonomous okrugs possess more autonomy than oblasts but less than republics; they are: Chukotka; **Khantiya-Mansiya**; **Nenetsiya**; and **Yamaliya**. Last, there are two federal cities that function as separate regions: **Moscow** and **St. Petersburg**.

During the 1990s, Prime Minister **Yevgeny Primakov** publicly declared his desire to see the administrative structure of the Russian Federation simplified, with a decrease in the number (and autonomy) of its federal subjects. Due to the weakness of Boris Yeltsin during his second term, this did not come to pass. Upon entering office, **Vladimir Putin** made reform of the **asymmetrical federal** system a tenet of his presidency. In 2000, he instituted a system of "super-regions" consisting of seven **federal districts**. In each, Putin appointed a plenipotentiary representative to serve as an overseer of national security issues, as well as the economic, social, and political well-being of the constituent subject; the presidential envoys were also charged with ensuring that regional laws adhered to those of the federation, somewhat reducing the disparities in Russia's asymmetrical federal system.

However, it was not until after the **Beslan** attacks of 2004 that Putin enjoyed the popular support to institute wide-ranging changes in the federal system. In creating what has been termed a **vertical of power**, Putin pushed through referendums that have begun to reduce the number of subjects, while simultaneously allowing him (and his successors) to appoint regional governors. In 2005, the Perm Oblast and Komi-Permyak Autonomous Okrug were united to form the Perm Krai. In 2007, Krasnoyarsk Krai absorbed two autonomous oblasts, **Evenkiya** and **Taymyriya**; also that year, the Kamchatka Oblast and Koryak Autonomous Okrug (**Koryakiya**) were merged to form the Kamchatka Krai. In 2008, the Ust-Orda Buryat Autonomous Okrug became part of the Irkutsk Oblast, while the Chita Oblast and Agin-Buryat Autonomous Okrug were combined as the Zabaykalsky Krai. A number of other proposed mergers have been raised but have yet to be approved at the federal or local level. *See also* POLITICS.

FEDERATION COUNCIL. Established by the 1993 **Constitution of the Russian Federation**, the Federation Council is the upper house of the Russia's bicameral legislature, the **Federal Assembly**. The body's principal task is the passage of laws drafted by the lower house, the **State Duma**. If the Federal Assembly refuses to pass a law within 14 days, the lower and upper house may choose to develop a compromise bill satisfactory to both houses. In addition to the right to impeach the president, the body's other powers include approval of the following: use of the armed forces on foreign soil, border changes, imposition of martial law, states of emergency, and nominations of judges to the country's highest courts, as well as the attorney general. The current chair of the council is **Sergey Mironov**. Each of Russia's 83 **federal subjects** sends two representatives to the assembly; with the decrease in administrative divisions in Russia under **Vladimir Putin**, the total number of senators has decreased in recent years. During his first term, Putin eliminated the possibility of senators concurrently serving as regional governors, resulting in an influx of more pro-Kremlin legislators. Despite this, there are no formal political fractions with the house, unlike the Duma. Senators enjoy immunity from prosecution and must be resident in the district for a period of at least 10 years before serving. Unlike the Duma members, who are elected, Federation Council members are chosen

by regional governors and approved by local parliaments. *See also*
CONSTITUTIONAL CRISIS OF 1993; POLITICS.

FEDERATION TREATY OF 1992. On 31 March 1992, **Boris Yeltsin**
adopted a series of agreements collectively known as the Federation
Treaty to address the concerns of regional elites and the new country's **national minorities**. The new relations weakened the power of
the federal government, and provided significant economic, cultural,
and legislative autonomy to the "constituent units" of the Russian
Federation. Moscow retained control of currency, finance and **banking**, communications, justice, and **space** exploration, while sharing
responsibility for the **environment**, historic preservation, **education**,
and key areas of the national **economy**. The **ethnic republics**, in
particular, gained substantive control of their own affairs, while the
oblasts received less independence, thus creating a system of **asymmetrical federalism**. Despite such dramatic devolution of power to
the periphery, **Tatarstan** and the self-declared **Chechen Republic of
Ichkeriya** refused to sign the new agreement, precipitating friction
between Moscow and both regions; Tatarstan subsequently signed a
"treaty of equals" in 1994, and Yeltsin ordered troops into **Chechnya**
to "restore constitutional order." After the **constitutional crisis of
1993**, the constituent units were renamed **federal subjects**, to reflect
a more centralized form of federation.

FEMINISM. In its Western form, the ideology of feminism entered
the discursive space of the Soviet Union and the minds of its citizens
during **perestroika**. However, a terminological distinction was made
almost immediately with the "**women**'s movement," which had been
part of the Russian political environment for more than a century.
As a concept, "feminism" generally signifies militant, often foreign,
forms of female liberation. Under the Bolsheviks, several prominent
female thinkers and activists emerged, most notably Aleksandra Kollontai. However, **Joseph Stalin** attempted to subvert the movement
by constructing Soviet women as ideological subjects. In the late
Soviet Union and post-Soviet Russia, the resurgence of the women's
movement unfortunately coincided with the **demographic** crisis,
the demise of the Soviet political and economic system, a surge in
pornography, and a rise in prostitution. As the representation and

consumption of sex and **sexuality** suddenly became possible after the relaxation of censorship, the public gravitated toward commercialization of sex rather than engaging in debate about **gender** issues and the political, social, and cultural roles and rights of women.

Despite such challenges, the number of activist groups increased to over 300 by the mid-1990s; the movement was particularly active in Tver and Petrozavodsk. These groups normally addressed practical issues, including domestic violence and harassment at work. Some of these groups, for example, the Union of **Committees of Soldiers' Mothers of Russia**, became politically active and increasingly important socially. Feminist leaders, such as **Mariya Arbatova**, were normally drawn from the Soviet **intelligentsia**, which had always enjoyed a more balanced and more informed approach to gender identity and associated social and familial roles. The work of such groups and centers was often sponsored and facilitated by foreign institutions, for example, the **Soros** Foundation, and in addition to social activism, it incorporated educational and artistic practices. Some female authors became phenomenally successful, including Lyudmila Ulitskaya working in elitist genres, and Daria Dontsova and Aleksandra Marinina devoting themselves to the more popular—and traditionally masculine—genre of crime fiction.

FILM. In 2008, Russian cinema celebrated its centenary, and in recent years, the post-Soviet film industry has blossomed. In 2003, Andrey Zviagintsev's *The Return* won the Golden Lion at the Venice festival. Russian films have received extensive international distribution and press coverage, especially Timur Bekmambetov's *Night Watch* (2003) and its sequel *Day Watch* (2004). Russian directors have also been involved in international productions: Bekmambetov produced *Wanted* (2008) for Universal Pictures, a film nominated for two Academy Awards, as well as the computer-generated film *9* (2009). Russia also now hosts 28 international and nationwide film festivals. Today, there are 47 distribution companies in the country, and Russia-made films are now outselling Hollywood productions among Russian filmgoers.

The recent success, however, follows a near death of the film industry in the 1990s. During **perestroika**, domestic Soviet feature films accounted for about 70 percent of ticket sales in the country's

5,257 permanent cinemas. By 1994, the figure had dropped to less than 10 percent, with a 73 percent share held by American-made films. Such a dramatic oscillation is rooted in a number of factors. First of all, the end of censorship and greater openness of Russian society induced a greater interest in foreign films—as well as in other art forms, including **literature** and **television**—that had been unavailable to the average Soviet citizen. On the other hand, because Soviet filmmakers had previously worked in conditions of central regulation and distribution, they were unprepared for the challenges of working under market conditions and often failed to understand domestic needs.

The processes of deregulation and decentralization resulted in the slowdown of the film industry, and the situation was exacerbated by the 1988 financial crisis and the diminishing role of the state as the provider of funds for the ailing film industry (in the 1990s on average only 6 percent of films received state subsidies). Furthermore, the deregulation of the market and fluctuating currency exchange rates, as well as decreasing supervision of production projects, created an ideal environment for currency speculation by some filmmakers and also for criminal activity by groups having nothing to do with the film industry. In 1990, per capita attendance was eight visits per year, a result of diminishing purchasing power of Soviet citizens and their interest in other activities such as the newly opened casinos and sex shops. The decrease in cinema attendance also reflected the growing video piracy market.

Video piracy had already been established as the dominant form of spectatorship in the early 1980s in the Union of Soviet Socialist Republics (USSR); it continued to dominate the post-Soviet distribution market until 2005, when the state launched a series of special measures fighting illegal video and DVD production. (It appears that while the state has managed to crack down on the sale of pirated DVDs on Russia's streets, illegal downloading of video materials from the **Internet** is thriving.) At the outset, numerous video salons appeared in Russia's largest cities, as well in the country's lesser-populated regions, showing the latest international productions as well as film classics. These video salons—often quite small and tastefully decorated—became a serious competitor to Soviet cinemas that in most cases had a capacity to sit over 500 people in cold, shabby auditoriums. As opposed to Soviet cinemas, video salons were managed by independent entrepreneurs, and to the Soviet mind they symbolized a new private, capitalist entertainment industry.

When video recorders became an affordable commodity (the USSR began producing its own video players in 1984), Soviet citizens began to enjoy their favorite films in the comfort of their homes, acquiring new releases and exchanging copies at specialized high street outlets. This process signaled a further **privatization** of the public sphere in the Russian Federation; it also induced an understanding of a film—or any other form of cultural activity—as a commodity that had its own value, something that had never occurred to Soviet citizens, who were raised in an atmosphere that art had no commercial value and belonged to everyone (the famous Stalinist slogan proclaimed that "art belongs to the people"). Despite its paradoxical emancipating value, video piracy drained the film industry from much-needed cash. In addition, government production subsidies decreased disproportionately, and the money that was available would be squandered by **corrupt** administrators. As a result, in 1996, only 34 films reached completion, compared with an average annual output of 150 films in the 1970s and early 1980s. In the early 1990s, even the most successful film barely drew 300,000 viewers.

The government intervened in 1996 when the Law on Cinema, initiated back in 1992, was finally signed by then-President **Boris Yeltsin**. The law addressed tax incentives and defined the responsibilities of Goskino, the state body regulating film production in the Russian Federation. The optimism of filmmakers and the industry in general soon evaporated with the 1998 **ruble crisis**. Most film projects under production were put on hold and major cinema construction projects came to a halt as state support plummeted to a meager 30 million rubles, which would be the budget of an average Hollywood production. Major film production companies were forced into subletting their property to create revenue to pay their bills. In order to save on costs, cinemas reduced their distribution capacity and used their premises as exhibition halls, casinos, and office space; many cinemas specializing in arthouse film or showing film retrospectives had to change their distribution policies to include at times Western semi-pornographic productions to fill the house with crowds.

These financial, legal, production, and distribution crises masked an artistic crisis. The artistic quality of screenplays in the 1990s was questionable. The scripts failed to engage with Russian contemporary society and constantly recycled plots and tropes borrowed from Hollywood. The production crisis also sparked a creative crisis as specialists—camera men, costume designers, makeup artists, and others—who had worked in the industry began to leave for better jobs in other sectors of the **economy**. The tradition of Russian-Soviet filmmaking began to deteriorate as film **educational** institutes found themselves in trouble as well. Finally, filmmakers struggled to come up with a new visual language that would represent a new Russia, which now seems to be an understandable difficulty since Russia itself was in transition, with its **national identity** trapped in a gestation period.

The cultural shift occurred around the start of the new millennium. Russia found itself awash with **oil** money; it was also a country with a better developed financial structure, an economy with a growing technological and cultural sector, and a population that was tired of perpetual changes and in need of a stable regime and a diverse leisure industry. As a result, Russians discovered the pleasures of consumerism. By 2000, urbanites had exhausted their interest in new home appliances, cars, and clothes, and turned their eye to more conspicuous consumption that would occur in public spaces. By this time, the first Russian multiplexes had been constructed, and over the next five years a number of new cinemas, furnished to the highest world standards and equipped with the latest visual and sound technology, opened in cities all over the country. These new cinemas, also known as leisure complexes, included shopping areas, restaurants, casinos, nightclubs, bowling alleys, and other forms of entertainment. Indeed, they projected the irresistible lure of an expensive and stylish night out, primarily targeting the new post-Soviet generation of Russian citizens who were quite keen to spend their rubles.

Efficient management of cinemas led to a diversification of prices that now vary from about a dollar to 10 dollars for the same film depending on the time of the show. This means that a cinema experience is now affordable not only to Moscow's successful executives, but also to poorly paid teachers and other public sector workers. As different crowds were drawn to cinemas in the late 2000s, the programming changed with more emphasis on family recreation, genre screenings, and domestic productions.

In 2002, Russian films sold more tickets than their American-made competition, and this trend has continued ever since. Another indicator that the crisis in the film industry was over was the fact that Sony Pictures and Disney productions began building film factories outside **Moscow** and **St. Petersburg** with the specific purpose of making films for the Russian market. Finally, a new cohort of film directors and film stars emerged, and filmmakers were able to create a set of new national narratives that have been well received by various sectors of the Russian viewing audience.

The main cinematic style of perestroika and the early 1990s is known as *chernukha*, translated as "black wave" or "black cinema." As a form of de-Sovietization, chernukha presented marginalized characters in disturbing settings, including filthy, overcrowded apartments, dirty streets populated by feral dogs, police stations and prisons, and hospitals. Dark imagery was meant to reveal the atmosphere of cruelty, violence, rape, **alcoholism**, and **drug use** that pervaded Soviet society at the time of its political demise. Film examples of chernukha include Vasily Pichul's *Little Vera* (1988), Yury Kara's *Kings of Crime* (1988), and Kira Muratova's *The Aesthenic Syndrome* (1990). These films display a few common features, including their focus on physicality and moral degradation; questioning the foundations of human existence; undermining the myths of the Soviet Union; and naturalism, decay, and fatalism.

In the 1990s, Russian cinema found itself at the crossroads of film genres. This was not only the effect of the postmodernist disavowal of the distinction between high and low culture—also noticeable in Russian literature and theater of the time—but also as a result of experimentation with genres that had not been allowed or often practiced in the Soviet Union, such as the thriller. Aleskey Balabanov created a synthesis of the intellectual genre with that of the thriller in his *Happy Days* (1991) and *The Castle* (1994). He also developed a new genre of *kriminal' nyi boevik* (crime action), including his internationally renowned films *Brother* (1997), *Brother 2* (2000), and *War* (2002), which tackled contemporary issues and expressed the social and psychological anxieties of the period. His films also presented a new type of national hero, a character, Danila, who—as the rest of Russia—was caught between the underworld of **crime** and the world of normalcy. Balabanov's films—like many other films of the period—represented the collapse of the socialist moral system in the new capitalist society, with an emphasis on the existential and philosophical foundations of the contemporary Russian society.

A number of films during this period also addressed the issue of national identity, imperial legacy, and Russia's relationship with the **near abroad**, including *The Muslim* (1995), *Peculiarities of the National Hunt* (1995), *The Prisoner of the Caucasus* (1996), and *The Barber of Siberia* (1998). These works explored the foundations of Russian culture in relation to its occidental and oriental, as well as internal other, in either a contemporary or a historical setting, by creating a new narrative, or producing a film adaptation of Russian classical works of literature.

Whereas the films produced in the 1990s presented a search for national identity from the perspective—or with constant awareness—of the Russian capital, many films made in the new millennium eschew Moscow to explore Russian life outside the core. This is, in fact, simultaneously a return to Russia's cultural roots, as well as an exploration of a cultural space that had remained largely unrecognized and unmapped throughout perestroika and the 1990s. This cinematic voyage is performed both by Russia's established directors as well as the new wave of film artists, namely, Andrey Zviagintsev's *The Return* (2003), Pyotr Buslov's *Bummer* (2003), Marina Razbezhkina's *Harvest Time* (2004), and Katya Shagalova's *Once Upon a Time in the Provinces* (2008). This cohort of new filmmakers enriches Russian cinema with new themes and conflicts and, most important, with an innovative cinematic language that on the one hand continues the Russian-Soviet tradition of filmmaking and, on the other, speaks to the cinematic experience of the whole world.

Since independence, many Russian films have focused on the figure of the absent father, whose disappearance signified the fact that the state had abandoned the Russian people in times of crisis. Abandoned and in despair, the characters either engaged in marginal or criminal activities, or sought a strong maternal figure, the recurrent symbol of the nation. The absent father, personified through the figure of a morally or physically impaired man, was a symbol of the national crisis, as well as the crisis of masculinity, which manifested itself in high mortality rates, alcoholism, and depression. In the new millennium, the father returns and attempts to reestablish relationships with his abandoned child, typically a son. Presented in a realistic, mythological, fantastic, or symbolic manner, this filial conflict may be resolved through the father's anguish and repentance. This motif of troubled father-son relationships demonstrates Russia's ongoing struggle to reconcile its own troubled past.

FINANCIAL CRISIS OF 1998. *See* RUBLE CRISIS.

FINANCIAL INDUSTRY. *See* BANKING.

FINLAND (RELATIONS WITH). Finland was incorporated into the **Romanov** Empire during the early 19th century. Formerly subjugated to Sweden, the region enjoyed substantial autonomy under tsarist rule and witnessed a national awakening in the 19th century. Benefiting from the chaos of the **Bolshevik Revolution**, Finland seceded in late 1917 and established a presidential republic two years later.

The nation fought two wars with the Union of Soviet Socialist Republics (USSR) during the 1940s, resulting in the loss of 10 percent of its territory and its access to the **Arctic Ocean**. After World War II, Finland adopted a liberal democratic political system, but coordinated its foreign policy with the Soviet Union, resulting in a form of political hegemony akin to the United States' relationship with its Western European allies. Officially on neutral terms, Helsinki and Moscow signed the Agreement of Friendship, Cooperation, and Mutual Assistance (also known as the YYA Treaty) in 1948. This new relationship gave birth to the concept of "Finlandization," whereby Moscow gained an ally against the Anglo-American alliance but generally refrained from meddling in the country's **foreign relations**. The resulting arrangement resulted in Helsinki's refusal of aid from the American-backed Marshall Plan.

During the **Cold War**, Helsinki carefully avoided public criticism of the Soviet Union, even during its widely condemned interventions in East Germany, Hungary, and Czechoslovakia. Despite political deference to Moscow, Finland adopted a free-market system and developed strong economic relations with the members of the

North Atlantic Treaty Organization (NATO), as well as **Warsaw Pact** countries. While eschewing full membership in the European Economic Community, the precursor to the **European Union** (EU), Finland did harmonize its economic system with European standards. This decision allowed the country to accede to the union in 1995, shortly after the **dissolution of the Soviet Union** removed concerns that EU membership would be a violation of neutrality.

In 1992, Finland and Russia signed a new friendship treaty that overhauled the hegemonic relationship in place since 1948, effectively eliminating an oversight of Moscow on Finnish foreign policy. Overreliance on markets in the **Eastern Bloc** (particularly Russia) resulted in an economic shock to the country's financial health in the early 1990s; however, Finland quickly rebounded and reassumed its role as an economic bridge linking Western and Eastern Europe. Under the overlapping presidencies of Tarja Halonen (2000–present) and **Vladimir Putin** (2000–2008), Helsinki has been particularly active in promoting economic integration between the Russian Federation and the European Union, including developing an improved customs infrastructure along the two countries' common border.

In 2006, Russia resumed its historic role as Finland's leading trading partner (Finland ranks eighth among Russia's partners). Joint projects in the Gulf of Finland and improved **transportation** infrastructure between Helsinki and St. Petersburg have been key areas of cooperation since the mid-1990s. **Tourism** is particularly important; nearly 1.5 million Russians visit Finland annually. Finland has invested extensive capital and resources in the Russian region of **Kareliya**, with which it has historic and ethnic ties. In 2004, Finland was joined by the **Baltic States** in sharing EU territorial borders with Russia, a development that somewhat lessened the diplomatic pressure Helsinki shouldered within the EU (especially in light of Finland's steadfast refusal to join NATO).

Areas of friction between the two countries include Finnish reticence over proposals for visa-free travel for Russians to the EU, a spy case in 1998 related to sensitive EU documents, and **environmental** concerns about Russia's expansion of its **oil** exports via the Gulf of Finland. In 2007, Finland scrambled its fighter jets after Russian violations of its airspace. However, the imbroglio was seen as symptomatic of Russia's more aggressive **military** posture around the globe, and not directed at Helsinki in particular.

FISHING INDUSTRY. With the world's fourth-longest coastline, access to the landlocked **Caspian Sea**, and more than 2 million rivers, Russia's fishing industry is one of the most important worldwide. Annually, Russia harvests more than 3 million tons of fish, with the salmon, cod, char, whitefish, pollock, halibut, and flounder hauls being the largest. The Russian fishing fleet is currently estimated at 2,500 vessels, including nearly 50 factory ships. The majority of the catch is exported to East Asian markets. Caviar, collected from Caspian and other sturgeons, is a historically important cash crop; however, the stocks are severely depleted. Poaching has emerged as a major problem; illegal sales of caviar are estimated at $40 million per year. In 2005, the federal government passed the law "On Fisheries and Protection of Aquatic Biological Resources" to regulate commercial, recreational, and indigenous fishing practices. Overfishing, marine **pollution**, and warming temperatures in the **Arctic Ocean** bode poorly for the future of the industry.

FLAG. The current state flag of the Russian Federation is known as the *Trikolor* (Tricolor), and consists of three equal-sized horizontal bands: white, blue, and red (from top to bottom). This new banner replaced the Soviet flag for the **Russian Soviet Federative Socialist Republic** (RSFSR), which consisted of a red background emblazoned with a vertical blue stripe on its left side, and a gold hammer, sickle, and star representing the Soviet Union. Prior to 1954, the Russian flag was a simple red background with the Cyrillic acronym for the RSFSR imprinted in the upper left-hand corner.

Traditionally, the color choice represents the coat of arms of the Grand Duchy of Moscow, which depicted a blue-clad St. George on a white horse against a red background; the colors are sometimes interpreted as symbols of **pan-Slavic** unity, representing the Belarusians (white), **Ukrainians** (blue), and **ethnic Russians** (red).

The flag of the Russian Federation was adopted on 22 August 1991, which is now celebrated as a national **holiday**; the flag had previously proved popular among anti-Soviet activists during the 1991 **August Coup**.

The current white-red-blue flag was adopted in lieu of the short-lived "coat of arms" flag (1858–1883) of the Russian Empire, which consisted of three horizontal stripes, black on top, yellow-orange in the middle, and white on the bottom; however, the imperial flag—sometimes embellished with the two-headed eagle of the **Romanov** dynasty—is often seen at demonstrations by ultranationalists and monarchists in contemporary Russia. The Soviet flag—with its bold red background and gold hammer, sickle, and star in the upper canton (the hammer represented industrial workers, the sickle stood for the peasants, and the star symbolized the **Communist Party of the Soviet Union**)—is also used as a political statement, particularly by members of the **Communist Party of the Russian Federation** and other left-wing groups. A version of the Soviet flag known as *Znamia pobedy* (banner of victory) was established in 2007 as the official representation of the victory in the Great Patriotic War, and is used during Victory Day celebrations on the 9th of May.

In addition to the national flag, each **federal subject** of the Russian Federation has its own standard that often evokes unique geographic, historical, or ethnic characteristics of the region in question. In the case of **Tatarstan** and some other **ethnic republics**, local governments often treat their own flag as superior to that of the federal flag, often to the dismay of the Kremlin. In August 2007, a Russian submarine team planted a titanium flag on the seabed near the North Pole, sparking fears of a land grab in the **Arctic Ocean** basin.

FOOD. The situation with food, restaurants, and diet changed from extreme scarcity in the late Soviet period to extraordinary abundance after 2000. Simultaneously, the food on offer transitioned from the stereotypically bland menus and inefficient Soviet service to the post-Soviet celebration of ethnic cuisines and acquisitions from international food purveyors, with **Moscow** becoming recognized as the European culinary capital of innovation in 2004.

As with other imperial states, Russian cuisine is a combination of foods and eating practices borrowed from Russia's former colonies: *borscht* (cabbage soup) and *golubtsy* (cabbage rolls) from **Ukraine**, wine from **Georgia**, pilaf and fermented dairy products from the **Tatars**, *chebureki* (filled deep-fried potato pockets) from the **Crimean** Tatars, herring and rye bread from the **Baltic Sea** region, ferns and pine nuts from **Siberia**, *shashlik* (shish kebob) and *plov* from **Central Asia**, salmon from the Pacific Rim, and so forth. It is this phenomenal ability to adopt and assimilate products coming from other cultures that characterizes Russian cuisine. However, the historical tradition makes some elusive categorizations possible. For Russians, grains (barley, buckwheat, rye, oats, and wheat) and cereals are of central importance. They form the basis of breads, savory pies, cakes, *bliny* (pancakes), dumplings, and fermented beverages such as *kvas*. Rice is a relatively recent introduction, a result of Russia's encounter with Central Asia in the 19th century; however, nowadays it is one of the staples of Russian cuisine, with rice porridge, *plov*, and all kinds of rice rolls being the most popular rice dishes.

Bread (*khleb*) forms the basis of the Russian diet; it is typically served with every meal and is consumed as an accompaniment to virtually every dish. Traditionally, bread symbolizes sustenance and hospitality; therefore, the Russian folk ritual of welcoming important guests involves bread and salt (one of the Russian words denoting hospitality—*khlebosol' stvo*—derives from the name of this practice). In Russian, there are numerous proverbs that emphasize the importance of bread in the culture, including "*khleb vsemu golova*," meaning "bread is the master of everything." It is not surprising that there are infinite variations of breads and similar baked goods, and the stereotypical division into black (*chornyi*) and white (*belyi*) breads is a gross simplification. In a similar fashion, *kasha* (porridge) comes in an immense variety: it may be produced from a number of grouts; it can be sweet or savory; it can be served for breakfast or as a side dish; it may be served with *smetana* (sour cream), eggs, mushrooms, sausage, fruits, cottage cheese, and so forth.

All vegetables, with the exception of cucumbers and tomatoes, are normally eaten cooked and served as a side dish, in soups, as a pickled dish (*solianka*), or as a main component of a salad. The salad that incorporates almost all customary vegetables and symbolizes Russian cooking par excellence is called *vinegret*. The name derives from the French word "vinaigrette," a seasoned oil-and-vinegar emulsion. The Russian variant contains potatoes, pickled cabbage or cucumbers, beetroot, carrots, and onions or spring onions, all finely sliced and dressed with oil and vinegar. This dish has secured a permanent place at the table both as an everyday dish as well as a dish for special occasions. On **holidays**, Russian women prepare vast amounts of *vinegret* and other salads and serve them in large bowls, not so much as a starter but rather as a form of main course. Leafy salads are gaining more popularity, and yet the term "salad" normally denotes a mixture of finely sliced cooked vegetables, meats and sausages, and a variety of other ingredients lubricated generously with *smetana*, or its spicier—and cheaper—alternative, mayonnaise.

Caviar is also a Russian culinary obsession. A great variety of **fish** roe is used—beluga black caviar, grey sevruga eggs, salmon roe, and so forth. Various types of caviar are served with bread and butter, on eggs, wrapped in *bliny*, or incorporated into a sauce. Purists prefer the finest caviar served chilled on very thin slices of white bread, garnished with some fine butter to achieve a smoother flavor of caviar. Due to poaching and caviar smuggling through the former Soviet republics, **Caspian Sea** sturgeon has now become an endangered species. Despite the government's attempts to control the population of fish in the sea, the future of the species is quite uncertain. Nonetheless, fish is still popular in Russia—salted Baltic herring is found in many cold salads, a mixture of cold smoked fish is served as an appetizer, and salmon is used to make fish soup (*ukha*) and can also be served grilled or baked. However, due to the rising prices of fish, meat and poultry are emerging as staples of the Russian diet.

Russia is one of the world's largest importers of meat: beef, pork, poultry, and mutton—listed in the order of preference and consumption—constitute the main source of protein in the Russian ethnic diet. Russians may use any meat to make *shashlik*, and the consumption of this food is associated with the start of spring when Russians move to their **dachas** to enjoy their meals in the open air. Another cultural import that has become a national staple is *kolbasa* (sausage). Varying in type, quality, and price, *kolbasa* prevails over Russian everyday consumption as a source of proteins and fats as well as a common form of fast food.

Russian food can be quite greasy; however, fats are important in a severe **climate** as they are an essential source of energy. Meat or *kolbasa* is consumed at least once a day and provides the necessary amount of fats; other substitutes, for example, *salo* (pig lard), are popular with Christian Russians and Ukrainians. Other common fats in the Russian diet are butter and sunflower oil (Russians use the same word for oil and butter—*maslo*). Russians make butter from the milk solids in cream and sour cream; butter produced in the north of the country is especially valued. Butter is one of numerous dairy products consumed in Russia, including *smetana*, yogurt, *slivki* (cream), *prostokvasha* (buttermilk), *kefir* and *riazhenka* (yogurt-type drinks), *tvorog* (cottage cheese), *syrki* (processed cottage cheese), and so forth. Cheeses were a rarity in the Soviet Union with just a handful of processed or semisoft cheeses available to average citizens, including such brands as *Rossiiskii* and *Gollandskii*. Cheeses exploded on the market after 1991, with many imported and locally produced cheeses becoming increasingly popular.

As for alcoholic beverages, recent trends indicate that beer is now more popular than vodka. Beer experienced a renaissance in the post-Soviet period, with the popular brand Baltika leading the market. Russians rarely drink cocktails, and consuming alcoholic beverages without food is believed to be unhealthy. Typically, an appetizer (*zakuska*)—a pickled cucumber, caviar on bread, a slice of herring, or a spoonful of salad—precedes and immediately follows each drink.

While statistically speaking, Russians consume large quantities of alcohol per capita, approaching the European average, their national drink is not vodka, as the stereotype suggests, but rather tea. *Chai* (tea) is consumed many times a day; it is served either black, or with a dash of milk, lemon and sugar, or honey and jam (*varen' e*). Russian tea is always served piping hot in mugs; however, the tradition indicates that it should be consumed out of porcelain cups with saucers and in some occasions—for example on board a train—in glasses with metal holders. Virtually everyone drinks tea; tea drinking involves a serving of chocolate, biscuits, cake, sweets, caramelized nuts, jam, or honey. Black tea—exported from India or the **Caucasus**, though some sorts are available from **Krasnodar Krai**—is the predominant style of tea; however, green tea is gaining more popularity, especially with younger Russian. Herbal teas—mint, linden flower, and so forth—are also extremely popular; in fact, many Russian families grow herbs on their dachas or pick them in woods and fields. However, this pastime, as well as using the samovar to make tea, is becoming a rarity. Instant coffee took off in the Union of Soviet Socialist Republics (USSR) in the 1970s and is a common alternative to tea. Nowadays filtered coffee is very popular with young people in urban centers, where such chains of coffeehouses as Coffee House, Shokoladnitsa, and others opened in the past decade.

The start of the new millennium also marked Russia's growing interest in eating out. The appearance of Russian cities has changed enormously with numerous cafes appearing in city centers, and on the outskirts restaurants are a compulsory element of shopping centers. While some traditional restaurants remain, the majority of food outlets are new cafes, either specializing in ethnic cuisine (particularly Georgian, Chinese, and Italian), or serving Russian versions of many popular international dishes. There has emerged what can be called "universal Russian food," or "Russian global food," which contains cliché dishes, as well as assorted ethnic foods. This type of food is ubiquitously served in cafes all across the country, on board airplanes, and so forth.

Though cafes and restaurants are very popular, Russians still prefer to eat at home, with cooking being the most consuming household chore, typically done by **women**. In multigenerational households, the *babushka* (grandmother) assumes the bulk of the cooking duties, while the wife and children help in preparation. Men rarely concern themselves with daily meals, as cooking is not viewed as a masculine pastime. Nor do men typically help their wives with shopping or cleaning up. However, the tendency seems to have changed in recent years, with more men cooking for their families. Families tend to cook soup and a main course that lasts for a few days; however, many Russian families are obsessed with fresh food, and so daily visits to markets and shops are quite normal. Unlike in other countries, both men and women work in the Russian commercial food sector, working as cooks and professional chefs. In the 1990s, Russians upgraded their kitchens so that now virtually every urban household boasts a wide range of electric appliances (though the dishwasher is still a rarity). More processed and semiprepared dishes are used in everyday life, raising health concerns. However, the situation in the Russian countryside has not changed as much, with many families living in villages with no running water or gas, making the process of food preparation even more arduous.

Many Russians, especially in **rural** areas, believe that Western-style fast food instead of the soup-centered meal causes health problems. However, a traditional Russian lunch consisting of cooked vegetables, meat broth, processed meat, full-fat dairy products, bread, and dessert cannot be called a healthy option either. Increasingly, people in Russia are concerned with their weight, though largely in regard to their appearance rather than associated health risks. This does not, however, prevent Russians from consuming fast food. The first McDonald's restaurant opened in **Moscow** in 1990 just a few hundred meters away from the Kremlin, thus symbolizing Russia's move toward Western market economies. There are now more than 250 McDonald's outlets operating in Russia.

There are a few types of restaurants in Russia: exclusive *haute cuisine* restaurants and private clubs (the majority of them are located in Moscow), international cuisine, fast-food chains (both international and Russian), independent middle-range restaurants, coffee shops and cafes, or cafeterias, and beer houses. Middle-range restaurants cater for the ever-expanding middle class, while fast-food outlets offer more dishes in response to increasing market demand. In 2005, there were 4,000 restaurants in Moscow (with a population of 11 million people), compared with 14,000 restaurants in Paris (2.3 million people). Paradoxically, about a third of the Russian population cannot afford basic food items, while another third visit expensive restaurants on a regular basis.

Food and food products have recently become cultural denominators: **Orthodox** Christians adhere to the rituals of fasting, while supermarkets now sell kosher and halal foods for the country's **Jews** and **Muslims**. Recently, food has also played an important role in Russian **foreign relations** with a partial ban on meat from **Ukraine** and discontinuation of wine and mineral-water imports from **Georgia** following these countries' respective **color revolutions**.

FOREIGN INVESTMENT. Under **perestroika**, the Kremlin sought to attract foreign investment into the Soviet **economy** for the first time since the 1920s. Under **Mikhail Gorbachev**'s premiership, the Law on Joint Ventures with Firms from Capitalist Countries, allowing up to 49 percent foreign ownership, opened the door to foreign investors. While modest in scope, the new laws allowed the Union of Soviet Socialist Republics (USSR) to acquire high technology and begin to modernize its manufacturing system. Under **Boris Yeltsin**, the new Foreign Investment Law of 1991 further opened the country to foreign capital, including natural resources, government-owned enterprises, and property. **Oil** and **natural gas** proved most attractive to foreign investors, and in 1995 a new law was passed giving greater protection to multinational corporations involved in Russia's hydrocarbon industries. Under **Vladimir Putin**, foreign investment increased dramatically, reaching an all-time high of $100 billion in 2007. Investors from **Great Britain**, the **United States**, **Germany**, Switzerland, the Netherlands, and Cyprus lead the pack, though much of the influx from the latter country is thought to be Russian investment returning after the "capital flight" of the 1990s. **China** is also an increasingly important player in foreign direct investment.

FOREIGN RELATIONS. Russia's foreign relations with its neighbors and even distant countries such as **Great Britain** and the **United States** are complex, often characterized by suspicion and rivalry. This is in part due to the country's historically fluid borders and projection of its power in all directions of the compass.

As the **Romanov** Empire, Russian territory steadily grew until it covered one-sixth of the earth's surface, a fact that did not sit well in foreign capitals. Under the new Bolshevik regime, Soviet Russia funded and directed the Comintern, an international organization dedicated to foment Communist revolution in Europe, Asia, and other parts of the world; as a result, the country became an international pariah during the 1920s. **Joseph Stalin**'s decision to build socialism in one country, rather than actively support world revolution, allowed for a normalization of relations with many countries by the mid-1930s, but most of the Soviet Union's neighbors remained hostile. During World War II, the Nazi invasion triggered a short-term alliance with the British and Americans; however, postwar differences regarding **Germany** soon precipitated the **Cold War** between the U.S. and its European allies and the Soviet Union and the **Eastern Bloc**. In 1955, the Soviets established the **Warsaw Pact** to provide collective security to its satellite states, which stretched from the **Baltic Sea** to the **Black Sea**.

The **Khrushchev** administration actively courted relationships with Third World countries, particularly in the **Middle East**, resulting in extremely poor relations with **Israel** and certain conservative regimes such as **Iran**, Saudi Arabia, and Pakistan. The Soviet military and economic support for left-wing regimes in Indochina, Latin America (especially **Cuba**), and sub-Saharan Africa created even more problems between Moscow and Washington. During this period, the fraternal relationship between the Union of Soviet Socialist Republics (USSR) and **China** disintegrated, resulting in a new global competition for the leadership of the Communist world. In the last years of **Brezhnev**'s regime, the Soviets invaded **Afghanistan** to prop up a friendly government against **Islamists**. The resulting bloodshed triggered worldwide condemnation, seriously harming the country's international standing.

Beginning in the mid-1980s, the new premier, **Mikhail Gorbachev**, initiated the so-called policy of "New Thinking" in international relations. His initial reforms aimed to limit the arms deployed in Europe, particularly **nuclear weapons**. Over the years, he developed cordial relations with U.S. President **Ronald Reagan**, British Prime Minister Margaret Thatcher, and German Chancellor Helmut Kohl. By the end of the decade, Gorbachev ordered Soviet troops out of Afghanistan and signaled to the Communist leaders of Eastern Europe that the Soviet Union would not repeat the military intervention of Hungary (1956) and Czechoslovakia (1968) if any of the members of the bloc moved to abandon socialism. Domestic problems forced Moscow to abandon its far-flung alliance system, resulting in the downgrading of its relations with **North Korea**, Cuba, **Mongolia**, Vietnam, and certain Arab states.

The **dissolution of the Soviet Union** resulted in massive changes in foreign policy. First, the Russian Federation was forced to develop peer relationships with the 14 newly independent states of the **near abroad**, that is, the other former Soviet republics. Second, **Boris Yeltsin** attempted to turn Russia into a "normal country" in terms of its foreign policy. This translated into an **Atlanticist** orientation under **Andrey Kozyrev**, whereby Russia sought to emulate the international behavior of North American and European nations. It quickly became apparent that the first and second directives were not wholly compatible, given Russia's historical relationships with

Ukraine, **Central Asia**, and other former republics. Russian **military** intervention in conflicts in the **Caucasus**, **Moldova**, and **Tajikistan** were defended under the so-called **Monroeski Doctrine**, while the presence of large numbers of **ethnic Russians** in **Estonia**, **Latvia**, and elsewhere provided Moscow with a lever of control over these states.

Hoping to maintain its influence as a regional power, Russia created a number of intergovernmental organizations like the **Commonwealth of Independent States**, **Collective Security Treaty Organization**, and **Eurasian Economic Community**, all of which it dominated. Russian troops were deployed across the former Soviet Union, including in **Armenia** and **Transnistria**, either as peacekeepers, border guards, or in **narcotics** interdiction. While Russia enjoyed improved ties to a number of states during the 1990s, particularly South Korea, Taiwan, and **Turkey**, lingering territorial issues dogged relations with **Japan**.

In the 1990s, several distinct schools of foreign policy developed in the Russian Federation that competed with Kozyrev's liberal, Westernizing orientation. The first school is the **Eurasianist** or **Slavophile** orientation, which was embraced by ultranationalists like **Vladimir Zhirinovsky** and certain conservative intellectuals. Eurasian foreign policy supports reintegration of the Russophone world (i.e., the former Soviet Union), and an alliance with other Asiatic powers to balance against the West, which is seen as hostile to Russia and its values. This approach shares some qualities with the National Communist or neo-Soviet school of foreign policy advocated by **Gennady Zyuganov** and other members of the **Communist Party of the Russian Federation** and the extreme left. This school is virulently anti-American in its posture, advocates imperialism, and supports a return to the ideological conflict between the socialist and capital worlds and a rejection of Western norms. The last school of thought can be described as statist or "great power" foreign policy, and is most closely associated with **Yevgeny Primakov**.

During the second Yeltsin administration, Primakov attempted to return Russia to great power (*derzhava*) status and sought to counterbalance American hegemony by strengthening ties to Iran, China, and **India**. Such moves found support among many Russian political elites, including the *siloviki*. During this period, Russia also took a strong stand against the **North Atlantic Treaty Organization**'s (NATO) actions in **Serbia** and against the military alliance's planned expansion into the Baltic region. Certain aspects of the **Primakov Doctrine** were expanded under **Vladimir Putin**, particularly the notion that Russia should not reject its unique geopolitical identity and civilizational messianism. However, the new president drew closer to the U.S. in the wake of the **September 11 attacks**, hoping to gain support for his actions in **Chechnya** and against Islamist **terrorists** on Russian soil. **George W. Bush**'s decision to invade Iraq precipitated a new axis of interest connecting Moscow-Berlin-Paris and a cooling relationship with the United States.

By 2005, Putin had rallied the **Shanghai Cooperation Organization** to force the Americans to begin the process of abandoning their bases in Central Asia, despite Putin's earlier acquiescence to the U.S. military presence in **Uzbekistan** and **Kyrgyzstan**. While Russia maintained excellent relations with **Kazakhstan** throughout the postindependence period, this event marked the return of Russian influence across the whole region. Under Putin, Russia assumed an increasingly aggressive posture in its economic and diplomatic relations with the former Soviet republics, including the suspension of **natural gas** shipments to Ukraine, threats directed at the **Baltic States**, and a partial embargo on goods from **Georgia**. While the rise of the *siloviki* certainly shaped this new posture, the increasing corporatization of the elite also played a role as **Gazprom**, **Transneft**, and other industrial giants gained a voice in foreign affairs. Buoyed by high **oil** and natural gas prices, Putin presided over a "proud" Russia, with representation in the **Group of Eight** (G8), a constituent part of the **BRIC** (Brazil, Russia, India, and China) grouping and a major player in the Asia-Pacific Economic Cooperation forum.

Fearful of the Western-backed **color revolutions**, the Kremlin began to develop its relationships with elites across post-Soviet space. This involved actively countering what it viewed as anti-Russian actions at home and abroad, backing its own form of "managed **democracy**" as a valid option for the larger region; this included an aggressive defense of **Belarus**'s authoritarian system. During this period, relations with Great Britain soured rapidly, particularly over **espionage** allegations and the **Litvinenko** case. Putin also began to engage in nationalist populism directed at the U.S., a country that he implied continues to seek the disintegration of Russia; his foreign minister **Sergey Lavrov** took an especially hard line against the proposed antimissile shield to be deployed in **Poland** and the Czech Republic.

Shortly after the ascent of **Dmitry Medvyedev**, Russia took its most dramatic military action since 1991, invading Georgia to secure its interests and citizens in the breakaway republics of **Abkhazia** and **South Ossetia** in 2008. Moscow's actions were condemned by the **European Union** and the U.S., though much of the developing world saw Russia's response as appropriate under the circumstances. In recent years, Russia has also sought to expand its claims to the **Arctic Ocean**, placing the country at odds with **Canada** and **Norway**. *See also* AZERBAIJAN; FINLAND; FOREIGN INVESTMENT; FOREIGN TRADE; FRANCE; IVANOV, IGOR; KOSOVO; LITHUANIA; POLITICS; SINATRA DOCTRINE, TURKMENISTAN; UNITED NATIONS; VENEZUELA.

FOREIGN TRADE. During most of the Soviet period, most of Russia's foreign trade was with its allies in the **Eastern Bloc** and friendly regimes in the Third World. However, the inefficiencies of the Council for Mutual Economic Assistance (COMECON), which functioned as a rudimentary common market for the socialist economies, became increasingly evident during the 1970s. While the Union of Soviet Socialist Republics (USSR) imported few goods from abroad, it did emerge as the world's largest **oil** producer under **Leonid Brezhnev**, and soon began selling its hydrocarbons to Western European nations. However, more than half of the USSR's foreign trade was still with COMECON nations when **Mikhail Gorbachev** came to power.

After independence, Russia opened its doors to imports from around the world (particularly technology, machinery, food, and textiles), while establishing new trade links with countries such as **Turkey**, **Japan**, and South Korea. Raw materials, such as oil, **natural gas**, metals, timber, and minerals, continued to dominate exports. Russia's **agricultural** and manufacturing industries suffered terribly under **Boris Yeltsin**, as did Russia's foreign trade with the **near abroad**, despite attempts to maintain economic links through the **Commonwealth of Independent States** and other post-Soviet schemes. Trade relations with **Belarus**, **Kazakhstan**, and **Ukraine**, however, remain strong. **Arms exports**, a mainstay of the Soviet economy, contracted sharply in the early 1990s but rebounded handily under **Vladimir Putin**. The dramatic increase in petroleum prices also helped balance the country's foreign trade. In 2007, exports totaled more than $350 billion, making it the world's 12th-largest exporter. The same year, its imports were an estimated $150 billion. The ratio of imports to exports has risen dramatically in recent years as the Russian **economy** has improved.

FRADKOV, MIKHAIL YEFIMOVICH (1950–). Politician. Born to a **Jewish** family from Samara, Mikhail Fradkov rose through the ranks of the Soviet Union's **foreign trade** bureaucracy during the 1980s. He received a steady string of promotions under **Boris Yeltsin**, ultimately becoming minister of trade. **Vladimir Putin** tapped him to head the Federal Tax Police in 2001; he was later chosen as the Russian Federation's representative to the **European Union**. On 1 March 2004, Putin nominated him to become the next prime minister in a surprise move given that he was not affiliated with any particular power base; he was approved by the **State Duma** four days later. Fradkov was replaced by **Viktor Zubkov** in 2007, and he took a position as head of Russia's Foreign Intelligence Service. The unexpected appointment, combined with Fradkov's earlier service in **India**, suggest he may have secretly held rank in the intelligence services. *See also* ESPIONAGE.

FRANCE (RELATIONS WITH). Despite their lack of a common border, France and Russia share a dynamic history of bilateral relations dating back to the Napoleonic Era. During the **Cold War**, France—particularly under the leadership of Charles de Gaulle—plied a middle ground between its **North Atlantic Treaty Organization** (NATO) allies, particularly the **United States** and **Great Britain**, and the Communist powers of the Union of Soviet Socialist Republics (USSR) and the People's Republic of **China**.

Warm relations between Moscow and Paris were characteristic of the Jacques Chirac presidency (1995–2007). Chirac, known to be sympathetic to many of Russia's concerns about Washington's dominance of the international system, often worked to assuage

Boris Yeltsin's fears regarding NATO expansion and to establish the Russian Federation as a partner to the military alliance. France's traditional pro-**Serbia** orientation also created a natural common front between Moscow and Paris during the 1990s. As permanent members of the **United Nations** Security Council, France and Russia often found common cause on issues related to **counterterrorism** and instability in South Asia and other troubled regions. Economic relations are robust; France is one of the largest exporters to Russia and a major source of **foreign trade** and **investment** (approximately $1.5 billion per year), particularly in developing the Shtokman **natural gas** field. There are also significant joint projects in the fields of aeronautics, chemicals, **nuclear energy**, and automobile manufacturing.

In advance of the U.S.-led invasion of Iraq, **Vladimir Putin** entered into a collaborative relationship with Chirac and **Gerhard Schröder**, known as the Yekaterinburg Triangle, in an effort to dissuade Washington from the use of force. French political elites, apprehensive about **George W. Bush**'s freedom agenda, sought to leverage a Paris-Berlin-Moscow axis to prevent a second Western-led invasion of a **Muslim** country, but to no avail. Russo-French relations cooled with the election of the decidedly pro-American Nicholas Sarkozy in 2007; in a diplomatic snub, Moscow noticeably delayed congratulations to the new leader, the only country to do so. In the run-up to his victory, Sarkozy had taken a particularly critical line on Putin's growing authoritarianism and **human rights** violations in **Chechnya**.

During the **South Ossetian War**, Sarkozy emerged as the principal peace broker between Moscow and Tbilisi, ultimately crafting the six-point plan for a cease-fire. Despite the tough rhetoric, Sarkozy's successful personal diplomacy with Putin demonstrated that relations were on the mend. However, a lingering issue remains regarding Western Europe's exposure to Moscow's aggressive use of pipeline politics in its **near abroad**. French energy security, often threatened by cuts in the distribution of **oil** and gas traveling via **Georgia**, **Ukraine**, **Belarus**, and other former Soviet states, remains a major issue in bilateral and **European Union**–Russian relations. An increasing divide between the two countries on how to deal with **Iran**'s nuclear program is also a major sticking point in Franco-Russian relations. *See also* KOSOVO.

FRIDMAN, MIKHAIL MARATOVICH (1964–). Oligarch. Born in Lvov, **Ukraine**, Fridman is a **Jewish** Russian businessman, who, according to *Forbes* magazine, was the 20th-richest man in the world in 2008. He made his fortune during the economic chaos of the 1990s by establishing the Alfa Group Consortium, which includes Alfa-Bank and Tyumen Oil (now TNK-BP), as well as several construction companies, food processing businesses, and supermarket chains. His career exemplifies the rapid rise of certain individuals under the **Yeltsin** regime, particularly those with close ties to the government. After studying at the Moscow Institute of Steel and Alloys, Fridman worked as an engineer at one of Moscow's factories until 1988. Under **perestroika**, he established a private company that specialized in window cleaning. From there, he dabbled in courier services, before setting up a photo cooperative and then a commodities trading firm. His success is largely due to his association with Pyotr Aven, minister of external economic relations in **Yegor Gaydar**'s government. Fridman managed to turn his Kremlin allegiance into a business model by recruiting members of his Alfa Group from high-profile Russian politicians and government officials. Though accused of money laundering several times, he has managed to stay out of jail and prosper in Russia's turbulent economic environment. In 1996, he established Russia's Jewish Congress and subsequently served as its vice president.

FSB/FEDERALNAYA SLUZHBA BEZOPASNOSTI. As the successor to the Federal Counter-Intelligence Service or FSK (*Federal'naia sluzhba kontrrazvedki*), which was itself the successor to the **KGB**, the Federal Security Service of the Russian Federation (FSB) is the country's primary security agency.

The FSB's responsibilities include counterintelligence, internal security, border security, **counterterrorism**, and **surveillance**, including **narcotics** trafficking, suppressing **Chechen separatists**, export control on dual-use technologies, anti-**corruption**, and organized **crime**. The agency is headquartered at Lubyanka Square in **Moscow**, formerly Dzerzhinsky Square after the founder of the Soviet secret police. The FSB was created by the federal law "On the Organs of the Federal Security Service in the Russian Federation" on 3 April 1995. At that time, its powers were expanded to allow agents to enter any home with sufficient reason to believe that a crime had been or is being committed. On 9 March 2004, it was subordinated to the Ministry of Justice.

Unlike the KGB, which operated abroad and at home, the FSB is mostly concerned with domestic security, while the Foreign Intelligence Service is charged with overseas **espionage**. The major exceptions are the **Newly Independent States**, where the FSB does engage in counterterrorism and other activities and maintains close relations with the **security services** of most of the **Commonwealth of Independent States**. The total number of FSB employees and agents is estimated at close to 500,000; however, these statistics, as well as the organization's budget, are state secrets. The FSB also controls the country's **nuclear weapons** and has significant influence over certain sectors of the economy such as the **oil** industry.

Throughout the 1990s and beyond, a number of Western and Russian scholars have posited a strong link between the FSB and the **mafia**, aimed at expanding the organization's economic and political influence in Russia. Since 2000, the FSB has been implicated in a number of high-profile murders or attempted murders of **journalists** and other critics of the Kremlin, including **Anna Politkovskaya**. Shortly before his elevation to prime minister, **Vladimir Putin**, a lifelong security agent, served as head of the FSB. High-ranking members of the agency represent a core group of the so-called *siloviki*, and have enjoyed substantial influence in Russian **politics** and the **economy** since Putin's ascendance. Spetsnaz, the FSB's Special Forces, which include the *Alfa* group and *Vympel* (Pennent), have been criticized for excessive use of force, particularly in the **Nord-Ost theater siege** and the **Beslan crisis**.

– G –

GAYDAR, YEGOR TIMUROVICH (1956–2009). The scion of a Soviet literary and **journalistic** family, Yegor Gaydar was educated at the prestigious **Moscow State University** where he gained his degree in economics. An active member of the **Communist Party of the Soviet Union**, he relinquished his membership in the early 1990s to work as an economist in the **Yeltsin** administration. Gaydar was an advocate of **shock therapy** and other controversial reforms. Yeltsin appointed him prime minister in June 1992; however, the conservative **Congress of People's Deputies** refused to confirm him, resulting in **Viktor Chernomyrdin** taking over the post in December 1992. Gaydar stayed on as a financial advisor to the president and played a critical role in the **constitutional crisis of 1993**. He continued to pursue **politics** as a member of the **Union of Right Forces**, and held a seat in the **State Duma** from 1999 to 2003. In 2006, Gaydar took ill in Ireland and later, following conspiracy theories surrounding the death of **Aleksandr Litvinenko**, accused his political adversaries of poisoning him, though he stopped short of accusing the Russian **security services** or anyone in the **Putin** administration. His daughter is the leader of a political youth movement called Yes (*Da*). Gaydar died of complications from a blood clot on 16 December 2009. *See also* PRIVATIZATION.

GAYNUTDIN, RAVIL ISMAGILOVICH (1959–). Also Ravil Gaynutdinov or Rawil Gaynetdin. Ravil Gaynutdin is the chairman of the Spiritual Administration of the Muslims of Central Russia and the Council of Muftis of the Russian Federation; he is also the grand mufti of Moscow. A Kazan **Tatar**, Gaynutdin's power base is built on alliance with Moscow mayor **Yury Luzhkov** and through support from **Tatarstan**'s Islamist elites. During the 1990s, he challenged Sheikh ul-Islam **Talgat Tajuddin** for leadership of the Russian *ummah* (Muslim community). His openness to **Wahhabism** (*vakhabizm*) and close relations with Saudi spiritual authorities have proved somewhat controversial. His strong support for **Chechen separatists** placed him at odds with the Kremlin, particularly after the rise of **Vladimir Putin** in 2000. In recent years, Gaynutdin has campaigned for greater understanding between the major faiths. *See also* ISLAMISM.

GAZPROM. With more than 445,000 employees and more than $100 billion in revenues, OAO Gazprom is the world's largest extractor of **natural gas**. It is also Russia's largest company and accounts for one-quarter of the country's **tax** revenues. Former Prime Minister **Viktor Zubkov** is the current chairman of the board of directors.

   After the discovery of large gas fields in **Siberia** and the **Volga-Ural region** in the 1970s, the Union of Soviet Socialist Republics

(USSR) developed the commodity for export. Under **Mikhail Gorbachev**, the Ministry of the Oil and Gas Industry oversaw the creation of a joint stock company that would become Gazprom in 1992. The company was privatized in 1994, with the Kremlin maintaining a sizable share. **Viktor Chernomyrdin** ran the company in the mid-1990s; when he lost his post as prime minister, the government demanded and received millions in back taxes. His replacement on the board of directors was the future Russian President **Dmitry Medvyedev**. On Medvyedev's watch, the company took over **NTV** in a move to create a more politically friendly **media** environment for the Russian president, **Vladimir Putin**. In addition to its media holdings, Gazprom is also active in **agriculture**, **banking**, construction, and the insurance industry.

In 2004, the state became the majority shareholder in the company; in the same year, foreign ownership of Gazprom shares became possible for the first time; the company is traded on the London and Frankfurt stock exchanges, as well as Russian markets. Gazprom's largest fields are located in **Yamaliya**. Annually, the company produced approximately 550 billion cubic meters of natural gas and more than 30 tons of crude **oil**. Gazprom is estimated to control 17 percent of the world's natural gas reserves. The Shtokman field in the **Barents Sea** is seen as the future of the company, as the field is estimated to contain 3.8 trillion cubic meters of natural gas and more than 37 million tons of gas condensate.

Gazprom is the dominant or exclusive provider of natural gas to Austria, Macedonia, **Moldova**, Bosnia, **Finland**, the **Baltic States**, Bulgaria, Hungary, **Turkey**, **Poland**, Slovakia, and the Czech Republic. The **European Union** (EU) as a whole gets a quarter of its gas from the company. Shipment is dictated by the company's Unified Gas Supply System subsidiary, which controls compressor stations and 159,500 kilometers of pipelines across Russia. The company is developing two new routes to European markets—Nord Stream (via the **Baltic Sea**) and South Stream (via the **Black Sea**), following disputes with **Ukraine** over pricing and allegations of theft of gas en route to Europe. The dispute resulted in the cutting of supplies in early 2009; this major disruption followed smaller service interruptions and spats in 2005–2006 and 2007–2008. Following gas shortages in the Balkans and elsewhere, the EU publicly stated that

Russia could no longer be considered a reliable partner in the field of energy provision.

GENDER. In the Soviet Union, gender identity was based on ideological paradigms and was projected on Soviet citizens through a system of social and cultural codes that were reinforced by **education**, **media**, **literature**, **art**, and **film**. While the early Bolshevik reforms promised gender equality and the emancipation of Soviet citizens (particularly **women**), conservative views on gender roles, family, and **sexuality** became embedded under **Joseph Stalin**. Conflation of these competing principles produced gendered asymmetries, resulting in the imperative to place the common goals and fulfilling state expectations before personal considerations. The state propagated the cult of masculinity that signified progress, (**military**) power, **industry**, and technology, eventually causing a masculinization of Soviet society. Women—when they were valorized—were represented in their roles as revolutionaries, shock workers, pilots, and, eventually, astronauts. The Soviet state dictated the form and extent of women's rights, continuously deferring a solution to the "woman's question."

The post-Soviet Russian general public has been actively involved in rethinking and reconceptualizing gender identities. A number of political, social, and cultural changes have generated the need for popular reconsideration. One of these causes was the collapse of Soviet ideology that had regulated the construction of gender identities and the subsequent withdrawal of the state from the private sphere. The import of Western consumer products that had been unavailable in the Soviet Union (including feminine personal care products) and the associated advertising, as well as the import of Western cultural products (especially in **television** and films), have resulted in a new set of gender relations. The emergence of **Runet**, an **Internet**-enabled space that facilitates anonymous—and ultimately—safe articulation of new gender identities, has also been a catalyst for change.

In the 1990s, a crisis of masculinity occurred in Russia, resulting from a number of factors: the mass emigration of women into countries with stronger economies; the trafficking of women into the global sex trade; declining fertility rates associated with poor health, **alcoholism**, and other social problems; and massive **unemployment** and poverty, which negatively impacted the ability of young men to establish and provide for families. This feeling coincided with Russian state failures in traditionally male arenas such as international **politics**, the **economy**, and military readiness. These failures were reinforced by a number of phenomena, including President **Boris Yeltsin**'s alcoholism and ill health, the 1998 **ruble crisis**, and Russia's poor performance in the first **Chechen War**.

In the new millennium, Russian masculinity was thoroughly reinvented, and a new, more forceful, stable, and virile male identity was established in mass media and popular culture. Since taking national office in 1999, **Vladimir Putin**, a teetotaler, has actively sought to present himself as a new male role model, appearing in settings and poses that enhance his macho image and physical prowess, including being photographed or filmed while hunting, exercising, engaging in martial arts, and fishing. In artistic film, a ruthless and socially disconnected Mafiosi hero of the 1990s has been replaced by a conscientious professional male, whereas in popular film productions, a type of Hollywood-inspired warrior/ protector has prevailed.

The post-Soviet Russian woman has been reimagined as a dominant consumer. If in the 1990s, in the absence of men, women were focused on the preservation of family and life itself, figuring in many roles, including that of the provider and protector, at the start of the new century Russian women affirmed their role through conspicuous consumption that symbolizes their new domain. As more women become entrepreneurs, bankers, and lawyers, while maintaining their near-monopoly position in education and **health care**, they have projected their new, more independent status through acquiring and enjoying expensive commodities and pastimes. A Russian woman simultaneously detests and adores **glamour** because it signifies her traditional feminine and new commanding roles.

Despite the new liberating process, the generational and geographical gap remains. While in Russian cities women attest their rights through militant consumerism, and **homosexual** communities create their own alternative identities, in the Russian provinces, women appear fully subjugated to men. Older women display characteristics of stereotypical Soviet citizens, who were solely focused on daily hardships and enduring loveless marriages to generally worthless male partners. *See also* FEMINISM.

GEOGRAPHY. Covering more than 17 million square kilometers, Russia is the world's largest country. The Russian Federation sits on two continents and occupies 13 percent of the earth's surface; it covers one-quarter of the European continent and nearly 30 percent of Asia. Russia is relatively synonymous with northern **Eurasia**, that is, the northernmost third of the Eurasian supercontinent. From the westernmost point in **Kaliningrad Oblast** to **Chukotka**'s easternmost islands, Russia is over 8,000 kilometers wide; from the northern reaches of Franz Josef Land to the country's southern border, the country is more than 3,500 kilometers long.

Despite the apparent monotony of the Russian landscape, it possesses every significant ecological environment except for tropical rainforests. The Russian landmass is divided between four principal biomes: **tundra**, found in the country's **Far North**; **taiga**, accounting for more than half of the country, and most of its Asian territory; temperate broadleaf forests and steppe-forests, found mostly in European Russia and along the **Kazakhstan** border; and semiarid **steppe**, which dominates extreme southern European Russia. Nearly one-quarter of the world's forests and half of its bogs are found in Russia, making the country vital to global biogeochemical cycles and the production of oxygen. Russia's **climate** is mostly continental; however, extremes exist in the country's higher and lower latitudes.

Due to expansive, varied, and sparsely populated territory, Russia—particularly Asiatic Russia—is home to a wide variety of **wildlife**, including many critically endangered species such as the Amur leopard, Saiga antelope, and Siberian white crane. Russia's sable and Beluga sturgeon are internationally known for their fur and caviar, respectively.

The country has a number of major mountain ranges; from west to east, the largest are: the **Caucasus**, the **Urals**, Altay, Sayan, Byrranga, Yablonovy, Stanovoy, Verkhoyansk, Chersky, Dzhugdzhur, Kolyma, Kamchatka, and Anadyr. Mount Elbrus, at 5,642 meters, is Russia's (and Europe's) highest point. The major lowlands are the East European Plain and the West Siberian Plain, which are divided by the Urals. The Central Siberian Plateau occupies much of the central part of Asiatic Russia.

A large portion of the Earth's freshwater reserves are also found in the country. **Lake Baykal**, the largest freshwater lake by volume, is located in Asiatic Russia; other important bodies of water include the lakes of Onega, Ladoga, and Peipus and the Kuybyshev and Rybinsk reservoirs. Russia's prodigious waterways include the European rivers of the **Volga**, Don, Kuban, Pechora, Kama, and Oka; its most important Asian rivers are the Ob, Irtysh, Yenisey, Lena, Amur, Indigirka, and Kolyma. These rivers empty into the various seas and oceans that lie on Russia's borders, including the **Sea of Azov**, the **Baltic Sea**, the **Black Sea**, the **Caspian Sea**, the seas of the **Arctic Ocean** (White, **Barents**, Kara, Laptev, and East Siberian), the Sea of Japan, the **Sea of Okhotsk**, and the Bering Sea. The country's major islands and island chains include Franz Josef Land, **Novaya Zemlya**, Severnaya Zemlya, the New Siberian Islands, Wrangel Island, the **Kuril Islands**, and **Sakhalin**. Important peninsulas include the Kola, Taymyr, Yamal, Kamchatka, and Chukchi.

Russia commands the largest share of the world's natural resources, including valuable commodities such as **oil**, **natural gas**, uranium, iron ore, aluminum, gold, silver, and diamonds, as well as other precious metals. Due to Leninist attitudes toward the natural world, the Soviet Union paid little attention to the negative aspects of industrialization, mineral resource extraction, and land use. This has resulted in extensive **pollution** of the country's rivers, lakes, air, and soil, including radioactive contamination associated with **Chernobyl** and other nuclear power accidents. Little has been done during the post-Soviet period to improve the situation, although Russia is party to a number of international agreements dedicated to **environmental** issues. However, the ecological situation in the European part of Russia improved significantly in the 1990s because of the collapse of many industries.

Less than 10 percent of the landmass—mostly in European Russia and along its southern Asiatic rim—is used for farming, as the taiga proves unsuitable for most forms of traditional **agriculture**. However, Russia is still one of the world's largest countries in terms of farmed land, despite suffering from soil degradation and erosion wrought by poor farming practices.

At the metalevel, Russia can be divided into the European core (including the most densely populated areas of Russia, which lie north of the Black Sea), the **Northern Caucasus** and its hinterlands, the Russian Far North, **Siberia**, and the **Russian Far East**.

In the contemporary Russian Federation, the highest level of internal political geographic division is the **Federal Districts**; from west to east, these seven units are the Northwestern, Central, Southern, Volga, Urals, Siberian, and Far Eastern. Each district is comprised of between 6 and 18 **federal subjects**. Each subject, whether **ethnic republic**, **krai**, **oblast**, autonomous oblast, **autonomous okrug**, or federal city, is then subdivided into smaller administrative districts, known as **raions**. Russia is home to the world's largest subnational political unit, **Sakha**, as well as the world's third largest, **Krasnoyarsk Krai** (the state of Western Australia is the second largest).

Russia's urban geography is dominated by its two historical capitals: **Moscow** and **St. Petersburg**. Other major cities include Novosibirsk, Nizhny Novgorod, Yekaterinburg, Samara, Omsk, Kazan, Ufa, and Chelyabinsk. Overall, Russia has approximately 150 urban areas with a population in excess of 100,000. In Asiatic Russia, proximity to the **Trans-Siberian Railway** is a key requirement for economic and demographic success.

With nearly 60,000 kilometers of international borders, Russia has more neighbors than any other country. Most of these countries are part of the so-called **near abroad**, or former Soviet republics, and include **Estonia**, **Latvia**, **Lithuania**, **Belarus**, **Ukraine**, **Georgia**, **Azerbaijan**, and Kazakhstan; its border with the latter is the longest unbroken territorial border in the world. Russia also neighbors **Norway**, **Finland**, **Poland** (via the Kaliningrad exclave annexed from **Germany** after World War II), **China**, **Mongolia**, and **North Korea**. Since its recognition of Georgia's breakaway republics of **Abkhazia** and **South Ossetia** in 2008, these states can also be considered to be on the Russian frontier. Russia's maritime boundaries abut those of the **United States** and **Japan** (and potentially **Canada**, based on recent Russian claims to the Arctic basin), and Russia shares jurisdiction of the Caspian with **Turkmenistan** and **Iran** (in addition to Kazakhstan and Azerbaijan).

As a result of a millennium-long history of territorial expansion, Russia incorporated a panoply of ethnic, religious, and linguistic groups in the fabric of the country. As a "settler empire," Russia's ethnic geography is shaped by the historic expansion of **Cossacks** and other **ethnic Russians** southward from the European (or Muscovy) core toward the Caucasus and eastward into Siberia and northeastern Eurasia, sometimes referred to by some geographers as the "boreal empire." In the **Volga-Ural region** and the North Caucasus, significant populations of **ethnic minorities** remain, while in Siberia and the Far East, Russian migration significantly diluted the former demographic dominance of indigenous peoples, with the exception of some ethnic republics such as **Tuva**.

In terms of **economic** geography, the cities of Moscow and St. Petersburg are the dominant nodes of activity, alongside Nizhny Novgorod, Yekaterinburg, Vladivostok, and other regional centers of finance, commerce, and **industry**. The central and southern parts of European Russia, formerly dominated by agriculture, experienced massive industrialization in the Union of Soviet Socialist Republics (USSR), while the Kuzbass enjoyed an expansion of **mining** during the 1930s. Subsequent wartime conditions—relocation of factories from occupied territories—contributed to the development of an industrial base in the Urals. It is in these areas that Russia's population density is the highest, upward of more than 100 persons per square kilometer in Moscow and parts of southern Russia. The vast majority of Russia, however, has a population density of fewer than one person per square kilometer, and migration patterns suggest that this statistic will only decrease in the coming decades except in areas associated with hydrocarbon exploitation such as Krasnoyarsk and **Khantiya-Mansiya**. Severe poverty afflicts certain regions of the North Caucasus, **Kalmykiya**, **Nenetsiya**, **Taymyriya**, and much of the Russian Far East, whereas the European part of Russia, especially Moscow, enjoys a high level of development. *See also* INDIGENOUS PEOPLES OF THE NORTH.

GEORGIA, REPUBLIC OF (RELATIONS WITH). Georgia, one of the oldest Christian nations in the world, was incorporated into the **Romanov** Empire at the beginning of the 19th century. During the Russian Civil War, Georgia declared itself an independent democratic republic under Menshevik rule. However, driven by the ambitions of **Joseph Stalin**, an ethnic Georgian himself, the Red Army invaded in 1921, setting the stage for the incorporation of Georgia into the Transcaucasian Soviet Federated Socialist Republic a year later. In 1936, Georgia became a **union republic**. During the 1970s, the republic was governed by the anticorruption campaigner

Eduard Shevardnadze, who would go on to become the last Soviet foreign minister. During the late 1980s, the anti-**Communist** movement developed rapidly in Georgia, placing strong centrifugal pressure on the Soviet Union itself. The push for independence, even among Georgian Communists, accelerated in the aftermath of a bloody suppression of a demonstration at Rustaveli Square in Tbilisi on 9 April 1989.

The country declared its independence in April 1991 and elected the former dissident Zviad Gamsakhurdia as president. He was quickly deposed, triggering the **Georgian Civil War**, which would last until 1993. Gamsakhurdia's nationalist rhetoric pushed many of the country's **ethnic minorities** (Abkhaz, **Ossetians**, **Armenians**, and Ajars) into the arms of Russia, which took an active interest in weakening Georgia as part of its larger strategy to maintain control in its **near abroad**. Responding to the overtures, Moscow passively— and sometimes actively—supported breakaway republics in **South Ossetia** and **Abkhazia** during the years after independence. In 1992, Gamsakhurdia was forced into exile; a year later he returned to the country to confront the new president, Shevardnadze.

Fearing further strife and interruptions in regional trade, Russia—along with Georgia's neighbors **Armenia** and **Azerbaijan**— backed the Shevardnadze regime. The quid pro quo was Georgia's agreement to join the **Commonwealth of Independent States** and to maintain Russian bases at Vaziani, Gudauta, Akhalkalaki, and Batumi. At a 1999 **Organization for Security and Co-operation in Europe** summit, Russia and Georgia agreed that all the bases would be evacuated by Russia before 1 July 2001; however, Akhalkalaki and Batumi were not evacuated until 2007, and Gudauta, which is in Abkhazia, still remains.

During the First **Chechen War**, relations between Tbilisi and Moscow grew progressively worse. **Boris Yeltsin** accused Georgia of sheltering **Chechen** guerillas in the Pankisi Gorge, a mountainous zone in the northeast of the country. Shevardnadze's vocal pro-American orientation further complicated bilateral relations. Under his leadership, Georgia declared its intentions to join the **North Atlantic Treaty Organization** (NATO) and the **European Union** and to participate in the strategic Baku-Tbilisi-Ceyhan pipeline intended to circumvent Russian and **Iranian** control over **oil** exports from the **Caspian Sea**. With the resumption of the Chechen War in 1999, the Georgian-Chechen border once again became a sticking point between Moscow and its Caucasian neighbor.

In the wake of the **September 11 attacks**, Georgia significantly expanded military cooperation with the **United States** under the Georgia Train and Equip Program (GTEP) intended to improve the country's **counterterrorism** capabilities and clear the Pankisi Gorge of radical **Islamists**. The close proximity of American Special Operations forces to Russia's sensitive border in the **North Caucasus** sparked a storm of criticism in the Russian **media**. In November 2003, Shevardnadze was pushed out of power in the so-called **Rose Revolution**. His successor, **Mikheil Saakashvili**, expanded military ties with the United States and directly confronted the Moscow-backed regime of Aslan Abashidze in **Ajaria**; both moves were ill-received in Moscow. After a tense standoff in the spring of 2004, Abashidze lost the support of his Russian patrons and fled the country, allowing a reassertion of central government control of the **Black Sea** region. In the wake of the Ajaria Crisis, Russo-Georgian relations plummeted.

The year 2006 was plagued by disputes between the two countries. In January, **natural gas** exports to Georgia were suspended after a series of pipeline explosions in **North Ossetiya**; the cessation of exports, however, was widely viewed in Georgia as sabotage to allow **Gazprom** to monopolize transit to the South Caucasus. In the spring, on the grounds of health and safety, Russia banned the import of Georgian wines and mineral water, two of the country's most important exports (Russian consumption accounted for more than three-quarters of Georgian wine production). In July, Emzar Kvitsiani, a local warlord, subverted Tbilisi's control of the Kodori Gorge, the only area of Abkhazia it controlled after the civil war. Russian and Abkhazian officials condemned Georgian actions to retake the region as incendiary and a possible violation of the cease-fire. At the end of the summer, Georgia arrested four Russian **military** officers on charges of **espionage**. In retaliation, Moscow placed a ban on all **transportation** and postal links between the two countries.

Russia also began a large-scale deportation of Georgian **immigrants**, many of whom were living and working legally in the Russian Federation. In November, the Russian energy giant Gazprom doubled prices just as winter was setting in; the move was condemned in Europe and the U.S. as a political tactic to keep Georgia in line with Russian interests in the region. In 2007, Russia violated Georgian sovereignty on several occasions, including Russian helicopter attacks on the Kodori Gorge, dropping an unexploded missile in the Gori District, and several violations of airspace. Saakashvili also accused the Russian secret services of being involved in an attempted coup d'état in November 2007. While Russia adjudicated a peaceful resolution to the standoff between the central government and Ajaria, **Vladimir Putin** signaled to Georgia that it would not brook Saakashvili's encroachment into the breakaway republics of South Ossetia and Abkhazia.

With significant numbers of **peacekeepers** (nominally CIS, but mostly Russian) in the republics, Moscow effectively functioned as a bulwark against reassertion of Georgian sovereignty. Despite the risk, Saakashvili ordered the Georgian military to retake Tskhinvali, South Ossetia's regional capital, on 8 August 2008, triggering the **South Ossetian War**. Russian troops, ostensibly to protect the lives of its peacekeepers, invaded Georgia proper, stopping only a few kilometers north of Tbilisi. After agreeing to a six-point peace plan negotiated by **France**'s President Nicholas Sarkozy, Russia implemented a cease-fire and slowly began withdrawal of its troops to "buffer zones" around Abkhazia and South Ossetia.

On 26 August 2008, Russian President **Dmitry Medvyedev** recognized Abkhazia and South Ossetia as independent states. Georgia suspended diplomatic relations with Russia in response (the ambassador had been recalled in July 2008), while much of the international community condemned the declaration as a violation of international law. Medvyedev subsequently promised military aid to the republics in the event of attack by a third party. *See also* FOREIGN RELATIONS.

GEORGIAN CIVIL WAR (1991–1993). As the Soviet Union unraveled in 1990–1991, **Georgia** was in the vanguard of the independence movement. The pro-Moscow orientation of certain autonomous regions of the Georgian Soviet Socialist Republic, however, created a volatile situation in the South Caucasian republic. In September 1990, relations between the central government and the South

Ossetian **Autonomous Soviet Socialist Republic** (ASSR) deteriorated rapidly, particularly after leaders in the regional capital Tskhinvali declared a **South Ossetian** Democratic Soviet Republic and appealed to **Moscow** for help against Georgian nationalists. In December, Georgian politicians negated South Ossetian autonomy. Fighting between South Ossetian and government forces broke out in early 1991, reaching its peak in April before a respite in the summer months.

Soviet Premier **Mikhail Gorbachev** attempted to calm the violence, but political challenges in the **Baltic States** and the ongoing conflict between **Armenia** and **Azerbaijan** weakened the position of the federal government. The presence of Soviet troops in South Ossetia did constrain Georgian military action against its breakaway region but proved ineffective against roaming bands of paramilitaries. The violence claimed nearly 1,000 lives and resulted in mass emigration of **Ossetians** across the Russian border to **North Ossetiya**.

In April 1991, in the midst of the conflict with South Ossetia, the Georgian Supreme Council unanimously passed the declaration of independence from the Union of Soviet Socialist Republics (USSR). On 26 May 1991, the former **dissident** and Georgian nationalist Zviad Gamsakhurdia was elected as president, winning 86 percent of the vote. However, his authoritarian style and refusal to address economic issues, as well as continued ethnic tensions, led to further instability across Georgia. Gamsakhurdia's ambiguous position on the **August Coup** and imprisonment of opposition leaders further sapped his popularity among reformists. Ready access to Soviet military hardware and the rising strength of paramilitary groups operating in the country came to a head in December when a group of military personnel, including the leader of the Georgian National Guard, Tengiz Kitovani, launched a coup against Gamsakhurdia. By the end of January 1992, the president had gone into exile, first fleeing to Armenia, then to **Chechnya**. **Media** reports suggested that Russian forces had assisted the plotters and aided anti-Gamsakhurdia activists to gain control of state television.

In March, **Eduard Shevardnadze**, who had been first secretary of the Georgian Communist Party from 1972 until 1985, returned to the country and was soon elected head of state. Shortly after coming to power, Shevardnadze was confronted with a new **separatist** challenge from the **Black Sea** region of **Abkhazia**. An ASSR during Soviet times, the region clamored for union with the **Russian Soviet Federative Socialist Republic** from the mid-1980s onward. As Georgia slipped into civil war, the Abkhaz, supported by local **Armenians** and **ethnic Russians**, turned against Georgia. In the summer of 1992, Abkhazian separatists attacked government buildings in Sukhumi, the regional capital. In an environment of threats and counterthreats, **Cossacks** from Russia and various volunteers from the **Confederation of Mountain Peoples of the Caucasus** rallied to defend the **Muslim** Abkhaz from Georgian aggression. Russian forces were ostensibly neutral in the conflict but supplied battlefield intelligence and weapons (missiles and SU-25 fighters) to the Abkhazians, and were found to have participated in the aerial bombing of Georgian-held Sukhumi in 1993. A number of Russian politicians including Vice President **Aleksandr Rutskoy** vocally supported the Abkhazians. Russian border guards also allowed the **Chechen** fighters, including **Shamil Basayev**, to cross into Abkhazia.

Ethnic cleansing reached epic levels, with some 200,000 Georgians being forced out of the region. Increasingly, Russia assumed the ambiguous role of **peacekeeper** in the region, but conflicting loyalties and reticence to send soldiers into harm's way actually contributed to a worsening of the security situation. Ultimately, Abkhaz forces were able to secure most of the region, with the exception of the Kodori Gorge, which remained under government control. From 1992 to 1993, pitched battles between the security forces, assisted by *Mkhedrioni* (Georgian: "Horsemen") paramilitaries, and Gamsakhurdia loyalists known as Zviadists wracked the country. Supporters of the ousted president were able to establish effective control over his home region, Samegrelo. This gave Gamsakhurdia the ability to launch an offensive against Shevardnadze's forces from the city of Zugdidi in the west of the country.

Under intense pressure, Shevardnadze begged Moscow for help, which came in the form of Russian support from the Black Sea. Gamsakhurdia's units were routed, and the ex-president died shortly thereafter under mysterious circumstances. In the midst of the strife, Aslan Abashidze sealed the borders to **Ajaria**, creating a semi-autonomous fiefdom that he would control for more than a decade. In addition to losing control of Ajaria, Shevardnadze was forced to join the **Commonwealth of Independent States** and accept long-term Russian deployments in his country and (temporary) subjugation of its foreign policy to Moscow. Other aftereffects of the civil war included long-term economic debilitation, frozen conflicts with South Ossetia and Abkhazia, and lingering social conflict. *See also* FOREIGN RELATIONS; IMMIGRATION.

GERMANS, ETHNIC. Germans began settling in Russia during the 16th century. Under the reign of Catherine the Great (1762–1796), German settlers were granted special rights, including exemption from conscription, precipitously increasing the number of **immigrants** from Central Europe. Many settled in the Volga region, then a buffer zone between the Slavs and nomadic peoples such as the **Kazakhs** and **Kalmyks**. In later centuries, Germans also settled in the **Black Sea** region, the **North Caucasus**, and other parts of European Russia. Following the establishment of the Soviet Union, Germans became the titular majority of the Volga German **Autonomous Soviet Socialist Republic**. The administrative region existed from 1924 until 1942, when it was permanently abolished (becoming part of the **Saratov Oblast** during World War II). Volga Germans were deported en masse to **Siberia** and **Kazakhstan** as a potential fifth column, suffering extremely high casualty rates in the process. Able-bodied Germans in other parts of European Russia were detained and placed in **gulags** where approximately one-third perished. Unlike other **punished peoples**, the ethnic Germans (along with Crimean **Tatars**) were not officially rehabilitated by **Nikita Khrushchev** after **Joseph Stalin**'s death, although their banishment was rescinded in 1964.

The right of return to European Russia was extended a decade later. Under **perestroika**, ethnic Germans began to take advantage of West Germany's Law of Return, which recognized *jus sanguinis* (Latin: "law of blood") and granted citizenship to ethnic German returnees. Emigration from Asiatic Russia continued after independence in 1991; however, the exodus has slowed due to more stringent language requirements being placed on prospective immigrants to **Germany**. Germans are still a sizable minority in the Russian Federation, numbering nearly 600,000. In 1992, **Boris Yeltsin**, as part of an agreement with Germany, made special concession for German resettlement in the Volga region. Some ethnic Germans have migrated to the historically German territory of **Kaliningrad**, which for a period of time was considered as the site of a German **ethnic republic** within the Russian Federation. Under a plan initiated by **Vladimir Putin**, **Moscow** intends to invest more than $100 million by 2012 in infrastructure and housing in **Novosibirsk** and the Volga region to encourage Russian Germans to return to the land of their birth. Returnees are granted €3,000, travel compensation, and free shipment of their belongings.

GERMANY (RELATIONS WITH). The modern era of Russo-German relations began during the partition of Poland in the late 18th century. First as Prussia and then as the Hohenzollern Empire, the two states shared a common border until World War I (1914–1918). After the cessation of hostilities, Weimar Germany and Soviet Russia were separated by a band of new states hostile to both countries; the two found common cause in the 1920s and signed the Treaty of Rappallo. The rise of Nazism created an ideological dilemma for the Union of Soviet Socialist Republics (USSR); however, the two parties did agree on spheres of interest during the interwar period, realized in the Molotov-Ribbentrop Pact (1939). However, mutual vilification, ideological opposition, and *Rassenkampf* (racial conflict) characterized the relationship between the two countries during World War II.

A victorious **Joseph Stalin** stripped Germany of its territory east of the Oder and Neisse rivers, dividing it between **Poland** and the **Kaliningrad Oblast** of the **Russian Soviet Federative Socialist Republic**. Stalin's postwar worldview involved either a crippled, neutral German state or a dismembered Germany. With the merger of the American, British, and French zones of occupation in 1949, he was forced to settle for the latter and oversaw the creation of the German Democratic Republic (GDR). East Germany was subjected to Soviet occupation and heavy reparations during the early **Cold War**, and eventually fell far behind its Western counterpart in terms of economic output. The GDR, after an anti-Stalinist uprising in 1953, proved to be a dependable Soviet ally within the **Eastern Bloc**. West German inclusion into the **North Atlantic Treaty Organization** (NATO) and its subsequent rearmament were ill-received by Moscow, while millions of West German *Vertriebenen* (German: "expellees" from Eastern Europe) turned the Federal Republic of Germany (FDR) into an anti-Soviet firebrand in the 1950s. However, relations between West Germany and the Soviet Bloc improved markedly with the advent of Chancellor Willy Brandt's (1969–1974) *Ostpolitik* (Eastern Policy), a policy of rapprochement based on cultural and economic collaboration.

During the fateful year of 1989, East German leader Erich Honecker began to crack down ever more violently on dissidents and all East Germans who tried to flee to the West. His refusal to implement policies complementary with **Mikhail Gorbachev**'s **perestroika** and **glasnost** further caused his popularity to plummet. His removal on 18 October 1989 and the enunciation of the so-called **Sinatra Doctrine** by the Kremlin several days later signaled the end of Soviet domination over its **Warsaw Pact** allies. After initially hedging on a unified Germany's membership in NATO, Gorbachev ultimately removed all barriers to the abolition of East Germany and incorporation of its territory into the FDR in the summer of 1990. The Soviet **military** withdrew from the region in 1991.

German Chancellor Helmut Kohl (1982–1998) oversaw the process of German unification and worked to develop strong relations with an independent Russia after 1991, including backing Russia's admission to the **Group of Eight** (G8). His personal relationship with Russian President **Boris Yeltsin** was particularly strong; however, the Russian **ruble crisis** of 1998 and Kohl's difficult (and ultimately unsuccessful) reelection campaign in the late 1990s caused the "strategic partnership" to stagnate, though the period saw the implementation of annual bilateral meetings known as the German-Russian Governmental Consultations. Angered by NATO's eastward expansion, Yeltsin tried to cobble together a Moscow-Bonn-Paris axis to counteract American hegemony during this period, to no avail.

When **Gerhard Schröder** came to power in 1998, he quickly moved to establish contacts with a wider array of Russian elites, effectively ignoring Yeltsin as a lame duck. While Schröder openly criticized the personalization of Russo-German relations during the Yeltsin-Kohl years (derisively called the "sauna friendship"), he eventually became very close to **Vladimir Putin**. Schröder actively engaged Russia as an arbiter of the conflict in **Yugoslavia** (however, Schröder, unlike his predecessor, adamantly condemned Russian actions during the second **Chechen War**), and worked to create a new era of diplomatic and economic relations bereft of the long-standing enmity that characterized the Cold War.

In 2001, Putin, a former **KGB** officer who had been stationed in Dresden, made history by addressing the Bundestag in German. In the wake of the **September 11 attacks**, Russo-German cooperation on **counterterrorism** increased rapidly. Expanding trade between the two countries (Germany is Russia's biggest trading partner, topping $50 billion in 2007) has continued to ensure that serious friction between the two states is averted. Germany—attracted to Russian markets in the Putin-era boom years and dependent on Russian energy to drive its own economy—pursued ever closer ties with Moscow, particularly after the **United States**' invasion of Iraq in 2003 (which was strongly condemned in both Berlin and Moscow). The next year, Germany was instrumental in bringing Russia on board with the **Kyoto Protocol**. However, relations were complicated by Putin's poor record on **democracy** and freedom of the press, as well as the Kremlin's worsening relationship with the **European Union**. As chancellor, Schröder strongly backed the proposed Nord Stream **natural gas** pipeline linking Russia directly to Germany via the **Baltic Sea** (Russia supplies nearly half of Germany's natural gas). This move infuriated **Poland** and the **Baltic States**, which viewed the route as an attempt to marginalize their positions within the EU's energy security regime.

Chancellor Angela Merkel (2005–), who grew up in the GDR as the daughter of a Lutheran pastor, has taken a harder line with the Kremlin on **democratization**, **human rights** issues, and the country's dealings with its neighbors in the **near abroad**. Furthermore, Merkel reversed Schröder's neglect of the American relationship, somewhat tempering the Berlin-Moscow bond of the early years of the new millennium. Despite the slight vector change, Germany's energy dependence demands a continuation of the strategic partnership between the former enemies. **Dmitry Medvyedev**'s decision to visit **China** on his first trip abroad as Russia's new president was viewed as a slight to Germany; however, Germany's top-tier role in Russia's diplomatic relations was assured when Chancellor Merkel became the first foreign head of state to visit President Medvyedev in Moscow. *See also* FOREIGN INVESTMENT; FOREIGN RELATIONS; FOREIGN TRADE; GERMANS, ETHNIC.

GLAMOUR. The phenomenon of glamour and celebrity in post-Soviet Russian culture ranges across **media** forms (**film, television, music, art, politics,** the **Internet,** and so forth) with a specific task of constructing new media personalities. Celebrity as a symbol of success has been manipulated by the dominant culture and has been embraced by the masses. In Russia, the process of "celebrification" coincides with the dizzying pace of social change and economic transformation of the past two decades, the latter enabling an unprecedented fascination with glamour and its requisite extravagance.

In the 1990s, celebrities moved beyond the established paradigms of *kinozvezda* (film star) and *zvezda sovetskogo televideniia* (Soviet TV star), straddling various media environments. Such figures also became independent of media moguls (principally, the **oligarchs**). The post-Soviet sociocultural climate has stimulated circulation of consumerist dreams, fantasies of social promotion, and self-aggrandizement. These cultural functions of glamour are similar to the social and economic expectations of the liberating movement of the late 1980s, known as **perestroika**. Ironically, the culture of glamour developed in Russia when the democratic vector of perestroika was replaced by the neo-traditionalist and restoration tendencies characteristic of the **Putin** era. To a large extent, the insidious spread of glamour in Russian culture of the 2000s has emerged as a substitute for the decreasing social mobility within Russian society.

It is not an exaggeration to suggest that under Vladimir Putin, the glamour and celebrity phenomenon became the dominant cultural discourse, a type of universal language, and a currency that has been used to address political, social, and cultural issues. In fact, Putin himself has actively promoted his status as a celebrity. He has enjoyed extraordinary popular support, with approval ratings of 70–80 percent. Until the 2008–2009 **global financial crisis**, he was revered as the savior not only of Russia's **economy**, but also of the country's national pride and its international status. Adoration of the Russian president during his term was not only ideological, but also romantic and quite creative. Russian citizens capitalized on the image of Putin by producing and selling official art and unofficial paraphernalia with Putin's image; depictions of Putin were featured in Russian popular music, while he also inspired Russian cuisine, sports competitions, and so forth. As a result, he appears as a glamorous, elite icon, whose image dominates the offices of Russian administrators, party leaders, and businesspeople. *See also* GENDER.

GLASNOST. Glasnost was the policy of introducing and maximizing openness, transparency, and publicity of government, **military**, and **media** institutions in the Soviet Union. It was introduced by **Mikhail Gorbachev** as part of his philosophy of the country's modernization known as **perestroika**, which also included such concepts as *uskoreniie* (acceleration) and **informatization**. Glasnost occurred as a result of relaxation of censorship and came to be viewed as a stride toward liberalization of the regime. The events that caused the change of course were the **Chernobyl disaster** and the **Soviet-Afghan War**, which collectively demonstrated the Soviet government's callous disregard toward and disconnection from the will and needs of its people. One of the main political objectives of glasnost was to lessen the power of the **apparatchiks**; however, the effects of glasnost were uncontrollable as it effectively changed the course of history in the **Eastern Bloc**.

The new glasnost environment provided Soviet citizens with greater freedom of access to information and greater freedom of speech. Glasnost was the first step in the process of **democratization** of the Soviet Union. At the outset, glasnost facilitated the processes of uncovering the truth about the Soviet past, especially about **Stalin-**era crimes. It was an ideological doctrine that was quickly accepted by the Soviet media and which eventually enabled criticism of the Soviet regime itself. Initially perceived with skepticism by the general public, glasnost quickly became a means of influencing local governments and the *nomenklatura*. Over time, increasing political openness caused decentralization of power in the Union of Soviet Socialist Republics (USSR), with the **union republics** taking the lead in multicandidate local and national elections. The rise of nationalism in Soviet republics stirred social and ethnic tensions, leading to **ethnic violence** in the late 1980s and early 1990s. The term "glasnost" may also be used to refer to the historic period of the late 1980s in the USSR when the principles of openness and transparency were introduced.

GLOBAL FINANCIAL CRISIS (2008–2009). The most serious financial downturn since the Great Depression, the global financial crisis began as a result of weakness in the **United States'** housing market, but quickly spread to world financial markets. As the economies of the U.S. and **European Union** contracted, the effect was felt in Russia, which had experienced an economic boom under **Vladimir Putin**. Plummeting **oil** and **natural gas** prices, the mainstay of the country's **foreign trade** disproportionately harmed the Russian **economy**. The precipitous decline in stock prices, particularly in September 2008, erased significant portions of the **oligarchs'** fortunes, allowing the Kremlin to acquire large stakes in formerly state-owned enterprises that had been **privatized** during the 1990s. This process has been called a reverse **loans for shares program**. The rapid rise in the value of the ruble prior to the crisis and a real estate boom further exposed the country to the global contagion. The Russian economic crisis was further compounded by investor uncertainty in the wake of the 2008 **South Ossetian War**, which sparked massive capital flight from Russia. Overall, the steel, real estate, construction, and automobile industries were hardest hit. **Unemployment** rose dramatically during the period, especially in the fields of metallurgy and finance. Prime Minister Putin moved to reduce the tax burden on companies, while the new president, **Dmitry Medvyedev**, worked with other world leaders, including those of the **Group of Eight** (G8) and **BRIC** (Brazil, Russia, India, and China) countries, to solve the global crisis.

GLOBALIZATION. Russia has an ambiguous position on globalization, which can be defined as the interdependency that results from commercial, cultural, **economic**, and political interaction between states and nonstate actors driven by sustained linkages of goods, people, communications, and **transportation** networks. Many believers in the Soviet system see **Mikhail Gorbachev**'s attempts to open the country to globalization through economic acceleration (*uskoreniie*) and **perestroika** as the immediate cause of the Soviet Union's demise, and thus the loss of Russia's status as a superpower. For such critics, Gorbachev allowed for "too much" globalization, particularly as it related to **glasnost** and **democratization**, unlike **China**, which opened to the world without extensive political reform.

During the **Yeltsin** era, Russia suffered first under the unrepentant **privatization** and **shock therapy** as it transitioned to a market economy, and later from international exposure related to the 1997 Asian economic "flu," which in turn triggered the **ruble crisis** a year later. The diminution of the social welfare system and impoverishment of many Russians during this period, combined with the soaring wealth of the country's **oligarchs** and the conspicuous consumption of so-called **New Russians**, further soured many on the fruits of globalism and generated nostalgia for the **Brezhnev** era. The perceived subjugation of Russian **culture**, including the weakness of the domestic **film** industry and the withering of the global appeal of the **Russian language**, further depleted Russians' appetite for globalization.

Russia's **industry**, in particular, has been harmed by openness to the outside world. This was particularly true given the Soviet Union's ideological preference for heavy manufacturing, much of which has since relocated to the developing economies of China, Southeast Asia, and elsewhere. In less than a decade, Russia's exposure to globalization transformed it from a world power into a country with a GDP that trailed Argentina and Austria.

In political terms, the new realities of the unipolar international system, often associated with the **United States**' attempts to impose its own form of neo-liberal globalization on the rest of the world, left Russia particularly cold, especially in relation to the expansion of the **North Atlantic Treaty Organization** (NATO). New insecurity associated with transnational **terrorism** and the instability of Russia's neighbors also impacted Russian views of the new world order. Taken together, these factors made antiglobalism an attractive ideology for many of Russia's political elites, particularly the **Communists**, supporters of Russian **Orthodoxy**, ultranationalists, and **neo-Eurasianists**.

During the **Putin** years, the rapidly rising price of **oil** and **natural gas** allowed the Russian Federation to benefit from the global marketplace. International investment firms soon began to speak of the **BRIC** (Brazil, Russia, India, and China) economies that increasingly determined the future of the global economic system. Putin ended further experiments in Western-style **democracy** and abrogated certain freedoms dating to the Gorbachev era, arguing that "Russia need not ape Western norms" and was able to determine its own "sovereign" path in the globalized world; he also sought for Russia to influence the process of globalization, not just be influenced by the phenomenon. Until 2008, the strong ruble, Moscow's new assertiveness in **foreign relations** (particularly in the **near abroad**), and a rapidly rising standard of living portended Russia's victory over the vagaries of globalization. However, Russia's overreliance on hydrocarbons led to severe difficulties during the 2008–2009 **global financial crisis**; the situation was further compounded by capital flight in the wake of the **South Ossetian War**.

GLONASS. Russia's Global Navigation Satellite System (*Global' naia navigatsionnaia sputnikovaia sistema*), or Glonass, is a satellite-based navigation system analogous to the **United States'** Global Positioning System (GPS), as well as **Chinese** and **European Union** variants. Originally developed in the late **Brezhnev** era as part of the country's **space program**, the system did not gain a global footprint until the mid-1990s; the success was short-lived, and the system soon fell into disrepair. Under **Vladimir Putin**, Russia diversified Glonass, adding the **Indian** government as a partner; Moscow plans to restore global coverage before 2011. In 2007, the system was made available for civilian and commercial uses. *See also* AIR FORCE; MILITARY.

GORBACHEV, MIKHAIL SERGEYEVICH (1931–). Born in a village in **Stavropol Krai**, Mikhail Gorbachev experienced both the privations of **Joseph Stalin**'s purges and World War II, losing relatives in both. He proved to be an excellent student and was awarded a law degree from **Moscow State University** in 1955. While at university, he met and married his wife, Raisa Titarenko, and joined the **Communist Party of the Soviet Union** (CPSU). After graduation, he retuned to his native Stavropol to take a position in the **Komsomol** youth organization. In the 1960s, he began to rise through the party ranks under the patronage of Mikhail Suslov, the CPSU's chief strategist.

In 1979, Gorbachev joined the Politburo and became its most influential member during the reign of **Yury Andropov**. During this period, he developed relationships with foreign leaders including Margaret Thatcher. Despite Andropov's wish that Gorbachev succeed him, the young Communist ideologue was passed over in favor of the ailing **Konstantin Chernenko** in 1984. A year later, on the event of Chernenko's death, Gorbachev became the general secretary of the CPSU. Gorbachev quickly embraced and expanded Andropov's policy of economic acceleration (*uskoreniie*), hoping to jump-start the stalled Soviet **economy**, which was no longer buoyed by high **oil** prices as was the case under **Leonid Brezhnev**.

His tentative first steps, largely based on semi-successful economic experiments conducted in the Baltic republics, soon gave way to a more aggressive reform agenda. Hoping to improve worker productivity, he launched an ill-received anti-**alcoholism** campaign that sapped the state of much needed tax revenue while doing little to stanch the abuse of spirits. By 1986, Gorbachev began to face off against so-called old thinkers within the party who were set on preserving the status quo. The incident at **Chernobyl**, among other crises, evinced increasing tensions between the old guard and Gorbachev's "Komsomol" generation. In order to promote genuine reform within the Soviet Union, Gorbachev instituted a grand policy known as **perestroika** (restructuring). In order to circumvent institutional barriers to change, he soon twinned this policy with one of **glasnost** (transparency), thus preventing the bureaucracy or other vested interests from blocking access to information about failures in the sprawling Soviet system.

By 1988, Gorbachev's economic reforms had gained steam; private ownership of certain types of businesses was legalized, creating the basis for an embryonic market economy, while also creating conditions that would lead to large-scale **corruption** in Russia's post-Soviet economy. In order to protect the progress made up until this point, Gorbachev began to systematically strip the CPSU of its monopolization on political power, though genuine **democratization** (*demokratizatsiia*) would not be embraced until 1990. Meanwhile, Gorbachev had adopted a new stance in **foreign relations**; under the rubric of "New Thinking," Moscow sought to redefine its relations with both Western Europe and the **United States**. His new orientation promoted respect for human and minority rights, as well as the inclusion of the **Eastern Bloc** (including the Soviet Union) into a "common European home"; the posture proved popular in European capitals. Through a series of agreements conducted with U.S.

President **Ronald Reagan**, the Union of Soviet Socialist Republics (USSR) also agreed to reduce its nuclear arsenal and conventional weapons.

Gorbachev also recognized the futility of continued participation in the **Soviet-Afghan War**, and set a timetable for withdrawal of troops; the last Soviet soldiers left **Afghanistan** in 1989. During that same year, Gorbachev radically altered the USSR's relationship with its satellite states, signaling an end to the threat of Soviet invasion if any member of the **Warsaw Pact** abandoned socialism. The institution of the so-called **Sinatra Doctrine** is seen as instrumental in the rapid transition of **Poland**, Czechoslovakia, Hungary, and other Central European states from one-party totalitarianism to liberal pluralism. Gorbachev's willingness to let the Soviet satellites go stemmed partially from difficulties at home.

Growing discontent—unintended outcomes of perestroika and glasnost—had created a volatile political situation in Russia proper, while centrifugal nationalism in the other **union republics** was reaching a boiling point. The situation was especially acute in the **Baltic States**, where the new liberalism had resulted in the rise of stridently anti-Russian elites within the political system; glasnost's uncovering of Stalin's crimes only fueled the fire in the region. Pro-independence movements were gaining ground elsewhere as well, including **Georgia** and **Ukraine**. In the southern **Caucasus**, **ethnic violence** erupted between **Armenians** and Azeris over the contested region of **Nagorno-Karabakh**. In **Uzbekistan**, a pogrom of **Meskhetian Turks** forced their evacuation, further suggesting that the Kremlin's hold on power in the regions was disintegrating. In early 1990, **Moldova** saw the trends of ethnic strife and centrifugal nationalism combined, as the republic's titular majority embraced unification with neighboring Romania while its Russophone population opted to create their own republic within the USSR to avoid such a contingency.

Hoping to weaken the tempest, Gorbachev stripped more control from the CPSU and began to go directly to the Soviet people to gain backing for a deepening of his reform agenda. Commensurate with these developments, he assumed a new position: president of the Soviet Union. However, his greatest competition by this point was no longer with the Soviet gerontocracy, but with the former Communist **Boris Yeltsin**. Despite gaining new powers as president, Gorbachev continued to lose ground to the nationalists, including Yeltsin, now president of the **Russian Soviet Federative Socialist Republic**. The situation in the Baltics, particularly Lithuania, proved Gorbachev's undoing. Unable to reign in anti-Soviet forces in the republic, he used force against the nationalists, resulting in international opprobrium and a diminution of his authority within the USSR.

In an effort to freeze the trend toward independence while simultaneously recognizing the inevitability of the loss of the Baltics, Gorbachev moved toward revising the treaty of union that had bound the USSR together for decades. His goal of creating a genuinely voluntary union of socialist republics triggered the **August Coup** of 1991, led by Soviet hard-liners who feared the ultimate **dissolution of the Soviet Union**. Gorbachev, vacationing at his **dacha** in **Crimea**, was held hostage during the crisis. Out of sight, he was quickly upstaged by Yeltsin, who turned the situation to his advantage and rallied the masses against the plotters. Ironically, the attempted coup produced exactly what it intended to avoid, the breakup of the USSR.

During the autumn of 1991, Gorbachev saw his influence marginalized at the expense of republican heads in Russia, **Belarus**, Ukraine, and the non-Slavic republics. In December, the **Belavezha Accords**—agreed to without Gorbachev's participation—signed the death warrant for the USSR. Gorbachev, recognizing the end of his tenure, resigned as general secretary on 24 December 1991. The following day, the Soviet Union passed out of existence, giving birth to a dozen new states (the Baltic States had gained their independence earlier that year). Boris Yeltsin, now the uncontested leader of Russia, occupied Gorbachev's offices shortly thereafter. In postindependence Russia, Gorbachev has maintained a high profile, though his popularity among average Russians remains low (as opposed to the sustained favor he enjoys in the West).

He proved a vociferous critic of the Yeltsin administration and a strong supporter of Russia's adoption of a social democratic model of government; he ran in the **1996 presidential elections** but garnered little popular support. He dedicates much of his time to the Gorbachev Foundation, established in 1992, and support of **environmentalism**. Gorbachev remained rather muted on Russia's domestic affairs under **Vladimir Putin**, though he did criticize the **electoral reforms of 2004–2005**. Conversely, he has been a vocal critic of U.S. foreign policy under **George W. Bush**, and even made his presence felt in local politics in America after the disaster precipitated by Hurricane Katrina in 2007. Shortly after the ascension of **Dmitry Medvyedev**, Gorbachev initiated a bid to return to Russian politics, hoping to field a major **political party** by 2010.

GRACHEV, PAVEL SERGEYEVICH (1948–). Military leader. Born in the **Tula Oblast**, Pavel Grachev served in **Lithuania** before coming to prominence as a commander in the **Soviet-Afghan War**. In 1991, he was appointed first deputy minister of defense during the **dissolution of the Soviet Union**. Owing to a close personal relationship with **Boris Yeltsin**, Grachev was ultimately appointed minister of defense in the new Russian Federation. He optimistically predicted a quick defeat of the **Chechen separatists** and was instrumental in Yeltsin's decision to use force against the self-declared **Chechen Republic of Ichkeriya** in 1994. He proved to be an incompetent commander during the first **Chechen War** and was sacked in 1996. He subsequently assumed the role of military advisor to Russia's **arms export** monopoly Rosoboronexport. His name was linked to multiple **corruption** scandals throughout the 1990s. *See also* MILITARY.

GREAT BRITAIN (RELATIONS WITH). Anglo-Russian relations date to the mid-16th century; however, the relationship has been more often characterized by rivalry and suspicion than by cooperation. From the Crimean War (1853–1856) until the Anglo-Russian Convention of 1907, the two empires were locked in a global competition across the Eurasian supercontinent. British troops invaded Russia during the civil war; however, after the Bolsheviks consolidated power, a modus operandi was established with Moscow, with the two states joining forces against Nazism in 1941.

With the advent of the **Cold War**, the Union of Soviet Socialist Republics (USSR) and Great Britain returned to an adversarial footing, dramatically initiated by Prime Minister Winston Churchill's condemnation of the Soviet "iron curtain" across Eastern Europe. After pursuing a stridently anti-**Communist** foreign policy in the early years of her premiership, Margaret Thatcher's government moved quickly to establish close ties to the USSR under **Mikhail Gorbachev**, even declaring the Cold War to be over in 1988. After independence, **Boris Yeltsin** pursued an **Atlanticist** policy that cultivated extremely close relations with Great Britain. In 1994, Queen Elizabeth visited Russia, the first royal visit by an English monarch since the execution of Nicholas II in 1918. While Yeltsin's relationship with British Prime Minister John Major did not reflect the camaraderie he shared with U.S. President **Bill Clinton** and German Chancellor Helmut Kohl, relations were generally friendly until 1996 when the first of many post–Cold War **espionage** cases came to light.

With the Labour Party victory in 1997, the relationship remained stable. The new prime minister, Tony Blair, primarily focused on economic issues between the two countries during the waning years of Yeltsin's presidency. Currently, Russo-British **foreign trade** turnover is in excess of $20 billion per year, with Britain ranking as a leader in **foreign investment** in the Russian Federation. British **oil** companies, such as BP and Royal Dutch Shell, have been particularly active in the Russian sector, as well as developing pipelines in Russia's **near abroad**. During the 1990s, London emerged as a principal site for investment (particularly English football clubs) and for capital flight by Russia's **oligarchs**.

Blair was an early international ally of **Vladimir Putin**, and the two leaders developed a vibrant relationship during Putin's first term, despite disagreements over **Chechnya**. Putin was even rewarded with a state visit to Albion, a perquisite denied both to his predecessor and all Soviet premiers. However, as Putin solidified his control on power and the schism over the **United States**–led war on Iraq rocked European relations, Britain and Russia began to drift apart. In 2003, London irked Moscow by refusing to extradite the oligarch **Boris Berezovsky** and the **Chechen** leader Akhmed Zakayev.

In 2006, a number of disputes boiled over, including accusations of British use of high-tech spying devices, London's financing of "antigovernment" organizations in the Russian Federation, and—most dramatically—the plutonium-related death of former KGB agent **Aleksandr Litvinenko** on British soil. British attempts to investigate the Litvinenko case were stymied by Russia, leading to a war of words between London and Moscow and mutual expulsion of diplomats in 2007. On 4 July 2007, Russia's out-of-hand refusal to extradite **Andrey Lugovoy**, Litvinenko's suspected murderer, drove relations to post-Soviet lows. In 2008, the Kremlin ordered offices of the British Council—an **educational** and cultural organization funded by the Biritish government—shuttered for tax violations while its officers were detained and interviewed by Russian **security service** personnel. Rows over visas for British executives working in Russia also worsened the feud.

Under Gordon Brown, Blair's successor, an even tougher line has been taken with the new president, **Dmitry Medvyedev**. In 2008, Foreign Secretary David Miliband, already unpopular among Russia's elite, signaled Britain's unqualified support for the **Georgian** people in the 2008 **South Ossetian War**, further exacerbating tensions. *See also* EUROPEAN UNION; FOREIGN RELATIONS.

GREENS. *See* RUSSIAN ECOLOGICAL PARTY.

GROUND FORCES. *See* ARMY.

GROUP OF EIGHT/G8. Originally the Group of Seven, or G7, the forum brings together the most economically important nations of the Northern Hemisphere: **Canada**, **France**, **Germany**, Italy, **Japan**, Russia, **Great Britain**, and the **United States**. Each year, the group holds a presidential summit in addition to regular meetings of the countries' finance ministers. Catalyzed by the 1973 **oil** embargo on Western countries supportive of **Israel**, the G7 formed to discuss financial policy. Over time, the issues covered were expanded to include **health care**, law enforcement, energy, **terrorism**, trade, and the environment. The association is informal in nature, and agreements are nonbinding. After three years of close collaboration with **Boris Yeltsin**'s government, the G7 formally admitted the Russian Federation in 1997 at the behest of British Prime Minister Tony Blair and U.S. President **Bill Clinton**. In recent years, the group has been moving toward a more inclusive model, recognizing the importance of countries such as **China**, **India**, South Africa, and Brazil. *See also* BRIC.

GRYZLOV, BORIS VYACHESLAVOVICH (1950–). Politician. Born in Vladivostok and raised in **Vladimir Putin**'s hometown of **St. Petersburg**, Boris Gryzlov entered public life in 1998 after a career in radio communications. He allied himself with **Viktor Zubkov** and joined the pro-Kremlin **Unity** party; he was subsequently elected to the **State Duma**. Two years later, he was appointed minister of the interior and tasked with the fight against **corruption** and **terrorism**. He particularly targeted those he deemed "werewolves in epaulets," that is, corrupt police officials affiliated with the country's **mafia**. After 2003, he returned to the legislature, assuming leadership of **United Russia**, and became chairman of the State Duma. He steadfastly supported Putin's initiatives as president, and as prime minister of the Russian Federation. *See also* POLITICS.

GUAM ORGANIZATION FOR DEMOCRACY AND ECONOMIC DEVELOPMENT. Intergovernmental organization. A regional organization comprised of **Georgia**, **Ukraine**, **Azerbaijan**, and **Moldova**, the GUAM Organization for Democracy and Economic Development takes its name from an acronym of its members. The group's charter was signed on 7 June 2001 in Yalta in **Crimea**. The organization originally included **Uzbekistan**, which at that time was positively oriented toward the **United States** and fearful of the Russian influence in the **near abroad** (Uzbekistan pulled out in 2005, following a bloody crackdown on protesters in Andijan). The goals of the organization include **democracy** promotion, developing common strategies for economic development, and enhancing regional security. Viewed as a counterbalance to Russia's dominance of the **Commonwealth of Independent States** and its affiliated agencies, GUAM enjoyed the support of Washington and the **European Union**. In its short history, GUAM has sought to improve energy cooperation, develop a joint **peacekeeping** force, and address the frozen conflicts in **Transnistria**, **Nagorno-Karabakh**, **Abkhazia**, and **South Ossetia**; however, little of substance has materialized. *See also* COMMUNITY OF DEMOCRATIC CHOICE.

GULAG. The term "gulag" refers to the government agency that administered the system of penal labor camps in the Union of Soviet Socialist Republics (USSR). The word is an acronym for "Chief Administration of Corrective Labor Camps and Colonies" (*Glavnoie upravlenie ispravitel' no-trudovukh lagerei*), a division of the NKVD, the predecessor of the **KGB**. Eventually, the term came to denote the entire Soviet penal labor system, which housed criminals of all types; however, the term gulag is predominantly used to describe Soviet political prisoners and to define the system of political repression in the USSR.

As a centrally administered unit and part of the Soviet secret police, the gulag system was established in the 1930s. Under **Joseph Stalin**, the gulag system expanded exponentially, absorbing individuals sentenced for corrective labor because of suspected counter-revolutionary activity, which could vary from taking membership in oppositional organizations to telling a joke about the regime. The growth of the camp system coincided with Stalin's great purges in the 1930s. The government quickly realized the economic potential of the gulags: the Soviet industrialization campaign required enormous labor and capital investments and the state sought them through building a system of slave labor. Therefore, gulag prisoners were used at the construction of many industrial developments in the Soviet Union, including hydroelectric stations in Siberia and the Moscow–White Sea canal. After Stalin's death in 1953, gulag laborers were freed, and many victims of the Soviet penal system were eventually rehabilitated after **Nikita Khrushchev**'s secret speech of 1956 denouncing Stalin and Stalinism.

In the West, the term "gulag" became known after the publication of *The Gulag Archipelago* by **Aleksandr Solzhenitsyn** in 1973, in which the author exposed the evildoing of the Soviet state. This work, as well as his earlier short novel *One Day in the Life of Ivan Denisovich* (1962), are based on the author's extensive research as well as his personal experience of spending eight years as an inmate of a Siberian prison camp.

At the height of the gulag system, there were about 500 camps; the majority of them were located in Russia's **Far North**. As with tsarist-era penal colonies, Soviet gulags were a method of colonization of sparsely populated northern areas of the USSR. As regards the number of people who served their sentence in the gulags, statistics vary from 14 million to 40 million. The official data presented by the Soviet authorities indicate that over a million people died in camps between 1934 and 1953. Independent analysts, however, estimate that the number of victims was at least 10 times higher than the official data.

Living and working conditions in gulags were unbearable; many laborers had meager food rations, inadequate clothing, insufficient (and sometimes nonexistent) **health care**, and primitive hygiene and housing. Prisoners were compelled to engage in harsh physical labor, sometimes working in temperatures well below freezing. A complex system of **surveillance** was implemented by Stalin's regime. The prisoners were completely disconnected from the outer world; very often, they would not be able to communicate with their families for years. Often, political prisoners fell victim to assaults by ordinary criminals who normally shared the same facilities. These factors account for an extremely high death rate among prisoners.

Gulags had an enormous influence on Russian culture, stretching from creating a new system of political and philosophical thought, as exemplified in the work of Solzhenitsyn, to providing the **Russian language** with new words and importing new practices into mainstream culture. A number of works of **visual art** and **literature** have been produced that commemorate the victims of political oppression and the gulag system. The Russian public are still divided in their attitudes toward the role of gulags, and particularly the role of Stalin and political repression. While there are local museums of gulags (one in **Moscow** opened in 2004), there is no national museum dedicated to the history of the political penal system and repression. This cultural gap signifies that the process of de-Stalinization in Russia is not complete and the society has not reconciled with its own past. A number of organizations continue looking for more evidence of the atrocities of the Stalinist regimes, with the group Memorial being the most prominent.

GUSINSKY, VLADIMIR ALEKSANDROVICH (1952–). One of the richest men in the world, Gusinsky is a former Russian media tycoon. In the 1990s, his media conglomerate Media-MOST included the **NTV television** channel, radio, the **newspaper** *Segodnia* (Today), and magazines known both for their high professional standards and for the critical stance they sometimes adopted toward the Kremlin. In 2001, Gusinsky lost control of his media empire at the end of what was often depicted as a Kremlin-inspired campaign to destroy him. He holds dual **Israeli** and Spanish citizenship and resides in Spain.

Gusinsky was born into a hardscrabble **Jewish** family in Moscow. He first studied at the Gubkin Institute of Petrochemicals and Natural Gas but never completed his coursework; after service in the **Russian army**, he finished at a theater school in Moscow and began his career as a theater actor and director in the regional capital of Tula. In the late 1980s, he entered the emerging private sector, first running a women's clothing business, then specializing in facilitating joint ventures between Soviet and American firms. Unlike many other **oligarchs**, he created his wealth without acquiring former state-controlled enterprises. In 1989, he established the MOST Bank, which handled accounts of the Moscow city government. Over time, he developed a close relationship with Moscow's mayor, **Yury Luzhkov**. A strong supporter of Luzhkov's presidential ambitions, Gusinsky was suspected of laundering money for the mayor; Luzhkov helped Gusinsky gain control of the television station Channel 4, which he used to criticize **Boris Yeltsin**'s actions in **Chechnya**. Fearing a return to **Communist** control of Russia, Gusinsky backed Yeltsin in the **1996 presidential elections** and was awarded control of NTV for his help managing the flagging image of the president.

After the **financial crisis of 1998**, Gusinsky borrowed money from **Gazprom** to keep his media empire afloat. He also resumed his previous anti-Yeltsin attacks. Gusinsky ill-advisedly took a critical stance against Yeltsin's successor, **Vladimir Putin**, ridiculing the new president on the satirical puppet show *Kukly* and criticizing the handling of the *Kursk* **submarine disaster**. In 2000, Gazprom began demanding repayment of its loans just as Gusinsky faced fraud charges. After spending three days in jail, Gusinsky signed a deal that kept him out of prison, which stipulated that he agreed to relinquish control of his media empire to Gazprom. The events surrounding Gusinsky's loss of his media holdings coincided with Putin's campaign against the Russian oligarchs. In the wake of the crisis, NTV was put under new management, while *Segodnia* was shuttered.

Gusinsky ultimately fled to Spain, where he was granted citizenship. Russia issued an international arrest warrant for Gusinsky; however, after being arrested in the luxury resort of Sotogrande, Spanish authorities released the billionaire, stating he was the victim of "political purges." He was similarly released after an arrest in Greece in 2003; **United States** diplomats reportedly intervened with Athens on his behalf. Gusinsky ultimately took up residence in Tel Aviv. In 1996, he was elected president of the Russian Jewish Congress. Today, Gusinsky runs RTVi, a satellite television station targeted at the **Russian diaspora** in the **Commonwealth of Independent States**, Israel, North America, and Europe.

GYPSIES. *See* ROMA.

– H –

HAKAMADA, IRINA MUTSUOVNA (1955–). Politician. The daughter of a prominent member of **Japan**'s Communist Party who fled his country in 1938, Irina Hakamada served in the **State Duma** from 1993 to 2003. She became known for moderate opposition to the Kremlin under the **Putin** administration, particularly for her criticism of the excessive use of force in **counterterrorism** operations. She ran against Putin in the 2004 presidential election on the **Union of Right Forces** ticket, garnering 4 percent of the vote. She subsequently founded the Our Choice **political party**, which later merged with the People's Democratic Union; she is also a member of **The Other Russia** coalition. *See also* POLITICS; WOMEN.

HEALTH CARE. Since 1991, the health care system in the Russian Federation has been in transition from a hierarchal, centrally controlled system of medical provision, wholly financed from Soviet government revenues, to a more decentralized, diverse, and insurance-based system. It has also been a shift away from a two-tier Soviet medical system, which had separate health care services for ordinary citizens and the *nomenklatura*, to a more market-based system that, on the one hand, provides free medical care and, on the other, does not prevent citizens from purchasing health care services from private medical establishments. The process of transformation began in the early 1990s but was abandoned under **Boris Yeltsin** due to the lack of funds and Yeltsin's disinterest in the nation's health problems, which partially accounts for the demographic problems Russia is facing today. Health care policies were reintroduced under **Vladimir Putin**; however, the process of transition has not been completed.

Russian health care suffered most in the transitional period of the 1990s with crumbling hospital infrastructure, lack of vital medicines, and poor-quality service. In the 1990s, it was not uncommon for Russian citizens scheduled to have surgery to purchase and bring the medical supplies on the day of the procedure. The social status of doctors was undermined as many of them were accused of **corruption**. Health care also became an arena for profiteering for entrepreneurs who managed to capitalize on the disintegration of the Soviet distribution system. Many talented medical students abandoned their careers and instead set up medical cooperatives.

The largely dysfunctional health care system accounts for many health-related **demographic challenges**, including a high mortality rate. These are caused by a number of factors, including **alcoholism**, malnutrition, and high levels of stress. Economic growth under Putin had little impact on the main indicators of human welfare; however, there are signs of improvement both in terms of the quality of medical care and life expectancy among average Russian citizens. Still, the number of deaths caused by malnutrition and infectious diseases, linked to poverty-related problems, remains very high. At the same time, the average life expectancy remains quite low for a country of Russia's level of economic and social development.

The Soviet health care system was an extension of the Stalinist industrialization project, favoring large centralized medical institutions, normally established in areas with high concentrations of Soviet factory workers. There was little emphasis on primary care, and quite often people were admitted to specialist and hospital care, putting unnecessary strain on the system. In post-Soviet Russia, general practioners have replaced *terapevts* (physicians), doctors with similar qualifications and focus on primary care; the name change, however, did not have any structural impact. Low prestige and poor payments of doctors and health workers encourage many doctors to join private hospitals and medical centers. Many health services are available only in private hospitals, resulting in the de facto **privatization** of health care. Russian health care carries the social burdens of the Soviet system, whereby access to certain medical services was available only to *nomenklatura* or required an informal payment for what is meant to be a free service. There also remains a huge divide between urban centers and **rural** areas: while people residing in provinces by law have access to large medical centers in urban centers, the sheer remoteness of many settlements prevents patients from accessing medical institutions. Access to private health care, especially to health care abroad (**Germany**, the **United States**, and **Israel** are popular destinations), has become an issue of social prestige, further undermining the principles of social equality and the very reputation of Russia's health care system. Therefore, access to the health care system in Russia is becoming significantly more unequal, irrespective of the free provisions guaranteed by the **constitution**.

To combat corruption and increase the quality of health care, the Russian government introduced the unified social tax in 2001, which is now the main source of financing health care. In principle, patients have the right to choose their insurer and medical service provider; however, in practice it is hard for them to exercise their right because of the complex bureaucratic system. As a result there is no real competition, and hospital and medical care providers are left with conflicting incentives. *See also* HIV/AIDS.

HERMITAGE. The State Hermitage is a museum of **visual art** and culture located in **St. Petersburg**. It is one of the largest and oldest museums in the world (it was founded in 1764 by Catherine the Great) and has been open to the public since 1852. The museum's collections comprise over 3 million items, including the largest collection of paintings in the world; however, like other museums, only a small collection of items is on permanent display.

The Hermitage displays Egyptian and Classical antiquities, prehistoric art, and Western and Oriental art up to the 20th century. The museum does not specialize in Russian art or contemporary art. The museum occupies a number of historic buildings in St. Petersburg, with the Winter Palace at the heart of the museum complex; it also operates a number of exhibition centers abroad. These include Somerset House in London, the Hermitage Center in Amsterdam, and the Guggenheim Hermitage Museum in Las Vegas. Mikhail Piotrovsky has been the director of the museum since 1991; he replaced his father, Boris Piotrovsky, who was the director of the Hermitage from 1964 until 1990.

In the 1990s, the museum was at the center of several restitution scandals. It emerged that the museum possessed a number of important works of art that were stolen from German private collections during World War II. In 2006, the museum came under scrutiny after it announced that over 200 items, valued at over 150 million **rubles**, had been stolen from its store. Though most of these items have been recovered, the reputation of the museum and its administration was severely tarnished. The Hermitage was central to the celebrations of the 300th anniversary of St. Petersburg in 2003. The museum featured as a setting and also as a character in Aleksandr Sokurov's film *Russian Ark* (2003): the director portrayed the Hermitage as a vessel that carries Russian cultural tradition throughout centuries and changes of the political regime.

HIV/AIDS. The Russian Federation has had an ongoing HIV/AIDS crisis since the **dissolution of the Soviet Union**. At times, the situation was described as epidemic, attracting the attention of global media, health, and financial institutions, including a **United Nations** conference on HIV/AIDS in **Moscow** in 2000. The majority of victims are **drug users** who become infected by sharing needles; these cases are followed by a second wave of infections spread by sexual contact. Some statistics show that there are about 40,000 new cases of infection every year. Particularly disturbing are figures showing the number of children infected with HIV.

In the 1990s, the **Yeltsin** government tended to ignore the problem of the pandemic, causing mass speculation and **media** frenzy, and leaving the problem for foreign agencies and foundations to tackle. In 2006, **Vladimir Putin**'s government for the first time allocated a significant allowance in its budget for HIV prevention schemes. Despite the increased spending and widening coverage of HIV prevention programs among populations who are at higher risk, the number of new cases has not declined. This is largely because people with HIV/AIDS are stigmatized in Russian society. The majority of the population—and especially religious people—views HIV/AIDS as proof of moral degradation, thus ignoring the reality of how the infection spreads. As a result, people take few precautions, which explains why the number of infected people has surged. The philistine attitude to sexual education results in many young people having unprotected sex.

With a few exceptions, popular culture and the mainstream media provide no explanation of the dangers of unprotected sex targeted to young people. Therefore, there is a contradiction between the official representation of the problem and its popular perception. At the same time, a number of documentary and feature **films** have been produced that truthfully represent the dangers of HIV/AIDS infection.

The HIV/AIDS crisis remains one of Russia's greatest **demographic challenges** and is a major impediment to the country's **economic**, social, and cultural development. The epidemic is also indicative of Russia's ailing **health care** system.

HOLIDAYS. Russian holidays present a mixture of Soviet-era celebrations, traditional **religious** holidays, and a host of new official and unofficial celebrations. National Unity Day (4 November) replaced the Soviet October Revolution Day (7 November) in 2005. Symbolically, this new holiday avoids direct reference to the Soviet past, at the same time providing an opportunity for national reconciliation. However, it is grounded in imperial legacy and in contemporary Russian nationalism. In 1612, Russian forces led by Kuzma Minin and Mikhail Pozharsky freed Moscow from the control of the Polish-Lithuanian Commonwealth. The holiday was celebrated in the Russian Empire until the Bolshevik Revolution of 1917. Therefore, the new post-Soviet holiday reaffirms Russian imperial aspirations and signifies Russia's troubled relations with new members of the **European Union** (EU). The holiday also legitimizes the dominance of the **Russian Orthodox Church** since the public holiday coincides with one of the main religious celebrations.

The new post-Soviet government institutionalized Russian Orthodox Christmas (7 January) as a national holiday. **Vladimir Putin**'s administration extended the winter celebrations from New Year's Day (1 January) until Christmas Day, providing the nation with almost a week of festivities. Promoted by the Soviets as an agnostic alternative to Christmas, New Year became Russia's most important and popular holiday and is celebrated by the whole nation irrespective of religious, social, or **political** denomination. Russia does not officially recognize **Jewish** or **Muslim** holidays as national holidays, nor does it prevent citizens from making alternative arrangements.

Most recently, Russian presidents Putin and **Dmitry Medvyedev** began publicly attending church services at Easter, thus signaling the political primacy of **Orthodox Christianity** in the Russian Federation.

Russia's most obscure holiday is Russia's Day (12 June), introduced by **Boris Yeltsin** as Russia's Independence Day in 1992 and renamed by Putin in 2002. Designed to copy the **United States'** Independence Day, the holiday lacked any historical resonance and was greeted without enthusiasm among Russian citizens. The government has found it difficult to promote this new holiday especially since its function is now replicated by National Unity Day and Constitution Day (12 December).

Three public holidays continue the Soviet tradition: the Day of the Defenders of the Motherland (23 February), International **Women**'s Day (8 March), and the Spring and Labor Day (1–2 May). The first was introduced in 1922 as Red Army Day. The other two have a common history with European and American holidays, celebrating the women's movement and worker solidarity, respectively. Postindependence, these holidays were stripped of their ideological content and rebranded for more popular appeal. The Day of the Defenders of the Motherland and International Women's Day are commonly referred to in Russia as "Men's Day" and "Women's Day," and thus serve primarily as a celebration of paternity and maternity, making them Russian equivalents of Father's Day and Mother's Day. The **gender**-biased foundations of these holidays are subject to permanent cultural debates, especially in a country that has a very confused attitude toward women's rights. Labor Day (1 May), a major holiday in the Union of Soviet Socialist Republics (USSR), once involved mass gatherings of workers in urban centers. In present-day Russia, **political parties** and associations use the occasion to demonstrate their strength in public. They, however, do not get much of an audience as the majority of the population celebrates the start of spring at their **dachas**.

The holiday that has survived post-Soviet cultural metamorphosis with little revision is Victory Day (9 May). This is indeed a sacred day for most of the Russian population, and remains a holiday that has escaped any political, social, or cultural controversy since 1991 (at least within the Russian Federation). The holiday serves many purposes: it is a day of national mourning and unity, a celebration of common European history, and a manifestation of endurance, love, and patriotism. On the international stage, however, Putin's glorification of the Red Army's performance in World War II has created controversy, particularly in the **Baltic States**.

Nostalgia has helped to retain some unofficial holidays that go back to the Soviet era or even pre-Christian times, namely, Maslenitsa ("Butter Week"), Ivan Kupala Day, Cosmonaut Day, and others. The First of September, also known as the Day of Knowledge and **Education**, is the official start of the academic year in all Russian schools and universities; unofficially, it symbolizes the end of summer and rites of passage. The celebrations of the day were tarnished after the **Beslan** school hostage crisis of 2004. Cosmonaut Day (12 April) marks the first space flight made by Yury Gagarin in 1961, and the day is a celebration of the Russian **space program**, as well as of science and masculinity. Maslenitsa and Ivan Kupala Day pay tribute to Russian pagan heritage, celebrating the cult of the sun and fertility (later adopted into **Christianity** as the Feast of St. John the Baptist).

Some Western holidays and celebrations have been appropriated into Russian culture, most prominently St. Valentine's Day (14 February) and Halloween (31 October). This type of holiday is celebrated predominantly by young people and involves Western-type consumerist practices. Halloween, however, has been criticized by the Orthodox Church as a manifestation of Satanism, creating some controversy.

HOMOSEXUALITY. The legal ban on homosexuality was repealed in the Russian Federation in 1993, and homosexuality was removed from the official list of mental disorders in 1999. Since then, Russia has seen an emergence of lesbian, gay, bisexual, and transgender (LGBT) communities, as well as the emergence of gay culture in urban centers.

In the early Soviet Union, homosexuality was viewed as a sign of bourgeois decadent culture and was roundly condemned. Under **Joseph Stalin**, homosexuality was also used as a pretext for legal and political oppression. Homosexuals who had hopes to join the **Communist Party**, the bureaucracy, or the **army** were forced to hide their sexual orientation and commit to heterosexual marriages.

Furthermore, those who remained single into middle age would raise suspicion among authorities as they would not conform to the official views on family life. This reflects the Stalinist project of nation building and the state's emphasis on reproductive sexuality as a means to attain political world dominance through a growing workforce. Homosexuals were often imprisoned under Article 121 of the Soviet legal code, and sent to **gulags** where they were routinely abused by inmates. This resulted in further stigmatization of homosexuality in the Union of Soviet Socialist Republics (USSR), as it became associated with the criminal world. In the late Soviet Union, homosexuality was primarily used as an excuse for ideological prosecution of **dissidents**; for example, in 1973 the world-famous **film** director Sergey Paradjanov was charged with homosexual activities and sentenced to five years of imprisonment.

The post-Soviet period is characterized by legal confusion, the increased visibility of gay culture, and the paradoxical combination of Russian mainstream society's acute homophobia and intense interest in LGBT lifestyles and alternative **gender** identities. While same-sex marriages or partnerships are not recognized by the state, there are no legal restrictions preventing single individuals, irrespective of their sexual orientation, from adopting children. Gay people can serve in the army; however, they are discouraged from displaying their sexual orientation in public.

Homosexual relationships are often stigmatized because of Soviet-era criminal connotations. At the same time, contemporary Russian culture, and especially **television** series, feature a number of high-profile LGBT individuals and present programs and films that display qualities and values of gay culture (though it is quite plausible many members of the audience interpret this type of content—for example, affectionate bonds between people of the same sex and cross-dressing—as merely eccentric). Unfortunately, these presentations do not deal with such important psychological and social issues as "coming out," **HIV/AIDS**, or adoption; rather, they promulgate a stereotype of flamboyant gay individuals who typically distance themselves from social and political concerns. Such flaws in mediated representation partially account for the failure to build the LGBT phenomenon as a political concern.

The struggle for equality and full legal rights continues in the cultural, rather than political, domain, possibly because the government is increasingly resistant to any form of political opposition. The mayor of **Moscow**, **Yury Luzhkov**, has consistently banned gay pride events, referring to such demonstrations as "satanic." When collective action is attempted, the police quickly disrupt the protests, sometimes violently, and arrest the participants; however, no legal actions follow. It is not yet clear whether Luzhkov is solely driven by antigay sentiment or whether his actions affirm the course of disallowing any form of political activism in Russia's capital. Nevertheless, the real criticism and danger to the LGBT community comes from ultranationalist and **neofascist** organizations, as well as ultrareligious groups, including **Christian** and **Muslim** organizations.

On **Runet**, however, LGBT citizens are free to exercise their opinions and demand political rights, as well as articulate their sexual orientation and lifestyle preferences. The Russian portal www.gay .ru is a platform for all Russian-speaking LGBT people in Russia, the **near abroad**, **Israel**, **Germany**, and the **United States**. It provides information on the history of the LGBT movement in Russia and abroad, LGBT regional communities, health concerns, and other related issues, including coverage of gay icons such as the Soviet-era singer Alla Pugacheva, the Russian-Ukrainian drag performer Andriy Danylko (also known as Verka Serduchka), and the author and photographer Yaroslav Mogutin.

HUMAN RIGHTS. While Russia is a signatory to many international conventions on human rights (including the Universal Declaration of Human Rights and the European Convention of Human Rights), the country is viewed in certain quarters of the West as a regular violator of individual and minority rights, as well as weak on freedom of the press. Moscow defends its record on the basis of the country's transition to **democracy** from totalitarianism and its unique **political**, social, and **religious** conditions. Indeed, the human rights situation in Russia varies widely across its vast territory, various social classes, numerous professional affiliations, and diverse cultural communities. The Kremlin often fires back at its European critics, citing evidence of abuses of the rights of **ethnic Russians** in **Estonia** and **Latvia**

(where they have been stripped of citizenship and pushed out of most public sector jobs) and decrying the hypocrisy of the international human rights monitoring system.

The fallout of the two **Chechen Wars** has had a particularly negative effect on the country's reputation. Extrajudicial killings, torture, rape, and attacks on civilian targets in the **North Caucasus** have resulted in a huge number of cases going before the European Court of Human Rights; in fact, nearly a quarter of all cases originate in the Russian Federation. The **military** culture of *dedovshchina* (i.e., violent and often deadly hazing), the low quality of care given to Russian orphans, and widespread trafficking in **women** for the **sex** trade are also major issues on the individual level.

In terms of minority rights, a number of religious groups complain of repression by federal and local authorities; this is particularly true for those religious sects that are not considered "native" faiths (**Orthodoxy**, **Islam**, **Judaism**, and **Buddhism**). Over the past decade, there has been a marked rise in attacks on **ethnic minorities**, **immigrants**, and **Jews** by **neofascist** youths. While it is improving, Russia's record on **homosexual** rights remains well below European standards.

In terms of press freedom, Russia's international ranking has plummeted under **Vladimir Putin**. Nationalization of most **television** stations, the use of selective prosecution for slander, libel, and **tax** evasion, a series of unsolved murders of prominent **journalists** (including **Paul Klebnikov** and **Anna Politkovskaya**), and new restrictions on covering **terrorist** attacks have all contributed to this situation.

Recognizing the overall problem, President **Dmitry Medvyedev** commented on his country's human rights record in September 2009, stating it was "far from perfect." His plans for improving the situation involve a larger reform of the Russian **judicial system**.

– I –

IBN AL-KHATTAB/SAMIR SALEH ABDULLAH AL-SU-WAILEM (1969–2002). Guerilla leader and terrorist. Born on the Jordan–Saudi Arabia border to an Arab father and **Circassian**

mother, he left the **Middle East** to fight on the side of the mujahideen resistance in the **Soviet-Afghan War**. He is then thought to have participated on the Azeri side in the **Nagorno-Karabakh** conflict, before joining the **Islamists** in the **Tajik Civil War**. He also claimed to have fought in Bosnia in defense of the Muslim population against **Serbia**. During the first **Chechen War**, he engaged in propaganda, fund-raising, and guerilla fighting against Russian troops. During the conflict, he became a friend of the **Chechen** commander **Shamil Basayev**. After the war, he established himself as the leader of a battalion of Arabs and other foreign **Muslim** fighters. He also came to the attention of Interpol and other international agencies as a supporter and perpetrator of acts of **terrorism**. In 1999, al-Khattab and Basayev launched an incursion into **Dagestan**, which in conjunction with the **apartment bombings** thought to be the work of al-Khattab, triggered the second Chechen War. He was killed on 20 March 2002, reportedly by a poisoned letter given to him by an **FSB**-employed hit man. *See also* CHECHEN REPUBLIC OF ICHKERIYA; COUNTERTERRORISM.

ICHKERIYA. *See* CHECHEN REPUBLIC OF ICHKERIYA.

ILYUMZHINOV, KIRSAN NIKOLAYEVICH (1962–). President of the Republic of Kalmykiya. Born to returnees of the 1943 deportation of the **Kalmyks**, Ilyumzhinov grew up in Elista, **Kalmykiya**, under modest circumstances. At the age of 14, he became the republic's chess champion. He is also a former Kalmyk boxing champion. Before studying Japanese language and culture at the Moscow State Institute of International Relations (MGIMO), Ilyumzhinov worked as a mechanic in Elista and served in the **military**.

Quick to embrace late Soviet capitalism in 1989, he worked as a manager at the Soviet-Japanese company Liko-Radugab and founded the SUN Corporation in **Moscow**. During those years, he became one of Russia's new elite, managing dozens of companies and making millions in the free-market economy created by **Anatoly Chubais** and **Boris Yeltsin**'s economic advisors. Concurrently, his political star was rising. In 1990 he was elected as a deputy of the Russian parliament for Kalmykiya, becoming a member of the Union of Soviet Socialist Republics (USSR) Supreme Soviet in 1991. In 1993, he was elected president of Kalmykiya. He actively marketed his wealth in the presidential campaign, using the slogan "a wealthy president is a safeguard against **corruption**." He also promised $100 for every voter and a mobile phone for every shepherd (reflecting a populist attempt to glean support from the traditionalist sector of society).

Once in office, he moved quickly to consolidate his power by abolishing parliament and the existing constitution as Soviet vestiges. Both institutions, once restored, served Ilyumzhinov's interests. The Steppe Code, based on 17th-century Kalmyk practices, all but guaranteed him autocratic power in the region. He also instituted a seven-year term for the presidency. Ilyumzhinov consciously models his system of rule on the Chinese, Korean, and Singaporean "Asian model" of governance, which values stability and collective responsibility over individualism. He proudly proclaimed an "economic dictatorship" over Kalmykiya in order to turn the country into a "second Kuwait." He makes decisions on minutiae other regional governors would quickly delegate to subordinates or local assemblies.

His public statements have often veered to the eccentric. He claims to have been transported to a distant galaxy aboard a UFO in 1997, and claims to communicate telepathically with his own nation and other peoples of the Russian Federation. He is also a strong supporter of the pan-ethnic ideology of **Eurasianism**, viewing Kalmykiya as a central node in the "world spirit." Ilyumzhinov's autobiography was published in 1998, entitled *The President's Crown of Thorns*; chapter titles include "Without Me the People Are Incomplete," "I Become a Millionaire," and "It Only Takes Two Weeks to Have a Man Killed." Since becoming president, he has encouraged a mild cult of personality within the republic through tireless self-promotion and lavish expenditures on pet projects, particularly relating to the game of chess.

In 1995, Ilyumzhinov engineered his election as head of the Fédération Internationale des Échecs (FIDE), the governing body of world chess. For the 1998 Chess Olympiad, Ilyumzhinov built the $50 million Chess City on the outskirts of Elista. The avant-garde village hosts national and international chess events, as well as visiting dignitaries, including the Dalai Lama in 2004. Ilyumzhinov has made chess a mandatory subject for three years of primary schooling, resulting in a number of international champions in the sport. He has also funded a spree of religious buildings, including **Buddhist** temples, **Islamic** mosques, and even a church for the republic's solitary practicing Roman Catholic. Although few Kalmyks express open discontent with his soft authoritarian rule, Ilyumzhinov's popularity has waned in the republic. In his last election, he only commanded a plurality of votes.

His professional ties to those implicated in the 1998 murder of Kalmykiya's leading opposition **journalist**, Larisa Yudina, have sullied his reputation as a munificent despot.

IMMIGRATION. With the **dissolution of the Soviet Union**, Russia faced an entirely new environment in terms of immigration. While the country had seen the mass exodus of **Jews** during the late tsarist period and significant emigration associated with the 1917 Bolshevik Revolution and ensuing civil war (1918–1922), few Soviet citizens had the opportunity to leave the country during its seven decades of existence. Due to the totalitarian nature of its government, even fewer people sought to immigrate to the Union of Soviet Socialist Republics (USSR). Immigration from the country has been a desirable aspect of social mobility in the USSR and post-Soviet Russia.

Under **Mikhail Gorbachev**, political reform allowed for a trickle of emigrants, while the comparative benefits of life in the USSR versus their homelands attracted a modest number of immigrants from Vietnam, **Mongolia**, the **Middle East**, and Africa. After 1991, however, millions of Russians quit the country for economic opportunities abroad, particularly in the **United States**, **Germany**, Italy, Australia, and **Canada**, while many of the country's Jews left for **Israel**. Economic success proved difficult for most migrants, with cases of former doctors, engineers, and professors taking menial jobs in the West to make ends meet, while at the same time harming Russia through a debilitating "brain drain." Concurrently, many **ethnic Russians** living in the **near abroad** "returned" to Russia when faced with the prospect of living as second-class citizens in their new states of residence; many other people of "Soviet identity" also migrated to Russia during the 1990s as the result of internal strife in former Soviet republics, particularly **Tajikistan**, **Georgia**, **Moldova**, and **Azerbaijan**.

The Russian Federation became the second most popular destination for immigration by 2005 (behind the U.S.), commanding more than 12 million foreign-born residents; of these, more than 10 million are considered to be in the country illegally. However, most of these people were born in the Soviet Union and would have been considered "internal migrants" until 1992. Thus, unlike most other countries where the immigrant population lacks knowledge of the local language, the majority of these migrants possess **Russian language** skills. The largest sending countries from within post-Soviet space are the **Central Asian** republics of **Kazakhstan**, **Uzbekistan**, and Tajikistan, but large numbers of immigrants also come from the South **Caucasus** and Moldova. Outside of the **Commonwealth of Independent States**, **China** and **North Korea** are the most important countries of origin for immigrants.

While immigrants undoubtedly contribute to Russia's gross domestic product (some estimates suggest they account for more than 10 percent of GDP), most Russians exaggerate their number and influence in the country and see immigrants as a drain on the **economy**. **Ethnic violence** against foreigners has skyrocketed in the past decade, with increasingly gruesome attacks on people of Central/East Asian or **Caucasian** appearance, including non-Slav citizens of the Russian Federation. Resentment toward internal immigration is also high, as large numbers of Russian citizens have left their **ethnic republics** or **oblasts** in Asiatic Russia or the **North Caucasus** to live and work in **Moscow**, **St. Petersburg**, or other metropolitan areas. Despite social problems, the Russian government recognizes the current **demographic crisis** and the need for workers, both legal and illegal.

As large immigrant communities flock to Russian cities, new immigrants from Russia have formed substantial communities in such countries as the United States, Germany, **France**, and particularly **Great Britain**, resulting in the BBC referring to London as "Moscow on the Thames" in 2004. These new immigrants rarely give up their citizenship; rather they see themselves as global citizens, who migrate to areas that are economically and culturally favorable. Some of these residents are very affluent and wield significant influence in their country of residence's economic and political life (e.g., **Roman Abramovich** in England).

In recent years, a number of schemes have been implemented to attract expatriate Russians, including **Old Believer** families who have not been resident on Russian soil for decades. However, forcing these "returnees" to settle in **Siberia** and other inhospitable locations has doomed the program. More aggressive suggestions include inviting Indian, Vietnamese, and Latin American guest workers to the country to alleviate the need for **Chinese** and Koreans, both of whom have territorial claims on the **Russian Far East**, and **Muslims**, who are seen as diluting the **Orthodox Christian** character of the new Russia. *See also* NAGORNO-KARABAKH; TAJIK CIVIL WAR; TRANSNISTRIA.

INDIA (RELATIONS WITH). Upon gaining its independence from **Great Britain** in 1947, India became the largest member of the Non-Aligned Movement. However, American overtures to its enemy Pakistan during the early years of the **Cold War** drove the country into a strategic relationship with the Soviet Union. In 1971, the two countries signed the Indo-Soviet Treaty of Peace, Friendship, and Cooperation, paving the way for a fraternal social, economic, and diplomatic partnership that continued for two decades.

After the **dissolution of the Soviet Union**, India strove to improve its relations with the West, including the **United States**; however, its possession of **nuclear weapons** and status as a nonsignatory of the Nuclear Non-Proliferation Treaty hampered its relations with Washington during the administrations of **George H. W. Bush** and **Bill Clinton**. Due to these complications, Russia remained a key partner in developing India's nuclear energy program and an important supplier of the country's **military** technology (although India has expanded its diplomatic contacts, adding **Israel** to its list of arms suppliers). During the latter years of **Boris Yeltsin**'s presidency, **Yevgeny Primakov** attempted to create a Russia-**China**-India counterweight to American hegemony, but the simmering Sino-Indian rivalry and disputes over Kashmir prevented the realization of any such plans.

Vladimir Putin made several visits to India during his presidency, typically focusing on practical matters such as **foreign trade**, energy, **counterterrorism**, scientific and **space program** cooperation, and improving trans-**Eurasian transportation** links; reflecting his focus on commercial ties, he often traveled with high-level business delegations. On his first visit in 2000, he signed the Declaration on Strategic Partnership between India and the Russian Federation, reworking the long-standing bilateral relationship for the 21st century. Trade between the two countries is robust, amounting to $3 billion in 2007 and projected to triple by 2010. As a provider of energy, Moscow also features prominently in New Delhi's long-term economic growth; Indian companies have made important investments in **Siberian oil** exploration in recent years.

While Indian-American relations only improved in the wake of **September 11**, with **George W. Bush** pushing for a normalization of ties with India despite controversy over nuclear proliferation issues, Russo-Indian ties remained strong and diversified. In 2003, the two **navies** conducted joint exercises in the Indian Ocean. India, a country with its own secessionist and **democratization** issues, has never leveled criticism against Russian actions in **Chechnya** or Moscow's spotty record on **human rights** and freedom of the press. Reciprocally, Moscow—unlike Washington—is not constrained by the demands of maintaining a cordial relationship with Pakistan. In 2008, **Dmitry Medvyedev** met with Prime Minister Manmohan Singh at the first Brazil, Russia, India, and China (**BRIC**) summit in Hokkaido, Japan, and made plans for a visit to India later that year.

INDIGENOUS PEOPLES OF THE NORTH. Known in Russian as the *korennyie malochislennyie narody*, or indigenous small-numbering peoples, the various ethnic groups of Russia's **Far North** engage in a loose confederation based on their common interests, which include **environmentalism**, antidiscrimination, control of local resources, self-government, and preservation of their indigenous **languages**, cultures, lifestyles, and **religions**. The native peoples of northern Russia include the Aleut, Dolgan, Itelmen, Koryak, **Mansi**, Nanai, **Nenets**, Nganasan, Nivkh, Oroki, Orochi, Sami, Selkup, Tofalar, Udegey, Ulchi, Chuvan, **Chukchi**, **Evenks**, **Even**, Enets, Yupik (Asiatic Eskimos), Yukagir, and **Sakha** (Yakuts).

In total, they number about 560,000, with the Sakha being the largest group. In recent decades, the Vod, Kamasinets, Kerek, and Omok nations have become extinct. In an attempt to use the benefit from the development of an embryonic **civil society** in the late Union of Soviet Socialist Republics (USSR), the northern peoples formed the Russian Association of the Indigenous Peoples of the North (RAIPON) in 1990. Lacking an effective lobby due to their endemic poverty and small numbers, these nations have seen few if any benefits from the 2001 Law on Territories of Traditional Natural Resources Use of the Small Indigenous Nations of the Russian North, Siberia and the Far East, as their interests are often arrayed against those of giant corporations such as **ALROSA**, **Gazprom**, **Lukoil**, **Norilsk Nickel**, and **Transneft**. In recent years, they have coordinated with foreign minority rights groups, hoping to use the power of the **European Union** to aid their cause.

Life expectancy is extremely low among the peoples of the north, and **alcoholism**, suicide, and infant mortality are widespread. Due to geographic challenges, the northerners suffer from lower levels of **education** and access to **health care**, while **unemployment** is high when compared to Russian society at large.

INDUSTRY. Russia's industrial infrastructure is dominated by the country's **Stalinist** experiment in rapid industrialization. During the 1930s, the **Communist Party of the Soviet Union** (CPSU) transformed the Union of Soviet Socialist Republics (USSR) from a primarily agrarian society into an industrial powerhouse. The use of Five-Year Plans, slave labor, and a command-and-control **economy** shaped Soviet industry for decades. Western Russia commanded the lion's share of this development. During World War II, a sizable portion of the country's industrial base was relocated to the **Ural Mountains**, southern **Siberia**, and other locations to avoid the German occupation. Adherence to Marxist-Leninist ideology under **Nikita Khrushchev** and **Leonid Brezhnev** dictated that the USSR remain attached to capital-intensive heavy industry (steel, electricity generation, machinery, cement, chemicals, aerospace, **military** equipment, etc.) as the economies of the First World shifted toward light industry and consumer products (and, later, economies based on finance and information).

Hoping to institute "acceleration" (*uskoreniie*) in the Soviet **economy**, **Mikhail Gorbachev** restructured the economy and industry to compete with **Japan**, the **United States**, and West **Germany**.

However, structural factors made this transition extremely difficult, particularly given the dependence of the workforce on heavy industry and the military-industrial complex. **Boris Yeltsin**'s administration oversaw a dramatic transformation of post-Soviet industry. By opening the country up to economic **globalization**, he rendered many of the country's factories obsolete. During the 1990s, Russian industry experienced a massive contraction, with concomitant **unemployment**. This drop was particularly acute in the defense industry, with missiles, tanks, and aircraft manufacturing nearly grinding to a halt. Shipbuilding, rail equipment, and heavy equipment manufacturing also took a tumble.

During this period, state-owned enterprises were transferred to private control through the controversial **loans for shares program** and other schemes. While steel production shrank considerably, the industry survived, and Russia remains a major exporter of the product. Russia's natural resources such as hydrocarbons (particularly **oil** and **natural gas** extraction, refining, and transshipment), timber, fisheries, and minerals served to buoy the economy as it recovered from the 1998 **ruble crisis**. With Russia's vast deposits of coal, nickel, aluminum, gold, and other metals and ores, metallurgy and **mining** continue to be important components of the economy. **Arms exports** and precision instruments also began to recover in the 2000s. Russia's pharmaceutical industry also experienced a modest revival, though the industry continues to suffer from technological backwardness.

Owing to a well-educated and **Internet**-savvy workforce, Russia has also emerged as a player in the computer software and outsourcing industries since the mid-1990s. Production of consumer goods and services, **foodstuffs** and beverages, textiles, and scientific and communications equipment also increased. The consolidation of the industrial base in the 1990s and **foreign investment** has allowed Russia to experience a period of moderate growth in the current decade, though many outdated factories are still in operation. Russia's **foreign trade** remains robust, particularly given the strength of its oil and natural gas exports. One benefit of the reduction in industry has been a drop in carbon emissions and other **pollutants** from late Soviet levels; this allowed Russia to easily meet its commitments under the **Kyoto Protocol**, and even benefit from the "cap-and-trade" system of international environmental regulation. However, such perquisites will be short-lived when new regulations are negotiated. *See also* FISHING; INFORMATIZATION.

INFORMATIZATION/INFORMATIZATSIIA. The Russian word *informatizatsiia* literally means "making use of information"; however, the term is used to refer to the use of information technologies in governmental, political, social, and cultural institutions. In its broader sense, the term and its derivatives denote the study, design, development, implementation, and support of computer-based information systems, and in its common use it is synonymous with the term "information technology" (IT). However, in Russia, the term has a political connotation that goes back to the **perestroika** period. As part of the modernization agenda, **Mikhail Gorbachev** attempted to create an information industry in the Union of Soviet Socialist Republics (USSR). In principle, *informatizatsiia* was meant to propel the Soviet **economy** to the forefront of world development by introducing new information technologies that would enhance the performance of the industrial sector, as well as to improve management and accountability of enterprise. On another level, the **politics** of *informatizatsiia* acknowledged that the USSR was no longer fit to compete on the global level because its overreliance on heavy industry and extensive exploitation of resources characteristic of the Stalin era had left the country behind its peers in the West (including **Japan**).

As part of *informatizatsiia*, the Soviet Union began to develop its own computer systems, including both hardware and software sectors. However, they were hardly competitive, and did not serve the purpose of advancing the country's economic capacity. With the **dissolution of the Soviet Union** and the economic collapse of the 1990s, the task of improving the information infrastructure of Russia was handed over to private enterprises, namely, **banks** and financial companies, which invested heavily in IT. Foreign companies and nongovernmental organizations (NGOs), for example, the **Soros** Foundation, also played an important role in developing the new infrastructure by creating computer and **Internet** centers in large urban areas. The move to new computer systems was possible because of the availability of cheap hardware from **China** and because of the common practice of pirating software and other forms of intellectual property.

The latest push to create a new information industry came under **Vladimir Putin** when the federal and local governments developed their own information systems and funded the proliferation of information technologies in the **education** system, postal service, and cultural institutions. Since 2000, the shift in the use of information technologies has been remarkable. At the moment, points of access to the Internet may be found in even the remotest parts of the country. Today, citizens of the Russian Federation are increasingly accustomed to using information technologies in their daily practices, including online commerce, banking, and personal communication. *See also* RUNET.

INGUSH. Ethnic group. With a population of some 400,000, the Ingush or Ghalghay are the smaller of the two Vainakh peoples of the **North Caucasus** (the **Chechens** being the larger). Their **language**, Ingush or Ghalghay, is a member of the Nakh subgroup of the Northeast Caucasian language family. They are an indigenous mountain people whose relations with the Turkic and Indo-European "foothill" peoples of the Caucasus have been checkered. However, unlike their Chechen cousins, they did not actively resist incorporation into the Russian empire. The Ingush are the titular majority of **Ingushetiya**; prior to 1991, they were one of two represented groups in the Checheno-Ingush **Autonomous Soviet Socialist Republic** (ASSR).

The Ingush are a Sunni **Muslim** people with a strong Sufi orientation, embracing the Naqshbandi and Qadiriyyah *tariqas* (paths). Due to its remote location, Ingushetiya was the last region of the North Caucasus to embrace **Islam**, occurring in the 19th century. The Ingush's identification with Islam is less dramatic when compared to the Chechens, who also have a history of using the faith as a tool of war. Unlike in **Chechnya**, **Wahhabism** is officially banned in the Ingush Republic. Vainakh society has traditionally been egalitarian and lacking the stratifications that characterize other Caucasian peoples, particularly the **Circassians**. Clans or *teips* remain central to political, professional, organizational, and social structures, even in urban areas.

During World War II, the entire nation (along with seven others) was deported to **Siberia** and Soviet **Central Asia** for alleged collaboration with Nazi Germany. Between 25 and 50 percent of the population perished as a result of the "forced evacuations." When they returned to their truncated ethnic homeland in the 1950s, many of their homes were in the hands of **Ossetian** settlers, a situation that triggered sporadic ethnic tensions over the next four decades, including a major uprising in 1973. Further clashes occurred in the early 1990s in the Prigorodny region of **North Ossetiya**. *See also* OSSETIAN-INGUSH CONFLICT.

INGUSHETIYA. An **ethnic republic** of the Russian Federation. The **Ingush**—along with their closely related neighbors, the **Chechens**—were incorporated into the Mountain People's Republic of Soviet Russia in 1920. After the establishment of the Union of Soviet Socialist Republics (USSR), each gained its own autonomous region within Russia. In 1934, through the merger of the Chechen and Ingush autonomous **oblasts**, a Checheno-Ingush Autonomous Oblast was established as a biethnic homeland for the two nationalities, becoming an **Autonomous Soviet Socialist Republic** (ASSR) two years later. The ASSR was abolished in 1944 when both groups were deported en masse to Central Asia for alleged collaboration with the Nazi invaders. Ingush lands were subsequently transferred to the **Ossetians**. The Checheno-Ingush ASSR was restored in 1957 by **Nikita Khrushchev**. However, upon their rehabilitation and return to the region, the Ingush were forced to purchase their old homes, land, and businesses from the Ossetian settlers. Furthermore, some traditionally Ingush lands remained within Ossetiya.

As the Soviet Union unraveled in 1991, **Chechnya** and Ingushetiya split apart. The dissolution of the republican condominium was precipitated by the rise of **Jokhar Dudayev**, whose declaration of Chechen sovereignty under the banner of the **Chechen Republic of Ichkeriya** prompted the Ingush to throw their support behind the federal authorities. Dudayev had previously predicted that the Ingush would side with Moscow in hopes of obtaining a slice of the much larger Chechen portion of their shared republic. The Ingush subsequently voted to form their own republic within Russia, a de facto reality recognized by **Moscow** in 1992. Contemporary Ingush-etiya comprised the western fifth of the Checheno-Ingush ASSR as it was demarcated in the late Soviet era. Ingush forces then moved to reclaim disputed portions of the Prigorodny district in **North Os-setiya**, specifically lands that had belonged to the pre-1944 Chech-eno-Ingush ASSR and were occupied by ethnic Ingush. The move precipitated a regional conflict that lasted two years. The intervention of federal troops on behalf of **Orthodox** Ossetians against **Muslim** Ingush permanently strained relations between the republic and the Kremlin. The conflict also prompted an influx of refugees from North Ossetiya, a problem compounded by the concurrent flood of Chechens fleeing the first **Chechen War**.

Today, the republic borders Chechnya in the east and north, North Ossetiya in the west, and **Georgia** in the south. Ingushetiya is part of the Southern **Federal District** and the North Caucasus **Economic Region**. As Russia's smallest **federal subject** (excepting the two federal cities), Ingushetiya covers approximately 4,000 square kilo-meters, although the exact area is unknown as the border between the republic and Chechnya has not been fully demarcated. The terrain is extremely mountainous, with some peaks reaching almost 4,500 meters. It is rich in natural resources and minerals, including marble, dolomite, plaster, limestone, gravel, granite, clay, rare metals, **oil**, and **natural gas**. The administrative capital is the newly founded city of Magas; there are only a few hundred permanent residents in the municipality. Magas is located less than 25 kilometers south of Nazran, the regional capital from 1991 to 2002.

The official population of the republic is 467,000 as of the 2002 census; however, this figure does not fully represent the semiperma-nent influx of refugees from neighboring Chechnya. Some estimates put the population at near 600,000, of which only half are native to the republic. Officially, ethnic Ingush account for more than three-quarters of the population, with Chechens making up 20 percent, though the actual ratio of Ingush to Chechens is likely much closer to parity. With only about 1 percent of its residents being **ethnic Rus-sian**, it is the least Russian administrative region in the country.

Ingushetiya is one of Russia's most **crime**-ridden, **terrorism**-prone, and economically depressed regions. Largely an agricultural society in the early 1990s, much of the land was transferred to private enterprises and joint-stock companies, reducing the percentage of the **labor force** involved in such work. Animal husbandry and the industrial sector are other major areas of jobs in the region. However, Ingushetiya's **unemployment** level, estimated at 65–70 percent, is the highest of any federal subject (excepting Chechnya due to lack of data). The region's **economy** began to improve in the late 1990s, but was again damaged by instability in the region resulting from the second Chechen War. **Corruption** has since skyrocketed and the republic now depends on subsidies from Moscow for nearly 90 percent of its annual budget.

In 1993, Ruslan Aushev, a Soviet war hero and parliamentarian, ran unopposed to become the first president of the republic. He was reelected two years later. During the Chechen conflict, he often upbraided Moscow for its actions and expressed some level of solidarity with the Chechens. His tenure saw amendments to federal law that conformed to the "national traditions" of the Ingush people (including polygamy), as well as certain aspects of *sharia* (Islamic law). He left office voluntarily in 2002 but returned to the public eye in 2004 when he served as a negotiator in the **Beslan** hostage crisis. His successor, former **KGB** and **FSB** agent Murat Zyazikov, won election under questionable circumstances, becoming the second president of the republic in 2002. He quickly became known for cronyism and nepotism. He has a close relationship with **Vladimir Putin**, who along with his successor, **Dmitry Medvyedev**, is popular in the republic.

On Zyazikov's watch, the level of violence in the republic has increased precipitously, often touching him personally. In 2004, Zyazikov was wounded in a car bomb attack. In 2006, his father-in-law was kidnapped, though later released. In 2007, his uncle was also kidnapped and then released. Zyazikov's motorcade was showered with bullets in July of that year as well. Hundreds of Ingush men have vanished without a trace in recent years and guerilla attacks by radical **Islamists** have often spilled over into the republic. A particularly deadly instance occurred in 2004 when nearly 100 people were killed in coordinated attacks on Nazran. The **security services** were specifically targeted; the acting interior minister and Nazran's chief prosecutor, as well as other high-ranking police officers, security officials, and prosecutors, were gunned down. Despite Moscow's support of the leader, he has faced increasing calls to step down because of corruption and failure to stem violence and crime. The only opposition media outlet, the website www.Ingushetia.ru, has been at the forefront of this campaign. Fearful of a **color revolution**, Zyazikov has frequently prevented public rallies since 2005. *See also* ETHNIC VIOLENCE.

INTELLIGENTSIA. The term derives from the Russian word *intelligentsiia*, which denotes a social class of people engaged in mental and creative labor directed at disseminating knowledge and cultural values. In the Russian imperial, Soviet, and post-Soviet traditions, the term "intelligentsia" typically refers to an intellectual class of people who think differently and who are critical of the existing political regime; as a manner of simplification, it is possible to suggest that the ultimate job of intelligentsia is to critique power.

In the Union of Soviet Socialist Republics (USSR), the term was used for self-definition of a certain category of intellectuals who did not find a niche in the **Marxist-Leninist** template of social classes. The ideology of the Bolsheviks—the majority of whom were, ironically, intellectuals—did not view intelligentsia as a social class; for them it was a stratum, encompassing individuals who did not belong to the established classes of exploiters and workers. This ambiguous status served the Soviet state in both practical and ideological ways. In the first instance, those in power were able to mask their real social affiliation under the mantle of intelligentsia and thus were able to escape the stigma of their nonproletarian backgrounds. In the second instance, individuals involved in **arts**, **music**, and other creative industries, as well as freethinking university lecturers and schoolteachers, could be branded as **dissident** intelligentsia, and purged. Therefore, the term intelligentsia simultaneously has negative and positive connotations in the Soviet political-speak, as well as everyday discourse, allowing the term to simultaneously refer to the best and worst of Soviet society.

Genuine intelligentsia should be differentiated from the "priviligentsiya," a concept that derives from two Russian words, "intelligentsia" and "privilege," and refers to sections of Soviet *nomenklatura*, who dominated cultural production and **education** in the USSR and who invariably had access to a high standard of living, **health care**, and other social privileges.

Intelligentsia were most affected economically and socially in the transient period of the 1990s as the state lowered its support to creative professions to a minimum and as the former system of social and cultural institutions collapsed. In addition, the role of intelligentsia as the moral anchor of Russian society was diminished in a country with a decentralized, disengaged, and morally bankrupt social system. A new class of intellectuals appeared at the dawn of the new millennium, encompassing individuals working in **media** industries who managed to find new ways to communicate their ideas to interested groups.

INTERNATIONAL ADOPTION. While collective responsibility for the raising of children (including those who have lost their parents due to war or disease) is common among some of Russia's **ethnic minorities**, historically speaking, the tradition of adopting orphans is culturally absent among **ethnic Russians**. During the Soviet period, unwanted births were rather rare, as free abortions were provided through the **health care** system and typically used as an ersatz form of birth control. With the crushing financial and social burdens that accompanied **shock therapy** under the **Yeltsin** administration and the dismantling of socialized health care, many single **women** and some married couples opted to give their infants and children over to state care during the 1990s and beyond.

The current preference for small families in Russia, combined with traditional social stigmas associated with adoption, has resulted in little demand for domestic adoptions, thus filling Russia's orphanages with parentless children. Lacking well-paid staff and even basic facilities, these orphanages quickly became unlivable, creating a generation of forgotten children who suffered from physical and mental neglect. Like several other post-Soviet countries (including **Kazakhstan** and **Ukraine**), the Russian Federation turned to international adoption to mitigate this problem. By 2000, the number of international adoptions of Russian orphans by **United States** citizens alone was averaging in excess of 4,000 per year; this figure represented approximately half of all annual international adoptions from Russia, with citizens of the **European Union** (EU) and **Israel** making up the remainder.

In recent years, the number has decreased by more than half, partly as a result of state-backed efforts to increase domestic adoption, but also because of improvements in Russia's health care and social support systems. Political pressure also contributed to the decline. The death of an adoptee in 2005, and several other documented cases of physical abuse of children adopted from Russia by American families, led Russian politicians to condemn the practice, particularly by Americans. New rules instituted in 2007, after a several-months-long moratorium on international adoptions, have made it increasingly difficult for foreigners to adopt. The most high-profile adoption occurred in 2004, when **Gerhard Schröder** and his wife adopted a three-year-old Russian girl from a children's home in **St. Petersburg**. There was speculation in the international media that Schröder chose the site of the adoption in an attempt to curry favor with **Vladimir Putin**, a native of the northern capital city; the couple later adopted a boy from the same orphanage.

INTERNET. Russia's first connections to the Internet occurred during the Soviet era. With the **dissolution of the Soviet Union** in 1991, the ability of average Russians to access cyberspace increased at a modest rate until the end of the 1990s. During this period, the concept of **Runet** evolved, which refers to the **Russian language** portions of cyberspace. Initially, Russophones outside of the Russian Federation dominated this space; however, this changed dramatically with the economic recovery that followed the 1998 **ruble crisis**. The Internet now figures prominently in Russian culture, the national **economy**, and the **media** environment. Both **Vladimir Putin** and **Dmitry Medvyedev** have made the promotion and regulation of the Internet in Russia part of their respective presidential administrations.

IRAN (RELATIONS WITH). Persian-Russian relations date to the 18th century as the **Romanov** Empire began to expand south of the **Caucasus**. During the 1800s, Russia annexed Persian-held **Azerbaijan** and displaced Iranian influence in **Central Asia**. During the Russian Civil War, a Soviet Republic was briefly established in the north of the country; though the Moscow-backed regime quickly collapsed, Tehran was left wary of Soviet influence.

During World War II, the Union of Soviet Socialist Republics (USSR) and **Great Britain** staged a joint invasion of the officially neutral country, occupying the north and south, respectively. **Joseph Stalin** reneged on a commitment to evacuate Persia within six months of cessation of hostilities, instead creating **separatist**, pro-Soviet states in the north of Iran with the help of local Azeris and Kurds. Soviet forces finally left in 1946 with promises of **oil** concessions from the Anglo-Iranian Oil Co., which were soon withdrawn by the shah, Mohammad Rezā Pahlavi. Outraged by the so-called Iranian method employed by the Americans and the British to limit Soviet influence, Stalin moved quickly to consolidate power in Eastern Europe, refusing to give even an inch to London or Washington. Fearing that leftist Prime Minister Mohammed Mossadegh might bring Iran into the Soviet sphere of influence in the early 1950s, the American Central Intelligence Agency (CIA) sponsored a royalist coup d'état, allowing Pahlavi to rule the country as a dictator until he was removed by the 1979 Islamic Revolution. As part of the American-allied "green belt" of Muslim states between the USSR and the Persian Gulf, Iran was stalwart in its anti-Soviet orientation, though economic relations were resumed after 1962.

While the Soviets were happy to see the shah go, the ascendency of Ayatollah Ruhollah Khomeini did little to improve relations; in fact, Moscow viewed the spread of revolutionary **Islamism** with such dread, it invaded **Afghanistan** within the year to put down an Islamist government on its long Central Asian border and when the Iran-Iraq War (1980–1988) broke out, Moscow liberally supplied Saddam Hussein with conventional arms until 1986 when relations between Moscow and Tehran improved. As the Soviet Union lurched toward denouement, Khomeini encouraged **Mikhail Gorbachev** to consider **Islam** as a substitute for the "failed" ideologies of **atheism** and **Communism**. While Russia did not adopt Islam en masse, the country markedly improved its relations with the Islamic Republic during the 1990s.

Economic and scientific exchange formed the core of this new relationship, with Russia agreeing to help develop the Iranian nuclear power plant at Bushehr in 1995. Involvement in supplying nuclear technology to a "rogue state" has been one of the most controversial aspects of Moscow's postindependence foreign policy. With the ascendency of **Yevgeny Primakov**, the Russo-Iranian relationship developed a political component, as the foreign minister sought to counteract American hegemony. Under **Vladimir Putin** and his successor, **Dmitry Medvyedev**, Russia has made cooperation rather than confrontation with Iran on the nuclear issue the policy standard, often using the country's permanent seat on the **United Nations** Security Council to scuttle or veto resolutions directed against Tehran. Russian intransigence on Iranian nuclear issue has negatively impacted relations with the international community (especially **France** and **Germany**), particularly since it has become obvious that Russia's relationship with Iran is not simply an economic one, but also a geopolitical strategy directed against the **United States'** interests in the **Middle East** (particularly against American allies **Israel, Turkey,** and Saudi Arabia).

Russia is one of Iran's largest trading partners, with a turnover of more than $2 billion per year (much of it in the form of **arms** and **military** hardware, sales of which were resumed in 1989 and expanded after 2000). While Russia and Iran do not share a territorial border, both states are washed by the **Caspian Sea**, a shared status that has led to competition over access to natural resources (oil and **natural gas**), shipping, and **fishing** rights. While the two countries have sparred over routes for transshipment of Caspian hydrocarbons, their deepening "strategic partnership" in the 1990s was a critical factor in developing the U.S.-backed Baku-Tbilisi-Ceyhan pipeline that skirted both countries. The two countries share common goals in **Central Asia** and Afghanistan. Despite its history of sponsoring transnational Islamism, Tehran is loath to see Saudi-influenced Sunni fundamentalism on its borders, a sentiment shared by the Russian Federation; similarly, both countries seek to limit America's extension of its influence into the region.

IRKUTSK OBLAST. An administrative region of the Russian Federation. Part of the Siberian **Federal District** and East Siberian **Economic Region**, Irkutsk is bordered by **Sakha, Buryatiya, Tuva, Zabaykalsky Krai**, and **Krasnoyarsk**. Enclosed within its borders is the formerly autonomous Ust-Orda Buryat Okrug, which was fully merged with Irkutsk on 1 January 2008. The move to merge the political entities was the result of a referendum that took place on 16 April 2006; the plebiscite showed strong support for eliminating Ust-Orda Buryatiya's status as an autonomous **federal subject**, especially among voters in Ust-Orda Buryatiya (98 percent supported a merger). In Irkutsk proper, 9 out of 10 voters approved the merger.

Irkutsk's geography is dominated by the hills and broad valleys of the Central **Siberian** and Patom plateaus. **Lake Baykal** is situated on Irkutsk's southeastern border; the lake contains 80 percent of Russia's freshwater resources. The Angara, Oka, Ilim, and the Lena are the major rivers in the region. The vast majority of the oblast is covered with coniferous forests. The region covers 767,900 square kilometers, and has a population of nearly 2.6 million. **Ethnic Russians** make up about 90 percent of the population. In Ust-Orda Buryatiya, **Buryats** account for 40 percent of the population, with Russians making up a majority (54 percent). The administrative capital is Irkutsk (pop. 593,000), one of the largest cities in Siberia. The emblem of the city is a Siberian tiger with a sable in its mouth, a symbolic reflection of the area's centrality in Russia's fur trade. Prior to the merger, the administrative center of Ust-Orda Buryatiya was Ust-Ordynsky.

The Irkutsk Oblast has a well-developed rail network and waterways for commercial transport. The **economy** is driven by metals, energy, logging, fossil fuels, machine-building, chemicals, and hydroelectricity, and commands a higher per capita income than most other regions. At times, relations between Irkutsk and Moscow have been strained as the former contributes significant tax revenues to the center but often receives few benefits from the federal government. In 1997, the regional governor, Yury Nozhikov, instituted a **tax** strike to force Moscow to pay greater attention to the needs of the **oblast**. The former engineer Aleksandr Tishanin was appointed regional governor by **Vladimir Putin** in 2005, replacing Boris Govorin, who served from 2001 to 2005.

ISLAM. Islam is the second largest of Russia's **religions**. Approximately 20 million or 14 percent of Russia's citizens are ethnic or legacy **Muslims**; of those, slightly fewer than half are active members of the faith. The vast majority of Russian Muslims are Sunni of the comparatively tolerant Hanafi school of jurisprudence; there is a small minority of Shiites in Russia. Russian Muslims are most prevalent in the **Volga** basin and the **North Caucasus**, as well as the historical capitals of **Moscow** and **St. Petersburg**. There are another 3–4 million **immigrants** in Russia who profess Islam, principally from **Central Asia** and **Azerbaijan**.

The presence of Muslims within the Russian Empire dates to the annexation of the Khanates of Kazan (1552) and **Astrakhan** (1556). The **Romanovs** steadily incorporated lands of Dar al-Islam over the next few centuries, culminating with the conquest of Central Asia in the late 19th century. Under **Joseph Stalin**, Islam—like other faiths—was suppressed, with Islamic schools (*maktabs*) being closed, bans on veiling, restriction of the *hajj* (pilgrimage to Mecca), the persecution of imams, and the abolition of *sharia* (Islamic law) and *waqfs* (religious land grants). Prior to the Bolshevik revolution, there were more than 25,000 mosques in the country; this was reduced to barely 1,000 by 1942 and then halved over the next 40 years. In the post–World War II period, religious training in the Union of Soviet Socialist Republics (USSR) was limited to two sites within Russia (Ufa and Orenburg) and to muftiates in Baku and Tashkent. By co-opting the Islamic *ulema* (religious scholars), the Soviets were able to procure a pro-statist "official Islam," though many Muslims continued to worship in secret.

During **perestroika**, there was a resurgence of Muslim identity in Russia, particularly among legacy Muslims who had been deployed to fight in the **Soviet-Afghan War**. In 1990, legal reforms allowed for nearly all aspects of Islamic life to flourish in the USSR. After 1991, **Middle Eastern** countries, especially Saudi Arabia, Egypt, and **Turkey**, began funding mosque-building, religious education, and Islamic charities in the Russian Federation; there are over 5,000 mosques now in operation. Many Russian Muslims also traveled abroad for pilgrimages or study at Islamic universities. **Islamist** political organizations sought to improve the plight of Russian Muslims and promote a resurgence of the faith after decades of enforced **atheism**. The **Chechen War** and the concomitant spread of jihadist **terrorism** have made the Russian state particularly wary of so-called fundamentalist Islam, often labeled **Wahhabism** (*vakhabizm*).

During the 1990s, conflicts, such as the one in **North Ossetiya**, have been colored by **Orthodox**-Muslim strife, further fanning the flames of the purported "clash of civilizations" within Russia. Efforts have been undertaken to assist in the development of a Russian form of "Euro-Islam" free of influence from the Arab World and South Asia; these are seen as radicalizing influences on Russia's Muslims, many of whom engage in Sufi practices, drink alcohol, do not fast during Ramadan, and embrace elements of Russian mainstream culture.

Finding common cause between Orthodox Slavs and Finno-Ugrics, Turkic and Caucasian Muslims, and Mongolic **Buddhists** remains a central tenet of **neo-Eurasianism**, thus making Russia's Muslims a key constituency for many political projects in post-Soviet Russia. Reflective of this, **Vladimir Putin** oversaw Russia's admission to the Organization of the Islamic Conference as a permanent observer in 2005. Under the competitive leadership of **Ravil Gaynutdin**, Chairman of the Council of Muftis of Russia, and Russia's supreme mufti, Sheikh ul-Islam **Talgat Tajuddin**, Russia's Muslim committee is seeking to create a place for itself within the larger society. However, anti-Muslim prejudices, particularly against **Chechens**, remain a major problem in the country. Generational and ideological differences also continue to internally afflict the community.

ISLAMISM. Political ideology. In Russia, Islamism—that is, the political ideology that, for **Muslims**, **Islam** and **politics** are inseparable—exists in a variety of forms. In its most extreme manifestation, Islamists advocate the institution of *sharia* (Islamic law) and support a *jihad* (holy war) to purge traditionally Muslim areas of Russians and other nonbelievers. For many, the ultimate goal is the establishment of a **Eurasian** caliphate that would stretch from western **China** to Anatolia. Such groups embrace a strict, Saudi-influenced form of Islam, often called **Wahhabism** (*vakhabizm*) by Russian authorities.

Many adherents of Islamism were deeply influenced by exposure to the mujahideen during the **Soviet-Afghan War** or to the teachings of clerics from the **Middle East** who were allowed to proselytize in Russia during the early **Yeltsin** era. This radical ideology is most prevalent in **Chechnya**, though it has found some adherents in other parts of the **North Caucasus**, particularly in the wake of the first **Chechen War**. In the **Volga-Ural region**, Islamism is much more pragmatic. Among **Tatars** and **Bashkirs**, there is a range of Islamist politics, from **neo-Jadidism**, which seeks to modernize Islam for the

21st century, to anticolonial movements that employ Islam as a tool for rallying Muslim minorities against the presence of **ethnic Russians** in the region.

Under **perestroika**, a number of cultural organizations were formed to revive Islamic identity across the Union of Soviet Socialist Republics (USSR), including the Union of Muslims of Russia, *Ittifaq* (Tatar: "Union"), *Nur* ("Light"), and the Islamic Renaissance Party (IRP) among others; by 1991, many of these had turned themselves into full-fledged **political parties**. Due to the structure of the new political system in the Russian Federation, none of these organizations was able to achieve traction on the national level; however, they have influenced policy in the Muslim republics, particularly **Tatarstan**, but also **Bashkortostan, Adygeya, Karachay-Cherkessiya, Kabardino-Balkariya, Ingushetiya**, and **Dagestan**.

Responding to a proliferation of jihadi **terrorism** in the late 1990s, **Vladimir Putin** pursued a multipronged strategy to weaken Islamism in the Russian Federation. At the regional level, Putin has given carte blanche to the republican leadership to deal with the Islamist "problem." In the North Caucasus, **security service** personnel often track mosque attendance and sometimes detain worshippers who visit "suspect" mosques or those who demonstrate outward signs of Wahhabism (including bearded men and veiled **women**). Putin has also attempted to marginalize more radical Islamic leaders, such as **Ravil Gaynutdin**, in favor of those who actively condemn Wahhabism and other "alien" forms of Islam.

ISRAEL (RELATIONS WITH). In the post–World War II era, **Joseph Stalin** was one of the strongest advocates for the creation of a Jewish state in Palestine; the Union of Soviet Socialist Republics (USSR) was the first country to recognize the existence of Israel in 1948. However, Stalin's hopes for a pliant, anti-British client state in the **Middle East** were dashed as Israel gravitated to the Western orbit by the mid-1950s.

Under **Nikita Khrushchev** and his successor, **Leonid Brezhnev**, the USSR and its **Eastern Bloc** allies steadfastly supported Israel's Arab neighbors in a series of wars and crises during the 1960s and 1970s. The turnabout allowed the Soviet leadership to return to its traditional anti-Zionist orientation, as well as to develop ideological, diplomatic, economic, and **military** ties with the Arab world, particularly Egypt, Syria, and Iraq; the **KGB** also surreptitiously supplied Palestinian **terrorist** groups with arms and training during the **Cold War**. During the late Soviet period, suppression of Jewish culture and refusal of emigration permits for Soviet **Jews** (*refuseniks*) further soured relations between Moscow and Tel Aviv, as well as emerging as a major stumbling block in Soviet-American diplomacy.

Under **Mikhail Gorbachev**, the ban on emigration was gradually lifted (resulting in a million Soviet Jews quitting the USSR in the last decade of its existence) and diplomatic relations were resumed. Moscow also began to retrench from its stridently pro-Arab orientation as relations with the **United States** improved. The new vector in Soviet Middle East policy pushed the Palestinian Liberation Organization (PLO) toward negotiation with Israel. With the **dissolution of the Soviet Union** in 1991, the Russian Federation restructured its relationship with Israel, abandoning ideological opposition in favor of a pragmatic approach. Israel's economic dynamism and cultural ties with the newly settled Russophone population of Israel provided the nucleus for this new era of relations.

Today, there are three major "Russian" parties in the Knesset, and the Russophone community has emerged as an important swing vote in national elections, a factor that allows Moscow some leverage in Israeli domestic politics. Conversely, Israel closely monitors the situation of Jews inside Russia, especially given the rising number of hate crimes on Jews that have been recorded in the past decade. Widely accepted political **anti-Semitism** in the **Russian State Duma** and elsewhere is also a concern. A number of Russian **oligarchs** who fell afoul of the state have fled to Israel, including the former **Yukos** executive Leonid Nevzlin; the failure to execute Russian and international arrest warrants remains an issue of contention in bilateral relations. Also troubling are Russian **arms sales** to and **nuclear** cooperation with **Iran**, a country where the political elite regularly commit themselves to the eradication of the Israeli state through military action. Sales of advanced missile systems to Syria are also a dampener on relations.

Despite such concerns, Russia and Israel have collaborated on joint military and technological initiatives. **Foreign trade** is also brisk (approaching $2 billion), with a large number of Israeli companies investing in Moscow and other parts of Russia. In 2002, Russia resumed its historical role of arbiter in the region through its membership in the Middle East Quartet, which also includes the **United Nations**, the **European Union**, and the U.S.; the group's aim is to mediate a peaceful resolution to the Israeli-Palestinian conflict. Israel, Russia, and the United States have all collaborated on **counterterrorism** issues since the **September 11 attacks**; Russia's difficulty in combating radical **Islamism** in the **North Caucasus** has allowed it to find some common ground on such issues with Israel, which has significant experience in combating transnational jihad groups (both countries have been reticent to condemn one another on the "internal" issues of **Chechnya** and Palestine).

In 2005, **Vladimir Putin** became the first Russian (or Soviet) head of state to visit Israel. He angered many Israelis, however, by inviting representatives of the Hamas movement to Moscow after their electoral victory in the Gaza Strip in 2006 and again in 2007, though Russian relations with the group were later downgraded. Shortly after **Dmitry Medvyedev** took office, Israeli-Russian relations grew cooler due to Israel's close relationship with **Georgia** and Moscow's decision to expand arms deals with Damascus.

ITAR-TASS. The Information Telegraph Agency of Russia (*Informatsionnoie telegrafnoie agentstvo Rossii*) or, as it is more commonly known, ITAR-TASS, is Russia's primary news agency. Currently headquartered in **Moscow**, the agency originated in late tsarist **St. Petersburg** (where it was known as the Petersburg Telegraph Agency), before being moved to the new capital under the Soviets and renamed the Telegraph Agency of the Soviet Union (TASS). Under **Boris Yeltsin**, the agency took its current name, abandoned its ideological orientation, and adapted to the new realities of the marketplace, though it remained state-owned. Similar to the Associated Press or Reuters, the agency distributes its stories and photos to newspapers and other **media** outlets, which cite ITAR-TASS as the source. ITAR-TASS has more than 70 bureaus in the Russian Federation and the **Commonwealth of Independent States**, and a presence in 75 other countries.

IVANOV, IGOR SERGEYEVICH (1945–). The successor to **Yevgeny Primakov**, Igor Ivanov served as the foreign minister of the

Russian Federation from 1998 until 2004. He was previously Russia's ambassador to Spain. Half Georgian, he played an important role in mediating between **Eduard Shevardnadze** and the opposition during the so-called **Rose Revolution** in **Georgia**. During his tenure, Russia took an increasingly critical opinion of **Iran**'s nuclear program, stating "the clock must be stopped"; he also spearheaded Russian condemnation of the **United States**–led invasion of Iraq. **Vladimir Putin** appointed Ivanov secretary of the Security Council in 2004; he was succeeded by **Sergey Lavrov**. In 2007, he stepped down from government service. *See also* FOREIGN RELATIONS.

IVANOVO OBLAST. An administrative region of the Russian Federation. Part of the Central **Federal District** and **Economic Region**, Ivanovo covers 21,800 square kilometers and has a population of over 1.1 million inhabitants. It is surrounded by the **Yaroslavl, Kostroma, Nizhny Novgorod**, and **Vladimir oblasts**. Though swampy in parts, half of its territory is forested and its main river is the **Volga**. Ivanovo is a major textile producer, and the historic center of Russia's cotton mill **industry**. **Agriculture**, light manufacturing, and handicraft production are also well represented in the regional **economy**. The region has failed to attract much **foreign investment** since Russia's independence. In 2000, the **Communist Party of the Russian Federation** (KPRF) candidate, Vladimir Tikhonov, defeated the incumbent, Vladimir Golovkov. Tikhonov was elected leader of the All-Russian Communist Party of the Future (VKPB) in 2004, a breakaway party of the KPRF that claims to be the "true" Communist party of Russia. In 2005, **Vladimir Putin** appointed Mikhail Men, a former deputy mayor of **Moscow** and ally of **Yury Luzkov**, to the post of regional governor; he declared his commitment to sustaining the region's focus on textiles as the major plank of his administration.

IZVESTIYA. **Newspaper**. *Izvestiya* is a high-circulation, quality daily newspaper and one of the oldest publications in Russia. In Russian, the word *izvestiia* means "messages," and is derived from the verb *izvesha'*, meaning "to inform" (the word *izvestiia* is, in fact, used in titles of many Russian news publications). During the Soviet era, *Izvestiya* presented the official views of the Soviet government and published copies of important official documents and laws, while

Pravda was the mouthpiece of the **Communist Party of the Soviet Union**. After the **dissolution of the Soviet Union**, *Izvestiya* remained one of the few newspapers with national coverage. **Vladimir Potanin** owned the newspaper until 2005, when **Gazprom** acquired it. At that point, the circulation of the newspaper was approximately 250,000 copies per day. The newspaper has a very well-developed website (www.izvestia.ru/) and positions itself as a multimedia news agency rather than a traditional newspaper. Since 2005, *The New York Times* has used *Izvestiya* to publish its Russian version. The newspaper is managed by Pyotr Godlevsky, and its editor-in-chief is Vladimir Mamontov. *See also* MEDIA.

– J –

JAPAN (RELATIONS WITH). Historically, Russo-Japanese relations have been plagued by territorial conflicts, beginning with the Russo-Japanese War of 1904–1905. Russia's defeat resulted in the virtual destruction of the country's naval fleet, an internal revolution, and the loss of the southern half of Sakhalin Island. Japan later intervened in the Russian Civil War (1918–1921) in an attempt to crush the **Bolsheviks** and exert control over the **Russian Far East**.

The Union of Soviet Socialist Republics (USSR) maintained neutrality toward the island nation during most of the Pacific War (1937–1945), only declaring war on Japan on 9 August 1945. With Japan's surrender less than a week later, the Soviets became an occupying force in its former imperial domains, including Manchuria and northern Korea. The Soviet Union annexed southern Sakhalin and the **Kuril Island** chain (including the four southernmost islands known as the Northern Territories in Japan), affixing them to the **Sakhalin Oblast** of the **Russian Soviet Federative Socialist Republic**.

As the **Cold War** set in, the status of the southern Kurils became a point of friction between the Kremlin and the **United States**, with the latter backing Japan's position that the Northern Territories were not part of the Kurils and thus not the legal property of the Soviet Union. In 1956, Moscow and Tokyo, in an effort to normalize relations, agreed on the transfer of the Habomai and the Shikotan islands to Japan once a permanent peace treaty was signed between the two countries; however, such a treaty has yet to be finalized primarily due to Japanese demand for the return of four rather than two islands.

During the 1990s, **Boris Yeltsin** regularly stated his intention to end the territorial dispute and sign a peace treaty, but to no avail. Relations between an independent Russian Federation and Japan developed rapidly under Yeltsin; however, the economic imbalance between the nations was characterized by Japanese dominance. Under the leadership of **Vladimir Putin**, Russia's economic turnaround allowed the country to restructure its previously subservient relationship with Japan; these new realities were reflected in January 2003 when Putin and Prime Minister Junichiro Koizumi signed the Russo-Japanese Action Plan to improve bilateral ties.

Trade between the two countries is growing rapidly (between 20–30 percent per year), standing at over $13 billion in 2006. Trade is expected to increase after the estimated 2012 completion of the Taishet-Nakhodka pipeline (currently, **oil** shipments are sent via rail from Skovorodino to the Pacific port of Nakhodka). In 2003, Koizumi pledged loans of $14 billion to finance the pipeline and additional economic support for projects in the Russian Far East to help secure the route, which bypasses **China**. New initiatives between the two countries also include the development of an energy bridge (electricity and **natural gas**) linking Sakhalin and Hokkaido. A number of large Japanese firms, including Toyota, have invested in the Russian Federation in recent years.

Cooperation in the high-tech field is also improving, with Russian software makers partnering with Japanese computer manufacturers. A high-level visit in 2007 to Japan by Prime Minister **Mikhail Fradkov** and 200 business leaders deepened economic linkages. In terms of international diplomacy, joint membership in the six-party talks on **North Korea**'s nuclear program has stimulated increased bilateral cooperation on security in northeast Asia. Cooperation on transnational **crime** fighting is also substantial, as both governments seek to stifle alliances between the Russian **mafia** and Japanese *yakuza*. *See also* FOREIGN INVESTMENT; FOREIGN TRADE.

JEWISH AUTONOMOUS OBLAST. An administrative region of the Russian Federation. The only autonomous oblast in the Russian

Federation, the Jewish Autonomous Oblast, or Birobijan (Birobidzhan), is part of the Far Eastern **Federal District** and **Economic Region**. It borders **Amur**, **Khabarovsk**, and northeastern **China**. The well-forested and mountainous region covers 36,000 square kilometers and has a population of just under 200,000.

The region was originally created as an ethnic homeland for Russia's Jewish population, where the Yiddish **language** and Eastern European Jewish culture could flourish within a Soviet framework. It was also meant as an ideological foil against Zionism. However, the region never attracted a large percentage of Soviet Jews (reaching a peak of one-quarter of the population in the 1940s), and an **anti-Semitic** political shift in Moscow resulted in Yiddish being banned after 1949, though it is one of two official languages of the **oblast** today. In 1991, the region was granted status as a **federal subject**, though it remains simultaneously subordinate to Khabarovsk.

Since 1991, the Yiddish language has experienced a modest renaissance, returning to the schools, airwaves, and newspapers. However, in the mid-1990s, the region only accounted for approximately 2 percent of Russia's Jewry, and **Jews**—the titular minority—make up less than 2 percent of the oblast's population. Furthermore, this number is declining rapidly, with Birobijan being the leading sending region in Russia of Jewish emigrants to **Israel**. **Ethnic Russians** are the majority, accounting for 90 percent of the inhabitants, with small minorities of **Ukrainians**, **Tatars**, and other nationalities forming the remainder.

Mining, **agriculture**, timber, and light manufacturing are the major economic activities. The region leads the country in per capita arrest for **narcotics** trafficking. The regional governor is Nikolay Volkov; he was appointed to head the region in 1991 and won elections in 1886 and 2000, before being nominated by **Vladimir Putin** in 2005 to continue his tenure. Under his watch, the gross regional product has risen dramatically since 2000, partly as a result of the resolution of long-standing insecurities about the status of the Russian-Chinese border. The improvement of the economic situation has reduced Jewish emigration from the region. Volkov also supported the refurbishment of a 100-year-old synagogue that opened in Birobijan in 2004. Volkov maintains good relations with the leadership of Khabarovsk Krai and has publicly supported full merger with the territory.

JEWS. Ethnoreligious group. At one time, Russia possessed the largest population of Jews worldwide; the country still has one of the largest Jewish communities in Europe. Historically, Jew (*ievrei*) was treated as an ethnonational category in Russia and the Soviet Union. Since 1991, Jewishness in Russia has come to be more closely associated with religiosity and cultural identification, and secular Jews may be treated as Russians for statistical purposes. Such was not the case during the Soviet era, as any citizen with two Jewish parents was automatically registered as Jewish on their internal passport (children of mixed marriages could adopt either ethnicity at the age of 16).

The Russian Federation's 2002 census recorded slightly fewer than 300,000 ethnic Jews in the country (down from 500,000 in 1989). External estimates put Russia's ethnic Jewish population at 1 million, suggesting that many Jews do not embrace their background for fear of discrimination. Most Russian Jews are Ashkenazi (literally, "German" Jews), though communities of Mizrahi ("Eastern") Jews can also be found in parts of Russia.

Not all Jews in Russia descend from diasporic Semites; in the 9th century, Khazaria, a Turkic empire that controlled parts of **Ukraine** and southern Russia, made **Judaism** its official religion, prompting the mass conversion of its subjects. While the effect of this on the composition of Russia's Jews is debated, it is thought that some percentage of Jews in the Russian Federation descend from Khazari rather than Ashkenazi Jews.

There is a long history of official **anti-Semitism** in Russia, going back to edicts establishing a Pale of Settlement (*cherta osedlosti*) for Jews and subsequent laws forbidding the settlement of Jews in agricultural communities and large cities. Mass pogroms and restriction of political and civil rights in the late 19th century prompted massive emigration of Russian Jews to the **United States** and elsewhere. The publication of *The Protocols of the Elders of Zion* in 1903 and the rise of the anti-Semitic Black Hundreds (*Chernaia Sotnia*) a few years later only compounded the situation. The 1917 revolutions, however, temporarily bettered the situation for Russia's Jews.

Ethnic Jews held key positions in the early Bolshevik and Menshevik parties' leadership, including the revolutionaries Grigory Zinoviev, Lev Kamenev, and **Vladimir Lenin**'s second-in-command, Leon Trotsky. However, under the reign of **Joseph Stalin**, much of the Soviet Union's *nomenklatura* was purged of Jews. While Stalin did not consider the Jews a genuine nation because they lacked a common language and were widely dispersed, he did oversee the creation of the **Jewish Autonomous Oblast** in the **Russian Far East**. Centered in the city of Birobijan, the inhospitable region was meant to be a "Soviet Zion" where Yiddish (as opposed to Hebrew) would evolve as the ultimate national **language** of the Jewish people. The creation of a Jewish homeland was also meant to offset the international allure of Zionism, which the **Communist Party of the Soviet Union** roundly condemned as a "socially retrogressive" and reactionary ideology. However, in the 1930s, a wave of anti-Semitic purges resulted in the suppression of Yiddish culture.

During World War II, 2 million Soviet Jews perished in the Holocaust, second only to Polish Jews. In the wake of **Israel**'s establishment, Stalin instituted another campaign of official anti-Semitism. Attacks on Jews reached their peak shortly before Stalin's death with the fabricated "Doctors' Plot," which, if seen to fruition, would have resulted in the internal exile of all Soviet Jewry to **Siberia**. The Soviet Union's close alliance with Arab states and Western support of Israel during the **Cold War** placed Russian Jews in an uncomfortable position within Soviet society. Following the Six Day War in 1967, large numbers of Soviet Jews petitioned to emigrate. Since they typically received perfunctory denials of emigrant visas, these aspirants were dubbed "refuseniks" (*otkazniki*) by the Western press.

After **Mikhail Gorbachev**'s rise to power, Jews were granted the right of exit, though a large number emigrated to the United States rather than opting for *aliyah* (Hebrew: "return" to Israel). Since Russia's independence, anti-Semitism has grown as a political force employed by **neofascists**, as well as the **Communist Party of the Russian Federation** and many in the **neo-Eurasianism** movement. As a result, Jewish emigration increased sharply in the early 1990s before beginning to ebb. In recent years, popular ire at the **oligarchs** has harmonized with anti-Semitism. Several of Russia's richest men are ethnic Jews, including **Roman Abramovich, Mikhail Fridman,** and **Viktor Vekselberg**, as are the imprisoned or exiled former tycoons **Mikhail Khodorkovsky**, **Boris Berezovsky**, and **Vladimir Gusinsky**.

Post-Soviet Russia's most important Jewish organizations include the Russian Jewish Congress, a rabbinical body dedicated to the renewal of Jewish life in the country, and the Federation of Jewish Communities of Russia, an orthodox organization focused on improving religious life for Russia's Jews. *See also* IMMIGRATION; KASPAROV, GARRY.

JOURNALISM. The freedom of the press is safeguarded by the **Constitution of the Russian Federation**. The 1991 law "On Mass Media" ensures the democratic character of the Russian press, including the freedom of speech and the right to publish in ethnic **languages**. Though censorship is constitutionally banned in Russia, many journalists apply self-censorship. This is done in order to avoid persecution, which is applied through a variety of measures including selective prosecution on charges of libel, disclosing of state secrets, and/or tax evasion, as well as physical intimidation and harassment by agents acting on behalf of the state. The failure of the judicial system to adequately investigate murders of journalists, the use of "black PR" and "compromising materials" (*kompromat*) against editors and reporters, and the subsidization of pro-state media outlets also negatively impacts press freedom in contemporary Russia.

Journalists were instrumental in the **glasnost** debates and it will not be an exaggeration to suggest that the press precipitated many political, social, and economic changes in the late 1980s. In the early 1990s, reporters emerged as an important player in postindependence **politics**, and the press one of the country's most respected institutions (alongside the **Russian Orthodox Church**). However, the image and importance of the press diminished with the rise of **television** in the mid-1990s, which—as an industry—was controlled by the **oligarchs**. Since 2000, the emergence of online journalism and the establishment of **Internet** publications, which do not suffer the same restrictions or limitations as television-, radio-, or print-based mediums, has helped to rehabilitate the professional press, particularly in contrast with state-influenced television journalists. However, new laws passed by the **Vladimir Putin** administration have made critical coverage of politics increasingly difficult, particularly after the **Nord-Ost theater siege** of 2004.

Russian journalists work independently; however, they also may choose to join the Russian Union of Journalists, a professional organization that aims to safeguard the interests of the profession in the Russian Federation. This is especially important in a climate where assaults on journalists are not infrequent. Since the early 1990s, reporters who have been vocally critical of the government, and especially of the war operations in **Chechnya**, have been subject to various assaults, including murder, kidnapping, threats, and blackmail.

Over 50 journalists, including the independent journalist **Anna Politkovskaya**, *Forbes Russia* editor **Paul Klebnikov**, and *Kommersant*'s military affairs reporter Ivan Safronov, have been killed since 1991, making Russia one of the most unsafe countries in the world for journalists; the situation is particularly dire in the **North Caucasus** and **Kalmykiya**, where media freedom is largely unknown. Though criminal investigations are always launched, it is extremely rare that the perpetrators are found and prosecuted. In 2009, President **Dmitry Medvyedev**, as part of his anti-**corruption** campaign, passed a new law providing journalists investigating government and corporate malfeasance in Russia with more protection.

JUDAISM. The Jewish faith has a long history in Russia, dating back to at least the 4th century. Casimir the Great's invitation to Ashkenazi **Jews** to settle in the Polish-Lithuanian Commonwealth made the religion an important minority faith across medieval Eastern Europe. While Jews were generally free to practice their faith under the **Romanovs**, they faced institutionalized discrimination and the almost constant threat of violence from the Slavic **Orthodox Christian** population.

During the Soviet period, vigorous antireligion campaigns during **Joseph Stalin**'s reign resulted in the shuttering of most of the country's synagogues (as well as churches and mosques). The Holocaust further weakened the status of Judaism in the Union of Soviet Socialist Republics (USSR). Under **glasnost**, a revival movement among Russian Jews began to grow, though many believers sought to immigrate to **Israel** or the **United States** rather than rebuild Judaic traditions in Russia. Cultural organizations established in the late

1980s such as Va'ad (Confederation of Jewish Communities and Organizations) attempted to reintroduce the celebration of Jewish **holidays**, offered instruction in Hebrew, and established contacts with Jewish religious organizations abroad.

In the post-Soviet period, rediscovery of Jewish identity has become common, and many young Russian Jews are embracing the faith of their ancestors. New synagogues have been built and old ones reopened, often with the financial support of Jewish **oligarchs**. Today, yeshivas for religious instruction operate in **St. Petersburg** and **Moscow**, and Jewish summer camps have become popular in recent years. Judaism is protected by the **Constitution of the Russian Federation** as a native or local religion, alongside Orthodoxy, **Islam**, and **Buddhism**. However, in 2009, two Hassidic rabbis from North America were deported for visa violations in a move that worried Jewish communities bereft of religious leaders after decades of state-sponsored **atheism**. Major Jewish groups in the Russian Federation include the Congress of Jewish Religious Communities and Organizations under **Adolf Shayevich**, the Federation of Jewish Communities of Russia, and the Russian Jewish Congress.

JUDICIAL SYSTEM. In the Soviet era, the legal system generally catered to the needs of the state, and more specifically, the **Communist Party of the Soviet Union** (CPSU). While the Union of Soviet Socialist Republics (USSR) displayed all the attributes of a typical legal system, judgments were often influenced by what was colloquially known as telephone law, that is, directives from Communist Party officials via the telephone. Frequent elections of judicial figures ensured that recalcitrant judges could easily be removed from office.

Mikhail Gorbachev initiated reforms weakening the CPSU's control over judges, gave them lifetime appointments, and instituted judicial review, thus creating an environment where the rule of law enjoyed greater levels of respect. However, the effects were moderate, and many citizens continued to distrust the judicial system. With the **dissolution of the Soviet Union**, **Boris Yeltsin** began a more far-reaching reform of the judiciary. Significant structural changes occurred in the wake of the 1992 Law on the Status of Judges. Further reforms followed with the passage of the 1993 **Constitution of the Russian Federation**. However, the low pay judges received and the failure to thoroughly implement the reforms precluded adherence to Western European norms.

The abolition of the death penalty and institution of trials by jury (at least for certain types of cases) were both introduced in the mid-1990s. However, the vast majority of cases continued to be tried by judges and "people's assessors" (lay judges). In the mid-1990s, the conviction rate was extremely high compared to other countries, especially when the case was tried by a judge (99 percent) rather than a jury (80 percent). Legal reforms passed under **Vladimir Putin** in 2002 were meant to solidify the presumption of innocence in criminal cases, but the legal culture has changed little in recent years. The highly politicized case of **Mikhail Khodorkovsky** undermined confidence abroad that the system was improving. In 2008, Prosecutor General Yury Chayka admitted that thousands of Russians are unlawfully put on trial every year, costing the country millions.

Administered by the Ministry of Justice, the Russian judicial system is divided between the regular court system (with the 23-member Supreme Court at its zenith), the arbitration court system (headed by the High Court of Arbitration), and the Constitutional Court (with no lower courts). During the early 2000s, the Constitutional Court oversaw a major harmonization of local and regional laws with federal statutes, thus undoing much of Yeltsin's system of **asymmetrical federalism**. There are approximately 2,500 public courts in the country, with a total of 13,000 judges.

JUST RUSSIA. *See* FAIR RUSSIA.

– K –

KABARDINO-BALKARIYA. An **ethnic republic** of the Russian Federation. Initially part of the Mountain Peoples' Autonomous Republic of Soviet Russia, the region was organized into the Kabardin-Balkar Autonomous Oblast in the early 1920s, becoming an **Autonomous Soviet Socialist Republic** (ASSR) in 1936. After being accused of collaboration with the Nazis in World War II, the **Balkars** were deported to Soviet **Central Asia**, and the region was renamed the Kabardin ASSR. Its prewar name was restored in 1957 after the post-Stalinist rehabilitation of the Balkars, who then began remigrating to their ethnic homelands. Kabardino-Balkariya declared itself a sovereign republic in 1991, becoming a **federal subject** of the Russian Federation in 1992.

The republic is part of the Southern **Federal District** and the **North Caucasus Economic Region**. Its geography is divided between the northern flank of the Greater Caucasus, foothills, and the Kabardin Plain, the latter being divided by the Terek River. It is bordered by **Karachay-Cherkessiya**, **Stavropol Krai**, **North Ossetiya**, and northern **Georgia**. A small republic, Kabardino-Balkariya covers 12,500 square kilometers and has a population of about 900,000. The capital, Nalchik, is a city of some 273,000 people. Mount Elbrus, the highest peak in Europe, is located in the region's western periphery. The republic is an ethnic condominium representing the Kabardins and Balkars, who account for 55 percent and 12 percent of the population, respectively. The Turkic Balkars live in the mountainous western zones, while the Caucasian Kabardins live in the central lowlands. Dominating the northeastern district of Prokhladnensky, **ethnic Russians**—including Terek **Cossacks**—represent a quarter of the population, and there are small communities of **Ossetians** and **Ukrainians** as well. Support for independence among the region's titulars is moderate (roughly 40 percent favor separation from Russia).

The regional **economy** is focused on **agriculture**, forestry, mineral extraction (**oil**, **natural gas**, and iron ore), and mechanical engineering. **Foreign trade** is low compared to other regions, though it does export raw materials to **Finland**, **Germany**, and **Turkey**, among other countries. **Unemployment** runs high in the republic, especially among rural Balkars.

The current president is Arsen Kanokov, a businessman and member of the **State Duma**. Since taking office in 2005, he has taken on **corrupt** officials, reduced the region's dependency on subsidies from **Moscow**, and made significant improvements in the republic's economic status by focusing on **tourism**, agriculture, and small-business development. Prior to the appointment of Kanokov, Valery Kokov served three terms as president before stepping down for health reasons in 2005 (he died from cancer later that year). Kokov maintained stability in the republic despite the troubling situations in neighboring Georgia and **Chechnya**. In 2002, he oversaw an increase in political and civil rights in the region, including a restriction of the authorities' ability to block public demonstrations.

After the **Beslan** tragedy in 2004, Kabardino-Balkariya began to experience greater levels of violence associated with **Islamist** extremism, which up until that point had found barren ground in the republic. In the wake of Beslan, the government began cracking down on suspected Islamic militants and closing some mosques and regulating others. In October 2005, militants, reportedly under the banner of the **terrorist** group Yarmuk, besieged government buildings in Nalchik. Dozens were subsequently killed in the fighting with security forces.

KABARDINS. Ethnic group. Closely related to the Adyghe, Kabardins or Kabards are the easternmost and the largest subgroup of the **Circassian** people, which also includes the **Adyghe, Cherkess,** Abazins, and Abkhaz. They speak a **language** from the Northwest Caucasian family which also includes Adyghe. The Kabardins number more than 500,000 and are the titular majority in the Republic of **Kabardino-Balkariya,** which they share with the Turkic **Balkars.**

Historically, the Kabardins have been the most pro-Russian of the Caucasian mountaineers. Unlike their western Circassian counterparts, their feudal elite were co-opted by tsarist Russia. Most Kabardins are Sunni **Muslims,** converting to **Islam** from **Christianity** under Ottoman influence; however, their identification with Islam remains comparatively low, even by Caucasian standards. Some noble families converted to Russian **Orthodoxy** after the **Romanov** conquest and still retain their Christian faith. Tsarist and Soviet policies of favoritism toward the Kabardins color interethnic relations in the republic, especially given the **Stalin**-era deportation of the Balkars.

Economically and politically, the Kabardins are the dominant force in post-Soviet Kabardino-Balkariya. Unlike the Balkars, the Kabardins possess a well-developed sense of **national identity** that is reinforced by traditional codes of loyalty and social hierarchy; as such, they are not generally attracted to pan-Islamic ideals. However, this has not prevented some Kabardins from joining **Islamist terrorist** groups like Yarmuk.

KADYROV, AKHMAD ABDULKHAMIDOVICH (1951–2004). Religious leader and politician. Akhmad Kadyrov was born in **Ka-**

zakhstan during the **Chechen** deportation; he later studied **Islam in Uzbekistan.** Kadyrov served as chief mufti of the breakaway **Chechen Republic of Ichkeriya** during the 1990s, famously calling for an international jihad against Russian federal forces during the first **Chechen War.** However, he later switched his loyalty to Moscow, and condemned the rising influence of radical **Islamists** in his country, particularly **Shamil Basayev**'s attempts to create a caliphate across the **North Caucasus.** Backed by the Kremlin, Kadyrov administered the republic from 2000 until 2003, when he won the Chechen presidency. In 2004, after escaping several assassination attempts, he was killed in a bomb blast that ripped through a victory parade commemorating the Soviet victory in World War II. In 2007, his son, **Ramzan Kadyrov**, followed in his footsteps, becoming the Chechen president. *See also* TERRORISM.

KADYROV, RAMZAN AKHMADOVICH (1976–). The son of **Chechnya**'s late grand mufti and former president **Akhmad Kadyrov**, Ramzan Kadyrov rose to prominence as a militia leader in the service of his father. His paramilitaries are popularly known as *Kadyrovtsy* (Kadyrov's men), and have been accused of **human rights** violations within and outside Chechnya, including torture, extrajudicial killings, and other **crimes. Vladimir Putin** began grooming the younger Kadyrov after his father's assassination in 2004. When Kadyrov attained the age of 30, the constitutional minimum for leadership of the republic, he replaced Alu Alkhanov as president under a decree issued by Putin. Kadyrov had previously served as Alkhanov's prime minister; however, the two were bitter political rivals.

As president, Kadyrov has overseen a period of increasing stability and the return of investment, particularly to the war-torn capital, Grozny. In addition to his role in human rights violations committed by his militia, Kadyrov has also been linked to the murders of rival warlords, the **journalist Anna Politkovskaya**, and the human rights activist Nataliya Estemirova, as well as illegal sales of Chechen **oil** and the construction of a vast personality cult. More recently, he has declared that Islamic law should reign in his republic and that the murder of **women** by their relatives for "loose morals" is socially acceptable. *See also* COUNTERTERRORISM.

KALININGRAD OBLAST. An administrative region of the Russian Federation. Part of the Northwestern **Federal District** and forming its own **economic region**, Kaliningrad is sandwiched between **Poland** and **Lithuania**, forming a Russian exclave on the **Baltic Sea**. The region is comprised of the northern half of East Prussia, which was annexed by the Soviet Union after World War II. The southern half of the German exclave was transferred to Poland after the war and confirmed in 1990 with the German-Polish Border Treaty.

Originally, the Poles were to gain control of Königsberg (Kaliningrad); however, **Joseph Stalin**'s desire for an ice-free port for the Russian navy, buttressed by ideological rationales, resulted in Moscow's decision to annex the region to the **Russian Soviet Federative Socialist Republic**. At the end of the war, the predominantly German population of some 2 million was forcibly removed and replaced by Slavic settlers.

Of the **oblast**'s nearly 1 million current inhabitants, there are 786,885 **ethnic Russians** (82 percent), 50,748 Belarusians (5.3 percent), and 47,229 **Ukrainians** (5 percent), according to the 2002 census. As the region is separated from Russia by members of the **North Atlantic Treaty Organization** (NATO) and the **European Union** (EU), Kaliningrad's political situation is often a point of contention between Moscow and the West. In 2004, Brussels and Moscow were at loggerheads over land travel between Kaliningrad and metropolitan Russia, with the former demanding visas for Russian citizens passing through the Schengen zone and the latter proposing the use of "sealed trains" for Russian citizens. Ultimately, a compromise solution established a controlled, visa-free travel corridor between the oblast and Russia proper.

The region's unique economic status within the Russian Federation (it singularly comprises the Kaliningrad Economic Region) gives businesses in the region priority status in trade with the rest of the federation. The proximity to European markets has also resulted in a flourishing black market of **narcotics**, cigarettes, alcohol, and other products passing through en route to Western Europe. Kaliningrad is one of only four locales in Russia permitting casinos after 1 July 2009. Per capita, the region suffers from one of the highest rates of **HIV/AIDS** in either Russia or Europe; with some 350 cases per

100,000 people, rates of infection are estimated at tenfold those of neighboring Lithuania.

During the 1990s, Kaliningrad had one of the highest rates of **unemployment** outside the **North Caucasus**; however, the demand for skilled labor has recently increased in the region. Amber extraction, **agriculture**, fisheries, shipbuilding, railcar manufacture, and **military** expenditures are also important economic drivers for the region. Kaliningrad Oblast is the most heavily militarized area of the Russian Federation, and the density of military infrastructure is the highest in Europe. Kaliningrad serves as the headquarters of the Russian Baltic Fleet, and also houses the Kaliningrad Chkalovsk, Chernyakhovsk, and Donskoye air bases.

In 1993 and 1998, regional leaders attempted to gain the status of a republic but were rebuffed by Moscow. In the latter case, the regional governor Leonid Gorbenko opposed the move, arguing instead for closer relations with **Belarus** (which, along with Lithuania, separates the region from Russia). Under his administration, Kaliningrad was able to command a level of autonomy rivaled only by Russia's **ethnic republics**, despite the region's official status as an oblast. His protectionist efforts stanched the flow of **foreign investment** into the region during the late 1990s (an abrupt departure from the region's status as a Free Economic Zone from 1991 to 1995), and prevented integration with the rest of the Baltic region.

Gorbenko was defeated by the former admiral of the Baltic Fleet, Vladimir Yegorov, in 2000. Yegorov stressed that Kaliningrad must function as a bridge between Europe and Moscow, and serve as a pilot project for Russia's integration into European economic space; however, such vectors were compromised by the row over transit visas. In 2005, Yegorov was replaced by **Putin** appointee Georgy Boos, a close ally of Moscow's mayor, **Yury Luzhkov**. In recent years, there has been an increase in German investment, as well as nostalgia **tourism** from Germany.

In July 2007, Foreign Minister **Igor Ivanov** declared that if the **United States** builds its defensive missile system in Poland and the Czech Republic, Moscow will possibly respond by deploying **nuclear weapons** in Kaliningrad. Previous reports suggest that tactical nuclear weapons are already present in the oblast; in late 2008,

Dmitry Medvyedev announced plans to deploy short-range missiles to the region as well. *See also* AIR FORCE; NAVY.

KALMYKIYA/KHALMG TANGCH. An **ethnic republic** of the Russian Federation. In 1920, the All-Russian Central Executive Committee formed the Kalmyk Autonomous Oblast within Soviet Russia. Five years later, the region was elevated to republic status, becoming the Kalmyk **Autonomous Soviet Socialist Republic** (ASSR). In response to the support given to the invading German army in World War II, **Joseph Stalin** ordered the wholesale deportation of the **Kalmyk** nation to Siberia in 1943. The ASSR was abolished and its lands were divided between the **Astrakhan** and Stalingrad oblasts and **Stavropol Krai**. The regional capital, Elista (along with other city and place names), was changed during the period.

After Stalin's death, the Kalmyks were allowed to return to their homeland, which was restored as an autonomous republic within the **Russian Soviet Federative Socialist Republic** in 1958, though it lost a sliver of productive land to the Astrakhan oblast. The republic declared its sovereignty in 1990, though it did not advocate separation from Russia, and retained its status of an ethnic republic in the new Russian Federation.

Located on the **Caspian Sea**, the republic borders Astrakhan, **Volgograd**, **Rostov**, Stavropol, and **Dagestan**. It is part of the Southern **Federal District** and the Volga **Economic Region**. The republic covers 76,100 square kilometers of mostly desert and **steppe** lands, and has a population of slightly less than 300,000. The Kalmyks recently gained majority status in the republic (53 percent); **ethnic Russians** make up a third of the population, down from 1991 due to a steady exodus from the republic. There are also significant numbers of **Kazakhs**, **Chechens**, and other **North Caucasian** minorities in the republic. The ethnic situation in the region is exceptionally calm, and there is little support for secession from Russia. Kalmykiya is the only predominantly **Buddhist** region in Europe; Kalmyks are Lamaist and revere the Dalai Lama, who has visited the republic a number of times since 1991.

Despite the rather unfavorable quality of the land, the regional **economy** is based on livestock and **agriculture**, in addition to some **oil** revenues. The legacy of Soviet agricultural schemes and disregard for **environmental** preservation has negatively impacted the region's ecosystem, making much of the landscape unsuitable for grazing or farming. Kalmykiya has the distinction of possessing Europe's only desert, the result of the Soviet-era importation of sharp-hooved merino sheep, which devastated the fragile steppe soils. As a result, part of the country is classified as an environmental disaster area by the **United Nations**. Water scarcity remains a major problem in much of the region. Kalmykiya is ranked next-to-last in Russia in terms of per capita monetary income, and **unemployment** runs high in the republic.

The presidential election in 1991 was inconclusive, and ultimately the final round of voting was delayed until 1993, when **Kirsan Ilyumzhinov** won office at the age of 31. He has held office since, expanding the role and power of the presidency at the expense of the region's unicameral legislature, the People's Khural. Of all of Russia's republican governors, Ilyumzhinov's control over his region is arguably the greatest. While he has avoided **Moscow**'s wrath by declaring Russian law the dominant legal code of the republic, he ran unopposed for reelection in 1995, thus contravening federal law. In 1998, Ilyumzhinov, playing on **Boris Yeltsin**'s weakness in the wake of the country's **ruble crisis**, threatened to sever ties with Russia and turn Kalmykiya into an independent **tax** haven (from 1995, Kalmykiya already served as a domestic-offshore zone for Russia, with all local taxes on companies registered in the republic replaced by a single $300 payment).

Despite Ilyumzhinov's independence from Moscow, he was recommended by **Vladimir Putin** to keep his post, a move quickly rubber-stamped by the Khural in 2005. Under his reign, the republic has become the global center of the sport of chess; in 1995, Ilyumzhinov was elected as head of the International Chess Federation (FIDE), and he has made chess mandatory in Kalmykiya's schools. For the 1998 Chess Olympiad, Ilyumzhinov built Chess City, a gleaming Olympic-style village on the outskirts of the capital, at a cost of nearly 50 million dollars.

KALMYKS. Ethnic group. The Kalmyks (or Kalmucks) are the western branch of the Oyrats, a Mongolic people whose origins lie in the Dzungaria region of western China. In the Russian Federation, there are approximately 174,000 ethnic Kalmyks. Arriving in the **Caspian** basin in the 17th century, the Kalmyks represent the last instance of nomadic Asians permanently migrating to the European continent.

After settling in the Volga **steppe**, they were integrated into the Russian empire and served as buffer between the **Orthodox** Slavs and the **Muslim** peoples of the **North Caucasus**. They are the titular majority of the Republic of **Kalmykiya**, but also live in small diasporic communities in Western Europe and the **United States**. The Kalmyk **language** is the only major member of the western branch of the Mongolian language family. Due to **Russification** policies and the social disruptions of the mid-20th century, many Kalmyks — including the president of Kalmykiya, **Kirsan Ilyumzhinov** — have limited mastery of the language; less than 10 percent of Kalmyk youth are fluent.

The Kalmyks are the only indigenous European ethnic group that professes **Buddhism**; like other Mongolic peoples of the Russian Federation, they are Lamaist. While the Kalmyk's **religious** infrastructure was almost totally destroyed by the 1940s, a revival, which began under **glasnost** and is now monetarily supported by Ilyumzhinov, is currently under way.

In 1943, the entire nation, some 92,000 strong, was deported from their homeland to various locales in southern **Siberia**; the mortality rate during transit or during the immediate aftermath of resettlement is estimated to be between one-third and half of all deportees. **Nikita Khrushchev** denounced the deportation in the 1950s, opening the way for repatriation to Kalmykiya. In recent years, Kalmyks emerged as a majority in their ethnic republic, partly as a result of **ethnic Russian** emigration.

KALUGA OBLAST. An administrative region of the Russian Federation. Part of the Central **Federal District** and **Economic Region**, Kaluga lies less than 100 kilometers south of the capital, **Moscow**. It is bordered by the **Smolensk**, **Bryansk**, **Oryol**, **Tula**, and **Moscow oblasts**. With just over a million residents, the oblast covers 29,900 square kilometers of plains and forests. Major international highways and railway lines connect European-bound traffic from Moscow to Kiev, Lvov, and Warsaw. The **economy** is mixed between **industry** (machine building, **food** processing, and chemicals) and **agriculture**.

Obninsk, Russia's "First Science City," is home to the country's largest scientific research complex and its oldest **nuclear energy** plant. The region showed strong support for the **Communist Party of the Russian Federation** during the early 1990s. The regional governor is Anatoly Artamonov; he replaced Valery Sudarenkov, who was the deputy prime minister of **Uzbekistan** in the 1980s. Artamonov was elected in 2000 with 56.72 percent of the vote; in 2004, he won re-election with a two-thirds majority and was reappointed by **Vladimir Putin** in 2005.

KAMCHATKA KRAI. An administrative province of the Russian Federation. Kamchatka Krai was created on 1 July 2007 through a merger of the Kamchatka Oblast and the Koryak Autonomous Oblast. The latter retains the status of an administrative division of the **krai** as the Koryak Okrug (**Koryakiya**), but is no longer a **federal subject** of the Russian Federation. The union resulted from a 23 October 2005 referendum that returned an 85 percent majority "yes" vote among the regions' populations. Kamchatka Krai is part of the Far Eastern **Federal District** and **Economic Region**.

Occupying all of the Kamchatka Peninsula and the Karaginsky and Commander islands, as well as part of the Chukotka Peninsula, the krai has an area of 472,300 square kilometers, making it the 10th-largest region in Russia. The peninsula, comprised of **taiga** and mountains, is home to a volcanic belt that is recognized by UNESCO as a World Heritage Site, as well as large numbers of rare flora and **wildlife**. Kamchatka Krai is bordered by **Chukotka** and **Magadan**, and is washed by the Bering Sea in the east and the Sea of Okhotsk in the west.

The administrative center is Petropavlovsk-Kamchatsky, which has a population of nearly 200,000; it is the world's second-largest city that is inaccessible by road. The city sits on the world's second-largest bay, Avacha, which is home to Russia's Pacific submarine fleet; during the Soviet era, the entire area was closed to foreigners.

Kamchatka has slightly more than 350,000 residents, with **ethnic Russians** making up approximately 80 percent of the population. In Koryakiya, the titular Koryaks account for 26 percent of the population, while Russians are a slight majority (51 percent); other ethnic groups include **Chukchis**, **Ukrainians**, Itelmens, and **Evens**.

The regional **economy** is driven by its **fisheries** (particularly crabbing), animal husbandry, mineral extraction (tin, coal, copper, nickel, and gold), and, more recently, eco-**tourism**. The region is one of Russia's poorest, and suffers from endemic energy shortages due to its lack of integration with the rest of the country's energy grid.

Politically, the region demonstrated strong support for the opposition **Yabloko** party in the 1990s. However, in 2000, the candidate of the **Communist Party of the Russian Federation**, Mikhail Mashkovtsev, was elected. The reformist, Yabloko-backed incumbent Vladimir Biryukov, did not stand in the election. In 2007, **Vladimir Putin** nominated the deputy governor, Aleksey Kuzmitsky, to head the new krai after Mashkovtsev tendered his resignation. Historically, **Moscow** has exercised significant control over the region's finances; whether this will change as a result of the administrative reorganization of the region remains to be seen.

KAMCHATKA OBLAST. *See* KAMCHATKA KRAI.

KARACHAY. Ethnic group. The Karachay are a Turkic ethnic group of some 190,000 inhabiting the **North Caucasus**. They form a plurality in **Karachayevo-Cherkessiya**, the **ethnic republic** that they share with the Circassian **Cherkess**. Karachays are closely related to the **Balkars**; both groups speak dialects of the same **language**, which is part of the Kypchak branch of the Turkic language family. Karachay are predominantly **Muslim**, often identifying less strongly with **Islam** than their Caucasian counterparts.

As one of the **punished peoples**, the Karachay were deported en masse during World War II to **Kazakhstan** and **Uzbekistan**; tens of thousands died on the journey or shortly thereafter. They were rehabilitated and returned to their reconstituted homeland in 1957. Today, ethnic identification remains tepid, crosscut by clan affiliation; however, Russophobia, a by-product of the deportation and exile, is a staple of the Karachay **national identity**.

While the collectivization and deportation disrupted traditional social structures, the Karachay continue to recognize three principal societal stratifications: the largely extinct *Bii* (barons), the subaltern *Uzden* (yeomen), and the *Kul* (serfs); the latter group gained political dominance under Soviet rule. Since 1991, the Karachay nationalist movement *Jamagat* (Karachay: "Renaissance") has advocated a separate Karachay republic; however, demographic superiority due to high birthrates and Russian emigration has sapped support for such plans in recent years.

KARACHAYEVO-CHERKESSIYA/KARACHAY-CHERKESS REPUBLIC. An **ethnic republic** of the Russian Federation. Formerly an autonomous **oblast** within **Stavropol**, the region was renamed the Cherkess Autonomous Oblast (AO) during World War II when **Joseph Stalin** ordered the deportation of the **Karachay** to Central Asia. The Karachay were rehabilitated by **Nikita Khrushchev** and permitted to return to a restored Karachay-Cherkess AO in 1957. Karachayevo-Cherkessiya gained republican status in 1992 in response to federal fears that ethnic **separatism** and **Cossack**-indigenous rivalries would lead to a Balkanization of the region.

The republic is part of the Southern **Federal District** and the North Caucasus **Economic Region**. Karachayevo-Cherkessiya is mostly mountainous, and borders **Krasnodar**, **Stavropol**, **Kabardino-Balkariya**, and the **Republic of Georgia**. The capital is Cherkessk, which was built on the site of a former Cossack *stanitsa* (settlement). It covers 14,100 square kilometers and has a population of 439,000. Collectively, the Turkic Karachay and Caucasian **Cherkess** account for about half the population of the republic, representing 39 percent and 11 percent of the population, respectively. **Ethnic Russians**, including large numbers of Cossacks, form about a third of the population. A number of Cossack organizations support secession from the republic and reincorporation in the Stavropol Krai or accession to Krasnodar. The other important ethnic groups are the Circassian Abazins (7 percent) and the Turkic Nogays (6 percent), as well as small numbers of **Ukrainians**, **Armenians**, and Greeks.

The predominant economic driver in the republic is **industry**, particularly petrochemicals, metalworking, and building materials. **Agriculture**, **mining** (coal, lead, zinc, copper, and gold), and timber are also important.

The republic's first president was the decorated Soviet **military** veteran Vladimir Semenov, an ethnic Karachay. His 1999 election victory stoked ethnic problems, as many Cherkess refused to accept the defeat of their candidate Stanislav Derev, who had secured

40 percent in the first round of voting compared to Semonov's 18 percent. In 2003 Semenov was replaced by the banker Mustafa Batdyyev, also an ethnic Karachay. Born in exile in **Kazakhstan** in 1950, Batdyyev and his family were repatriated six years later. He has been at the forefront of Russia's embrace of separatist leaders in the breakaway Georgian regions of **South Ossetiya** and **Abkhazia**, the latter bordering the republic.

Expressions of pan-**Circassian** solidarity have colored relations between the republic and Abkhazia, as well as attempts at greater co-ordination and cooperation with **Adygeya** and Kabardino-Balkariya. Batdyyev has also curtailed press freedoms in the republic by forbidding government employees from speaking with the **media**. In 2004, he was forced to flee when an angry mob stormed a government building and ransacked his office over the murder of seven prominent businessmen, all of whom were leaders of powerful clans in the region; his son-in-law Ali Kaitov was previously linked to the killings. The high-profile murders were symptomatic of a larger epidemic of **crime** and violence in the **North Caucasian** republic.

KARELIANS. Ethnic group. The Karelians or Karjalaiset live in the borderlands of southeastern **Finland** and northwestern Russia, and are the titular minority of **Kareliya**. In their home republic, they account for less than a 10th of the region's population; there is also a small community in the **Tver Oblast**. In Russia overall, there are slightly fewer than 100,000 Karelians.

Ethnically related to the Finns, Estonians, and other Finnic peoples of northeastern Europe, Finnish Karelians generally speak dialectical Finnish, while their Russian counterparts speak Russian and Karelian. The latter is a Russian-influenced Finnic **language** created by Soviet authorities in the 1930s to foster a separate identity from Finns across the border. It is written with the Cyrillic script and is based on the Olonets dialect. Russian Karelians, unlike their Finnish cousins, are almost exclusively Russian **Orthodox**.

During the early Soviet era, Soviet Kareliya experienced an influx of Finnish **immigrants** who dominated the political scene and prepared the way for an eventual merger of the Karelian and Finnish nationalities; this situation changed drastically in the late 1930s as **Joseph Stalin**'s purges and the Soviet Union's Winter War (1939–

1940) with Finland made Finns persona non grata in the Union of Soviet Socialist Republics (USSR). While the Karelian culture and language were officially supported by the **Communist** regime, the ultimate outcome was a steady Slavicization of the republic.

Nationalist and cultural autonomy movements sprouted during the final years of **glasnost**, including the radical Karelian Congress, which advocated the region's accession to Finland with autonomous status or joint Russian-Finnish administration of the republic, and the Union of Karelian People, which advocates greater cultural and political rights for the titular minority. Karelian (along with Finnish and Veps) was elevated to official status alongside the **Russian language** in the waning days of Soviet rule. However, the linguistic renaissance of Karelian has been limited: only 1 out of 10 young Karelians is fluent in their ancestral language, and Karelian is frequently listed among Europe's most endangered languages.

KARELIYA. An **ethnic republic** of the Russian Federation. Covering lands annexed from Sweden in the 18th century, Kareliya was created as an **Autonomous Soviet Socialist Republic** (ASSR) in 1923. In 1940, the region was enlarged with territory from **Finland** and renamed as the Karelo-Finnish Soviet Socialist Republic (SSR) as part of a larger effort to reincorporate all territories lost to Russia after World War I (1914–1918).

Kareliya holds the distinction of the only **union republic** to be downgraded to an ASSR within Russia (**Abkhazia** was demoted to an ASSR of **Georgia** in 1931), which occurred in 1956. Kareliya is part of the Northwestern **Federal District** and the Northern **Economic Region**. It is bordered by the **Murmansk**, **Archangel**, **Vologda**, and **Leningrad oblasts**, as well as sharing a 723-kilometer-long international border with Finland.

It is washed by the White Sea, and sits on Lake Ladoga and Lake Onega. Kareliya covers 172,400 square kilometers. Half of the territory is forested **taiga**, and the northwestern areas are generally marshy. It is considered one of the most pristine areas of the Russian Federation and has attracted an increasing number of eco-**tourists** from Europe. The regional capital is Petrozavodsk (pop. 266,000). Kareliya's **economy** is dependent on forestry (particularly pulp and paper manufacture) and animal husbandry. It is also a site of rare ores such as chromium, titanium, molybdenum, vanadium, and uranium.

Its population of more than 700,000 includes **ethnic Russians** (77 percent), **Karelians** (9 percent), Belarusians (5 percent), **Ukrainians** (3 percent), Finns (2 percent), and Vepsians (1 percent). Many "Red Finns" came as settlers from Finland after the Bolshevik Revolution, occupying an important political niche until **Joseph Stalin**'s political purges of the 1930s. Further internal migrations of Finns from Murmansk and Leningrad occurred during the 1940s and 1950s, swelling the Finnish population of the region. While Finnish was once an important **language** in the republic, it was dropped from officialdom in the 1950s. **Russian** has long been the dominant language in the republic, but Karelian—a Finnic tongue closely related to Finnish, but written in Cyrillic—has seen a revival since 1989.

The first premier of the republic was Viktor Stepanov, a member of the Soviet *nomenklatura*; he was succeeded by the current head of the republic, Sergey Katanandov. The former mayor of Petrozavodsk (1990–1998) and the region's prime minister from 1998 to 2002, Katanandov was reappointed by **Vladimir Putin** in 2006. His recent efforts have focused on establishing a reliable legal climate in the republic. He is a close ally of **Yury Luzhkov**, and has signed a number of lucrative deals with Moscow, particularly on construction materials. **Unemployment** has been reduced to 3.3 percent, one of the lowest rates in the Russian Federation. He has taken a strong stance against the return of portions of Finland annexed to Kareliya during World War II (about 12 percent of Finland's pre-1940 territory), a policy advocated by some right-wing Finns but not endorsed by Helsinki. Regardless, nearly half of all residents of Kareliya (Russians included) favor **separatism** for the republic.

KARELOVA, GALINA NIKOLAEVNA (1950–). Born in the **Sverdlovsk Oblast** and educated at the Department of Economics of the Ural University, Galina Karelova made a career in Soviet academia. She earned a PhD in social studies and worked in higher **education** until 1990, when she was elected deputy of the Oblast Soviets. In the 1990s, she worked in the federal councils and ministries, focusing on social programs. Since 2000, she has been deputy of the **State Duma**, and she has been in charge of social programs, taxation, and budget committees.

Karelova is also an active member of several prominent **women**'s organizations, including the Russian Association of Businesswomen and the Association of Russian Women's NGOs. She has represented Russian delegations on **demographic issues** at the **United Nations**. Her work with homeless children is particularly renowned.

KASPAROV, GARRY (1963–). Given name: Garrik Kimovich Vaynshteyn. Born to a **Jewish** father and an **Armenian** mother in Baku, **Azerbaijan**, Garry Kasparov rose to international prominence as an international chess champion, capturing the world title in the 1980s. He announced his retirement from major competition in 2005, dedicating himself to writing and **politics**. Kasparov had been a member of the **Communist Party of the Soviet Union** and leader in the **Komsomol** youth movement in the late Soviet period, but had participated little in political activity during the **Yeltsin** era. In 2005, he established the United Civil Front with the aim of preserving **democracy** in Russia. He regularly condemned **Vladimir Putin**'s neo-authoritarian reforms, often doing so in English for international **media** audiences. He helped organize the 2007 **Dissenters' March** and the anti-Kremlin coalition, **The Other Russia**. He entered the 2008 presidential race against Putin's hand-picked successor, **Dmitry Medvyedev**, though he later withdrew his candidacy due to difficulties in recruiting supporters.

KASYANOV, MIKHAIL MIKHAILOVICH (1957–). After serving in **Boris Yeltsin**'s administration, Mikhail Kasyanov became prime minister of the Russian Federation in May 2000 under **Vladimir Putin**. During his tenure, he supported fiscal reforms, a reorganization of the pension system, and modernization of the country's infrastructure. He also supported **Yukos** plans to develop an **oil** pipeline to the Pacific Ocean via **China**, a route that was unpopular among Putin loyalists. Putin dismissed Kasyanov and his entire cabinet on 24 February 2004, signaling a trend toward a nationalistic and conservative approach to governance. A year later, Kasyanov declared his intention to run in the next presidential elections, a bid supported by certain **oligarchs** and anti-Kremlin figures such as **Garry Kasparov**. Kasyanov established the People's Democratic Union as a vehicle for his political ambitions; the group also joined **The Other Russia** coalition. Kasyanov's criticism of Putin's **vertical of power** soon triggered investigations of possible past **corruption**, and he was regularly lambasted in the popular **media**. His hopes to challenge **Dmitry Medvyedev** in the 2008 presidential race were derailed when a percentage of the signatures he obtained were declared invalid by the Central Election Commission. *See also* POLITICS.

KAZAKHS. Ethnic group. The Kazakhs are a mixture of various peoples of inner Asia, primarily Turkic, Mongol, and Indo-Aryan nomads who coalesced as a unified ethnicity in the late Middle Ages. Their **language** is part of the Kypchak branch of the Turkic language family. Kazakhs are nominally **Muslim** with a strong Sufi orientation; however, a significant minority converted to Russian **Orthodoxy** under tsarist rule. While they are the titular majority in **Kazakhstan**, Kazakhs are also an important **ethnic minority** in the Russian Federation, numbering over 650,000. In regions contiguous to Kazakhstan, they make up a significant portion of the local population: **Astrakhan** (14 percent); **Altay Republic** (6 percent); **Orenburg** (6 percent); **Omsk** (4 percent); and **Saratov** (3 percent). Since the **dissolution of the Soviet Union**, Kazakhstan's president, Nursultan Nazarbayev, has encouraged ethnic Kazakhs to return to their ethnic homeland in an effort to promote indigenous demographic dominance of the country, a strategy that resulted in ethnic Kazakhs obtaining a clear majority in the mid-1990s. Kazakhs, along with other Central Asian peoples, have been targeted for **ethnic violence** by neo-Nazi and other racist groups, particularly in **Moscow**. Timur Bekmambetov, the director of Russia's first post-Soviet blockbuster **film**, *Nightwatch* (2004), and the Oscar-nominated Hollywood production *Wanted* (2008), is an ethnic Kazakh.

KAZAKHSTAN (RELATIONS WITH). The incorporation of the Kazakh Steppe into Russia began nearly 300 years ago with the first alliance between the **Kazakh** Hordes and the tsar. Over the centuries, large numbers of Slavic settlers quit European Russia for Kazakhstan. After a brief period of autonomy during the Russian Civil War (1918–1922), Kazakhstan was incorporated into the **Russian Soviet Federative Socialist Republic** (RSFSR); it was awarded the status of **union republic** in 1936. **Stalinist** collectivization and **immigration** of Slavic settlers under **Nikita Khrushchev**'s 1950s Virgin Lands program both depleted the number of native Kazakhs and increased the nonindigenous population to the point that Kazakhstan was the only union republic where the titular population did not possess majority status.

In 1986, the Soviet-era capital of Alma-Ata (Almaty) was the site of the first widespread **ethnic violence** that presaged the fractious centrifugal **nationalism** that would help tear apart the Soviet Union. Replacing his unpopular **ethnic Russian** predecessor, Nursultan Nazarbayev came to power in the last days of Soviet rule. Nazarbayev played a critical role in the **August Coup** of 1991 as a behind-the-scenes mediator between the conspirators and **Boris Yeltsin** (Yeltsin was visiting Kazakhstan when the coup began and narrowly averted assassination upon his return to **Moscow**).

In the wake of the coup, Nazarbayev became one of the principal architects of the **Commonwealth of Independent States** (CIS), hosting its creation at a summit in Alma-Ata on 21 December 1991. The loss of Kazakhstan (along with **Ukraine**) proved to be a painful pill to swallow for many Russians during the 1990s. The existence of millions of **ethnic Russians** in Kazakhstan prompted many nationalists, including **Aleksandr Solzhenitsyn**, to advocate annexing the northern part of the country. Cognizant of its 7,000-kilometer border with the Russian Federation, the central role of ethnic Russians in the workforce, centuries of shared culture, and myriad common economic interests, Nazarbayev has sought to maintain as positive a relationship as possible with Moscow.

On 25 May 1992, Russia and Kazakhstan agreed to a treaty of friendship, cooperation, and mutual assistance, representing one of the first of such treaties to be signed between Moscow and its former Soviet Republics. In 1994, relations were deepened through commitments to further economic integration and expansion of **military** cooperation; the two countries also adopted an agreement on the continued use of the Baikonur cosmodrome for Russia's **space program**. Along with **Belarus**, Kazakhstan has proved itself to be one of the strongest supporters of Russian initiatives within the CIS.

Despite his desire to remain cordial with Russia, Nazarbayev undertook the creation of a multivector approach to **foreign relations** shortly after independence. As the veritable "president for life" in a republic dominated by the executive branch, Nazarbayev has exercised near-total control of the country's foreign policy. Kazakhstan joined the **North Atlantic Treaty Organization** (NATO) **Partnership for Peace** program, expanded trade links with **Germany** and the **European Union** (EU), and developed new ties with **Muslim** countries (particularly other Turkic polities) and East Asian states. Economic dominance of Kazakhstan by Russian businesses during the late 1990s led to a series of ups and downs in the countries' relationship. Kazakhstan was also a pivotal player in the development of the Baku-Tbilisi-Ceyhan pipeline.

Nazarbayev, who views his country as the "Eurasian Bridge," hoped to provide an alternative route for the export of **oil** and **natural gas** to Europe, rather than exclusively relying on the Soviet-era infrastructure that runs through the Russian Federation. In the 1990s, Boris Yeltsin's obsession with the Euro-**Atlantic** community and active diplomacy in the region by the **Clinton** administration gave Nazarbayev enough political protection to step out from Moscow's shadow. Kazakhstan voluntarily transferred its **nuclear weapons** to the Russian Federation, with the financial support of the **United States**. The country, ravaged by decades of Soviet nuclear testing at Semipalatinsk, also ratified the Nuclear Non-Proliferation Treaty (NPT).

In an effort to solidify his authority over Kazakhstan—the world's ninth-largest state—and stave off revanchist calls for Russia's annexation of the northern tier of his country, he moved his capital to the north-central city of Aqmola (Tselinograd) in 1997; the city was subsequently renamed Astana. While the central government's efforts at "Kazakhization" of the state through the imposition of pro-Kazakh language laws and the indigenization of the highest posts in firms, education, health care, and so forth was often ill-received by the local Russian community (roughly 25 percent of the national population) and their self-appointed protectors in Moscow, ethnic relations have remained remarkably amiable, unlike the situation in the **Baltic States**.

In 1996, Kazakhstan and Russia were co-founders of the Shanghai Five (later the **Shanghai Cooperation Organization** or SCO) in 1996, alongside **China**, **Tajikistan**, and **Kyrgyzstan**. In the wake of the **September 11 attacks**, coordination on **counterterrorism** issues between the SCO members increased. Kazakhstan has sought to use Russia as a buffer against an increasingly powerful China, a country with potential geopolitical designs on eastern Kazakhstan. **Vladimir Putin**, in his support for the United States' efforts on the "war on terror," made clear he would not stand in the way of the expansion of Washington's presence in **Central Asia**. This decision was a key turning point in Russia's historical treatment of the region as solely within its sphere of influence. While Kazakhstan did not accept the presence of U.S. troops on its soil (unlike Tajikistan, Kyrgyzstan, and **Uzbekistan**), Nazarbayev did provide logistical support to coalition forces in the war in **Afghanistan**. Nazarbayev was careful to expand links with Russia as the U.S. made inroads into Central Asia, and was quick to support Moscow and Beijing's calls for Washington to set a timeline for withdrawal from its bases in the region in 2005.

Nazarbayev and Putin developed a solid working relationship that resulted in the two countries working closely on security, border issues, **narcotics** interdiction, and other critical issues in the first decade of the millennium; however, sensitivities over the division of **Caspian Sea** resources remains a sticking point. In 2005, the Russian **Federation Council** ratified an agreement between Russia and Kazakhstan extending Russia's lease of the Baikonur spaceport until 2050 at an annual fee of $115 million dollars. In 2008, as Russia's new president **Dmitry Medvyedev** made Kazakhstan the first destination on his first foreign visit, he also included a stop in Beijing. Nazarbayev, speaking at a joint press conference with Medvyedev, stated that Russia "was, is, and will be" the priority in Kazakhstan's foreign policy. Trade between the two countries reached $20 billion in 2008.

KEMEROVO OBLAST. An administrative region of the Russian Federation. Part of the Siberian **Federal District** and the West Siberian **Economic Region**, Kemerovo borders **Tomsk**, **Krasnoyarsk**, **Khakasiya**, **Altay Krai**, **Novosibirsk**, and the **Altay Republic**. The region is also known as Kuzbass, after the Kuznetsk basin, one of the world's largest coal deposits. It covers an area of 95,500 square kilometers and has a population of nearly 3 million, the vast majority of whom are **ethnic Russians**, though minorities of **Ukrainians**, **Tatars**, and ethnic **Germans** are also present.

The region is heavily urbanized (87 percent) and industrialized, with major centers being Kemerovo, Novokuznetsk, Prokopyevsk, and Kiselevsk. Its mineral resources—particularly coal—drive the regional **economy**, with more than a third employed in the industrial sector. Symptomatic of the regional focus on heavy **industry**, Kemerovo has strongly supported Communists in the postindependence era, receiving a plurality of votes in the 1995 federal election (the second highest in any region in the Russian Federation).

In the late 1990s, **Boris Yeltsin** appointed Amangeldy Tuleyev, a Communist with strong protectionist leanings, to head the region after dismissing the widely disliked Mikhail Kislyuk in a dispute over pension payments. Tuleyev, a railway engineer of **Kazakh** and **Tatar** parentage, had previously run for the presidency of Russia in 1991 and 1996. Despite being born an ethnic **Muslim** and making a journey to Mecca, Tuleyev was rumored to have been baptized as a **Russian Orthodox** Christian in 1999. He denied **media** reports to that effect but was issued a death sentence for apostasy by **Chechnya**'s Majlis al-Shura council.

The regional government came under intense pressure from workers in 1998 over wages, a conflict that affected the rest of Russia due to a blockade of a portion of the **Trans-Siberian Railway**. Despite the controversy, Tuleyev remained extremely popular in the region and won a majority of votes in Kemerovo when he stood against **Vladimir Putin** for the 2000 federal presidential election. While losing his bid for president of Russia, he did secure more than 90 percent of the vote when he ran for regional governor again in 2001.

In recent years, he has shored up his relations with Moscow; he broke with the **Communist Party of the Russian Federation** in 2003, later joining **United Russia**. In 2007, a methane blast at the Ulyanovskaya mine made international headlines when over 100 miners lost their lives; since the explosion, Tuleyev has campaigned for improved safety regulations across the Russian Federation. *See also* MINING.

KGB/KOMITYET GOSUDARSTVENNOY BEZOPASNOSTI. The Committee for State Security, most commonly known by its **Russian language** acronym KGB, was the Soviet Union's premier secret police, internal security, and **espionage** agency. Established in

1954 out of the NKVD and other **Stalin**-era **security services**, the organization controlled many aspects of life in the Union of Soviet Socialist Republics (USSR) until its demise in the immediate wake of the 1991 **August Coup**, which had been perpetrated by several high-ranking members of the organization including KGB chief **Vladimir Kryuchkov**.

The KGB's responsibilities were subsequently divided between the newly created Inter-republican Security Service, the Central Intelligence Service, and the Committee for Protection of the State Border. With the **dissolution of the Soviet Union** in December 1991, these organizations underwent further reforms and division of responsibilities; in 1995, **Boris Yeltsin** clearly delineated the lines between domestic security and foreign spying by creating the **FSB** and the Foreign Intelligence Service of the Russian Federation. However, these organizations are deeply influenced by the culture and organization of their predecessor, the KGB. Abroad, the KGB ran a massive international spy ring of ideological sympathizers, as well as paid informants and agents. Within the **Eastern Bloc**, the agency carefully monitored opposition to local Communist Party and Soviet domination, often infiltrating anti-Soviet organizations. At home, the security agency was charged with suppressing ideological subversion and "counterrevolution," which included disinformation campaigns and the monitoring and censoring of **dissidents**, **national minority** leaders, and anti-Communist activists.

Despite its fearsome reputation, the agency maintained a high level of prestige and commanded a great deal of political influence in the late Soviet period. Many observers noted that the KGB was the only major state institution that was not afflicted by the **corruption** that had become rampant by the mid-1980s. The KGB proved a valuable ally for **Mikhail Gorbachev** during his rise to power and early years of reform. By the late 1980s, however, Gorbachev's move toward **democratization** (*demokratizatsiia*) soured relations with the KGB's leadership. While the military aspects of the KGB's spy programs were toned down under Gorbachev's "New Thinking" in **foreign relations**, the agency ratcheted up its industrial espionage, creating a legacy that influenced policy under both Yeltsin and **Vladimir Putin**, the latter a former KGB agent himself. *See also* UNITED STATES.

KHABAROVSK KRAI. An administrative province of the Russian Federation. Part of the Far Eastern **Federal District** and **Economic Region**, Khabarovsk is a prorupt province that stretches from the Sea of Okhotsk in the north to the Amur River in the south. Within Russia, it is bordered by **Magadan, Sakha, Amur,** and **Primorsky.** It shares an international border with **China,** contains the **Jewish Autonomous Oblast,** and is separated from the **Sakhalin Oblast** by only a few kilometers at the Strait of Tatary.

Khabarovsk's northern geography is dominated by the **taiga**; in the south, it is temperate broadleaf forest. Much of the province is mountainous, with the Jugjur and Bureya being the largest ranges. It is Russia's fourth-largest **federal subject,** covering 788,600 square kilometers, and has a population of approximately 1.5 million. **Ethnic Russians** make up 90 percent of the population; **ethnic minorities** indigenous to the area include Nanays, **Evenks,** Ulchi, Nivks, Udege, Negidals, and Orochs. Other minorities include **Ukrainians,** ethnic Koreans, **Yakuts,** and **Tatars.**

Forestry and **fishing** are the region's major economic drivers; petroleum refining and shipbuilding are also key components of the **economy.** The region is an important transit zone for air traffic to and from **Japan.** Khabarovsk has well-developed trading relationships with Japan, **Canada,** and **China,** as well as other Pacific Rim countries.

Viktor Ishayev, a former engineer at a shipbuilding plant, is the region's long-standing, pro-market executive. In September 1991, he became head of the regional administration. In 2001, he gained the post of regional governor, to which he was reelected in 2004 and then reappointed by **Vladimir Putin** in 2007. He was one of the last popularly elected regional governors in Russia and was able to win Moscow's favor despite his strong regionalist orientation. Ishayev has been vocal about China's poor environmental record and its deleterious effects on Khabarovsk. His condemnations of Chinese **pollution** of the Amur River have been especially harsh, suggesting that his southern neighbor is destroying the livelihoods and traditional culture of the region's indigenous ethnic minorities, who depend on subsistence fishing.

Despite his opposition to Beijing's environmental record, Ishayev did not publicly decry Moscow's decision to relinquish control of

Tarabarov (Yinlong) Island and approximately half of Bolshoy Us-
suriysky (Heixiazi) Island, both formerly part of Khabarovsk, to
China in 2004. Despite **North Korean** propaganda to the contrary,
the Khabarovsk village of Vyatskoye was the birthplace of **Kim
Jong-il**, whose father was the commander of Soviet-controlled Korean military units stationed in the province.

KHAKAS. Ethnic group. The Khakas or Khakassians were known
as Yenisei or Minusinsk Tatars until the 20th century. A formerly
nomadic Turkic people, they formed a separate ethnic group and
national identity as a result of remaining in **Siberia** when their
counterparts departed for the mountains of Central Asia, ultimately
becoming the Kyrgyz. Khakas number about 75,000 and are found
mostly in their **ethnic republic** of **Khakasiya** where they make up 12
percent of the population, though more than 4,000 live in neighboring
Krasnoyarsk Krai.

The Khakas **language**, which was developed in its literary form
after the 1917 Bolshevik Revolution, is a member of the Northeastern (Siberian) Turkic family, related to Yakut and Tuvan. Under
Romanov rule, the Khakas adopted Russian **Orthodoxy**, though
animism, **shamanism**, **Islam**, and **Buddhism** still have resonance
in Khakas culture. As part of **Joseph Stalin**'s national delimitation
scheme, five ethnic groups (Beltir, Sagai, Kachin, Koibal, and Kyzyl) were consolidated to form the Khakas nation in the 1920s. As a
result of the above factors, Khakas national identity remains rather
weak compared to other **ethnic minorities** of the Russian Federation
(evidenced by the Khakas' gravitation toward **pan-Turkism** in the
1930s). Intermarriage with Russians runs very high, and **Russian**
is the dominant language of communication among ethnic Khakas,
though a vast majority of Khakas are fluent in the native tongue.

Demographically, the Khakas have experienced strong growth,
both in the late Soviet era and postindependence. Under **perestroika**
and **glasnost**, a modest cultural revival occurred with the emergence
of the Khakas Cultural Center and the Tun (Renaissance) Association
of the Khakas People; however, few Khakas and virtually no **ethnic
Russians** favored **separatism**, opting instead for a republican option
within the Russian Federation. Much of the renaissance has focused
on religious practices including reviving traditional shamanism as

well as establishing new forms of non-Christian worship, principally mysticism and Burkhanism, an import from the **Altay Republic**.

KHAKASIYA. An **ethnic republic** of the Russian Federation. An area known for its archeological relics, the Khakas National Okrug was converted into an autonomous **oblast** with **Krasnoyarsk** in 1930. While never having been an **Autonomous Soviet Socialist Republic** during the Soviet era, Khakasiya nonetheless became a republic under the terms of the **Federation Treaty** in 1992.

Khakasiya is part of the Siberian **Federal District** and the East Siberian **Economic Region**. It is bordered by **Kemerovo**, Krasnoyarsk, **Tuva**, and the **Altay Republic**. Its geographic area is 61,900 square kilometers and it has a population of slightly less than 550,000. In terms of ethnic makeup, **ethnic Russians** form a majority of the population (80 percent); the titular minority, **Khakas**, make up 12 percent of the population, with ethnic **Germans** (1.7 percent) and **Ukrainians** (1.5 percent) also being represented. The regional capital is Abakan (pop. 165,000), a major industrial center situated near the Krasnoyarsk Reservoir. Processing natural resources (coal, iron ore, aluminum, etc.) and forestry are the major components of the local **economy**.

Geographically, the region consists of black-earth (**chernozem**) **steppe**. Its eastern boundary is formed by the upper Yenisei River; in the west and south, it is hemmed in by the Kuznetsk Alatau and Sayan ranges. As a result of numerous fast-flowing rivers, the region has a surplus of hydroelectric power, much of which is generated at the 6.4-million-kilowatt Sayano-Shushensk hydroelectric power plant, the largest in Russia. Well connected to other regions, Khakasiya has one of the highest rail densities in Asiatic Russia.

Aleksey Lebed, the younger brother of General **Aleksandr Lebed**, has ruled the republic since 1996. His policies were frequently coordinated with his brother, governor of neighboring Krasnoyarsk, from 1998 until his death in 2002 (the younger Lebed briefly ran to replace his brother, but dropped out before the poll). In the midst of the **financial crisis of 1998**, Aleksey Lebed declared he would no longer transfer funds to the federal budget, taking the opportunity to liken **Boris Yeltsin** to Adolf Hitler. The impasse, however, was quickly resolved when Moscow agreed to increase financial transfers to Khakasiya.

Under **Vladimir Putin**'s tenure as president, Lebed joined the pro-Kremlin **United Russia** party; however, he refused to openly seek Putin's endorsement for reinstatement after the **electoral reforms of 2004–2005**, which impacted regional governors. Failure to do so was viewed as a catalyst for the opening of criminal proceedings against Lebed for "misappropriation of authority" in 2006. In the late 1990s, the region drew international attention when the Khakasiya Supreme Court ordered the closure of a Lutheran mission, a decision later overturned on appeal. Khakasiya has long been a refuge for marginal religious groups including Catholics, Pentecostals, Baptists, and **Old Believers**. *See also* HUMAN RIGHTS.

KHANTIYA-MANSIYA/KHANTY-MANSI AUTONOMOUS OK-RUG-YUGRA. An administrative district of the Russian Federation. As an **autonomous okrug** (AOk), Khantiya-Mansiya is both a **federal subject** of the Russian Federation and a subject of the **Tyumen Oblast**, which lies on its southern border. The region also shares a border with **Yamaliya**, **Tomsk**, **Sverdlovsk**, and the **Komi Republic**. It is part of the Urals **Federal District** and the West Siberian **Economic Region**. The administrative center of the region is Khanty-Mansiisk, a city buoyed by **oil** wealth that has emerged as a showcase among Russian cities; despite its small size (pop. 60,000) it will soon boast a 280-meter diamond-shaped tower meant to signify the region's wealth.

Khantiya-Mansiya occupies a land area of 523,100 square kilometers and has a population over 1.4 million. Unlike most of **Siberia**, Khantiya-Mansiya has experienced a population boom since 1991, with an increase of nearly 100,000 residents. The major ethnic groups include **ethnic Russians** (66 percent), **Ukrainians** (9 percent), **Tatars** (8 percent), and **Bashkirs** (2.5 percent). The region's dual titular minorities, the **Khanty** and the **Mansi**, make up 1.2 percent and 0.7 percent, respectively.

The territory is divided between **tundra**, swampland, and **taiga** and has several major rivers, including the Ob and the Irtysh. During the late Middle Ages, the region was known as Yugra. When the region fell to invading **Cossacks**, the indigenous Ugrian peoples, known as the Ostyaks (Khanty) and Voguls (Mansi), were subjected to **Russification** and forced to convert to Russian **Orthodoxy**. In the early Soviet period, **Moscow** established an East Vogul National Autonomous Okrug, which became the Khanty-Mansi Autonomous Okrug in 1943, an appellation that survived the transition from Soviet to post-Soviet control. The region's name was officially altered to include the historical name "Yugra" in 2003. Like its sister district Yamaliya, Khantiya-Mansiya is partially administered by Tyumen; however, the exact constitutional relationship of the Khanty-Mansi AOk to Moscow and Tyumen remains contentious.

In the 1990s, Khantiya-Mansiya sought relief from the federal constitutional court regarding what it saw as Tyumen's illegal attempts at exercising control over oil revenues. Khantiya-Mansiya is Russia's leading producer of oil, representing 57 percent of the country's oil production and 7.5 percent of global output (approximately 5 million barrels per day). It is Russia's second-largest producer of electrical energy and its third-largest **natural gas** producer. Despite its location and relatively small population, the region accounts for more than one-tenth of Russia's **tax** income. Oil revenues account for 90 percent of the regional economy, but natural gas fields are also undergoing massive development. Forestry and **fishing** are also important to the region.

Aleksandr Filipenko has served as the elected head of the regional administration since 1996 (he was appointed to the post by **Boris Yeltsin** in 1991). His early administration was characterized by attempts to secede from Tyumen in order to keep a larger percentage of revenues within the AOk; over time, he has been forced to simply work toward greater autonomy. He has signed numerous deals with energy producers such as **Lukoil**, **Rosneft**, and Slavneft, many of which have clauses that promote local social development, ecologically sound approaches to fossil fuel extraction, and protection of indigenous cultures.

Reappointed by **Vladimir Putin** in 2005, he has sought to diversify the regional **economy** by attracting highly trained scientists and academics to the region. By focusing on telecommunication and information technology, Filipenko hopes to turn the district into a "Silicon Taiga" that will retain its young people and attract talent from around Russia. The district's oil boom has created a magnet for legal and illegal **immigrants** from all over the Russian Federation and other post-Soviet countries, particularly **Tajikistan**.

KHANTY. Ethnic group. Formerly known as the Ostyaks, the Khanty are an Ugrian people of western **Siberia**. They are closely related to the **Mansi** people, and together they represent the titular minorities of **Khantiya-Mansiya**, which collectively represent less than 2 percent of the region's population. They can also be found in **Yamaliya** and **Tyumen** proper. The Khanty number fewer than 30,000 and are considered to be an endangered ethnolinguistic group.

The Khanty **language** is a member of the Ob-Ugric subdivision of the Finno-Ugric branch of the Uralic language family; roughly 60 percent of ethnic Khanty possess fluency in their ancestral language. The Khanty are distantly related to Hungarians, Estonians, and Finns. Clan (*syr*) affiliation remains an important part of Khanty society and governs land-use rights in the Ob River basin. Their historic territory is known as Yugra, which was part of the Siberia Khanate until falling under Russian control in the 17th century.

Despite attempts to force the Khanty to accept Russian **Orthodoxy**, many Khanty continued to practice **shamanism** into the 20th century. Traditional beliefs—specifically the sacred bear hunt and its associated rituals—were not tolerated by the Soviet authorities until the **glasnost** era. In recent years, shamanistic practices have become more common, including the communal reindeer sacrifice (*myr*) and other pre-Soviet rituals. The Khanty have possessed a national homeland in the form of an **autonomous okrug** for more than 60 years; however, most Khanty have adhered to traditional lifestyles centered on **fishing**, hunting, and reindeer herding (and more recently, the fur trade).

Soviet attempts at collectivization, persecution of shamans, and forced attendance at boarding schools for Khanty children in the 1930s sparked the Kazym Rebellion, which was violently crushed by the Red Army. As is the case with other **indigenous peoples of the north**, many Khanty suffer from **alcohol** addiction and there is a high suicide rate. Political identity based on membership in the nation remains weak due to poor communication between the various communities that comprise the Khanty people.

Development of the region's petroleum resources negatively impacted Khanty culture during the Soviet period, **polluting** rivers and destroying grazing lands and sacred groves alike. However, since Russia's independence, the Khanty and Mansi have gained additional land-use rights and have modestly benefited from social programs associated with oil profits. A small group of **intelligentsia** has also been established that lobbies for greater protection of the Khanty's traditional practices. Along with the Mansi and the **Nenets**, the Khanty form the core of the Association to Save Yugra, a political organization dedicated to protecting indigenous ecosystems from natural resource exploitation. They also have links to the international Finno-Ugric Congress, a transnational organization that develops closer ties between the various Uralic peoples of Europe and **Eurasia** and works against language death in the Russian Federation.

KHASAV-YURT ACCORD. Signed on 30 August 1996, the Khasav-Yurt Accord produced a cease-fire marking the end of the first **Chechen War**. During the meeting in the **Dagestan** town of Khasavyurt, the federal representative, General **Aleksandr Lebed**, and **Aslan Maskhadov**, who represented the breakaway **Chechen Republic of Ichkeriya**, agreed to the mutual withdrawal of troops from the Chechen capital of Grozny; there was also a commitment that federal troops would vacate the entirety of Chechnya by the end of the year. Delineation of the relationship between Ichkeriya and Moscow would be delayed for five years. **Shamil Basayev**'s incursion into Dagestan in 1999, however, triggered the second Chechen War, resulting in the restoration of federal authority over the region. *See also* DUDAYEV, JOKHAR.

KHASBULATOV, RUSLAN IMRANOVICH (1942–). Politician. As an ethnic **Chechen**, Ruslan Khasbulatov suffered deportation to **Kazakhstan** as a toddler. After secondary school, he moved to the capital where he studied at **Moscow State University**. He joined the **Communist Party of the Soviet Union** in the mid-1960s, and developed a reputation as a scholar of foreign capitalism. He partnered with **Boris Yeltsin** during the early 1990s and was elected to the **Congress of People's Deputies** in 1990. However, the two politicians fell out during and after the **dissolution of the Soviet Union** in December 1991. As chairman of the **Supreme Soviet of the Russian Federation**, Khasbulatov was arguably the most important opposition figure in the **constitutional crisis of 1993**. After the violent assault on the White House, Khasbulatov was arrested, though the newly elected **State Duma** pardoned him later that year. Though he has spoken of returning to **politics**, since 1993, Khasbulatov has generally maintained a low profile as an economics professor at the Plekhanov Russian Academy of Economics in **Moscow**.

KHODORKOVSKY, MIKHAIL BORISOVICH (1963–). Oligarch. Once the wealthiest man in Russia, Mikhail Khodorkovsky is currently an inmate of a **Siberian** prison, where he is serving an eight-year sentence.

Khodorkovsky was born into a **Jewish** family in **Moscow**; his parents were factory workers and he grew up in a communal apartment. As a young man he was active as a **Komsomol** (Communist Youth League) leader, envisaging a future career of an **apparatchik**. Through his Komsomol associates, he managed to build up a network of friends who had access to the Soviet government, and particularly to Russia's **banking** sector. In the late 1980s, he and several friends from the Medeleeva Chemical Technical Institute started a private business, selling computers and software. In 1989, he established the Menatep Bank to finance his growing trading business (the bank later collapsed during the 1998 **ruble crisis**). It is rumored that the financial institution operated as a front for diverting state funds from Komsomol, **KGB**, and other state sources. Khodorkovsky managed to obtain a license to handle accounts of the victims of the **Chernobyl** nuclear accident, which provided him with an opportunity to evade taxes and import duties. In the immediate post-Soviet period, Menatep provided bridge credit and capital to state enterprises when **Boris Yeltsin**'s new Russian government was unable to do so. He also set up a market for purchasing state-issued vouchers, allowing him to expand his holdings of various companies across Russia.

In 1993, as a result of a controversial **privatization** gamble under the umbrella of his Rosprom holding company, Khodorkovsky created the **Yukos** oil company, a conglomerate of a number of former Soviet state-owned **oil** companies. It became one of the world's largest private oil companies, producing 20 percent of Russian oil. In 2003, Khodorkovsky attempted a merger of Yukos with Sibneft, hoping to create a supersized oil agglomerate. However, during the same year, Khodorkovsky was arrested on charges of fraud. Shortly thereafter, the Russian government froze shares of Yukos as a result of allegations of tax evasion, resulting in the collapse in Yukos share price and eventually in the sell-off of the company. In 2005, Khodorkovsky was found guilty of fraud and sentenced to 10 years in prison (ultimately reduced to eight).

In 2003's parliamentary elections, Khodorkovsky had funded several **political parties**, including the liberal **Yabloko** and **Union of Right Forces**, as well as the **Communist Party of the Russian Federation**; he had also hinted at a possible run for the presidency in 2008. As a result, Khodorkovsky's prosecution has been viewed as political. In February 2000, **Vladimir Putin** had informed the oligarchs that they were to refrain from **politics** if they wanted to preserve their economic empires. Even before his arrest, Khodorkovsky was viewed as failing to live up to his part of the bargain. While it is doubtful Khodorkovsky managed to gain his capital by obediently following Russian law, it is evident that he was singled out for his political activities. The Kremlin's involvement in his prosecution has not been proven, but many Russian and Western observers dispute the validity of the investigation process and court proceedings. *See also* LEGAL SYSTEM.

KHRUSHCHEV, NIKITA SERGEYEVICH (1894–1971). Politician. Nikita Khrushchev served as chairman of the **Communist Party of the Soviet Union** (CPSU) from 1953 to 1964, making him the de facto leader of the Union of Soviet Socialist Republics (USSR). He conducted a partial de-Stalinization of the country, oversaw major advances in the country's **space program**, backed the erection of the Berlin Wall, and expanded the scope of the **Cold War** to Latin America, Africa, and other parts of the globe. His ill-conceived Virgin Lands project wreaked havoc on **agriculture** and the **environment** in **Kazakhstan** and the **Altay** region. He did not die in office, but was instead removed by a group of senior CPSU figures, including **Leonid Brezhnev**, his successor. He died of a heart attack on 11 September 1971. *See also* STALIN, JOSEPH.

KIM JONG-IL (1941–). Korean politician. Born in Vyatskoye, **Khabarovsk Krai**, Kim Jong-il is the de facto leader of the Democratic Republic of **North Korea** and the son of the country's first ruler, Kim Il-sung. The younger Kim returned to Korea in 1945 as the country gained independence from **Japan**. Benefiting from his father's cult of personality and totalitarian control of the hermit state, Kim Jong-il, as leader of the Korean Workers' Party, emerged as the heir apparent in the late 1980s. While not taking the title of president, the younger Kim assumed total control of the country upon his father's death in 1994.

Under **Mikhail Gorbachev** and **Boris Yeltsin**, North Korea's relations with the Soviet Union and Russia degenerated rapidly. Russia's support of the impoverished Stalinist regime prevented economic and diplomatic relations with its wealthier neighbor, South Korea, and harmed relations with the **United States** and Japan; as a result, ties with Kim's regime were dramatically scaled back, as was **military** support. However, with the ascendance of **Vladimir Putin**, Kim was partially rehabilitated.

The two leaders were frequently photographed together, and Kim paid a previously unthinkable visit to **Moscow** via the **Trans-Siberian Railway** in 2001; he later visited the **Russian Far East**. Russia, along with the People's Republic of **China**, has attempted to persuade Kim's government to abandon its nuclear weapons program, but to little avail. In 2009, reports of Kim's ill health have led to fears in the region of instability associated with any change in leadership. *See also* FOREIGN RELATIONS.

KIRILL I, PATRIARCH (1946–). Religious leader. Born Vladimir Mikhailovich Gundyayev, Kirill I is the current Patriarch of Moscow and All Rus and the Primate of the **Russian Orthodox Church** (ROC). He was enthroned on 1 February 2009 in the wake of his predecessor, **Alexius II**'s death; the event was attended by President **Dmitry Medvyedev** and Prime Minister **Vladimir Putin**. Kirill previously served as Bishop of Vyborg, from which he oversaw **Finland**'s **Orthodox** community, and the Metropolitan of Smolensk and Kaliningrad, as well as the chair of the ROC's Department for External Church Relations. Despite his purported openness to dialogue with the Roman Catholic Church, he is viewed as highly conservative and opposed to any major changes in religious doctrine. *See also* RELIGION.

KIRIYENKO, SERGEY VLADILENOVICH (1962–). Politician. Sergey Kiriyenko was born in Sukhumi, **Abkhazia**, and grew up in the **Black Sea** resort town of **Sochi**. Of mixed **Jewish**-**Ukrainian** heritage, he adopted his mother's Slavic surname as a young man. He achieved national prominence in 1998 when he was nominated to succeed **Viktor Chernomyrdin** as prime minister. Though the Communist-dominated **State Duma** initially refused to confirm him, **Boris Yeltsin** ultimately succeeded in gaining his appointment. He served from 23 March 1998 until 23 August 1998. His short tenure was the result of a government default on bond coupons, which in turn led to a devaluation of the Russian currency and the 1998 **ruble crisis**. After leaving the government, he helped form the liberal **Union of Right Forces political party** and unsuccessfully challenged **Yury Luzhkov** for mayor of **Moscow**. Since 2005, he has served as the head of Rosatom, the federal atomic agency. *See also* POLITICS.

KIROV OBLAST. An administrative region of the Russian Federation. Part of the Volga **Federal District** and the Volga-Vyatka **Economic Region**, the Kirov Oblast is bordered by **Komi**, **Perm Krai**, **Udmurtiya**, **Tatarstan**, **Mari El**, and the **oblasts** of **Archangel**, **Vologda**, **Kostroma**, and **Nizhny Novgorod**. Kirov is located at the eastern edge of the East European Plain, which turns to uplands and ridge in the north and northwest of the oblast. The region has a land area of 120,800 square kilometers and a population of 1.5 million. Nine out of 10 inhabitants are **ethnic Russians**; the significant minority populations are **Tatars** (3 percent), **Maris** (2.6 percent), and **Udmurts** (1.2 percent). Unlike most oblasts, the capital city, Vyatka, does not share its name with the region due to a name change in 1992. A failed attempt to reorganize the province into the Vyatka Krai failed in 1994 due to a veto by **Moscow**. The region is named after the Old Bolshevik and revolutionary Sergey Kirov (born Kostrikov).

During the 1990s, both Communists and **Vladimir Zhirinovsky** enjoyed popularity in the region. The **Communist Party** candidate Vladimir Sergeyenkov won election in 1996 with a majority of votes cast; he immediately set about renationalizing portions of the regional **economy**. Sergeyenkov was reelected in 2000 but was prevented from running for a third term by local legislation. In 2004, he was succeeded by a former deputy general prosecutor and **Duma** member, Nikolay Shaklein. Shaklein has focused on introducing innovative technology, improving regional **transportation** infrastructure, and developing new industries such as biofuels.

The regional economy has experienced growth in the areas of nonferrous metal **industry**, cellulose and paper production, construction materials, and furniture manufacture in recent years. Forestry and the **military**-industrial complex are also important drivers of the local economy. Peat deposits in the region are substantial; discovery of **oil**, gold, and other natural resources in recent years also show promise. Recently, the destruction of chemical weapons stored in the Maradykovsky Arsenal, Russia's second-largest stockpile of such weapons, has become a hot-button issue on the local and international stages. *See also* WEAPONS OF MASS DESTRUCTION.

KLEBNIKOV, PAUL (1963–2004). Journalist. Paul Klebnikov (sometimes spelled Khlebnikov), was an American journalist of Russian descent. He was educated at the University of California, Berkeley, and the London School of Economics; he wrote his doctoral thesis on Russian pre-Soviet **economic** reforms. In 1989, he joined *Forbes* and gained a considerable reputation by investigating controversial financial dealings in post-Soviet Russia. He investigated Russian **corruption** and made many influential enemies. He rose to the position of *Forbes'* senior editor and became the first editor of *Forbes'* Russian edition when it was launched in 2004. He authored a number of publications, including a biography of **Boris Berezovsky** and a series of interviews with a **Chechen** guerilla commander.

In 2004, Klebnikov was assassinated in **Moscow**, and although he survived the initial attack, he died in the hospital. His murder was linked to his professional activities and was one in a series of political assassinations of Russian journalists, including **Anna Politkovskaya**. Russian officials rejected U.S. help in investigating the case, which has been brought to trial but has not been resolved yet. Russian investigation has focused on Klebnikov's links with **Chechnya**. Since his death, his widow, Musa Klebnikov, has established the Paul Klebnikov Fund to support the growth of **civil society** in the Russian Federation.

KOMI. Ethnic group. The Komi are a Finno-Ugrian people who reside in the extreme northeastern European Plain. While they consider themselves to comprise a single nationality, they are divided into Komi-Zyrians (or Komi proper), Komi-Izhems, and Komi-Permyaks. Collectively known simply as Komi, the first two groups are the titular minority (25 percent) of the **Komi Republic**, while the latter—sometimes called simply Permyaks—are the titular majority (59 percent) of the formerly **autonomous okrug** of **Permyakiya**. Komi are also found in **Nenetsiya**, **Khantiya-Mansiya**, **Kirov**, **Murmansk**, and **Perm Krai**. In all, there are some 434,000 Komi in the Russian Federation: 68 percent are Komi-Zyrians, 29 percent are Komi-Permyaks, and 3.6 percent are Komi-Izhems (who live around the Izhma River and are ethnically and culturally linked to the **Nenets**).

The Komi **languages** (Komi-Zyrian and Komi-Permyak) are mutually intelligible; along with Udmurt, they are the only living members of the Permic group of Finno-Ugric languages, part of the Uralic language family. Forcibly converted to Russian **Orthodoxy** in the 14th century, many Komi retain strong vestiges of pre-Russian **shamanism** and animism. While Russification significantly weakened Komi **national identity** during the Soviet period, the last years of **perestroika** saw the introduction of greater cultural rights for the indigenous population and the rise of political organizations dedicated to fostering national identity among the Komi. The first of these organizations was *Komi Kotyr* ("Komi Community"); however, the party soon dissolved into competing factions, including the Committee for the Revival of the Komi People and the more radical *Doriam Asnõmös* ("Let's Defend Ourselves"). Another organization, the Komi Stav (Association for the Defense of the Komi People) advocated for union with Permyakiya, an outcome that looks ever more remote given the subsumption of the **oblast** into Perm Krai.

After the power-sharing agreement of 1996, new measures were introduced protecting indigenous ecosystems for **fishing**, hunting, and reindeer herding. The status of the Komi language has also been greatly improved among Komi since Russian independence, gaining official status in 1991, the first Finno-Ugric tongue in the Russian Federation to receive such a designation. Demographically, the ratio of Komi to non-Komi is rising due to a steady exodus of nonindigenous inhabitants after 1991. Symbolic violence against the Russian **flag** (and its replacement with the republican tricolor) is a central manifestation of Komi nationalism, a phenomenon known as the "War of the Flags." While Komi identify strongly with their locality and republic, Komi national identity remains quite low compared to other **ethnic minorities** of the Russian Federation.

KOMI-PERMYAK AUTONOMOUS OKRUG. *See* PERMYA-KIYA.

KOMI REPUBLIC. An **ethnic republic** of the Russian Federation. The Komi Republic covers part of the Russian Plain in extreme northeastern Europe. Established as the Komi-Zyrian Autonomous Oblast in 1929, the region was transferred to the Northern Territory before being reassigned as its own **Autonomous Soviet Socialist Republic** (ASSR) in 1936. In 1990, republican leaders declared Komi sovereignty before settling on existence as a republic of the Russian Federation in 1992.

Encompassing a portion of the Arctic Circle, the republic is bordered by **Nenetsiya**, **Yamaliya**, **Khantiya-Mansiya**, **Perm Krai**, and the **oblasts** of **Sverdlovsk**, **Kirov**, and **Archangel**. During the Soviet era, the region served as a major site of the Arctic **gulag**; as such, most of the region's northern cities are former prison encampments. Komi is part of the Northwestern **Federal District** and the Northern **Economic Region**. The regional capital is Syktyvkar, a riparian city of 230,000. Much of the region is forested; however, much of the northern reaches of the region is permanently frozen wooded **tundra**.

Komi also has significant reserves of hydrocarbons, gold, diamonds, and other minerals. The regional **economy** is dependent on energy production, specifically the coal fields of the Pechora basin and **oil** and **natural gas** extraction in the Timan-Pechora basin. Komi is an important supplier of energy to **St. Petersburg**, and has export relationships with 40 foreign countries. Forestry also accounts for an important portion of the regional economy; however, a significant portion of the region's forests are protected as they generate much of the oxygen supply of the European continent. UNESCO has designated the Pechora-Ilych Preserve and the Yugyd Va National Park, the largest remaining tract of virgin forest in Europe, as a World Cultural and Natural Heritage site.

The republic has a land area of 415,900 square kilometers and a population of slightly more than 1 million. The republic's titular nationality, the **Komi**, make up a quarter of its population; **ethnic Russians** comprise 60 percent, while **Ukrainians** are 6 percent. Support for **separatism** is low among the Russians (less than 25 percent), while about one-third of the republic's Komi favor independence.

During the 1990s, the head of the republic, Yury Spiridonov, established semi-authoritarian rule in the region, expanding his power and gaining substantive autonomy from Moscow with a 1996 power-sharing agreement. Under his watch, a disastrous oil spill made international headlines, only after his administration tried to silence local **media** and downplay the severity of the event. In 2001, Komi was forced to repudiate its declaration of sovereignty after a federal court ruling found that a significant portion of its laws contravened the Russian **Constitution**. Later that year, Spiridonov, a member of the pro-government **Our Home—Russia** party, was defeated by a former physics teacher, Vladimir Torpolov.

Supported by the liberal **Yabloko** party, Torpolov won 40 percent of the vote; he was one of only a few candidates to unseat an incumbent in the last years of popularly elected regional governors. As an ethnic Komi, Torpolov's ethnicity played a role in victory against Spiridonov, an ethnic Russian. Torpolov was reappointed by **Vladimir Putin** in 2005. In 2007, the region was removed from the list of **federal subjects** receiving subsidies from Moscow, a signal of the economic well-being of the republic. Under both the Spiridonov and Torpolov administrations, Komi demonstrated a tendency to favor deals with fellow Finno-Ugric partners, specifically **Finland** and Hungary.

KOMMERSANT. Newspaper. *Kommersant* is a high-circulation quality daily business newspaper. In Russian, the word *kommersant* means "businessman" or "merchant." The newspaper provides information on international and Russian business, financial news, and general reporting on **politics**, **economy**, society, culture, and **sport**. The newspaper was initially published in 1909 but was closed by the Bolsheviks in 1917.

At the height of **perestroika**, in 1989, the newspaper was re-launched under the ownership of businessman and correspondent for *Ogoniok* magazine, Vladimir Yakovlev. In order to demonstrate the link to Russia's pre-Bolshevik cultural tradition, Yakovlev introduced a letter ъ at the end of the newspaper's title: this letter, the terminal hard sign, was abolished during the postrevolution Russian spelling reform. This letter is also incorporated into the newspaper's logo.

In 1997, **Boris Berezovsky** bought the Kommersant publishing house, which in addition to the *Kommersant* newspaper, included two magazines: one focusing on Russian politics, *Kommersant-Vlast'*, and one specializing in finance, *Kommersant-Den' gi*, as well as other publications such as the popular family magazine *Domovoi*. In 2005, Berezovsky sold the newspaper to Badri Patarkatsishvili, who then sold it to Alisher Usmanov, the head of a **Gazprom** subsidiary. Changes in ownership incurred numerous resignations, including multiple editors-in-chief. In 2009, the newspaper manager was Demian Kudriavtsev and the editor-in-chief was Azer Mursaliev.

Originally a weekly publication, the paper expanded in 1992, styling itself as Russia's first business daily. In 2005, the circulation of the newspaper was 131,000 copies per day. Since February 2009, the paper has also been published in **Great Britain**. The newspaper has employed some innovative publishing practices, including publishing its articles upside down as a form of political protest. The newspaper's multimedia website (www.kommersant.ru/) is linked to other Kommersant publishing projects, making it one of the largest multimedia platforms in Russian **media**.

In 2007, Ivan Safronov, *Kommersant*'s **military** affairs **journalist** and columnist, fell from the fifth floor of his **Moscow** apartment; although his death was ruled a suicide, it is widely assumed he was murdered for his critical coverage of the military.

KOMSOMOL. Nongovernmental organization. The Communist Youth League (*Kommunisticheskii soiuz molodiozhi*) or Komsomol was established in 1918 to train future generations of leaders of the **Communist Party of the Soviet Union** (CPSU) and inculcate the values of **Marxism-Leninism**. Members ranged from 14 to 28 years of age; younger children joined the affiliated Pioneers organization.

At its height in the early 1980s, there were more than 40 million members. Under **Mikhail Gorbachev**'s twin policies of **glasnost** and **perestroika**, Komsomol came under criticism as an overly bureaucratic, **corrupt**, and bloated organization that did not adequately represent the interests of the country or the needs of Soviet youth. Market-oriented reforms introduced in the late Soviet period, however, granted special privileges to Komsomol members, enabling valuable networks of influence (*blat*) that shaped the development of capitalism in post-Soviet Russia. Reflecting the end of the CPSU, the organization held its last congress in September 1991 before disbanding. The media outlet of the youth league, the *Komsomolskaia Pravda* newspaper, survived the organization. *See also* CIVIL SOCIETY.

KORENIZATSIYA. Taking its name from the Russian word for "putting down roots," *korenizatsiia* is traditionally translated as "indigenization" or "nativization." Originally a Leninist policy intended to accelerate the spread of Bolshevism to Soviet Russia's **ethnic minorities**, the program eventually was directed at the indigenous populations of the Soviet Union's 14 non-Russian **union republics**, as well as the titular groups in the **Russian Soviet Federative Socialist Republic**'s **Autonomous Soviet Socialist Republics** (ASSRs). Though it was no longer an official policy after the 1930s, indigenization remained the de facto policy in the non-Russian regions of the Union of Soviet Socialist Republics (USSR). *Korenizatsiya* solidified **national identity**, promoted the use of local **languages**, and created an indigenous *nomenklatura*. While linguistic and cultural **Russification** remained a major issue and **ethnic Russians** generally commanded the secondary position in every political, industrial, educational, and scientific hierarchy, *korenizatsiya* laid the groundwork for the flowering of nationalism in the 1980s under **perestroika** and **glasnost**. With the introduction of **democratization** (*demokratizatsiia*), many of these national elites abandoned Communism and embraced populism and Russophobia in order to secure office or promote their own political-economic agendas.

KORYAKIYA. An administrative division of **Kamchatka Krai**. Formerly a **federal subject** and known as the Koryak **Autonomous**

Okrug, Koryakiya was subsumed with the newly formed **krai** of Kamchatka on 1 July 2007 after a 2005 referendum on merging the Kamchatka Oblast and Koryakiya. The region, which occupies the upper portion of the Kamchatka Peninsula in northeastern Asia, is now officially known as the Koryak okrug. Out of a population of 25,157, **ethnic Russians** form a slim majority (51 percent), while indigenous peoples account for four-fifths of the population. The major groups include the titular ethnic group, the **Koryaks** (27 percent), as well as **Chukchis** (6 percent), Itelmens (5 percent), and **Evens** (3 percent). Koryakiya was formerly the smallest federal subject in terms of population, despite ranking 17th in size. The former administrative capital was the village of Palana. The last governor of the region was Oleg Kozhemyako.

KORYAKS. Ethnic group. Numbering fewer than 9,000, the Koryaks are an indigenous Asiatic people who live in the Kamchatka Peninsula. They identify themselves as either Nymylan (Koryak: "village dwellers") or Chavchu ("reindeer herders"). The Koryak **language** is a member of the Chukotko-Kamchatkan language family and is related to Chukchi. Koryaks practice animism and **shamanism**, often alongside Russian **Orthodoxy**. In the **Gorbachev** era, the Koryaks established a special nationality commission to deal with the federal government on indigenous issues such as the fur trade. They were also represented in the Association of the Peoples of the North, a nongovernmental organization (NGO) formed to protect the traditional rights and lands of Russia's northern **national minorities**. Since 1991, the **privatization** and marketization of Russia has weakened the Koryaks' position against environmentally unsound practices, although they have found some success through cooperation with international NGOs committed to **environmental** protection. Until 2007, Koryaks possessed their own **autonomous okrug** called **Koryakiya**; however, after the results of a 2005 referendum, the region was merged with Kamchatka Oblast to form **Kamchatka Krai**.

KORZHAKOV, ALEKSANDR VASILYEVICH (1950–). Politician. Born in **Moscow** to a proletarian family, Aleksandr Korzhakov rose through the ranks of the **KGB** during the 1970s. After serving in the **Soviet-Afghan War**, he was assigned to **Yury Andropov** as a personal bodyguard. In 1985, he assumed the same role for **Boris Yeltsin**, the leader of the **Communist Party of the Soviet Union** (CPSU) in Moscow. He remained close with Yeltsin after his dismissal from the CPSU, becoming head of the Presidential Security Service when Yeltsin took control of the **Russian Soviet Federative Socialist Republic** in 1991. On the occasion of the 1991 **August Coup** and the constitutional crisis of 1993, Korzhakov assumed personal responsibility for the leader's safety. Over time, he emerged as a key advisor to Yeltsin, particularly on security issues such as the **Chechen War**. As a key member of the antidemocratic "Party of War" within the presidential administration, Korzhakov strongly opposed Yeltsin's decision to permit the **1996 presidential election** to be conducted. In a position with little external oversight, Korzhakov naturally became the subject of criticism for supposed **corruption** and embezzlement. He was sacked during a turf war within Yeltsin's cabinet after **media** reports planted by his rival **Anatoly Chubais** suggested he was attempting a coup. He later won election to the **State Duma** representing **Tula**; the seat had opened in the wake of the untimely death of the incumbent **Aleksandr Lebed**. Korzhakov recounted his time in government in his biography *Boris Yeltsin: From Dawn to Dusk* (1997).

KOSOVO. During the late 1990s, Kosovo became an important issue in Russian **foreign relations** and the country's domestic **politics**. The intervention of the **North Atlantic Treaty Organization** (NATO) in the former Yugoslavia was deeply unpopular in the Russian Federation, due to **United States** and **European Union** (EU) support for Catholic Croatia and Muslim Bosnia against Orthodox **Serbia**, a historical ally of Russia.

With the ascent of **Yevgeny Primakov**, the Kremlin became increasingly critical of U.S. policy toward Belgrade, and in 1999, **Boris Yeltsin** warned **Bill Clinton** not to intervene militarily in the region. However, when negotiations between the Kosovar leadership and Slobodan Milošević's government failed to produce results, NATO began a bombing campaign of Serbia and occupied Kosovo in an effort to stop the forcible removal of ethnic Albanians. In an attempt to save face, Russian troops entered Kosovo shortly before the NATO force. The Kosovo crisis underscored Yeltsin's lack of influence with the United States and NATO and soured many Russians' view of the West in general.

Over the next decade, the Kosovars moved steadily toward full secession from Serbia, under the aegis of NATO and later EU protection. **Vladimir Putin** emerged as a vocal critic of Pristina's goal of independence, arguing that such a move—if recognized by the international community—would trigger similar outcomes in the frozen conflict zones of the former Soviet Union, specifically **Nagorno-Karabakh**, **Transnistria**, **Abkhazia**, and **South Ossetia** (the latter two were, in fact, recognized by President **Dmitry Medvyedev** in the summer of 2008).

On 17 February 2008, the Assembly of Kosovo formally declared independence; the decision was ultimately recognized by more than 50 foreign nations, including most members of the EU, **Turkey**, and the United States. Russia described the move as "illegal," and used its permanent seat on the **United Nations** Security Council to prevent UN recognition. No member of the **Commonwealth of Independent States** has recognized Kosovo's independence.

KOSTROMA OBLAST. An administrative region of the Russian Federation. Part of the Central **Federal District** and **Economic Region**, the Kostroma Oblast borders **Yaroslavl**, **Vologda**, **Kirov**, **Nizhny Novgorod**, and **Ivanovo**. The region's population is 736,600 and its land area is 60,100 square kilometers. The region is heavily wooded, and forestry and woodworking are major **economic** drivers. **Agriculture** (grain, legumes, and potatoes) and animal husbandry (cattle, pigs, and sheep) are also important. Its capital, Kostroma, is situated on the **Volga River** and forms part of the Golden Ring of Russian cities, and thus is popular with tourists. Economically, the **oblast** has long been dependent on federal subsidies, an outgrowth of its creation as a hodgepodge of lands left unclaimed by neighboring regions. Kostroma was a **Communist Party of the Russian Federation** (KPRF) stronghold in the early 1990s; in fact, the regional leadership was removed after supporting the parliament in the **constitutional crisis of 1993**. In 1996, the KPRF candidate Viktor Shershunov won office; he was reelected in 2000 and reappointed by **Vladimir Putin** in 2004. He died in a car crash in **Moscow** during the early hours of 20 September 2007. His deputy governor, Yury

Tzikunin, briefly served as acting governor until he was replaced by Igor Slyunyayev, formerly the **Altay Krai** representative in the **Federation Council**.

KOZYREV, ANDREY VLADIMIROVICH (1951–). Diplomat and politician. Born the son of a Soviet diplomat in Brussels, Belgium, Kozyrev graduated from the Moscow State Institute of International Relations (MGIMO). He joined the Soviet Ministry of Foreign Affairs in 1968, holding various posts, including head of the Department of International Organizations. Kozyrev served directly under Foreign Minister **Eduard Shevardnadze** in the waning years of the Union of Soviet Socialist Republics (USSR).

As a radical reformer, he campaigned against ideologically driven overreach in areas of the world where the USSR did not possess strategic interests. He became **Boris Yeltsin**'s chief **foreign relations** advisor in 1990, a position that allowed him to assume the role of foreign minister of the Russian Federation upon independence. In his new position, he oversaw Russia's economic divorce from its various client states around the world, including **Cuba** and **North Korea**. As foreign minister, he oriented Russia toward **Atlanticism**, making integration in the community of Western nations his utmost goal.

Under the "Kozyrev Doctrine," Russian foreign policy operated under the assumption that the **United States** and other Western democracies were as much natural friends and potential allies of the Russian Federation as they were natural enemies of a totalitarian Soviet Union. Consequently, foreign policy centered on developing a strong transatlantic partnership and Russian integration into the West. By the mid-1990s, Kozyrev's orientation was roundly condemned as naively pro-American and deleterious to Russia's national interests. His pro-Western reputation earned him the derogatory nickname "Mr. Yes" in the Russian **media**.

Despite being criticized for allowing Russia to lose its great-power status, he vigorously defended **ethnic Russians** in other former Soviet republics and Moscow's interests in the **near abroad**, especially in relation to regional conflicts in **Tajikistan**, **Georgia**, and **Moldova**. His failure to support the Orthodox Serbs against their Muslim and Catholic adversaries in the Bosnian War (1992–1995) and acquiescence of eastward expansion by the **North Atlantic Treaty Organization** (NATO) severely impacted his popularity among Russia's nationalists. Shortly after winning a seat in the **Duma**, Kozyrev was forced to resign in 1996 amid growing criticism of his fealty to the West; he was replaced by **Yevgeny Primakov**.

KRAI. Political subdivision of the Russian Federation. Derived from the Russian word that means "an end of something" or "a far distance," the term is usually rendered in English as "province" and carries subtle undertones of the frontier, annexation, and historical imperialism. Out of Russia's current 83 **federal subjects**, there are a total of nine krais: **Altay**, **Kamchatka**, **Khabarovsk**, **Krasnodar**, **Krasnoyarsk**, **Perm**, **Primorsky**, **Stavropol**, and **Zabaykalsky**. With the exception of Perm and Krasnoyarsk, the krais are all located at the periphery of the federation, especially the **Russian Far East**. The distinction between krais and **oblasts** is largely historical, and the two entities are fairly similar in administrative terms.

KRASNODAR KRAI. An administrative province of the Russian Federation. Krasnodar is a southern borderland for Russia proper, occupying the northwestern corner of the Caucasian Isthmus and washed by the **Black Sea** and the **Sea of Azov**. It is unofficially referred to as the Kuban, a historical appellation stemming from the territory's principal river, which divides the **krai** into two parts. The northern zone, called the Kuban-Azov lowlands, is part of the Pontic Steppe; the area possesses a continental **climate**. The southern or seaward part is historically known as Circassia, a mountainous zone with a Mediterranean climate.

Due to its mild climate, the region attracts a large number of Russian pensioners, many of them former **military**, thus giving the region a politically conservative character. It is also a major holiday destination thanks to its beaches, mineral springs, and resorts. In the west, Krasnodar is separated from **Crimea** by the Strait of Kerch by less than 10 kilometers. In the south, it borders **Abkhazia**, a breakaway republic of **Georgia**. In the west, the province is bordered by **Rostov**, **Stavropol**, and **Karachay-Cherkessiya**. The Republic of **Adygeya**, formerly an autonomous **oblast** of Krasnodar, is completely enclosed within the krai. A part of the Southern **Federal**

District and the **North Caucasus Economic Region**, Krasnodar Krai has an area of 76,000 square kilometers.

The region has a population of 5.1 million, making it the third-largest region in the Russian Federation (preceded only by **Moscow** and the **Moscow Oblast**). The region was once predominantly inhabited by **Adyghe** (also known as **Circassians**), Greeks, and **Armenians**. However, after Russian conquest in the 19th century, many Adyghe quit the region for the Ottoman Empire while a massive influx of settlers flocked to the region from central Russia and **Ukraine**. **Cossacks**, in particular, established a strong presence around the Kuban basin. During the Soviet period, further Slavic settlements occurred, establishing Russian demographic dominance in the territory. Today, **ethnic Russians** account for 86 percent of the population (roughly a quarter of those consider themselves to be Cossacks, which has been officially delimited as a distinct "people" but not a "nationality"). Armenians are the next-largest group at 5.4 percent, followed by **Ukrainians** (2.6 percent), Greeks (0.5 percent), and **Tatars** (0.5 percent). Overall, some 30 **ethnic minorities** registered populations of more than 2,000 persons each, making Krasnodar one of Russia's most ethnically diverse regions.

Unlike most nonrepublican regions, the population is almost evenly divided between **rural** and urban settlements. Villages (*stanitsy*) are often characterized by the dominance of an ethnic group or a historical Cossack affiliation. In addition to the regional capital, Krasnodar, the region also includes the important cities of Novorossiysk and **Sochi**; the former is Russia's principal Black Sea port and the latter is one Russia's premier resort towns and the site of the 2014 Winter Olympiad.

The regional **economy** is driven by **chernozem**-based **agriculture** in the north, producing grains, sugar beets, rice, tobacco, and tea. Other **industries** include **food** processing, metalworking, construction materials, and power generation. Petroleum extraction, refineries, and hydrocarbon transit, as well as **banking** and **tourism**, are also important to the regional economy.

Immigration is a highly politicized issue in the krai; the resettlement of the **Meskhetian Turks** in the region in the late 1980s and, more recently, the influx of Armenians fleeing a 1988 earthquake and the **Nagorno-Karabakh** War (1988–1994) and other refugees from conflicts in the **North Caucasus** has stimulated fear among the Russian population of a demographic shift favoring "non-Slavs." The situation has been especially acute among the Cossack population. As the historic site of the Kuban Host, Krasnodar has served as the epicenter of the neo-Cossack revival in post-Soviet Russia. In fact, Krasnodar is viewed by many in the country as the "ethnic home-land" of the Cossacks, who are in turn viewed as an informal titular nationality in the krai.

Since 1989, a number of Cossack political organizations have flourished, ultimately being consolidated in the mid-1990s under the banner of university professor Vladimir Gromov's Kuban Cossack Host (KKV). Over time, an unofficial policy developed in which the ataman of the KKV (and its predecessor, the Kuban Cossack Rada) serves as a de facto deputy governor of the province. Cossacks have formed volunteer policing units to defend *Kubantsy* (indigenous, i.e., pre-1980s residents of the Kuban) from criminality typically associ-ated with "foreigners"; as a result, these groups have frequently been linked by the Russian **media** to intimidation and violence against im-migrants and ethnic minorities. Cossack organizations, which view Cossack paramilitary units as a "state within a state," have created Cossack secondary schools and cadet academies, and lobbied for greater levels of self-government within the krai.

Krasnodar was a Communist stronghold throughout the first half of the 1990s; during the **constitutional crisis of 1993**, the local leadership took a decidedly anti-**Yeltsin** position despite the fact that the regional governor, Nikolay Yegorov, was a Yeltsin supporter. In 1996, the last leader of the Krasnodar Soviet, Nikolay Kondratenko, was elected governor on an antireform platform. Under **perestroika**, Kondratenko had vociferously denounced the "**Gorbachev**-Yeltsin-Masonic-Zionist" plot to bring down the Union of Soviet Socialist Republics (USSR); upon entering his new office, he drew interna-tional condemnation for making **anti-Semitic** remarks and stirring up xenophobia against Meskhetian Turks and other non-Slavic minorities. In 2000, he was defeated by Aleksandr Tkachev, who despite his opposition to **Vladimir Putin**'s land reform policies has maintained his position as regional governor, being reappointed in 2007. Tkachev has continued Kondratenko's anti-immigrant policies (particularly the prevention of land sales to Armenians and other "nonindigenous" residents) and has implemented stringent border control measures. Tkachev has also complicated Russo-**Ukrainian** relations by constructing a dike in the Kerch Strait in 2003, which was viewed by Kiev as an attempt to annex Tuzla Island.

KRASNOYARSK KRAI. An administrative province of the Russian Federation. Covering over 2.3 million square kilometers, Krasnoyarsk is the second-largest **federal subject** in Russia (after **Sakha**) and the country's largest **krai**. Approximately the same size as Algeria or the Democratic Republic of Congo, Krasnoyarsk occupies one-tenth of Russia's landmass. The province, which includes the Severnaya Zemlya archipelago in the **Arctic Ocean**, stretches across central **Siberia** from the Kara and Laptev seas to the Sayan Mountains in the south. It is bordered by Sakha, **Irkutsk, Tuva, Khakasiya, Kemerovo, Tomsk, Khantiya-Mansiya,** and **Yamaliya,** and includes the formerly **autonomous okrugs** (AOk) of **Evenkiya** and **Taymyriya.** During the Soviet era, it also administered Khakasiya as an AOk.

The regional geography includes ice deserts and **tundra** in the extreme north, **taiga** in its vast middle band, and temperate forests and **steppe** in the south. Its main geographic features include the Byrranga Mountains in the Taymyr Peninsula, the Central Siberian Plateau, much of the Yenisei River system, and the Sayan Mountains.

The krai's population is slightly less than 3 million, making it one of Russia's most sparsely populated regions (one-quarter of the national average). **Ethnic Russians** dominate the region's multiethnic population, comprising nearly 90 percent of its inhabitants. In their okrug, **Evenks** are 21 percent of the population, while in Taymyriya, the two titular groups—the Dolgans and **Nenets**—make up 14 percent and 8 percent of the population, respectively. The krai is also home to a number of other **indigenous peoples of the north**, including the Kets, Nganasans, Chulyms, and Enets.

Much of the region was closed to foreigners during the Soviet era due to the location of nuclear and defense installations, excepting the areas transversed by the **Trans-Siberian Railway**. The plutonium-producing city of Zheleznogorsk, previously known as Krasnoyarsk-26, effectively remains closed today, as a visit requires government authorization. On 30 June 1908, the region witnessed the Tunguska Event, a theorized midair meteoric explosion that leveled 80 million trees. There is still speculation about the exact cause of the event, which was equivalent to a nuclear explosion.

Despite its harsh **climate** and vast size, Krasnoyarsk has the capacity to develop into one of Russia's richest regions. After a period of economic decline in the 1990s, the regional **economy** rebounded and today is one of Russia's top 20 regions in overall economic terms, performing even higher in terms of investments and exports. More than two-thirds of commodities exchange is conducted with foreign partners. The principal **industry** is nonferrous metallurgy, which accounts for nearly three-fourths of economic output. Bauxite, nickel, gold, palladium, platinum, copper, cobalt, zinc, and iron ore are all found in abundance.

The region houses the key **mining** operation of one of Russia's largest transnational corporations, **Norilsk Nickel**, which accounts for more than 1 percent of Russia's gross national product. Norilsk Nickel's regional operations are centered in Norilsk, one of the world's ten most polluted cities. The city, though geographically part of Taymyriya, was under the direct control of the krai prior to the Taymyr AOk's subordination to Krasnoyarsk. Norilsk is the world's second-largest city above the Arctic Circle (after Murmansk) and the northernmost city of more than 100,000 residents. The krai is also home to Krasnoyarsk Aluminum, which operates the world's second-largest aluminum smelter (after the facility in Bratsk, Irkutsk). Aluminum smelting in the region has produced extensive environmental degradation and **pollution** across the Arctic Circle, particularly damaging to **Norway**'s ecosystem.

In addition to mining and smelting, power (particularly hydroelectric) generation is also an economic driver in the region. While much smaller in terms of percentage of economic output, forestry and **agriculture** are also important. The region is home to a significant portion of Russia's fur industry, particularly Arctic fox, sable, and squirrel. As a result of its financial independence, the krai possesses significant control over its own affairs at the budgetary level and in regard to interregional and international commercial relations.

Valery Zubov, a strong supporter of **Boris Yeltsin**, became the region's first popularly elected governor in 1992. Due to a poor record in terms of paying wages, he became quite unpopular in the mid-1990s. In 1998, Zubov was unseated by the nationally known figure General **Aleksandr Lebed**, who had previously served as commander of the 14th Army in the War of **Transnistria** and had negotiated the **Khasav-Yurt Accord**. Lebed was backed by the **oligarch Boris Berezovsky** and the head of Krasnoyarsk Aluminum, Anatoly Bykov, though he later fell out with both supporters. Relations with Bykov were particularly problematic after the magnate was accused and later convicted of a murder plot against a business associate (he received a six-and-a-half-year suspended sentence). Despite Lebed's international stature, he proved to be a rather lackluster governor, often bickering with the region's economic elites. In 2002, Lebed's helicopter crashed in the Sayan Mountains under somewhat controversial circumstances.

He was replaced by former Norilsk Nickel director Aleksandr Khloponin, who had won the governorship of Taymyriya only a year earlier, defeating the longtime incumbent Gennady Nedelin. The 2002 gubernatorial election, which proved to be one of Russia's most expensive and divisive, pitted the region's two largest taxpayers— Norilsk Nickel and Russian Aluminum—against one another, as the latter had thrown its support behind the chairman of the regional legislature, Aleksandr Uss. The results of the runoff election were initially set aside due to irregularities; however, Khloponin's victory was later sanctioned by the courts (shortly after he was appointed acting governor by **Vladimir Putin**). Once in office, Khloponin oversaw Krasnoyarsk's consolidation of Evenkiya and Taymyriya, a goal that had previously been endorsed by Lebed and the Kremlin.

In accordance with the results of the 2005 referendum on merging of the three **federal subjects**, the Evenk and Taymyr Autonomous Okrugs were downgraded from federal subjects to autonomous districts of Krasnoyarsk Krai on 1 January 2007. In Krasnoyarsk proper, 93 percent supported the merger, with 7 percent voting against it; in Evenkiya, 79 percent of registered voters gave their support, while 20 percent voted against consolidation; in Taymyriya, the poll was 70 percent against and 30 percent in favor. In 2007, Putin reappointed Khloponin to his post as regional governor; later that year, rumors surfaced that he was being considered to succeed the outgoing president.

KRYUCHKOV, VLADIMIR ALEKSANDROVICH (1924–2007).

Politician. Born in Volgograd, Vladimir Kryuchkov's early career was in the diplomatic service. He later joined the **KGB** and enjoyed support from his powerful patron **Yury Andropov**. Under **Mikhail Gorbachev**, he rose to the rank of general and assumed control of the KGB; in 1989, he became a member of the Politburo. Fearing that further reforms would lead the Union of Soviet Socialist Republics (USSR) into political and economic calamity, he soon emerged as a voice against liberalization of the Soviet system. He was particularly critical of acceptance of Western aid, suggesting it was a mechanism to destabilize the country. In June 1991, Kryuchkov and other hardliners had failed in their attempt to sap Gorbachev's powers and transfer them to then–Prime Minister Valentin Pavlov. In August 1991, Kryuchkov and other conspirators formed the State Committee for the State of Emergency, precipitating the **August Coup** against Gorbachev. In the wake of the failed putsch, Kryuchkov was arrested and charged with high treason. His actions indirectly led to **Russian Soviet Federative Socialist Republic** President **Boris Yeltsin**'s decision to disband the KGB and outlaw the **Communist Party of the Soviet Union**. In 1994, Kryuchkov was granted amnesty, along with the other surviving conspirators. He kept a low profile until the **Putin** administration, when he became a frequent guest at Kremlin events. In his memoirs, he criticized Russia's leaders for subjugating the country to the West and admonished the political elite for their internal feuding. He died in **Moscow** on 25 November 2007. *See also* DISSOLUTION OF THE SOVIET UNION.

KUMYKS. *See* DAGESTAN.

KURGAN OBLAST. An administrative region of the Russian Federation. Part of the Urals **Federal District** and **Economic Region**, Kostroma is often called the "gateway to **Siberia**" due to its use as a rail junction for European and Asiatic Russia. The oblast is internally bordered by **Chelyabinsk**, **Sverdlovsk**, and **Tyumen**, and shares an international border with **Kazakhstan**. The regional topography is defined by forests and **steppes** with numerous lakes. Kurgan Oblast's most important waterway is the Tobol River, which flows from Kazakhstan's Qostanay region (also spelled as Kostanai) through the administrative capital of Kurgan, before joining the Irtysh River.

With a warm, moist **climate**, the region functions as the key **agricultural** center for the Urals region, with over 60 percent of its territory being arable. In addition to agriculture, the **oblast**'s industries include mechanical engineering, pharmaceuticals, electricity generation, and manufacturing of building materials. In 2006, 600 million tons of **oil** reserves were located. The region is 71,000 square kilometers and has a population of approximately 1 million inhabitants. **Ethnic Russians** account for more than 90 percent of the population, with small minorities of **Tatars**, **Bashkirs**, **Kazakhs**, and **Ukrainians**.

The region was a reliable supporter of the **Communist Party of the Russian Federation** (KPRF) in the 1990s, with some support shown for **Vladimir Zhirinovsky**'s **Liberal Democratic Party of Russia** as well. In 1996, the KPRF candidate Oleg Bogomolov won the gubernatorial election in the oblast. He was reelected in 2000 and 2004. In the last election, he switched to **Vladimir Putin**'s **United Russia** party; despite having the Kremlin's backing, he only narrowly escaped defeat by Yevgeny Sobakin, a candidate of the liberal **Union of Right Forces**. His weakness was reflective of the region's worsening economic plight during a period of overall growth in Russia. In the late 1990s, Bogomolov took an active role in trying to resolve the diplomatic standoff between **Abkhazia** and **Georgia**. He has also established close contacts with other members of the **Commonwealth of Independent States** including Kazakhstan and **Azerbaijan**.

KURIL ISLANDS. A volcanic archipelago of more than 50 islands, the Kuril Islands, or Kuriles, stretch some 1,300 kilometers from the tip of the **Kamchatka** Peninsula to just north of **Japan**'s Hokkaido Island and function as the southeastern boundary of the **Sea of Okhotsk**. The entire island chain is administered by the Russian Federation, but Tokyo lays claim to the four southernmost islands (Iturup, Kunashir, Shikotan, and Habomai), which the Japanese refer to as the Northern Territories. The islands were occupied by Soviet forces at the end of World War II and were not returned due to **Cold War**–era disputes with **United States**–allied Japan. The island chain's current population of 16,000 includes **ethnic Russians**, **Ukrainians**, Koreans, and indigenous peoples such as the Nivkhs and Orochs. *See also* GEOGRAPHY.

KURSK OBLAST. An administrative region of the Russian Federation. Part of the Central **Federal District** and Central Black Earth **Economic Region**, Kursk borders **Bryansk**, **Oryol**, **Lipetsk**, **Voronezh**, **Belgorod**, and northeastern **Ukraine**. Kursk Oblast has a land area of 29,800 square kilometers and a population of 1.2 million. Generally, the region is hilly, with an average elevation of between 175 and 225 meters. There are nearly 1,000 rivers and streams in the **oblast**, endowing the region with extensive water resources. Much of the forest has been cleared, making the region suitable for farming the rich **chernozem** soil; key crops include wheat, corn, sunflowers, and sugar beets.

The region was the scene of the pivotal Battle of Kursk during 1943, one of the turning points in the Soviet-Axis conflict. The region is one of Russia's most industrially developed with nearly 10,000 firms in operation (more than 90 percent of which are privately owned). Manufacturing accounts for nearly half of the regional GDP, with engineering, nuclear energy, metalworking, and chemicals being the most important sectors. The oblast is on the site of the Kursk Magnetic Anomaly, the world's largest iron ore basin; both open-pit and underground **mining** of dolomite, copper-nickel ores, and bauxite are prevalent in the region.

Kursk, one of Russia's oldest cities, is an important scientific, cultural, and **industrial** center, with **transportation** links to Eastern Europe and the **Caucasus**. The **Communist Party of the Russian Federation** drew strong support from Kursk in the early 1990s. In 1996, former Russian Vice President **Aleksandr Rutskoy** was elected governor with 76 percent of the vote; however, he was prevented from standing for office in 2000 for failure to properly register his car. A Communist, Aleksandr Mikhailov, won the election in 2000 with a campaign that smacked of **anti-Semitism**; he left the KPRF in 2005 to join **United Russia** and was quickly reappointed by **Vladimir Putin**. Mikhailov has greatly expanded his oblast's relationship with Ukraine and **Belarus** while in office.

KURSK SUBMARINE DISASTER. The Russian submarine K-141 *Kursk* sank in the **Barents Sea** on 12 August 2000. The accepted theory of the explosion is that a gas leak led to a detonation of a torpedo-based warhead, which in turn triggered the explosion of six other warheads. This second explosion was so powerful that it registered on seismographs across northern Europe. Despite a rescue attempt by British, Norwegian, and Russian teams, all 118 sailors and officers aboard perished. The Russian government commissioned a Dutch firm to recover the wreckage, and all of the bodies were later buried in Russia.

The explosion was reported on Russian **television** channels and soon became a mass **media** event that riveted the nation, as it was believed the sailors were alive for a few days after the explosion. The Russian government's slow reaction to the disaster and subsequent misinformation campaign caused anger among the Russian public; the Kremlin's approach was viewed as similar to the Soviet failure to inform the population of the **Chernobyl nuclear disaster** in 1986. The event was also the first and only genuine political challenge faced by **Vladimir Putin** while holding the office of president of the Russian Federation. His decision to remain in the vacation resort of **Sochi** during the early days of the crisis caused his popularity ratings to drop markedly, and he subsequently apologized for what he characterized as a bad "public relations" decision.

KYOTO PROTOCOL. With Russia being one of the world's largest **polluters**, **environmental** activists diligently campaigned for the Russian Federation to sign up to the Kyoto Protocol of the **United Nations** Framework Convention on Climate Change. The international agreement was designed to reduce greenhouse gases and carbon emissions by members by 5.2 percent from 1990 levels. While **European Union** (EU) members were expected to reduce their output by a larger metric (12 percent), Russia was not required to make any reductions, only needing to keep the country's pollution at 1990 levels. Initially, **Vladimir Putin** had taken an ambivalent position on signing up to the protocol, with some advisors suggesting that, due to its cold **climate**, Russia might benefit from global warming, while others worried about its impact on the Russian **economy** and **industry**. American President **George W. Bush**'s decision not to ratify the treaty had placed the entire scheme in jeopardy, since it required that members' emissions account for 55 percent of all emissions. The participation of Russia, which accounted for 17 percent of global greenhouse and carbon gases, thus became an absolute necessity for the protocol to come into force. Putin ultimately agreed to join Kyoto on 4 November 2005, putting the emissions count over the 55 percent threshold (the **United Russia**–dominated **State Duma** ratified the Kyoto Protocol on 18 November 2004). The decision was seen as a political one, since, at the time, Putin was looking to shore up his relations with key EU members **France** and **Germany**, while isolating the **United States**.

KYRGYZSTAN (RELATIONS WITH). The territory of modern Kyrgyzstan was occupied and annexed by the Russian Empire in the late 1800s. During the **Stalinist** era, the Kirghiz **Autonomous Soviet Socialist Republic** (ASSR) was elevated to the status of a **union republic**. In 1990, Askar Akayev, the liberal-minded president of the Kyrgyz Academy of Sciences, assumed the highest post in the country. After an attempt to remove him from power during the **August Coup**, he moved rapidly to declare the republic's independence from the Union of Soviet Socialist Republics (USSR) on 31 August 1991. Kyrgyzstan, along with most other **Central Asian** republics, strongly supported the formation of the **Commonwealth of Independent States** (CIS) in 1991.

After independence, Kyrgyzstan sought to maintain friendly relations with the new Russian Federation, including joining the Russian-backed **Collective Security Treaty** in 1992. Russian aid in the wake of a disastrous 1992 earthquake also helped bilateral relations. Heavily dependent on evaporating Soviet-era subsidies, Akayev strove to develop the Kyrgyz economy along free-market lines and sought investment from Western as well as Russian firms during the 1990s. Educational, cultural, and scientific ties remained strong during the 1990s and have only deepened since that time.

While other Central Asian states turned away from Russia during the early years of **Boris Yeltsin**'s rule, Bishkek maintained close ties with Moscow, in part due to the country's need for cheap energy and also as a bulwark against **Uzbekistan**, a country that possesses a large diaspora in south Kyrgyzstan. Kyrgyzstan and Russia are both founding members of the **Shanghai Five**; the two countries, in concert with the other members of the organization, work closely on combating **terrorism** and **narcotics** trafficking, and border security. In 2000, Russia and Kyrgyzstan signed the Declaration of Eternal

Friendship and Partnership, further solidifying their political and economic bonds.

In the wake of the **September 11 attacks**, Akayev agreed to host a **United States** military base at the Manas International Airport; the installation serves as the primary regional hub for coalition operations in **Afghanistan**. In response to the American presence in Central Asia, Moscow secured rights to base the Fifth Air Army's 999th Air Base in Kant, only 30 kilometers from the American base. **Vladimir Putin** personally opened the base in October 2003, triggering talk of a new "Great Game" in Central Asia. On 24 December 2001, an amendment to the constitution gave the **Russian language** official status, a move welcomed by the country's sizable **ethnic Russian** population and lauded by the Kremlin as a model for other CIS countries to follow. In the spring of 2005, protests in the cities of Osh and Jalal-Abad followed by disputed parliamentary elections precipitated the "Tulip Revolution" in which marginalized elites (principally from the poorer south of the country) ousted Akayev and his allies from power.

According to published reports, the United States actively aided the opposition forces, while Russia issued criticism of their actions, fearful of a loss of influence reminiscent of the pro-Western reorientation that occurred in the wake of **Ukraine**'s **Orange Revolution**. In the midst of the uprising, Akayev fled to **Kazakhstan** and then to the Russian Federation, where he remains to this day. On 4 April 2005, he issued his resignation from the Kyrgyz embassy in Moscow. Hoping to improve relations with Russia, the leader of the opposition and new president, Kurmanbek Bakiyev, made his first international visit to Moscow where he actively sought investment from Russian energy companies. He subsequently declared that the Russian presence is the "guarantor of the Kyrgyz Republic's security," ostensibly against irredentist threats from Uzbekistan or **China** (Kyrgyzstan lies within an area controlled by the Tang Dynasty during the 8th century; in 2002, Akayev made the controversial decision to cede 900 square kilometers of territory to his eastern neighbor).

Bakiyev has developed strong ties with **Yury Luzhkov**, who is involved in expanding the country's transportation and tourism infrastructures. In 2007, Russia announced plans to invest $2 billion in the economy and to boost its **military** presence in the country. Russia is Kyrgyzstan's second-largest **foreign trade** partner, only narrowly outstripped by neighboring Kazakhstan. Remittances from economic migrants working in the Russian Federation are a key component of the national economy. The pro-Russian reorientation has been met with popularity: a 2008 poll showed strong support for further ties to Moscow, though a surge in nationalism and resentment at the dominance of the Russian language has also been evident in the country.

Dmitry Medvyedev visited Bishkek in 2008 amid the crisis over **South Ossetia**; he and Bakiyev heralded new agreements on **oil**, **natural gas**, electricity, and the **mining** sector. In 2008, shortly after **Barack Obama** was inaugurated as U.S. president, Bakiyev announced while in Moscow that he planned to close the air base at Manas; the statement came during a meeting with Medvyedev on debt forgiveness and $2 billion in new loans. Bishkek ultimately relented on its demands for closure of the base and signed a more lucrative deal with Washington that would allow the U.S. presence to continue.

– L –

LABOR FORCE. Due to the Soviet legacy, the Russian workforce is highly educated and enjoys nearly universal literacy. Nine out of 10 Russian workers have completed secondary **education** or higher. **Gender** equality is also high, with **women** making up nearly half of the workforce in the mid-1990s, though this figure has dropped in the past decade. However, ideological concerns during the Soviet period left a negative legacy as well, with most Russian workers being trained for careers in heavy **industry** (construction, manufacturing, chemicals, etc.) and **agriculture**.

With little to no focus on the service sector until the late 1980s, the transition to a market-based **economy** required extensive retraining for many workers and left others in untenable positions. During the 1990s, economic hardship hit certain sectors particularly hard, including scientists, educators, and other professions dependent on the public sector. **Unemployment** emerged as a major social ill during this period, particularly given the fact that the Union of Soviet Socialist Republics (USSR) enjoyed universal employment, at least in theory. As a result, participation in the "black" or "gray economies" became a necessary evil for many.

Due to the control of the **Communist Party of the Soviet Union** and the perpetuation of the myth of the "worker state" under Communism, **trade unions** wielded little power in the Soviet and immediate post-Soviet eras. As such, wage arrears, poor working conditions, and other labor problems proved pernicious during the **Yeltsin** era. Russia's labor force is currently estimated at 75 million out of a total population of 140 million.

As president, **Vladimir Putin**'s plans to double the country's gross domestic product resulted in a renewed commitment to improving the quality of the workforce, particularly through training and improved education. **Demographic challenges**—particularly the aging of the workforce, lowered life expectancy, massive commitments to pensioners, and low fertility rates—are expected to cause a dramatic, if not catastrophic, decline in the labor force over the coming decades. As a result, Russia is becoming increasingly dependent on **immigration**—particularly from the **Caucasus** and **Central Asia**—to maintain its workforce, though this has led to increasingly acute social and political problems in the Russian Federation. *See also* ETHNIC CHINESE.

LABOR UNIONS. *See* TRADE UNIONS.

LAKE BAYKAL. Located in southern **Siberia**, Lake Baykal is the world's oldest, deepest, and largest freshwater lake by volume. The 600-kilometer-long and 1,740-meter-deep lake is shared by **Buryatiya** on its eastern shore and **Irkutsk Oblast** on its western shore; it has a surface area of 31,500 square kilometers. A body of water with religious significance to the indigenous **Buryats**, the lake also attracts visitors from around the world. Known as the "Galapagos of Russia," Lake Baykal is home to a wide variety of species unique to its ecosystem (including the Baykal Seal), and was declared a UNESCO Heritage Site in 1996. In the early decades of the **Trans-Siberian Railway**, cargo and passengers were off-loaded and transported via ferry or, during winter, on sleds across the lake; later rail lines circumvented the lake altogether. International concerns about **pollution** and waste from **nuclear energy** have been raised in the past decade, given the fact that the lake possesses 20 percent of the world's unfrozen freshwater reserves.

LAMAISM. *See* BUDDHISM.

LANGUAGE IN THE RUSSIAN FEDERATION. While the **Russian language** is the dominant medium of communication in **education**, **media**, **literature**, public life, and the **economy** of the Russian Federation, the country is home to dozens of languages spoken nowhere else in the world. While only 80 percent of the population is **ethnic Russian**, 97 percent of all Russian citizens are fluent in Russian.

In the **ethnic republics** and **autonomous okrugs**, certain languages enjoy equal status with Russian, while the nongovernmental organization Russian Association of the **Indigenous Peoples of the North** and other cultural groups attempt to provide support to tongues that lack the political protection of one of Russia's **federal subjects** (particularly Paleo-Siberian and Manchu-Tungus languages). Linguistic diversity is particularly high in the **Volga-Ural region**, the **Far North**, and the **North Caucasus**, and especially **Dagestan**, where Russian, Agul, Avar, Azeri, Chechen, Dargin, Kumyk, Lak, Lezgian, Nogai, Rutul, Tabasaran, Tat, and Tsakhur all enjoy the status of official languages.

Besides Russian, the indigenous languages spoken in Russia can be allocated into four major groups: Finno-Ugric (Karelian, Mari, Udmurt, Erzya, Moksha, Nenets, Komi, Khanty, and Mansi); Turkic (Tatar, Bashkir, Karachay-Balkar, Nogay, Altay, Sakha, Tuvan, Khakas, and Chuvash); Mongolic (Kalmyk and Buryat); and Caucasian (Adyghe, Kabardian, Chechen, Ingush, and the languages of Dagestan). Other languages include Ossetic, Yiddish, Romany, Ukrainian, Polish, Kazakh, Uzbek, Tajik, Chinese, Korean, and Armenian.

In terms of foreign language study, English is the most popular, accounting for 80 percent of foreign-language speakers; German, French, and Turkish are also spoken by a significant portion of the Russian population. *See also* IMMIGRATION; NATIONAL MINORITIES.

LATVIA (RELATIONS WITH). Latvia was incorporated into the Russian empire during the 18th century and later became one of the most developed areas within the empire. During the Russian Civil War, Latvia secured Russian and international recognition of its independence; however, like the two other **Baltic States**, it was invaded and annexed by the Union of Soviet Socialist Republics (USSR) during World War II. The **United States**, **Great Britain**, and other Western countries did not recognize Latvia's incorporation into the USSR.

During the Soviet era, the republic suffered from the deportation of a significant portion of its **intelligentsia** and political elites. Latvia experienced significant Russian **immigration** during the next several decades, alongside unpopular **Russification** efforts conducted by Moscow. Under **Mikhail Gorbachev**'s policy of **glasnost**, a number of nationalist organizations flowered. From 1989 to 1991, Latvia inched toward restoring its independence, which was obtained on 6 September 1991. Alongside **Estonia** and **Lithuania**, Latvia set itself on a course for admission to the **European Union** and the **North Atlantic Treaty Organization** (NATO); both accessions occurred in 2004. During the presidency of **Boris Yeltsin**, Russia employed a number of mechanisms—including the delay of the withdrawal of Russian forces until 1994—to prevent the country's efforts to join the organizations, but to no avail.

The republic's desire to enter the U.S.-dominated Atlantic alliance, in particular, created problems with Moscow. However, the most contentious issue between the two states remains Riga's treatment of its sizable **ethnic Russian** minority. Fearful that Russians and other non-Latvian immigrants (and descendents of immigrants) would function as a fifth column for the Russian Federation and/or prevent the country from revitalizing its language and culture in the post-Soviet era, Latvia did not automatically grant citizenship to residents whose ancestors were not citizens prior to 17 June 1940 (the date of the Soviet invasion). Those persons rendered noncitizens by the law were ultimately declared legal residents and eligible to apply for Latvian citizenship, which required knowledge of the Latvian language and an oath of loyalty to the state.

Official limitations on the use of the **Russian language** in public life also followed. As more than a third of the population was ethnic Russian or non-Latvian Russophone, this policy created controversy within the country, as well as strident condemnation from politicians in Russia, particularly among the ultranationalists and **Communists**. Protection of "compatriots" in Latvia, seen as part of the **near abroad** and thus within Moscow's sphere of influence, became an important tool for foreign policy elites from the mid-1990s onward.

During the **Putin** administration, Russo-Latvian relations worsened. Recognizing the inevitability of NATO membership, Moscow sought to isolate Latvia through its energy policy. In 2003, **Transneft** stopped delivering **oil** to the Latvian port of Ventspils in favor of a more northerly (and Russian-controlled) route to the Gulf of Finland. The cessation of transshipment revenues was a major blow to Latvia since, during the 1990s, Ventspils was the second-largest export port for foreign-bound Russian crude, accounting for more than $150 million per year in revenue. Latvia—in conjunction with Poland and its Baltic neighbors—has strongly criticized Russian plans to develop an undersea **natural gas** pipeline from Vyborg to Germany as an attempt to weaken its voice within a united Europe; in theory, bypassing these states will allow the Kremlin to exert influence over them via energy control without interrupting flows to Western Europe.

On the 60th anniversary of the end of World War II, a war of words erupted between Putin and Latvian President Vaira Vike-Freiberga over the Soviet Union's role in "liberating" the Baltics from German occupation, further souring relations. Russia continues to accuse Latvia of rehabilitating fascists and of Russophobic historical revisionism. Also that year, a poll taken in Russia found that Latvia ranked as the country's greatest enemy, with half the respondents affirming such a position. **George W. Bush**'s strong support of Latvian democracy, particularly in the wake of the **color revolutions**, also put a strain on the country's bilateral relations with Russia. Tensions began to ease in 2007 when Latvia abandoned its lingering border dispute with Russia over the Abrene District, a decision that was officially commended by the Russian Foreign Ministry.

At $2 billion per year, Latvian-Russian **foreign trade** is brisk, particularly in the raw materials sector. However, unlike other post-Soviet republics, Latvia is not economically dependent on Russia; the European Union collectively accounts for three-fourths of Latvia's exports and imports. *See also* LENINGRAD OBLAST; UKRAINE.

LAVROV, SERGEY VIKTOROVICH (1950–). Diplomat. Born in **Moscow** to an **Armenian**-Russian family, he studied at the prestigious Moscow State Institute of International Relations (MGIMO) before being sent to Sri Lanka as a diplomat in the 1970s. When he returned from abroad, he was posted to the Department of International Organizations within the Soviet Ministry of Foreign Affairs. In 1994, Lavrov was appointed Russia's representative to the **United Nations** (UN), where he served as president of the UN Security Council on several occasions. He took a strong stance against the war in Iraq and the situation in **Kosovo** during his tenure. **Vladimir Putin** tapped him to replace **Igor Ivanov** as foreign minister on 9 March 2004. During the second Putin administration, Lavrov was tasked with managing Russia's more aggressive posture in **foreign relations**, including disputes with **Ukraine** over **natural gas**, the militarization of Russia's **Arctic Ocean** basin, **espionage**-related complications with **Great Britain**, and the 2008 **South Ossetian War** against **Georgia**. In 2009, he met with American President **Barack Obama**'s secretary of state, Hillary Clinton, in order to help "reset" the **United States**–Russia relationship after **George W. Bush**'s presidency. Unfortunately, the "reset button" gift that was presented to him as a gimmick, stated "overcharge" (*peregruzka* instead of *perezagruzka*), thus leading to embarrassment on the part of the American diplomats, whose lack of knowledge of the **Russian language** became immediately apparent. Lavrov is not considered to be particularly close to Putin or his successor, **Dmitry Medvyedev**, but is recognized as a tough negotiator and an effective bureaucrat with a keen intellect. *See also* MIDDLE EAST.

LAZAR, BEREL (1964–). Religious leader. A member of the Chabad-Lubavitch, an ultraorthodox Hassidic movement currently headquartered in Brooklyn, New York, Rabbi Berel Lazar is recognized by the Russian government to be the leader of the country's **Jewish** community. A native of Milan, Italy, Lazar studied at Central Lubavitch Yeshiva in the **United States**, and worked clandestinely with the refusenik movement to abet Jewish migration to **Israel** during the late 1980s. His appointment to an advisory board in 2000 demonstrated that the new president, **Vladimir Putin**, sought to marginalize the previously recognized Chief Rabbi **Adolf Shayevich**, an ally of **Vladimir Gusinsky**, an **oligarch** and critic of Putin. Lazar's appointment was criticized by a number of prominent Jewish organizations, which worried that Moscow was seeking to exert control over the practice of **Judaism** in Russia; his foreign birth and poor **Russian language** skills have also been criticized.

LEBED, ALEKSANDR IVANOVICH (1950–2002). Military commander and politician. Born in Novocherkassk, a **Cossack**-dominated area of **Rostov Oblast**, Aleksandr Lebed descended from a line of military veterans. He joined the Soviet **army** in 1970 and served with distinction in the **Soviet-Afghan War**, before being deployed to the **Caucasus** during the ethnic turmoil of 1989–1990. In 1991, he defied orders by the leaders of the **August Coup** to move on **Boris Yeltsin**'s position at the White House, issuing a crippling blow to the putschists. After Russia's independence, he was dispatched to **Transnistria**, where he gained national prominence for his support of **ethnic Russians** and other Slavs in the breakaway Moldovan province.

After years of simmering tension with Minister of Defense Pavel Grachev, Lebed resigned his commission on 30 May 1995 and entered **politics** as leader of the nationalist Congress of Russian Communities. While his party underperformed, he won a seat in the **State Duma**. He challenged Yeltsin in the **1996 presidential election**, finishing third with 14.5 percent of the vote in the first round. In an attempt to win away nationalist voters from **Gennady Zyuganov** in the runoff, Yeltsin placed Lebed in charge of the Security Council of the Russian Federation two days after the first poll; Lebed endorsed Yeltsin a few days later. Lebed represented the federal government at the **Khasav-Yurt Accord**, thus ending the first **Chechen War**.

After his dismissal from Yeltsin's cabinet over a dispute with the Interior Minister Anatoly Kulikov, Lebed entered regional politics, winning the governorship of **Krasnoyarsk Krai** in 1998. During the next year, he maintained a high profile nationally, and was widely assumed to be the front-runner in the coming presidential elections. However, Yeltsin outmaneuvered him by choosing the unknown **Vladimir Putin** as his successor. On 28 April 2002, Lebed's helicopter crashed in the Sayan Mountains, triggering conspiracy theories that still persist. His biography, *General Alexander Lebed: My Life* *and My Country* (1997), reflected his strong belief in the importance of the military but evinced his lack of a cogent political platform for Russia during its most troubled period.

LEBEDEV, ALEKSANDR YEVGENYEVICH (1959–). Politician and **oligarch**. According to *Forbes* magazine, Aleksandr Lebedev is one of the richest men in Russia, with an estimated fortune of $3.1 billion. He built his fortune in the **banking** industry, and is recognized as one of the country's more influential oligarchs. He has a 30 percent stake in **Aeroflot** and controls 39 percent of *Novaya Gazeta*. On 21 January 2009, Lebedev purchased the London-based *Evening Standard* for the symbolic fee of £1 in an effort to prop up the failing newspaper. He previously served in the **KGB** in **Great Britain**, and was a member of the **State Duma** from 2004 until 2008. He maintains a personal friendship with **Mikhail Gorbachev** and former British Prime Minister Tony Blair.

LEGAL SYSTEM. *See* JUDICIAL SYSTEM.

LENIN, VLADIMIR ILYICH (1870–1924). Politician. Born Vladimir Ilyich Ulyanov. Lenin led the 1917 Bolshevik Revolution establishing Soviet Russia. He oversaw the creation of the Union of Soviet Socialist Republics in 1922, and became its first leader. His contributions to Marxism—specifically his ideas on how to govern a "workers' state," the creation of a vanguard **political party**, the effects of imperialism, and promotion of world revolution—led to the creation of the ideology of Leninism. **Marxism-Leninism**, in turn, became the governing ideology of the **Communist Party of the Soviet Union**. Against Lenin's dying wishes, he was succeeded by **Joseph Stalin**, who emerged as the uncontested leader of the Soviet Union in 1928. After Lenin's death in 1924, his body was preserved and placed on permanent display in the Lenin Mausoleum in Red Square, **Moscow**; **Boris Yeltsin** failed to have the leader's body buried in the late 1990s, due to a popular backlash. While many streets in Russia were renamed in the 1990s, returning them to their pre-Soviet appellations, certain major streets in **Moscow** and other urban areas still bear the name of Lenin; his sculptures continue to decorate squares of provincial cities, especially in the

Red Belt. Lenin remains a revered figure within Russia's extreme left, especially the **Communist Party of the Russian Federation**. His image continues to figure prominently in marches and political propaganda, as well as being displayed in the homes of many older Russian citizens.

LENINGRAD OBLAST. An administrative region of the Russian Federation. Leningrad Oblast, unlike the original source of its name, **St. Petersburg**, has maintained its Soviet-era designation. Leningrad is part of the Northwestern **Federal District** and **Economic Region**. The **oblast** is 84,500 square kilometers and has a population of slightly fewer than 1.7 million. Leningrad Oblast surrounds the federal city of St. Petersburg; since 1931, the oblast has been administratively separate from the city itself. Important cities in the oblast proper include Gatchina, Vyborg, and Volkhov. Over the past 50 years, certain outer suburbs of St. Petersburg (Leningrad) have been transferred from the oblast to the city as it has grown in size.

The region shares international borders with **Finland** and **Estonia**, and is internally bordered by **Pskov**, **Vologda**, **Novgorod**, and **Kareliya**, with which it shares jurisdiction over Lake Ladoga. In the southwest, the oblast occupies the Pribaltiyskaya Lowlands; its northwestern part is located on the Karelian Isthmus, while the eastern parts rise to the uplands of the Valday Hills. The oblast is washed by the Gulf of Finland, which opens up into the **Baltic Sea**, and thus includes the strategic islands of Gogland, Moshchny, and Lesnoy and the Birch Islands off the coast of Vyborg (though not Kronshtadt, which is administered as part of St. Petersburg). In the 1930s, the region's Ingrian Finns were forcibly relocated to other areas of the Union of Soviet Socialist Republics (USSR). During the Winter War (1939–1940) and the Continuation War (1941–1944), Finnish-Soviet conflict saw further evacuation of ethnic Finns from the area. Under the terms of the Moscow Peace Treaty (1940) and reaffirmed by the Moscow Armistice (1944) and the Paris Peace Treaty (1947), Finnish Karelia was ceded to the Soviet Union, with the southwestern zones being transferred to Leningrad Oblast. Today, **ethnic Russians** make up 90 percent of the population, with **Ukrainians** and Belarusians being the largest minorities; Finns account for less than one-half percent of the current population.

Unlike many Russian regions, Leningrad Oblast possesses few natural resources, bauxite being the important exception. However, water resources and timber reserves abound in the region. The maritime industry, particularly transshipment of hydrocarbons, is vital to the oblast, with the Primorsk seaport at Vyborg being the most important. The major industries are metallurgy, **oil** refining, petrochemicals, and light manufacturing.

In 1996, the region formally delimited its status vis-à-vis **Moscow** (though the power-sharing agreement was annulled in 2002) and elected its first popularly chosen governor. Vadim Gustov, who ran as an independent although he was backed by the **Communist Party of the Russian Federation**, replaced the Yeltsin appointee Aleksandr Belyakov. Gustov stepped down in 1998 to become deputy prime minister under **Yevgeny Primakov**. Valery Serdyukov was chosen as his replacement; Serdyukov, competing against 15 other candidates, was elected to the post in 1999 with 30 percent of the vote. Four years later, he won a slim majority; he was reappointed by **Vladimir Putin** in 2007. Under his administration, **foreign investment** in the region has increased dramatically.

LEZGINS. Ethnic group. The Lezgins are an ethnic group comprising roughly half a million living in **Dagestan** and northern **Azerbaijan**. They are the fourth-largest ethnic group in Dagestan, after the **Avars**, Dargins, and Kumyks. Their **language**, Lezgin or Lezgi, is a member of the Northeast Caucasian language family. They are predominantly a Sunni **Muslim** people, though some follow Shi'a **Islam**. Under tsarist and Soviet rule, the Lezgin people enjoyed contiguity within the same state; however, the impending breakup of the Union of Soviet Socialist Republics (USSR) at the end of the 1980s triggered the development of a national movement intended to preserve the territorial integrity of Lezgin-inhabited lands on both sides of the Samur River (which serves as an international border between the Russian Federation and Azerbaijan). The political organization Sadval (Lezgin: "Unity") unsuccessfully advocated the creation of Lezgistan, an autonomous region that would stretch across Dagestan (Russia) and Azerbaijan. Failing to achieve such ends, Sadval became increasingly radical in the early 1990s and was implicated in **terrorist** bombings in Baku and with establishing links with the security services of

Armenia, a development that had the potential to widen the conflict over **Nagorno-Karabakh**. However, in 1996, Sadval retracted its call for Lezgian statehood, fearing such rhetoric could place Azeri Lezgins in a precarious position in their state of residence.

LIBERAL DEMOCRATIC PARTY OF RUSSIA (LDPR). Political party. Known in Russian as *Liberal' no-Demokraticheskaia Partiia Rossii*. Established in December 1989 as the Liberal Democratic Party of the Soviet Union (LDPSU), the LDPR has been led by the eccentric, and often unpredictable, nationalist politician **Vladimir Zhirinovsky** since its inception. According to some reports, the genesis of the party lay in a **KGB** attempt to establish a pseudo-party to compete with the **Communist Party of the Soviet Union** during the last days of **Mikhail Gorbachev**'s premiership; despite its origins, the LDPSU was the first political party to compete with the CPSU under **perestroika**, receiving legal status in 1990.

Despite its name, the party is often described as illiberal and undemocratic due to its adoration of **Joseph Stalin** and objections to Western-style political pluralism and free-market capitalism. Its platform includes certain leftist planks, including the right to work, price controls, support of pensioners, state ownership of key **industries**, and state control of **agricultural** lands; however, the party is also known for its ultranationalism, geopolitical revanchism, and **anti-Semitism**. Reincorporation of **Belarus** and **Ukraine** as well as some other portions of the former Soviet Union is party doctrine. The party's motto is "Freedom, Law, Russia." Zhirinovsky's "patriotic" or "national liberalism" promotes statism, lauds law and order (including the death penalty), and supports the **military** and neo-imperial adventurism, giving the party a quasi-fascist patina.

The LDPR is particularly condemnatory of the **oligarchs**, linking them to Zionism and Western conspiracies to undermine Russia. However, the party has softened its harder edges, which were readily apparent in the first administration of **Boris Yeltsin**, placing some distance between the LDPR and the radical right-wing groups of **neofascists**, monarchists, and extreme nationalists. Rather than promoting the "Russian idea" based on a blood-based Russian nationalism, the LDPR borrows aspects of **neo-Eurasianism** to advocate for solidarity among all peoples united by the Union of Soviet Socialist Republics (USSR) and the **Romanov** Empire before it, including Turkic **Muslims**, Mongolic **Buddhists**, and Finno-Ugric **Christians**. The LDPR, however, rejects exogenous, "fanatical" sects, particularly Protestant denominations, as incompatible with Russian civilization and lacking allegiance to the Russian state.

The LDPR's approach to respecting the diversity of Russophone Eurasia, while guaranteeing the **ethnic Russians**' role as *primi inter pares* within that space, has been described as imperial liberalism. However, the party's stated aim of dismantling Russia's system of **ethnic republics** and other sovereign subjects is unpopular with many of the country's **national minorities**. The LDPR rose to national prominence in 1991 when Zhirinovsky ran for the Russian presidency, placing third behind Yeltsin and Nikolay Ryzhkov with 7.8 percent of the vote. Two years later, the party's fortunes reached their zenith, as popular discontent with Yeltsin's actions during the **constitutional crisis of 1993** benefited the bombastic Zhirinovsky. His advocacy of militarism and rejection of Russia's **Atlanticist** course proved especially attractive to the Russian military.

In the 1993 elections for the **State Duma**, the LDPR won a plurality of the vote (23 percent) at the national level, and was the most popular party in nearly three-quarters of Russia's regions. The 1995 elections, however, saw that number cut in half. Still riding high as an individual political actor, Zhirinovsky represented the LDPR in the **1996 presidential election**; however, despite a lead over Yeltsin in early polling, he finished in a disappointing fifth place. During the mid-1990s, the LDPR steadily transitioned from political nihilism toward moderate accommodation with the Kremlin. The first major shift occurred with its backing of the invasion of **Chechnya**. Yeltsin's newfound enthusiasm for Russian military action, particularly when directed at the "South," meshed well with Zhirinovsky's geopolitical worldview, which dictated a push toward the Indian Ocean.

The LDPR emerged as a major critic of the **North Atlantic Treaty Organization**'s (NATO) expansion and the war in Yugoslavia during the late 1990s, with both positions being echoed in the Kremlin by **Yevgeny Primakov**. Moderation failed to produce results, and the LDPR—running as the Zhirinovsky Bloc—returned a pitiful 6 percent of the vote in the 1999 Duma elections. With the presidency of **Vladimir Putin**, a second **Chechen War**, Russia's return to great-power status, and the rise of the *siloviki*, much of the LDPR's political platform became reality. This proved a mixed blessing for the LDPR as it adjusted to its uncomfortable role as a pro-government party; however, the party did see its popularity rise in the 2003 Duma elections, doubling its take from 1999.

In 2007, the LDPR once again dropped below the 10 percent threshold. In the 2008 presidential election, Zhirinovsky won a respectable 9.35 percent against the victorious **Dmitry Medvyedev** and the second-place finisher, **Gennady Zyuganov**. The LDPR remains one of Russia's few genuine political parties, with over 500,000 members nationwide and a well-organized party infrastructure. The membership is comparatively young, with half being between the ages of 16 and 29. *See also* NEAR ABROAD; POLITICS; SERBIA.

LIGACHEV, YEGOR KUZMICH (1920–). Politician. A member of the Soviet Politburo and protégé of **Mikhail Gorbachev** during the late Soviet period, Yegor Ligachev broke with his former mentor over the direction of reforms within the Union of Soviet Socialist Republics (USSR). Critical of certain aspects of **glasnost** and **perestroika**, Ligachev railed against Gorbachev for abandoning **Marxism-Leninism**, circumventing the **Communist Party of the Soviet Union** (CPSU), and governing the country by popular mandate. In 1990, he ran against Gorbachev in the first genuine competition for leadership of the party since its creation. After losing his bid for power, he retired from public life for some time. After the **dissolution of the Soviet Union**, he returned to **politics** and was instrumental in founding the **Communist Party of the Russian Federation** (KPRF) in 1993. He won election to the **State Duma** in the mid-1990s, holding a seat until 2003, when he lost to a candidate from the pro-Kremlin **United Russia** party. His memoir *Inside Gorbachev's Kremlin* (1993) paints an intimate picture of power and governance in the waning days of the Soviet Union. *See also* POLITICAL PARTIES.

LIMONOV, EDUARD (1943–). Given name: Eduard Veniaminovich Savenko. Writer, **dissident**, and **political party** leader. Born on 22 February 1943 in Dzerzhinsk to a career NKVD officer and an educated homemaker, he grew up in Kharkiv, **Ukraine**, before moving to

Moscow in 1967 where he became a poet. Due to the graphic nature of his writings and his counterculture leanings, he was stripped of his citizenship and expelled from the Union of Soviet Socialist Republics (USSR). Limonov lived in New York City and Paris before gaining French citizenship. Returning to Russia after having his Soviet citizenship restored by **Mikhail Gorbachev** in 1989, he soon became active in **politics**, establishing the ultranationalist, antigovernment **National Bolshevik Party** in 1993. Limonov gained international notoriety for his unabashed support of the Bosnian Serbs, even being filmed with indicted war criminal Radovan Karadžić and firing a machine gun at Muslim-held Sarajevo. Limonov was jailed on **terrorism** and weapons charges in 2001 stemming from an article in his newspaper, *Limonka*, stating his intention to form an army, invade **Kazakhstan**, and create a "second Russia." He was paroled after two years for good behavior. He was arrested again in 2007 for participating in an antigovernment rally in Moscow. *See also* SERBIA.

LIPETSK OBLAST. An administrative region of the Russian Federation. Lipetsk is part of the Northwestern **Federal District** and **Economic Region**. Deep in the **chernozem** region of Russia, the **oblast** is bordered by **Ryazan, Tambov, Voronezh, Kursk, Oryol,** and **Tula**. Lipetsk was formed from the breakup of several other regions in 1954. Its defining geographic features are the Galichya Mountain Reserve and the Usman Pine Forest, part of the larger Voronezh Biosphere Preserve. The regional capital is a **tourist** destination as a result of its salubrious mineral waters. The oblast is 24,100 square kilometers and has a population of slightly more than 1.2 million.

The region is thoroughly industrialized and suffers from high levels of air **pollution**. Nonferrous metallurgy—driven by the industrial giant Novolipetsky Metallurgical Combine—is a major **industry** in the oblast, accounting for 60 percent of the gross regional product. The region produces a significant portion of the country's concrete, refrigeration equipment, tractors, and cast iron.

Lipetsk was one of only eight territorial units permitted to hold gubernatorial elections in late 1992. The **Communist Party of the Russian Federation** candidate, Mikhail Narolin, defeated the federally supported contender. As a result, there was strong support for the anti-Yeltsin forces during the **constitutional crisis of 1993** and for **Gennady Zyuganov** in both the 1996 and 2000 presidential elections. He was replaced by the current governor, Oleg Korolyov, who won convincing majorities in 1998 and 2002 before being reappointed by **Vladimir Putin** in 2005. Korolyov has been praised by **Jewish** groups for promoting interfaith relations in the oblast since coming to power. He has also expanded commercial ties with the city of **Moscow** through good relations with **Yury Luzhkov**, as well as **Finland** and Italy (Korolyov hosted Italian Prime Minister Silvio Berlusconi in 2004). Lipetsk is one of Russia's few "donor regions," contributing more to the federal budget than receiving from it.

LITERATURE. The history of post-Soviet Russian literature is defined by the changes introduced by **Mikhail Gorbachev** as part of the **perestroika** process, as well as the long-ranging effects of the **dissolution of the Soviet Union**. The period of **glasnost** led to a dramatic easing and eventual abolishing of censorship. Russian literary authors gained the opportunity to express their thoughts freely and to publish their works openly without the need to resort to **samizdat** practices. Citizenship was restored to émigré writers, and as a result, **Aleksandr Solzhenitsyn**, Russia's most famous living writer, returned to the country. Literary works such as Boris Pasternak's *Doctor Zhivago* and Yevgeny Zamyatin's *We*, banned under the Soviet regime, were finally published in Russia during the same period. The return of these works into the public domain had an immediate aesthetic effect on contemporary writing as the cultural tradition of Russian literature had finally been fully established. The division between official and unofficial literature, and between Soviet and émigré literature, became redundant. Russian literature suddenly lost its long-established status of political opposition, while simultaneously failing to any longer provide a moral compass for the Russian society.

With the end of the Union of Soviet Socialist Republics (USSR), the status of the **Russian language** and Russian literature had to be addressed. Furthermore, Russian readers gained access to literatures of other countries and they desired to absorb large parts of the world literary tradition that had previously been unavailable to them. During this period, writers and readers sought to understand the past, both historic and literary, and to comprehend the chaotic and often threatening present. Finally, both the readers and the authors found themselves in the new conditions of the market **economy**, whereby a financial viability of an artistic project mattered just as much as its aesthetic or ideological quality. If in the Soviet Union, the literary process was regulated through the means of political control of the **Communist Party of the Soviet Union** and the aesthetic control of the Writers' Union, in post-Soviet Russia, these have been replaced by the control of the market and the politics of various literary prize committees.

The end of the 1980s saw a boom in literary publications as authors attempted to rethink the past and provide accounts of reality that was in constant flux; literary journals became extremely important as they facilitated the speedy publications of new and newly discovered works. Ironically, this boom coincided with heated debates about the purported end of Russian literature; the debates took place in the same literary journals. Such pessimism accounted for the urgent need to produce a new literary style that would suffice to represent the new reality. It seemed for a while that postmodernism, with its interest in rewriting and reinventing the past, ironic discourse, obsession with cultural allusions, unreliable narratives, and so forth, would serve the purpose. Indeed, the most important authors of the period, including Vladimir Sorokin, Viktor Pelevin, and the poet Dmitry Prigov, utilized the aesthetic principles of postmodernism, producing a number of remarkable literary texts.

The aesthetic pluralism that postmodernism propagated represented adequately the social and cultural disarray of the 1990s. New names quickly appeared on the literary horizon and disappeared equally fast; new publishing houses opened and closed, and new journals were launched and soon discontinued. However, some giants of the literary business prevailed such as *Novoie Literaturnoie Obozreniie*, an independent professional journal of literary studies, and *Inostrannaia Literatura*, a journal specializing in the publication of contemporary foreign literature. The publishing crisis of the early 1990s was soon replaced by a new publishing boom as there was an increasing interest in contemporary Russian literature. However, an aesthetic revolution did not occur; instead, Russian popular literature was reinvented as a lucrative business. Detective stories and thrillers proved a very successful genre of new Russian literature. Serial detective novels by Aleksandra Marinina, Polina Dashkova, and Daria Dontsova sold millions of copies. In the next decade, a more highbrow author, Boris Akunin (under the nom de plume Grigory Chkhartishvili), with his series about the 19th-century spy Erast Fandorin, became widely popular. Fantasy and science-fiction literature became increasingly marketable, with such best-selling authors as Sergey Lukyanenko and Maria Semionova gaining popularity.

In the new millennium, Russian authors continued the postmodern project of questioning the boundaries of literary genres and the boundaries of literary activity, and, as a result, it is often hard to distinguish between writing proper and social activism. However, the realist tradition has also witnessed a revival, especially in its representation of the conflict in **Chechnya** (as in works by Vladimir Makanin), **rural life** (represented by the works of Aleksandr Titov and Lidiya Sychova), and the existential crisis of the new post-Soviet generation (best exemplified by Nikolay Kononov and Mikhail Shishkin). A wave of neo-sentimentalist authors emerged as well, including playwright Yevgeny Grishkovets, poet Timur Kibirov, and novelist Lyudmila Ulitskaya.

While **Moscow** remains the center of the Russian literary process, there have also been regional groupings, most notably in **St. Petersburg** and Yekaterinburg. There also appeared a new space for Russian literature: the Russian **Internet** (**Runet**). The financial constraints of the 1990s, as well as Russia's lenient policy regarding intellectual property, resulted in a post-2000 shift of Russian literature toward cyberspace, with www.lib.ru (also known as the library of Maksim Moshkov) being the major portal where Russian classics and new titles have been published. There are also websites where alternative literary movements publish their manifestos and Russian literary critics examine theoretical issues of literary studies. However, the most important development of the recent decade is the active integration of new **media** into literary practice.

Russian authors persistently engage with new media, especially the Internet, to create new cross-media, cross-genre forms. Most of these literary experiments take place in *LiveJournal*, which has been described as the primary web-based resource of the Russian intellectual elite. For example, Linor Goralik's blog contains general postings related to her literary activities, but also samples of her writing, **visual art**, and other materials. It is virtually impossible to distinguish between her creative work posted in the blog and unrelated postings, prompting many literary scholars to speak about a new form of literary work that utilizes new media as a form of writing, publication, and distribution. This practice is destined to have a profound effect on Russian literature as it blurs the boundaries between the author and the reader, and conditions new temporal qualities of creative work.

LITHUANIA (RELATIONS WITH). During the late 18th century, most of modern-day Lithuania was annexed by the Russian Empire as part of the larger dismantlement of the Polish-Lithuanian Commonwealth. An independent Lithuania emerged in the 1920s after wars with both **Poland** and Soviet Russia. Along with the other **Baltic States**, Lithuania was annexed by the Soviet Union in 1940 and became one of the **union republics**. Under **perestroika**, a Lithuanian reform movement known as Sąjūdis emerged as the dominant political force in the republic. Lithuania began to emerge as the leading force for political change within the Union of Soviet Socialist Republics (USSR) by 1989. During that year, Lithuanians along with Estonians and Latvians created a nearly 600-kilometer human chain known as the Baltic Way to protest against the actions of the USSR 50 years before at the signing of the Molotov-Ribbentrop Pact, which paved the way for annexation of the Baltics. After World War II, the Kremlin ordered the deportation of more than 100,000 Lithuanians to **Siberia** and other parts of the USSR.

In 1990, the opposition Democratic Labor Party of Lithuania declared the republic's independence and suspended the Soviet Constitution, laying the groundwork for the ultimate dissolution of the USSR in 1991. Vytautas Landsbergis, the new president, emerged as the popular face of struggle against Moscow, particularly after **Mikhail Gorbachev** ordered Soviet troops to seize communication installations in Vilnius during the so-called January Events of 1991. The subsequent bloodshed impugned Gorbachev's international image, allowing Landsbergis and other independent-minded local politicians to push for international recognition and hold a referendum on independence (in an election that polled three-fourths of the voters, 90 percent favored cutting ties with Moscow).

Shortly after the **August Coup**, Vilnius was granted full independence by the Russian government, now under the direction of **Boris Yeltsin**. Russia completed its troop withdrawal on 31 August 1993, a year ahead of Russia's Northwestern Group of Forces evacuation of the other Baltic republics. The country's post-Soviet relations with Russia deteriorated sharply in the 1990s as Lithuania moved toward accession to the **European Union** (EU) and the **North Atlantic Treaty Organization** (NATO); Lithuania joined both organizations in 2004. Since admission to NATO, a number of events have chilled relations, including the crash of a Russian spy plane near Kaunas in 2005 and the arrest of a Russian official on charges of **espionage** for Lithuania in 2006.

Unlike its northern Baltic counterparts—**Estonia** and **Latvia**—Lithuania chose not to pass restrictive citizenship laws on its **ethnic Russians**, who comprise less than 10 percent of the population. Due to its geopolitical situation within the Schengen zone of visa-free countries, Lithuania's policy on the transit of Russian citizens between **Kaliningrad Oblast** and Russia proper remains a critical issue on the bilateral and European levels; Kaliningrad's dependence on Lithuania for foodstuffs and energy is also a factor in the Moscow-Vilnius relationship. Lithuania's criticism of **Belarus**'s political leadership also complicates matters, as the latter is a stalwart ally of the Russian Federation. Vilnius, backed by the **United States** and European powers, has sought to assist the development of a new, oppositionary political elite in Belarus through educational exchanges and support of nongovernmental organizations, as well as support for opposition media.

Lithuania's support for NATO admission of **Ukraine** and **Georgia** has rankled Moscow; however, in early 2009, Vilnius became the first EU state to push for warmer relations with Russia in the wake of the **South Ossetian War**. Unlike Latvia to its north and Belarus to its south, Lithuania is not a major transshipment partner for EU-bound Russian **oil** and **natural gas**, thus allowing a certain level of normalcy in energy relations between the two states. Vilnius has, however, backed a common Baltic strategy to avoid Russian hegemony on energy, in part due to the Kremlin's iron-fisted negotiations over the purchase of refineries in 2006, which resulted in a Lithuanian portion of the Druzhba pipeline being shut down.

LITVINENKO, ALEKSANDR VALTEROVICH (1962–2006). Security officer and **journalist**. A former **KGB** agent from Voronezh, Aleksandr Litvinenko skyrocketed to international notoriety in 2006 when he fell ill in London, England. He had been granted asylum by **Great Britain** after alleging that his superiors had ordered the assassination of the Russian **oligarch Boris Berezovsky**. As a journalist operating in the West, he made further allegations against the Kremlin, most notably that the 1999 **apartment bombings** had been perpetrated by the Russian **security services** and that **Vladimir Putin** was complicit in the murder of the journalist **Anna Politkovskaya**. On 1 November 2006, Litvinenko was hospitalized; the cause of his sickness was later determined to be poisoning by polonium-210, a rare radioactive substance. He died on 23 November 2006. An investigation by British authorities implicated **Andrey Lugovoy** in Litvinenko's death; however, a request for his extradition from Russia was denied, sending Anglo-Russian relations into their worst state since the Soviet period. Litvinenko was posthumously demonized in Russia as a criminal, a spy, and a traitor. *See also* ESPIONAGE.

LOANS FOR SHARES PROGRAM. Part of the overall program of **privatization** under **Boris Yeltsin**, the "loans for shares" scheme saw the regime auction off large bundles of stock shares of formerly state-owned enterprises. Payment was made in the form of loans, which, if unpaid by 1996, would be converted into ownership stakes in the firms in question. The **industries** particularly affected were energy, telecommunications, and metallurgy. Only a small number of **banks** were allowed to participate, thus creating conditions where transparency was absent. The prices for these "shares" were surprisingly low, allowing well-connected individuals access to extremely valuable assets. In effect, the loans for shares program expanded the fortunes of Russia's main **oligarchs** overnight. **Boris Berezovsky, Mikhail Khodorkovsky, Vladimir Potanin**, and other tycoons emerged from the scheme with both economic and political clout that could be matched by few in Russia. *See also* CORRUPTION.

LUGOVOY, ANDREY KONSTANTINOVICH (1966–). Politician. A former member of the **KGB** and its post-Soviet Russian counterparts, Andrey Lugovoy left the **security services** in 1996 to serve as head of personal security for **Yegor Gaydar**. In the ensuing years, he built a large private security firm. On 1 November 2006, he met with **Aleksandr Litvinenko** in London; Litvinenko fell ill from polonium poisoning later that day and died shortly thereafter. A subsequent investigation resulted in a request that Lugovoy be extradited to **Great Britain** to give evidence in the case. Russian law does not permit extradition and so Russia did not comply with the request, and Lugovoy, who denied his guilt but claimed British intelligence had attempted to recruit him to kill Litvinenko, converted the publicity around the case into a successful run for the **State Duma** on the ticket of the **Liberal Democratic Party of Russia**. In office, he has lobbied for stricter punishments against **dissidents** in Russia.

LUKOIL. Founded in 1991 through the merger of the firms Langepasneftegaz, Uraineftegaz, and Kogalymneftegaz, Lukoil is Russia's largest company and its largest producer of **oil**. It is the world's second-largest publicly traded company in terms of proven reserves of oil and **natural gas** (behind ExxonMobil), and controls 1.3 percent of the world's reserves. Headquartered in **Moscow**, Lukoil has operations in over 40 countries and produces nearly 2 million barrels of oil per day. Within Russia, its major fields lie in western **Siberia**, the **Volga-Ural region**, and the Timan-Pechora basin. Internationally, Lukoil is engaged in exploration and/or production in the **Middle East**, **Central Asia**, **Azerbaijan**, Columbia, and **Venezuela**. Besides oil, the company also has major gas processing plants across the Russian Federation and is also invested in energy generation. Lukoil owns Getty Oil, giving it a major platform for distribution in the **United States**. It also has retail operations in much of Central Europe and the **Newly Independent States**. The company is controlled by **Vahid Alakbarov**, the former Soviet deputy minister of oil production. Unlike other major enterprises in the Russian energy sector, Lukoil has generally avoided being dragged into domestic or international **politics**, though the company's interests in Iraq and **Iran** have colored the Kremlin's policies toward those states.

LUKYANOV, ANATOLY IVANOVICH (1930–). Politician. Born in Smolensk, Anatoly Lyukanov graduated from **Moscow State University**. He rose through the ranks of the **Communist Party of the**

Soviet Union, becoming a candidate member of the Politburo in the late **Gorbachev** era. As chairman of the Supreme Soviet of the Union of Soviet Socialist Republics (USSR), he was arrested in connection with events of the 1991 **August Coup**, but during his 18-month-long incarceration maintained that he was not part of the putsch. In the early 1990s, Lyukanov—along with **Gennady Zyuganov** and **Yegor Ligachev**—was instrumental in the formation of the **Communist Party of the Russian Federation**. He earned the reputation of being the "Deng Xiao Ping" of the party for innovative thinking. Lyukanov won election to the **State Duma** in 1993, 1995, and 1999. He left public service in 2003.

LUZHKOV, YURY MIKHAYLOVICH (1936–). Politician. Born in **Moscow**, the city he would ultimately come to govern, Yury Luzhkov joined the **Communist Party of the Soviet Union** in 1968. He worked as a manager in several chemical and scientific firms before moving into **politics**. He was elected to the Moscow city council in 1977, where he served in a number of senior positions during the 1980s.

Boris Yeltsin appointed Luzhkov to replace Gavril Popov, Moscow's first democratically elected mayor, in 1992 after Popov resigned. Luzhkov proved popular with voters due to his expansion of the **transportation** system and public works projects, though he has been criticized for his demolition of significant historical buildings in the city center. He is also credited with Moscow's dramatic increase in wealth as compared to other parts of the Russian Federation, particularly in the area of attracting **foreign investment**. He has drawn criticism for keeping the permit-based (*propiska*) residence registration system in effect in the capital, and for his harsh stance against **immigrants**, particularly those from **Central Asia** and the **Caucasus**.

As mayor of Moscow, Luzhkov has amassed a prodigious fortune and vast array of business interests including **media** outlets; he is frequently described as one of the country's **oligarchs**. His political ambitions have grown with his wealth. In the late 1990s, he formed the Fatherland **political party**, which soon merged with All Russia to form the **Fatherland—All Russia** party. Allied to **Yevgeny Primakov**, he sought to challenge Boris Yeltsin for control of the federal government. However, the emergence of **Vladimir Putin** dashed his plans for national influence; Luzhkov ultimately reconciled himself to supporting the new president. His party was soon absorbed by the pro-Putin **Unity**, which ultimately became **United Russia**.

He has created international controversy over the status of the Russian naval port of Sevastopol, resulting in him being declared persona non grata in **Ukraine**. He maintains economic interests across many Russian regions (primarily to guarantee privileged access to **foodstuffs**, energy, and other necessities), and has recently expanded into international real estate as a major investor in improving **Kyrgyzstan**'s **tourism** infrastructure around Lake Issyk Kul.

Luzhkov is an avowed **Orthodox Christian** and a strong supporter of the **Russian Orthodox Church**. His opposition to **homosexuality** is well known, and he has denied permission to gay pride parades on several occasions.

– M –

MAFIA. Sometimes known as the "Red Mob" (*krasnaia mafiia*) or the "Brotherhood" (*bratva*), the Russian mafia (sometimes spelled "mafiya" in the Western press) has rapidly expanded its international presence since the collapse of Communism and the **dissolution of the Soviet Union** in 1991. Organized **crime** in Russia is differentiated by its extremely close relationship with the government, particularly members of the *siloviki*. There are several reasons for this historical development. The totalitarian structure of the Union of Soviet Socialist Republics (USSR) allowed for few criminal enterprises to exist without the complicity of officials. The proliferation of the black market under **Leonid Brezhnev** created expansive networks of procurers who needed protections that could be afforded through contacts with the **Communist Party of the Soviet Union**. Economic privations and the shortage economy of the late **Gorbachev** era gave further impetus to the developing criminal underworld.

With the withering of the police state in the 1990s, many members of the **KGB** found themselves out of work, or existing on meager incomes. With their connections abroad and across the Russian Federation, some allied themselves with criminal gangs to engage in money laundering, extortion, illegal arms sales, **narcotics** trafficking, prostitution, and other illicit activities. Through **immigration** and the effects of Russia's exposure to **globalization**, Russian mafiosi established links with the Japanese *yakuza* and the Italian *Cosa Nostra*, as well as Chinese and Latin American criminal syndicates.

Corruption, which reached to the highest levels of government, allowed the situation to worsen over time, particularly during periods of economic crisis. Russia's dangerous business climate during the early 1990s further compounded the problem, as local entrepreneurs and foreign investors became dependent on private security firms and alliances with disreputable figures to assure their own safety. Each major city saw the rise of its own criminal gang, while certain **Chechens**—displaced from their homeland and scorned across the country—established a widespread network of criminal activity known as the *obshchina* (Community).

While railing against the growth of organized crime under his predecessor **Boris Yeltsin**, **Vladimir Putin** made stamping out the mafia a major plank of his presidency. However, critics of the new regime regularly suggested that the state had simply co-opted organized crime rather than eradicating its control of important sectors of the country's **economy**. In fact, contract killings—a common occurrence under Yeltsin—rose dramatically in 2008, sullying Putin's "law and order" legacy.

MAGADAN OBLAST. An administrative region of the Russian Federation. Magadan occupies an area historically known as Kolyma, situated in extreme northwestern Asia on the **Sea of Okhotsk**. The **oblast** borders **Kamchatka Krai, Chukotka, Sakha,** and **Khabarovsk Krai** (until 2007, the oblast also shared a border with **Koryakiya Autonomous Okrug** until it was subsumed by the newly created Kamchatka Krai). Magadan is part of the Far Eastern **Federal District** and **Economic Region**. At 461,400 square kilometers, Magadan is Russia's fourth-largest oblast and 11th-largest **federal subject**. However, with fewer than 200,000 inhabitants, it is Russia's smallest oblast in terms of population.

The vast majority (92 percent) of Magadan residents live in urban areas; in the decade after Russia's independence, this trend was increased by a rapid decline in the number of rural settlements in the oblast. **Ethnic Russians** make up 80 percent of the population, a rather low number for an oblast. **Ethnic minorities** include **Ukrainians** (10 percent), **Evens** (1.4 percent), Belarusians (1.2 percent), and **Tatars** (1.1 percent). Indigenous populations of **Koryaks**, Itelmen, and **Sakha** are also located within the region.

Geographically, the region is defined by mountainous **tundra** and **taiga**, though it turns to swamps and bogs near the coast; the major river is the Kolyma, which flows northward to the **Arctic Ocean**, providing significant hydroelectric power to the region. The regional **economy** is centered on **mining** (gold, silver, tin, tungsten, mercury, copper, antimony, and coal) and **fishing**, particularly for export. Gold mining was long conducted by prisoners of the **gulags** (under **Joseph Stalin**, nearly 1 million were exiled to the Kolyma basin) and continues to be conducted under the auspices of the state; however, a significant number of local residents illegally mine for the precious metal as well. Exploitation of **oil** and **natural gas** reserves is expected in the near future. **Agriculture** is underdeveloped in the region.

Since 1999, the region has functioned as a Special Economic Zone (SEZ) for export, although the law only explicitly applies to the city of Magadan. Valentin Tsvetkov, a gold-mine proprietor, became the regional governor in 1996; he was backed by the Popular-Patriotic Union of Russia, a leftist-nationalist coalition chaired by **Gennady Zyuganov**. In 2000, Tsvetkov, nicknamed "the Bulldozer" for his ham-handed tactics, defeated **Duma** deputy Vladimir Butkeyev with 70 percent of the votes cast. On 18 October 2002, the governor was gunned down in the Arbat district of **Moscow**.

Crime and **corruption** are traditionally higher in Far Eastern territories, including Magadan; the Japanese *yakuza* are reported to have connections with local **mafia** in smuggling of fish and precious metals. In the wake of Tsvetkov's assassination, numerous federal cases were opened against members of his administration. In 2003, Nikolay Dudov, then acting governor, was elected to head the region for a five-year term, defeating the mayor of Magadan. A member of the pro-Kremlin **United Russia** party, Dudov was reappointed by **Vladimir Putin** in 2008.

Economically, the region has stagnated in recent years, seeing limited growth in **foreign investment** and enjoying little in the way of socioeconomic development. Magadan suffers from some of the highest **unemployment**, **alcoholism**, and suicide rates in the country. Due to its remote location, the region has one of the highest costs of living in Russia. Since the end of Soviet subsidies, Magadan has come to be colloquially referred to as an "island," cut off from the rest of Russia by prohibitively high **transportation** costs, which also translates into expensive goods. According to local estimates, more than half of the population has incomes below the minimum subsistence level.

MAGNITOGORSK. Roughly translated as "Magnetic Mountain City," Magnitogorsk is a city of over 400,000 located in the **Chelyabinsk Oblast**. It is one of the largest cities in Russia that does not serve as the administrative capital of its corresponding province. The city was built atop a mountain comprised almost completely of iron. Meant to rival Pittsburgh, Pennsylvania, and other famous industrial cities, the city emerged as a showcase of Stalinist industrialization. During the late 1930s, the city was closed to foreigners and not reopened until the 1980s. Having depleted its local iron, the Magnitogorsk Iron and Steel Works has come to depend on materials shipped in from **Kazakhstan**. In post-Soviet times, the city—which suffers from high levels of **crime**, **pollution**, and **unemployment**—has emerged as a symbol of the ills of Soviet urban planning.

MANSI. Ethnic group. Formerly known as the Voguls, the Mansi are an Ugrian people of western **Siberia**, and one of two titular nationalities of **Khantiya-Mansiya**, the other being the **Khanty**. The Mansi are considered to be an endangered ethnolinguistic group, numbering fewer than 12,000. They represent less than 1 percent of the population of their ethnic homeland. Like the Khanty, a significant percentage of the community observes a traditional lifestyle based on reindeer herding, trapping, hunting, and **fishing**. However, the Mansi tend to be more Russified (often intermarrying with Slavs) than their Khanty counterparts, with only a tiny minority using their **language** in everyday situations.

Many Mansi still work on collective-style farms and engage in trade with the nonindigenous community, unlike their Khanty cousins, who have opted to return to a seminomadic lifestyle. The Mansi language is a member of the Ob-Ugric subfamily of the Finno-Ugric languages. While some Mansi practice Russian **Orthodoxy**, many retain their traditional **shamanistic** beliefs. **Oil** and **natural gas** extraction has accelerated the cultural decline of the Mansi people through destruction of their traditional hunting grounds and pastures. However, since 1991, the Mansi and their Khanty cousins have gained additional land use rights; at the same time, they have also been the victims of high-pressure tactics by petroleum companies seeking access to their lands.

Life expectancy among the Mansi is drastically lower compared to that of other ethnic groups in the Russian Federation, partly a result of **alcoholism** and lack of regular **health care**. Politically, the Mansi are party to the Association to Save Yugra, a nongovernmental organization focused on the protection of indigenous lands, and the Cultural Congress of the Mansi People, which in the early 1990s sought to declare a separate Mansi **okrug** under the jurisdiction of the **Sverdlovsk** (rather than **Tyumen**) Oblast.

MARI. Ethnic group. Previously known as Cheremiss, the Mari are a Finnic people whose traditional homeland lies in the **Volga** and Kama river basins. They are the titular nationality of **Mari El**, where they form 43 percent of the population, but also live in **Bashkortostan**, **Kirov**, **Sverdlovsk**, and **Tatarstan**, as well as other parts of the Russian Federation.

The distribution of the Mari among the **Muslims** of the Volga is, in part, the result of an exodus after the Cheremiss Wars (1552–1584); many Mari left their homeland to avoid Slavicization and forced conversion to Russian **Orthodoxy**. In total, they number over 600,000, more than half of whom live in Mari El. Mari are divided among three principal groups: Meadow (*Olyk*) Mari, Hill (*Kuryk*) Mari, and Eastern (*Üpö*) Mari. The Meadow Mari are by far the largest of the three. Literary **languages** exist for Hill and Meadow Mari, though the two languages might be classified as dialects of the same tongue.

The Mari languages are members of the Volga-Finnic branch of the Finno-Ugric language group, which is part of the Uralic language family. Native language use remains high among the Mari, who tended to resist urbanization during the 20th century; a recent study suggests that 80 percent use Mari as their first language and that a third of the Mari lack fluency in the **Russian language**. Seventy percent of Mari El's rural population is ethnic Mari.

Modern Mari **national identity** was forged in the 1870s as a result of open resistance to **Russification**. The catalyst was the *Kugu Sorta* (Mari: "Great Candle") movement, a nationalistic religious sect with anti-Russian and anti-Orthodox orientations. The group's activities focused on literacy campaigns and a revival of Mari animism and **shamanism**. As a result, many Olyk and Üpö retained their traditional beliefs; highland Mari, however, generally embraced Russian Orthodoxy. In the early 20th century, Mari nationalists coalesced under the umbrella organization Mari Ushem (Mari Union). The radical fringe ultimately came under Bolshevik influence after the 1917 revolution. **Moscow**'s creation of an ethnic territory for Mari did little to protect them from **Joseph Stalin**'s tender mercies. The Mari language was steadily pushed from the public realm during midcentury; however, a revival of Mari culture and language characterized the **Gorbachev** era. Mari Ushem was reconstituted during the period; the organization pursued a moderate platform, working with the Soviet (and later, Russian) federal system.

In 1992, Mari Ushem organized the First Congress of the Mari Nation, which called for greater Mari representation in government. In 1993, a new, more radical organization, Kugeze Mlande (Land of Our Ancestors), also became active under the leadership of animist priests. The movement advocated limits on migration into Mari El and promoted secession and/or the formation of a Volga Federation independent of Russia, but failed to attract many adherents and was forced to merge with Mari Ushem by 1995.

Mari identity remains rooted in traditional religious practices, which are sanctioned both at the republican and federal levels. Since 1991, Mari paganism, which has strong anti-Russian overtones, has achieved a level of respectability within Mari El, with *karts* (shamans) often exercising political influence among their followers. The first post-Soviet president of Mari El was publicly blessed by Aleksandr Yuzykain, the leader of Oshmari-Chimari (White Mari-Pure Mari), Russia's first registered pagan organization. Religiously oriented **environmentalism**, protection of sacred groves, and public support for pagan festivals such as Agavairem has become a basic element of political life in contemporary Mari El. Mari animism is not confined to the republic, however; Mari in Bashkortostan, in particular, are more militantly attached to their pagan faith than those in the **ethnic republic**.

Like the **Mordvins**, the Mari national movement is divided on how to address the issue of territoriality, that is, whether activism should be confined to Mari El or extended to diasporic Mari across Russia. Under Leonid Markelov's presidency of Mari El (2004–present), Mari organizations, **media** outlets, and gatherings have faced growing government restrictions.

MARI EL. An **ethnic republic** of the Russian Federation. Incorporated into Russia in the 16th century, the Finnic **Mari** people often resisted attempts at **Russification**, maintaining a separate ethnic and religious identity. The Soviets established the Mari Autonomous Oblast in 1920; it became an **Autonomous Soviet Socialist Republic** in 1936. The republic declared its sovereignty in 1990 and elected a president in December 1991. The republican constitution was adopted in 1995; the Mari word for "land" was added to the name, creating the current Republic of Mari El. A power-sharing agreement with **Moscow** was agreed in 1998.

Located in the Volga region, the Mari El Republic is bordered by **Nizhny Novgorod**, **Kirov**, **Tatarstan**, and **Chuvashiya**. Mari El is part of the Volga **Federal District** and the Volga-Vyatka **Economic Region**. The land area of the republic is 23,200 square kilometers. The regional geography is mostly defined by plains rising to the Vyatka Hills in the northeast, with numerous plunge basins and other types of lakes. The region has a fairly well-developed **tourism** infrastructure based on trains and share cabs (*marshrutki*); holy sites of the Mari traditional **religion** are major destinations for tourists. The capital of Mari El is Yoshkar-Ola (Red City); the city was closed to foreigners during the Soviet era due to its proximity to a rocket factory. Other major towns include Sovetsky, Volzhsk, and Kozmodemyansk.

The republic has a population of 728,000. Mari—the titular nationality—account for 43 percent of the population, while **ethnic Russians** form a plurality (47.5 percent); other minorities include **Tatars**, **Chuvash**, and **Udmurts**. The Hill and Mountain variants of Mari are official **languages** alongside Russian; furthermore, the laws of the republic require protection of the language, culture, and **national identity** of the Mari people. Mari El recognizes both Russian **Orthodoxy** and paganism as major religions in the republic. With virtually no mineral resources, the **economy** is dependent on forestry, animal husbandry, **agriculture**, and **industry** (machine construction, metalworking, food processing).

The republic has developed commercial relations with the Finno-Ugric states of **Finland**, **Estonia**, and **Hungary**, as well as **Belarus**, **Kazakhstan**, and other European states. In a 1991 referendum, a majority of the republic's residents voted against the introduction of private property; as such, it is not surprising that the **Communists** dominated the first State Assembly (parliamentary) elections in 1993. The first president of the republic, formally known as head of state, was Vladislav Zotin, a Hill Mari who was supported by the nationalist organization Mari Ushem. His pro-Mari political appointments engendered fear among many ethnic Russian managers and public employees, who feared for their jobs.

Zotin was replaced by Vyacheslav Kislitsyn, an ethnic Russian, in the late 1990s, after Kislitsyn overcame Zotin's presidential decree barring the election and successfully appealed to Moscow to circumvent local regulations that presidential candidates pass a Mari language exam (imposed in 1995 by Zotin to ensure his reelection). During his tenure, he provoked the ire of the Kremlin and was linked to criminal gangs. In 2000, Kislitsyn, a self-described authoritarian ruler who ended popular election of city and district administrators, was defeated by Leonid Markelov, deputy head of the Rosgossstrakh insurance company; Markelov ran on the **Liberal Democratic Party of Russia** ticket. Markelov's initial goal upon entering office was to rid the republic of the **corruption** and nepotism that had flourished under Kislitsyn's reign.

During the first several years of Markelov's leadership, he presided over a dramatic rise in personal income in the republic, as well as growth in the **industrial** sector; these are positive developments for the region, which has long been dependent on federal subsidies. Markelov was reelected with 57 percent of the vote in 2004, defeating an ethnic Mari, Mikhail Dolgov; however, the electoral process was criticized by outside observers due to Markelov's extensive use of administrative resources and intimidation of public employees, as well as postelection retribution against districts that voted for Dolgov.

In 2005, Markelov got into a row with **Estonian** Prime Minister Andrus Ansip over the treatment of ethnic Mari in the republic and the status of the Mari language. Markelov, a Moscow-born ethnic

Russian, upbraided Ansip for not visiting Mari El, and defended his republic's record by stating that, out of 379 schools, 43 primary schools taught all subjects in the Mari language while the tongue is studied in 196 schools. He further suggested that Estonian criticism was a "smokescreen" to cover the country's poor treatment of its own ethnic Russians. However, Markelov has voiced a desire to have the republic's status downgraded, which would effectively reduce or eliminate the need to protect the Mari language and culture. In recent years, the republic has gained international infamy as the site of **Internet** scam artists who prey on prospective grooms from abroad seeking to marry local women.

MARITIME KRAI. *See* PRIMORSKY KRAI.

MARXISM-LENINISM. In the wake of **Vladimir Lenin**'s departure from active politics, the term "Marxism-Leninism" came to describe the ideological orientation of the **Communist Party of the Soviet Union** (CPSU) and the Soviet state. The ideology combines social and economic aspects of Karl Marx and Friedrich Engel's theories put forth in *The Communist Manifesto* and *Das Kapital*, combined with the political and revolutionary prescriptions of Lenin (particularly in his works *What Is to Be Done?*; *Imperialism, the Highest Stage of Capitalism*; and *The April Theses*). Marxism-Leninism remains a popular ideology among certain Russians in the post-Soviet period, particularly members of the **Communist Party of the Russian Federation** (KPRF) and other leftist **political parties**. The ideology, in an adapted form, also serves as the governing force in Vietnam, **North Korea**, and the People's Republic of **China**.

MASKHADOV, ASLAN ALIYEVICH (1951–2005). Guerilla leader and politician. Born in exile, Alsan Maskhadov returned from **Kazakhstan** to his ancestral homeland of **Chechnya** as a young boy. He served in the Soviet **army** in **Georgia**, Hungary, and **Lithuania**, winning several accommodations before retiring in 1992. During the first **Chechen War**, Maskhadov organized Chechen defenses against federal troops, including operations in the capital, Grozny. In 1996, he ended the conflict during negotiations with General **Aleksandr Lebed** through the **Khasav-Yurt Accord**.

On 17 October 1996, he was appointed prime minister of the **Chechen Republic of Ichkeriya**, though he retained his position as minister of defense. He then ran successfully for the presidency, handily beating his main rival, **Shamil Basayev**. He served as president of the breakaway republic from 1997 until his death on 8 March 2005. During that period, Maskhadov signed a formal peace treaty with **Boris Yeltsin**, attempted to rebuild the shattered local economy, and worked to stanch the growing tide of **Wahhabism** in his country. Despite his allegiance to the nationalist cause, he eventually capitulated to the **Islamists** and instituted *sharia* (Islamic law) in the late 1990s.

Following **Ibn al-Khattab** and Shamil Basayev's armed incursion into neighboring **Dagestan**, Maskhadov put his country on a war footing against the imminent Russian invasion, which came in late 1999. Pushed out of Grozny, he conducted a long-running guerilla campaign against federal troops and the pro-Russian government of Chechnya, led by **Akhmad Kadyrov**. Accusing Maskhadov of acts of international **terrorism**, the Kremlin ultimately put a $10 million bounty on his head. In 2005, he effectively ordered an end to guerilla operations. One month later, it was reported that he died when Russian Special Forces threw a grenade into his bunker in Tolstoy-Yurt, Chechnya; however, the actual cause of his death remains a mystery. *See also* DUDAYEV, JOKHAR.

MATVIYENKO, VALENTINA IVANOVNA (1949–). Politician. The only **woman** to lead one of Russia's **federal subjects**, Valentina Matviyenko, a former ambassador to Malta and Greece, was elected the governor of the federal city of **St. Petersburg** in 2003. She is a member of the pro-Kremlin **United Russia** party. She is also closely linked to **Vladimir Putin**, who created controversy by formally backing her as president. Despite the endorsement, she failed to win the first election outright, capturing only a plurality of votes despite strong support in the **media**. However, in the second round, she defeated her opponent, Anna Markova, and replaced the former governor, Vladimir Yakolev, who had stepped down over charges of mismanagement of funds. In office, she has worked to attract **foreign investment** to the region and to increase the former capital's share of federal power vis-à-vis **Moscow**. Under the new electoral laws imposed in 2004–2005, Putin nominated her to retain her seat in 2006. On 19 May 2007, the **FSB** reported a plot to assassinate the governor, as well as the detention of several members of an unidentified religious group. In 2008, *Forbes* magazine named her number 31 among the world's most powerful women.

MEDIA. The term "media," and its descriptive derivative *medial'nyi*, meaning "pertaining to media," is a new addition to the **Russian language**. A more common term used both in academia and popular discourse is *sredstva massovoi informatsii* (SMI), which can be literally translated as "means of mass communication," or even "means of informing the masses." Unlike the English concept of "mass media," SMI puts emphasis on a one-to-many type of communication, which is obviously an extension of the Soviet notion of media as a tool of political propaganda. In the Soviet Union, **journalism** was subject to governmental and, more specifically, **Communist Party** control, including censorship of and editorial control over **newspapers**, **radio**, and **television**. Political censorship was exercised through the Central Publishing Agency (Glavlit), as well as through editorial policies, which allowed only a small degree of editorial autonomy on matters that were not politically sensitive.

In addition to censorship, Soviet media was controlled financially as all media outlets were funded by the state. Centralized economic planning often did not reflect local economic and social needs, and media consumers had no opportunity to support production or distribution costs, or directly participate in media production. Furthermore, Soviet citizens were not permitted to establish their own media outlets, resulting in quite passive attitudes toward media among the general public. Soviet authorities were focused on control of media production, being especially paranoid about print media and television, and they largely ignored media consumption, which resulted in the rise of the underground culture with its **samizdat** (self-published) practices. In the Union of Soviet Socialist Republics (USSR), especially in the 1970s and 1980s, audience involvement was simulated through the practice of *stengazety* (wall newspapers) or community bulletins, released by citizens and communities at their place of work or study. These publications were usually amateurish versions of state media like ***Pravda***, but at times displayed some degree of autonomy and criticism. Soviet authorities were not equipped to control new electronic media. In the 1970s, tape recorders were used to deliver oppositional messages, often taking the form of counter-cultural expressions.

Mikhail Gorbachev's **perestroika** occurred at the time when electronic media, including computers and video recorders, were first becoming available to Soviet citizens. Gorbachev's ideas about modernizing the economic structure of the Soviet Union with the purpose of creating an information industry— often referred to as the policy of *informatizatsiia*—overhauled Soviet practices of media control. One of the main outcomes of **glasnost** was the reintroduction of live television broadcasts. In 1986, a youth television program called *12 etazh* (The 12th Floor") permitted critical statements that were aired live; it was a new practice that was immediately replicated by regional television programmers. In the mid-1980s, prompted by the **Chernobyl disaster**, which the Soviet public first learned about from foreign media, Soviet press and television were flooded with information about current and past technological, natural, and social disasters that the state had kept secret from the nation for decades. The revelatory mode of the perestroika media soon spread to political and ideological issues, including the atrocities of the **Stalin** era. Eventually the media became the public arena for debates about how to modernize the country and its political regime.

The previously apathetic Soviet public now displayed an extraordinary enthusiasm about social and political changes that was projected onto the media. The increasing flow of information, facilitated by new means of reproduction and distribution and permitted instances of live broadcasting, prevented the state censorship apparatus with its ailing technological base from effectively controlling media and information at large. The monopoly of the state was undermined, and further availability of information, especially in **union republics**, contributed to the **dissolution of the Soviet Union** in 1991. Indeed, perestroika enabled a media revolution, and when the Law on Press was adopted in 1990, there were 600 periodicals, many of which were already privately owned.

The new law prohibited censorship and allowed organizations and individuals to establish media outlets independently from the state. It also enabled citizens to privatize existing media outlets. Unfortunately, this law and the following "Law on Media" of 1991 did not properly regulate media ownership or the relationships between the media owners and staff, which led to widespread scandals and ownership battles of the later period. If the period before 1995 was characterized by mass **privatization** of media outlets and the emergence of a large number of new publications, television programs, and even new television channels, the period after 1995 was defined by the redistribution of media outlets among major business groups and corporations. While the preceding period, when the state continued to finance but no longer controlled media outlets, was marked by unprecedented freedom and glasnost euphoria, the period after the mid-1990s saw greater economic dependence in the absence of state control.

The new conditions, including skyrocketing inflation as well as the sudden drop in living standards, significantly altered Russia's media landscape. Circulation of newspapers and magazines was now defined not by mandatory subscription but rather by public demand, and decreased dramatically (in five years, the circulation of *Trud* dropped from 20 million copies to just 1 million, and *Izvestiya* plummeted from 1.2 million to 600,000).

National and regional television channels were broken up into a number of small independent studios; production studios were rented to private businesses to enable media outlets to survive financially. Many media personnel left their jobs and started business careers; this brain drain resulted in a lower quality of media production in the mid-1990s. Television channels and especially print media were now dedicated to commercial success through advertising, promotion, and branding, rather than journalistic integrity. This shift resulted in the redistribution of content, with less attention being paid to political and social issues. In order to increase sales, media outlets began to adopt the sensationalist approach to news and topic coverage, causing disappointment in many audiences. Despite these negative tendencies, the overall number of media outlets continued to grow because new players, especially the **oligarchs**, were happy to support financially unprofitable media institutions as their commercial or propaganda resources.

In the second half of the 1990s, giant media holdings were established as a result of the redistribution of the ever-expanding media market. For example, **Yury Luzhkov** established a number of media organizations including TV-Center; the alliance of **Boris Berezovsky** and **Roman Abramovich** resulted in the control over the previously state-monitored Channel 1 (later renamed ORT); **Vladimir Gusinsky** set up the Media-MOST holding company, which included **NTV** among other large media outlets. All of these individuals utilized their media institutions to their own advantage, staging public relations wars against their economic or political rivals. As a result, the media environment of the late 1990s was characterized by information wars, while discrediting and compromising materials (*kompromat*) were circulated endlessly in print and on television. Eventually, the Kremlin grew weary of the media situation—in practice, the government did not have any loyal media outlets at its own disposal—and with the rise of **Vladimir Putin** in 2000, it decided to extend its control over all television, as the most popular medium, and other media establishments.

The government specifically attempted to regain two media-related political losses it sustained during the late 1990s. The first was the loss of control over the media coverage of the first **Chechen War**. Putin's government now wanted to exercise effective management of the media with the purpose of creating a positive image of state agents, especially the *siloviki*. The other was the unpredictability of the press during times of political crisis. Boris Yeltsin had to rely heavily on the financial and media support of Russian oligarchs during the **1996 presidential election**, which resulted in the diminution of his powers as he promised to guarantee their economic privileges. In addition to these concerns, Putin's government recognized the economic potential of media exploitation. With the decline of the era of oligarchs and consolidation of state power after 2000, Russian media saw more stable rules of the game and the capitalization and rationalization of media, which were introduced with the purpose of maintaining the Kremlin's influence over major media institutions.

Russian media and the Russian government, which is so much invested in the media, face two major challenges in the opening decades of the new millennium. The first challenge is that they must operate in the global media environment. Russian television channels need to compete with BBC World, CNN, and Euronews, which are widely available to Russian viewers in English on satellite television and in Russian through their Russian-language services. To counteract these global media outlets, the Russian government has adopted a strategy of intervention: it exercises greater control over television and other mass media establishments and it has boosted its presence on the **Internet**. The Kremlin also launched its **Russia Today** television channel, which broadcasts the state's "official" views abroad in English and other major languages. As Russian media can no longer ignore information available to Russian audiences through Western media, nor suppress oppositional views, it often applies the technique of sensationalism to undermine other voices. Still another approach is the insistent depoliticization of Russian media, especially television, achieved through replacement of analytical programs with entertainment shows (the neologism "petrosianization" is derived from the name of a Russian stand-up comedian, Yevgeny Petrosian, whose programs are being constantly aired on Russian television in primetime with the purpose of distracting the audiences from political activity).

The other challenge is the rise of user-generated media that circumvents any previously known forms of media-audience relationships and undermines the Russian traditional centripetal attitude to media. Technologically and socially, the Russian Internet, most commonly known as **Runet**, develops according to the patterns of traditional media, especially television. However, Runet has a completely different cultural currency and enjoys a privileged status in terms of state control compared with other media. For example, whereas satirical shows are virtually nonexistent on television, on the Internet political satire continues to thrive. In this sense, Runet continues the Soviet political and cultural project of samizdat. Unfortunately, the democratizing potential of Runet has been undermined in recent years by the commercialization of online content. Russia's online advertising market alone grew by 67 percent in 2004 and by a further 71 percent in 2005. There has also been a tendency toward monopolization of the web environment, which has to do with the underdeveloped technical infrastructure that enables the concentration of information flows—and associated capital—in just a few nodes.

The popularity and effectiveness of the Internet has prompted the Kremlin to devise approaches to use the new technology more effectively with the purpose of controlling public opinion. A set of new legislation was established between 2002 and 2004 that aims to combat **terrorism**-related activities online, but in practice is targeted at sites of political resistance. Despite this new legislation, Runet remains the most open medium on the Russian media landscape, with individuals and activist groups enjoying remarkable freedom of expression. At the same time, there has been a negative impact resulting from government intervention into the web space, namely, a higher degree of self-censorship that is applied by Internet activists. Furthermore, on the one hand, the government interference has hindered the technological development of Runet as many small private Internet providers have closed down; on the other, the government has facilitated the provision of web technologies to underprivileged social groups, especially in remote **rural** areas of Russia, as the government now provides points of access to the Internet in schools, post offices, and other regional administrative institutions.

Unfortunately, the Russian public maintains a high degree of skepticism in relation to media: its nature is in the Soviet practices of media control and the post-Soviet experience of media manipulation for economic and political purposes. The lack of media awareness is apparent; media studies are not a standard part of school or university **education** and are normally only available to students who are planning to start careers as journalists. However, media literacy has improved in the past few years thanks to the use of media outlets, especially the Internet, in private spaces.

MEDVYEDEV, DMITRY ANATOLYEVICH (1965–). Politician. The son of a professor, Dmitry Medvyedev grew up in comfortable fashion in Leningrad (now **St. Petersburg**). He graduated from law school in 1987, and later received his PhD in private law from the Leningrad State University. Through his academic connection to **Yeltsin**-era politician **Anatoly Sobchak**, Medvyedev subsequently entered public life. During the first half of the 1990s, he worked in the St. Petersburg City Administration on legal issues related to gambling, real estate, and joint stock ventures.

In the middle part of the decade, he began working for a timber company as well. Upon St. Petersburg native **Vladimir Putin**'s political ascendance in 1999, Medvyedev—along with a coterie of other "Petersburgers"—made the move to **Moscow** to join the new government. He supported Putin's election campaign and was appointed deputy head of the presidential staff in 2000; he was promoted to chief of staff in 2003. In 2001, he was tapped as chair of **Gazprom**'s board of directors. In 2005, *Ekspert* magazine named him "Person of the Year." In the midst of fervid speculation on whom he would choose as his successor (assuming the president chose to step down after two terms), Putin appointed Medvyedev first deputy prime minister, setting the stage for Putin's 10 December 2007 endorsement of Medvyedev's candidacy for the highest office in the nation.

In a secret ballot, Medvyedev won the nomination to represent the dominant **United Russia** in the upcoming election. He also enjoyed the support of **Fair Russia** and the **Agrarian Party of Russia**, two smaller pro-Kremlin parties. In January 2008, he stepped down from Gazprom and formally registered his candidacy. Commanding enormous popularity among Russian voters (more than 75 percent), Medvyedev declared his intention to nominate Putin as prime minister after his victory, evidencing a carefully managed transition that would allow the outgoing president to retain significant influence after the election.

As Putin—legally barred from a third consecutive term—could run again for the presidency after Medvyedev's first term, many assumed that the new president would simply be a figurehead, which sat well with Russia's pro-Putin majority.

Medvyedev's campaign reflected his training and experience in law, focusing on protection of private property, anti-**corruption**, defense of personal freedom, and eradication of "legal nihilism." He also advocated economic deregulation and lower taxes. In a **media** environment where pro-Putin/pro-Medvyedev coverage was ubiquitous, Medvyedev sailed to victory with 63 percent of the vote, though the election was criticized abroad for being less than fair. On 7 May 2008, Medvyedev became the Russian Federation's third popularly elected president. The following day, he appointed Putin as prime minister.

Since taking office, Medvyedev has been tasked with enormous challenges at home and abroad. In August, the **South Ossetian War** broke out when Russian troops, responding to **Georgia**'s attacks on **South Ossetia**, threatening Russian **peacekeepers**, invaded the Black Sea country. Following backing in the **Federal Assembly**,

Medvyedev issued formal recognition of the independence of South Ossetia and **Abkhazia** on 26 August 2008. The decision was met with criticism in Europe and the **United States**, sending relations with both the **European Union** and the **North Atlantic Treaty Organization** (NATO) into a deep freeze for months. Relations were further exacerbated by plans to station missile and radar-jamming facilities in **Kaliningrad** to counter American missile defense systems in **Poland** and the Czech Republic.

The 2008–2009 **global financial crisis** struck the country particularly hard in the late summer, as plummeting commodity prices undercut Russian **oil** and **natural gas** profits. The Russian stock market dropped precipitously, deepening the country's financial woes, which had started with massive capital flight in the wake of the invasion of Georgia in August. Medvyedev and Putin have sunk substantial state funds into the flagging **economy**, while simultaneously reacquiring government stakes in many enterprises that were privatized under Boris Yeltsin. When not engaged in **foreign relations** and economic policy, Medvyedev has dedicated his early administration to combating corruption, targeting the bureaucracy; his plan, which covers 2009–2013, aims to introduce technology and improve efficiency in the civil service, mirroring reforms that occurred in the U.S. under President **Bill Clinton**. In a sop to the nationalists, Medvyedev has also backed a special commission to extirpate "unfavorable" treatment of Russia in history books and popular culture.

His sharpest departure from the Putin era came in April 2009 when he issued a call for more cooperation between the state and **civil society**; the statements were taken as implicit criticism of Putin's attempt to marginalize, co-opt, or eradicate nongovernmental organizations under his presidency. Medvyedev is also seen as extremely tech-savvy, and is a fan of **Runet** and a regular video blogger, a trait that has allowed him to market himself to younger Russians. Medvyedev has been married to Svetlana Medvyedeva (neé Linnik) since 1982, and has a son, Ilya, who was born in 1996.

MESKHETIAN TURKS. Ethnic group. Often simply called Meskhetians, the ethnic group is comprised of **Muslim** inhabitants of **Georgia** who were deported to **Central Asia** by **Joseph Stalin** during World War II. In 1989, a pogrom against the Meskhetians in the

Fergana Valley of **Uzbekistan** resulted in their evacuation to other parts of the Soviet Union, particularly **Krasnodar**. Ethnic tensions with local **Cossacks** within the **krai** resulted in an internationally formulated program to relocate more than 10,000 Meskhetians to the **United States** in the post-Soviet period. Numbering approximately 300,000 worldwide, significant populations of Meskhetians can also be found in **Kazakhstan**, **Azerbaijan**, and **Turkey**. *See also* ETHNIC VIOLENCE.

MIDDLE EAST (RUSSIAN ROLE IN). In the pre-Soviet era, Russia's relations with the Middle East were colored by the long-running rivalry with the Ottoman Empire, most notably the Crimean War (1853–1856), which began over the treatment of **Orthodox** Christians in Palestine. During the Soviet era, **Nikita Khrushchev** expanded Moscow's relations with the nationalist and socialist Arab regimes to offset Western backing of the new state of **Israel** and the anti-Communist regime of pre-revolutionary **Iran**, including providing **arms**, logistical support, and economic aid.

During the 1960s and 1970s, the Union of Soviet Socialist Republics (USSR) developed particularly close ties with Egypt, Libya, Iraq, Syria, and the People's Democratic Republic of Yemen. The Kremlin has also been a longtime supporter of Palestinian statehood and Kurdish separatist movements. During the Iran-Iraq War (1980–1988), the USSR officially adopted a policy of neutrality, though fear of spreading **Islamism** and losing Iraq to the West tempered this position. In the last days of **Mikhail Gorbachev**'s rule, the **United States**–led Persian Gulf War against Saddam Hussein created a crisis within the foreign policy community, as well as domestic problems for Gorbachev, who attempted to maintain his promises to the **United Nations** while satisfying economic and political interests at home.

After the **dissolution of the Soviet Union** in 1991, **Boris Yeltsin** adopted a strongly **Atlanticist** foreign policy orientation, effectively eschewing the ideological support for local potentates that had characterized his predecessors; however, established interests in the region—particularly arms exports—ensured that Russia would continue to play a role in regional politics. Yeltsin also normalized relations with **North Atlantic Treaty Organization** (NATO) member **Turkey**. Under the influence of **Yevgeny Primakov**, Russia began to renew its political—rather than just economic—ties to the region, particularly Syria and Iran, both major critics of Washington. With a generation of foreign policy specialists trained in Arabic and Middle Eastern affairs, the new posture was welcomed by many *siloviki*. **Gazprom** and other corporate interests also backed the return of Russian interest in the region.

Such trends continued under **Vladimir Putin**, who condemned the U.S.-led invasion of Iraq in 2003, brought Russia into the Organization of the Islamic Conference as a permanent observer in 2005, and invited a senior delegation of Hamas officials to visit the country after their 2006 electoral victory in the Gaza Strip. In 2007, Putin was the first Russian leader ever to visit Saudi Arabia. He also reinvigorated Russian participation in the Middle East peace process as part of the Quartet, which also includes the U.S., the **European Union**, and the United Nations. Putin's rejection of a "one-size-fits-all" model of Western democracy proved exceptionally palatable to many of the region's leaders, especially monarchs and long-serving autocrats like Muammar al-Gaddafi. Russia's relations with Israel have also been in flux, partly due to the large Russophone diaspora in the country and increased economic ties between Moscow and the **Jewish** state.

MIGRANYAN, ANDRANIK (1949–). Diplomat. Considered to be one of Russia's premier **foreign relations** experts, Adranik Migranyan served on **Boris Yeltsin**'s advisory council on **foreign relations** in the early 1990s. He is credited with developing the concept of the **Monroeski Doctrine**, which articulated Russia's preeminence in the **near abroad** following the **dissolution of the Soviet Union**. He was highly critical of **Mikhail Gorbachev**'s actions leading to the breakup of the union, producing numerous regional wars and **ethnic violence**. He is currently head of the **United States** division of the Russian think tank the Institute for Democracy and Cooperation; he is based in New York. *See also* ARMENIANS.

MILITARY. The Armed Forces of the Russian Federation (*vooruzhenniie sily Rossiiskoi federatsii*) is the collective name for the Russian military. On 7 May 1992, **Boris Yeltsin** established the Russian Ministry of Defense, and placed all Soviet Armed Forces in the territory of the **Russian Soviet Federative Socialist Republic** under the control of the Russian Federation. The president of the Russian Federation, currently **Dmitry Medvyedev**, holds the title of Supreme Commander of the Armed Forces.

The Armed Forces are divided between the three branches: Ground Forces (or **army**), **navy**, and **air force**. Additionally, there are three independent arms of the service: Strategic Rocket Forces, which manage Russia's **nuclear weapons**; Space Forces, which participate in the country's **space program**; and the Airborne Troops, an elite force for rapid response to national emergencies. In terms of active troops, the Russian Federation ranks second in the world with more than 1.5 million soldiers, sailors, and aviators. Military expenditures in 2009 were just under $50 billion, a figure that has risen dramatically since the **ruble crisis** of 1998, when spending fell to its nadir. Russia trails both the **United States** and **China** in military spending. Nearly three-quarters of military procurements come from Russia's domestic defense industry.

The military is currently in the midst of a massive upgrade, funded, in part, by Russia's booming **economy** prior to the 2008–2009 **global economic crisis**. The Russian military has been deployed in a number of **peacekeeping** operations since its creation, and engaged in its first interstate conflict in 2008 during the **South Ossetian War** with **Georgia**.

MINING. With its vast and varied **geography**, Russia possesses more mineral resources than any other country in the world. The sector is considered to be a strategic part of the **economy**, and many of Russia's largest companies are mining concerns, including Rusal, **Norilsk Nickel**, and **ALROSA**. Russia is the world's top producer of palladium and nickel, and ranks second in aluminum. It is also a world leader in coal, gold, copper, iron ore, diamonds, lead, potash, cobalt, zinc, uranium, and various rare earth metals. Most the country's mines are located in Asiatic Russia, particularly in eastern **Siberia** and the **Russian Far East**, though the **North Caucasus** region yields various minerals. **Kaliningrad** commands the vast majority of the world's amber deposits. Historically, **foreign investment** in the mining sector has remained underdeveloped due to concerns about high **taxes** and the unreliability of the **judicial system**. Nonetheless, expenditures and inward foreign investment rose dramatically under **Vladimir Putin**. However, the Kremlin's decision to nationalize gold mining in 2008 underscored preexisting concerns about foreign investment. Increasingly, Russian companies and the state have shown interest in outward investment. Most dramatically, **Gazprom** announced a $4 billion deal with **Venezuela** in 2009. *See also* NATURAL GAS; OIL.

MINISTRY OF INTERNAL AFFAIRS (MVD). Maintaining the same name since the **Romanov** Empire, Russia's Ministry of Internal Affairs (*Ministerstvo vnutrennikh del*) is a key part of the country's **security services**, with duties including administering the Federal Migration Service, the Criminal Militia Service, the Public Security Service, and other divisions. The MVD is tasked with combating white-collar **crimes**, **tax** evasion, and the **mafia**, as well as managing highway safety and the issuance of passports and visas. The MVD Internal Troops help maintain internal security, guard prisons, and assist with the transport of sensitive materials. The agency is headed by General Rashid Nurgaliyev, a veteran of the **FSB**. Alongside the FSB, the **military**, and the GRU (military intelligence), the MVD is considered one of Russia's "power industries" associated with the *siloviki*.

MINOR PEOPLES OF THE NORTH. *See* INDIGENOUS PEOPLES OF THE NORTH.

MIRONOV, SERGEY MIKHAILOVICH (1953–). Politician. Currently the chairman of the **Federation Council**, Sergey Mironov established himself on the **St. Petersburg** political scene during the mid-1990s. In 2001, he gained a seat in the upper house of parliament representing the former capital. He led the short-lived Russian Party of Life before it was folded into the pro-Kremlin **Fair Russia** party. In 2006, he took up the leadership of Fair Russia, making him the ostensible leader of the opposition. However, his strong support of **Vladimir Putin** sapped this distinction of any real meaning. (In 2004, Mironov ran for president, but publicly stated that Putin would be victorious, thus undermining his own campaign.) He has consistently lobbied for an end to the two-consecutive-term limit on the president's office and an extension of the presidential term. *See also* POLITICS.

MOKSHA. *See* MORDVINS.

MOLDOVA (RELATIONS WITH). The present-day territory of the Republic of Moldova, historically known as Bessarabia, was incorporated into the Russian Empire at the end of the Russo-Turkish War (1806–1812). After World War I (1914–1918), much of the region was granted to Romania, though the lands east of the Dnestr River were an autonomous region within the Ukrainian Soviet Socialist Republic. Following the 1939 Molotov-Ribbentrop Pact, the Union of Soviet Socialist Republics (USSR) occupied Romanian Bessarabia and created a new **union republic**, which was reconstituted after World War II and lasted until 1991.

Under **glasnost**, a strong nationalist movement emerged among the republic's titular majority, ethnic Romanians also known as Moldovans. Fearful of Romanianization and/or reunification of the republic with Romania, the country's Slavs—who dominated the **Transnistria** region—declared independence in September 1990. Fighting soon broke out between republican authorities and the **separatists**; a cease-fire was brokered in July 1992, several months after the Republic of Moldova gained its independence from the Soviet Union.

Dispatched to the region in the summer, **Aleksandr Lebed** loudly denounced the Romanian "fascists" and Transnistrian "bandits," making a name for himself politically while ending the violence. Acting as a **peacekeeping** force, the Russian 14th Army, known as the Operational Group of Russian Forces in Moldova after 1995, has remained in Transnistria since that time.

Relations between the two states reached their nadir during the first **Yeltsin** administration in the midst of a Russian-imposed trade embargo. After Moldova joined the **Commonwealth of Independent States** (CIS), Moscow committed to a withdrawal; however, opposition in the **State Duma** made such an outcome impossible as protection of Russian "compatriots," that is, Russophones in Moldova, had emerged as a key domestic policy issue in the Russian Federation. During the late 1990s, the Transnistrian conflict became frozen, with the breakaway republic governing itself as a wholly sovereign entity. In 2004, a proposal to make the Russian **military** presence permanent sparked outrage across Moldova proper; the

North Atlantic Treaty Organization (NATO) has condemned Russia for not living up to its 1999 commitment to remove its troops from the region. **Ukraine**, Romania, the **European Union** (EU), and the **Organization for Security and Co-operation in Europe** have all sought to resolve the situation, without success.

Moldova is committed to neutrality and has not participated in any of the CIS's military structures; likewise, although it is a member of the **GUAM Organization for Democracy and Economic Development**, the country is not party to any common defense initiatives within the group. As Europe's poorest country, Moldova has sought to attenuate its disputes with Moscow since the economic successes of the **Putin** administration have become apparent. President Vladimir Voronin (2001–present), a vocal supporter of the CIS, head of the country's Communist Party, and a Transnistrian by birth, has declared that his country is on good terms with Russia, with the only issue dividing Chişinău and Moscow being the status of Transnistria.

Relations have improved markedly since 2006: annual trade exceeds $1 billion, Russian **foreign investment** in the country is on the rise, and Moscow is allowing increasing numbers of Moldovan **agricultural** products to enter the country, including wine, which was barred until 2007. In the spring of 2009, violent pro-Western, youth-led demonstrations against the Communist government complicated the country's international situation as it became clear that Moscow had little influence over the country vis-à-vis the EU. *See also* FOREIGN RELATIONS.

MONGOLIA (RELATIONS WITH). In the decade after independence from Qing China, Mongolia steadily gravitated into the sphere of influence of Soviet Russia. In 1924, a Mongolian People's Republic was established under Soviet protection, becoming the first of many Soviet satellites during the **Cold War**. Mongolian-Soviet relations remained close (including during the Sino-Soviet split) until **the dissolution of the Soviet Union** in 1991.

Under **perestroika**, **Mikhail Gorbachev** dramatically reduced Soviet subsidies to Ulan Bator and began the withdrawal of Soviet troops. Recognizing the loss of its longtime protector, Mongolia concurrently improved relations with the People's Republic of **China** and the **United States**. Mirroring reforms in the Soviet Union, Mongolia abandoned one-party totalitarianism and began market reforms, maintaining friendly but diminished relations with Russia in the process. The new relationship—built on principles of equality—was solidified with the 1993 Treaty of Friendship and Cooperation; however, pernicious disputes over Mongolia's debt to Russia and the latter's abolition of visa-free travel for Mongolian citizens weakened the relationship. Recently, Mongolia has again entered into Russia's geopolitical strategy. **Vladimir Putin** has sought to leverage Mongolia as an ally in northeast Asia, and made one of his first foreign visits to Ulan Bator, signifying an unwillingness to let China act as the sole great power in the region.

Mongolia was also positioned as an important player in maintaining stability in **Central Asia** and given observer status within the **Shanghai Cooperation Organization**. The Kremlin wrote off nearly all of the impoverished country's debt and has expanded trade, energy, and cultural linkages in the past decade. With nearly 3,500 kilometers of shared border between the two countries, Russia's regional governors in the districts of Chita, **Buryatiya**, **Tuva**, and the **Altay Republic** have emerged as important players in bilateral relations, particularly on issues of **foreign trade**. *See also* FOREIGN RELATIONS.

MONROESKI DOCTRINE. The "Monroeski Doctrine" was a colloquial description of **Boris Yeltsin**'s foreign policy strategy in the **near abroad**. Adapted from the **United States**' 19th-century Monroe Doctrine, which prohibited European colonization of the newly independent Latin American republics, the Monroeski Doctrine affirmed the Russian Federation's position as the dominant power in the entire former Soviet Union. Moscow often invoked the doctrine when it intervened in post-Soviet conflicts in the **Newly Independent States** of Eurasia, such as the **Tajik Civil War** and the **separatist** conflicts in **Nagorno-Karabakh**, **Transnistria**, **Abkhazia**, and **South Ossetiya**. Articulated by **Andranik Migranyan**, the Monroeski Doctrine used historical and geopolitical logic to argue that Russia—rather than **Turkey**, **China**, **Iran**, or the U.S.—was better equipped to solve issues in its "backyard," particularly through organizations like the **Commonwealth of Independent States**. Political elites in the former Soviet Republics, particularly in the **Baltic States**, **Georgia**,

Moldova, and **Uzbekistan**, criticized the policy as neo-imperialist. The term fell out of favor by the end of the 1990s, but the concept still girds the **foreign relations** theories of Russia's **Eurasianists**.

MONTENEGRO. *See* SERBIA.

MORDOVIYA. An **ethnic republic** of the Russian Federation. The historic region of Mordoviya (or Mordvinia) was fully incorporated into Russia during the reign of Peter the Great. After the defeat of the anti-Bolshevik forces in the Russian Civil War, Moscow established an **autonomous okrug** in the region. Mordoviya became an **Autonomous Soviet Socialist Republic** of the **Russian Soviet Federative Socialist Republic** in 1934, an appellation the republic only abandoned in 1994. Mordoviya's retention of its Soviet nomenclature longer than **federal subjects** of the Russian Federation was emblematic of the conservative nature of the republican leadership in the early 1990s.

Mordoviya is a member of the Volga **Federal District** and the Volga-Vyatka **Economic Region**. It is surrounded by **Chuvashiya**, **Ulyanovsk**, **Penza**, **Ryazan**, and **Nizhny Novgorod**. Mordoviya includes part of the **Volga River** basin; it is divided between forests and **steppe** lands. In the west, the Oka-Don Plain is the defining geographic feature; the Volga Highlands dominate the republic's eastern landscape. The regional capital is Saransk (pop. 304,000), located at the confluence of the Saranka and Insar rivers. The republic is one of Russia's smaller regions, covering only 26,200 square kilometers. The population of 889,000 inhabitants is divided between **ethnic Russians** (61 percent), **Mordvins** (32 percent), **Tatars** (5 percent), and others (2 percent). While Mordoviya is the ethnic homeland of the Mordvins, only about a third of the nationality resides in the republic. The republic's official **languages** are **Russian**, Erzya, and Moksha, the latter two being languages of the Finno-Ugric indigenous population. Russian **Orthodoxy** is the dominant faith of the region, with the Tatars representing a small **Muslim** minority.

The regional **economy** is focused on woodworking, mechanical engineering, pharmaceuticals, petrochemicals, and **agriculture** (animal products, grains, sugar beets, and vegetables). Mordoviya is the center of Russia's luminescence **industry**; major companies include

Saranskkabel (fiber optics), Elektrovypryamitel (power converters), Lisma-KETZ (halogen lamp), and Orbita (integrated circuits). As the site of numerous medicinal springs and a unique cultural heritage, the region is also a **tourist** site for Russians and foreign visitors. With a focus on innovative products that can compete in global markets, the regional economy has proved stable since independence, and continues to grow.

The head of the regional government since 1995, Nikolay Merkushkin, an ethnic Mokshan Mordvin, is close to **Moscow** mayor **Yury Luzhkov**, a relationship that has produced economic dividends for the republic. An engineer by training, Merkushkin began his career in **politics** as the head of the republic's **Komsomol** youth organization before assuming control of the state property committee. Originally a member of the **Communist Party of the Soviet Union**, Merkushkin joined the **Agrarian Party** in the 1990s before opting for Luzhkov's **Fatherland—All Russia** bloc at the end of the decade. In 1998, he ran virtually unopposed after disqualifying his major rivals from participating in the poll. Rarely taking on Moscow during the **Yeltsin** administration, he proved to be one of the most loyal republican governors. In fact, many Russians in the regional leadership backed devolution of republican sovereignty and the creation of Saransk Oblast, including the eradication of the special cultural rights of the Mordvins.

While Merkushkin was a rather docile vassal of Boris Yeltsin, he did oppose **Vladimir Putin**'s plans to centralize decision making by implementing the system of **federal districts** in 2000. Despite such criticism, he was reappointed by Putin in 2005. In recent years, freedom of the press in the republic has sunk to new lows, even by Russian standards. However, Merkushkin remains popular among parliamentarians and the general populace.

MORDVINS. Ethnic group. Mordvins are a composite nationality of the Russian Federation comprised of Erzyans and Mokshans, both being Finno-Ugrian peoples of the **Volga** basin. The description "Mordvin" is an exonym imposed on the Erzyans and Mokshans by the Russians; the term has been described as a "pseudo-ethnonym" by some nationalistic Mordvins, who prefer to be described separately from one another or, collectively, as Moksherzians.

Both the Erzyan and Mokshan **languages**, along with Mari, form the Finno-Volgaic subgroup of the Uralic language family. The two Mordvinian languages are distinct, and speakers do not possess full mutual intelligibility. On these grounds, certain Mordvin nationalists (especially among the Erzyan community) argue that the two groups should be recognized as separate ethnic groups. There are cultural differences as well; the Erzyans came under Russian domination earlier than their Mokshan cousins, who lingered under Kazan **Tatar** rule, absorbing a greater level of Turkic influence. Erzyans are estimated to account for two-thirds of the Mordvin population, while Mokshans constitute one-third; however, Mokshans possess a slight demographic edge in Mordoviya. Mordvins generally espouse Russian **Orthodoxy**; however, **shamanistic** and animist elements still pervade their folkways.

Collectively, Mordvins represent the fifth-largest indigenous **national minority** in the Russian Federation. Out of a total of 843,000 in the Russian Federation, only 284,000—roughly one-third of all Mordvins—reside in their ethnic homeland, **Mordoviya**. Significant numbers reside in the following regions: **Samara** (86,000), **Penza** (71,000), **Orenburg** (52,000), **Ulyanovsk** (50,000), **Bashkortostan** (26,000), **Nizhny Novgorod** (25,000), **Tatarstan** (23,000), and **Moscow** (23,000). Unlike most other nationalist movements among Russia's **ethnic minorities**, most Mordvin organizations seek to promote policies that are confined not simply to the ethnic homeland, but to all of Russia (and the Soviet Union before it). Under **perestroika** and **glasnost**, the first major Mordvin organization was Mastorava (Mother Earth). The organization, led by writers and linguists, lobbied for a republican governor who was fluent in the Mordvinian language, petitioned for the right to draft laws, and sought controls on migration. Mastorava also had a strong ecological orientation and was supportive of Mordvins embracing Protestantism like their Finnish relatives. The organization lost influence after 1995, being replaced by the moderate Executive Committee of the Congress of the Mordvin People.

During the mid-1990s, a more radical group, Erzyan Mastor (Erzyan Land), also emerged. Erzyan Mastor campaigned for a separate national homeland for the Erzyans within Mordoviya, as well as citizenship of the Mordvin Republic for all ethnic Mordvins, regardless of place of residence. The organization also eschewed Russian Orthodoxy as a tool of **Russification**, and embraced a politicized form of **neo-paganism**, which attempted to revive traditional Mordvin practices such as animal sacrifice, communing with the dead, and food blessing. Despite efforts at national revival, language loss and assimilation of Mordvins into Russian culture remain high.

MOSCOW, CITY OF. Moscow is the capital and largest city of the Russian Federation; it is also the largest metropolitan area in Europe. The city is the major political, economic, financial, cultural, **religious**, **educational**, and **transport** center of Russia. Known as *Moskva* in the **Russian language**, its name derives from the eponymous river on the banks of which there have been human settlements since prehistoric times. The city was first mentioned in the Russian Chronicles in 1147, and became the center of Russian political power in the 14th century. Moscow lost its status as the capital of the **Romanov** Empire when Peter the Great moved the capital to the newly founded city of **St. Petersburg** in the country's northwest in the early 18th century. Following the Bolshevik Revolution, Moscow once again became the capital, first of the **Russian Soviet Federative Socialist Republic** in 1918, and then the Union of Soviet Socialist Republics (USSR) several years later.

As the seat of power for the Russian Federation, the Moscow Kremlin (from the word for "fortress" or "citadel") houses the home of the president of Russia, as well as many other agencies of the national government, including **military** headquarters. Moscow is also home for the Russian **State Duma** and other national and international organizations. However, in recent years, there has been a move to transfer some of the government institutions to St. Petersburg, with the purpose of revitalizing Russia's northern capital and of decentering Russia's judicial, financial, and cultural life.

The longtime mayor of the city of Moscow is **Yury Luzhkov**. The local government is called the City Duma. Moscow is a federal city and thus one of Russia's **federal subjects**. Moscow is part of the Central **Federal District** and **Economic Region**. It covers an area of 1,081 square kilometers. Moscow and its suburbs, which are part of the **Moscow Oblast**, form one of the largest urban conglomerates in the world. Roughly 1 out of 10 Russian citizens resides in the greater Moscow area.

Moscow has one of the largest city **economies** in Europe, providing approximately a quarter of Russian gross domestic product on an annual basis. Primary **industries** include chemicals, **foodstuffs**, textiles, software development, and machinery. In 2008, Moscow was home to Russia's 74 billionaires; however, that figure has decreased dramatically in the wake of the 2008–2009 **global financial crisis**.

Moscow proper is defined by its seven administrative divisions (**okrugs**), and also by the Moscow Circle Road (MCR), a major highway that encircles the city and provides access to the capital's main roads. Because of the MCR, Moscow proper is easily defined. There are five main airports (including Sheremetyevo and Domodedovo International Airports) and seven large train stations serving the metropolitan area. The MCR is part of Moscow's circular geographical and transportation system. With the walls of the Kremlin forming the city's innermost circle, the inner core of the city is bounded by the Boulevard Ring (which encloses a series of parks in the city center), then the Garden Ring, Moscow's major thoroughfare, and, finally, the MCR, from which highways and train lines stretch in a radial fashion all across the country, symbolically securing Moscow's dominant position in the Russian Federation.

In 2009, the population of Moscow was estimated at 10.5 million people (a century ago it was only 1 million people, suggesting that on average the population of Moscow grows by a million every decade). However, this estimate includes only officially registered residents of the city; in order to reside in Moscow, individuals need to obtain a writ of permission (*propiska*) from Moscow's authorities who, through this practice, are able to partially regulate migration to the capital. Lack of such paperwork prevents Russian citizens (and **immigrants** from other countries) from applying for mortgages and gaining access to **health care** and other services. As it is virtually impossible to obtain such a *propiska* for residency in the capital, many people continue to live in the city as unregistered residents or as temporary visitors, which means that the real population of Moscow is a few million larger. The registration practice applies to the Russian capital only, making it a unique place in the Russian Federation, socially and culturally.

Moscow is a multicultural, multiconfessional city; however, in Moscow, the number of people who define themselves as **ethnic Russians** is higher than Russia's average. The city is home to large communities of **Ukrainians**, **Tatars**, **Armenians**, **Jews**, Georgians, and other **ethnic minorities**. The city's ethnic population increased significantly after the **dissolution of the Soviet Union**, when many citizens of the former Soviet republics, especially from **Central Asia** and the **Caucasus**, came to live in Russia's capital. While in Moscow there are areas that are named after Russia's ethnic minorities, for example, the *Armianskii pereulok* (the Armenian street), they refer to a settlement practice of imperial Russia. Generally, Moscow's ethnic minorities do not live in communities as they do in other large cities in the world (for example, in New York's Chinatown); instead, social stratification in Moscow is based on people's class, with higher classes gravitating to the city center or living in the suburbs. However, it is still possible to find communal flats (*kommunalki*) in Moscow's center, occupied by poorer families that cannot afford other accommodation.

Moscow's living costs are among the highest in the country: in 2009, renting a studio apartment cost between $1,000 and $5,000 per month, and an average square foot of Moscow's property was valued at $1,000. While property is very expensive, public services are cheap, for example, London's underground is five times more expensive than Moscow's metro. Furthermore, Moscow retains a system of state subsidies for unprivileged citizens, including cheap commercial outlets, keeping the capital affordable for many. At the same time, the city's center and Moscow's suburbs, especially the Rubliovka Highway (*Rubliovskoie shosse*), are dominated by Russia's new political and economic elites, featuring multimillion-dollar apartments and mansions of Russian **oligarchs** and **celebrities**.

As with other world capitals, Moscow is a highly fashionable and desirable place to live, which accounts for the annual drain of a great number of young people from Russian provinces to the country's capital. They are motivated by the hopes of social mobility, particularly opportunities associated with Moscow's world-class institutions of education, such as the **Moscow State University**, as well as cultural sites such as the Tretiakov Gallery and the Bolshoy Theater,

St. Basil's Cathedral and the Cathedral of Christ the Savior, **sports** arenas, and **music** venues, which attract **tourists** and new residents. Numerous parks and green areas also dot the city's landscape. Moscow has a vibrant nightlife, which is certainly a post-Soviet addition: in the early 1990s, new luxurious restaurants, nightclubs, and shops appeared in and in the vicinity of Tverskaya Street.

These outlets provide escape and entertainment during Moscow's long and bleak winters. Because of the changing **climate**, heavy snowfalls and low temperatures are now a rarity in the winter, while the summer normally features a series of punishing heat waves. Moscow suffers from serious air **pollution**, due to the city's industry, automobiles (the number of private cars in Moscow trebled in less than a decade), and congested road system (**Joseph Stalin** built new highways in the capital, thus destroying many historical districts; however, their purpose was more military than civic and so they do not meet the needs of Moscow's bulging population). The capital has become notorious for its smog, which explains why many Muscovites prefer to take to their **dachas** when possible.

MOSCOW OBLAST. Administrative region of the Russian Federation. The second most populous **federal subject** after the Federal City of **Moscow**, Moscow Oblast has a population of 6.6 million. More than 90 percent of the population is **ethnic Russian**, but the region is highly cosmopolitan, with nearly every ethnic group from the former Soviet Union represented. At a smallish 45,000 square kilometers, it also one of the most densely populated and urbanized regions in the country; there are more than 70 cities in the region, with 15 that have more than 100,000 residents.

The region is highly industrialized; metallurgy, chemicals, **oil** refining, energy production, engineering, and **food** services are the main sectors. Well connected by rail and roads, the region serves as a hub for travel into and out of Moscow proper. The **oblast** also possesses significant academic and scientific infrastructure and is a national center of research and development. Despite its urban character, the area is also known for its **agriculture** and rivers. The region is part of the Central **Economic Region** and the Central **Federal District**. It is bordered by **Tver**, **Yaroslavl**, **Vladimir**, **Ryazan**,

Tula, **Kaluga**, and **Smolensk oblasts** and is perforated by the Federal City of Moscow.

The current governor is Boris Gromov, a popular veteran of the **Soviet-Afghan War** and the last Soviet soldier to quit the country, passing over the Friendship Bridge separating the Union of Soviet Socialist Republics (USSR) from **Afghanistan** on 15 February 1989. Prior to his 2000 election to the governorship, he served in the **State Duma**. Gromov, who had the backing of Moscow's influential mayor, **Yury Luzhkov**, won the election in a heated battle for power. Gromov has focused on improving living standards for public sector workers, increasing the number of small and medium-sized businesses, and attracting **foreign investment** to the region. He succeeded Anatoly Tyazhlov, who had governed since 1991 but had seen his popularity decline amid criticism of his **alcoholism** and poor governance.

MOSCOW STATE UNIVERSITY. M. V. Lomonosov Moscow State University (MSU) is Russia's oldest and largest university and the premier university in Eastern Europe. It is the most important and prestigious center for **education** and research in the Russian Federation. It was founded in 1755 by Mikhail Lomonosov, Russia's most prominent Enlightenment figure. Since 1953 its main campus has been on the Sparrow Hills (known as Lenin's Hills during the Soviet period) in **Moscow**. Its main building is one of seven tiered neoclassical towers that **Joseph Stalin** ordered built after World War II. It remained the tallest building in Europe until the 1990s.

In 1992 the university was granted a unique status in the Russian educational system: it is funded directly from the state budget, bypassing the Ministry of Education and thus ensuring a significant degree of independence. The rector of the university is Viktor Sadovnichy. Since 2005, he has used the university's special status to oppose Russia's educational reforms and integrate MSU into the pan-European Bologna process.

MSU has 30 schools and over 300 departments, as well as a large number of research centers. The university has an undergraduate population of 40,000, and 90 percent of students do not pay any tuition fees. It also possesses one of the largest libraries in Russia.

MOSCOW THEATER HOSTAGE CRISIS. *See* NORD-OST THE-
ATER SIEGE.

MURMANSK OBLAST. An administrative region of the Russian
Federation. Murmansk occupies the Kola Peninsula and its hinter-
land on the Fenno-Scandinavian Peninsula of northeastern Europe.
Murmansk is washed by the **Barents Sea** in the north and the White
Sea in the east. It shares international borders with **Norway** and **Finland**; the latter was forced to cede Petsamo (now Pechenga District)
to Soviet Russia after World War II, thus denying the Finns access
to the Barents Sea and establishing a Soviet-Norwegian land border.
Internally, Murmansk borders only **Kareliya**.

Murmansk Oblast has a population of 892,500 and a land area of
144,900 square kilometers. It is part of the Northwestern **Federal
District** and the Northern **Economic Region**. Due to competing
influences of the **Arctic** and Atlantic oceans, the region possesses a
dichotomous **climate** with **tundra** in the north and maritime **taiga** in
the south (two-thirds of the region is forested). The region is one of
Russia's more economically developed areas, possessing vast mineral reserves of quartz, cobalt, titanium, copper, nickel, zirconium,
and other precious metals. Nonferrous metallurgy is the dominant
sector of the economy, followed by power generation, the **food** industry (including fish), and petrochemicals.

Nickel smelting in the region is responsible for environmental degradation and **pollution** in the Nordic countries and has been regulated
since 1996. **Oil** and gas reserves are being developed in the Barents
Sea, particularly by **Lukoil**. The region's fisheries (cod, halibut,
flounder, herring, and salmon) are some of the most productive in the
world. While animal husbandry is well developed, the region does not
support a sufficient crop yield due to its northern geography. The site
of a large number of **nuclear** reactors, the region generates all of its
own electricity and also exports to Finland and Kareliya; wind power
generators have also been installed in the region in recent years. The
region also possesses a significant **military** presence, including the
nuclear submarine base at the closed town of Ostrovnoy.

Ethnic Russians account for 85 percent of the population. The
Saami, a group indigenous to Sápmi (Lapland), of which the Kola
Peninsula is a part, account for less than 1 percent of the population.

The regional capital, Murmansk, is Russia's largest ice-free port and a central location of the country's **fishing industry**. The region's first and only popularly elected governor is Yury Yevdokimov. He took office in 1996 and soon signed a power-sharing deal with **Moscow**. Yevdokimov was reelected in 2000 and 2004 and reappointed by **Vladimir Putin** in 2007 (he had strongly defended Putin's handling of the *Kursk* **submarine disaster** in 2000). The governor's bid to have Murmansk designated as a Special Economic Zone like **Khabarovsk** was rejected by the Kremlin in 2008; however, Yevdokimov has expanded the power of the regional administration during a period when Moscow has been sapping authority from its **federal subjects**.

In 2008, Murmansk residents gained visa-free travel rights to northern Norway. With the annual decrease of ice in the Arctic Ocean, Murmansk is poised to play a pivotal role in Russia's economic and political expansion in the northern polar region in coming decades; Yevdokimov has emerged as an international advocate for Russia's national interests in this domain.

MUSIC. Russia's diverse ethnic composition accounts for the country's complex, multifaceted music scene. **Ethnic Russian** music is closely tied with **rural life** and its traditions. It is primarily vocal, with the Russian folk song being an integral part of daily life in a village. With the demise of rural life in the 20th century, the traditions of singing and performing have been maintained through professional music ensembles, choruses, and singers. No musical instruments are used in **Orthodox** churches, following the ban on musical instruments that dates back to the middle of the 17th century. Liturgy music is normally performed by a female chorus with male voices of the clergy leading the ritual.

In post-Soviet Russia, there is declining interest in traditional Russian folk music, and performances by folk artists are increasingly rare. However, acts such as Lyudmila Zykina, the Piatnistky Russian Folk Chorus, and the Aleksandrov Song and Dance Ensemble of the Soviet army enjoy a devoted audience of music connoisseurs. More recently, Russian folk music instruments and *chastushky* (a short song of humorous or satirical nature that is rapped) have been successfully incorporated into contemporary music.

Russia's **ethnic minorities** each possess a rich musical culture. For example, **Buryats** are known for their distinct folk music that uses a two-stringed fiddle (*morin khuur*). As in other historically oral cultures, Buryat music is heavily focused on narration, evoking heroic deeds of the past. Contemporary Buryat music combines traditional styles with lyrics in the **Russian language**. **Tatar** music employs the pentatonic scale, which indicates links to East Asian musical traditions. Tatars employ musical instruments such as the *kubyz* (Jew's harp) and the *zurna*, a double-reed wind instrument.

In the Soviet Union, musical concerts by Russia's **national minorities** were a common feature of state **holidays** and a staple of the all-Union festivals of arts and music. They were regularly broadcast on **television**, and the state supported musical education and preservation of musical traditions in the **ethnic republics**. In post-Soviet Russia, while the state continues to support ethnic traditions, public musical performances are confined to philharmonic concerts and special programs on the Kul'tura television channel.

Despite some interest in ethnic traditions of music, the market in Russia is dominated by the Russophone and Anglophone popular music. Popular, mainstream music had an ambivalent status in the Soviet Union. On the one hand, the state propagated "ideologically correct" songs (for example, songs from the **Stalin**-era **film** musical *Volga-Volga*) and was willing to allow for popular tunes at times of national hardship (like during World War II, when the famous ballad *Katiusha* was sanctioned by the state). On the other hand, the state opposed any form of popular music that seemed to be outside the accepted ideological and aesthetic canon (for instance, jazz, labeled as the music of the bourgeoisie, was banned for decades until it was "rehabilitated" in the 1970s) or hinted at market conditions necessary for the proliferation of a popular music industry. Music distribution was controlled by the state through **radio** and television channels as well as the state recording monopoly, Melodiia. During the **Brezhnev** era, music played a pivotal role in maintaining a cheerful spirit and hopes for a "brighter future," and generally was used by the state to distract the population from critically examining social and political issues. This resulted in the emergence of genuinely popular stars like Alla Pugacheva, who dominates the contemporary Russian pop scene even now through her network of hand-picked "starlets."

Classical music was always seen by Soviet officials as a safe option for popular entertainment as, first of all, it symbolized the Soviet notion of enlightenment, and second, it rarely contained elements that aimed to critique the regime. The traditions of classical music have been maintained in post-Soviet Russia, with every major urban center having a philharmonic orchestra and one or two concert halls and music **education** institutions. **Moscow** and **St. Petersburg** remain the country's centers of classical music, with the Moscow Conservatory and other institutions producing world-famous performers. The Kul'tura television channel and the Orpheus radio channel specialize in broadcasting classical music. Russian contemporary classical music composers include Boris Philanovsky and Anton Batagov, among many others. While Philanovsky's music is highly experimental and combines complex abstract forms and evocations of Russian postmodern literature, Batagov's music is a synthesis of European notation and **Buddhist** spirituality.

Rock music played a crucial role in undermining the Soviet regime. Genealogically linked to the Soviet **intelligentsia** tradition of the bard song, Soviet rock formed an important stratum of Soviet unofficial culture. Underground concerts and **samizdat** copies of musical albums served as a channel of dissemination of free thinking and as a form of social mobilization. It is not an exaggeration to suggest that rock music brought about the changes associated with **perestroika** and **glasnost**, with one of the songs by Viktor Tsoi, *Peremen!* ("We expect changes!"), becoming the unofficial anthem of the period. In post-Soviet Russia, rock music is as diverse as in any Western country. Other genres of popular music are equally represented, with a variety of music festivals dedicated to every genre occurring across contemporary Russia.

The dramatic change from a highly regulated music scene of the 1970s to a thriving music culture of the new millennium has to do with a few factors. First of all, the abolishing of censorship under **Mikhail Gorbachev** and **Boris Yeltsin** enabled musicians to express themselves freely, using the style that they thought was most appropriate for their work. Second, Russia's lenient intellectual property laws permit almost unbarred circulation of musical content on- and offline. Paradoxically, this disrespect of authorship facilitated creativity during the national crisis of the 1990s as musicians and fans were still able to remain attuned to Russian and foreign music developments despite the lack of economic means to purchase music. Furthermore, as Russian musicians have little hope of making money by selling music recordings because of widespread piracy, they are forced to perform live, which in the end serves as a boost to the music industry. Third, with economic stabilization under **Vladimir Putin**, Russian teenagers, who have no experience of life in the Union of Soviet Socialist Republics (USSR), have fully embraced the new market conditions and view music culture as part of their personal independence and freedom.

While Russia's contemporary music market caters to all kinds of audiences and tastes, the state has continuously failed on the music front. In 1991, Yeltsin's government adopted the new Russian anthem, Mikhail Glinka's "Patriotic Song" (1833). Unfortunately, the anthem did not contain any lyrics, and despite the popular demand for lyrics, the national anthem remained wordless. Putin's government replaced the 1990s-era hymn with an adaptation of the Soviet anthem originally composed by Aleksandr Aleksandrov in 1944. Although Putin's choice contains new lyrics that do not refer to the Soviet regime, it invariably taps a lingering nostalgia for the Stalin era.

In the past few years, music has been used for other political purposes. Valery Gergiev, the artistic director of the Mariinsky Theater in St. Petersburg and the principal conductor of the London Symphony Orchestra, came to Tskhinvali in South Ossetia in the aftermath of the 2008 **South Ossetian War**, and performed a concert near the ruined building of the Ossetian parliament to pay tribute to the victims of the war. An Ossetian himself, Gergiev made no secret of his political intentions.

In 2007, the Ukrainian entry for the Eurovision Song Contest caused a scandal when a song by Verka Serduchka (a female persona portrayed by Andriy Danylko) contained the lyrics "Dancing Lasha Tumbai," which, in the context of **color revolutions**, were interpreted in Russia as "Dancing Russia Good-Bye." Danylko had made his career in Russia and in fact remains a Russian celebrity; however, his performance at Eurovision cost him access to Russia's major television channels. In 2009, when Moscow hosted the Eurovision Song Contest, the Russian entry for the competition was a song performed by Ukrainian pop star Anastasiya Prikhodko. Her song

"Mamo" (Ukrainian for "mother") was composed by a Georgian musician and featured lyrics in both Russian and Ukrainian. Many viewed this entry as Russia's attempt to reconcile with its neighbors, at least in the field of popular music.

MUSLIMS. Religious group. While the estimates vary, the number of Muslims in the Russian Federation is in excess of 20 million and may be as high as 23 million. The ambiguity of the figure stems from a number of factors: there is a large presence of illegal **immigrants** from Muslim countries (particularly **Central Asia** and **Azerbaijan**); only about half of all ethnic or legacy Muslims practice **Islam**; and a significant minority of some traditionally Muslim ethnic groups have embraced Russian **Orthodoxy**.

Russian Muslims are most prevalent in the **North Caucasus**, the **Volga-Ural region**, and western **Siberia**, as well as the historical capitals of **Moscow** and **St. Petersburg**. Numbering more than 5.5 million, Russia's largest and most influential Muslim **national minority** is the **Tatars**; the second-largest group is the closely related **Bashkirs**. **Chechens**, who number 1.4 million, are the largest Muslim population from the North Caucasus; other groups from the region include **Avars**, **Kabardins**, Dargins, Kumyks, **Ingush**, **Karachay**, and **Adyghe**, among others. Distinct from recent immigrants, diasporic populations of **Kazakhs**, Azeris, and Uzbeks are also significant.

Since the **dissolution of the Soviet Union**, the number of Russian Muslims has increased by one-third. Compared with the national average of 1.5, the fertility rate among Russia's Muslims is extremely high, with some ethnicities averaging upward of 10 children per family. As a result, the percentage of Muslims to **Christians** in Russia is in flux, triggering fears among many ultranationalists.

Fears among many Slavs that Muslims will embrace radical **Islamist** ideologies, as was the case in **Chechnya**, have also soured communal relations in the country. In contemporary Russia, deep-seated religious prejudices and **media** portrayals of Muslims as either terrorists or criminals make life difficult for many Muslims, ethnic and observant. As a religious minority, Muslims often complain of poor treatment in the **military**, for example, bans on Islamic services, being fed non-*halal* meals such as pork, and so forth. However, since 1991, Russian Muslims have enjoyed greater freedom to worship and organize than at any other time in modern Russia. *See also* CRIME; RELIGION; TERRORISM.

– N –

NAGORNO-KARABAKH. The region of Nagorno-Karabakh, which translates as "Black Garden Highlands," was established as an autonomous **oblast** of **Azerbaijan** in the 1920s. Predominantly populated by ethnic **Armenians**, the region emerged as a site of ethnic clashes in 1988. After the region's autonomy was stripped away by Moscow in 1989, **Armenia** proclaimed a union with the territory. Ethnic cleansing and emigration of the Azeri population soon followed.

In a late 1991 referendum boycotted by the minority Azeri population, residents of Nagorno-Karabakh supported a declaration of independence from Azerbaijan, thus creating the internationally unrecognized Republic of Nagorno-Karabakh on 6 January 1992. In the wake of the dissolution of the Union of Soviet Socialist Republics (USSR), both sides scrambled to acquire **military** hardware as clashes turned into full-scale war. Linked by their **Orthodox** faith, many Russian military officers funneled weapons and equipment to the Armenians, effectively counter-balancing the Soviet-era military superiority of Azerbaijan. Armenia, fearful of invasion by **Turkey**, quickly joined the **Commonwealth of Independent States** in order to provide itself with safeguards under Russia's collective security umbrella.

Volunteers from the former Soviet Union rallied to both sides, and a significant number of former **Soviet-Afghan War** mujahideen came to the defense of the Azeris. Fighting between Karabakh Armenians, supported by Armenian forces, and Azerbaijani troops raged for more than two years, until a Russian-brokered cease-fire froze the conflict. In addition to controlling Nagorno-Karabakh, Armenian forces ultimately occupied a significant portion of Azerbaijan including the Lachin Corridor connecting Armenia to Nagorno-Karabakh. While Armenia emerged as the territorial victor, the conflict triggered an embargo from Turkey and has kept Armenia out of regional energy development schemes, such as the Baku-Tbilisi-Ceyhan pipeline.

More than 25,000 perished in the conflict, and 200,000 Armenians from Azerbaijan and 800,000 Azeris from Armenia and Karabakh have been displaced by the chaos. Russia, **France**, and the **United States** co-chair the **Organization for Security and Co-operation in Europe**'s Minsk Group, which has been attempting to end the dispute since the mid-1990s. However, the transfer of $800 million in weapons from Russia to Armenia in 2008 complicated Russia's role as a fair arbiter and scuttled the recent improvement in relations between Moscow and Baku.

NARCOTICS. Narcotic addiction and illicit drug sales in Russia are, to a large extent, the result of the economic and social crises of the 1990s. The problem of **drug use** has been exacerbated by a lack of control over use and movement of narcotic substances and the continual laxity of the country's southern borders. Analysts believe that the Russian Federation has the largest per capita narcotics market of all the former Soviet republics. **Criminal** organizations (**mafia**) are thought to control most of the narcotics trafficking and distribution. Most narcotics are brought into Russia through **Central Asian** republics, the **Caucasus**, and **Ukraine**; however, domestic production of narcotics and other illicit drugs is on the rise. The situation has worsened since the American "war on terror" in **Afghanistan**, when Russia became the main destination for Afghan exports of heroin. In the Russian Federation, crimes related to narcotics, particularly among **ethnic minorities** and **immigrants**, are increasingly viewed as an impediment to the country's development. Narcotics are closely related to Russia's **demographic challenges** and the spread of **HIV/ AIDS**. The government attempts to fight narcotics use through social advertising and by supporting popular culture, principally **films** and **music** that depict individual and societal problems caused by narcotics addiction.

NASHI. Political movement. Known in Russian as *Molodezhnoie demokraticheskoie antifashistskoie dvizheniie "Nashi,"* the Youth Democratic Anti-Fascist Movement "Ours!" is a government-funded youth movement established at the behest of senior members of the **Putin** administration. Modeled on the Soviet-era **Komsomol** youth organization, the group's membership, aged between 17 and 25, numbers in excess of 100,000.

Nashi grew out of the "Walking Together" movement, which was established in 2000 as a post-Soviet version of the Komsomol's Young Pioneer movement. Reacting to **Ukraine**'s Orange Revolution, the group's founder, Vasily Yakemenko, envisaged Nashi as a bulwark against any youth-led **color revolution** in Russia. While its origins were influenced by the threat of Western influence in Russia's domestic affairs, Nashi is equally opposed to pro-Nazi and right-wing groups like the **National Bolsheviks**, which it labels "enemies of the state." Despite its vociferous denunciation of fascism, many internal and foreign commentators have expressed concern that Nashi is itself a proto-fascist organization abetting a personality cult for Putin, hence the pejorative nickname, the *Putinjugend* ("Putin Youth"). Nashi members have engaged in street battles with their political enemies on a number of occasions; members gain **military** training during Nashi's annual summer camps, which also serve to indoctrinate new recruits to the group's statist ideology.

The group has also made its presence felt in international affairs, particularly during the 2007 **Estonian Cyberwar**. Since 2007, the threat of a color revolution in Russia has abated, resulting in the Kremlin's decision to scale down its support of the group in favor of consolidation of political power via **United Russia**. Many of Nashi's older members have moved on to government positions in the **Dmitry Medvyedev** administration or the **State Duma**. *See also* NEO-FASCISM.

NATIONAL BOLSHEVIK PARTY (NBP). Banned ultranationalist **political party**. Founded in 1993 by émigré writer **Eduard Limonov**, **neo-Eurasianist** philosopher **Aleksandr Dugin**, and rock musicians Yegor Letov and Sergey Kurikhin, the NBP, or NatsBols, began as a counterculture youth movement before embarking on a mission of antiregime violence, which it refers to as "velvet terror." The party platform exudes anti-**globalization**, glorifies the accomplishments of the Soviet Union, and advocates the restoration of Russian power over its historical domains, thus putting it at the nexus of the anti-**Yeltsin**, "red-brown" coalition of the mid-1990s. Due to its somewhat esoteric origins, the movement attracted an eclectic mix of intellectuals, disaffected youth, and skinheads in its early years. After Dugin's departure in 1998, the party lurched to the far left, accusing Dugin and his neo-Eurasianists of fascism. Since **Vladimir Putin**'s rise to power, the NatsBols have been targeted by the **FSB** and other **security services**; as a result the party has abandoned its glorification of the Stalinist police state and has begun advocating the building of **civil society** and an end to **media** restrictions, though the organization remains extremist, continues to employ direct action, and promotes a cult of violence. The NBP possesses a membership of approximately 15,000 members, with its largest contingent in **Moscow**.

NATIONAL IDENTITY. In contemporary Russia, the question of identity is multifaceted and controversial. It is important to first distinguish between Russian national identity and national identities among the Russian Federation's 175 **ethnic minorities**. Slightly less than one-quarter of Russia's population is non-Russian. Among these 23 million, there are vibrant ethnic movements that include political projects, as well as attempts at linguistic, cultural, and religious revival. Groups such as the **Tatars**, **Chechens**, and **Kalmyks** have well-developed histories that allow their political leaders to employ historical identity as a tool against **Russification**. Smaller groups have been forced to navigate between their minority identity and identification as Russian citizens. As for the Russians, the four principal categories of Russianness are as follows: ethnically defined Russianness granted solely through familial bloodlines, that is, **ethnic Russians** (*russkie*); culturo-linguistically defined Russianness, primarily determined by membership in the community of **Russian language** speakers (*russkoiazychnyie*); civic Russians or Rossians (*rossiane*) constituted through citizenship and loyalty to the Russian Federation; and a form of Russian identity based on the Soviet Union's seminal role in building a multiethnic "nationality" among those people living inside its former borders, that is, the post-Soviet person (*homo post-Sovieticus*). The struggle over which identity is dominant in post-Soviet Russia remains a highly politicized issue, particularly among ultranationalist **political parties**. See also LANGUAGE.

NATIONAL MINORITIES. In Russian, the concept of an ethnic or national minority (*natsional' noie men' shinstvo*) is rendered through the use of the term *natsional' nost'*, which is often confusingly translated into English as "nationality." Rather, the term refers to an ethnic formation, or an **ethnic minority** with a distinctive cultural identity. The concept of nationhood and ethnic minorities is further complicated by Russia's weak **national identity** and Russia's complicated—both tsarist and Soviet—imperial past.

The concept of national minority was fully developed under the Soviets but has its roots in the tsarist-era notion of *inorodets* and *inoverets*. The first term, meaning "foreigner," was a loose denomination that included not only all foreigners living in the country but also non-Slavic peoples who in fact were indigenous to the Russian lands. The second term, meaning "person of other faith," had to do with the notion of autochthonous non-**Orthodox** peoples, who were targeted for gradual assimilation, that is, embracing the Orthodox **religion** and cultural traditions. Tsarist Russia—and the Soviet Union after it—contained sizable indigenous populations of Finnic, Ugric, Baltic, Caucasian, Iranian, Turkic, Mongolic, and Tungusic peoples. The situation was further complicated by the need to distinguish between **ethnic Russians** and other Orthodox Slavs, such as **Ukrainians** and Belarusians, which was primarily a cultural distinction.

Under **Joseph Stalin**, the Union of Soviet Socialist Republics (USSR) was reorganized along ethnonational lines giving many (but not all) of the union's ethnic minorities their own homelands. For instance, at the highest level, the **union republics** such as the Ukrainian Soviet Socialist Republic were established; however, in most cases these were multiethnic, multiconfessional formations that simultaneously recognized the cultural and political autonomy of the titular nation. These entities were reserved for the most linguistically and historically developed ethnic groups (despite well-established linguistic, political, and cultural traditions, the **Tatars** were denied this status for strategic reasons). Smaller ethnic groups gained **Autonomous Soviet Socialist Republics** (ASSRs), and other groups received **autonomous okrugs** or **oblasts**.

This process of Soviet nation building (*natsiona' noie stroitel' stvo*) enshrined ethnic identity in Soviet society, a fact that was underscored by the listing of a person's ethnic origins (*natsional' nost'*) on all Soviet citizens' internal passports, the so-called fifth line. The term "Soviet" was used as an umbrella term to refer to all citizens of the USSR, irrespective of their ethnic origins. Ethnic Russians had an uncertain position in this order; on the one hand, the **Russian language** and culture were used as a template for the Sovietization of all ethnic minorities, and on the other hand, ethnic Russians did not have their own titular ethnic republic since the **Russian Soviet Federative Socialist Republic** was in itself a conglomerate of ethnic republics and ethnically determined autonomous administrative units.

Under **glasnost**, national minorities, which have endured intermittent **Russification** and Sovietization and seen their political identities quashed, embarked on cultural revivals that took on an increasingly political patina by the end of the 1980s. With the **dissolution of the Soviet Union** in 1991, the titular majorities of the 15 union republics—including the Russian Federation—gained independent states. Certain national minorities within Russia, such as the **Chechens** and Tatars, declared their sovereignty and in some cases moved toward full-fledged independence. Other ethnic minorities such as the **Mordvins** and **Chuvash** sought to secure their newfound privileges of language use and republican autonomy. Those minorities in Russia that were granted their own **ethnic republics** (**Komi**, **Ingush**, **Udmurts**, etc.) tend to have the most developed national identities.

Under **Boris Yeltsin**, a linguistic distinction was made to differ between various ethnic groups of the Russian Federation: while the term *russkii* refers to ethnic Russians, the term *rossiiskii* includes all citizens of the Russian Federation, irrespective of their ethnic origins. Both terms are translated into English as "Russian," thus causing categorical confusion. *See also* ETHNIC VIOLENCE.

NATIONAL-PATRIOTIC FORCES OF THE RUSSIAN FEDERATION (NPSRF). Political party. Established in 2001, the National-Patriotic Forces of the Russian Federation (*Natsional' nopatrioticheskie sily Rossiiskoi federatsii*) grew out of the Assembly of National-Democratic and Patriotic Forces, a movement dating to the mid-1990s. Although strongly leftist in its orientation, the party does embrace the role of an opposition party and avers its patriotism.

The NPSRF is led by Shmidt Dzoblayev. The party platform supports friendship and equity of all peoples of the Russian Federation, consolidation of public and political forces in order to maintain the country's security and territorial integrity, and improved interethnic relations. The party strongly supported **Vladimir Putin**'s attempt to create a **vertical of power** to weaken **asymmetrical federalism** and protect the country from **terrorism**. The National-Patriotic Forces are avowedly antiliberal, condemning center-right parties' economic policies as debilitating and against Russia's national interest. Normative in its approach to governance, the party hopes to purge the Russian political system of **corrupt** and incompetent officials. Evoking shades of **neo-Eurasianism**, the NPSRF aims to use Russia's mineral wealth and geopolitical location to put an end to the country's purported subservience to the West. Support for Russia's scientific and **educational** development also figure highly in the party's ideology. In 2004, the party joined a coalition of nine other nationalist, left-wing parties called the People's Patriotic Union of Russia. The party did not register significant support in either the 2003 or 2007 parliamentary elections.

NATURAL GAS. Russia is the world's leader in natural gas production, easily outstripping its closest competitors, the **United States** and **Canada**. Each year, the country produces 654 billion cubic meters of natural gas, or more than 20 percent of global output. Of this, 173 billion cubic meters are sold abroad, making Russia the leading exporter of the product. The country also leads the world in proven reserves, with 44.6 trillion cubic meters (one-quarter of world totals).

In recent years, the Kremlin has pushed for the creation of an OPEC-like cartel for natural gas, bringing together the countries with the largest reserves (Russia, **Iran**, and Qatar); accounting for more than half of the world's reserves, these countries regularly meet to discuss pricing and supply-related issues.

Gazprom holds a monopoly on extraction of natural gas. In Russia, major fields are found in eastern **Siberia**, the East Siberian Sea and **Sakha**, around the southern **Urals**, and in the Barents and Kara seas in the **Far North**; the Shtokman Field in the **Barents Sea** promises to generate 3.8 trillion cubic meters of gas in the future. In the **Russian Far East**, Sakhalin-II, a major liquefied natural gas project, has just been initiated. With the **European Union** functioning as the primary market for exports, the principal pipelines (Yamal-Europe and Blue Stream) cross European Russia, including transmission routes bringing gas from **Turkmenistan** to Europe.

This transshipment bottleneck, combined with Gazprom's desire to charge market prices to countries in the **near abroad**, has led to severe disputes with **Belarus** and **Ukraine** in recent years, occasionally resulting in gas shortages to customers farther west, which are highly dependent on Russian exports. As a result, new routes are planned or currently in development, including a **Baltic Sea** route (Nord Stream) and a **Black Sea** pipeline (South Stream). A new route from the Kovykta field in eastern Siberia to **China** and other East Asian markets is also under consideration.

NAVY. The Military Maritime Fleet of Russia (*voienno-morskoi flot Rossii*) is the naval arm of the Russian **military**. The current fleet evolved out of the short-lived navy of the **Commonwealth of Independent States**, which was created out of the Soviet navy.

The maritime forces are divided between the following units: the Northern Fleet (based in Severomorsk, **Murmansk**, and deployed in the Atlantic and **Arctic** oceans); the Pacific Fleet (based in Vladivostok, **Primorsky Krai**); the **Black Sea** Fleet (based in Sevastopol, **Ukraine**); the Baltic Fleet (headquartered in **Kaliningrad**); the Caspian Flotilla (based in **Astrakhan**); Naval Aviation; and the Coastal Troops. The Russian navy includes a wide variety of warships, including an aircraft carrier (the *Admiral Kuznetsov*), 15 ballistic and 8 cruise missile submarines, more than 40 other submarines, 17 destroyers, 4 cruisers, dozens of patrol ships, and more than 100 patrol craft.

With 170,000 sailors, Russia has the world's third-largest navy in terms of personnel, behind the **United States** and **China**. Beyond Russia's borders, the navy maintains a presence at Tartus, a port in Syria. Redeployment of Russian naval forces to Yemen is also under consideration. Naval forces participated in the **South Ossetian War** in 2008, blockading Georgian ports. However, their primary activity since 1991 has been devoted to antipiracy operations. Russia has conducted joint exercises with China, **India**, South Korea, and **Japan** in the past decade.

The Russian navy has suffered a number of embarrassments in recent years (including high-profile failed missile launches and a rescue of Russian submariners by the British navy in 2005), as well as the tragic loss of the *Kursk* **submarine** in 2000. However, a major overhaul of the fleet is currently under way, with new vessels being launched and older ones retired. Since 11 September 2007, Admiral Vladimir Vysotsky has served as commander-in-chief of the Russian navy. *See also* MIDDLE EAST.

NEAR ABROAD. The term "near abroad" (*blizhneie zarubezh' ie*) is commonly used by Russians both inside and outside the Russian Federation to refer to the **Newly Independent States**, which formerly comprised the Soviet Union (excepting Russia itself), and which contain some 19 million **ethnic Russians**. This geographic space is differentiated from the "far abroad," a concept that refers to the rest of the world. The term contains imperialistic overtones for many non-Russian residents of the former Soviet Union, who see its use as emblematic of Russia's reticence to fully abandon its empire. Advanced by a number of Kremlin theoreticians, the notion of the near abroad as Russia's "backyard" and within its exclusive sphere of influence has been growing since the early 1990s. *See also* MONROESKI DOCTRINE; NATIONAL IDENTITY.

NEMTSOV, BORIS YEFIMOVICH (1959–). Politician. Born in **Sochi** to **Jewish** and Russian parents, Boris Nemtsov was raised as a Christian in the **Orthodox** faith. He holds a PhD in mathematics and physics. His start in **politics** came when he organized a protest in response to the **Chernobyl disaster** in 1986. Four years later, he ran for office in Sochi on a radical reform platform; his bid for the Soviet **Congress of People's Deputies** failed, but a year later he won a seat in the **Supreme Soviet** of the **Russian Soviet Federative Socialist Republic** as a representative of Gorky (**Nizhny Novgorod**).

During the **August Coup** of 1991, he forged a profitable alliance with **Boris Yeltsin**. In the early 1990s, he turned Nizhny Novgorod into a "laboratory of reform" through innovative and dramatic economic programs. Running as an economic liberal, he won a seat in the **Federation Council** in 1993. During the mid-1990s, his political star rose and he was well positioned to assume the presidency in

2000, until the **ruble crisis** of 1998 struck. In 1999, he helped found the **Union of Right Forces**, and won election to the **State Duma** on the party's ticket.

Nemtsov became deputy speaker the next year, but was constrained from fully articulating his ideas due to **Vladimir Putin**'s overwhelming popularity as president. He resigned his leadership of the party in 2004 after its poor performance in parliamentary elections. After leaving the Duma, he became a strident critic of the Putin administration. In 2004 he supported Viktor Yushchenko, the pro-Western candidate, in the 2004 **Ukrainian** presidential elections, and was appointed to his cabinet after the Orange Revolution. This created controversy in both **Ukraine** and Russia, and he was ultimately forced to step down. After returning to Russia, he resumed his criticism of the Kremlin, and landed himself in jail in 2007 for taking part in an unauthorized protest. He has more recently joined forces with **Garry Kasparov** and made an unsuccessful run for mayor of his hometown and site of the 2014 Winter Olympiad, Sochi. *See also* COLOR REVOLUTIONS.

NENETS. Ethnic group. The Nenets are an indigenous Uralic people of Russia's **Far North**. According to the most recent census, they number fewer than 50,000 and reside mostly in the Nenets Autonomous Okrug (**Nenetsiya**), the Yamalo-Nenets Autonomous Okrug (**Yamaliya**), and the Dolgan-Nenets Municipal District (**Taymyriya**). Previously known as the *Samoyed*, a corruption of the plural of *Saami* that translates in Russia as "self-eater" or "cannibal," the Nenets were distinguished from other northern Uralic peoples during the early 20th century. The Nenets are divided between the Tundra Nenets and the Forest Nenets (*Khandeyar*), both of whom possess their own dialect, though the literary version of Nenets is based on the former. Nenets is a member of the Samoyedic branch of the Uralic **language** family, which also includes the Finnic and Ugric languages. Slightly more than half of ethnic Nenets are fluent in their native language.

During the 1920s and 1930s, the Nenets were subjected to a collectivization campaign by the Soviets that brought traditional reindeer herding under state control. The establishment of permanent "cultural bases" for the seminomadic Nenets led to sedentarization and some level of **Russification**. The Soviets also continued the tsarist campaign to eradicate indigenous animist practices, as well as outlawing **Russian Orthodox** ceremonies among the Nenets. Cultural imperialism, including the forced adoption of Nenets children by the state, led to a series of uprisings in the 1950s.

NENETSIYA/NENETS AUTONOMOUS OKRUG. An administrative district of the Russian Federation. As an **autonomous okrug** (AOk), Nenetsiya is both a **federal subject** and part of **Archangel Oblast**, with which it shares a border. As an administrative unit of Archangel, Nenetsiya is part of the Northwestern **Federal District** and the Northern **Economic Region**. Nenetsiya was originally created as an AOk of Soviet Russia in 1929. During the 1990s, local political elites persisted in referring to the region as the "Nenets Republic," despite the **Yeltsin** administration's opposition to raising the region's status within the federation.

The district is bordered by **Komi** to the south and **Yamaliya** in the east. Nenetsiya is washed by the White, **Barents**, and Kara seas, and includes the Kolguyev and Vaygach Islands, but not Franz Josef Land or **Novaya Zemlya**, which lie to its north in the **Arctic Ocean**. Nenetsiya's land area is 176,700 square kilometers of swampy plains, **tundra**, and eroded mountains, much of it covered in permafrost. The region's major river is the Pechora, which connects the administrative center Naryan-Mar (pop. 18,600) to the Arctic Ocean via the Pechora Gulf and the Barents Sea. With only 41,500 residents, Nenetsiya is the smallest Russian region in terms of population. The titular nationality, **Nenets**, make up 19 percent of the population, while **ethnic Russians** form a majority (62 percent); **Komi** are the other major group at 11 percent of the population.

The Nenets **language**, along with the **Russian language**, has official status in the district. In 1996, independent candidate and businessman Vladimir Butov became the regional head. He was reelected in 2001 but shortly faced an arrest warrant for abuse of power. The warrant was later cancelled. His successor, Aleksey Barinov, however, was not so lucky. He was charged with extortion and embezzlement and taken into custody in 2006. This was the first time in post-Soviet Russian history that a governor in office was arrested. *See also* CORRUPTION.

NEO-EURASIANISM. *See* EURASIANISM.

NEO-FASCISM. Political ideology. Since the collapse of the one-party state, neo-fascism has emerged as a major social and political force in Russia. In the waning years of the Soviet Union, the **Pamyat** movement attracted significant support and created a new generation of radical, sometimes neo-Nazi political activists. Since 1991, a host of new "brown" parties have been established around the principles of **anti-Semitism**, anti-Communism, and Russian racial supremacy.

The movement is intellectually rooted in the doctrine of **neo-Eurasianism**, which presupposes global domination by whichever country possesses the heartland of the "world continent," that is, Russia. Nearly all neofascist ideologies hold that Russia has long been the victim of a global conspiracy to suppress the Russian people; the supposed perpetrators include Freemasons, **Jews**, capitalists, Westerners, and Bolsheviks. Groups such as the **Russian National Unity** party and Igor Pirozhok's "Werewolf Legion" are consciously modeled on German Nazism. Within this category, organizations such as Roman Perin's Russian National Liberation Movement, Viktor Korchagin's Russian Party of Russia, and Ilia Lazarenko's National Front/Church of Nav also incorporate the ideologies of **neo-paganism** and **Aryanism** into the fabric of their movements.

Some groups have tried to enter the political mainstream, the most successful of which is **Vladimir Zhirinovsky**'s **Liberal Democratic Party of Russia**. More radical and peripheral **political parties** that have sought seats in the **State Duma** include Nikolay Lysenko's National-Republican Party of Russia, as well as the splinter group of the same name led by Yury Belyaev. During the mid-1990s, despite conflicting ideological orientations, many of these groups entered into loose coalitions with radical left-wing parties such as the **National Bolshevik Party** and the **Communist Party of the Russian Federation**, forming a "red-brown" alliance against **Boris Yeltsin**. In the post-Yeltsin era, the red-brown coalition weakened as many of its members gravitated to a pro-**Putin** political orientation. *See also* NASHI.

NEO-JADIDISM. Political ideology. Plotting a path between the traditionalism of "old" Hanafi interpretations of **Islam** and "new" streams of thought such as **Wahhabism**, many **Tatar** and some **Bashkir** elites have embraced neo-Jadidism as a solution for the 21st century. Jadidism, from the Arabic *usul ul-jadid*, or "new method," was a socioreligious movement that dominated Russian Islamic thought in the late tsarist era. Its proponents sought to reform *sharia* (Islamic law) through forward-looking interpretation (*ijtihad*) that accommodated the demands of modernity and stressed acquisition of knowledge from all sources, especially the West. Recognizing their position as a **religious** minority in the Russian Federation, neo-Jadidists see accommodation with their **Russian Orthodox** neighbors as necessary, while at the same time supporting a moderate **Islamist** political platform for the country's 20 million **Muslims**. They often brand their movement as a political expression of "Euro-Islam" that can provide a desirable model for other countries with large Muslim minorities. Neo-Jadidists tend to be strongly nationalistic at the regional level and support **neo-Eurasianism** at the federal level. *See also* TATARSTAN.

NEO-NAZISM. *See* NEO-FASCISM.

NEO-PAGANISM. Social movement. Although Russian neo-paganism functions as a quasi-**religion** and shares some traits with Western "New Age" movements, it is primarily an intellectually driven sociopolitical movement. Sometimes called Vedism, Slavic neo-paganism takes many of its popular rituals and beliefs from Hinduism. In terms of indigenous influences, the sacred text of the religion is the Book of Veles, a tome of questionable origins that recounts the pre-**Christian** history, morals, and social practices of the 7th- and 8th-century Eastern Slavs.

Neo-pagans reject the imposition of **Orthodox** Christianity in 988 as a cataclysm that subjected the Slavs to a millennium of **Jewish** and "Western" domination. As such, neo-pagan publications and theories, in conjunction with the closely allied ideology of **Aryanism**, have served the interests of Russian ultranationalists and **anti-Semitic** movements. Under **glasnost**, the neo-Pagans were most closely allied with the racist **Pamyat** party. However, in the mid-1990s, a significant portion of the neo-pagan community allied itself with the rebranded **Communist Party of the Russian Federation** (KPRF), clearly demonstrating its power as a political force in the country. **Gennady Zyuganov**'s populist anti-Semitism meshes well with the neo-pagan worldview; however, the relationship with the KPRF is problematic given the strong pro-environment orientation of many neo-pagans.

In addition to Russian neo-paganism, there has been a resurgence of paganism, **shamanism**, and animism among many of the country's **ethnic minorities**. This is particularly true in **Siberia** and the Volga regions where a certain percentage of Russia's Turkic (**Chuvash, Khakas, Altay**, and **Tuvans**), Mongolic (**Buryats**), and Finno-Ugrian (**Mari, Khanty, Mansi, Mordvins, Udmurts**, and **Komi**) peoples have begun to return to traditional religious practices, often in synthesis with Russian **Orthodoxy** or **Buddhism**. A significant portion of Russia's Turkic and Mongolic peoples (as well as **Kazakhs** and Kyrgyz) have also embraced a politicized form of Tengrism, or sky worship. To some, the religion presupposed and does not contradict **Islam**, while to other adherents it functions as an ethnic faith in opposition to the Semitic belief systems of **Judaism**, Christianity, and Islam.

NEWLY INDEPENDENT STATES. The Newly Independent States (NIS) of **Eurasia** constitute those 15 republics that gained independence from the Union of Soviet Socialist Republics (USSR) in 1991, though sometimes Russia is excepted from this group due to its long history as an independent state and as the governing force in the Soviet Union. The NIS can be regionally grouped as follows: the **Baltic States** (**Estonia, Latvia**, and **Lithuania**); the Western Republics (**Ukraine, Belarus**, and **Moldova**); the Caucasian Republics (**Georgia, Armenia**, and **Azerbaijan**); and **Central Asia** (**Kazakhstan, Uzbekistan, Turkmenistan, Kyrgyzstan**, and **Tajikistan**). With the exception of the Baltic States, all are members of the **Commonwealth of Independent States**. The inclusion of the Baltic countries is sometimes rejected as these states were fully independent during the interwar period (1918–1939).

NEW RUSSIANS. A derogative term, "New Russians" (*novye russkiie*) is used to refer to the nouveau riche in post-Soviet Russia. The concept of "New Russian" is defined by conspicuous consumption, an absence of good taste, and unfamiliarity with high culture. New Russians emerged as the dominant social class in the 1990s, as **privatization** created opportunities for social mobility, sweeping aside the old *nomenklatura*. Stereotypical New Russians can be recognized by their expensive mobile phones, jewelry, cars, and clothes; they frequent tony nightclubs and overpriced cafes. Many are connected with the **mafia** and often employ (or affect) the Russian **criminal** argot. *See also* OLIGARCHS.

NEWSPAPERS. As in other countries, consumption of newspapers is decreasing in Russia. Many Soviet-era newspapers, such as *Pravda* and *Trud*, enjoyed a special status as required reading for **Communist Party** members and **apparatchiks**. Furthermore, libraries and other cultural institutions of the Union of Soviet Socialist Republics (USSR) had a compulsory subscription to these newspapers, which explains their high circulation rates. Under **Mikhail Gorbachev**'s **perestroika**, Soviet citizens abandoned their tendency to read a single newspaper, and began comparative reading of several newspapers to glean meaning from minor divergences in news coverage. **Glasnost** allowed for increasing levels of editorial independence by the end of the Soviet era.

In the 1990s, the role of newspapers diminished as political and social debates migrated to **television**. With the rise of the **Internet**, especially with the user-generated platforms of the last decade, Russian readership is largely attracted to online media outlets. Furthermore, the majority of national newspapers are generally too expensive for Russian readers residing in **rural** areas. As a result, many opt to read local newspapers, which are cheaper.

During the first decade of independence, Russian **oligarchs** played a pivotal role in the establishment of new newspapers and **media** in general. However, under **Vladimir Putin**, many of these publications were acquired by state-controlled firms or companies that are loyal to the state, such as **Gazprom**, raising concerns about the freedom of the press in the Russian Federation. Nevertheless, Russian newspapers provide a more diverse range of views than Russian national television channels.

In 2009, a large number of national newspapers were available in the Russian Federation. *Rossiiskaia Gazeta* (The Russian Newspaper) is the mouthpiece of the Russian government. It was established in 1990 and has the authority to publish all new Russian laws in full at the point when the new legislation comes into force. The newspaper is a powerful source of information for national and local governments; it has been known for its critique of executive power, especially different ministries that often conflict with each other. *Trud* and *Pravda* are two of the few survivors of the Soviet period. Both pay special attention to international and national news as well as to issues of social concern. Established in the 1990s, **Kommersant**, *Nezavisimaya Gazeta*, and **Novaya Gazeta** are known for their criticism of the regime. Some Russian newspapers, for example, *Vedomosti* (The News), are either associated with Western media outlets—in this case, with the *Wall Street Journal* and the *Financial Times*—or model themselves on Western business publications. The circulation of most newspapers varies from 100,000 to 250,000 copies.

A much larger circulation is found among the popular press. The most famous tabloid newspapers are *Argumenti i fakty* (The Arguments and the Facts), a weekly with over 2 million subscribers; *Komsomolskaia Pravda* at 660,000 copies; and *Moskovskii Komsomolets* (Moscow's Komsomol Member) at 1.2 million copies. These and other Russian newspapers still use their Soviet-era titles; however, they have been completely reinvented and rebranded for the post-Soviet era. For example, *Komsomolskaia Pravda* used to be a youth version of the party-oriented *Pravda*. Today, it is a popular tabloid that publishes sensational news, scandalous reports, and entertainment reporting.

In post-Soviet Russia, the Soviet tradition of trade newspapers remains in effect: *Uchitel' skaia gazeta* (Teachers' Newspaper)—as the title suggests—publishes materials that may be of interest to Russian teachers and all people involved in Russian **education**. There are also lifestyle publications, such as *Sovestskii Sport* (Soviet Sport) and *Mir Sadovoda* (The World of the Gardener), which caters to the interests of Russian **dacha** enthusiasts. Unlike in the Union of Soviet Socialist Republics (USSR), it is common for contemporary Russian newspapers to contain classified sections. In fact, a few newspapers, for example *Iz ruk v ruki* (From Hands to Hands), specialize in the publication of classified sections and various private advertisements.

Important web-based newspapers include www.utro.ru, www .vesti.ru, and www.gazeta.ru. There are also English-language newspapers, with the *Moscow Times* and *St. Petersburg Times* being the most popular. *See also* RIA NOVOSTI.

NEW UNION TREATY. Also called the All-Union Treaty or the Union Treaty, the New Union Treaty was the proposed replacement for the original Treaty on the Creation of the Union of Soviet Socialist Republics (USSR) in 1922. During 1991, independence movements in the **Baltic States**, **Georgia**, and elsewhere prompted **Mikhail Gorbachev** to allow devolution of power to the **union republics** in an effort to hold the country together. While the majority of Soviet citizens supported preserving the union, the republican leadership, including **Boris Yeltsin** as the leader of the **Russian Soviet Federative Socialist Republic** (RSFSR), backed a loosening of the ties between the Soviet Socialist Republics. The new entity, tentatively titled the Union of Sovereign States (originally the Union of Soviet Sovereign States to preserve the **Russian language** acronym of the USSR), was to be created on 20 August 1991 but was preempted by the **August Coup** one day before the treaty-signing ceremony (Georgia, **Estonia**, **Latvia**, **Lithuania**, **Moldova**, and **Armenia** were not signatories to the agreement). In the wake of the failed putsch, the leaders of **Belarus**, **Ukraine**, and the RSFSR (now the Russian Republic) established the **Commonwealth of Independent States**, effectively bringing about the **dissolution of the Soviet Union**. *See also* ALL-UNION REFERENDUM.

NIZHNY NOVGOROD OBLAST. An administrative region of the Russian Federation. Home to Russia's third-largest city, Nizhny Novgorod, a historical trading, cultural, and spiritual center (formerly known as Gorky), the **oblast** dominates the Volga-Vyatka **Economic Region**; it is within the Volga **Federal District**. Nizhny Novgorod Oblast is bordered by the oblasts of **Ryazan**, **Vladimir**, **Ivanovo**, **Kostroma**, and **Kirov**, as well as the ethnic republics of **Mordoviya**, **Chuvashiya**, and **Mari El**.

With a population of 3.5 million, it is 10th in terms of administrative districts; it covers an area of 76,900 square kilometers. While it does not possess significant natural resources, the region is one of

Russia's most economically active, particularly in the financial sector, and maintains trade relations with many foreign governments. The region is considered to be Russia's most capitalist-oriented and is known for economic experimentation, land **privatization**, and the proliferation of small businesses, which is not surprising as the oblast has a long-established tradition of merchant trade dating back several centuries.

This reputation was solidified under the rule of **Boris Nemtsov**, whose wide-ranging economic reforms in the early 1990s earned the region a reputation as a "laboratory of reform." During his tenure, Nemtsov gained levels of autonomy for the region akin to those granted only to **ethnic republics**. In 2001, the **Communist Party of the Russian Federation** candidate Gennady Khodyrev won the governorship, and promptly suspended his membership in the party for fear that the federal authorities were planning to sap the region of its privileged position. The current governor is Valery Shantsev, a former deputy mayor of **Moscow** and the mastermind of the city's failed 2012 Olympic bid.

Situated in the **chernozem**, the region is also **agriculturally** productive, focusing on grains, sugar beets, and onions. The oblast is an important automobile manufacturing site, owing to the Soviet-era Gorky Automobile Plant (GAZ); it is now the region's largest company. Dzerzhinsk, the region's second city, was once a secret scientific city, and continues to be an important center of chemical production due to its **Cold War** heritage as a manufacturer of chemical weapons; it is considered to be one of the world's most **polluted** cities. The city of Nizhny Novgorod has a large river port with access to the White, **Baltic**, **Black**, and **Caspian** seas and the **Sea of Azov**; shipbuilding continues to be an important driver of the local **economy**. The region and the city are often considered the gateway from European to Asiatic Russia, and function as a major **transportation** hub via its international airport. *See also* ENVIRONMENTALISM.

NOMENKLATURA. From the Latin *nomenclatura* (list of names), the term denotes a small elite subset of the general population of the Soviet Union and other **Eastern Bloc** countries. Members of *nomenklatura* held key administrative positions in all spheres of society, that is, they were **apparatchiks** and were its de facto ruling class. They were members of the **Communist Party of the Soviet Union**, with the Politburo being the core of this social stratum. *Nomenklatura* enjoyed social, monetary, and other privileges unattainable to the majority of the population (for example, special shops, foreign travel, and cars). In ideological terms, some Soviet **dissidents** opposed the *nomenklatura*, criticizing them for the perversion of Soviet socialist principles.

NONGOVERNMENTAL ORGANIZATIONS. *See* CIVIL SOCIETY.

NORD-OST THEATER SIEGE. Also called the Moscow theater hostage crisis or the Dubrovka theater hostage crisis. On the evening of 23 October 2002, 42 gunmen who claimed allegiance to the **Chechen separatist** movement stormed a crowded theater in the Dubrovka area of **Moscow** during a performance of the musical *Nord-Ost*. After taking hostage some 900 spectators, the terrorists, under the leadership of Movsar Barayev, demanded the withdrawal of Russian forces from **Chechnya**. Frantic negotiations involving a number of preeminent Russian politicians ensued, and despite an offer to let the terrorists depart for a third country, no resolution of the crisis could be achieved.

In a predawn raid on the third day of the crisis, Spetsnaz forces of the **FSB** entered the building after filling it with an unknown airborne agent that rendered hostages and their captors unconscious. All of the terrorists were killed (most were shot), along with 130 of the hostages, almost all of whom died of gas poisoning; there were no Spetsnaz casualties. The principal cause of fatalities was the mysterious aerosol anesthetic used by Spetsnaz rather than gunfire or explosives. The government blamed the terrorists for the loss of life, arguing that they had begun assassinating hostages when the Kremlin failed to meet the 6:00 a.m. deadline on 26 October 2002 for withdrawal of federal forces from Chechnya. However, it is clear that the assault was planned well before its execution, as was evidenced by the notification given to foreign diplomats in advance of the siege.

The people of Russia strongly supported **Vladimir Putin**'s harsh response to the crisis. The terrorist and guerilla leader **Shamil Basayev** subsequently claimed responsibility for planning the attack. In the wake of the crisis, the **United States** added several additional

Chechen groups to its list of international terrorist groups. The long-term consequences of what was framed as "Russia's 9/11" included a crackdown on **media** reporting of ongoing national emergencies, an increase in the intensity and brutality of **counterterrorism** operations in Chechnya, and changes in Russian **military** doctrine that permitted strikes on foreign soil to prevent future acts of **terrorism**. *See also* CHECHEN REPUBLIC OF ICHKERIYA; SECURITY SERVICES.

NORILSK NICKEL. One of Russia's largest publicly owned companies, Norilsk Nickel is a nickel and palladium smelting company jointly headquartered in **Moscow** and Norilsk-Talnakh in **Taymyriya**. The company also runs the Kola Mining and Metallurgical Company in **Murmansk**. It is the largest producer of nickel in the world. Internationally, it has interests in Australia, South Africa, and Botswana; it also holds a majority stake in the American company Stillwater Mining. The company's **mining** operations also include extraction of platinum, copper, and cobalt, as well as several rare earth elements. After Norilsk's acquisition of the Russian mining company Polyus in 2002, it became the country's largest gold producer. The country's origins are rooted in the **gulag** system, which employed slave labor during the 1930s. Despite the harsh **climate** and inhospitable conditions, in later years, high wages attracted workers to the mines. In 1993, the firm was reorganized into a joint-stock company. Norilsk Nickel operations are of concern to **environmentalists**, as its smelting operations contribute to high levels of **pollution** in the sensitive **Arctic** ecosystem; **Norway** has been acutely affected by the company's activities. Aleksandr Voloshin was named chairman of Norilsk Nickel on 26 December 2008. The **oligarch Vladimir Potanin** owns 30 percent of the company. *See also* ARCTIC OCEAN.

NORTH ATLANTIC TREATY ORGANIZATION (NATO). Established on 4 April 1949, the North Atlantic Treaty Organization is a collective security arrangement backed by the **United States** and its allies. Its principal function is to provide mutual defense if any member state is attacked by a third party. The treaty is a vestige of the **Cold War**, and was originally established to protect **Canada**, Iceland, **Norway**, Portugal, Italy, **France**, Denmark, **Great Britain**, and the Benelux countries from Soviet invasion; in 1952, Greece and **Turkey** joined. After West **Germany** was admitted in 1955, the Union of Soviet Socialist Republics (USSR) created the **Warsaw Pact** to provide common defense against any potential offensive action by NATO.

After the breakup of the **Eastern Bloc** in 1989, a number of former Soviet allies moved toward joining the union, beginning with East Germany in 1990. The Russian Federation and many members of the **Commonwealth of Independent States** joined NATO's **Partnership for Peace** program during the 1990s in an effort to reduce the threat of military confrontation in northern **Eurasia**. **Poland**, the Czech Republic, and Hungary were admitted in 1999, and plans were announced around the same time for the inclusion of the **Baltic States** into the group. **Boris Yeltsin**'s government, which had been growing increasingly anti-American after the perceived failure of its early 1990s **Atlanticist** orientation, condemned the new direction of the organization as inherently hostile to Russia and its interests. Disputes between NATO and the Kremlin during the breakup of Yugoslavia—particularly the NATO bombing campaign against **Serbia** in 1999—further hampered relations.

However, in 2002, the NATO-Russia Council (NRC) was established to provide an opportunity for cooperation and partnership between the 28 members of the treaty and the Russian Federation. The NRC builds on bilateral ties established by the 1997 NATO-Russia Founding Act. **Vladimir Putin**, who had established closer relations with the U.S. and NATO, particularly on **counterterrorism**, in the wake of the **September 11 attacks**, reluctantly acceded to the admission of **Estonia**, **Latvia**, and **Lithuania** in 2004, alongside the other post-Communist states of Slovenia, Slovakia, Romania, and Bulgaria. However, during the second Putin administration, relations with NATO cooled over the U.S. plan to incorporate two members of the Commonwealth of Independent States, **Georgia** and **Ukraine**, into the organization.

The crisis reached its peak during the 2008 **South Ossetian War** when Russia condemned the deployment of NATO vessels in the **Black Sea**. Relations were strained during the waning days of **George W. Bush**'s administration over the issue of missile defense sites in Poland and the Czech Republic in response to veiled threats from Russia against these states. In 2008, the North Atlantic Council, the highest governing body within NATO, criticized **Dmitry Medvyedev**'s recognition of the breakaway republics of **South Ossetia** and **Abkhazia** as a violation of Georgia's territorial integrity and dangerous to the stability of the **Caucasus**. In March 2008, NATO-Russian relations were normalized after more than six months of heated exchanges, despite the Kremlin's obdurate position against Ukrainian or Georgian admission to the treaty. The rapprochement was short-lived, however, as NATO announced its plans to expel two Russian diplomats from its Brussels headquarters due to suspicion of **espionage**. Russia's envoy to NATO, **Dmitry Rogozin**, promised retaliatory actions to the "provocation."

NORTH CAUCASUS. Geographically, the North Caucasus, or Ciscaucasia, includes the foothills and mountains north of the Greater **Caucasus** Range's watershed, and is bounded by the **Black Sea** in the west and the **Caspian Sea** in the east. Politically, the area denotes extreme southern European Russia, and specifically refers to the **ethnic republics** of **Adygeya**, **Karachay-Cherkessiya**, **Kabardino-Balkariya**, **North Ossetiya**, **Ingushetiya**, **Chechnya**, and **Dagestan**, as well as the **krais** of **Krasnodar** and **Stavropol**. These **federal subjects** border the southern Caucasian—and thus geographically Asian—states of **Georgia** and **Azerbaijan**, as well as the breakaway republics of **Abkhazia** and **South Ossetia** (though the latter two are sometimes included in the North Caucasus for political purposes).

Along with **Rostov Oblast**, these territories comprise the North Caucasus **Economic Region**. The area has a long history of civilizational conflict, particularly during imperial conquest (1817–1864) when forced conversion to **Christianity** and ethnic cleansing created endemic resentments among the indigenous Turkic and Caucasian peoples against their **ethnic Russian** and **Cossack** conquerors. During the early Soviet period, the region was briefly united as the Mountainous Republic of the Northern Caucasus before being delimited into its constituent ethnic elements during the 1920s. **Joseph Stalin**'s World War II–era deportations of the **Chechens**, **Ingush**, **Balkars**, and **Karachay** to **Siberia** and **Central Asia** severely disrupted the social fabric of the region and sowed the seeds of future ethnic friction. In the late 1980s and early 1990s, the region became a hotbed of conflict and strife.

In 1989, **ethnic violence** flared between **Orthodox Ossetians** and **Muslim** Ingush, resulting in a three-year, low-intensity conflict. The region was the site of the formation of the **Confederation of Mountain Peoples of the Caucasus**, a paramilitary organization that intervened in the Abkhaz-Georgian conflict, resulting in accusations of war crimes. In 1991, Chechnya declared independence from the Russian Federation, setting the stage for the first **Chechen War** in 1994, which proved detrimental to the region as a whole. During the second **Yeltsin** administration, the North Caucasus was afflicted by increasing **Islamist terrorist** attacks coordinated by **Shamil Basayev**. Hoping to create a regional caliphate, Basayev ultimately attempted an invasion of Dagestan, precipitating the second Chechen War in 1999.

Vladimir Putin used federal troops to crush Chechen insurgents and urged the regional governors to crack down on **Wahhabism** (*vakhabizm*). Terror attacks and some guerilla actions, most notably the 2004 **Beslan hostage crisis** and the 2005 siege on Nalchik, continued until 2005 when the level of violence across the region dropped dramatically. Despite the relative calm, the regional **economy** remains in shambles and **tourism** is almost nonexistent. As a result, the North Caucasus remains one of Russia's most underdeveloped and politically unstable regions.

NORTH KOREA (RELATIONS WITH). Korean-Russian relations have been largely determined by Moscow's geopolitical interests in northeastern Asia. During and after World War II, **Joseph Stalin** supported the first leader of the Democratic People's Republic of Korea (DPRK), Kim Il-sung, against both Japanese imperialists and the **United States**–backed regime in the south, the Republic of Korea. Relations cooled after Stalin's death but grew closer in the wake of the Sino-Soviet split.

As part of **perestroika**, **Mikhail Gorbachev** dramatically reduced the Soviet subsidization of the **Kim Jong-il** regime, and, in 1990, recognized the Republic of Korea (South Korea). A policy of divestment from the PDRK was also pursued by **Boris Yeltsin** after Russia's independence; lack of support from Russia and Pyongyang's mismanagement of its centralized economy sparked an economic crisis in the country, resulting in a famine in the mid-1990s that claimed upward of 3 million lives. Yeltsin sought to distance the Russian Federation from North Korea in an effort to gain admittance to a number of international organizations that considered the DPRK a rogue state; he terminated a bilateral defense treaty and suspended all non–hard currency **foreign trade** with the republic. Much to the chagrin of Pyongyang, Yeltsin also rapidly expanded **economic**, **political**, and cultural links with Seoul.

With the ascension of **Yevgeny Primakov** in the second Yeltsin administration, Pyongyang reentered Russia's geopolitical strategy in the region. Upon his election to the presidency, **Vladimir Putin** moved quickly to rehabilitate North Korea and pushed through a Treaty on Friendship and Good-Neighborly Relations in 2000. Trade expanded rapidly, though still below late Soviet norms. In 2001, Kim made the 9,330-kilometer journey across Russia in a specially armored train to meet with Putin in **Moscow**, marking a significant departure from his isolationist stance. Through quiet and pragmatic diplomacy, Moscow used its reinvigorated influence to urge reconciliation between the two Koreas, with the ultimate aim of developing **transportation** and energy links to Seoul via the **Trans-Siberian Railway**–Trans-Korean Railroad (TSR-TKR) project.

Following North Korea's withdrawal from the Nuclear Non-Proliferation Treaty on 10 January 2003, Russia became a key player in the Six-Party Talks meant to keep the Korean Peninsula free of **nuclear weapons**. Russia became a strong advocate for North Korea and critic of any possible military action to remove Kim, particularly after **George W. Bush**'s inclusion of the pariah state in his "axis of evil" in 2001. However, in 2007, Putin prohibited Russian companies from supplying the DPRK with materials for its weapons program; the decision was made in response to Pyongyang's 2006 nuclear test. In 2008, Moscow and Pyongyang completed a border demarcation project begun in 2000, finally settling the 17.5-kilometer frontier between the two countries. In early 2009, Moscow condemned Pyongyang's increasingly threatening military posture vis-à-vis its southern neighbor as "intolerable." *See also* CHINA; FOREIGN RELATIONS; JAPAN.

NORTH OSSETIYA-ALANIYA. An **ethnic republic** of the Russian Federation. Incorporated into the **Romanov** Empire during the early 19th century, the region constituted a portion of the Mountain **Autonomous Soviet Socialist Republic** (ASSR) during the early Soviet period. It became an ASSR of the **Russian Soviet Federative Socialist Republic** in 1936; North Ossetiya declared its sovereignty in mid-1990, the first ethnic republic to do so.

The titular majority of the republic are **Ossetians**, an Iranian-speaking, predominantly **Orthodox** people who also reside in **South Ossetia** (although a significant **Muslim** minority exists). **Joseph Stalin** saw fit to expand the republic in the wake of the deportation of the neighboring **Ingush** in 1944, planting the seeds for continuing ethnic conflict and territorial disputes between the peoples of the two republics; from 1991 to 1992, open conflict between the two communities raged and **Boris Yeltsin** was forced to send in federal troops to quell the violence. In 1994, Alaniya—the medieval place-name of Ossetia—was added to the republic's name, and has gained popular use among the Ossetians.

North Ossetiya covers 8,000 square kilometers of heavily forested and mostly mountainous territory, making it one of the smallest administrative regions in the country. The republic borders **Kabardino-Balkariya**, **Chechnya**, **Ingushetiya**, and **Stavropol Krai**, and shares an international border with **Georgia**. It is part of the Southern **Federal District** and the North Caucasus **Economic Region**. It has a population of slightly more than 700,000 inhabitants, 63 percent of whom are ethnic Ossetians; **ethnic Russians** comprise a quarter of the population, followed by Ingush, **Armenians**, and **Ukrainians**. The regional capital is Vladikavkaz (pop. 315,000), one of the most populous cities in the **North Caucasus**.

North Ossetiya has suffered intensely from the regional instability caused by the **Chechen Wars**. Since 1999, Vladikavkaz has been a regular target of bomb attacks, and in 2008, two successive mayors were gunned down by unknown assailants. The most dramatic development, however, was the September 2004 hostage taking at School Number One in **Beslan** perpetrated by militants under the direction of **Shamil Basayev**. The ensuing gun battle resulted in the deaths of more than 300, including 186 children. Developments in Georgia have also impacted the republic. Conflict between the **separatist** South Ossetians and Tbilisi in 1990–1992 and 2008 has resulted in massive flows of refugees into North Ossetiya's Prigorodny raion; the first influx triggered the **Ossetian-Ingush conflict** of 1991–1992.

Unlike much of the rest of the North Caucasus, North Ossetiya is mostly urbanized, and benefited from industrial development during the Soviet era; the republic's **economy** is strong when compared to its neighbors in the region. The region is rich in natural resources, including lead, silver, zinc, and untapped fossil fuels. Major **industries** include radio electronics, hydroelectrical power, metallurgy, alcohol manufacture, and light industry. Despite concerns about **terrorism**, the region is also a **tourist** destination and is developing its skiing infrastructure; half of the republic is covered by the Alaniya National Park and other national preserves.

The republic is a bastion of the **Communist Party of the Russian Federation**, and elected Aleksandr Dzasokhov, a former Politburo member, as president in 1998. His relations with Ingushetiya's president, Ruslan Aushev, which began as friendly, grew strained over the disputed Prigorodny raion. After completing a second term, Dzasokhov was replaced by the **Putin** loyalist Taymuraz Mamsurov in 2005. Mamsurov is a native of Beslan, and his son and daughter were both taken hostage during the crisis. Since taking office, he has raised the geopolitical temperature in the region by speaking of the "integral" nature of the two Ossetiyas and warning of **North Atlantic Treaty Organization** (NATO) conspiracies to incorporate North Ossetiya to Georgia. *See also* ISLAMISM.

NORWAY (RELATIONS WITH). As a result of the Soviet annexation of **Finland**'s Petsamo (*Pechenzhskii raion*) region, Norway and the Union of Soviet Socialist Republics (USSR) gained a common border in 1946. Three years later, Norway abandoned four decades of neutrality and joined the **North Atlantic Treaty Organization** (NATO) as an original member, creating a tense relationship with the USSR. This rivalry grew in intensity with the establishment of the **Warsaw Treaty Organization** in 1955 and the discovery and exploitation of **oil** in the **Barents Sea**. However, Oslo generally pursued a pragmatic approach to the Kremlin during the **Cold War**, deemphasizing the defense of its Finnmark region adjacent to the **Murmansk Oblast** and rejecting proposals to host **nuclear weapons**

on its soil (though Norway was and is a major site for radar installations monitoring Russian **military** movements).

Under **glasnost**, Russian-Norwegian exchanges greatly expanded,
being based upon cultural commonalities of the Fenno-Scandinavian
Peninsula and resumption of cross-border trade. Cooperation on
joint energy projects has helped improve relations between the two
counties since 1991. Norway has also proved to be an effective fa-
cilitator of improved NATO-Russian relations in the post-Soviet era.
During the *Kursk* **submarine disaster** in 2000, the Norwegian navy
provided substantial aid to Russia. Recently, competition for **Arctic
Ocean** resources (particularly fossil fuels and fisheries) and delimitation of maritime borders has come to the fore in bilateral relations.
Environmental concerns also impact relations; Oslo is particularly
sensitive to transborder **pollution** from **Norilsk Nickel**'s smelting in
Russia's extreme northwest.

A significant number of **ethnic Russians** and **Ukrainians** reside
in the Norwegian archipelago of Svalbard on Spitsbergen, a situation
allowed under the Paris Treaty of 1920. Under the **Putin** administration, settlement and investment has increased after a decade of stagnation. In 2008, the Russian **navy** conducted war games off the coast
of Bergen, much to dismay of NATO and Norway. Conservative
politicians in Norway have been particularly critical of Moscow's actions in the **Caucasus**, suggesting such moves represent a resurgence
of Russian imperialism that might eventually be directed at Norway.
See also BALTIC STATES.

NOVAYA GAZETA. **Newspaper**. Founded in 1993, *Novaya Gazeta*
is a Russian daily newspaper, and is famous at home and abroad
for its critical coverage of Russian political and social affairs. The
name of the newspaper in Russian means "A New Newspaper." It is
published three times a week (Mondays, Wednesdays, and Fridays)
in **Moscow**, and is available in some Russian regions and foreign
countries. The online version of the newspaper is published at www
.novayagazeta.ru/. The newspaper is owned by billionaire **Aleksandr
Lebedev** and former Soviet premier **Mikhail Gorbachev**; the latter
used the money from his 1990 Nobel Peace Prize to establish the
publication. Dmitry Muratov is the chief editor. In 2009, the circulation of the newspaper was 171,000 copies. Because of its critical

stance and focus on **corruption** and the violation of **human rights**, the newspaper has been called "the last truly independent national newspaper in Russia." Four *Novaya Gazeta* **journalists** were murdered between 2001 and 2009, including **Anna Politkovskaya**, Yury Schekhochikhin, Stanislav Markelov, and Anastasiya Baburova. The newspaper was involved in a series of scandals: in 2004, it accused **Sergey Kiriyenko** of embezzling $8 billion during the **ruble crisis** when he was the prime minister; it was later discovered that the accusations were based on a prank posted on the **Internet**. When this was revealed, Kiriyenko sued the newspaper for libel and won the case. *See also* MEDIA.

NOVAYA ZEMLYA. An archipelago in the **Arctic Ocean**, Novaya Zemlya ("New Land") separates the **Barents** and Kara seas. The island chain, which covers an area of 90,000 square kilometers, is administered by **Archangel Oblast**. The two main islands—Severny (Northern) and Yuzhny (Southern)—are separated by the narrow Matochkin Strait, the site of dozens of underground **nuclear** tests during the Soviet period and, more recently, subcritical nuclear experiments. This, combined with the Rogachevo Air Base on Yuzhny, made the area militarily sensitive during the **Cold War**. Novaya Zemlya has a population of about 2,500, including a small community of indigenous **Nenets**. The area featured prominently in Aleksandr Melnik's science-fiction film *Terra Nova* (2008), which portrayed a dystopian penal colony where prisoners administered themselves, leading to such atrocities as cannibalism; the film was not shown in many foreign countries, including **Great Britain**, due to its controversial content.

NOVGOROD OBLAST. An administrative region of the Russian Federation. Home to several of Russia's oldest cities including the UNESCO World Heritage site Great Novgorod, the oblast is a center for **tourism** as well as science and engineering. Surrounded by the **Leningrad**, **Tver**, **Vologda**, and **Pskov oblasts**, the region is proximate to the **Baltic States** and **Belarus** and is well connected to both **St. Petersburg** and **Moscow**.

Novgorod Oblast covers an area of 55,300 square kilometers and is part of the Northwestern **Economic Region** and **Federal District**.

Novgorod's population is slightly less than 700,000, making it the least populous **federal subject** in European Russia. At 95 percent, it has one of the most homogenously **ethnic Russian** populations in the federation. The regional capital, Novgorod (pop. 241,000), was once a key city in the **Baltic-Volga** trade route, and sports ancient monasteries, icons, and frescoes reflecting its centrality to early **Orthodoxy** in the region.

The **geography** of the region is characterized by **taiga** and forested marshland, and numerous glacial lakes, Ilmen being the largest, dot the countryside. The attractive Valdai National Park is located in the southeast of the oblast. Novgorod is rich in shale, clay, limestone, and quart deposits, as well as mineral springs. In addition to tourism, regional **industries** include woodworking, fertilizers, forestry, and electricity production. In the 1990s, the regional **economy** enjoyed five times the national amount of **foreign investment** due to **tax** incentives, which attracted more than 200 companies including Cadbury Schweppes (**Great Britain**), Dansk Tyggegummi Fabrik (Denmark), and Dresser (**United States**).

Under the leadership of the popular governor Mikhail Prusak, the regional government pursued a policy of economic pragmatism combined with reform. Prusak revived medieval traditions of so-called northern self-government and pushed for greater levels of private land ownership and localized authority; he detailed his strategies in the 1999 book *Reform in the Provinces*. Prusak's inability to stop the rising popularity of the **Communist Party of the Russian Federation** led to his purportedly voluntary decision to step down as governor. The current governor is Sergey Mitin; he was appointed by **Vladimir Putin** in 2007. He immediately launched a campaign to improve housing, **health care**, **agriculture**, and **education** in the region. However, Mitin's campaign against **corruption** has been criticized for its draconian enforcement of tax collection, including targeting **women** selling homemade pies on the roadside of the St. Petersburg-Moscow highway.

NOVOSIBIRSK OBLAST. An administrative region of the Russian Federation. Located in the very center of Russia on the Siberian Plain, Novosibirsk Oblast is bordered by **Omsk**, **Tomsk**, **Kemerovo**, and **Altay Krai**; it shares an international border with

Kazakhstan. The **oblast** is part of the West Siberian **Economic Region** and the Siberian **Federal District**. As a **federal subject**, the oblast ranks 18th in both population (2.7 million) and territory (178,200 square km). While the vast majority of the population is **ethnic Russian**, a significant ethnic **German** community is resident in the oblast, though many have quit the area for **Germany** since 1991.

The regional geography is a mix of **taiga**, **steppe**, bogs, and numerous rivers (the Ob and Om) and lakes, including Chany Lake, one of the world's largest. A relatively sunny **climate** allows for extensive **agriculture**, with the primary crops being potatoes, flax, mustard, and sunflowers; the region's forests are also abundant in berries. The capital, Novosibirsk (pop. 1.4 million) has grown extremely rapidly in the past century, owing to its location on the **Trans-Siberian Railway** as well as its internationally recognized university community at Akademogorodok. Sometimes known as the Soviet Union's "City of Science," Novosibirsk has a strong reputation for physics, math, and informatics. The Tolmachevo International Airport is the largest in **Siberia**, and connects to destinations across the **Commonwealth of Independent States** and farther afield. Engineering and metalworking are the primary drivers of **industry**; the region's export **economy** is oriented toward metals, machinery, chemical products, and timber.

Despite being dismissed by **Boris Yeltsin** in 1993 after he publicly sided with Vice President **Aleksandr Rutskoy** in the **constitutional crisis of 1993**, Vitaly Mukha was able to regain his post as a candidate for the **Communist Party of the Russian Federation** by 1995. A contentious relationship existed between the oblast and the federal authorities during the late 1990s. With the waning popularity of the Communists, Viktor Tolokonsky, former mayor of the regional capital and an ally of the **oligarch Boris Berezovsky**, replaced Mukha in 2000; he was reappointed by **Vladimir Putin** in 2007. Improving the **transportation** network, specifically the construction of a metro, has been Tolokonsky's key issue since taking office. He has also focused on expanding cross-border trade with Kazakhstan. In 2001, Igor Belyakov, the deputy mayor of Novosibirsk, was gunned down, purportedly for his support of transferring control of the city's largest open-air market to government control.

NTV. In Cyrillic, the channel's name is HTB, whereby TB stands for **television**, while the letter H may stand for the word *novoie*, meaning "new," as well as for the word *nezavisimoie*, meaning "independent." The television channel was a pioneer of post-Soviet independent television **media**; however, it was later taken over by state-owned **Gazprom**, causing a major controversy in Russia and abroad. The channel was founded in 1993 by **Vladimir Gusinsky**, a Russian **oligarch**, who managed to hire Russia's best news **journalists** and news anchors, including Leonid Parfenov, Mikhail Osokin, Tatyana Mitkova, and others. The channel set extremely high professional standards, giving live coverage and critical analysis of events as well as displaying innovative studio and program design. The channel was home to many successful programs, including *Segodnia* (Today), a prime-time news show, *Itogi* (Summary), a weekly commentary program, and *Kukly* (Puppets), a satirical program. The channel was also popular for its creative entertainment programs. By the end of the millennium, NTV's audience was over 100 million, covering about 70 percent of the federation. However, since the Gazprom takeover, the station's reputation has diminished as has the quality of its programming, which is now entertainment-centric. The fate of the network is seen as a barometer of independent media in **Vladimir Putin**'s Russia. NTV is also available in the other countries of the **Commonwealth of Independent States**.

NUCLEAR ENERGY. The Union of Soviet Socialist Republics (USSR) established the world's first nuclear power plant in Obninsk, **Kaluga**, in 1954. An outgrowth of the Soviet-era **nuclear weapons** program, Russia has a robust, if out-of-date nuclear energy program. Approximately one-sixth of the country's electricity is generated by its 31 nuclear reactors. In an attempt to reduce its consumption of profitable **natural gas**, the figure is to be doubled by 2020. All civilian reactors are operated by the state-controlled firm Energoatom, which currently receives loans from the **European Union** (EU) to upgrade and monitor its facilities. The EU is wary of a repeat of the 1986 **Chernobyl disaster**, which released nuclear radiation across the continent. A number of Russia's current reactors are of the same type as the one at Chernobyl. Most of Russia's reactors are located in the industrialized west of the country; however, the Kola and

Bilibino plants are in the **Far North**. Russia also supports nuclear power programs in foreign countries, including **Turkey** and Ecuador. Such assistance is most controversial in **Iran**, where Russia's nuclear agency has assisted in the development of the Bushehr reactor. Exporting nuclear fuel is an integral part of the country's **foreign trade**. Russia also benefits economically as a processor of spent nuclear fuel, though this has generated intense criticism from local and international **environmental** groups. Failure to properly secure such materials is also a concern among **foreign relations** experts, who fear that the fuel can be converted into **weapons of mass destruction** by terrorists.

NUCLEAR WEAPONS. In 1991, the Russian Federation emerged as the legal successor to the Union of Soviet Socialist Republics (USSR), including the defunct nation's right to possess nuclear weapons under the 1968 Nuclear Non-Proliferation Treaty (NPT). At the time of the **dissolution of the Soviet Union**, the country had approximately 27,000 nuclear weapons. During the 1990s, **Belarus**, **Ukraine**, and **Kazakhstan** transferred their weapons to Russia with economic support provided by the **United States**. All nuclear missiles deployed in the **Eastern Bloc** or other areas of the former Soviet Union had been relocated to Russia by 1992.

Today, Russia has more than 6,000 strategic nuclear weapons (primarily intercontinental ballistic missiles, or ICBMs) and more than 10,000 nonstrategic nuclear warheads. Washington continues to provide funding to Russia to help it secure its nuclear weapons and other **weapons of mass destruction** to prevent "loose nukes" and chemical and biological weapons from falling into the hands of international **terrorists**. Despite years of monitoring and improvement of security, there is still intense concern about the safety of the country's weapons. The unresolved question of the existence of so-called suitcase bombs is particularly worrying, especially after General **Aleksandr Lebed** publicly stated in the 1990s that Russia was no longer in control of some of these weapons.

Command and control of Russia's nuclear weapons is located in **Moscow**. The Strategic Rocket Forces are a special division of the Russian **military** dedicated to protecting and deploying nuclear weapons. Russia's military doctrine permits the limited use of nuclear weapons to protect Russia and its allies—namely, **Serbia**, **Armenia**, Belarus, Kazakhstan, **Kyrgyzstan**, and **Tajikistan**—from political pressure, an assertion that is of deep concern to many in the international community.

– O –

OBAMA, BARACK HUSSEIN (1961–). American politician. Barack Obama possessed little **foreign relations** experience prior to his election as the 44th president of the **United States**; however, as U.S. senator, he had traveled to Russia and other parts of the former Soviet Union, focusing on ways to prevent the proliferation of **weapons of mass destruction**. His early administration was characterized by attempts to "reset" the relationship with Moscow; however, a number of gaffes, including demeaning comments about Russia made by Vice President Joe Biden, have undermined this strategy.

While Obama and **Dmitry Medvyedev** have a congenial relationship, Prime Minister **Vladimir Putin** has made his disdain for the new president obvious. The Russian public proved to be the only foreign audience the charismatic president could not woo in the summer of 2009 when he spoke at the New Economic School in **Moscow**; commentators suggested that the resurgence of American popularity abroad—itself an outgrowth of Obama's election in 2008—posed a threat to Russia's newfound influence in much of the non-Western world. Obama also suffered a setback in **Central Asia** when **Kyrgyzstan** demanded that American military forces vacate the country, a position that had been urged by the Kremlin and other **Shanghai Cooperation Organization** members (ultimately, the U.S. was allowed to maintain a stripped-down presence in the country and received permission to use Russian airspace to assist in its mission in **Afghanistan**).

Despite a major change in American foreign policy under Obama, certain disputes, such as that over **Georgia** and **Ukraine**'s eventual admission to the **North Atlantic Treaty Organization** (NATO), remain. In September 2009, however, Obama announced his decision not to move ahead with a missile defense shield in **Poland** and the Czech Republic, somewhat improving relations with the Kremlin.

OBLAST. The most common administrative division among Russia's **federal subjects**, *oblast'* is generally translated as "region" or "area." Unlike the **ethnic republics**, oblasts are not associated with titular ethnic groups; however, they differ little from **krais**, which are virtually the same in administrative terms. Oblasts are subdivided into **raions**.

OIL. Russia is the largest producer of oil outside of the Organization of the Petroleum Exporting Countries (OPEC) and currently the second-largest producer after Saudi Arabia. Recent declines in Saudi production contrasted with steady gains in Russia since 1998 suggest that the latter will soon regain the leadership position (the Soviet Union was the world leader from the late 1970s until 1991). However, Russia ranks only seventh in terms of proven oil reserves, so such a peak will only be temporary. Globally, Russia produces 12 percent of oil and accounts for the same figure in terms of exports. Russia exports 5 million barrels per day, as well as 2 million barrels per day of refined petroleum products.

Russia's major fields are located in the **Volga-Ural region**, the **North Caucasus**, Timan-Pechora in **Nenetsiya**, and western **Siberia**; a new field is being developed in northern **Sakhalin**. Due to its vast **geography** and the legacy of Soviet-era transshipment routes, Russia is also an important transit country, particularly for oil sent from **Kazakhstan** to European markets. The state-owned firm **Rosneft** is Russia's largest petroleum company; the company purchased **Yukos**'s assets after they were seized by the state, thus surpassing **Lukoil**. Other major companies include TNK-BP, Surgutneftegas, and **Gazprom** Neft.

Established by presidential decree in 1992, **Transneft** is the state-owned firm that controls Russia's nearly 50,000 kilometers of pipelines. The Russian **economy** is highly dependent on oil and **natural gas** exports. Rising prices during the 2000s led to a markedly improved economic situation in the country as well as strong popularity ratings for **Vladimir Putin**. High demand has also allowed Russia to expand its exports in recent years as rail and river shipments have become more cost effective.

The **European Union** (particularly **Germany** and **Poland**) and other European states serve as the main market for Russian oil exports. Most of this oil is shipped via the 4,000-kilometer Druzhba (Friendship) pipeline, which passes through **Belarus** (northern spur) and **Ukraine** (southern spur), though a percentage is transported from the **Far North** to the **Baltic Sea** via the Baltic pipeline. In recent years, **China** and **Japan** have also become major customers. Prospective pipelines from the Siberian oil fields to East Asia have become critical political issues in bilateral relations and have impacted Russia's domestic **politics** as well (particularly vis-à-vis the **oligarchs**).

OKRUG. Usually translated as "district," an *okrug* is an administrative division in the Russian Federation. After the **dissolution of the Soviet Union**, a number of **autonomous okrugs** were downgraded to okrugs within their corresponding **federal subjects**, including Aga Buryatiya, Komi-Permyakiya, **Koryakiya**, and Ust-Orda Buryatiya. In **Samara Oblast**, the lowest-level territorial division is the okrug rather than the traditional **raion**; **Belgorod**, **Murmansk**, and **Krasnodar Krai** also use okrugs to designate internal geopolitical divisions. Russia's federal cities, **Moscow** and **St. Petersburg**, are similarly subdivided into okrugs.

OLD BELIEVERS. The Old Believers (*starovery* or *staroobriadtsy*) separated from the mainstream of the **Russian Orthodox Church** (ROC) at the end of the 17th century in a protest against church reforms. Specifically, these concerned new liturgical rites introduced by Patriarch Nikon, including the visual canon of Russian icons and everyday rituals. In effect, Old Believers were the most conservative branch of Eastern **Orthodox Christianity**, resisting even the slightest changes in the religious practices. In tsarist Russia, the Old Believers were persecuted, tortured, and executed. To escape such harsh treatment, many moved to peripheral parts of Russia or fled the country altogether. Consequently, they helped to colonize some of the most remote parts of Russia (including **Siberia**, **Latvia**, and Alaska), and therefore continued the Russian imperial project. The ROC viewed them as a threat to the Russian state until 1905 when Tsar Nicholas II signed an act allowing freedom of **religion** and ending the persecution of religious minorities in Russia. Many Old Believers were Russia's main merchants and philanthropists. In the

1970s, the Orthodox Church apologized for its discrimination of Old Believers and accepted them into the fold once again. In recent years, the Russian state has reached out to Old Believers in the Americas and elsewhere, hoping to partially alleviate the country's endemic **demographic challenges** through remigration to the Russian Federation. *See also* ROMANOVS.

OLIGARCH. During the late Soviet period, private enterprise returned to the Soviet Union, allowing a number of well-connected entrepreneurs to benefit from the introduction of a limited market **economy**. In some cases, these individuals were veterans of the **perestroika**-era black market, while others moved into the business world from academe, the sciences, or other occupations. Through the use of political and social connections (*blat*), these budding capitalists began to develop small commercial empires in a number of fields, including **banking**, **industry**, and computers. During the Soviet period, they were dependent on ties to the **Communist Party of the Soviet Union** (CPSU), the *nomenklatura*, and/or the **Komsomol** network. However, under **Boris Yeltsin**'s administration, a small clique of businessmen became corporate tycoons through voucher **privatization** under the direction of **Anatoly Chubais** and **Yegor Gaydar**. The corrupt **loans for shares program** further transferred large amounts of the country's wealth into the hands of a small economic elite, which included **Boris Berezovsky**, **Vladimir Gusinsky**, **Mikhail Khodorkovsky**, **Roman Abramovich**, **Vladimir Potanin**, **Vahid Alakbarov**, **Viktor Vekselberg**, and **Mikhail Fridman**, among others. While these mostly **Jewish** oligarchs were loathed by the Russian masses, their influence over the country's economy, **media**, and **political** system made them nearly untouchable in the mid-1990s. Good relations with Yeltsin and his inner circle, colloquially known as "the Family," certainly aided the rise of certain oligarchs, but there were anti-Yeltsin oligarchs as well. During the **1996 presidential election**, a number of wealthy businessmen—particularly Berezovsky—shifted their allegiance to Yeltsin, fearing the alternative, that is, **Gennady Zyuganov** and the **Communist Party of the Russian Federation** (KPRF). The 1998 **ruble crisis** severely impacted the fortunes of these magnates; however, most survived the economic turmoil. The rise of **Vladimir Putin** presented an existential challenge to their political influence in Russia. Early in his first term, Putin demanded that the tycoons abstain from politics if they wanted to preserve their economic empires. Gusinsky and Berezovsky soon fell afoul of the new president and were forced into exile. Khodorkovsky, the richest man in Russia, took on Putin, and was arrested on charges of fraud and **tax** evasion in 2003. A new cadre of pro-Kremlin oligarchs saw their fortunes rise during the Putin years, including **Oleg Deripaska**, while others—like Abramovich and Fridman—were able to establish cordial relations with the new president. The 2008–2009 **global financial crisis** saw the oligarchs' fortunes wane, with Moscow scooping up many of their most lucrative assets in what some have called a "deprivatization." Despite this, a small number of economic high-flyers continue to dominate the Russian economy today.

OMSK OBLAST. An administrative region of the Russian Federation. Bisected by the **Arctic**-bound Irtysh River, this **Siberian oblast** is situated at the frontier with **Kazakhstan** and borders **Tyumen**, **Tomsk**, and **Novosibirsk** oblasts. The oblast is part of the West Siberian **Economic Region** and the Siberian **Federal District** and covers an area of 139,700 square kilometers. The region has a population of 2 million, more than half of whom live in the administrative capital Omsk (pop. 1.1 million).

As a site for relocation of the defense industry during World War II, much of the region was closed to foreigners; the recent decrease in defense production has negatively impacted the regional **economy**, though Omsk remains a leading city in terms of **industrial** production. Major regional industries include electricity generation, mechanical engineering, glass, and petrochemicals. **Oil** refineries built during the 1950s and now owned by Gazprom Neft, the oil arm of **Gazprom** formerly known as Sibneft, are an important source of employment for the region; a large number of pipelines carry petroleum across the region.

In 2008, Gazprom Neft announced support for a number of social projects including aid to orphanages and local schools. Nearly 20 percent of the population is engaged in **agriculture**, owing to the rich **chernozem** found in the region. The region was a dependable supporter of the **Communist Party of the Russian Federation**

(KPRF) during the 1990s; however, Leonid Polezhayev, a **Yeltsin** appointee, was able to maintain the post of governor despite challenges from the KPRF. Polezhayev won reelection in 1995, 1999, and 2003 before being reappointed by **Vladimir Putin** in 2007. During his tenure, he has developed a robust level of **foreign trade** with Slovakia amounting to nearly $100 million per year by 2005. The region's relationship with Kazakhstan has also greatly expanded through the development of more than 30 new joint enterprises. *See also* ABRAMOVICH, ROMAN.

OORZHAK, SHERIG-OOL DIZIZHIKOVICH (1942–). Politician. Born in the village of Shekpeer in the Tuvinian People's Republic, Oorzhak studied agriculture in Moscow and became active in the **Communist Party of the Soviet Union**, ultimately rising to the highest position in the Tuvan **Autonomous Soviet Socialist Republic** (ASSR). During the early 1990s, he pursued a more accommodating line toward Moscow compared to his nationalist rivals in the "Free Tuva" movement. Despite this, he stressed a desire to reverse the half-century of forced Europeanization of his nation, and took the oath of office clad in traditional garb and wearing a Tuvan knife.

As president of Tuva from 1992 to 2002 and prime minister from 2002 to 2007, he pursued a pro-Russian policy that effectively weakened the local drive for secession from the Russian Federation. He oversaw amendments to the republican constitution that contravened the federal **constitution**, as well as the negation of the clause that stipulated Tuva's right to secede from Russia. Oorzhak remained on good terms with **Boris Yeltsin** during the 1990s and was able to preserve his office under **Vladimir Putin**'s first administration.

However, in 2007, he was forced to step down amid allegations of **corruption**. More importantly, Oorzhak, who had promised to deliver 80 percent of his republic's voters for **United Russia**, had failed to produce a majority for the party in the 2006 parliamentary elections. His inability to command local elites proved intolerable to Moscow; Putin dismissed Oorzhak in 2007 and replaced him with Sholban Kara-ool. After losing the governorship, Oorzhak was rewarded with a position in the office of the chief of the presidential staff, Sergey Sobyanin, alongside a number of other loyal former governors.

ORANGE REVOLUTION. *See* COLOR REVOLUTIONS.

ORENBURG OBLAST. An administrative region of the Russian Federation. Orenburg Oblast is a prorupt region in southern Russia that narrowly separates the **ethnic republics** of **Tatarstan** and **Bashkortostan** from **Kazakhstan**; it is also bordered by **Samara** and **Saratov** in the west and **Chelyabinsk** in the northeast. The **oblast** rises into the foothills of the **Ural Mountains**. Like Russia itself, Orenburg is geographically **Eurasian** as it is divided by the Ural River, one of the traditional dividing lines between the two continents.

Orenburg is part of the Urals **Economic Region** and the Volga **Federal District**. It occupies an area of 124,000 square kilometers and has a population of 2.1 million inhabitants. While **ethnic Russians** enjoy a clear majority (72 percent), **Tatars** (8 percent), **Kazakhs** (6 percent), and **Bashkirs** (2.5 percent) give the region a decidedly Turkic character. Approximately 20 percent of the population is **Muslim**, while the remainder is Eastern **Orthodox**. More than a half-million reside in the regional capital, Orenburg, a former **Cossack** outpost that served as the launching point for Russia's conquest of **Central Asia**. The city was also the capital of the Kirghiz **Autonomous Soviet Socialist Republic** (ASSR), the forbearer of Soviet Kazakhstan, during the 1920s.

Orenburg Oblast is an important donor region within the federation, with extensive natural resources and a well-developed agroindustrial complex. However, **oil** and **natural gas** exploration have taken their toll on the soil, and erosion is a major issue in the region. Likewise, widespread industrialization makes the region one of Russia's most polluted. The region was also the site of five underground **nuclear** tests, and thus suffers from high levels of radiation in localized areas. Major **industries** include metallurgy, mechanical engineering, petroleum production, animal husbandry, and farming. **Mining** of nickel, copper, dolomite, quartz, gold, marble, and jasper is also important. A large number of small businesses are in operation, and **unemployment** is comparatively low.

The region supported the **Communist Party of the Russian Federation** during the 1990s, though its governor, Vladimir Yelagin, was a backer of **Boris Yeltsin**'s administration. In 1996, Orenburg signed a power-sharing agreement with Moscow that recognized its importance as a border region with Kazakhstan. In 1999, Aleksey Chernyshev, a member of the **Agrarian Party of Russia** and former chair of the **State Duma**'s Committee on Agrarian Issues, defeated Yelagin; he was reelected in 2003 and reappointed by **Vladimir Putin** in 2005. Chernyshev has actively promoted cross-border **foreign trade** with neighboring Kazakhstan, as well as joint projects such as natural gas extraction and the development of a **China–European Union** transit corridor. Trade turnover between the region and Kazakhstan is nearly $500 million per year. In the early 1990s, there was a brief effort on the part of Tatar and Kazakh nationalists to redraw the borders of the region to allow contiguity between the Muslim, Turkic ethnic republics of the Volga region and the Central Asian republics. *See also* PAN-TURKISM.

ORGANIZATION FOR SECURITY AND CO-OPERATION IN EUROPE (OSCE). Founded in 1973, the Organization for Security and Co-operation in Europe is one of the world's largest intergovernmental organizations (IGO). The Russian Federation, as well as the other former Soviet republics, is a member of the organization. Originally created as a forum for East-West dialogue during the **Cold War** (known as the Helsinki Process), the OSCE's charter has expanded greatly over time.

Today, it is dedicated to regional security, freedom of the press, fair elections, arms control, and the protection of **human rights**. Russia's relationship with the organization is complex. The OSCE monitored and reported on the situation inside the **Eastern Bloc** during the late Soviet period, increasing the pressure on the region's one-party regimes to **democratize** and protect human rights, particularly those of **ethnic minorities**. Since Russia's independence, the OSCE has criticized Russia for its activities in **Chechnya**, as well as a number of post-Soviet conflict zones where it maintains **peacekeeping** forces, including **Transnistria**, **Tajikistan**, **Nagorno-Karabakh**, and **Georgia**. **Boris Yeltsin** returned the criticism, condemning the OSCE for not doing enough to protect the rights of **ethnic Russians** in the **near abroad**, particularly in the **Baltic States** and **Central Asia**.

Under **Vladimir Putin**, the clampdown on nongovernmental organizations received strong criticism from other OSCE members, and created demands that Moscow live up to its commitments as a member of the IGO. In 2004, Russia and several other members of the **Commonwealth of Independent States** issued a joint statement chiding the OSCE for its politicization, "double standards," and disregard for the "national sovereignty" of its member states. The statement was taken as a defense of the growing prevalence of "managed democracy" in the **Newly Independent States** of Eurasia and pushback against OSCE election monitoring in the region. *See also* CIVIL SOCIETY.

ORGANIZATION OF CENTRAL ASIAN COOPERATION (OCAC). *See* EURASIAN ECONOMIC COMMUNITY.

ORTHODOXY. Also known as Eastern Orthodox Christianity. Following the Great Schism in 1054, western Christendom (Catholicism) and Eastern Orthodox **Christianity** grew into distinct faiths. Within the latter, a number of nationally distinct but theologically unified churches developed, the largest of which today is the **Russian Orthodox Church** (ROC). Other Eastern Orthodox Churches include the Ukrainian, Belarusian, Serbian, Romanian, Bulgarian, Georgian, Albanian, and the Greek Orthodox Churches. Worldwide, there are approximately 225 million Orthodox Christians. Within Russia, the ROC is the dominant church, though there are adherents of most—if not all—of the other branches of Eastern Orthodoxy. Orthodox Christianity, alongside **Islam**, **Judaism**, and **Buddhism**, is recognized as one of the native **religions** of the Russian Federation, and enjoys the status of *primus inter pares* in relation to these other faiths. Following the rise of **Vladimir Putin**, there has been an increase in the role Russian Orthodoxy plays in **education** and public life in Russia. However, despite a rise in the **political** status of the religion, many Russians continue to declare **atheism**.

ORYOL OBLAST. An administrative region of the Russian Federation. Oryol is a small, particularly riverine **oblast** in the Central **Economic Region** and **Federal District**. Seventieth in size among federal subjects, the region covers an area of 24,700 square kilometers and has a population of 860,000. It is bordered by the **Bryansk**, **Kaluga**, **Tula**, **Lipetsk**, and **Kursk** oblasts. At its closest point, the oblast is less than 60 kilometers from the **Ukrainian** border. Its geography is dominated by **steppe** and forest steppe, and it is part of the **chernozem** belt of European Russia.

The regional **economy** is balanced between **agriculture** and heavy **industry**. The oblast is a center of milk production for European Russia, as well as an exporter of sugar beets, potatoes, and grains. Post–World War II reindustrialization endowed the region with steel-rolling plants and other large factories. Instrument making, metallurgy, **food** processing, and light **industry** are major sources of employment. There are significant, but undeveloped iron ore deposits in the region, which is part of the Kursk Magnetic Anomaly. Much of the oblast's energy needs are met by **nuclear energy** plants in neighboring regions. Along with its western neighbors, the oblast continues to suffer the effects of the **Chernobyl disaster**, including high levels of thyroid diseases among the population.

Oryol supported **Communist Party of the Russian Federation** (KPRF) candidates during the 1990s, making it a dependable **Red Belt** region (the region is home to KPRF leader **Gennady Zyuganov**). In the wake of the **constitutional crisis of 1993**, the KPRF governor was dismissed and replaced by **Yeltsin** appointee Nikolay Yudin. He was quickly unseated by Yegor Stroyev, a former member of the Soviet Politburo; Stroyev advocated a statist approach to economic reform based on the model employed by the People's Republic of **China**. During much of his governorship, Stroyev held a senior position within the **Federation Council** until he was forced to step down from national office due to new legislation. Despite his leadership of the oblast, Stroyev was a vehement critic of power-sharing agreements between Moscow and its **federal subjects**. After several reelections, including one in 2001 where Stroyev won 90 percent of the vote, **Vladimir Putin** reappointed the governor in 2005.

As early as 2000, Stroyev publicly endorsed Putin's plans to create a **vertical of power** within the Russian Federation after having urged Yeltsin to step down in 1999; he was later elected to an executive position with the pro-Putin **United Russia** party. Stroyev maintained an international profile by meeting with heads of state from **Finland**, Nigeria, Romania, and other countries. In early 2009, he stepped down along with several other regional executives; President **Dmitry Medvyedev** appointed Aleksandr Kozlov to replace him.

OSSETIAN-INGUSH CONFLICT (1991–1992). Poor relations between the **Orthodox**, Indo-European **Ossetians** and the Caucasian **Muslim Ingush** date back centuries; however, recent disputes are the outgrowth of **Joseph Stalin**'s deportation of the Ingush to **Central Asia** during World War II (1939–1945). Upon the rehabilitation and return to the ethnic homelands in the **North Caucasus**, many Ingush found themselves spatially and **economically** displaced by Ossetian settlers. The depopulation of the Prigorodny District of the Checheno-Ingush **Autonomous Soviet Socialist Republic** and its transfer to **North Ossetiya** was also a major issue in interethnic relations. Post-Soviet reforms provided the displaced Ingush with legal grounds to attempt to reclaim the region just as North Ossetiya was absorbing large numbers of their co-nationals fleeing the **Georgia–South Ossetia** conflict (1991–1992).

In an environment where weapons were readily available, the dispute between the Ingush and Ossetians soon turned violent. In November 1992, open warfare broke out, requiring the deployment of Russian **peacekeepers**. More than 500 died in the skirmishes, with tens of thousands of people displaced. Moscow's apparent support of the Christian Ossetians riled many Caucasian Muslims in the region, making North Ossetiya a target for **Islamist** terror attacks. The **Beslan** hostage crisis, which targeted Ossetian schoolchildren, reopened communal prejudices in the region when it was discovered that a majority of the hostage takers were ethnic Ingush.

OSSETIANS. Ethnic group. An Indo-Iranian group of the **Caucasus Mountains**, the Ossetians are divided between Russia's **North Ossetiya-Alaniya** and the **Georgian** breakaway republic of **South Ossetia**. Ossetians, or Ossetes, self-declare as Iristi or *Iræ ttæ*, and descend from the Sarmatian Alans. Their ancestral **language** is the last surviving member of the northeastern family of Iranian languages, which also include Persian, Pashto, and Kurdish; it employs a Cyrillic orthography. Most Ossetians in the Russian Federation use the **Russian language** as a lingua franca, while those in South Ossetia use Georgian in their everyday activities. They are predominantly Eastern **Orthodox**; however, a significant number are **Muslims**, especially among the Digor subgroup. In total, they number 725,000, of which more than a half-million reside in the Russian Federation.

The Ossetians, who were favored by tsarist as well as Communist authorities, benefited from World War II–era deportations of their Muslim neighbors; subsequent historical disputes with the **Ingush** have triggered **ethnic violence** since 1991. Attempts by authorities in North Ossetiya and South Ossetia to unify have been a major source of friction between Moscow and Tbilisi. *See also* CHECHNYA; IRAN; SOUTH OSSETIAN WAR.

OTHER RUSSIA, THE. Political organization. An umbrella organization that includes a variety of liberal and extreme right-wing **political parties** and organizations, The Other Russia (*Drugaia Rossiia*) emerged in the late **Putin** administration, calling itself a "national forum" dedicated to providing an alternative to the pro-Kremlin parties. The group's most well-known personalities include **Garry Kasparov**, **Mikhail Kasyanov**, and **Eduard Limonov**. The Other Russia rose to national prominence as the organizer of the 2007 **Dissenters' March**. The coalition operates a website in English, where it collects donations from abroad. Both The Other Russia and its leaders have been criticized by the Kremlin for being a "fifth column" for Western control of the country. *See also* POLITICS.

OUR HOME—RUSSIA (NDR). Political party. Known in Russian as *Nash Dom—Rossiia*, the NDR operated during the second half of the 1990s. The pro-**Yeltsin** party was founded by then–Prime Minister **Viktor Chernomyrdin** as an economically liberal, centrist movement. In the mid-1990s, Our Home functioned as Russia's "party of power," enjoying support from the Kremlin, **oligarchs**, the **media**, and major Russian corporations, including **Lukoil** and **Gazprom**. The party platform focused on greater levels of personal freedom, expansion of private property, and better observance of the law. The NDR also supported lower **military** spending, increased **agricultural** subsidies, anti-**corruption** campaigns, and pro-family legislation. In the 1995 election to the **State Duma**, the party won 10 percent of the vote, second only to the **Communist Party of the Russian Federation**. Our Home—Russia played a central role in supporting Yeltsin's reelection during the **1996 presidential election**. The party's fortunes were closely tied to those of Chernomyrdin, and when he failed in his bid for a second term as prime minister, the NDR faltered accordingly. Yeltsin switched his support to **Unity** prior to the 1999 parliamentary elections, effectively banishing the NDR to the political wasteland.

– P –

PAMYAT. Ultranationalist **political party**. Led by Dmitry Vasilyev from 1985 until his death in 2003, the group, officially known as the Pamyat ("Memory") Patriotic Association, was once the most powerful right-wing organization in Russia. Established under **glasnost**, the organization viewed itself as a spiritual successor to the Union of Russian People, a proto-fascist mass movement that emerged in response to Russia's disastrous war with **Japan** (1904–1905). While Pamyat generally supported the Soviet state, the group was antidemocratic, opposed to **Gorbachev**'s reforms, and virulently **anti-Semitic**.

As a result of its late 1980s push for a "renaissance" of environmental awareness, spirituality, and national pride among the Russian peoples, the movement won the support of a significant number of intellectuals and members of the **Communist Party of the Soviet Union**, even holding a 1987 meeting with future Russian president **Boris Yeltsin**. In 1990, the new, even more anti-Semitic party platform declared the organization to be at war with "aggressive Zionism, Talmudic **atheism**, and cosmopolitan usury." Also that year, more violent activists under the leadership of **Aleksandr Barkashov** split off, forming the **Russian National Unity** party.

After the collapse of Soviet power in 1991, the organization abandoned its support of national Communism in favor of monarchism, as well as **pan-Slavism**. Despite its strong support of Russian **Orthodoxy**, the party's main theoretician, Valery Yemelyanov, author of the infamous *Dezionization* (1979), urged its membership to embrace **neo-paganism** and neo-Nazism, and built links with like-minded organizations. The group's influence precipitously weakened in the late 1990s as it competed with a raft of **neofascist** parties. After Vasilyev's death, the party experienced a minor revitalization and participated in the right-wing Russian March in 2006.

PAN-SLAVISM. A 19th-century politico-cultural ideology that advocated the unity of all Slavic-speaking peoples, pan-Slavism functioned as a tool of Russian influence across Central Europe and the Balkans under both the tsars and the Soviets. Since the **dissolution of the Soviet Union** in 1991, pan-Slavism has had influence in the former **Eastern Bloc** as most states have focused on membership in the **European Union** and the **North Atlantic Treaty Organization** (NATO) with some, like **Poland**, fearful of Russian intentions. Pan-Slavism was used by certain Russian politicians, particularly those at the extreme right and left of the political spectrum, to advocate anti-Western policies during the breakup of Yugoslavia and the NATO bombing campaign against **Serbia**. Pan-Slavism has also been invoked as a rationale for the exceptionally close relations between the Russian Federation and **Belarus**, and for continued Russian involvement in the internal affairs of **Ukraine**. In a modified form, pan-Slavism is also employed by **Eurasianist** ideologues who stretch the meaning of the concept beyond its ethnic and etymological roots to embrace all Russophone peoples of the former Soviet Union. *See also* NATIONAL IDENTITY; RUSSIAN LANGUAGE.

PAN-TURKISM. Originally a religious and cultural project of Volga and Crimean **Tatars** against **Russification**, pan-Turkism expanded beyond the **Romanov** Empire in the late 19th and early 20th centuries. The movement was loosely linked to Jadidism, a modernizing reform movement within **Islam**. During World War I (1914–1918), elements within the Ottoman Empire advocated pan-Turkism across **Central Asia**, the **Caucasus**, and southern Russia in an attempt to turn the Turkic peoples against **St. Petersburg**. Under **Joseph Stalin**, pan-Turkism was targeted as a dangerous ideology and its supporters were ruthlessly purged. In the wake of the **dissolution of the Soviet Union**, pan-Turkism experienced a modest rival in the Russian Federation, **Azerbaijan**, and Central Asia. Tatars, **Bashkirs**, **Chuvash**, **Tuvans**, **Khakhas**, **Altays**, **Sakha**, and the Turkic peoples of the **North Caucasus** and the Central Asian republics began to reembrace their common cultural and linguistic heritage. During the early 1990s, **Turkey** actively supported such informal initiatives, often with the backing of the **United States**, which hoped to mitigate influences from Saudi Arabia, **Iran**, and Pakistan. However, Turkey's financial crisis at the end of the decade weakened its ability to promote such transnational cultural projects. Today, support for pan-Turkism remains tepid as many Russian Turkics resent the Tatars' dominant position in terms of both **culture** and **language** across the Russian Federation. **Tatarstan**'s failed effort to convert to the Latin alphabet was viewed as a linguistic manifestation of pan-Turkism, as it would have allowed greater communication with speakers of Turkish, Azeri, and Uzbek, who all now employ a similar script.

PARTNERSHIP FOR PEACE (PfP). A security partnership operated by the **North Atlantic Treaty Organization** (NATO), the Partnership for Peace aims to create military-to-military cooperation, trust, and good relations between the **United States**, **Canada**, Europe, and the former Soviet republics. Launched in 1993, the PfP currently includes all members of the **Commonwealth of Independent States**, **Serbia**, Macedonia, Bosnia and Herzegovina, and the traditionally neutral states of Western Europe (Ireland, Austria, Malta, Switzerland, Sweden, and **Finland**). A number of former members—including the **Baltic States**—later joined NATO. During the 1990s, Russia's relationship with the PfP was ambiguous: on the one hand, membership was supported by the country's **Atlanticists**, who saw it as a first step to eventual NATO membership, while on the other, Moscow viewed Washington's budding military relations with the former **Eastern Bloc** and the **Newly Independent States** with suspicion, and the prospect of an alliance with Washington was viewed with derision by the nationalists and Communists. NATO's eastward expansion effectively marginalized the pro-Western voices within Russia, turning much of Russia's political elite against cooperation. However, Russia signed the PfP Status of Forces Agreement in 2004, and it was ratified by parliament in 2007. The relationship has served as a mechanism for Russia's assistance to NATO in its operations in **Afghanistan**.

PEACEKEEPING. Following the **dissolution of the Soviet Union** in 1991, the Russian military remained ensconced in a number of conflict zones across post-Soviet space. While Russia no longer had the legal right to intervene in the security of its neighbors, **Boris Yeltsin**, under the umbrella of the **Commonwealth of Independent States**, developed a robust system of peacekeeping operations, allowing Russia to maintain security and protect its interests in **Tajikistan, Transnistria, Abkhazia, South Ossetia**, and **Nagorno-Karabakh**. (A Russian contingent was also sent to **Kosovo** during the late 1990s, and Russia has participated in **United Nations** peacekeeping operations in other locations.) In most cases, the majority of troops (usually in excess of 1,000 in each conflict zone) are not Russian citizens but are under the command of Russian officers. Such personnel became integral to the so-called **Monroeski Doctrine** of the 1990s, which posited a "special role" for Russia in **Central Asia**, the **Caucasus**, and other parts of the **near abroad**.

International observers leveled regular criticism against Russian peacekeepers for actively and passively supporting one side against another in regional conflicts, including providing logistical support, **arms**, and/or intelligence. Furthermore, the peacekeepers have often been found to be ignoring abductions, murders, and arms trafficking, which they are charged with fighting in conflict zones. In the summer of 2008, Russian peacekeepers in South Ossetia came under fire from **Georgian** forces attempting to reclaim the province. This event served as a pretext for the Russian invasion of Georgia and the wider **South Ossetian War**.

PENZA OBLAST. An administrative region of the Russian Federation. Located within the Volga **Federal District** and **Economic Region**, Penza occupies 43,200 square kilometers of territory in the Volga uplands. It has a population of 1.4 million, 86 percent of whom are **ethnic Russians**, with a significant minority of **Tatars** and **Mordvins**. Its neighbors include the **Republic of Mordoviya, Ryazan, Ulyanovsk, Saratov**, and **Tambov**. The regional capital, which sits on the Sura River, is a major transit hub for Russia and the **Commonwealth of Independent States**. The **economy** is driven by **agriculture** (grains, vegetables, and livestock), engineering, woodworking, and light **industry**. Part of the **Red Belt**, voters supported Communist candidates in the early 1990s. In 1998, Vasily Bochkarev was elected on a platform of pragmatic reform; he was reelected in 2002, narrowly defeating his Communist opponent. **Vladimir Putin** reappointed Bochkarev in 2005. He has signed deals with **Gazprom**

and **Lukoil** to support the region with energy and maintained an international profile with visits abroad, including a trip to **Great Britain** to lure English farmers to the region. In the wake of **Dmitry Medvyedev**'s recognition of the independence of **South Ossetia** and **Abkhazia**, he moved to establish economic relations with the breakaway Georgian republics in 2008.

PEOPLE'S UNION. Political party. Known in Russian as *Narodnyi Soiuz*, the People's Union is a nationalist party with a strong conservative orientation. Veteran politician **Sergey Baburin** founded the party in 2001 as the People's Will; the party changed its name after incorporating more than a dozen **Orthodox Christian** groups in 2007. While the party was closely allied with **Rodina**, it chose not to become part of **Fair Russia**. The party has established contacts with other nationalist parties across Europe, and includes **Aleksandr Rutskoy** among its members. Failing to meet the requirements for participation in the 2007 **State Duma** elections, the party backed the **Communist Party of the Russian Federation**.

PERESTROIKA. Originally rendered as "restructuring" to convey the meaning of the word in Russian, the term "perestroika" was eventually adopted into the English language. Perestroika, put forth at the 27th Congress of the **Communist Party of the Soviet Union** (CPSU) in 1986, formed the central plank of **Mikhail Gorbachev**'s multivariate reform policy of the late 1980s. The original goal of Gorbachev's restructuring was to introduce "acceleration" (*uskoreniie*), efficiency in production and management, mass initiative, and entrepreneurialism into the Soviet **economy**, which was stagnating after the drop of **oil** prices in the early 1980s.

Hoping to catch up with (or overcome) the West, Gorbachev introduced reforms that were meant to move the Soviet economy away from its overreliance on heavy **industry** and **military** spending, and toward light industry, information, and finance. Gorbachev used Leninist framing to market the plan to the masses, calling perestroika the uniting of socialism with **democracy**. However, such a massive transformation required significant political change and the removal of **corruption** within the quasi-totalitarian state. Realizing that perestroika was doomed to fail without self-criticism and new voices, the comparatively young Gorbachev eventually introduced two other policies, **glasnost** and **democratization**, which proved highly controversial with the CPSU old guard.

In 1988, Gorbachev emerged victorious in a power struggle with the entrenched *nomenklatura* and antireform contingent, allowing him to deepen and broaden perestroika. Perestroika attacked the command-and-control system of state capitalism, which had been the bedrock of the Soviet economy since the time of **Joseph Stalin**. Limited forms of private ownership were introduced through the Law on the Cooperatives in 1987, and **foreign trade** and **foreign investment** were courted. Gorbachev took his campaign directly to the Soviet people that same year with his book *Perestroika: New Thinking for Our Country and the World*. The reforms ultimately resulted in chaos, however, as tax revenues decreased (particularly during the anti-**alcoholism** campaign) as the government tried to maintain price controls.

The situation was made worse by the fact that the Soviet Union suffered from a shortage economy during the 1980s, which resulted in rationing and a brisk trade in black market goods, particularly in the consumer sector. However, by the end of the 1980s, the situation extended to foodstuffs as well. Furthermore, Soviet **media** played a crucial role by publishing truthful materials about the atrocities of the Soviet regime. Overall, perestroika was viewed as a historical necessity for the Union of Soviet Socialist Republics (USSR); however, many historians have compared the situation to **China**'s late-1970s economic reforms, suggesting that the combination of unpredictable economic and political reforms ultimately led to the **dissolution of the Soviet Union**.

PERM KRAI. An administrative province of the Russian Federation. Perm Krai came into existence on 1 December 2005 as a result of a 2004 referendum in the former Perm Oblast and **Permyakiya** on merging the two **federal subjects**. The province is bordered by **Kirov**, **Sverdlovsk**, **Chelyabinsk**, **Bashkortostan**, **Udmurtiya**, and the **Komi Republic**. It is part of the Volga **Federal District** and the Urals **Economic Region**. It covers 160,600 square kilometers of territory, and has a population of slightly less than 3 million.

Ethnic Russians make up a majority (83 percent), with minority communities of **Tatars** (5 percent), **Komi** (4 percent), and other nationalities also comprising the population. Perm is known both for its artistic traditions, particularly **ballet**, and as a gateway to the **gulag** (Perm-36 was one of the Soviet Union's most infamous detention facilities). Situated on the western slopes of the **Urals** with a population in excess of 1 million, the regional capital, Perm, is considered to be the easternmost city on the European continent. Known as Molotov during the late **Stalin** era, the city was restricted to foreigners until 1989.

The region is heavily industrialized, focusing on artillery, ship-building, aviation, and chemicals. Other sectors include coal, petro-leum, **natural gas**, and forestry. The province is attractive to **foreign investors** and enjoys a good number of small businesses. The province is bisected by the Kama River, which enables shipping to ports on the **Baltic**, **Black** and **Caspian** seas without off-loading. In 2000, Perm's mayor, Yury Trutnev, won election as the regional governor; he quickly announced plans to merge the oblast with the **autonomous okrug** of Permyakiya. In 2004, **Vladimir Putin** appointed economist Oleg Chirkunov as acting governor, with Trutnev taking the position of minister of natural resources of the Russian Federation. Chirnokov was confirmed as the governor of the **krai** in 2005 after the merger; he is touted as Russia's most **Internet**-savvy governor.

PERM OBLAST. *See* PERM KRAI.

PERMYAKIYA. Formerly known as the Komi-Permyak **Autono-mous Okrug** (AOk) within the Perm Oblast, Permyakiya was down-graded to an **okrug** of the newly constituted **Perm Krai** in 2005. The 2002 census recorded a population of 147,800, of which a majority was Komi-Permyaks (60 percent). Permyakiya served as one of two ethnic homelands for the **Komi**, the other being the **Komi Republic**. **Ethnic Russians** comprise slightly more than one-third of the terri-tory's population. The district's administrative center is Kudymkar, a city of 31,000; barely one-quarter of the population resides in urban areas. With few paved roads, almost no small businesses, and little **industry**, the okrug is one of the poorest and most underdeveloped regions in European Russia; much of the population still depends on small-scale farming, animal husbandry, and hunting. Permyakiya is heavily dependent on federal subsidies, though these have been reduced in the wake of its subordination to Perm. In 1996, the AOk signed a treaty with Moscow delimiting respective powers in the territory. Beginning in 1999, a movement to abolish Permyakiya's autonomous status began to gain steam, reversing the post-1993 trend that saw the autonomous okrug and its "host," the Perm Oblast, drifting apart. This came to pass under the new leadership of Gennady Savelyev, who supported **Vladimir Putin**'s goal of simplifying the federal structure of Russia. The results of the plebiscite in 2004 showed 83 percent of the electorate supporting unification of the AOk with Perm.

POLAND (RELATIONS WITH). Polish-Russian relations remain mired in four critical historical events: the partitions of the Polish-Lithuanian Commonwealth (1772–1795); the Molotov-Ribbentrop Pact (1939); the Katyń Massacre (1940), and the Red Army's failure to intervene in the Warsaw Uprising (1944). With the inclusion of a Communist Poland in the **Eastern Bloc**, discussion of these and other fractious issues was stanched until the 1980s.

With the relegalization of the *Solidarność* (Solidarity) movement in 1989, Poland moved toward ending its subordinated relationship with Moscow, culminating in the dissolution of the **Warsaw Pact** in 1991. With the emergence of a genuinely independent Poland, bilateral relations remained frosty, particularly given post-Soviet Russia's reticence to address World War II–era issues related to Poland. As part of the Visegrád group of east-central European countries, Poland moved quickly to improve relations with the **United States** and Western Europe, culminating in admission to the **North Atlantic Treaty Organization** (NATO) in 1999 and the **European Union** (EU) in 2004.

The rapidity of Warsaw's embrace of the West unnerved many politicians in Russia; Poland's new orientation, however, inspired ordinary citizens, especially entrepreneurs who regularly traveled to Poland to import commodities for resale in Russia and witnessed the country's economic and social changes on the grassroots level. Russian elites condemned Poland for failing to recognize Soviet munificence during the **Cold War**, particularly in relation to Moscow's support for the westward shift of Polish borders, economic subsidies, and the country's status as the "freest barrack in the socialist camp."

The Russian Federation has also condemned the establishment of **Chechen** information centers in Poland as well as Warsaw's active support of opposition (and generally anti-Russian) movements in **Ukraine** and **Belarus**. Many Russians view this so-called Eastern Partnership as an effort by Warsaw to restore its domination over the territories that once comprised the *Rzeczpospolita* (the late medieval Commonwealth). Warsaw's support for the various **color revolutions** sparked a Russian embargo on certain agricultural products in 2005. Despite the row, bilateral **foreign trade** is robust at more than $20 billion per year, and Poles invested more than $350 million into the Russian **economy** in 2007 alone.

Under the presidency of Aleksander Kwaśniewski (1995–2005), Poland pursued an ever closer relationship with the **United States**, including assuming a major role in the U.S.-led invasion of Iraq, despite strong Russian diplomatic efforts to avoid war in the **Middle East**. Kwaśniewski also made public his strong desire for Ukrainian admission to NATO, against the explicit wishes of the Kremlin. Poland has been particularly critical of Moscow's heavy-handed energy policies vis-à-vis its **near abroad** (particularly Belarus, Ukraine, and **Georgia**). Acting in concert with the **Baltic States**, Poland has lobbied the EU against agreeing to an undersea route for **oil** and **natural gas** from the Gulf of Finland to **Germany** as such a route would jeopardize "new Europe's" energy provision and make the region more susceptible to Russian neo-imperialism. If the plans for the **Baltic Sea** route are realized, Poland stands to lose millions in transit revenue. With Poland and **Lithuania**'s admission to the Schengen visa-free zone, the issue of the **Kaliningrad** exclave has also colored bilateral relations with Russia, and special exceptions were made for residents of this **oblast**.

In 2005, relations hit a nadir with assaults on Polish diplomats in retaliation for the mugging of several Russian youths — themselves children of diplomatic personnel — in Warsaw. The latter event did not seem politically motivated; however, **Vladimir Putin** and other members of Russia's political elite seized on the robberies as if they were. The atmosphere between the two countries had already been poisoned by Putin's refusal to apologize for any actions conducted by the Union of Soviet Socialist Republics (USSR) in the lead-up to the 60th anniversary of the end of World War II in 2005 (by contrast,

Boris Yeltsin visited the Katyń site but did not issue a state apology for Soviet misdeeds). The relationship was further harmed by the announcement in 2008 that Poland had agreed to host a portion of Washington's missile defense shield, including interceptor missiles. Russia proposed moving the site to **Azerbaijan**; however, this option was rejected by **George W. Bush**, triggering a hostile stance by Moscow including veiled threats of **military** action against Poland. Since his election, **Barack Obama** has slowed the deployment process, and given the post-Kwaśniewski Polish leadership's reticence, it is unclear if the program will be completed.

POLICE. *See* SECURITY SERVICES.

POLITICAL PARTIES. Owing to the country's seven decades as a one-party totalitarian state, the status of political parties in Russia is complex and protean. In 1990, the **Communist Party of the Soviet Union** (CPSU) abandoned its monopoly on political representation, opening the door to opposition parties in the Soviet Union. The domain that experienced the most rapid growth was nationalist parties; in each of the non-Russian **union republics** and some of Russia's **ethnic republics**, the lifting of the ban on opposition parties resulted in a flurry of ethnically oriented political organizations, many of which had been previously established as cultural organizations. Other parties such as Democratic Russia, the Green Alternative, and the Ukrainian Beer Lovers' Party were also founded during this period.

The **dissolution of the Soviet Union** in late 1991 disrupted the embryonic multiparty system in Russia. The inherent weakness of Russia's **civil society** and comparative lack of economic factors reflecting real social divisions amongst the masses provided few bases on which to develop political platforms in such a short period of time. In the political vacuum, the old Soviet *nomenklatura* were rather effective in maintaining their status as political elites, though they rebranded themselves for the rapidly evolving system. **Boris Yeltsin**, who was elected as the Russian Federation's first president, was able to build a personal power base that did not rely on political parties. Following Yeltsin's example, other prominent political figures used weak pseudoparties to advance their own political agendas during the first two years of independence.

During this period, avidly pro-democratic parties were critically undermined by infiltration by the **KGB**. Yeltsin's simmering rivalry with members of Russia's parliament boiled over during the **constitutional crisis of 1993**, sending further shocks through the anemic protoparties of the Russian Federation. Out of the chaos, Yeltsin's reforms provided some impetus for the development of a stronger, more coherent party system, though many political analysts argue that the changes actually weakened party **politics**. The new system for electing the 450 **State Duma** members, introduced in late 1993, was evenly split between a party list system of proportional representation and a single-member system that precluded the listing of the political party of the candidate on the ballot.

Much to the president's chagrin, this reorganization significantly aided **Vladimir Zhirinovsky**'s ultranationalist **Liberal Democratic Party of Russia** (LDPR), originally formed in 1989, and **Gennady Zyuganov**'s newly constituted **Communist Party of the Russian Federation** (KPRF). In the party list poll, the LDPR, which finished first, won 23 percent of the vote in elections for the new Duma, while the KPRF ranked third, taking 12.4 percent of the vote. **Yegor Gaydar**'s pro-Yeltsin Democratic Choice of Russia placed second, with 15.5 percent of the vote; in terms of single constituencies, the party placed first, winning 24 single constituencies. The **Agrarian Party of Russia**, which genuinely represented the interests of a well-defined constituency, namely farmers, also performed well. In the subsequent period, the use of political parties as fronts for individual political aspiration grew, resulting in the evolution of "parties of convenience."

Yeltsin unsuccessfully attempted to impose a two-party system from above through the creation of **Viktor Chernomyrdin**'s **Our Home—Russia** (NDR) and a competing loyal opposition party led by Ivan Rybkin, further fragmenting the political party system. In the 1995 Duma elections, the KPRF emerged as the most popular party, outpacing the NDR by more than two to one and capturing 157 seats. The liberal **Yabloko** party also did well. Four years later, electoral reform made it more difficult for small parties to contest for the election, due to imposed monetary requirements of the one-year advance registration. The KPRF narrowly edged out the pro-government **Unity** (*Iedinstvo*) party, which, along with third-place finisher

Fatherland—All Russia, was formed exclusively for the elections. The **Union of Right Forces**, formed out of the Democratic Choice of Russia, placed fourth.

With the rise of **Vladimir Putin**, the steady growth of the KPRF was reversed, and in the 2003 parliamentary elections, the pro-Kremlin **United Russia**, which was formed in 2001 as a merger of Unity and Fatherland—All Russia, captured 37.5 percent of the vote. The Communists finished a disappointing second with only 12.6 percent, while Zhirinovsky's LDPR won a respectable 11.5 percent of the vote. Liberal parties fared poorly, losing most of their seats in the Duma. In 2007, Putin instituted reforms making the elections by party list only, resulting in a further diminution of the number of political parties in the Russian Federation. Backed by a pliant **media** and enjoying support from regional governors fearful of losing their seats under the new system of presidential appointment that was established by the 2004–2005 **electoral reforms**, United Russia, as expected, took first place with a commanding 64 percent of the vote.

Putin, in an attempt to maintain power, put himself on the United Russia ballot in preparation for assuming the office of prime minister in 2008. The cowed KPRF and the now pro-Kremlin LDPR generally held their positions, while a new "working man's" party, **Fair Russia**, took fourth place. The parliamentary elections were criticized within and outside Russia as a carefully orchestrated vote of confidence in Putin's leadership and totally lacking in genuine political competition. Marginal political figures like **Garry Kasparov** and radical groups like the **National Bolshevik Party**, which were barred from standing for office, represented the only anti-Putin voices in the campaign.

With the ascendency of **Dmitry Medvyedev**, United Russia, now under Prime Minister Putin's leadership, gave its full support to the new president. While the KPRF has enjoyed some level of political rehabilitation with the 2008–2009 **global financial crisis**, most political parties in Russia have been thoroughly sapped of influence, while the pro-government "party of power" continues to dominate the parliament. However, United Russia no longer acts as a rubber stamp for the president due to Putin's dramatic increase in the power of the premiership since 2008. *See also* EURASIA PARTY; ORGANIZATION FOR SECURITY AND CO-OPERATION IN

EUROPE; OTHER RUSSIA, THE; PAMYAT; RODINA; RUS-
SIAN ECOLOGICAL PARTY; RUSSIAN PENSIONERS' PARTY;
SOCIAL DEMOCRATIC PARTY OF RUSSIA; UNION OF RIGHT
FORCES.

POLITICS. Historically, Russian politics has been shaped by those
close to the head of state, whether the tsar, the general secretary of
the **Communist Party of the Soviet Union** (CPSU), or the president. During the late Soviet period, the Union of Soviet Socialist
Republics' (USSR) governing ideology of **Marxism-Leninism** and
the utter dominance of the CPSU over all aspects of society began
to wane.

Recognizing the difficulties of the Soviet system without the benefit of the high **oil** prices that had characterized the long rule of **Leonid
Brezhnev**, the CPSU's idealistic new leader, **Mikhail Gorbachev**,
instituted a series of reforms under the title of **perestroika** (restructuring). His ultimate goal was the acceleration (*uskoreniie*) of the
Soviet **economy** so that it would be able to compete with the industrialized nations of the so-called First World, particularly the **United
States**, **Germany**, and **Japan**. In order to achieve this restructuring,
Gorbachev was forced to open up the political structure of the Soviet
system, which had stagnated over the previous decades.

Soviet one-party rule, mild totalitarianism, and the state's suffocation of **civil society** had bred a generation afflicted by political apathy. In order to stimulate the change he desired, Gorbachev
instituted a new era of **glasnost** (transparency) into all aspects of
the Soviet bureaucracy, government, and society. The press began
to actively investigate and criticize the state, and **media** freedoms
increased greatly during this period. Such reforms, however, were
not welcomed by many political elites. The membership of the CPSU
enjoyed substantially better living standards than the masses, and the
apparatchik system guaranteed employment to the politically well-
connected, regardless of talent. Despite opposition from within the
party, Gorbachev's experiment in economic and political liberalization continued throughout the late 1980s.

In 1987, Gorbachev moved forward on his boldest plan, the introduction of **democratization** (*demokratizatsiia*) of the one-party
system. While opposition **political parties** were not permitted until

late 1990, democratization did allow for competitive elections to take place, with multiple candidates on the same ballot. For the first time since 1918, Russians had a genuine choice in the selection of their leaders. During this period, Gorbachev went over the heads of the CPSU "old guard" in the Politburo and directly to the people, triggering a new interest in political life among the Soviet citizens.

Cultural and social organizations began to flourish without the support of the state or the Party. In the **Russian Soviet Federative Socialist Republic**'s (RSFSR) **Autonomous Soviet Socialist Republics** (ASSRs) and the **union republics**, nationalist politicians—still operating as nominal Communists—began to gain ground against the *nomenklatura*. Political developments in the **Eastern Bloc** kept pace with the USSR's reforms, and by 1989, Gorbachev, preoccupied with **ethnic violence** in **Nagorno-Karabakh** and other parts of the **Caucasus**, signaled the Kremlin's intent to let the Soviet satellites abandon one-party rule. **Poland**, Czechoslovakia, Hungary, and other **Warsaw Pact** allies of the USSR moved quickly to institute free elections and dismantle the Communist Party's monopoly on power. The "loss" of the Soviet empire proved deeply unpopular among the old-guard politicians, the **security services**, and certain members of the **military** elite. More troubling to these centers of political influence, however, was the increasing centrifugal forces within the USSR.

The **Baltic States** and **Georgia** took their lead from the new democracies of Eastern Europe and began to move toward ultimate secession from the Soviet Union. By the 28th Party Congress in July 1990, the Soviet political system was in a state of rapid flux. Nationalist and liberal elements within the **Supreme Soviet** of the RSFSR, led by the ex-Communist **Boris Yeltsin**, had undermined the authority of the CPSU. Under Yeltsin's guidance, Russian institutions were strengthened at the expense of Soviet ones, including the federation's vast natural resources. Yeltsin rode a wave of support based on the idea of "Russia for the Russians," which condemned decades of subsidies to the country's "internal empire" (the 14 other union republics) and its "external empire" (the Eastern Bloc, **Mongolia**, **Cuba**, Vietnam, etc.).

In 1991, the CPSU was stripped of its central role in the government of the Soviet Union, and a host of opposition parties clamored for influence in the newly democratic country. Gorbachev, meanwhile, had relocated his base of political power out of the CPSU and assumed the presidency of the USSR. He was unable, however, to stop the unraveling of the union, and by the summer, it was readily apparent that the Baltic States (and perhaps Georgia, **Moldova**, and **Armenia** as well) were lost. In an effort to preserve what remained of the Soviet Union, Gorbachev called for the establishment of a Union of Soviet Sovereign Republics (later the Union of Sovereign States) that would allow for legal secession of its constituent members under certain conditions, thus abrogating the 1922 treaty of union.

The signing of the proposed **New Union Treaty** by members of the RSFSR government triggered the ill-planned **August Coup**. Disaffected members of the old guard and the **KGB** detained Gorbachev in his **Crimean dacha** while they tried to reverse democratization and reintegrate the secessionist republics. Yeltsin, however, rallied popular elements and won over key members of the military, crushing the putsch. Events moved quickly in the autumn, with the center of political gravity shifting to Yeltsin, with Gorbachev being marginalized. In December, Yeltsin and the leaders of **Ukraine** and **Belarus** effectively dismantled the USSR with the **Belavezha Accords**. The formal **dissolution of the Soviet Union** occurred later that month in Alma-Ata, **Kazakhstan**, as the Soviet successor states (excluding the Baltics) joined the new **Commonwealth of Independent States**, an organization that allowed Russia to maintain some level of control over its so-called **near abroad**.

After a brief honeymoon period in early 1992, Russia transitioned into a turbulent period in its domestic politics as competition between the executive branch, headed by President Yeltsin, and the legislative branch, which consisted of the **Congress of People's Deputies** and the Supreme Soviet of the Russian Federation, raged. The principal dispute was over the limits of presidential power, which were ambiguous given the limited applicability of the 1977 constitution to the Russian Federation. Yeltsin's powers had been beefed up in the wake of the August Coup; however, the legislature steadily stripped these new powers away over the next two years. The president's failure to secure the election of his prime ministerial appointee, **Yegor Gaydar**, further poisoned relations with the legislature, which was growing increasingly nationalistic and conservative.

In 1993, tensions continued to rise over power sharing and the drafting of the new constitution. During this period, known as the **constitutional crisis**, **Ruslan Khasbulatov** and **Aleksandr Rutskoy** emerged as Yeltsin's most vociferous critics in the parliament. Confident of public support, Yeltsin ultimately used military force against the legislature. The anti-Yeltsin forces were arrested, the parliament dissolved, and the new **constitution** pushed through. In the wake of the crisis, the Russian political system was substantially recrafted. Claiming that Russians preferred a strong hand and a **vertical of power**, Yeltsin preserved the post of prime minister, retaining the greater share of powers. The legislature was shortly reconstituted as the **Federal Assembly of Russia**, divided between the upper house, known as the **Federation Council**, and the lower house, or **State Duma**.

In an attempt to buy off allies in the provinces during this period, Yeltsin instituted a policy of **asymmetrical federalism** for Russia's regions, particularly the **ethnic republics**. This radically shifted the balance of power away from the center, turning Russia into a genuine federation while simultaneously gifting the regional governors with extraordinary powers; rent seeking and rampant **corruption** soon followed. Yeltsin was unable to buy off the **Chechens**, however, and launched the first **Chechen War**. What had promised to be a quick public relations victory turned into a bloody civil war tinged with growing **Islamist** radicalism. Simmering discontent with Yeltsin translated into strong support for the ultranationalist **Liberal Democratic Party of Russia** (LDPR) and the newly formed **Communist Party of the Russian Federation** (KPRF). Over the next few election cycles, Yeltsin orchestrated "parties of power" to buttress his support in the Duma and the Federation Council; however, the extreme right- and left-wing parties continued to win a significant percentage of the electorate in parliamentary elections.

During the **1996 presidential election**, Yeltsin faced down impossible odds to keep his post. His alliance of convenience with the media and the **oligarchs** is seen as having negative impacts for the country's nascent **democracy** despite having preserved it in the face of an almost guaranteed Communist victory. Clearly weakened by his unpopularity, Yeltsin placated conservative and patriotic elements in the country during his second administration. **Yevgeny**

Primakov, appointed as foreign minister (1996–1998) and prime minister (1998–1999) in the aftermath of the **ruble crisis**, reversed the country's **Atlanticist** orientation in **foreign relations**, opting instead for a **Eurasianist** approach combined with contestation of American hegemony of the world system. During this period, eastward expansion of the **North Atlantic Treaty Organization** (NATO) and the war in **Serbia** turned Russian domestic opinion against the United States and Western European nations, while the ruble crisis soured Russians on **globalization**, free markets, and financial reform.

In ill health and fabulously unpopular, Yeltsin orchestrated the rise of the hitherto-unknown KGB agent and St. Petersburger **Vladimir Putin** through his appointment as prime minister. Putin's hard line on the second Chechen War and strong distinctions from Yeltsin in terms of fitness and youth won over enough of the electorate to give him the presidency. After a rocky start marred by the *Kursk* **submarine disaster**, Putin began to gain popularity. In the wake of the **September 11 attacks**, he gained international support for his crackdown on Chechen **terrorism**, though Russia would suffer scores of deaths over the next four years culminating in the **Beslan** hostage crisis.

From the very beginning of his administration, Putin expressed a desire to truly implement the vertical of power, and used every opportunity to reduce asymmetrical federalism including enacting a presidential appointment system for regional governors. He also reduced the influence of the powerful oligarchs, allowing them to keep their fortunes as long as they refrained from politics; **Boris Berezovsky** and **Mikhail Khodorkovsky** failed to observe the "new rules" of the game and were forced into exile and imprisoned, respectively. Putin carefully orchestrated Russia's political party system to ensure a pliable Duma, while using appointments and political favors to weaken the KPRF and the LDPR. His two administrations were defined by a sharp rise in oil and **natural gas** prices, resulting in a buoyant Russian economy and a return to great-power (*derzhava*) status. Meanwhile, he curtailed media freedoms, undermined civil society, and increased the influence of *siloviki* within the government and **industry**, prompting criticism at home and abroad.

Steadfast in his commitment to serve only the constitutionally mandated two terms, Putin oversaw the transfer of some presidential power to the office of the prime minister before stepping down to take up the premiership as the leader of the **United Russia** party in 2008. His hand-picked successor, **Dmitry Medvyedev**, has done little to deviate from the path set by Putin, though some signs demonstrate a growing rift between the old and new presidents, particularly given Putin's ever-growing portfolio as the new prime minister.

Generally speaking, most Russians disdain politics, the result of decades of the Soviet monopolization of power, followed by Yeltsin-era "politricks" and Putin's creeping authoritarianism. Since 1991, the country's anemic civil society, cowed media, and debilitating economic transition have done little to improve this attitude.

POLITKOVSKAYA, ANNA STEPANOVNA (1958–2006). Journalist. Born Anna Mazepa to Soviet **Ukrainian** parents in New York (both of whom served as diplomats to the **United Nations**), Politkovskaya was a Russian journalist, author, and **human rights** activist, known for her strong opposition to the war in **Chechnya** and **Vladimir Putin**'s administration. She authored a number of publications on Chechnya, as well as a book entitled *Putin's Russia: Life in a Failing Democracy* (2004), for which she received prestigious international awards. She was assassinated in her Moscow apartment building in 2006. The Russian police have failed to find her murderers. Politkovskaya held dual citizenship of the Russian Federation and the **United States**. She grew up in Moscow and completed a course in journalism from the **Moscow State University**. She first worked for *Izvestiya* newspaper, and then for *Novaya Gazeta*. In her reports on the second **Chechen War**, she focused on the human tragedies, and chronicled human rights abuses and policy failures of the Russian **military** forces, **Chechen terrorists**, and the Russian-backed republican administration. She was involved in negotiating the release of hostages during the **Nord-Ost theater** (2002) and **Beslan** (2004) crises. Her exposure of atrocities during the Chechen War is believed to have been related to her murder.

POLLUTION. The effects of environmental degradation and pollution in the Russian Federation are particularly acute due to the low priority placed on ecology by the Soviet and post-Soviet governments. **Joseph Stalin**'s industrialization projects had an incredibly harmful impact on the environment, leading to the disruptions of entire ecosystems (e.g., the Aral Sea). During the **Cold War**, the Soviet government invested hugely in **space** exploration, **mining**, **nuclear weapons**, and massive building schemes, while ignoring the impact of such activities on the environment. Areas such as the Kuznets basin, the Kola Peninsula, the **Urals**, **Kalmykiya**, **Lake Baykal**, and the **Caspian Sea** all suffer from unacceptable levels of pollution. Grandiose projects such as the diversion of rivers for irrigation and canal building rarely took into account the long-term effects; the same can be said for nuclear testing in **Kazakhstan** and other areas of the former Soviet Union.

Further compounding the problem, the Soviet government treated environmental disasters as an issue of state secrecy. The prime example is the **Chernobyl disaster** of 1986, which led to radiation poisoning in **Ukraine**, **Belarus**, and elsewhere. Some areas of the former Union of Soviet Socialist Republics (USSR) have become dangerous to live in because of nuclear experiments or intensive industrial use. In Russia itself, the main rivers in the European part of the country, including the **Volga** and Don, have very high levels of water contamination due to industrial waste, sewage, and use of pesticides and fertilizers. Aluminum smelting in the **Far North** — and its accompanying pollution — has emerged as a transnational issue, creating problems with **Norway** and other Arctic states.

The economic turmoil of the 1990s diverted public interest and funds from nascent ecological problems to everyday survival issues. A number of powerful interests were arrayed against the environmental movement, including the **military** and Russian and multinational corporations, thus making environmental management during the 1990s a difficult task. The improved economic situation of the 2000s resulted in more cars appearing on Russian roads, leading to high levels of air pollution, despite new initiatives to support **environmentalism**. For instance, recycling is virtually nonexistent in the Russian Federation, and when it is used it is driven by financial rather than ecological interests (rather than having a compulsory regime, Russian citizens receive monetary compensation for recycling paper, glass, and metals). Pollution and environmental problems are one of the main causes of poor health and low life expectancy in Russia, thus contributing to overall **demographic challenges**.

POTANIN, VLADIMIR OLEGOVICH (1961–). Oligarch. Unlike most oligarchs, Vladimir Potanin comes from a prestigious **Communist Party of the Soviet Union** (CPSU) pedigree. During the Soviet era, he studied at the elite Moscow State Institute of International Relations (MGIMO), which trained Soviet diplomats and **KGB** agents and educated the children of the **apparatchiks**. Upon graduation he worked under his father at the Ministry of Foreign Trade, where he created an extensive network of business contacts. In 1991, he started the metals-trading company Interros.

With his partner, Mikhail Prokhorov, Potanin built his fortune by winning over the corporate clients of two large Soviet-era banks in 1992. Eventually they took control of metal giant **Norilsk Nickel** and Sidanco Oil Company as a result of the controversial **privatization** of the 1990s. His empire also includes various **media** outlets, including *Izvestiya*, *Komsomolskaya Pravda*, and *Expert*, as well as insurance firms, agribusinesses, and power companies. Potanin was involved with **George Soros** in Russia's telecommunications monopoly Sviazinvest; Soros considered the nearly $1 billion he put into the enterprise to be his worst investment. He briefly worked for the Russian government as first deputy prime minister, overlooking economic policies. Potanin is recognized as one of the architects of the controversial **loans for shares program**. He is also one the key oligarchs who supported **Boris Yeltsin** in the **1996 presidential election**.

Since 2003, he has headed the National Council on Corporate Governance, whose main aim is to improve legislative regulations in Russia and to introduce ethical standards of corporate governance into the operations of Russian companies. He has been an active patron of various charitable organizations, funding **sports**, educational, and **visual arts** institutions, including the State **Hermitage** Museum in **St. Petersburg**. His daughter, Anastasiya Potanina, is a famous athlete and celebrity in Russia. *See also* BANKING.

PRAVDA. **Newspaper**. Founded by Leon Trotsky in 1908, *Pravda* ("Truth") was originally published in Vienna, Austria, and was smuggled into Russia. Following the Bolshevik Revolution, the newspaper moved to **Moscow** and became the principal mouthpiece of the **Communist Party of the Soviet Union**. During the

Soviet era, subscription to the newspaper was compulsory for party members, state-run firms, **military** units, libraries, and many other organizations. There were also republican and regional versions of the newspaper (such as *Ukrainskaia Pravda* in **Ukraine**). After the **dissolution of the Soviet Union** in 1991, *Pravda* was seized by the new government by writ of Russian President **Boris Yeltsin**. Some of the editorial staff moved to found a new paper with the same title. In 1991, the new paper was sold to Greek entrepreneurs Theodoros and Christos Giannikos. In print, the relaunched *Pravda* tended to analyze events from a leftist-nationalist point of view. The paper was shuttered in 1996 after years of falling subscriptions, though the Giannikos brothers continued a tabloid version of the publication. Subsequently, a group of **journalists** launched Pravda Online; still in operation today, the website often takes a sensationalist approach to news reporting.

PRESS. *See* JOURNALISM.

PRIMAKOV, YEVGENY MAKSIMOVICH (1929–). Politician and diplomat. Born on 29 October 1929 in Kiev to parents of purported Jewish origin (his original family name has been reported as either Finkelstein or Kirschenblatt), he grew up in Tbilisi, **Georgia**. He received his degree from the Moscow State Institute of Oriental Studies in 1953. A fluent Arab speaker, he worked for *Pravda* in various Arab countries during the 1960s, ultimately cultivating personal relationships with Muammar Gaddafi, Yasser Arafat, and Hafez al-Assad, among others. He returned to Moscow to take up a career in academe, leading the Institute for World Economy and International Relations (IMEMO).

Primakov exercised significant influence over Soviet relations with the **Middle East** and South Asia in the 1970s, including providing the authoritative ideological justification for the invasion of **Afghanistan** in 1979. A reformer under **Mikhail Gorbachev**, he quietly worked to reorient the Union of Soviet Socialist Republics' (USSR) **foreign relations**. He assumed the leadership of the **KGB** shortly before the dissolution of the USSR, overseeing the department's transition to Russian control; he served as director of the Foreign Intelligence Service (SVR) until 1996 when he replaced **Andrey Kozyrev** as the country's chief diplomat.

As foreign minister (1996–1998) and prime minister (1998–1999), Primakov was the highest-ranking anti-Western politician during the Yeltsin administration. Under his leadership, he oversaw Russia's "turn to the East," which involved strengthening relations with **China**, **Japan**, and ASEAN countries to counterbalance American power. As part of his drive to end unipolarity in world politics, he also advocated the eventual creation of a "strategic triangle" linking **India**, China, and Russia in areas of mutual interest. This shift in foreign policy was subsequently labeled the **Primakov Doctrine**; his nascent development of a multidirectional foreign policy for Moscow continued under the Putin administration.

Domestically, he was known for his desire to reduce the complexity of Russia's regional structure and to rein in the power of the presidents of the **ethnic republics**. He lost his job as prime minister during the tense period of **United States**–Russian relations stemming from the 1999 **North Atlantic Treaty Organization**'s (NATO) bombing campaign in **Kosovo**. Given his popularity, determination to take on the **oligarchs**, and strong anti-Western orientation, he was considered the front-runner to replace **Boris Yeltsin** as president before the **security services**, **military**, and other vital factions of the establishment rallied around Yeltsin's hand-picked successor, **Vladimir Putin**. He abandoned the race shortly before the election and soon became an ally of the new president. In 2001, he became the president of the Russian Chamber of Commerce and Industry. Reprising his role as a personal mediator between Saddam Hussein and the outside world prior to the first Gulf War, he returned to Iraq in 2003 in an unsuccessful bid to avert the U.S.-led invasion of the country.

PRIMAKOV DOCTRINE. Foreign relations doctrine. In the latter half of the Yeltsin administration, Russia turned away from the **Atlanticist** foreign policy that had existed under Foreign Minister **Andrey Kozyrev**. Named after the politician and diplomat **Yevgeny Primakov**, the three principal planks of this new orientation included 1) integrating Russia into the world **economy**; 2) establishing a multipolar world; and 3) counteracting key **United States**–led initiatives including **North Atlantic Treaty Organization** (NATO) enlargement, the Iraqi economic embargo, and military intervention in **Kosovo**. Both as foreign minister and later as prime minister, Primakov expanded Russian ties to East Asia and the **Middle East** to counterbalance American dominance of world politics. The inherent weakness of Russia under **Boris Yeltsin**'s administration ultimately served to isolate Russia, and precluded the successful outcome of Primakov's primary goal of returning the country to great-power status. However, Primakov's embrace of a multidirectional foreign policy and opposition to unipolarity are seen as strongly influencing the **Putin Doctrine**.

PRIMORSKY KRAI. An administrative province of the Russian Federation. Sometimes known in English as the Maritime Krai, Primorsky is situated in extreme southeastern Russia, bordering **Khabarovsk Krai**, **North Korea**, and **China**. The area was part of the Qing Empire until the mid-19th century. Washed by the Sea of Japan, the province is an entrepôt for goods from **Japan** and other Pacific Rim countries, as well as an export hub. It is part of the Far Eastern **Federal District** and **Economic Region**. The mostly mountainous and heavily forested territory covers some 165,900 square kilometers, with 1,350 kilometers of sea coast. The current population slightly exceeds 2 million. **Ethnic Russians** comprise 90 percent of the **krai**'s inhabitants; indigenous Tungusic minorities include Udege, Nanai, and Oroch.

The **fishing industry** drives the regional **economy**, followed by machine building and the defense **industry**; livestock, fur, and forestry are also important sources of employment. The province is the center of **banking** and finance for Russia's **Far East**, as well as a major outpost of the Russian **mafia**. Vladivostok (pop. 594,000), once a closed city, is the provincial capital and home to Russia's Pacific Fleet. As the terminus of the **Trans-Siberian Railway**, the region is well-connected to European Russia and China. The international ports of Vladivostok and Nakhodka-Vostochny are key drivers of the regional economy. The province possesses an immense diversity of **wildlife**, including rare Siberian or Amur tigers and half of all the bird species found in the former Soviet Union.

Under the governorship of the China-baiting demagogue Yevgeny Nazdratenko, the krai declared itself a republic during the **Yeltsin** era; however, this declaration was not recognized by the federal authorities. Nazdratenko continuously sparred with Yeltsin's chief of staff, **Anatoly Chubais**, and local proponents of economic liberalism, particularly over subsidies relating to energy, resulting in major power outages in the mid-1990s. In 2001, Nazdratenko resigned in response to criticism from **Vladimir Putin** and was replaced by businessman Sergey Darkin; the new governor was the first person to be appointed under the 2004–2005 **electoral reforms** that gave the Russian president power to pick regional governors.

In recent years, the administration has moved to develop a special economic zone in the region and attract **foreign investment**, especially from South Korea. In 2009, protests broke out in Vladivostok against cost-prohibitive duties on used cars imported from Asia. Security forces were brought in from **Moscow** to quell the discontent, much of which was directed at Prime Minister Vladimir Putin. Primorsky will be one of only four locales in Russia where casinos will be legal after 1 July 2009.

PRIVATIZATION. Under **Boris Yeltsin**, the newly independent Russian Federation initiated a mass privatization scheme meant to transfer the assets of the now-defunct Soviet state to the people in whose name the property nominally was held. However, incipient privatization efforts in the late Soviet period, targeting smaller industrial concerns, had already determined that, in practice, assets would be transferred to political and economic elites rather than the masses. Under Yeltsin, state-owned enterprises proved to be the major target of this undertaking, excepting strategic assets in the defense **industry**.

In the early stages of this plan, **Anatoly Chubais** spearheaded privatization through the State Committee for State Property Management of the Russian Federation. Adapting the voucher privatization plan that had been employed in Czechoslovakia, Chubais distributed vouchers to employees of small and medium-sized state firms and some large enterprises from 1992 to 1994. These vouchers were quickly bought up by industry insiders and others with access to large amounts of capital (including members of the **security services** and the **mafia**).

This concentration of ownership laid the groundwork for the emergence of the **oligarchs** in the mid-1990s, and, after a brief flurry of enthusiasm, turned much of the populace against the government and further privatization efforts. Despite public opposition, Yeltsin, in desperate need of funding, expanded privatization to larger firms and strategic sectors of the **economy** in 1995. Through the **loans for shares program**, the state auctioned off what would become ownership stakes in some of Russia's largest enterprises, transferring control of the country's telecommunications, **mining, oil, natural gas**, and other key industries to a handful of well-connected tycoons. The lack of transparency and low prices paid for the assets, as well as the program's intensification of the country's wealth gap, soured most of the citizenry on the entire idea of privatization. The process also gave rise to the slang *prikhvatizatsiia*, a portmanteau of the Russian word for "grab" and the English word "privatize," producing the concept of "grab-it-ization" to criticize the emerging kleptocracy and **corruption** of the state.

Ignored during the Yeltsin era, the Land Code of 2001 opened the door to privatization of the large swaths of land that remained under state control. Despite **Vladimir Putin**'s push for land reform, few businesses or individuals took advantage of the new opportunity to buy land, in part due to long-standing traditions of publicly held lands, but also as a result of high levels of taxation and insecurity about the legal status of such purchases. In the wake of the 2008–2009 **global financial crisis**, the Kremlin has bought up controlling stakes in a number of strategic assets, suggesting a concerted effort at "reverse privatization," that is, renationalization. Such actions follow the widely criticized seizure of **Yukos** from **Mikhail Khodorkovsky**.

PSKOV OBLAST. An administrative region of the Russian Federation. The westernmost contiguous region of the Russian Federation, Pskov Oblast borders the **European Union** countries of **Estonia** and **Latvia**, as well as **Belarus**, making it the only region to administer three separate international borders. Nearly one-tenth of Russia's exports travel through the region on their way to Europe and farther afield. Its total international border is more than 600 kilometers in length. Within Russia, its neighbors are the **Leningrad**, **Smolensk**, **Novgorod**, and **Tver oblasts**. It is part of the Northwestern **Eco-**

nomic Region and **Federal District**. The regional capital, Pskov (pop. 202,000), is one of Russia's oldest cities and was once part of the Hanseatic League. It covers an area of 55,300 square kilometers and has a population of 760,900.

Mostly covered by boreal and mixed forests, the region is considered to be Russia's most ecologically pristine. Along with Estonia, it sits on the shore of one of Europe's largest lakes, Pskov-Chud (Peipsi-Pihkva) Lake. Major crops include flax, wheat, sunflowers, and sugar beets; livestock and fishing are also a key part of the local economy.

Important industries include small electronics, engineering, and communications equipment. Private and mixed ownership of enterprises is comparatively high in the region. Due to its location, a vibrant **banking** sector has grown since 1991. **Foreign investment** is also robust, and includes a Russian-Italian industrial zone in Velikiye Luki; however, the region trails its neighbors Leningrad and Novgorod in attracting investments from abroad, and **unemployment** is a perennial problem. **Tourism** and recreation are also drivers of the regional economy. The region is plagued by **demographic challenges**, including one of the highest death rates in the Russian Federation.

Disputes over the border with Latvia were an issue for the region in the 1990s; however, the issue was resolved in 2007. Estonia renounced its territorial claims to the area in the mid-1990s.

In the 1990s, the region's **politics** tended toward the extreme, and the ultranationalist **Vladimir Zhirinovsky** found ample support in the region during his run for the presidency. The potential encroachment of the **North Atlantic Treaty Organization** (NATO) on the region's borders and the oblast's function as the first stop for returning Russian soldiers from the **Baltic States** is seen as the catalyst for right-wing support. In 1996, a member of the **Liberal Democrat Party of Russia** (LDPR) and representative in the **State Duma**, Yevgeny Mikhailov, won the governorship by defeating the **Yeltsin**-appointed incumbent, Vladislav Tumanov, of the **Our Home—Russia** political party.

In the mid-1990s, Mikhailov secured the border and increased customs revenues; he was also a strong advocate of the union with Belarus. By 2000, however, Mikhailov abandoned the LDPR for the pro-government **United Russia** party, and won reelection. In 2004, he lost a runoff election to local businessman Mikhail Kuznetsov. During his tenure, he sought to attenuate local conditions in order to increase investment from the Baltic States as well as **China**. **Dmitry Medvyedev** appointed Andrey Turkchak in early 2009, following Kuznetsov's dismissal after a disagreement with the head of the Kremlin administration Sergey Naryshkin. Turkchak is a high-ranking member of the United Russia party and brother of a personal friend of **Vladimir Putin**.

PUNISHED PEOPLES. Coined by the **dissident** historian Aleksandr Nekrich in his *Punished Peoples: The Deportation and Fate of Soviet Minorities at the End of the Second World War* (1978), the term refers to those **ethnic minorities** that were deported en masse during World War II. At the behest of **Joseph Stalin**, himself ethnically **Georgian** and **Ossetian**, **Chechens**, **Ingush**, **Kalmyks**, **Balkars**, **Karachay**, **Meskhetian Turks**, Crimean **Tatars**, and Volga **Germans** were packed onto cattle cars and relocated to **Siberia** and **Central Asia**; the rigors of the journey resulted in a 30–40 percent mortality rate.

Under **Nikita Khrushchev**, these ethnic minorities were politically "rehabilitated," but only the Chechens, Ingush, Kalmyks, Balkars, and Karachay were allowed to return to their ethnic homelands. Economic dislocation and memories of the trauma continued to plague these communities after their return to the **North Caucasus** and **Kalmykiya**; both would figure in the **Ossetian-Ingush Conflict** and the first **Chechen War**. With the coming of **glasnost**, more information about the deportations came to light and the Crimean Tatars, in particular, began to push for the right of return to **Crimea**, now in **Ukraine**.

Ethnic violence between Uzbeks and the Meskhetian Turks in 1989 created a unionwide fear of general ethnic struggle, coinciding as it did with the **Nagorno-Karabakh** War and other incidents. Throughout the 1990s, ethnic Germans employed **Germany**'s law of return based on ethnicity to relocate to Europe.

The term is sometimes extended to include minorities that are not indigenous to Russia, but which suffered the same fate, including Koreans, Greeks, Bulgarians, Poles, and the peoples of the **Baltic States**. *See also* GORBACHEV, MIKHAIL; UZBEKISTAN.

PUTIN DOCTRINE. Foreign relations doctrine. Strongly influenced by the multidirectional foreign policy of Yeltsin-era politician **Yevgeny Primakov**, **Vladimir Putin** reoriented Russian foreign policy away from its **Atlanticist** approach of the early 1990s and toward more developed relations with Arab and Asian states, especially **China**. Furthermore, it stressed a number of goals beyond traditional security concerns, including the establishment of conditions favorable to Russia's economic growth; the creation of a belt of friendly states along Russia's perimeter; the comprehensive protection of the **human rights** and interests of Russian citizens and co-nationals abroad; and the promotion and support of the **Russian language** and culture in foreign countries. It appears that **Dmitry Medvyedev** will continue in his predecessor's footsteps. In his first visit abroad as the newly elected president, Medvyedev abandoned established protocol, which demanded an inaugural call on Berlin, and used his maiden foreign trip to visit **Kazakhstan** and China, one month before visiting Russia's principal European partner, **Germany**.

PUTIN, VLADIMIR VLADIMIROVICH (1952–). Politician. Born in Leningrad on 7 October 1952, Vladimir Putin grew up in humble surroundings as the son of a former Soviet sailor and member of the NKVD (the forbearer of the **KGB**). In his early life, he took up *sambo*, a Soviet form of martial arts, before moving into judo. At the Leningrad State University, Putin studied international law, and became a protégé of **Anatoly Sobchak**. During his college years, Putin became a member of the **Communist Party of the Soviet Union** (CPSU); he would remain in the party until it was outlawed under **Boris Yeltsin**.

In 1975, he joined the KGB, where he began **surveillance** on foreign visitors to Leningrad. Ten years later, he received a foreign posting in Dresden, East **Germany**. In 1990, he returned to his hometown and became reacquainted with Sobchak, then mayor of the city, for whom he served as an advisor on international affairs. During the **August Coup**, Putin resigned his commission in the **security services**. During the first half of the 1990s, Putin controlled the Committee for External Relations, handling **foreign investment** and **St. Petersburg**'s relations with foreign governments. Unlike many of his peers, Putin reputedly never succumbed to the attraction of **corruption** during the period of intense economic chaos (while his actual wealth is opaque, officially, Putin's financial situation is modest for a former world leader).

During the latter half of the 1990s, Putin rose through the ranks of St. Petersburg politicians, assuming the leadership of the local branch of **Our Home—Russia** in 1995. In 1998, he attracted the attention of Yeltsin, who appointed him to manage negotiations between the federal government and the regions. Shortly thereafter, he was tapped to head the **FSB**, bringing the former KGB agent back to his roots, and became a member of the Security Council of the Russian Federation. During 1999, Yeltsin, with the help of the business tycoon **Boris Berezovsky**, began preparing the ground for Putin's election as the next president of the Russian Federation.

On 16 August 1999, the **State Duma** approved Putin's appointment for the office of prime minister. His principal rivals at the time included **Moscow** mayor **Yury Luzhkov** and former Prime Minister **Yevgeny Primakov** (though neither challenged him in the 2000 presidential election). Putin, though not a member, backed the **Unity** party in the 1999 State Duma elections, thus guaranteeing himself strong parliamentary support in the upcoming presidential poll. Despite his status as a relative unknown, Putin's backers deftly used the 1999 **apartment bombings** and **Shamil Basayev**'s armed incursion into **Dagestan** to position the heir apparent as the "law and order" choice at the time when the country lurched toward the second **Chechen War**.

On 31 December 1999, Yeltsin stepped down from office, leaving Putin as acting president. The news was broadcast on national television channels as part of the holiday celebrations, and at first, many people thought the announcement was a prank. As a quid pro quo, Putin issued a decree protecting Yeltsin and his family from corruption charges. Three months later, on 26 March 2000, Putin won the presidential poll with 53 percent of the vote, becoming the second popularly elected President of the Russian Federation. He immediately began building what he referred to as a **vertical of power** through the tempering of Yeltsin's **asymmetrical federalism**. He gained the right to dismiss the heads of the country's **federal subjects** and began the process of bringing regional laws into harmony with federal laws.

In 2000, Putin also called a meeting with the country's **oligarchs**, demanding they avoid direct involvement in Russian **politics** in return for the safety of their vast fortunes. Subsequently, Putin began supporting the rise of a competitive clique of pro-Kremlin magnates with close ties to the "power ministries" (FSB, the **military**, and the **Ministry of Internal Affairs**) and affiliated *siloviki*. His popularity, however, took its first hit with the *Kursk* **submarine disaster** of 2000. In the eyes of ordinary Russians, his mishandling of the situation seriously marred his presidency: Putin's attempt to keep the details of the incident from the public reminded the nation of the **Chernobyl disaster** and an earlier period when the government did not properly inform the citizenry of catastrophic events. During the remainder of his first term, Russia would suffer from a spate of spectacular acts of **terrorism**, with especially deadly effects in Moscow and the **North Caucasus**. Putin's use of force, however, met with wide approval, as did his reining in of the **media** after the **Nord-Ost theater siege** in 2002.

Prior to his election for a second term, Putin swept out the remaining members of the Yeltsin administration, including **Mikhail Kasyanov**, demonstrating his intent to govern more aggressively in the future. On 14 March 2004, Putin won 71 percent of the vote. **Gennady Zyuganov**, the perennial **Communist Party of the Russian Federation** (KPRF) candidate for the presidency, chose not to run, citing the inevitability of the popular incumbent's reelection. Putin's approval ratings as president rarely dropped below 65 percent and often ran as high 85 percent. A commercialized "cult of personality" also swept the country, with Putin-themed products and songs, as well as emulations of his active, teetotaler lifestyle. Putin's "strong hand," when combined with high **oil** and **natural gas** prices, proved irresistible to the electorate, especially given his favorable coverage in the press. At the same time, the Russian press, especially **Runet journalists**, have increasingly featured Putin through caricature drawings, which, on the one hand, carry a critical stance, and on the other, help promote his popularity among the people.

In the wake of the **Beslan hostage crisis**, Putin enacted his sweeping 2004–2005 **electoral reforms**, which gave the president the right to appoint regional governors (though they must still be confirmed by regional legislatures), as well as consolidating the **political party** system in the Duma. Collectively, these reforms strengthened

Russia's executive branch and expanded Putin's personal power. Putin also began using fiscal surpluses to rebuild the country's anemic welfare and **health care** systems. Plans for improvement in **agriculture**, housing, **education**, and the military were also instituted.

In October 2004, federal authorities arrested **Mikhail Khodorkovsky**, Russia's richest man and the owner of **Yukos**; his subsequent trial for **tax** evasion was viewed as punishment for violating the terms of the oligarch behavior stipulated by Putin in 2000. While Putin denied he was responsible for the arrest and prosecution, citing the independence of the **judicial system**, many at home and abroad viewed the case as a show trial and the first salvo in a war on anti-Kremlin factions (Khodorkovsky had given money to a number of political parties and was exploring running for president in 2008).

During his second administration, Putin became more strident in his defense of "sovereign **democracy**"—usually labeled "managed democracy" or "neo-authoritarianism" in the West—suggesting that Russia (and other members of the **Commonwealth of Independent States**) enjoyed the right to move toward political pluralism at its own pace. Under Putin, Russia's weak **civil society** withered further, particularly after the Kremlin began funding its own youth movements and pseudo-nongovernmental organizations (NGOs) while simultaneously disrupting the activities of foreign-backed NGOs. His continued campaign to control the media—either through state acquisition of **television** stations or censorship, intimidation, and/or prosecution of journalists—also weakened Russia's social fabric.

Putin's effective use of nationalism, however, blunted criticism of his actions inside the country even as he suffered criticism as a crypto-fascist abroad. His partial "rehabilitation" of **Joseph Stalin**, long a hero of the KPRF and older Russians, and campaign to remake the Soviet Union's role in World War II won him accolades from most Russians, though it rankled many in the **Baltic States** and **Ukraine**.

In terms of **foreign relations**, Putin demonstrated himself to be a pragmatist, but also a shrewd defender of Russia's national interest and advocate for Russia's return to great-power status in **Eurasia**. Shortly after **George W. Bush**'s election as president of the **United States**, Putin met the leader in Slovenia, where they established what was marketed as a fast friendship. In the wake of the **September 11**

attacks on New York and Washington, Putin—acting against the advice of his cabinet—established substantive **counterterrorism** links with Washington and backed American plans to deploy military bases in **Central Asia** to support the war in **Afghanistan**. In return, Putin won the Bush administration's support of Russia's often brutal campaign in **Chechnya** (which was brought to a satisfactory, if incomplete, resolution by 2006).

Not willing to pass up an opportunity, Putin sided with **France** and **Germany** against the American- and British-led war in Iraq, strengthening Russia's position within the **European Union** without doing much damage to Russia's ties to Washington. Russia's ratification of the **Kyoto Protocol** won him more kudos from Berlin and Paris. U.S.-Russian relations would, however, worsen during Putin's last year in office over U.S. antimissile installations in **Poland**, and spats with **Great Britain** over **espionage** and the **Aleksandr Litvinenko** case also marred Putin's record abroad, if not at home.

Through a combination of economic power and geopolitics, Putin expanded Russia's influence over the **near abroad**, especially during his second term when **Uzbekistan**—long suspicious of Moscow—returned to the fold after Western criticism of its actions during a 2005 crackdown in its Andijan province. He was not totally effective in expanding Russian power, however; due to worsening relations with the Baltics after their admission to the **North Atlantic Treaty Organization** (NATO) and the **color revolutions** in **Georgia** and **Ukraine**, the Kremlin's political clout in its former possessions was reduced dramatically. Skillful use of petropolitics, conducted through the proxy of **Gazprom**, has kept Kiev within the Russian sphere of influence.

Through the **Shanghai Cooperation Organization**, Putin developed closer ties with **China**, and marginalized American influence in Central Asia. Globally, Putin resurrected the superpower image of Russia by expanding **arms exports** and diplomatic support to a number of unpopular regimes including **Venezuela**, Syria, and **Iran**, while simultaneously resuming long-range bomber missions and seeking to control large portions of the resource-rich **Arctic Ocean**. He was also instrumental in winning the 2014 Winter Games for **Sochi**, one of his favorite vacation destinations, and Russia's so-called southern capital.

As he prepared to leave office in 2008, Putin enjoyed immense support at home, in no small part due to his stewardship of the **economy**. Russia's gross domestic product had doubled during the Putin years. **Industry** grew, as did salaries, while **unemployment** noticeably decreased. A new middle class had developed, though the wealth gap remained a problem and inflation remained a perennial issue. Furthermore, Russia's so-called national champions (large enterprises such as Gazprom, **Lukoil**, and **Norilsk Nickel**) had become major players in the global economy. Consequently, Putin faced little resistance to his choice as the next president, **Dmitry Medvyedev**.

As promised during the election campaign, Medvyedev appointed Putin his prime minister after being sworn in. As head of the government, Putin has had to deal with severe challenges to his country and flagging popularity among the masses. The 2008 **South Ossetian War**, though undeniably popular at home, weakened the economy due to massive capital flight in the wake of Russia's invasion of Georgia. Shortly thereafter, the effects of the 2008–2009 **global financial crisis** struck Russia, sending oil and natural gas prices, as well as the Russian stock market, plummeting. In December 2008, Putin—condemned as "Putler" (playing on images of Adolf Hitler)—became the focus of protestors in Vladivostok, **Primorsky Krai**; new duties on imported used cars angered many residents whose livelihoods depended on reselling the vehicles in other parts of the federation.

While it is clear that Putin remains the most important figure in national politics, Medvyedev has begun slowly building a power base independent of Putin and has implicitly criticized his predecessor's actions in some areas, particularly the stifling of civil society. Regardless of Medvyedev's ability to rally support moving forward, Putin, who was recognized as *Time* magazine's "Person of the Year" in late 2007 for his ability to bring Russia out of chaos and put the country on solid footing, is well situated to run for president in the next elections.

Putin married his wife, Lyudmila Shkrebneva, in 1983; the couple has two daughters, both of whom grew up in East Germany. Putin speaks nearly fluent German and is learning English. He embraced the **Russian Orthodox Church** after a near-death experience in the early 1990s, but rarely talks about **religion** in public. His fondness for dogs and **Eurasian** wildlife is well documented. *See also* PUTIN DOCTRINE.

– R –

RAION. Largely unchanged since Soviet times, the raion is a second-level administrative division, used within **federal subjects** or large cities. Usually translated as "district," the raion is roughly equivalent to a county in the **United States**. **Sakha** and **Tuva** use indigenous terminology—*ulus* and *kozhun*, respectively—to denote similar divisions.

REAGAN, RONALD WILSON (1911–2004). American politician. The 40th president of the **United States** (1981–1989), Ronald Reagan began his administration by sending U.S.-Soviet relations into one of their coolest periods of the **Cold War**. During the short-lived premierships of **Yury Andropov** (1982–1984) and **Konstantin Chernenko** (1984–1985), Reagan maintained minimal diplomatic relations with the Union of Soviet Socialist Republics (USSR), while aiding Moscow's adversaries—the mujahideen—in the **Soviet-Afghan War**.

On 8 March 1983, Reagan referred to the USSR as an "evil empire," reflecting his view of the country as a dangerous and imperialistic adversary that must be defeated. This coincided with his proposed Strategic Defense Initiative (SDI), a space-based system to intercept Soviet nuclear missiles, thus preventing the threat of mutually assured destruction. While SDI never came to fruition, it was one of many defense programs that put pressure on the Soviet **economy** during a period of intense contraction related to flagging **oil** revenues. (During his tenure, Reagan increased military spending by 35 percent.)

With the ascendency of **Mikhail Gorbachev**, Reagan—while continuing his "peace through strength" approach to bilateral relations, opened the door to negotiations, which resulted in a treaty that would ultimately eliminate medium-range **nuclear weapons**. Responding to Gorbachev's "New Thinking" in Soviet **foreign relations**, Reagan worked closely with the Soviet premier to reduce tensions and promote international cooperation, while consistently urging him to expand his reform agenda at home. Famous for his 12 June 1987 declaration at the Brandenburg Gate, "Mr. Gorbachev, tear down this wall!" (referring to the Berlin Wall in East **Germany**), Reagan is often described as the "man who beat Communism," though his contributions to the downfall of the **Communist Party of the Soviet Union** and the **dissolution of the Soviet Union** are exaggerated, particularly in American and Western sources. *See also* BUSH, GEORGE H. W.

RED BELT. The term refers to a group of **oblasts** stretching across the European part of Russia that supported the **Communist Party of the Russian Federation** in the parliamentary elections of the 1990s and **Gennady Zyuganov** in the **1996 presidential election**. Those regions demonstrating the greatest loyalty to the Communist Party of the Russian Federation included **Bryansk, Oryol, Lipetsk, Penza, Tambov,** and **Ulyanovsk; Voronezh** and **Volgograd** are often associated with this group as well. The Red Belt included impoverished cities and largely agrarian areas of Russia, which benefited little from the **economic** reforms of the **Yeltsin** era. The Red Belt was characterized by highly conservative local administrations that opposed changes to the country's welfare system, **foreign trade,** and **privatization**. The term has fallen out of use in the new millennium as the Russian Federation has enjoyed the benefits of high **oil** and **natural gas** prices, a popular president, and a renewed position in the global community.

RELIGION. Given Karl Marx's trenchant criticism of religion as the "opium of the masses," it is not surprising that the Soviet state diligently promoted scientific **atheism** during its seven decades of existence. The Soviet Union's four principal faiths—**Orthodox Christianity, Islam, Judaism,** and **Buddhism**—all suffered under **Joseph Stalin**'s reign, with houses of worship closed, clerics imprisoned, and funding sources blocked. Where the Kremlin could not destroy organized religion, it co-opted it, such as forcing the patriarchy to pledge its allegiance to the state and strictly controlling the **education** and appointment of **Muslim** leaders.

Under **perestroika**, religious organizations began to flourish under the mantle of "informal" (*neformal'nyie*) cultural groups. With the end of the **Communist Party of the Soviet Union**'s monopoly on power in 1990 and the chaos associated with the **dissolution of the Soviet Union** a year later, many Russians turned to religion to fill the gap left by the abandonment of the secular faith of **Marxism-Leninism**.

In **Siberia** and the **Russian Far East**, indigenous peoples rediscovered ancestral faiths such as **shamanism**, animism, and Tengrism. Buddhism enjoyed a revival in **Kalmykiya**, **Buryatiya**, and **Tuva**, while neo-Buddhist beliefs combined with "New Age" principles, such as the **Rerikh Movement**, gained appeal among **ethnic Russians**. For other Russians seeking spirituality, **neo-paganism** and Vedism proved attractive.

Of all Russia's faiths, Islam has experienced the most dramatic revival. Across the **North Caucasus** and the **Volga-Ural region**, Russia's traditionally Muslim **ethnic minorities**—including the **Tatars**, **Bashkirs**, **Chechens**, and others—rediscovered their Islamic roots and began to build religious connections to other parts of the Dar al-Islam, including the **Middle East** and South Asia. In some instances this went far beyond spirituality, with many Russian Muslims embracing **Islamism** in both its pragmatic and extremist forms.

Judaism has also benefited from the new environment, with many Russians conducting family histories and reconnecting with their **Jewish** heritage.

While the early-1990s predictions of ethnic Russians' wholesale return to Orthodoxy failed to materialize, the church is thriving. Support from politicians, particularly **Boris Yeltsin**, **Vladimir Putin**, and **Yury Luzhkov**, endowed the patriarchy with a new authority. Even the **Communist Party of the Russian Federation** supports the centrality of the **Russian Orthodox Church** in the country's identity. Religiosity is now worn as a badge of patriotism in the contemporary Russian Federation, and is often used as a tool for establishing corporate networks and business contacts. Despite this flurry of enthusiasm for faith, a majority of Russians believe that there is no God, roughly comparable with the highly secular outlook of Western Europeans. *See also* OLD BELIEVERS.

RERIKH MOVEMENT. The Rerikh religious movement originated in the 1920s, when Nikolay Konstantinovich Rerikh (1874–1947), Russian stage designer, theosophist, and Nobel Prize nominee, and his wife, Elena Ivanovna Shaposhnikova-Rerikh, authored the philosophical and spiritual treatise *Agni Yoga*, which included many **Buddhist** ideas and principles, such as reincarnation and karma. Rerikh believed that culture, in its secular, artistic, and especially ecclesiastical forms, has a sacral role. His thoughts were a continuation of the mystical tradition that prevailed in Russia at the turn of the 20th century, particularly **Eurasianism**. The Rerikh Society prophesied the idea of a cosmopolitan brotherhood and denounced war and human suffering, ultimately endowing the Rerikhs with international repute.

Under **perestroika**, the Soviet Rerikh Foundation (*Sovetskii fond Rerikhov*) was established to revive the Rerikh movement in its homeland. After the **dissolution of the Soviet Union**, Rerikh's ideas became incredibly popular, with most bookstores stocking his publications and retrospective exhibitions of his art enjoying acclaim. The Rerikh movement is exemplary of the ethical and spiritual confusion of the 1990s, when anything anti-Soviet was valued irrespective of its qualitative value. Theosophy proved a convenient middle ground for the disappointed and disillusioned Soviet **intelligentsia**. However, in some quarters, neo-Rerikhism has taken on an extremist nationalist patina, condemning **Jewish**-Masonic plots to destroy Russia. The belief system has also found other adherents, including leading members of the **Communist Party of the Russian Federation** and **shamanists** among Russia's **national minorities**.

RIA NOVOSTI. RIA Novosti, or the Russian Information Agency Novosti (from Russian: *Rossiiskoie agentstvo mezhdunarodnykh novostei "RIA Novosti"*), is a state-owned news agency based in **Moscow**. It publishes news and analytical reports on social, political, economic, financial, **sport**, and cultural issues on the **Internet** and through e-mail service and RSS in the main European **languages** and in Arabic, Japanese, and Mandarin. It has a network of correspondent agencies in the Russian Federation, the **Commonwealth of Independent States** (CIS), and over 40 non-CIS countries. In Russia, the news agency provides information for the presidential administration, Russian government, **State Duma**, government departments and main ministries, administrations of Russian regions, diplomatic missions, and public organizations. RIA Novosti was created in 1991 on the basis of two information agencies that had operated in the Soviet Union since the end of World War II. The new establishment became a state news and analytical agency. In 1997, the **television** channel Kul'tura was founded on the basis of the RIA Novosti TV channel. In 1998, the growing **media** firm was renamed the Russian Information Agency Vesti (in Russian, *vesti* means "news" or "reports"), while the news agency section retained the name of RIA Novosti. *See also* RUSSIA TODAY.

RODINA/MOTHERLAND-NATIONAL PATRIOTIC UNION. **Political party**. Rodina (Motherland) was a coalition of nationalist, left-wing political parties and organizations formed to win seats in the **State Duma** under the **Putin** administration. The party was originally led by **Dmitry Rogozin**, a well-known member of Russia's foreign policy elite and a longtime supporter of **ethnic Russians** living in the **near abroad**. With its curious motto "For Putin, but against the government," the party performed well in the 2003 parliamentary elections, winning 37 seats and garnering nearly 10 percent of the vote. Criticized by the **Communist Party of the Russian Federation** and reformist parties as a Kremlin-backed pseudoparty, Rodina chose not to field a candidate for the 2004 presidential election, creating an internal split in the party in which Rogozin marginalized his rival, Sergey Glazyev. The following year, another split in the party triggered Glazyev's return to the party. In 2005, the party was barred from **Moscow** elections due to its virulently anti-**immigrant** campaign. Rogozin unexpectedly stepped down in 2006 and was replaced by businessman Aleksandr Babakov. Shortly thereafter, Rodina merged with the Russian Party of Life and the **Russian Pensioners' Party** to form **Fair Russia**. The combined party went on to a fourth-place showing in the 2007 Duma elections.

ROGOZIN, DMITRY OLEGOVICH (1963–). Politician. A vocal advocate for the rights of **ethnic Russians** in the **near abroad**, Dmitry Rogozin rose to prominence as a member of General **Aleksandr Lebed**'s Congress of Russian Communities **political party** in the early 1990s. He was elected to the **State Duma** in 1997, representing **Voronezh** on the **Rodina** party ticket. As the leader of Rodina, he oversaw the party's shift toward strident nationalism, racism, and anti-**immigration** advocacy. He left the party when it merged with two other parties to form **Fair Russia**. Rogozin left the Duma in 2007 and formed the Great Russia Party, which closely reflected his own ultranationalism. Since 2008, he has served as Russia's envoy to the **North Atlantic Treaty Organization** (NATO). The bombastic Rogozin made international headlines regarding **Georgia**'s and **Ukraine**'s prospective admission to NATO, as well as recent **espionage** disputes between Moscow and the organization. *See also* ETHNIC VIOLENCE.

ROMA. Ethnic group. According to the 2002 census, there are nearly 190,000 Roma, or Gypsies (*tsygane*), in the Russian Federation, thus making them a significant **ethnic minority**. The major subgroups are Ruska Roma, who arrived in Russia from Central Europe in the 18th century, and Vlach Roma, who came to Russia from the Balkans in the mid-19th century. Roma are originally of Indian origin; however, a millennium of residence in Europe has diluted or erased any links to the subcontinent. Many Russian Romani speak a dialect of Romanes, the Romani **language**, which is Indo-European in origin and is related to Panjabi, Hindi, and other Indic languages. Most Roma profess Russian **Orthodoxy**.

Sedentarized and culturally marginalized during the Soviet era, some Roma have reestablished their cultural identity in postindependence Russia. However, their difference in physical appearance from Slavs and their popular association with street **crime** have made Roma frequent targets of **neofascists**, including a particularly violent spate of pogroms in the early 1990s. Discrimination against Roma remains high, and unlike in the case of Roma in the **European Union**, Romani political identity is almost nonexistent. At the same time, there are well-established Roma cultural institutions that date back to the **Stalin** era. Certain aspects of Roma culture are quite popular with Russian people, with many concert halls presenting traditional singing and dance performances, and there is currently a popular television series based on Roma culture.

ROMANOVS. The House of Romanov ruled the Russian Empire from 1613 until 1917 when Tsar Nicholas II abdicated in the aftermath of the February Revolution. The former emperor, his wife Aleksandra, and their children were shot by Bolsheviks in Yekaterinburg on 16 July 1918 on the orders of **Vladimir Lenin**. In 1991, their remains were exhumed and kept in a local laboratory until 1998 when they were interred in the Peter and Paul Cathedral in **St. Petersburg**, an event attended by dozens of descendents of the line. Patriarch **Alexius II** refused to officiate at the ceremony, citing concerns over the authenticity of the remains. On 30 April 2008, new forensic evidence proved the remains of the heir apparent, Tsarevich Aleksey, were among those recovered from Yekaterinburg. Following the **dissolution of the Soviet Union**, roughly one-fifth of Russians supported a reinstitution of the monarchy, but this sentiment quickly dissipated.

ROSE REVOLUTION. *See* COLOR REVOLUTIONS.

ROSNEFT. Following the company's 2004 purchase of **Yukos**'s assets following a state-run auction related to the criminal proceedings against **Mikhail Khodorkovsky**, Rosneft emerged as Russia's largest **oil** producer and refiner. The company, formed in 1995 from Rosneftegaz, which was the successor to the Soviet Union's Ministry of Oil and Gas, is state controlled (75 percent ownership), though **Sberbank** and private investors maintain minority stakes. A number of Russian **oligarchs** including **Roman Abramovich** and **Oleg Deripaska** purchased large numbers of shares in the company's 14 June 2006 initial public offering. Igor Sechin, a close ally of **Vladimir Putin**, is the chairman. The company's major fields are located in **Siberia**, southern and central Russia, Timan-Pechora, and the **Russian Far East**. In 2008, the company refined 985,000 barrels of oil per day and produced more than 2 million barrels of oil per day. It has a significant retail operation with more than 1,700 service stations and proprietary port facilities at Tuapse on the **Black Sea**, De-Kastri in **Sakhalin**, Nakhodka in **Primorsky Krai**, and **Arkhangelsk**. Rosneft also produces significant quantities of **natural gas**. *See also* LUKOIL.

ROSTOV OBLAST. An administrative region of the Russian Federation. Situated on the head of the Taganrog Bay in the **Sea of Azov**, Rostov Oblast is Russia's gateway to the **Caucasus Mountains**. The **oblast** has an international border with **Ukraine**, as well as internal borders with the oblasts of **Volgograd** and **Voronezh**, the **krais** of **Stavropol** and **Krasnodar**, and **Kalmykiya**. It is part of the North Caucasus **Economic Region** and the Southern **Federal District**.

The region covers an area of 100,800 square kilometers; its **geography** is characterized by its **chernozem** soil and the rivers Don and Severny Donets, as well as three large water reservoirs. The regional capital, Rostov-na-Donu (pop. 1,068,000), is well connected to the **Commonwealth of Independent States** and Europe via air, rail, and shipping links; it is considered the unofficial capital of southern Russia. The city, a former Greek colony, is economically vibrant and ethnically diverse. Other major cities include Taganrog, Shakhty, Novocherkassk, and Volgodonsk. With more than 4.4 million inhabitants, the oblast is the fourth most populous region and one of the more densely populated areas of the federation. Many of Russia's **ethnic minorities** are represented in the region; while **ethnic Russians** are the majority (89 percent), there are sizable communities of **Ukrainians**, **Armenians**, and Turks, as well as many **Cossacks**.

The regional **economy** is diversified. In terms of **agricultural** production, it is the second-largest producer in the country, focusing on grains, melons, vineyards, corn, rice, and soybeans; more than 80 percent of the oblast's land is dedicated to farming. **Fishing**, animal husbandry, and fur farming are also widespread. Engineering and heavy manufacturing are also key components of the regional economy, including production of aircraft and equipment for nuclear facilities. Coal **mining**, though in decline, is also an important regional **industry**. There are more than 25,000 small businesses in operation in the region. Revenue from shipping and **tourism** also add to the oblast's output. Azov City, one of only four sites in Russia where casinos are permitted as of 1 July 2009, is expected to further contribute to tourism spending and possibly deepen the region's already high **crime** problem.

The region disproportionately supported the liberal **Yabloko** bloc during the 1990s; in recent years, the regional administration has been dominated by local business interests, with the Communists making rather poor showings. In 1996, Vladimir Chub, a late Soviet-era appointee, was popularly reelected as governor. He was reelected again in 2001 before his reappointment by **Vladimir Putin** in 2005. He has a close working relationship with **Gazprom**, owing to the numerous pipelines that cross the oblast heading toward Europe; Chub also served in the **Federation Council**. In 2007, he was awarded with **Chechnya**'s highest recognition, the Order of **Akhmad Kadyrov**, for his efforts at securing stability in southern Russia; more than 15,000 **Chechens** reside in the region. Chub is also the chair of Russia's Federal Antiterrorism Commission. *See also* NUCLEAR POWER.

RUBLE. The ruble (*rubl'*), sometimes spelled "rouble," is the main unit of currency in the Russian Federation. One ruble is divided into 100 kopecks (*kopeika*). The word "ruble" derives from the Russian verb *rubit'*, which means "to chop off," and refers to the ancient practice of slicing an amount of silver off an ingot. The ruble coins include 1, 2, 5, and 10 rubles, and are usually minted with special insignia. The ruble banknotes include 10, 50, 100, 500, 1,000, and 5,000 rubles, featuring images of national heroes and important national sites such as the Bolshoy Theater (which appears on the 100 ruble banknote). In the Soviet Union, the foreign exchange value of the ruble was controlled by the state; the ruble was liberalized in the early 1990s, thus exposing the currency to devaluation in 1998 when a global economic downturn triggered the **ruble crisis**. With economic stabilization under **Vladimir Putin**, the ruble began to feature in foreign currency exchange offices around the world. Plans are under way to introduce a globally recognized symbol for the ruble to promote confidence in the currency and place it on the same plane with the dollar ($), yen (¥), pound (£), and euro (€). In 2009, one U.S. dollar was worth about 30 Russian rubles.

RUBLE CRISIS (1998). Also known as the Russian financial crisis of 1998, the ruble crisis was an outgrowth of the Asian financial crisis of the previous year. Falling commodity prices—which accounted for more than three-quarters of Russia's gross domestic product—brought down the **economy** beginning on 17 August 1998.

Tax revenues, which were highly dependent on **oil** and **natural gas**, suffered as well, and the situation was exacerbated by huge deficit spending, wage arrears, and a national economy wracked by the first **Chechen War** and transition to the free market.

Boris Yeltsin's ineffective response to the crisis led investors to flee the **ruble** and Russian assets, depleting confidence in the overall economy and sapping the stock market of two-thirds of its value. In the chaos, stabilization loans from the World Bank and the International Monetary Fund were misused and went missing. Between August and November, massive devaluation of the currency occurred, with accompanying street protests opposing the trebling of food prices overnight. **Military** units were brought in to quell potential violence, and certain regions were forced to take extreme measures to ensure the safety and security of **food** shipments. Responding to intense political pressure and calls to step down, Yeltsin dismissed his prime minister, **Sergey Kiriyenko**, hoping to replace him with **Viktor Chernomyrdin**, but was ultimately forced to accept the more nationalistic **Yevgeny Primakov**.

After Primakov's appointment, the situation stabilized rapidly, and the Russian economy entered a period of growth that lasted until the 2008–2009 **global economic crisis**. As a result of the 1998 crisis, the Russian population turned against further experiments of economic reform and exposure of the economy to **globalization**. The fallout of the ruble crisis was felt across post-Soviet space, with the **Baltic States** going into recession and economic slowdowns and currency devaluations in **Kazakhstan**, **Belarus**, and other members of the **Commonwealth of Independent States**.

RUNET. In Russian, "Runet" is an acronym for *russkii Internet*, or the Russian Internet. Despite its territorial connotation, the term includes all Russophone sectors of the World Wide Web, as well as online activity of Russian-speaking communities in Russia proper, the **near abroad**, **Israel**, the **United States**, and other countries.

The first remote electronic connections between computers were established in the Soviet Union in 1989 between nodes located in **Moscow** and **Siberian** universities. Originally, such websites used the extension .su, which was replaced with .ru in 1994 following the **dissolution of the Soviet Union** and the emergence of the **Internet** as we know it today. In its early days, Runet existed in English or in the transliterated form of the **Russian language** until Microsoft's Windows 95, with its standard for the Cyrillic alphabet, became available. The introduction of programming in Russian increased the number of computers and users during the mid-1990s; however, the economic privations associated with the 1998 **ruble crisis** interrupted incipient development of Russian online activity within the Russian Federation.

In the post-1998 time frame, Runet grew rapidly in the traditional centers of technological innovation—Moscow and **St. Petersburg**—as well as portions of the Russian provinces, particularly in large urban centers like Nizhny Novgorod, Volgograd, and Yekaterinburg. While Russian cyberspace started out as an environment dominated by members of the "old diaspora" of Russians in Western Europe and North America, the dawn of the new millennium saw Russian-language Internet traffic come to be dominated by Russians inside of Russia; **ethnic Russians** and Russophones in the comparatively more "wired" **Baltic States** also contributed to Runet in the early 2000s.

In an environment where the **oligarchs** and the state dominated traditional **media**, Runet came to serve as a "do it yourself" publishing tool for those who did not have access to their own media outlet and yet sought to express their beliefs in public. In this sense, the Russian Internet continued the Soviet tradition of **samizdat** (self-publishing), providing the Russian **intelligentsia** and especially the political opposition with a publishing and distribution tool. Between 1994 and 2004, the number of users grew to include 10 percent of the population, a figure that typically signifies the emergence of the Internet as a mass medium (in 2004, 55 percent of users relied on a dial-up connection to the Internet, accounting for 40 percent of traffic). Runet is one of the leading sectors of the World Wide Web in terms of the speed of growth of the number of web users, websites, and web content. This trend indicates that by 2010, up to 50 percent of the population of the Russian Federation may have regular access to the Internet. While the digital gap between Russian cities and **rural** areas remains, it is likely to be bridged in the future as the state now provides access to the Internet in small settlements through its postal and educational systems.

The Kremlin's attitude to Runet has changed from complete ignorance of the medium in the early days, to attempts to control the medium using **Cold War** technologies of censorship and **surveillance** at the start of the most recent decade. More recently, the government has taken an active role online, including political interventions during **Vladimir Putin**'s second term and supporting the rise of **Dmitry Medvyedev**. As the Russian government tightened its grip on traditional media following Putin's recentralization of executive power through the 2004–2005 **electoral reforms** and the expansion of the **vertical of power**, the **State Duma** passed a series of laws aiming to codify and standardize the use of digital technologies in the Russian Federation. The impetus has been to shift the responsibility from Internet users to Internet and content providers, which in the long run may hinder the technological development of Runet as small players may be squeezed out of the web market. Generally, this legislation demonstrates the government's mistrust of **civil society**, especially nongovernmental organizations (NGOs) and any independent organizations that may strengthen **democracy** in the country. It also demonstrates the government's interest in monitoring new forms of communication that may threaten its control of information. Finally, it shows the government's lack of comfort with horizontal democratic structures that might challenge the existing hierarchal administrative and political system.

Despite these retrograde tendencies, Runet remains Russia's most democratic and open medium. While political satire is banned on Russian **television**, it continues to thrive online, with some sites offering textual and visual parodies of the government and its leaders. In addition to political activity, Runet is the space for artistic expression. Since the mid-1990s, digitized **visual art** has thrived on the Russian Internet in the form of flash animation, online gaming, and other digital projects. LiveJournal has been the main platform for communication among Russian-speaking bloggers; the proportion of Russian users of LiveJournal is so large that the portal was purchased by a Russian Internet company in 2007. There are Russian versions of other networking sites such as www.Odnoklassniki.ru and http://Vkontakte.ru, both specializing in provision of technology for social networks. Additionally, the video sharing site RuTube has emerged as a national version of YouTube.

In the past few years, there has been greater commercialization of Runet with annual online advertising revenues exceeding tens of millions of dollars. The service sector of Runet has also expanded with more state-owned and private companies selling goods and providing services online. As the Internet becomes more ubiquitous—the number of Internet cafes in Russian cities has gradually decreased, indicating that more and more users have access to broadband Internet from the privacy of their homes—some social issues have been raised. One of them is the proliferation of pornography on Runet. In 2009, the Duma discussed the challenges as regards the protection of minors while using the Internet. The other important issue is the rapid spread of file-sharing sites that facilitate illegal copying of **films**, **music**, and other intellectual property.

RURAL LIFE. The sheer size and diversity of the Russian Federation make describing the country's rural life problematic. While there are highly developed rural settlements in European Russia, other parts of the country—particularly in **Siberia**, the **North Caucasus**, the **Far North**, and the **Russian Far East**—may appear quite backward. The same region of Russia may contain sections with a complex rural infrastructure and, at the same time, almost derelict outposts. Therefore, the geographical location of a specific place, especially in relation to major transport links and urban centers, are definitive in terms of economic potential, social development, and cultural life. The Russian word *glubinka* (remote place) denotes distant settlements where life continues without much interference from or contact with the modern world. Rural life is paradoxical: while some villages may not have access to running water, they will have access to and use satellite **television** and the **Internet**.

At the end of the 19th century, 87 percent of the Russian population lived in the countryside; in 1913, 82 percent; in 1970, 38 percent; and in 2007, only 27 percent. Such a dramatic drop in the rural population was the result of a series of agrarian reforms, each of which was intended to meet specific economic, political, or social needs in rural society. During the course of these reforms, Russia was transformed from a backward, peasant society to one that is increasingly urban and modern. The reforms not only made Russian peasants leave for cities, but also educated them and mechanized agricultural production.

However, even in the 21st century, in many rural areas there are households that use quite primitive forms of **agriculture** and animal husbandry, and horse-driven carriages are not uncommon.

Late tsarist-era reforms attempted to change the land and class structure of the Russian countryside, which had existed largely unchanged for centuries. Under **Joseph Stalin**, state (*sovkhozy*) and collective (*kolkhozy*) farms were introduced, forcing peasants to form communal holdings. Soviet agrarian policy favored large mechanized collective farms that exercised political and social control over the rural population. **Nikita Khrushchev** relieved the rural population from high taxation on private plots that had been introduced by Stalin, which boosted production of farm goods on privately owned plots. Under **Leonid Brezhnev**, massive funds were allocated for rural development; rural cultural institutions such as cinemas and libraries became common during this period. In the late 1980s, **Mikhail Gorbachev** allowed average Soviet citizens to own small plots of land that were called **dachas**; many of these were used for essential farming rather than for leisure activities often connoted by the term.

In the postindependence period, economic reforms were introduced with the purpose of creating a private agricultural sector to replace the collectivist structures inherited from the Stalin era. The main outcomes of the reforms are the **privatization** of farmland, the development of commercial real estate, and changes in the **food** distribution systems. Incentives introduced in 1992–1994 resulted in a tremendous increase in the number of private farms. However, the **Yeltsin** government failed to replace the organizational structures of the Soviet era with a new set of institutions to support village communities, and it was only under **Vladimir Putin** that considerable investments into **education**, **health care**, and local **transport** systems were made. Yeltsin's failures in the Russian countryside were partially attributable to his inability to secure the political support of the rural population. Federal attempts at agrarian reform eventually deteriorated; as a result, in 1999, for example, meat production was less than 60 percent of its 1992 level and the country came to rely heavily on food imports (in large urban centers, up to 75 percent of food was imported in 1997). At the same time, the economic reforms of the 1990s and the more stable economic environment of the 2000s has encouraged many rural citizens, especially young families, to establish small businesses that rely on farming and also production of foods such as butter and oil, and to construct high-standard housing in rural areas that were bypassed throughout decades of development.

Russian village life maintains many aspects of traditional country living, including family and work relationships, pastimes, and rituals. The running of the country house is a responsibility of **women**. Men traditionally use machinery, while women work the private plot by hand. Rural families tend to be larger. At the same time, across Russia there are the so-called dying villages, that is, settlements with just a dozen elderly citizens who reside in quite remote areas. They typically rely on the support of their children who reside in urban centers, and who travel often enough to provide them with essential goods and services.

Russian villages traditionally consisted of wooden houses, a church, windmills and storage sheds, and other buildings spaced around to prevent the spread of fire. Until recently, wood was the most common building material; however, it has now been replaced by brick and concrete constructions. The spacing between houses is no longer used as a fire prevention technique but rather indicates the boundaries of private property. Historically, the term *derevnia* describes a small village without a church, while a *selo* possesses both a church and a market. This distinction is maintained these days through educational and health institutions: a *selo* will have a school, while a *derevnia* will not; the same applies to postal services, banks, and other institutions.

RUSSIAN ALL-PEOPLE'S UNION. *See* PEOPLE'S UNION.

RUSSIAN CONSTITUTIONAL CRISIS. *See* CONSTITUTIONAL CRISIS OF 1993.

RUSSIAN DIASPORA. The global community of **ethnic Russians** who live beyond the borders of the Russian Federation is approximately 30 million, making it second only to overseas **Chinese** in total numbers. The "old" Russian diaspora dates to the early 20th century, when large numbers of Russian émigrés fled the civil war and persecution by the Bolshevik regime. During this period, they principally settled in the **United States**, **France**, **Serbia**, **China**, and **Great Britain**. Prior to 1917, most Russian immigrants were religious minorities, such as **Jews** and **Old Believers**. During World War II, a second wave of Russians, including many **Cossacks**, fled the Soviet Union, fearing reprisals from **Joseph Stalin** for real or imagined acts against the state.

The **Communist Party of the Soviet Union**'s totalitarian controls on society precluded mass emigration during most of the **Cold War**, and most who left the country were **dissidents** or defectors. In the 1970s, the "refusenik" movement saw many Russian Jews attempting to quit the country for **Israel** or the U.S. Under **perestroika**, Soviet citizens enjoyed hitherto unavailable opportunities to travel abroad, and many used this new freedom to emigrate.

The nature of the Russian diaspora was dramatically altered in December 1991, when the **dissolution of the Soviet Union** left 25 million ethnic Russians out of the newly independent Russian Federation. **Ukraine**, **Kazakhstan**, **Belarus**, and **Uzbekistan** possessed the largest communities of Russians, though Russians also represented nearly a third of the population of the **newly independent states** of **Estonia** and **Latvia**. The political situation of these so-called co-fatherlanders quickly became an important domestic issue in Russian **politics** and determined Russia's **foreign relations** with its post-Soviet neighbors.

Since 1991, the number of ethnic Russians in the **near abroad** has decreased by 6 million, but still remains the core of the diaspora. During the 1990s, large numbers of Russians relocated to **Germany** as guest workers alongside a flood of Russophone ethnic **Germans** returning to their ancestral homeland; smaller communities of **economic** immigrants formed in the U.S., UK, **Canada**, Australia, and other wealthy countries. The continued immigration of Russian Jews to Israel has altered the country's political fabric, including the proliferation of **Russian language** newspapers and other media, as well as the emergence of a political party dedicated to the interests of Russophone Jews from the former Soviet Union.

RUSSIAN ECOLOGICAL PARTY—"THE GREENS." **Political party**. Known in Russian as *Rossiiskaia ekologicheskaia partiia "Zelionyie,"* the Russian Ecological Party (REP) is Russia's leading political party dedicated to **environmentalism**. Initially established as Cedar (*Kedr*) in the early 1990s, the REP is dedicated to protecting the environment from the destructive effects of contemporary civilization. The party platform stresses ecological responsibility, health and social security, reduction of **pollution**, protection of animal and plant species, and energy conservation. The party's political support has remained rather low in Russia, a country shaped by decades of Leninist use and abuse of the environment, rarely breaking the 1 percent mark. Due to electoral reforms, the REP has been virtually eliminated from contention for seats in the **State Duma** since 2003; however, it won seats in the **Samara**'s regional parliament in 2007. The party now works to help implement the Russian Ecological Doctrine, a state-based commitment to implement ecological reform.

RUSSIAN FAR EAST. Though the region is often viewed as part of **Siberia**, the Russian Far East (*dal'nii vostok Rossii*) is a historically and geographically distinct region of the Russian Federation. The area is comprised of the northeastern extremities of the **Eurasian** supercontinent, and borders on or near **China**, the Korean Peninsula, **Japan**, and the American state of Alaska. In the **Russian language**, the region is simply referred to as the Far East, and is differentiated from the non-Russian parts of the Far East that are called East Asia (*vostochnaia Aziia*) or the Asia Pacific Region (*Aziatsko-tikhookeanskii region*).

The region is roughly synonymous with the Far Eastern **Federal District**, and includes the **federal subjects** of **Sakha**, **Amur**, **Kamchatka**, **Khabarovsk**, **Magadan**, **Chukotka**, **Primorsky**, **Sakhalin**, and the **Jewish Autonomous Oblast**. Covering an area of more than 6,000,000 square kilometers with a population of less than 7 million, the Russian Far East is one of the most sparsely populated areas of the globe. While **ethnic Russians** are the majority (82 percent) in the region, there are large numbers of **ethnic minorities**, particularly **indigenous peoples of the north**. Traditional occupations such as reindeer herding and **fishing** continue to employ a sizable percentage of the autochthonous population. The region's flora and **wildlife** are extremely diverse, and there have been efforts to protect the region's pristine **environment** in recent years. However, newly discovered reserves of hydrocarbons, as well as continued exploitation of diamonds and precious metals, are making preservation of the ecosystem increasingly difficult.

Due to its distance from **Moscow** and poor **transportation** links with the rest of the country, the Russian Far East is afforded a high level of autonomy compared to other regions of the Russian Federation. China's historic claims to the region, combined with the steady flow of **Chinese** immigrants into the area, are of concern to many Russian politicians. *See also* IMMIGRATION; NORTH KOREA.

RUSSIAN FAR NORTH. *See* FAR NORTH.

RUSSIAN LANGUAGE. Russian (*russkii iazyk*) is part of the East Slavic branch of the Indo-European language family. It is mostly closely related to Ukrainian and Belarusian, and more distantly related to Polish, Serbian, Bulgarian, and the other Slavic tongues. As with the majority of other Slavic **languages**, Russian has a flexible word order: nouns, adjectives, pronouns, and numbers change their endings (the case system) to reflect the relationships between words in a sentence. A specific feature of the Russian sound system is the use of palatalized, or soft consonants, which, when transliterated, are indicated with an apostrophe: *vlast'*—"power." The Russian language has an enormous ability to generate new meaning with the help of prefixes, suffixes, and other morphological tools.

Worldwide, there are approximately 275 million speakers of the language, with 160 million speaking it as their native tongue. The language is spoken by 97 percent of Russian citizens; outside of Russia, it is spoken in the former Soviet republics (particularly **Ukraine**, **Belarus**, and **Kazakhstan**), as well as in **Israel**, **Germany**, **Mongolia**, **Great Britain**, and the **United States**. It is an official language in Russia, Belarus, Kazakhstan, and **Kyrgyzstan**, as well as the breakaway republics of **Abkhazia**, **South Ossetia**, and **Transnistria**. The Russian hybrids of *Surzhyk* (Ukrainian-Russian) and *Trasianka* (Belarusian-Russian) attest to the language's importance beyond Russia's borders. Russian employs the Cyrillic alphabet, originally adapted from the Greek alphabet by Byzantine missionaries. It is one of the six official languages of the **United Nations**, and—until

1991—enjoyed popularity among many second-language learners in the **Eastern Bloc** and the Third World.

The Russian language, and especially its vocabulary system, reflects the religious, political, and imperial history of the nation. Abstract notions are often words of Greek or Latin origin. Russian poetic language derives from the Old Church Slavonic; these words have common Russian equivalents (for example, *mlechnyi* and *molochnyi*, both referring to milk). Words for **food** products and everyday objects come from a host of neighboring cultures, often reflecting their original nature as imports from abroad (for example, the Russian word for apple jam—*povidlo*—is of Polish origin, whereas the word for money—*den'gi*—is Turkic).

In the 19th century, the Russian aristocracy communicated in French, and so a large part of the Russian vocabulary consists of coinages derived from French words. English vocabulary units began entering the Russian language from the end of the 19th century; however, this process has increased in the past several decades due to the import of technologies and rapid modernization of the country. A special stratum of the Russian language is *mat*, or *maternyi iazyk*, a system of profanities that have Slavic or Indo-European roots and are reserved for specific uses: *mat* is used as a sign of social distinction—among criminals, army recruits—and designates power relations among speakers. *Mat* is a language in its own right and its uses are highly tabooed and ritualized in the Russian culture.

The nature of Russian is such that despite it being spoken across a vast geographical space, its dialectic variation, especially pronunciation, is not significant, which means it is easily understood by all speakers of Russian, irrespective of their background. Though Russian displays a great capacity for adapting and adopting new vocabulary and speech patterns, there have always been fears among Russian nationalists that the Russian language is under threat. Although no equivalent of the French Academy exists in the Russian Federation, the **State Duma** from time to time discusses legislation aimed at the protection of the Russian language; however, little has been done to advance any specific policies. Major transformations in the language system occurred after the Bolshevik Revolution (1917) and in the wake of Russian independence (1991). In the early 20th century, the alphabet was simplified, with several redundant letters being phased out. More recently, with the arrival of digital technologies, such as the **Internet**, new forms of communication have precipitated new linguistic patterns. One such recurrent system is the "language of scum," a deliberately rude form of Russian that proliferated in the blogosphere of **Runet** in the 2000s. This "digital dialect" uses an innovative system of spelling that, ironically, effectively denotes the sound system of the language. Increasing dual use of the Roman alphabet in electronic environments is also a by-product of the shift to digital technologies.

In recent years, the Russian government realized the political potential of the Russian language as an identity formation tool. Cultural centers like *Russkii Mir* (The Russian World) were established with the aim of disseminating knowledge of Russian across the globe. **Media** outlets, which are widely available in the **Commonwealth of Independent States**, also support knowledge and use of the language. Russian remains one of the few mandatory examinations that Russian students must take to graduate and in order to gain access to higher **education**. The knowledge of Russian is compulsory for individuals seeking Russian citizenship. In the former Soviet republics, for example, **Latvia**, the status of Russian is ambivalent, causing concerns among members of Russian **ethnic minorities** and providing the Russian government with political leverage.

RUSSIAN NATIONAL UNITY (RNU). Banned ultranationalist **political party** and paramilitary group. Under the leadership of **Aleksandr Barkashov**, Russian National Unity (*Russkoe national'noe edinstvo*) grew out of the radical **Pamyat** party in 1990. The neo-Nazi party was legalized in 1993 and began publishing its propaganda vehicle *Russian Order* (*Russkii poriadok*). Most of its members have a strong **Orthodox** orientation, but the group also includes a following of **neo-pagans**, who collectively oppose what they call the "Jewish-Communist yoke" on Russia. The party condemns ethnically mixed marriages and promotes forced birth control for Russia's **ethnic minorities**. They also demand the expulsion of all **immigrants** and minorities possessing a homeland outside Russia, such as the Azeris,

Armenians, Uzbeks, and so forth. The group is hierarchically organized by length of membership, including the ranks (from lowest to highest) of "supporter," "co-worker," and "comrade-at-arms." During the Russian **constitutional crisis of 1993**, the RNU participated in the defense of the White House. Despite the group's swastika-adorned uniforms, Vice President **Aleksandr Rutskoy** granted them the right to bear arms to defend the building from "intruders." While the use of violence is not currently part of the group's charter, a subgroup known as the Russian Knights are organized as a "volunteer self-protection unit" and trained in the use of small arms and explosives. In 1999, the same year it was banned, the group reached its peak in popularity, with some 100,000 members. In 2000, Barkashov lost influence over the organization and established an alternative organization known as Barkashov's Guards or the RNU of A.P. Barkashov. *See also* JEWS; NEO-FASCISM.

RUSSIAN ORTHODOX CHURCH (ROC). Also known as the Moscow Patriarchate, the Russian Orthodox Church is the largest autocephalous or self-governing Eastern Orthodox Church. With approximately 135 million followers, the ROC is second only to the Catholic Church in terms of total adherents within the Christian faith. **Ethnic Russians** within and outside the Russian Federation make up the bulk of the Church's membership, but the ROC also has significant followers among **Ukrainians** and Belarusians, as well as smaller contingents of **Chuvash**, **Mordvins**, **Kazakhs**, **Tatars**, **Armenians**, and other non-Slavic peoples of the Russian Federation and the former Soviet Union.

The ROC claims more than 1,290 dioceses, nearly 30,000 parishes, and over 800 monasteries. These institutions fall under the jurisdiction of the Patriarch of Moscow, who also oversees more than 200 bishops and 27,000 priests. Unlike the Catholic pope, the **Moscow** patriarch does not have full authority to render decisions for his flock, and must coordinate some actions with other Eastern and Oriental Orthodox patriarchs.

The Ukrainian Orthodox Church (UOC) exists under the ecclesiastic jurisdiction of the ROC. The UOC competes with the Ukrainian Autocephalous Orthodox Church Canonical and the Ukrainian Orthodox Church—Kiev Patriarchate (UOC-KP) for parishioners in

Ukraine; in 1997, Patriarch Filaret of the UOC-KP was excommunicated by the Hierarchical Council of the Russian Orthodox Church as part of a five-year dispute over religious authority. The ROC also has authority over the Orthodox Church of **Estonia**, though nationalism-infused disagreements during the 1990s led to a split among the various congregations, with a minority favoring subordination to the Ecumenical Patriarchate rather than Moscow.

In the 1920s, much of the **Russian diaspora** split with the ROC and formed the Russian Orthodox Church Outside of Russia (ROCOR) after refusing to submit to the authority of the Soviet-backed Patriarch of Moscow, Sergius I. The two branches of Russian **Orthodoxy** reunited on 17 May 2007 with the Act of Canonical Communion with the Moscow Patriarchate, though the ROCOR retains a high level of autonomy. Other affiliated churches include the Chinese Orthodox Church, which serves the small Russian diaspora in **China**, the Latvian Orthodox Church, the Moldovan Orthodox Church, the Japanese Orthodox Church, the Orthodox Church in America, and various **Old Believer** churches around the world.

Under Soviet rule, the Russian Orthodox Church, like the spiritual administrations of Russia's other faiths (**Islam**, **Judaism**, and **Buddhism**), came under intense pressure from the state, which espoused secularism and scientific **atheism**. Church-held lands were nationalized and many churches were destroyed or converted for other uses. Priests and bishops were executed, imprisoned, and subjected to intimidation and psychological abuse. During and after World War II, the Church enjoyed a lessening of repression, though a new antireligion campaign was initiated under **Nikita Khrushchev** and continued under **Leonid Brezhnev**. By the 1980s, the **KGB** had thoroughly infiltrated the ranks of the priesthood and co-opted elements of the Church hierarchy. Under **perestroika**, church-state relations improved, marked by the public celebrations of 1,000 years of Russian **Christianity** in 1988.

The ascension of **Alexius II** to patriarch in 1990 signaled a new era in the history of the ROC. As the **Communist Party of the Soviet Union** crumbled, the Church moved to fill the vacuum left by Russia's abandonment of the secular faith of **Marxism-Leninism**. The Church's high approval rating in the mid-1990s ensured that Russian politicians, including then-President **Boris Yeltsin**, would gravitate to the ROC to shore up their support among the masses. Likewise, the Church has benefited from an increasingly close relationship with the Kremlin, and is enjoying ever greater levels of political influence across the country and access to state agencies such as the **military**.

Throughout the 1990s and the current decade, the ROC has overseen the restoration of existing churches and the building of new ones. In collaboration with Moscow Mayor **Yury Luzhkov**, the Church oversaw the reconstruction of Moscow's Christ the Savior Cathedral, which was originally built to commemorate the victory over Napoleon's army in the 19th century, and then destroyed by **Joseph Stalin** in the 1930s. The Church has also expanded its charitable work and lay organizations. After some brief attempts at reconciliation with the Catholic Church, Alexius's relations with the Vatican became strained over the 2002 formalization of an administrative structure for Russia's Catholic community. Alexius's death on 5 December 2008 resulted in the appointment of **Kirill I** in early 2009, an event attended by Prime Minister **Vladimir Putin** and President **Dmitry Medvyedev**.

RUSSIAN ORTHODOXY. *See* ORTHODOXY.

RUSSIAN PENSIONERS' PARTY (RPP). Political party. Known in Russian as *Rossiiskaia partiia pensionerov*, the RPP was established in 1997 by Sergey Atroshenko. In the 1999 **State Duma** elections, the party claimed nearly 2 percent of the vote. While the party increased its share of the vote to 3 percent in 2003, the RPP failed to win any seats. Atroshenko was subsequently dismissed for failure to improve electoral performance; he was replaced by Valery Gartung, though a subsequent dispute between the two led to fractures within the party. The party has performed comparatively better in regional polls, particularly in **Magadan** and **Tomsk**. On 28 October 2006, the RPP merged with the Russian Party of Life and **Rodina** to form **Fair Russia**, which went on to place fourth in the 2007 Duma elections.

RUSSIAN SOVIET FEDERATIVE SOCIALIST REPUBLIC (RS-FSR). As part of the reorganization of Soviet Russia following the October Revolution of 1917, the Bolsheviks created the Russian Soviet Federative Socialist Republic, colloquially known abroad as

Soviet Russia. With the creation of the Union of Soviet Socialist Republics (USSR) in 1922, the RSFSR became the largest and most populous of all the **union republics**. The RSFSR was the **industrial** and **economic** core of the Soviet Union; however, it lacked commensurate political dominance as most powers lay with the party organ of the **Communist Party of the Soviet Union** rather than with RSFSR leadership.

During the period of national delimitation (1919–1936), large swaths of the RSFSR's territory were transformed into **Autonomous Soviet Socialist Republics** (ASSRs) or elevated to the status of Soviet Socialist Republics, such as **Kazakhstan**. During World War II, the RSFSR saw territorial aggrandizement through the annexation of the Tuvan People's Republic and portions of East Prussia (renamed **Kaliningrad Oblast**); in 1954, the administration of **Crimea** was transferred to **Ukraine**.

Under the leadership of the ex-Communist **Boris Yeltsin**, the RSFSR began to acquire greater sovereignty from 1990 to 1991. After the **August Coup** of 1991, Yeltsin moved rapidly to strip power from Soviet President **Mikhail Gorbachev** and expand his own powers beyond those set forth in the 1978 Constitution of the RSFSR. Affirming the plan set forth in the **Belavezha Accords** between the RSFSR, Ukraine, and **Belarus**, the Congress of Soviets of the RSFSR voted to leave the Soviet Union on 12 December 1991; the RSFSR was renamed the Russian Federation on 25 December 1991. Geographically, the RSFSR was the world's largest subnational political entity during its existence, being succeeded by its largest province, **Sakha**, upon independence from the USSR.

RUSSIA TODAY (RT). Television station. Launched in 2005, Russia Today is a Russian news channel that broadcasts globally in English and Arabic (the latter is known as Rusiya Al-Yaum). It is sponsored by the state-owned news agency **RIA-Novosti**. The main objective of the channel is to project Russian official views on international and domestic **politics**, while providing stories on cultural life in Russia for international audiences. Similar to Al Jazeera English (AJE), France 24, Iran's Press TV, and Germany's Deutsche Welle (DW-TV), RT is an attempt to provide an alternative perspective on international news on the Anglophone **media** market dominated by

CNN International and the BBC World News. RT's programming consists of Russian and world news, business and **sports** programs, feature documentaries, and travel, history, and culture shows. In the Arabic language satellite television marketplace, Rusiya Al-Yaum competes with Al Jazeera (Qatar), al-Hurra (**United States**), al-Arabiya (United Arab Emirates), and Hizbullah's al-Manar.

Russia Today is also the first Russian all-digital channel. It is transmitted on 15 satellites covering Europe, Asia, the Americas, southern Africa, and Australia. The channel is transmitted for free, enabling viewing without a subscription. However, in some countries, such as **Great Britain**, the channel is available as part of some television packages, which signifies national control over foreign television broadcasters. RT has a significant web presence with news clips and free live streams available from the channel's homepage as well as on YouTube. The channel has been criticized for applying positive spin to reports about the **Putin** and **Medvyedev** governments and aggressively promoting a pro-Kremlin political agenda. Despite such concerns, RT broadcasts are highly professional and sleekly designed, and have won numerous industry awards.

RUSSIFICATION. Unofficially and officially, Russification (*rusifikatsiia*) of the country's **ethnic minorities** has been a part of Russian rule for centuries. Russification is the forced adoption of the **Russian language**, mores, dress, religious beliefs, **culture**, and/or civilization. The concept can be distinguished from the more neutral "Russianization," which implies a passive or voluntary embrace of Russianness. Under the tsars, cultural and linguistic Russification of **Orthodox** Slavs (including **Ukrainians** and Belarusians) and Finno-Ugric peoples (such as the **Mordvins**, **Mari**, **Karelians**, and **Udmurts**) existed side-by-side with forced conversions of **shamanist indigenous peoples of the north** and **Muslim Tatars**, **Bashkirs**, and **Caucasian** nations.

After the creation of the Soviet Union in 1922, official policies of *korenizatsiia* (rooting or indigenization) were imposed to prevent so-called Great Russian nationalism from eradicating local cultures. **Joseph Stalin** chose the Russian culture as the model for the creation of the common Soviet culture, which was imposed on all Soviet

national minorities. The established **educational** and politico-bureaucratic structure of the Union of Soviet Socialist Republics (USSR) naturally led to the dominance of Russian as the "language of interethnic communication," a trend that was only increased with the **Khrushchev**-era policy of *sblizheniie* (drawing together) of ethnic groups and cultures. Fluency in Russian, with all its accompanying cultural effects, became the norm for nearly all peoples of the **Russian Soviet Federative Socialist Republic** and the urban areas of the other 14 **union republics**. Theorized in the 24th Congress of the **Communist Party of the Soviet Union** in 1971, the end result of such phenomena was the evolution of a unique Soviet *narod* (people), comprised of multiple ethnic backgrounds but unified in language and culture.

With **perestroika** and then the **dissolution of the Soviet Union**, the titular nations of the non-Russian republics, as well as the various ethnic minorities of Russia, moved to reverse decades and even centuries of Russification through support of local **languages**, cultural practices, and **religions**. While the **Baltic States** have effectively extirpated the effects of post–World War II Russification, use of Russian in daily life remains a fact among economic and political elites across much of **Central Asia** more than 15 years after independence. In **Belarus** and **Ukraine**, novel hybrid languages—*Trasianka* and *Surzhyk*, respectively—have evolved as a response to intense Russification and the relative similarities of the indigenous languages to Russian. Dialectal differences also function as political markers of cultural and linguistic difference between traditionally Russian and non-Russian communities. However, census data in both countries show a steady reversal of Russianization since 1991 as more citizens reject "Russian" as their ethnic identity as time goes by.

Within the Russian Federation, the results have also been mixed. Groups like the **Tatars**, **Sakha**, and certain peoples of the **North Caucasus** are enjoying linguistic, cultural, and religious revivals, while the autochthonous peoples of the **Far North** and **Russian Far East** and traditionally Orthodox peoples of the **Volga-Ural region** continue to exhibit the effects of Russification.

RUTSKOY, ALEKSANDR VLADIMIROVICH (1947–). A veteran of the **Soviet-Afghan War**, Aleksandr Rutskoy's war record included being shot down and interrogated by Pakistan's Inter-Service Intelligence and being offered the chance to defect by the **United States Central Intelligence Agency**. He was awarded the title of Hero of the Soviet Union for his bravery, and was subsequently chosen by **Boris Yeltsin** as a running mate for the 1991 Russian presidential election. A strong supporter of **ethnic Russians**, he backed the independence of **Transnistria** and **Crimea**. He also railed against **Yegor Gaydar**'s economic reforms and Russian weakness in the wake of the **dissolution of the Soviet Union**.

In part due to his unpredictable and populist methods, a rift soon developed between Rutskoy and Yeltsin. Following the **Congress of People's Deputies**' attempted "soft coup" against Yeltsin in March 1993, the relationship worsened, and in September, the president suspended Rutskoy from his duties as vice president over allegations of **corruption**. Defending Rutskoy, the **Supreme Soviet of the Russian Federation** declared the move unconstitutional, thus precipitating the **constitutional crisis of 1993**. Rutskoy, now a conspirator, assumed the role of acting president of the Russian Federation, and allied himself with **Ruslan Khasbulatov**.

In the wake of the crisis, Rutskoy was arrested and imprisoned in **Moscow**'s Lefortovo prison until 26 February 1994 when he was granted amnesty by the newly formed **State Duma**. He subsequently founded the *Derzhava* (Great Power) **political party**. In 1996, he was elected governor of his home province, **Kursk Oblast**. He was banned from running for reelection in 2000 on a technicality, reportedly on the orders of **Vladimir Putin**. *See also* POLITICS.

RYAZAN OBLAST. An administrative region of the Russian Federation. Ryazan Oblast is located in the Central **Economic Region** and **Federal District**. It has an area of 39,600 square kilometers and a population of 1.2 million, placing it in the lower midrange of Russia's **federal subjects** in both categories. The region shares borders with **Moscow Oblast**, as well as **Vladimir**, **Nizhny Novgorod**, **Penza**, **Tambov**, **Lipetsk**, **Tula**, and **Mordoviya**. Due to its proximity to **Moscow**, the region enjoys well-developed **transportation** links to other parts of Russia and the **Commonwealth of Independent States**. One of Russia's oldest towns, Ryazan (pop. 520,000) is home to Russia's Higher Airborne Command academy, and a strategic **air force** base is found just outside the city at Dyagilevo.

The region is well forested; the Oka River and Don tributaries are its major rivers. Much of the region was exposed to radiation during the **Chernobyl disaster**, though **agriculture** continues to be an important part of the regional **economy**, thus sustaining a **rural**-urban cleavage that has long characterized the oblast's economic character. The area is heavily industrialized and enjoys a number of institutions of higher **education**. Principal **industries** include automotive, **oil** refining, electronics, agricultural equipment, glass, and petrochemicals. The economy has grown steadily in recent years, and the region has attracted more than 50 **foreign investment** projects; **unemployment** is not a major problem in the **oblast**.

Reflecting the industrial-agrarian nature of the region, rural interests entered into a junior partnership with the **Communist Party of the Russian Federation** (KPRF) in the 1990s, placing it squarely within the so-called **Red Belt**. The KPRF candidate, Gennady Merkulov, won the 1996 gubernatorial elections, after having secured dominance in the regional Duma the year before. Federal authorities, however, removed the KPRF candidate, replacing him with Igor Ivlev; Moscow's man, however, was not able to fend off Vyacheslav Lyubimov, the KPRF candidate with strong backing from **Gennady Zyuganov**, who won the ensuing election.

Lyubimov emerged as a staunch defender of **Serbia** in the late 1990s, advocating the country's admission to the Russia-**Belarus** Union. In 2004, Lyubimov failed to advance to the runoff in the gubernatorial elections; he was replaced by former Commander-in-Chief of Russia's Airborne Troops Georgy Shpak. The former general ran on the **Rodina** ticket defeating a pro-Kremlin candidate, becoming his party's first regional governor. In 2008, **Vladimir Putin** put forth Oleg Kovalev as governor in March 2008. The region is a bastion of the **Russian National Unity** (RNU) party and other far right-wing organizations, and has been the site of attacks on **Jews** and other **ethnic minorities**.

– S –

SAAKASHVILI, MIKHEIL (1967–). Georgian politician. Elected as president of **Georgia** in the wake of the **Rose Revolution** that swept his predecessor Eduard Shevardnadze from power, Mikheil Saakash-vili immediately set to work integrating his country into the fabric of Europe and purging Russian influence over Georgian politics. His first victory came when he successfully reclaimed control of **Ajaria**, which, with Russian backing, had claimed de facto autonomy for several years.

Russia, while dissatisfied with the result, accepted the situation. Saakashvili's attempts to reintegrate **South Ossetia** and **Abkhazia**, however, were met with scorn in Moscow, due to robust economic interests in the regions and the presence of Russian **peacekeepers**. Saakashvili's attempts to gain entry for his country into the **North Atlantic Treaty Organization** (NATO) further displeased the Kremlin, which considered the **Commonwealth of Independent States** member within its exclusive sphere of influence. Tension came to a head in the summer of 2008 when Saakashvili ordered his troops to reclaim Tskhinvali, the capital of South Ossetia.

Russia responded to the actions by launching the **South Ossetian War** against Georgia. Prime Minister **Vladimir Putin** saw the war as a way to permanently deal with the nettlesome Georgian leader, telling President Nicholas Sarkozy of **France**, during mediation of the cease-fire, that he wanted to "hang Saakashvili by the balls." Saakashvili, who traveled to the conflict zone, narrowly escaped with his life. In Georgia, despite plummeting popularity ratings and criticism of creeping authoritarianism, he remains in power.

SAKHALIN OBLAST. An administrative region of the Russian Federation. Located within the Far Eastern **Economic Region** and **Federal District**, the **oblast** is comprised entirely of islands, including the **Kuril Islands** and Sakhalin Island. The elongated island of Sakhalin is nearly 1,000 kilometers from north to south, and only 150 kilometers at its widest point. Sakhalin's closest neighbor is **Khabarovsk Krai**; the two oblasts are separated by less than 10 kilometers at the Strait of Tartary. A rail ferry connects Sakhalin Island to the mainland. Sakhalin Island and the Kurils are separated by the **Sea of Okhotsk**; the Sea of Japan washes the western shores of Sakhalin and the Pacific Ocean is to the east of the Kuril chain. The four southernmost islands of the Kurils are claimed by **Japan**; at their closest point, these islands are less than 10 kilometers from the island nation.

The region covers an area of 87,100 square kilometers and has a population of 547,000. Though it is one of Russia's least populous regions, it is highly urbanized with nearly 90 percent of the population living in cities. The regional capital is Yuzhno-Sakhalinsk (pop. 175,000); the city, as well as the southern half of Sakhalin Island, was under Japanese control from 1905 until 1946.

Approximately 85 percent of the population is **ethnic Russian**; other minorities include Koreans and **Ukrainians**, as well as the indigenous Nivkhs and Oroks. Another autochthonous population, the Ainu, was deported to Japan after World War II. Sakhalin Island's **geography** is dominated by numerous lakes and rivers, boreal forests, and two parallel mountain ranges separated by the Tym-Poronaiskaya Valley. The Kuril Islands are volcanic in nature, and 40 volcanoes are currently active. The oblast was created comparatively late in Soviet history when the Khabarovsk Sakhalin region was joined with newly acquired Japanese territory after World War II. Ethnic Japanese were deported from the region, while Koreans and some indigenous populations were allowed to remain.

Despite its reputation as a budding destination for snowboarding and eco-**tourism**, the movement of foreigners within the oblast remains partially restricted by the Federal Security Service (**FSB**) and border control. The region is a key part of Russia's fur trade, with large populations of bear, fox, sable, raccoon, ermine, and other animals. The Sea of Okhotsk and surrounding bodies of water are some of Russia's richest **fishing** grounds. Sakhalin is also endowed with extensive natural resources, including **oil**, **natural gas**, coal, gemstones, and certain rare metals.

Hydrocarbons account for more than half of the region's industrial output. In addition to the energy complex and fishing, forestry is also a major local **industry**. Most **agriculture** is conducted on the family or village level. Due to its location in the northern Pacific Rim, the region is well situated for **foreign trade**; air links connect the region to Japan, South Korea, and the **United States**. The region has two international schools, the Russian-American Business Education Center and the Russian-American School of Business Management of Portland State University.

A significant number of foreign companies have invested in the oblast, including Exxon Mobil (U.S.), Mitsui (Japan), and the Oil and

Natural Gas Corporation Ltd. (India). In recent years, **Gazprom** has muscled its way into the region, buying majority stakes in development projects such as the Sakhalin-2 oil and gas project. Due to preferential treatment of Gazprom by the Kremlin, foreign corporations such as BP and Royal Dutch Shell have been faced with difficult operating conditions. Despite the wealth generated by the energy industry, much of the local population remains mired in poverty, and **unemployment** remains a problem.

Igor Farkhutdinov governed the oblast from 1995 until his death in a helicopter accident in 2003. On his watch, the oblast signed a power-sharing treaty with **Boris Yeltsin**'s federal government in 1996. He was a strong supporter of production-sharing agreements with foreign oil companies, which facilitated the development of the region's ample natural resources under a free-market-type economic regime. Farkhutdinov sought to maintain vibrant economic relations with Japan during his tenure, despite controversy over the Kuril Islands following **Vladimir Putin**'s rise to power.

Farkhutdinov was succeeded by Ivan Malakhov, who won reelection in late 2003. Malakhov's policies attracted even greater levels of **foreign investment**, particularly in the field of mineral extraction; however, he proved to be a less effective defender of foreign firms' interests vis-à-vis Moscow than his predecessor. He stepped down amid Putin's criticism of his handling of the aftermath of a 2007 earthquake in southern Sakhalin Island. Putin appointed the mayor of the northern Sakhalin town of Okha, Aleksandr Khoroshavin, to replace him. Since taking office, Khoroshavin has courted Japanese investment in the Kuril Islands' special economic zone.

SAKHA REPUBLIC. An **ethnic republic** of the Russian Federation. Formerly known as Yakutiya, the Sakha Republic is Russia's largest **federal subject**. Only slightly smaller than **India**, the republic spans three time zones and covers an area of 3,100,000 square kilometers. Globally, Sakha is the largest subnational political region, and it would be the world's eighth-largest country if it were independent of Russia. Sakha is washed by the Laptev Sea and the Eastern Siberian Sea, and has an **Arctic Ocean** coastline of 4,500 kilometers.

Sakha administers the Anzhu, Lyakhovsky, and De Long Islands, which are collectively known as the New Siberian Islands. More than one-third of the region lies above the Arctic Circle. Much of the republic is covered by permafrost, with **tundra** in the north and **taiga** in the south. The Lena, which empties into the Laptev Sea, is the region's major river; there are currently no bridges in the region spanning the river, though one is due to be completed in 2013. Other rivers include the Kolyma, Indigirka, and Yana, and the Vilyuy and Aldan, both tributaries of the Lena.

Sakha is part of the Far Eastern **Economic Region** and **Federal District**. The administrative capital is Yakutsk (pop. 210,000), also known as Dyokuuskay. Yakutsk is one of the coldest cities on earth. The republic shares borders with **Chukotka**, **Magadan**, **Khabarovsk Krai**, **Amur Oblast**, **Zabaykalsky Krai**, **Irkutsk**, and **Krasnoyarsk Krai** (prior to 1 January 2007, it bordered the federal subjects of **Evenkiya** and **Taymyriya**, both of which are now part of Krasnoyarsk).

Despite its vast geography, the republic has fewer than 1 million inhabitants. The titular plurality, **Sakha** (Yakuts), accounts for 46 percent of the population; the second-largest group is **ethnic Russians**, who comprise 41 percent of the republic's population. Other statistically significant **ethnic minorities** include **Ukrainians** (3.5 percent), **Evenks** (2 percent), and **Evens** (1 percent). The official **languages** of the republic are Sakha (Yakut) and **Russian**; Evenk, Even, Yukaghir, Dolgan, and Chukchi are recognized as official languages in local areas where these ethnic groups predominate. Most of the population resides in its 10 cities; about one-third of the population lives in village settlements numbering fewer than 700. Eastern **Orthodoxy** is the dominant faith in the republic, though many indigenous peoples continue to observe pagan rites.

The region is particularly rich in natural resources and precious metals, including gold, diamonds, antimony, silver, **oil**, and **natural gas**; the republic holds 45 percent of Russia's coal reserves and is a major exporter of the product to the Pacific Rim. Sakha is the center for diamond **mining** in Russia, accounting for 95 percent of the country's production; the diamond industry is controlled by ZAO **ALROSA**. A number of alternative fuels also exist in the region but are as yet underdeveloped. Consumer goods, fruits, and vegetables are highly priced in the region due to the region's harsh **climate** and remote location as well as its limited **transportation** infrastructure;

however, **unemployment** is comparatively low and Sakha's per capita income is among Russia's highest.

Foreign trade turnover in 2007 was $2.6 billion; economic relations are particularly strong with **Japan** and **China**. Yakutiya was first granted autonomy as an **Autonomous Soviet Socialist Republic** (ASSR) in 1922 under the leadership of the poet Platon Oyunsky. During the period of **glasnost**, a resurgence of Yakut identity combined with a strong **environmental** and localist movement intent on wresting control of the region's vast resources from Moscow produced a particularly vibrant nationalist program in the region. On 27 April 1990, local leaders declared a Yakut-Sakha SSR; Yakutiya's declaration, like those of Gorno-Altay and **Chechnya-Ingushetiya**, was not recognized by the leadership of the **Russian Soviet Federative Socialist Republic**, precipitating a temporary halt on diamond exports from the region.

However, the region's status was changed to a republic on 15 August 1991. The region was officially renamed the Sakha Republic in March 1992, and an Agreement on Economic Relations with **Boris Yeltsin**'s government was signed, providing extensive local control over the region's natural resources and state-owned property; one of the provisions allowed for sales of 20 percent of all extracted diamonds to be controlled by the regional authorities. Sakha's parliament, Il Tumen, adopted a new constitution in April 1992.

Elected shortly before the **dissolution of the Soviet Union**, Mikhail Nikolayev, an ethnic Sakha and a former veterinarian, oversaw the republic's post-Soviet transition, as well as the republic's power-sharing arrangement with Moscow on 28 June 1995. He proved to be one of Yeltsin's staunchest supporters among the regional governors, particularly during the **constitutional crisis of 1993**. As one of the "little fathers," that is, one of the Russian Federation's **ethnic republican** presidents, he emerged as a powerful voice for Russia's need to envision itself as a "federation of nation-states," rather than a simple federal state. Nikolayev exerted almost unquestioned control over the regional **economy** during his tenure, appointing prominent businesspeople to key posts to ensure synergy between the state and local corporations. He established economic relations with 50 foreign governments, including **Great Britain**, Belgium, **Israel**, and the **United States**.

Nikolayev also sought to utilize the region's vast and underpopulated territory for animal conservation, establishing partnerships with other northern countries such as **Canada**. The region possesses some of the best-preserved mammoth skeletons in the world. Federal rules prevented Nikolayev from running for a third term in 2001, despite republican statutes to the contrary and strong support from the local population.

He was replaced by Vyacheslav Shtyrov, head of ALROSA, who won nearly 60 percent of the vote. Shtyrov, who had served as vice president of the republic in the early 1990s, was backed both by **Vladimir Putin** and the outgoing president, Nikolayev; he was reappointed by Putin in 2007 for a second five-year term. With a net worth of $410 million, he is considered one of Russia's richest citizens. Economic relations with South Korea have expanded under his watch, and he has worked closely with **Gazprom** to expand the region's export of its natural gas to East Asia. Support for **separatism** in Sakha is among the highest in the federation, only exceeded by **Tatarstan**. More than half of all Sakha support independence, as do nearly one-third of ethnic Russians. *See also* INDIGENOUS PEOPLES OF THE NORTH; NEO-PAGANISM; NORTH KOREA; PAN-TURKISM.

SAKHA/YAKUTS. Ethnic group. The Sakha, formerly known as the Yakuts, are the Turkic ethnic group who comprise the titular nation of the **Sakha Republic** (Yakutiya); they are the largest ethnic group among the **indigenous peoples of the north**. Across Russia, there are approximately 470,000 Sakha; 430,000 of these reside in Sakha, thus comprising a plurality (45 percent) of the population of the republic.

The Sakha **language** (*Sakha tyla*), despite borrowing heavily from Mongolic and Tungusic languages, is a member of the Northern Siberian subgroup of the Northeastern branch of Turkic languages; it is most closely related to the Dolgan language of **Taymyriya**. While only a limited number of **ethnic Russians** speak Sakha, it is used as a lingua franca among the republic's non-Russian **national minorities** (particularly **Evenki** and **Evens**); since 1991, Russians have increasingly learned Sakha, even sending their children to kindergartens that use the language.

Historically, northern Sakha were seminomadic hunters and fishers, while southern Sakha were pastoralists; the Sakha also have a strong tradition of blacksmithing. Sakha religious practices combine Russian **Orthodoxy**, Turkic paganism, animism, and **shamanism**. The Association of Folk Medicine and the Kut-Sür (Sakha: "Soul-Reason") have served as key organizations for the revival of traditional spiritual practices in Sakha. Reverence for sacred groves is a central aspect of Sakha **neo-paganism**.

Beginning in the **Gorbachev** era, Sakha nationalism asserted itself through language revival and calls for high levels of autonomy and resource control for the ethnic homeland, as well as irredentist claims for territory reaching as far as the **Sea of Okhotsk**. The principal cultural organizations dedicated to the national revival include Sakha Keskile (Sakha Perspective) and Sakha Omuk (Sakha People). Many Sakha organizations marry ethnic nationalism with **environmentalism**.

SAMARA OBLAST. Known as Kuybyshev Oblast during the Soviet era, Samara is part of the Volga **Economic Region** and **Federal District**. Samara Oblast borders **Saratov**, **Ulyanovsk**, **Orenburg**, and **Tatarstan**. At its southern tip, the region is adjacent to **Kazakhstan**, and the regional capital of Samara (pop. 1.1 million) is a transit gateway to the Kazakhstani city of Uralsk and other points in **Central Asia**.

Samara was once a closed city due to its role in the defense and aerospace **industries**, but it is now one of southern Russia's most thriving industrial centers. From 1941 to 1943, the city was the seat of Soviet government as **Moscow** was threatened with **German** conquest. The city is also the site of a large number of **educational** and cultural institutions. The region's second city, Togliatti, is a center of automobile manufacturing. In 2007, the government-owned spa town of Volzhsky Utyos near Togliatti hosted the **European Union**–Russia summit.

The region covers 53,600 square kilometers and has a population of 3.2 million. **Ethnic Russians** form a majority (83 percent); **Tatars** (4 percent), **Chuvash** (3 percent), and **Mordvins** (2.7 percent) are the largest **national minorities** in the region. The region's varied topography is divided between uplands (Zhiguli Mountains), forests, and the Kazakh **steppe**; the region is one of Russia's warmest. Natural resources include coal, **oil**, and **natural gas**. Deposits of various minerals important to the building industry are also found in the area. Local crops include corn, sugar beets, grapes, and melons. Samara also produces wool, meat, and sturgeon. The region has a comparatively lengthy history of industrialization within Russia's south.

A number of hydroelectric power plants are found in the region, as well as factories relating to the chemical, mechanical engineering, and **military** industries. The largest company in the region is AvtoVAZ, the Volga automobile plant, Russia's leading car manufacturer. AvtoVAZ is the maker of Lada cars, and, through a joint venture with the American automaker General Motors, of the Chevrolet Niva sport utility vehicle. With ample local financing through **Sberbank** and the European Bank for Reconstruction and Development, the region has attracted a number of foreign companies, including Coca-Cola, Alcoa, and Nestlé. In 2007, **foreign investment** rose to over $2.3 billion, up from $260 million in 2001. The number of small businesses in the region is in excess of 25,000.

Boris Yeltsin removed the local leadership in the wake of the **constitutional crisis of 1993**. In 1996, the centrist economic reformer **Konstantin Titov** assumed the governorship. As one of Russia's longest-serving regional governors, Titov exerted a great deal of influence over the local **economy**, turning it into one of Russia's most vibrant and sophisticated; he also dismantled many Soviet-era social programs. In 2007, facing high disapproval ratings in rural Samara, he stepped down after having lost the confidence of **Vladimir Putin**. Titov was replaced by Vladimir Artyakov, former managing director of AvtoVAZ. Since taking office, he has worked to expand ties between the region and **Belarus**.

SAMIZDAT. The term *samizdat*, from the Russian *sam* (myself) and *izdat'* (to publish), denotes the clandestine practices of generating, copying, and distributing texts that were otherwise forbidden in the Soviet Union and the former **Eastern Bloc**. It is also an umbrella term for other forms of unofficial information distribution, including *magnitizdat* (the duplication of records using tape recorders) and *tamizdat* (the publication of materials from abroad, or, literally, "over there"). Samizdat was an oppositional political activity since the state persecuted anyone involved in illegal distribution of political or artistic **media**. Those individuals who received a copy were normally expected to produce and distribute more copies, and thus join the unofficial network of the opposition. Samizdat was particularly widespread in the post-**Stalin** Union of Soviet Socialist Republics (USSR) and contributed to the ultimate demise of totalitarianism. Samizdat materials were integral to the early days of **glasnost**, as numerous "forbidden" texts were published in official media organs. In the 1990s, and especially in the 2000s, samizdat practices have been continued in a modified form on **Runet**: Russian literary authors use it as a main platform for publication of their works, and oppositional political views are expressed with a larger sense of freedom online.

SAMOBYTNOST. The term *samobytnost*, from the Russian *sam* ("myself") and *bytnost'*, which is a derivative of *byt* (everyday practices), is a term central to Russian debates about **national identity**. Used in early Russian literature to mean individuality and by the **Russian Orthodox Church** to mean independence, the term became politically charged in the 19th century during the debates between **Slavophiles** and **Westernizers**. The term defines a specifically Russian way of living and emphasizes the originality, uniqueness, and messianic role of the Russian people. The term was used in the Soviet Union to denote local culture and unique everyday practices. The term's 19th-century meaning was resurrected in the 1990s when the newly independent Russia embarked on a journey in search of a new national identity and role in the world.

SARATOV OBLAST. Straddling the **Volga River**, the Saratov Oblast shares an international border with **Kazakhstan** and internal borders with **Volgograd, Voronezh, Tambov, Penza, Ulyanovsk**, and **Samara**; it is adjacent to **Orenburg Oblast**. The **oblast** forms part of the Volga **Economic Region** and **Federal District**. The regional capital, Saratov (pop. 873,000), is a major port located on the western bank of the Volga; once a closed city, it is now a major academic, scientific, and industrial center of southern Russia. Saratov Oblast includes areas that once comprised the Volga German **Autonomous Soviet Socialist Republic** (1924–1941), including its old capital, Engels; however, the region's ethnic **Germans** have, for the most part, been permanently resettled elsewhere in the former Soviet Union or repatriated to **Germany**.

The region covers an area of 100,200 square kilometers of mountainous territory in the west and **steppe** land in the east. Out of a total population of 2.7 million, **ethnic Russians** account for 86 percent of all inhabitants; other **national minorities** include **Kazakhs** (3 percent), **Ukrainians** (2.5 percent), and **Tatars** (2 percent). The region has long been a center of **agricultural** activity, owing to the centuries of settlement of skilled farmers from Europe, particularly Germany. Today, Saratov is a major producer of wheat, as well as rye, sunflowers, sugar beets, and meat. However, industrialization, which began in the late 19th century, has endowed the region with **oil** refineries, petrochemical plants, and numerous mechanical engineering factories.

During the **Cold War**, Saratov Oblast was a major producer of chemical weapons; in 2002, federal authorities opened a chemical weapons destruction plant at Gorny. The first person in space, Yury Gagarin, studied in the region and landed there upon his return from space; the oblast remains an important center for aerospace research and development. There is low **unemployment** in the region, and a large number of small businesses. Exports from the region totaled $2.4 billion in 2008; major **foreign trade** partners include **Turkey**, the Netherlands, Switzerland, and the **United States**. The largest companies in the region are Saratov Refinery, Balakovo Mineral Fertilizers, and **Lukoil**-Neftekhim.

During the 1990s, the **Yeltsin** gubernatorial appointee Dmitry Ayatskov introduced significant reforms in the agricultural and **industrial** sectors of the regional **economy**, including passing one of Russia's first laws on land **privatization**. He also backed the legalization of prostitution. During the 1990s, Ayatskov developed close ties with **Moscow** Mayor **Yury Luzhkov** and signed a number of bilateral agreements with the region. His popularity began to wane after his 2000 reelection as governor. In 2004, charges of misappropriation of funds were brought against him, forcing a leave of absence.

In 2005, he was replaced by Pavel Ipatov, a director of a **nuclear energy** plant and a member of the pro-Kremlin **United Russia** party. Ayatskov has since moved to develop closer relations with **Belarus**. Ironically, Belarusian President Aleksandr Lukashenko blocked the appointment of Ayatskov as ambassador to Minsk in 2005 after the former Saratov governor made light of Belarusian sovereignty vis-à-vis Russia. *See also* CORRUPTION; SPACE PROGRAM; WEAPONS OF MASS DESTRUCTION.

SBERBANK. Tracing its origins to 1841, Sberbank is the oldest and largest credit insitution in Russia, controlling one-quarter of the country's **banking industry**. The company controls 50 percent of retail deposits and has a 30 percent share of the Russian loan market The bank is the primary lending institution for Russia's major **industries** including **oil**, **natural gas**, and **mining** companies. The Central Bank of the Russian Federation is the majority shareholder in the company. Sberbank has approximately 20,000 branches with 261,000 employees and revenues of $20 billion. It also operates in **Kazakhstan** and **Ukraine**. The current president and CEO of Sberbank is German Gref, who also headed the Ministry of Economics and Trade from 2000 to 2007.

SCHRÖDER, GERHARD FRITZ KURT (1944–). German politician. Gerhard Schröder served as **Germany**'s chancellor from 1998 to 2005. During that time, he developed a close personal relationship with **Vladimir Putin**. Putin's fluency in German and Schröder's strident opposition to the **United States**–led invasion of Iraq in 2003 allowed the two to cement a mutually beneficial "strategic partnership." Schröder and his wife's adoption of two orphans from Putin's hometown of **St. Petersburg** created further bonds of comradeship between the two world leaders. Schröder was criticized at home for extolling Putin's "flawless" commitment to **democracy**, as well as for his willingness to sacrifice his nation's energy security and the economic stability of **Poland** and the **Baltic States** to secure direct **natural gas** pipelines from Russia to Germany, notably **Gazprom**'s Nord Stream project. After he stepped down from power, he accepted the position of chairman of the board at Nord Stream AG, a consortium of investors backing the controversial pipeline. Since leaving office, he has criticized the recognition of **Kosovo** and blamed **Mikheil Saakashvili** for the **South Ossetian War**, positions that are quite popular in Russian political circles. *See also* EUROPEAN UNION; FOREIGN RELATIONS; MIDDLE EAST.

SEA OF AZOV. The world's shallowest sea, the Sea of Azov is separated from the **Black Sea** by the Strait of Kerch. The surface area of the Sea of Azov is 37,600 square kilometers. It washes southeastern **Ukraine**, **Crimea**, **Rostov Oblast**, and **Krasnodar Krai**; the Ukrainian and Russian coastlines are roughly equal in length at approximately 500 kilometers each. Both the Don and Kuban rivers flow into the sea, resulting in low levels of salinity; however, late Soviet-era damming projects caused the salinity to spike, thus reducing the variety and quantity of **fish** populations. Both the Russian **navy** and Ukrainian navy are active in the shared waters. In 2003, rumored plans to extend Russia's Kerch Peninsula toward Crimea via a new causeway riled Ukrainian politicians, who feared a Russian attempt to reincorporate the peninsula into Russia. Three years later, Russo-Ukrainian talks on the permanent status of the sea broke down over whether to divide the sea on a bilateral basis or to internationalize the waters; the Ukrainians favored the latter position, but this was opposed by Russia on the grounds that such a decision would allow third-party navies, particularly **North Atlantic Treaty Organization** (NATO) ships, to enter the sea.

SEA OF OKHOTSK. Part of the western Pacific Ocean, the Sea of Okhotsk is bounded in the north by the Russian territories of **Khabarovsk** and **Magadan**, the **Kamchatka** Peninsula in the east, **Sakhalin** Island in the west, and the **Kuril Islands** and the Japanese island of Hokkaido in the south. It connects to the Sea of Japan via the Strait of Tartary and the La Pérouse Strait. The sea has a surface area of 1,528,000 square kilometers. Due to the predominance of Russian coastline along the sea's basin, Moscow historically treated the body of water as a "Russian lake," and continues to maintain the Sea of Okhotsk as a **naval** bastion of Russia's Pacific Ocean Fleet. Due to its low salinity from the Amur River's discharge, the sea is prone to freezing in the winter. The sea is of particular importance to Russia's **fishing industry**, and beginning in the 1990s, Russia sought to ban commercial fishing in certain areas of the sea, creating disputes with **China**, **Poland**, and other states. The seabed was recently discovered to contain approximately 3.5 billion tons of hydrocarbons.

SECURITY SERVICES. Since the tsarist era, the Russian security services have played an important part in the country's **politics**, social and cultural life, and—at times—**economics**. Under the **Romanovs**, the Third Department was established in 1825 as a secret organization charged with **surveillance** of aliens, combating enemies of the regime, and censorship. In 1880, the organization was disbanded and replaced with the Okhrana, or Department for Defense of Public Security and Order, which was a specialized subunit of the Ministry of Internal Affairs (**MVD**). The Okhrana monitored the activities of Russian subjects, as well as Russians abroad, thus giving the Russian secret police an international as well as a domestic role.

Following the Bolshevik Revolution in 1917, the Soviet leadership established the Cheka (or All-Russian Extraordinary Committee to Combat Counter-Revolution and Sabotage) under the leadership of the Polish Bolshevik, Feliks Dzerzhinsky. In 1922, the organization was restricted and divided between the NKVD (People's Commissariat for Internal Affairs) and the GPU (State Political Directorate). The latter was delinked from the NKVD a year later, and made into OGPU (Joint State Political Directorate). Following another series of name changes during World War II, the NKVD and other state security apparatus were merged into the Soviet MVD under **Joseph Stalin**'s ally Lavrenty Beria. In 1954, in conjunction with the purge of the Beria, the **KGB** was created, and would last until shortly before the **dissolution of the Soviet Union** in 1991.

During the **Yeltsin** era, the KGB's functions were assumed by the Federal Counterintelligence Service (FSK). However, in 1995, the FSK was reorganized into the **FSB**, or Federal Security Service. The FSB headquarters are located at Lubyanka Square in Moscow, which until 1991 was known as Dzerzhinsky Square (a monument honoring the Chekist known as "Iron Felix" was removed as part of the de-Sovietization process; it was placed on the outskirts of **Moscow**, though **Yury Luzhkov** has proposed that it be returned to its original plinth).

In addition to the FSB, which manages **espionage** and internal surveillance, other security services include the MVD's special forces (*Spetsnaz*) such as the Alfa, Vitiaz, and Vympel **counterterrorism** units, as well as internal troops that deal with **military** issues, such as guarding **weapons of mass destruction** (historically, the MVD also managed the **gulag** system). These troops often support the civilian police (*militsiia*) in crowd control and other politically sensitive activities. Russia's Special Purpose Police Unit (OMON), originally formed to protect the 1980 Olympics from a potential **terrorist** attack, is also considered part of the security apparatus. Today, OMON is often deployed against antigovernment protestors, including **The Other Russia** and the **National Bolshevik Party**.

Since **Vladimir Putin**'s rise to power, members of the security apparatus have seen their political influence expand greatly. They form a key component in the so-called *siloviki*, and have also enjoyed increased control over Russian **industry** and natural resources.

SEPARATISM. Given Russia's history with separatist movements during World War I and the ensuing Civil War—which gave birth to the **Baltic States**, **Finland**, and the short-lived independent states of **Ukraine** and **Georgia**—and the **dissolution of the Soviet Union** in 1991, the fear of separatism runs high in Moscow. **Chechnya**'s declaration of independence and **Tatarstan**'s decision to pursue diplomatic relations with foreign states in the early 1990s forced the **Yeltsin** administration to treat the question of regional autonomy with kid gloves.

While making it clear that the Kremlin would not tolerate secession from the Russian Federation (even going to the lengths of military invasion to preclude such actions), Boris Yeltsin's policy of **asymmetrical federalism** allowed Russia's **ethnic republics** to enjoy nearly all aspects of sovereignty. Despite such liberal policies, support for separatism remained high among the titular nationalities of these regions through the next decade (in **Komi** and **Sakha**, **ethnic Russians** are also generally supportive of separatism). The reasons behind such support are varied, and include resentment toward the center on resource-sharing; competition among elites for jobs and political influence; conflict between ethnic Russians and the indigenous populations; religious disputes (particularly related to **Islamism**); and historical grievances.

Chechnya and Tatarstan remain the bastions of such sentiment, but **Bashkortostan**, **Adygeya**, and **Tuva** are also predisposed to separatism. Under **Vladimir Putin**, centrifugal trends were reversed, particularly through legislative reforms that allowed the president to appoint regional governors. Putin's successful postconflict management of the second **Chechen War** dramatically decreased local calls for independence, while sustained economic growth related to rising **oil** and

natural gas prices mitigated separatist sentiment in other parts of the federation. The question of secession still remains very much a part of the fabric of **politics** in the ethnic republics, but it appears that the federal government has successfully averted another round of territorial losses that many geopoliticians predicted during the 1990s.

SEPTEMBER 11 ATTACKS (RUSSIAN REACTION TO). Vladimir Putin was the first world leader to console **George W. Bush** in the wake of the September 2001 attacks on the World Trade Center in New York and the Pentagon in Washington, D.C. Putin also called a meeting of the most influential members of the **State Duma** to ascertain how to respond; while the vast majority argued for neutrality or even condemnation of American foreign policy, Putin decided to unequivocally support the Americans in their plight against international **terrorism**. His subsequent televised address made clear his intentions to frame Russia also as a major victim of terror: "Russia knows directly what terrorism means and because of this we, more than anyone, understand the feelings of the American people. In the name of Russia, I want to say to the American people—we are with you."

In the coming months, Putin even took the unprecedented step of permitting **United States** military bases in **Kyrgyzstan, Tajikistan,** and **Uzbekistan**. Moscow also began an unprecedented program of **counterterrorism** information sharing with Washington in an effort to root out transborder networks that connected former mujahideen from the **Soviet-Afghan War** to **Chechen** terrorist cells. Putin referred to September 11 as a "turning point" in Russian relations with the rest of the world, and particularly the U.S. Putin's sophisticated response to 9/11 allowed him to refashion, temporarily, his country's **foreign relations** by placing **Chechnya** at the "epicenter of the global war on terror." Russia quickly reaped a host of benefits including an expanded role for the country in European security through the **North Atlantic Treaty Organization** (NATO)–Russia Council, a pledge of full membership in the **Group of Eight** (G8), and commitments of greater Western consumption of Russia's **oil** and **natural gas**.

SERBIA (RELATIONS WITH). Based on a shared antipathy to the Ottoman Empire, a common faith, and **pan-Slavism**, Serbia and

Russia have a long history of relations. After World War II, the Union of Soviet Socialist Republics (USSR) supported the establishment of the Socialist Federal Republic of Yugoslavia under Josip Broz Tito (while the multiethnic state included a dozen nationalities and six republics, Serbs and Serbia dominated the state apparatus). Fraternal relations, however, quickly dissolved into a rivalry over the direction of Communism in southeastern Europe, with Tito breaking with **Joseph Stalin** and the rest of the **Eastern Bloc**.

Under **Nikita Khrushchev**, relations were restored with Moscow recognizing Yugoslavia as a stable, nonaligned Communist state, although Moscow continued to exercise pressure on Belgrade via its Balkan satellite Bulgaria. During the 1980s, **Mikhail Gorbachev** introduced a period of "new thinking" about Soviet-Yugoslav relations, with some aspects of Tito's economic model being adapted for **perestroika**. Shortly after the **dissolution of the Soviet Union**, the Russian Federation under the leadership of **Boris Yeltsin** established relations with Yugoslavia.

In 1991, both Slovenia and Croatia had seceded from the federation against the wishes of the **United States** and Russia. When the West backed the breakaway republics against Yugoslavia, Yeltsin initially followed suit, preferring to let the **European Union** manage the situation. The early agreement between Washington, Brussels, and Moscow steadily evaporated as war and ethnic cleansing spread across Yugoslavia, fomented by the policies of Slobodan Milošević (Serbia) and Radovan Karadžić (Bosnia).

By the mid-1990s, Russia emerged as the primary defender of **Orthodox** Serbs against the Catholic and **Muslim** populations of a disintegrating Yugoslavia. Recognizing vehement pro-Serb sentiment among Russian politicians, particularly **Vladimir Zhirinovsky**, and the masses, Yeltsin assumed an increasingly belligerent stance on the breakup of Yugoslavia, culminating in the tacit support of Milošević's policies in the formerly autonomous Serbian province of **Kosovo**. Yeltsin, however, was ultimately forced to abandon Belgrade or risk direct confrontation with the **North Atlantic Treaty Organization** (NATO); the crisis over the Kosovo intervention produced the greatest challenge to Western-Russian relations during the Yeltsin administration. In 2000, a popular uprising backed by the military removed Milošević from power. Serbia's new leader

Vojislav Koštunica and **Vladimir Putin** quickly moved to normalize Russo-Serbian relations, with Putin visiting Belgrade in 2001.

In 2006, Yugoslavia was officially dissolved, with Montenegro and Serbia—the remaining republics—declaring their independence (Russia was the first country to establish diplomatic relations with Montenegro). While recognizing the de facto situation in **United Nations**–governed Kosovo during his tenure, Putin vociferously condemned any moves to recognize the independence of the province. He also threatened that international recognition of Kosovo's independence would lead to similar outcomes in other zones of frozen conflict, such as **Transnistria**, **Nagorno-Karabakh**, **Abkhazia**, and **South Ossetia**.

Since Kosovo's unilateral declaration of independence, Russia has led the international campaign to protect Kosovo's ethnic Serbs and return Kosovo to Serbian rule. Russo-Serbia **foreign trade** is vital to Belgrade, with over $2.75 billion annually. Russia is also a critical supplier of energy to Serbia; in 2008, **Gazprom** acquired Serbia's **oil** monopoly in exchange for the right to build a **natural gas** pipeline through the country, a deal that provoked controversy abroad due to its purported linkages to the Kosovo question.

SEVASTOPOL. A port city on **Ukraine**'s Crimean Peninsula, Sevastopol was formerly the home of the Soviet Union's Black Sea Fleet. Today, the city is shared by both the Russian and Ukrainian **navies**. The city has a population of 342,000, approximately 25,000 of whom are Russian **military** personnel. Russia leases several harbors around the city for naval use under an agreement that expires in 2017. **Ukraine** has signaled that it will not renew the lease, thus forcing Russia to begin the transfer of its naval facilities to its own **Black Sea** port cities. In the early postindependence period, Moscow refused to recognize Ukrainian sovereignty over militarized portions of the city; however, a 1997 agreement saw Russia abandoning any territorial claims to Sevastopol. Despite this, certain ultranationalists within Russia continue to lobby for its integration into the Russian Federation or the granting of Russian citizenship to the city's residents.

With a pleasant climate, scenic quays, and art nouveau architecture, Sevastopol is an attractive **tourist** destination; however, during the Soviet period, it was a closed city due to its military significance.

Like the rest of **Crimea**, the **Russian language** is the dominant medium of communication. **Ethnic Russians** form a majority (71 percent), while **Ukrainians** make up slightly less than a quarter of the city's population.

SEXUALITY. Russia's transition from a totalitarian state to a market **economy** and democratic society in the late 1980s and 1990s was marked by a concurrent cultural and sexual revolution. In the Soviet Union, representations of sex in **literature**, **visual art**, **television**, and **film** were highly regulated and even taboo. Foreign films that contained sexual scenes were heavily edited. Textbooks did not contain any references to sexual intercourse, although a study of the human reproductive system was part of the curriculum. This created a sense of a sexless, prudent society, which was often mocked in the West. It is not surprising that during one of the television link-ups between Soviet and American youth, co-hosted by **journalists** Vladimir Pozner and Phil Donahue, a Soviet lady famously declared that there had never been any sex in the Soviet Union. The lack of official information about sex had many negative impacts: for example, Soviet shops did not stock condoms and so the Union of Soviet Socialist Republics (USSR) had one of the highest abortion rates in the world, leading **demographic problems**.

In contrast to the bland official culture, Soviet unofficial culture was quite sexualized. First, the use of *mat*—a substratum of the **Russian language** containing vocabulary describing sexual organs and activities—was extensive, though unofficial, in the Soviet **army** and **industry**. Second, Soviet-era informal commercial networks, known as *blat*, enabled the circulation of certain consumer goods such as lingerie that were unavailable in state stores. Finally, folk traditions, for example, the Russian *chastushka*, contained powerful erotic manifestations that the state was unable to control.

Mikhail Gorbachev's **perestroika** enabled public discussion on many previously taboo subjects, including sex. As part of the broader **education** reform, sex education was introduced in Soviet schools during the 1980s. This shift promulgated a view that a romantic relationship was a precondition to sexual intercourse (always in a marriage). Several popular Western books were translated into Russian during this period, serving as one of the main sources of sexual education. Soviet **media** began to discuss matters of sex and sexual education. For example, the youth-oriented talk show *12th Etazh* ("The 12th Floor") addressed the issue of sexual development among Soviet young people in new and illuminating ways. In 1988, Vasily Pichul's *Little Vera* (*Malen' kaia Vera*) premiered, becoming the first motion picture to contain explicit sexual scenes. This and other films shocked Soviet audiences, who were generally unaware of the country's burgeoning social and sexual revolution.

The post-Soviet sexual revolution, however, had all the characteristics of a sexual revolt. In the course of just a few years, the Russian media marketplace was flooded with low-quality pornography. The **newspaper** *Spid-Info* started as a publication whose goal was to draw public attention to the threat of the **HIV/AIDS** pandemic (hence the title, which in Russian means "information about AIDS"); however, it was soon converted into a tabloid, publishing semipornographic stories and images. While finding an erotic image in a public space was unthinkable in 1980, a decade later magazines with explicit images of sexual intercourse were sold openly at every metro station in **Moscow**. Sex clubs proliferated, pornographic films were shown on cable television networks, and video salons stocked rows of erotic films, with little to no state regulation. Prostitution became a common profession, and many Russian **women** were smuggled out of the country to become sex slaves.

Meanwhile, the AIDS pandemic drew the attention of the public to **homosexuals**. In the absence of an effective hygienics policy, public health officials and media personalities began to blame male homosexuals for the spread of HIV, as well as linking them to other societal problems. However, the public controversy surrounding homosexuality did not stop **Boris Yeltsin**'s government from decriminalizing homosexuality in 1993. Fifteen years later, many Russian homosexuals prefer to keep their identity secret from their families and colleagues for fear of being stigmatized. Gay pride parades and demonstrations in Moscow have been consistently banned by the city authorities, largely because of the religious beliefs of the mayor, **Yury Luzhkov**.

The **Russian Orthodox Church** remains the fountainhead of moral codes that regulates sexual behavior in the Russian Federation.

Like many other traditional **Christian** denominations, the Church promotes reproductive sex as the only acceptable form of intercourse, denounces abortions, and condemns homosexuality. Russia's **ethnic minorities** often follow their own cultural traditions, which sometimes may be at odds with the federal law. For example, there have been attempts to reintroduce polygamy in certain Muslim communities. In **Chechnya**, tribal law, which allows women to be kidnapped and forced into marriage, still trumps state law regulating sexual and marital relationships.

SHAMANISM. Until the arrival of **Cossacks** in **Siberia** and the **Russian Far East**, shamanism reigned as the dominant faith in the region. Even when **Buddhism, Islam,** and **Christianity** began to attract converts, most indigenous peoples of Asiatic Russia continued to employ shamans for purposes of **health care** and as spiritual guides, creating unique syncretic forms of faith. The word *shaman* is, in fact, of Tungusic origin and thus native to Russia's extreme eastern periphery; it has been adopted in many European languages to describe intermediaries between humans and the spirit world.

During the late **Romanov** period, the **Russian Orthodox Church** expanded its reach among the **Sakha, Chukchi, Evenks,** and other non-Russian peoples of the **taiga** and **tundra** zones; however, shamanism was not eliminated. Even in European Russia, the **Mari** continued to preserve folkloric traditions, venerate sacred groves, and observe pagan rites, even as they ostensibly embraced Christianity, exemplifying the so-called double faith (*dvoeveriie*). Under the Soviets, a vigorous anti-**religion** campaign weakened the influence of shamans and forced many practices underground.

With the introduction of **perestroika** in the late 1980s, cultural groups among the **indigenous peoples of the north** and other traditionally shamanistic **ethnic minorities** blossomed. Since the **dissolution of the Soviet Union**, shamans have begun to accrue political, as well as cultural, influence among certain nationalities, including the **Altays, Buryats, Tuvans,** and Mari. In the post-Soviet period, the Russian government created the Shamans Register of Russia to provide some level of oversight over the practice of "neo-shamanism" and to prevent charlatanism.

In recent years, some **ethnic Russians** have gravitated to **neopaganism**, which employs the use of Slavic shamans, who are more likely to be "New Age" enthusiasts as opposed to hereditary inheritors of shamanistic knowledge. In 2009, the country saw its first "Top Shaman" contest where adherents to shamanism could vote for their favorite candidate.

SHANGHAI COOPERATION ORGANIZATION (SCO). Established in 2001, the Shanghai Cooperation Organization assumed the role played by Shanghai Five, which had been founded in 1996 as an intergovernmental mutual security organization linking Russia, **China**, and certain **Central Asian** republics (in 2001, **Uzbekistan** joined **Kazakhstan**, **Kyrgyzstan**, and **Tajikistan** as members of the organization). The original grouping grew out of regional efforts to reduce **military** tensions on the countries' respective borders. Over time, the Shanghai grouping broadened its focus to include cooperation on **counterterrorism**, suppression of **separatism** and other forms of extremism, interdiction of **narcotics** trafficking, and regional security. Joint military exercises were initiated in **Chelyabinsk** in 2007. The following year, the SCO signed an agreement with the **Collective Security Treaty Organization** to expand cooperation on cross-border security and transnational **crime**. Future economic cooperation has also been proposed by China, the only member that is not part of the **Eurasian Economic Community**. Current observers of the organization include **India**, **Iran**, **Mongolia**, and Pakistan; Tehran applied for full membership on 24 March 2008. The group also has relations with Sri Lanka, **Afghanistan**, and **Belarus**. While the **United States** initially was suspicious of the organization as a counterbalance to the **North Atlantic Treaty Organization** (NATO), Washington saw increasing value in the existence of the SCO after the **September 11 attacks**.

SHAYEVICH, ADOLF (1938–). Religious leader. One of two claimants for the title of Chief Rabbi of Russia, Adolf Shayevich is a native of Birobijan in the **Jewish Autonomous Oblast** and the chief rabbi of **Moscow**. The rabbi's claim to be Russia's supreme authority on **Judaism** is recognized by the Russian Jewish Congress, a rabbinical council established in 1996 and supported by many of Russia's most prominent **Jews**. In a move closely tied to **Vladimir Putin**'s attempt to marginalize the influence of Jewish **oligarch Vladimir Gusinsky**, the Kremlin recognized Italian-born rabbi **Berel Lazar** as the leader of Russia's Jewish community in 2000; Shayevich, an ally of Gusinsky, previously held that distinction.

SHAYMIYEV, MINTIMER SHARIPOVICH/ŞÄYMIEV, MINTIMER ŞÄRIP ULI (1937–). Politician. Mintimer Shaymiyev, an ethnic **Tatar**, was born in the village of Anyakovo, Tatar **Autonomous Soviet Socialist Republic** (ASSR). Beginning his political career as manager of irrigation, he worked his way up the ranks of the **Communist Party of the Soviet Union** before assuming leadership of the republic in 1990. During the last years of **glasnost**, Shaymiyev emerged as a powerful voice for pan-Tatar nationalism and regional autonomy.

Once **Tatarstan** declared its sovereignty in 1990, he began to adopt a more conciliatory attitude toward both **ethnic Russians** and nationwide **political parties**. However, his decision not to ratify the 1992 **Federation Treaty** and to adopt his own constitution led to fears of a civil war between the republic and Russia. Unlike **Chechnya**'s leadership, Shaymiyev carefully avoided an embrace of independence in favor of asserting that Tatarstan was fully sovereign, albeit "associated with the Russian Federation." In 1994, he assured Tatarstan's special relationship with the central government through the signing of the first bilateral treaty between Moscow and one of its **federal subjects**.

Given his role as the face of ethnic regionalism within the federation and a well-known actor on the international stage, particularly in the **Muslim** world, Shaymiyev has come to be considered to be one of the most important politicians in Russia. His policies have kept Tatarstan on an even economic keel and prevented the erosion of the social programs taken for granted during the Soviet era. His push for free markets and new housing has been especially popular among the people of Tatarstan, whose unofficial motto is "Buldirabiz!" ("We can!") Shaymiyev was popularly elected in 1996 and 2001. **Vladimir Putin** reappointed Shaymiyev in 2005; at the time of his reappointment, Shaymiyev commanded 70 percent approval ratings. As the dominant political force in the republic for nearly two decades, Shaymiyev's rule has been described as a post-Soviet form of "boss politics" based on clientelism.

In 2008, Shaymiyev issued a stinging criticism of Putin's **vertical of power**, and condemned "Great Russian chauvinism" as equally dangerous to the federation as any form of centripetal minority nationalism. He condemned the encroachment of Russian **Orthodoxy** into the region's **education** system, as well as the proliferation of anti-**immigrant** groups in the capital and **St. Petersburg**. He also advocated for a return to the popular election of regional governors, a policy abolished after the **Beslan** attacks. Shaymiyev's attack on Putin was the first major sign of the prime minister's weakening popularity. Recognizing the need to maximize production of heavy **oil** in his republic, Shaymiyev has partnered with companies in **Canada** to apply innovative techniques for extraction. *See also* SEPARATISM.

SHEVARDNADZE, EDUARD (1928–). Georgian diplomat and politician. As minister of foreign affairs of the Soviet Union from 1985 to 1990, Eduard Shevardnadze was charged with implementing **Mikhail Gorbachev**'s "New Thinking" in **foreign relations**. He presided over the Soviet departure from **Afghanistan**, the termination of Soviet domination of the **Eastern Bloc**, the decision to allow the reunification of **Germany**, and the end of the **Cold War** with the **United States**.

Following Zviad Gamsakhurdia's flight from **Georgia** during the **Georgian Civil War**, Shevardnadze won the presidency of his homeland. Shevardnadze, who had led the country before becoming foreign minister, faced challenges on all sides, including **separatist** movements, as well as from Gamsakhurdia, who attempted to return to power. Ultimately, Shevardnadze gained control of the country but was forced to accept de facto independence of **South Ossetia** and **Abkhazia** as well as limited control over **Ajaria**.

He assumed a decidedly pro-Western orientation and won economic support from the U.S., as well as a strategic partnership that was intended to lead to eventual **North Atlantic Treaty Organization** (NATO) membership. This created friction with the Kremlin, which saw the **Caucasus** as part of its exclusive sphere of influence. Problems between Tbilisi and Moscow were exacerbated after the initiation of the second **Chechen War**, as anti-Russian fighters began taking refuge in northern Georgia. Following Washington's decision to distance itself from his regime due to rampant **corruption**, Shevardnadze was swept from power by the 2003 **Rose Revolution**. He refused asylum in Germany, and returned to private life in Georgia.

SHOCK THERAPY. Promoted by the world-renowned economist Jeffrey Sachs as the most efficient mechanism for transitioning from a state-controlled **economy** to the free market, "shock therapy" was applied to Russia in the early years of the **Yeltsin** administration. The process, conducted under **Yegor Gaydar**, included elimination of price controls and subsidies, mass **privatization** through the sale of state assets, and floating the **ruble** on the international currency market. While the program had worked fairly well in post-Communist **Poland**, the effects on the Russian Federation were disastrous. In early 2009, the respected British medical journal *Lancet* estimated that millions of Russians—mostly late-middle-aged men—died as a result of the withering of the country's welfare and **health care** systems, **unemployment**, **alcoholism**, and rise in **crime** that accompanied shock therapy.

SHOYGU, SERGEY KUZHUGETOVICH (1955–). Politician. An ethnic **Tuvan**, Sergey Shoygu rose through the ranks of **Boris Yeltsin**'s government, ultimately heading up the Ministry for Emergency Situations (EMERCOM), which handles the aftermath of **terrorism**, earthquakes, and other national disasters. In 1999, he emerged as one of the leaders of the newly formed **Unity** party, a vehicle for ensuring **Vladimir Putin**'s election as Russian president in 2000. When Unity merged with **Fatherland—All Russia** in 2001, Shoygu retained a leadership position in the new **United Russia** hierarchy. A competent manager and well liked by the Russian citizenry, Shoygu retained his post as head of EMERCOM throughout the Putin years. In 2009, he visited **South Ossetia** to assist the recently recognized state with reconstruction efforts in the wake of the 2008 **South Ossetian War**. *See also* POLITICAL PARTIES.

SIBERIA. Occupying a vast swath of northern **Eurasia**, Siberia (*Sibir'*) constitutes more than half of the territory of the Russian Federation.

Siberia stretches from the **Ural Mountains** in the west to the watershed Arctic and Pacific drainage basins in northeastern Eurasia. The northern border of the region is the **Arctic Ocean**, while its southern border is geopolitically fixed by **Mongolia** and **Kazakhstan**. Historically, Siberia once comprised lands of the **Russian Far East**; however, the two regions are now distinct. Siberia includes all members of the Siberian **Federal District** (**Altay Krai**, **Altay Republic**, **Buryatiya**, **Zabaykalsky Krai**, **Irkutsk**, **Khakasiya**, **Kemerovo**, **Novosibirsk**, **Omsk**, **Tomsk**, and **Tuva**), as well as portions of the Urals Federal District (**Khantiya-Mansiya**, **Kurgan**, **Tyumen**, and **Yamaliya**); **Sakha** is sometimes included as well, though the **ethnic republic** has been included in the Russian Far East since the 1960s.

Historically, Siberia has been home to many of the great nomadic civilizations including the Huns, Scythians, and Mongols. **Romanov** Russia began the incorporation of the region in the 16th century as **Cossacks** moved eastward from Europe. **Ethnic Russians** have been settling in Siberia for centuries and now represent about 85 percent of the population; however, sizable indigenous minorities remain, including Siberian **Tatars**, **Tuvans**, **Khakas**, **Altays**, and **Buryats**, as well as smaller native groups known collectively as the **indigenous peoples of the north**. There are also an estimated 1 million ethnic **Chinese immigrants** in the region and neighboring Russian Far East.

In the late tsarist era, the **Trans-Siberian Railway** opened up the zones of the region to further European settlement and tied Siberia more closely to the imperial core; the region's population centers remain near the railway. During the Soviet period, Siberia became a human dumping ground for the **punished peoples** and the site of many of the regime's **gulags**.

The region's **climate** ranges from **tundra** in the north to temperate broadleaf forests in the south, with a wide band of **taiga** in between. The absence of east-west mountain ranges translates into severe exposure to Arctic weather patterns, and thus brutally cold winters.

Siberia is rich in mineral resources as well as **oil** and **natural gas**. In the south, **agriculture** is also a key source of employment and revenue. Heavy **industry** has mostly collapsed since the **dissolution of the Soviet Union** in 1991. Novosibirsk (pop. 1,500,000) is the largest city in the region. Due to its insalubrious climate and distance from major population centers, Siberia is currently facing severely negative **demographic challenges**, which the federal and local governments are working to counteract.

SIBNEFT. *See* GAZPROM.

SILOVIKI. The term *siloviki* is a recent coinage derived from the Russian word *sila* (power). The notion designates governmental power institutions and agencies such as the police, **army**, and various **security services**. The term first appeared in the 1990s, when it was used in colloquial speech to refer to new state power instruments that had often confusing and contradictory jurisdictions. The term eventually became common in the Russian **media** and officialdom, being used to denote Russian governmental culture after the rise of **Vladimir Putin**. In the West, the word is used in relation to the individuals who command the state power institutions and who are close to the president of the Russian Federation. The influence of such individuals is often contrasted with the power of the **apparatchiks** in the late Soviet context and with the **oligarchs** in the **Yeltsin** era.

SINATRA DOCTRINE. The "Sinatra Doctrine" was a tongue-in-cheek description of **Mikhail Gorbachev**'s 1989 shift in policy that allowed the **Warsaw Treaty Organization** (WTO) nations to determine their own path toward socialism, effectively triggering the abandonment of one-party totalitarian systems in Eastern Europe. Alluding to the Frank Sinatra song "My Way," the new orientation eliminated the threat of Soviet military intervention if one of Moscow's **Eastern Bloc** satellite states chose to abandon its **military** and diplomatic alliances with the Union of Soviet Socialist Republics (USSR). The threat of such action stemmed from the 1968 WTO invasion of Czechoslovakia during the "Prague Spring," and was generally labeled the **Brezhnev** Doctrine in the West. The phrase came into wide usage after Foreign Ministry spokesman Gennady Gerasimov uttered it on a popular American morning talk show on 25 October 1989. Gerasimov's appearance was meant to provide greater context to a seminal speech on the Soviet Union's changing stance in its **foreign relations** made by **Eduard Shevardnadze** two days earlier.

SLAVOPHILES. In 19th-century Russia, Slavophiles were intellectuals who emphasized Russia's unique historic and cultural identity (often called *samobytnost*); they contrasted sharply with the **Westernizers**, who believed that Russia had a common history with Europe and was ultimately destined to adopt Western economic and social practices. The term derives from the Russian word *slavianophil*, which signifies someone who supports Slavs, the ethnolinguistic group to which Russians belong, along with Ukrainians, Belarusians, Serbs, Poles, and others. Slavophiles emphasized Russian traditional forms of commonality and unity as well as an individual's spiritual development. The term is mostly out of use in contemporary **Russian language**; however, ideas of **pan-Slavism** and the messianic role of the Russian nation are instrumental in **neo-Eurasianism**, an ideology that carries on the Slavophile opposition of the Westernizers, now personified by the **Atlanticists**.

SMALL PEOPLES OF THE NORTH. *See* INDIGENOUS PEOPLES OF THE NORTH.

SMOLENSK OBLAST. An administrative region of the Russian Federation. Smolensk Oblast is located on the Eastern European Plain along Russia's western frontier with **Belarus**. Within the federation, it borders the **oblasts** of **Pskov**, **Tver**, **Moscow**, **Kaluga**, and **Bryansk**. Smolensk is part of the Central **Federal District** and **Economic Region**. With approximately 1 million inhabitants, the region's territory covers 49,800 square kilometers. The regional capital, Smolensk (pop. 325,000), lies on the Dnepr, which roughly divides the oblast into northern and southern halves.

Regional **agriculture** is focused on animal husbandry and grain production. Smolensk was severely ravaged by the German invasion; however, postwar reconstruction allowed the region to develop into an important **industrial** center. Major industries include metalworking, computer manufacturing, power generation, chemicals, printing, and clothing. The region is comparatively poor in terms of natural resources, though coal and peat are mined. Smolensk Kristall, Russia's leading diamond polisher and exporter, is located in the region. **Gazprom** is also a key part of the regional economy, as the oblast is a major transit zone for European-bound **natural gas** exports.

Regional trade with Belarus is quite high, and the oblast controls the Moscow-Minsk highway, which serves as a route for **Polish** and **German foreign trade** with Russia.

In the 1990s, Smolensk was part of the **Red Belt** of regions that supported the **Communist Party of the Russian Federation** (KPRF). The KPRF's **Gennady Zyuganov** won a majority of the regional poll in the **1996 presidential election**. The KPRF dominated the regional Duma, while its allies controlled the governorship, including Anatoly Glushenkov (1993–1998) and Aleksandr Prokhorov (1998–2002). In 2002, the pro-Kremlin candidate, Viktor Maslov, a **security services** officer, was elected to lead the region, thus demonstrating a new trend in regional politics; the election was marred by reports of intimidation of Prokhorov supporters by Maslov and his agents. Maslov was reappointed by **Vladimir Putin**. Since 2007, the governor has been Sergey Antufiev, who previously managed relations between the **State Duma** and compatriots in the **Commonwealth of Independent States**. In 2009, Antufiev welcomed the new patriarch **Kirill I** to the region, where the head of the **Russian Orthodox Church** was made an honorary citizen of the oblast. The Russian-American science-fiction author Isaac Asimov and the first person to orbit the earth, Yury Gagarin, were both born in the region. *See also* ALROSA; SPACE PROGRAM.

SOBCHAK, ANATOLY ALEKSANDROVICH (1937–2000). Politician. The first democratically elected mayor of **St. Petersburg**, Anatoly Sobchak taught for several years at the Leningrad State University where his students included two future presidents, **Vladimir Putin** and **Dmitry Medvyedev**. As an independent (non-**Communist**) member of the **Congress of People's Deputies** in the late Soviet period with a legal background, Sobchak contributed greatly to the rewriting of law in the country, as well as crafting the Russian **Constitution** after independence when he served on **Boris Yeltsin**'s Presidential Council.

In June 1991, he won the race for mayor of his hometown in an election that also restored the historic name of the former capital (St. Petersburg). He served as mayor until 1996, overseeing the city's revival as a major international **tourism** destination and the site of important **sporting** events. He fled to Paris in 1997 in the midst of **corruption** allegations relating to **privatization** of real estate. Upon his ascendency, Vladimir Putin arranged for the charges to be dropped, and Sobchak returned to Russia. The former mayor died of a heart attack under somewhat suspicious circumstances on 20 February 2000. He had been campaigning for Putin in **Kaliningrad**.

Sobchak's daughter, Kseniya, is a Russian **media** celebrity who has worked on many popular **television** projects. She is known for her provocative **sexual** behavior and she has undermined Russia's **feminists** by asserting **women**'s traditional role as sexual objects.

SOCHI. A resort city in **Krasnodar Krai**, Sochi is the site of the 2014 Winter Olympiad. The federal government has committed $12 billion in investment to the region to prepare for the games. While the city enjoys warm weather and access to **Black Sea** beaches, it is quite close to the **Caucasus** Mountains, making it an ideal destination for **tourism**. Under **Vladimir Putin**, who has a **dacha** in the region, the city experienced a major revival, capturing tourism dollars that would otherwise be spent in **Crimea**. Sochi has a population of 320,000 and stretches for 145 kilometers along the coast. Less than 15 kilometers from **Abkhazia**, the resort's location is of some concern to Olympic organizers in the wake of the 2008 **South Ossetia War**, which resulted in Moscow's recognition of the breakaway **Georgian** republic's independence; a spate of unexplained bombings in the city since 2008 have also unnerved the Olympic Committee. *See also* SPORT.

SOCIAL DEMOCRATIC PARTY OF RUSSIA (SDPR). Political party. Known in Russian as *Sotzial-demokraticheskaia partiia Rossii*, the SDPR was established by former Soviet premier **Mikhail Gorbachev** in 2001. Commanding about 12,000 members, the party united a number of social democratic **political parties** under a single banner. Gorbachev left the party in 2004 over a dispute regarding the party's support of a deal with the pro-**Putin** "party of power," **United Russia**. The party's membership dwindled under the leadership of Vladimir Kishenin, Gorbachev's successor, and ultimately lost its official status in 2007 due to attrition. Many of the party faithful have reorganized as the Union of Social Democrats, a new party under the leadership of Gorbachev, which abstained from the

2007 **State Duma** elections to focus on becoming a major opposition party by 2011.

SOLZHENITSYN, ALEKSANDR ISAYEVICH (1918–2008). Novelist, historian, and nationalist ideologue. Born to a young widow in Kislovodsk on 11 December 1918, Solzhenitsyn's youth was shaped by the Russian Civil War and the subsequent collectivization of his family's farm. He studied mathematics at Rostov State University before serving in the Red Army during World War II. In 1945, in a personal letter, a passing reference to **Joseph Stalin**'s conduct of the war resulted in Solzhenitsyn's arrest for distributing anti-Soviet propaganda; he was sentenced to eight years of hard labor and internal exile thereafter. His experiences in the **gulag** served as inspiration for his novels *The First Circle*, *The Cancer Ward*, *The Gulag Archipelago*, and *One Day in the Life of Ivan Denisovich*. While the latter text was published with the backing of Soviet Premier **Nikita Khrushchev**, Solzhenitsyn was ultimately declared a nonperson in response to the international controversy generated by his novels. He was deported to West **Germany** in 1974; he then moved to Vermont in the **United States**, where he lived in semi-isolation, railing against the dangers of Communism while harshly condemning Western culture as spiritually bankrupt. In 1990, his citizenship was restored; he returned to Russia in 1994. His polemic views on Soviet history, **anti-Semitism**, condemnation of **democracy**, and belief in Russian supremacy kept him in the political spotlight long after the dismantling of the gulags. Solzhenitsyn, while not actively involved in **politics**, has served as an intellectual anchor for the resurgence of Russian **Orthodoxy**, rejection of Western values, and a reconstitution of an all-Russia state including **Ukraine**, **Belarus**, and northern **Kazakhstan**. For several years, he headed a Sunday morning **television** show that discussed the issues of morality and nationalism; the program became quite controversial and was discontinued. Solzhenitsyn died from heart failure at the age of 89.

SOROS, GEORGE (1930–). Hungarian-American philanthropist and currency speculator. Listed by *Forbes* magazine as one of the 30 richest people in the world, George Soros runs Soros Fund Management and the Open Society Institute (OSI), which supports economic and political transition of post-totalitarian states in Europe and Eurasia. His support of democratization led him to fund the Rose Revolution and other **color revolutions** across post-Soviet space. He emerged as a biting critic of **Vladimir Putin**'s attacks on **civil society** in Russia, particularly after the arrest of **Mikhail Khodorkovsky**, whom Soros viewed as a major asset to the country's social fabric. Soros has connections to a number of other Russian **oligarchs**, including **Vladimir Potanin**.

SOUTH OSSETIA. An autonomous republic of Georgia. The region of South Ossetia, indigenously known as *Khussar Iryston*, existed as an autonomous oblast (AO) within **Georgia** during the Soviet period. Ethnic **Ossetians** enjoyed privileged status in the AO, and their Indo-European language was recognized as co-equal with **Russian** and Georgian. Under **perestroika**, a South Ossetian movement known as Ademon Nykhas (Ossetic: "Popular Shrine") formed to protect the interests of the Ossetians who opposed the Georgian leadership's move toward independence from the Union of Soviet Socialist Republics (USSR) and the increasingly nationalistic rhetoric emanating from Tbilisi. Ademon Nykhas proclaimed the South Ossetian Democratic Republic on 20 September 1990 (seen as the first step toward ultimate unification with **North Ossetiya**), prompting the Georgian president Zviad Gamsakhurdia to abolish the region's autonomous status.

Mutual suspicion between Ossetians and ethnic Georgians turned to violence in 1991, initiating the South Ossetian–Georgian War (1991–1992). More than 100,000 fled the region and there were upward of 1,000 deaths in skirmishes over the next year. In the summer of 1992, the Russian parliamentarian **Ruslan Khasbulatov** threatened Russian **military** intervention if the attacks on the regional capital Tskhinvali and other South Ossetian targets did not stop. The new Georgian president, **Eduard Shevardnadze**, met with **Boris Yeltsin** and agreed to a cease-fire shortly thereafter. Russian **peacekeepers**, supported by the **Organization for Security and Co-operation in Europe** (OSCE), took up positions in the region, which remained relatively peaceful for the next decade.

In 2004, tensions began to rise again. The election of **Mikheil Saakashvili** and his reincorporation of the breakaway region of

Ajaria led to fears that Tbilisi was ready to move again on South Ossetia. Two years later, South Ossetia held a referendum on independence that nearly unanimously supported secession from Georgia. Subsequently, South Ossetian President Eduard Kokoity stated his country's intention to join the Russian Federation, though he recanted after an upbraiding from his patrons in Moscow. Georgian criticism of Russia's increasing military and economic control of the region (Russia is estimated to contribute two-thirds of the region's annual budget) via its peacekeepers and mutual charges of **espionage** worsened relations between Tbilisi and the Kremlin.

In 2008, Georgian military forces began shelling Tskhinvali in what was seen as a prologue to reincorporation of the province, in hopes that the **United States** would intervene. However, the American help did not arrive and the attack prompted a full-scale Russian invasion. After the short but decisive **South Ossetian War**, Russian President **Dmitry Medvyedev** recognized the breakaway region as an independent state (along with the Georgian region of **Abkhazia**); Guatemala and **Venezuela** later followed suit. In 2009, a deal was signed between Moscow and Tskhinvali that allowed Russian border guards to patrol the region's frontier with Georgia proper.

South Ossetia is a mountainous area in the southern **Caucasus** covering 3,900 square kilometers; it has a population of 70,000. The regional economy is mostly based on **agriculture**, with some industry around Tskhinvali; unlike Abkhazia, the region has few prospects for economic development other than its role as a transit zone for Russian-Georgian **foreign trade**.

SOUTH OSSETIAN WAR (2008). In an atmosphere colored by worsening relations between Russia and **Georgia** over the former's military support of the breakaway republics of **Abkhazia** and **South Ossetia** and the latter's talks to join the **North Atlantic Treaty Organization** (NATO) alliance and significant cooperation with the **United States** military, Georgian President **Mikheil Saakashvili** ordered his military to attack the South Ossetian capital of Tskhinvali on the night of 7 August 2008.

Responding to casualties among Russian **peacekeepers** deployed in the region, Moscow immediately responded by ordering a full-scale invasion of South Ossetia. The **military** action was Russia's first offensive deployment outside its borders since independence. The Russian **navy** quickly moved to block Georgian ports, and, acting in conjunction with Abkhazian **separatists**, the Russian army opened a second front in the Kodori Gorge in northwestern Georgia. After five days of fighting, Russian forces had secured the breakaway regions and moved on the Georgian cities of Poti and Gori.

As the Russian military drew closer to the Georgian capital of Tbilisi, the international community—led by French President Nicholas Sarkozy—put pressure on Moscow to agree to a cease-fire, which was brokered on 12 August 2008. Over the next week, Russia evacuated most of its positions in Georgia proper but retained control of so-called buffer zones around Abkhazia and South Ossetia; this allowed the separatist governments to consolidate control of certain territories that had been under Georgian control prior to the conflict. Russian President **Dmitry Medvyedev**, at the behest of the **Federation Council**, recognized Abkhazia and South Ossetia as independent states on 26 August 2008, a move mirrored by only two other **United Nations** members, Nicaragua and **Venezuela**.

A final pullout from Georgian territory occurred in early October. Approximately 400 soldiers died in the fighting and more than 150,000 civilians were displaced. The U.S. and other countries committed substantial funds to rebuilding Georgia's infrastructure in the wake of the summer war, while Moscow has plowed money into Abkhazia and South Ossetia and signed deals to establish military bases in the regions. Since the war, Medvyedev has described Transcaucasia as a "zone of privileged interest" for Russia, prompting fears of future military actions.

SOVIET-AFGHAN WAR (1979–1989). In response to a request made by the **Marxist-Leninist** government of **Afghanistan**, the Soviet Union committed troops to the country on 27 December 1979 with the aim of destroying an Islamist mujahideen insurgency. On the same day, **KGB** Special Forces assassinated the sitting Afghan president Hafizullah Amin, paving the way for the ascension of the more pliant Babrak Karmal.

In the preceding months, Moscow had been building up the Afghan military, while the **United States** was covertly supplying the mujahideen with various forms of aid with the strategic goal of "handing the Soviets their own Vietnam." Unable to quickly smash the mujahideen, the Soviet **military** was soon drawn into urban warfare and clashes with tribal militias. While the Soviet **air force** was able to dominate the skies and the **army** controlled the cities and main communication routes, a guerilla war, directed by local warlords, raged across the country and proved almost impossible to quell. The U.S. Central Intelligence Agency (CIA), working in conjunction with Saudi, Pakistani, and other intelligence services, steadily increased its support of the rebels and backed the creation of a mostly Arab volunteer army that infiltrated Afghanistan via the Pakistani border.

By the mid-1980s, Pakistan's involvement in the war had increased to such an extent that a regionwide conflict loomed. Upon coming to power in 1985, **Mikhail Gorbachev** implemented a long-term exit strategy, which began by shifting the bulk of the engagement to Afghan forces. In the last two years of the war, Soviet forces participated in few military actions. Under protocols established by the 1988 Geneva Accords, the last Soviet troops left the country on 15 February 1989. In the wake of the Soviet withdrawal, the country descended into a civil war, which ended with the victory of the Islamist Taliban in 1996.

During the course of the war, nearly 14,000 Soviet military personnel lost their lives, with nearly 500,000 being wounded or falling ill to serious diseases. More than 100 aircraft and over 300 helicopters were downed, often by U.S.-supplied Stinger antiaircraft missiles. The war had significant international and domestic consequences for the Soviet Union. American President Jimmy Carter placed a trade embargo on the Union of Soviet Socialist Republics (USSR) and led a Western boycott of the 1980 Moscow Olympic Games in protest of the initial invasion. The poor conduct of the war and reports of atrocities severely harmed the Soviet Union's reputation, particularly in the Third World.

The trauma the war left on the home front jolted much of Soviet society from the political apathy that had characterized the late **Brezhnev** era. The conflict inflamed Muslim sensibilities across **Central Asia**, **Azerbaijan**, and the **Muslim** portions of the **Russian Soviet Federative Socialist Republic**. Most importantly, the conflict drained much-needed funds during a difficult period in the Soviet

economy, hampering Gorbachev's efforts to promote reform and reinvigorate Marxism-Leninism.

SOVIET SOCIALIST REPUBLICS (SSRs). *See* UNION REPUBLICS.

SOVIET UNION. *See* DISSOLUTION OF THE SOVIET UNION.

SPACE PROGRAM. As the first country to launch a satellite (Sputnik) and send a manned spacecraft into orbit (piloted by Yury Gagarin), the Union of Soviet Socialist Republics (USSR) long held the lead in the **Cold War**–era space race against the **United States**. However, with the **dissolution of the Soviet Union** in 1991 and the subsequent economic hardships under **Boris Yeltsin**, Russia's space program fell into disrepair, and came to rely on space **tourism** to supplement state funds. In order to maintain the Soviet space station *Mir* (Peace), the Russian Federal Space Agency (FSA or Roscosmos) was forced to collaborate with NASA, its American counterpart. *Mir* was de-orbited on 23 March 2001.

In 1998, the two agencies, along with the space programs of **Canada**, **Japan**, and 10 **European Union** countries, started construction on the International Space Station (though the U.S. later signaled its desire to abandon the project). Under **Vladimir Putin**, the federal government has committed a massive investment toward expanding the space program, including replacing Soyuz spacecraft with the new Kliper model, expanding the **Glosnass** network, and sending unmanned flights to the moon and Mars.

While Russia signed a deal to maintain its lease on the Baikonur Cosmodrome in **Kazakhstan** until 2050, it is simultaneously developing its Plesetsk Cosmodrome in **Arkhangelsk** and Vostochny (formerly Svobodny) Cosmodrome in **Amur Oblast** for future launches. The general director of the FSA is Anatoly Perminov. Roscosmos's headquarters are located in Moscow, while the space flight operations center is located in the suburb of Korolev. The Yury A. Gagarin Cosmonauts Training Center (GCTC) is in Star City in **Moscow Oblast**. The Russian Space Forces are a special division of the **military** dedicated to extraterrestrial operations.

SPETSNAZ. *See* FSB.

SPORT. As was the case with **visual art**, **literature**, and the **media**, sport in the Soviet Union was a matter of ideological significance. In the 1930s, **Joseph Stalin** used sport as a means of constructing the new socialist man (*homo Sovieticus*), with regular sporting events taking place in Soviet cities and **rural** areas, and athletic performances being incorporated into the **military** parades on Red Square in **Moscow**. Sport, and physical culture in general, was used as a means to mobilize masses, and, together with aviation, it formed the bedrock of Soviet mythology and symbology. Despite this, the Soviet Union did not participate in the Olympic Games until 1952 in Helsinki, **Finland**.

Under **Nikita Khrushchev**, the Union of Soviet Socialist Republics (USSR) rapidly emerged as an athletic superpower. During the **Cold War** the ideological battles between the **United States** and the USSR also took place on the field. In protest to the **Soviet-Afghan War**, the U.S. boycotted the 1980 Summer Olympic Games in Moscow; the Soviet Union and much of the **Eastern Bloc** reciprocated by not attending the 1984 Los Angeles Games. In a different vein, the chess tournaments between Anatoly Karpov and Viktor Kortchnoi were viewed as a battle between two systems, with the former representing the socialist world and the latter being an émigré from the USSR who had settled in the West. In the Soviet Union, athletes could earn sport titles that, to some extent, were similar to ranks used in the military forces or in academia.

Deideologization of sport in the late 1980s was part of **Mikhail Gorbachev**'s **perestroika** initiative. Consequently, sport lost its preeminent ideological status and was marginalized in the public arena as political and economic debates commenced in the press and on **television**. In the 1990s, plummeting state support resulted in the deterioration of sporting facilities and mass exodus of athletes from the Russian Federation. At the same time, new athletic activities, such as weight lifting and jogging, were introduced into the country. Many sporting facilities were **privatized**, often being transformed into health spas and exclusive clubs. Despite the withering of state subsidies for international competition, Russia remains one of the world's leading sporting nations (Russia has never finished below third place in the Olympic Games). Russia remains particularly strong in such sports as ice hockey, gymnastics, figure skating, orienteering, wrestling, chess, tennis, and swimming. Russia's achievements on the world stage have not translated into the popularity of sport among Russian citizens. Few people exercise regularly, leading to health problems.

In the 1990s, as a result of the commercialization of Russian **economy** and cultural life, professional—that is, commercial—sport emerged as a reality. Newly established professional sporting associations began searching for funds outside the realm of the Ministry of Sport, Tourism, and Youth Culture. Recently, Russian **oligarchs** have begun funding the national and international sport scene. **Dmitry Medvyedev** included development of sport facilities and sport associations in one of his federal programs, aimed at the modernization of Russian society. In 2014, Russia will hold the Winter Olympic Games in **Sochi**, an event that is meant to boost Russia's national image and improve sporting facilities in the south of the country. *Sport-Express* is one of Russia's most popular **newspapers**, covering sporting news around the world, while the television channel Sport (established in 2003 under the auspices of the state radio and television broadcasting company) is the primary source for live sporting news. *See also* KASPAROV, GARRY.

STAROVOYTOVA, GALINA VASILYEVNA (1946–1998). Politician. Born in Chelyabinsk, Galina Starovoytova achieved national recognition as an ethnographer before entering **politics**. Her fieldwork took her to **Nagorno-Karabakh** and other zones of **ethnic violence**. She became an advocate for minority rights and was elected to the **Congress of People's Deputies** in 1989, representing **Armenia**. After the **constitutional crisis of 1993** and abolition of the Congress of People's Deputies, she worked in a number of nongovernmental organizations before returning to parliament as a member of the **State Duma** in 1995. She was highly critical of **Boris Yeltsin**'s conduct of the first **Chechen War**, dubbing him "Boris, the Bloody," as well as **Yury Luzhkov**'s anti-**immigrant** policies as mayor of **Moscow**. In 1998, as members of the **security services** were ascendant in Yeltsin's government, she was gunned down in the entryway of her apartment building. In 2005, Yury Kolchin and

Vitaly Akishin were convicted of the murder; however, the case remains under investigation.

STALIN, JOSEPH (1878–1953). Real name: Ioseb Besarionis Jugashvili, also known as Iosif Vissarionovich Stalin. Politician. Born to a poor family in Gori, **Georgia**, Stalin rose through the Bolshevik ranks to become **Vladimir Lenin**'s successor. He assumed the role of general secretary of the **Communist Party of the Soviet Union** (CPSU) in 1922, and held that office until his death more than 30 years later. He industrialized Russia through the imposition of a command **economy**, while simultaneously collectivizing **agriculture**.

In the late 1930s, he conducted a purge of the CPSU that resulted in the deaths of approximately a million Soviet citizens and sent countless more to the **gulag**. As the Soviet leader during World War II, he brought the country into alignment with the **United States** and **Great Britain** to defeat Nazi **Germany**. Fearful of treasonous fifth columns, he also ordered the mass deportation of the so-called **punished peoples** to **Central Asia** and **Siberia**. In the postwar period, he incorporated the **Baltic States** into the Union of Soviet Socialist Republics (USSR), annexed large portions of interwar **Poland** and Romania, and established Soviet dominance over what came to be known as the **Eastern Bloc**. As disputes between Washington and Moscow regarding the future of Europe intensified, Stalin led his country into the **Cold War** against the U.S. and its **North Atlantic Treaty Organization** (NATO) allies. He died on 5 March 1953 of cerebral hemorrhage, though speculation remains that he was poisoned.

In the wake of Stalin's death, **Nikita Khrushchev** conducted an anti-Stalinism campaign to do away with the worst abuses of the regime, though the effects ultimately proved lackluster. Many Soviet citizens continued to revere Stalin for his ability to bring stability and prosperity after the civil war, for defeating the forces of fascism, and for turning the USSR into a global power. With **Mikhail Gorbachev**'s institution of **glasnost**, the full extent of Stalin's crimes against the Soviet people came to light; however, this did little to diminish his reputation in certain quarters of the population. During the 1990s, as political chaos, **shock therapy**, and economic crises robbed older Russians of their pensions, apartments, and **health care**, many waxed nostalgic for the days of the firm hand and meager, but reliable guarantees of the Stalin era.

Shortly after coming to power in 2000, **Vladimir Putin** signaled that he planned to rehabilitate Stalin within the Russian Federation. History books were rewritten to accentuate his accomplishments and whitewash or delete his misdeeds. Surveys conducted throughout the late 1990s and early 2000s regularly demonstrated that, if he were still alive, approximately one-quarter of all Russians would vote for him for president. Interestingly, many young Russians now have a positive or ambivalent attitude toward the dictator, a trend that likely reflects the general support for Putin's neo-authoritarian style, which has accompanied Russia's economic growth and return to great-power status. In a recent nationwide campaign to select the greatest Russian figure in history, Stalin placed third; however, it was later discovered that **Internet** activists had rigged the process by generating automated votes.

STATE DUMA. Formed in the wake of the **constitutional crisis of 1993**, the State Duma replaced the defunct **Congress of People's Deputies** as the lower house of the Russian parliament. The **Federation Council** is the upper house; collectively the two are known as the **Federal Assembly**. The use of the word "Duma"—derived from the Russian verb *dumat'* (to think)—reflects an attempt to resurrect the pre-Soviet democratic heritage of Russia (the first Duma was seated in 1906).

As Russia's primary legislative body, the State Duma has a number of duties under the **Constitution of the Russian Federation**: confirmation of the president's choice for the office of prime minister; appointment and dismissal of the chairman of the Central Bank; bringing charges of impeachment against the president; and amnesty. All bills in the legislature must be written by the Duma's deputies, before being debated and either approved or rejected by the Federation Council. If a bill is rejected, a compromise version may be agreed between the two houses.

The Duma consists of 450 deputies, who serve four-year terms; the minimum age requirement is 21. The current chair of the State Duma is **Boris Gryzlov**; he has held the leadership position since

29 December 2003. Previous chairs include Gennady Seleznyov (1996–2003) and Ivan Rybkin (1994–1996).

Since the 2004–2005 **electoral reforms**, election to the Duma is based on **political party** lists, with the seats being filled by the party electors. Prior to these changes, half of all candidates could stand for election in single member districts, needing a simple plurality to win the seat.

The first Russian legislative election occurred in 1993 in the wake of the constitutional crisis. The ultranationalist **Liberal Democratic Party of Russia** (LDPR) showed the best performance, winning 64 seats. The **Communist Party of the Russian Federation** (KPRF) also fared well, placing third. In 1995, the two parties switched places, with the KPRF winning 157 seats. The pro-**Yeltsin** party **Our Home—Russia** came in second. Four years later, the KPRF again placed first, though only receiving 90 seats, while the LDPR—running as the **Zhirinovsky** Bloc—dropped to sixth. The pro-**Putin** party **Unity** took second, while **Fatherland—All Russia**, a party backed by presidential aspirants **Yevgeny Primakov** and **Yury Luzhkov**, placed third.

Following Vladimir Putin's consolidation of power, **United Russia** emerged as the uncontested master of the Duma, winning 223 seats in the 2003 election. The KPRF and the LDPR placed second and third, respectively. A new threshold requirement of 5 percent prevented smaller parties from winning proportional representation in the house, though single-member candidates did capture some seats for the lesser parties. In 2007, United Russia added 92 seats for a total of 315, while a threshold requirement of 7 percent—combined with the new party-list-only system—limited the number of parties receiving seats to four (United Russia, KPRF, LDPR, and **Fair Russia**). The elections were widely criticized in the international community—and the **Organization for Security and Co-operation in Europe**, in particular—as neither free nor fair.

STAVROPOL KRAI. An administrative province of the Russian Federation. Previously called the Ordzhonikidze Krai, Stavropol was given its current name in 1943. Situated in the central **North Caucasus**, the **krai** borders **Kalmykiya, Dagestan, Chechnya, North Ossetiya, Kabardino-Balkariya, Karachay-Cherkessiya, Krasnodar**

Krai, and **Rostov Oblast**; Karachay-Cherkessiya was formerly an autonomous **oblast** within the region. The krai covers a territory of 66,500 square kilometers, and is part of the Southern **Federal District** and the North Caucasus **Economic Region**.

The province has over 2.7 million inhabitants; only a small majority reside in urban areas. With more than 30 statistically significant ethnic groups, Stavropol is one of Russia's most multicultural regions. While **ethnic Russians** are the dominant group (81 percent), many of these continue to self-identify as **Cossacks**. **Armenians** are the second-largest group at 5.5 percent; other **ethnic minorities** include **Ukrainians** (1.7 percent), Dargins (1.5 percent), **Roma** (1.5 percent), and Greeks (1.2 percent), as well as a number of Turkic and Caucasian peoples indigenous to the region.

The provincial capital is Stavropol (pop. 354,000); the city's name is adapted from the Greek "city of the cross." The city served as a base of operations for the **Romanov** Empire's conquest of the **Caucasus**; today, it is an important **education** center in the Russian south. Other cities in the province include Kislovodsk, Piatigorsk, and Nevinnomyssk. The regional topography changes from a mixture of plains and foothills to mountains as one moves south; the highest point is Mount Dombay-Ulgen (4,046 m).

The provincial **economy** is diversified, and includes **agriculture**, **industry**, **tourism**, and **transport**. Major crops include grain, sunflowers, sugar beets, citrus, and legumes; the province supplies half of the country's vegetable oil and is also an important livestock region. Stavropol, when compared to other Russian regions, is comparatively underdeveloped in terms of industrialization; however, key sectors include **food** processing, chemicals, and electricity. **Natural gas**, **oil**, and **coal** are all found in the region. Due to its salubrious **climate** and mineral waters, the region has a long history of medicinal tourism.

Stavropol continues to develop its recreation infrastructure to appeal to tourists from Russia and other parts of the **Commonwealth of Independent States**; as a crossroads for many ancient empires, the region also has strong historical appeal. In terms of international transit, the region is an important crossroads for **foreign trade** with the **Middle East**, as well as a conduit for oil and natural gas from the **Caspian** basin.

In the mid-1990s, the **Communist Party of the Russian Federation** candidate Aleksandr Chernogorov defeated the pro-**Yeltsin** incumbent Petr Marchenko. Chernogorov later came under federal investigation after butting heads with the local pro-**Putin Unity** party (now **United Russia**). The region bucked the national trend by failing to vote United Russia in the first decade of the 21st century, thus allowing the party **Fair Russia** to claim the top spot. Chernogorov was able to hang on to his post until 2008, when he became one of the first regional governors to be removed from his post by the new president, **Dmitry Medvyedev**. Medvyedev nominated Valery Gayevsky to replace him.

In 1995, a group of **Chechen** militants under the leadership of **Shamil Basayev** took control of a hospital in Budennovsk; in the ensuing siege, 166 perished and the hostage takers escaped. Bomb attacks in Pyatigorsk and Nevinnomyssk claimed more lives in 2000, and smaller attacks continued throughout the first Putin administration. During this period, the provincial leadership backed restricting **immigration** into the krai, culminating in a 2002 law that was declared to be in contravention of federal statutes on movement within the Russian Federation. The province was the scene of ethnic unrest in 2007 after the murders of Dmitry Blokhin and Pavel Chadin, both of Slavic descent, who were killed allegedly in response to the death of an ethnic Chechen, Gilani Atayev, a week earlier. Federal authorities detained members of the **Russian National Unity** to prevent the violence from spreading. The region is considered to be one of the most prone to Russian **neo-fascism**. The last premier of the Soviet Union, **Mikhail Gorbachev**, was born in Privolnoye, and ultimately became leader of the Communist Party in the province. *See* CHECHEN WAR; ETHNIC VIOLENCE; TERRORISM.

STEPPE. From the Russian *step'*, the word means a "flat and arid land." While the steppe is unique to **Eurasia**, it shares many characteristics with the North American prairie. Russia's steppe is divided between transitional forest-steppe and the classic variant, that is, grassland plains nearly bereft of trees (except near water sources). The latter is known as the Great Steppe, and stretches from Hungary's Pannonian Plain to the deserts of western **China**; in Russia, this includes the lower Don River basin, the Transvolga, and **Stavropol**. The **climate** of the steppe is continental, allowing for large fluctuations in temperature between the summer and winter months. Much of Russia's forest-steppe has been converted to **agricultural** usage in the past centuries. Under the direction of **Nikita Khrushchev**, an attempt to turn **Kazakhstan**'s northern steppe into farmland failed miserably, creating environmental degradation and soil erosion. Historically, the steppes have served the nomadic conquerors well, including the proto-Indo-Europeans, Huns, Mongols, and Turkic peoples.

ST. PETERSBURG. St. Petersburg (*Sankt-Peterburg*) is a Russian city situated on the Neva River, which empties into the Gulf of Finland on the **Baltic Sea**. The city was founded in 1703 by Peter the Great as the new capital of the Russian Empire. St. Petersburg (known as Petrograd during World War I) remained the Russian seat of power until 1918, when the Bolsheviks moved the capital to **Moscow**. In 1924, following the death of **Vladimir Lenin**, the city was renamed Leningrad. The original name was restored in 1991 as part of the process of de-Sovietization of Russian culture. The name of the surrounding area—Leningrad Oblast—remained in place as a symbol of reconciliation between the Soviet and post-Soviet generations. Informally, the city is known as Piter.

The city is one of Russia's **federal subjects**, and is located in the Northwestern **Federal District** and **Economic Region**. Its administrative jurisdiction is 1,439 square kilometers, while the city proper accounts for less than half of this area. The current mayor is **Valentina Matviyenko**, the only **woman** governor in the country. The regional government is known as the Legislative Assembly.

St. Petersburg is situated far in the north, which results in great variation in the **climate**. In the summer, the city experiences heat waves, whereas in the winters, the weather can be quite damp and cold. Around the summer solstice, it never becomes totally dark, a natural phenomenon that is colloquially referred to as the "White Nights." Historically, the city has suffered from serious floods (in the city center, marks indicating past water levels are common and are used as a reminder of previous disasters). Today, a number of architectural barriers have reduced the risk of flooding.

St. Petersburg is Russia's second-largest city and one of Europe's largest metropolises. Approximately 5 million people live in St. Petersburg proper, with another 2 million in its environs. The city is a large **industrial** center, specializing in shipbuilding, aerospace, software and computers, heavy machinery, and weapons production. St. Petersburg is an important financial center and Russia's second-largest center for the construction industry. The city is also home to many international brands, including Baltika beer. The city serves as an important **foreign trade** gateway; the city's port connects the rest of Russia to Baltic and Nordic Europe via the Volga-Don Canal.

As a **tourism** destination, cultural capital, and **educational** center, St. Petersburg is Moscow's main rival. As a home of the **Romanov** dynasty, the city boasts an extraordinarily rich history and culture, memorialized in the city's landscape, architecture, museums, and arts centers. The **Hermitage** houses the richest collection of art in the world; the Russian Museum specializes in the Russian **visual arts**; the *Kunstkamera*, founded by Peter the Great to house collections of curiosities from around the world, is considered to be Russia's first museum. The royal palaces in the city and its suburbs, such as Tsarskoye Selo, are unique examples of landscape art. A number of world-renowned authors are associated with St. Petersburg, including Aleksandr Pushkin, Fyodor Dostoevsky, Anna Akhmatova, and Joseph Brodsky. Russia's world-famous **ballet** and avant-garde art originated in the northern capital as well.

Unlike Moscow, St. Petersburg is characterized by careful city planning, including numerous canals, straight avenues, and well-orchestrated architectural arrangements. The city's architecture combines baroque, neo-classical, rococo, art nouveau, and modernist styles. Often referred to as the "Northern Venice," St. Petersburg rivals the Adriatic port in terms of its cultural wealth and an obsession with history. While contemporary Moscow is defined by rapid modernization, sometimes-brutal transformation, and unceasing intensity, St. Petersburg is characterized by preservation, memory, and nostalgia, which is especially ironic given that the city was founded in an attempt to promote modernity.

Though St. Petersburg was central to Russian history during the Romanov and early Soviet periods, its role was downplayed in the second half of the 20th century, largely as a result of **Joseph**

Stalin's fear of the city's tendency to produce political opposition. Compared with Moscow, St. Petersburg is somewhat influenced by provincialism, though this is changing as much of Russia's current political elite are Petersburgers (both **Vladimir Putin** and **Dmitry Medvyedev** are from the city). In political terms, the history of St. Petersburg is principally linked to monarchy and Bolshevism, as well as to **democratization**. In fact, many of the social and economic reforms of **perestroika** were conceived in the northern capital. In the 1990s, St. Petersburg gained the unfortunate title of Russia's **crime** capital, partly because of a number of successful crime drama television series such as *Banditskii Peterburg*; in recent years, the crime rate has decreased dramatically.

In 2003, the city celebrated its 300th anniversary. Shortly before this, the historical center underwent a full-scale renovation project, and the history of the city was recollected through a number of art projects, including Aleksandr Sokurov's film *Russian Ark*, set in the Hermitage. The film celebrates the grandeur of the northern capital as well as anticipates its demise. In 2006, the **Group of Eight** (G8) summit was held in the city, which served to showcase further beautification projects and promote the role of city's favorite son, then-President Putin.

SUPREME SOVIET OF RUSSIA. Previously known as the Supreme Soviet of the **Russian Soviet Federative Socialist Republic**, the Supreme Soviet was the highest power in Russia from 1938 until 1990. The body was elected in a secret ballot by the **Congress of People's Deputies**. As the result of legislative changes in the 1990s, the Supreme Soviet became subjugated to the power of the Congress of People's Deputies. From this point onward, the Supreme Soviet was nominally divided between two bodies: the Soviet of the Republic and the Soviet of Nationalities. The parliamentary body was abolished in wake of the **constitutional crisis of 1993**, partly as the result of its leader **Ruslan Khasbulatov**'s role in the crisis. *See also* STATE DUMA; YELTSIN, BORIS.

SURVEILLANCE. Russia is one of many countries in the world that exercises a high degree of government surveillance over its citizens. Western obsessions with the **KGB** (and the tsarist secret police in an earlier era) have exaggerated the myth of the watchful Russian state. Despite this notorious reputation, Russia scores very low in terms of the proliferation and especially efficiency of surveillance technologies when compared with other developed countries.

The Soviet Union was infamous for its elaborate system of surveillance and **espionage**, which was frequently portrayed in the Western press and romanticized by Hollywood filmmakers. The regime did maintain a massive spy network at home and abroad. Attempts at information control often smacked of the absurd, including the registering of all typewriters with the **security services** to ensure that authors of "forbidden" writings could be tracked down and incarcerated. Upon his ascent to power, **Mikhail Gorbachev** condemned the established practices of spying and reporting that had proliferated in all spheres of Soviet society. The new climate of transparency (**glasnost**) made many aspects of the Soviet surveillance system redundant, especially in such nonmilitary areas as museums and archives. The late 1980s and 1990s saw a radical transformation of the system of surveillance, its purposes, and the means of conduct.

In contemporary Russia, surveillance is used for **military** purposes (particularly in **counterterrorism**) and espionage, as well as for data protection in **banking** and for safety reasons in public **transport**. The presence of uniformed police and plainclothes security personnel in Russian public places is dramatically higher than in other European countries, and even most of the **Commonwealth of Independent States**. Russia uses its satellite system to monitor activities in outer **space**, as well as targets on the surface of the planet, including both moving and static objects. The 2008 **South Ossetian War** demonstrated certain flaws in Russia's reconnaissance drones and resulted in the country—one of the world leaders in military exports—having to purchase surveillance technologies from other countries, including **Israel**.

While in the **European Union**, especially in **Great Britain**, video surveillance is widely used for traffic management, in Russia traffic authorities still rely on individual observers. The need to incorporate new surveillance technologies was recently highlighted by **Dmitry Medvyedev** as part of his fight against a high death toll on Russian roads. Though trains are the most popular means of transportation in the country, they are not equipped with CCTV; instead, on long-haul trains, police are used to safeguard passengers (the **Moscow** metro and other underground systems do employ CCTV). CCTV and other surveillance technologies are widely used in banking and other financial industries as well as in retail and service outlets.

SVERDLOVSK OBLAST. An administrative region of the Russian Federation. Lying on the eastern slope of the Urals, Sverdlovsk Oblast is a mineral-rich region with a strong sense of identity. Sverdlovsk is bordered by **Komi**, **Khantiya-Mansiya**, **Tyumen**, **Kurgan**, **Chelyabinsk**, **Bashkortostan**, and **Perm**. The **oblast** is part of the Urals **Federal District** and **Economic Region**. It has a population of 4.8 million and covers an area of 194,800 square kilometers. The topography consists of mountains in the west and **taiga** in the east. **Ethnic Russians** account for 90 percent of the population with Tatars being the largest minority in the region. The regional capital, Yekaterinburg (pop. 1.3 million), is Russia's fifth-largest city; Yekaterinburg saw the restoration of its historical name in 1991 after more than 60 years as Sverdlovsk.

The region is one of only a handful of oblasts that does not share its name with its regional capital. The city's name lives in infamy as the site of the execution of the last members of the **Romanov** dynasty. The city is home to the Uralmash, one of the Soviet Union's largest manufacturing plants. Since 1996, the plant has been part of OMZ (Uralmash-Izhora Group), Russia's largest heavy **industry** company. Sverdlovsk is one of Russia's wealthier regions, and has exceptional economic potential. Other cities include Nizhny-Tagil, Kamensk-Uralsky, Pervouralsk, and Serov. The oblast is heavily forested and has nearly 20,000 rivers (the Ob and the Kama being the largest), allowing for both forestry and hydroelectric power.

Reserves of **oil** and **natural gas** have both been located in the region. Raw materials for the construction industry abound, as do deposits of gold, platinum, and other rare metals, making **mining** a key sector of the regional economy. Key industries include power generation (including **nuclear energy**), engineering, steel production, chemicals, and the manufacture of turbines, generators, and other industrial equipment.

The region possesses a well-developed **banking** and financial industry. Sverdlovsk has been able to attract significant amounts of **foreign investment** since 1991, including from Philips, Coca-Cola, Pepsi, Ford, Audi, and Volvo.

Sverdlovsk's population is highly educated and the region has a long history of scientific research and development; plans are currently under way to develop a so-called Big Eurasian University that will attract talented students and academics from across the **Commonwealth of Independent States** (CIS). The region, which straddles the divide between Europe and Asia, is a key **transportation** hub with the CIS; the international airport has connections to **Finland**, **Germany**, **Great Britain**, and other countries in the far abroad.

In January 1996, Sverdlovsk was the first ethnically Russian region to sign a bilateral treaty with the federal government. The agreement allowed the region to establish direct relations with the Ministry of Defense and Ministry of Finance without going through federal authorities in **Moscow**, though these contacts were later terminated under **Vladimir Putin**'s **vertical of power**. Sverdlovsk took the lead among the non-**ethnic republics** in assuming sovereignty from the center in the early 1990s with its attempted self-redefinition as the Ural Republic (initially, the plan included six oblasts).

The campaign was led by the regional administrator and later governor, Eduard Rossel, an ethnic **German** whose parents were both victims of the **gulag**. Rossel's "Transformation of the Urals" movement outpaced, at least for a time, national **political parties** in terms of local support (though it failed to find favor outside Sverdlovsk). In the early 1990s, he was a supporter of **Boris Yeltsin**, a native of the region, but relations cooled over Rossel's campaign for complete sovereignty. Yeltsin, however, eventually lauded Sverdlovsk's autonomy as a model for establishing genuine federalism in the country. During the **Putin** administration, Rossel adopted a more pro-Kremlin stance and joined the **United Russia** party; he was reappointed by Putin in 2005. With the ascension of **Dmitry Medvyedev**, Rossel's position became tenuous, though he was able to avoid the first round of gubernatorial purges in 2009. *See also* EDUCATION; SIBERIA.

– T –

TAIGA. A Russian word of Turkic origin, *taiga* refers to an ecosystem characterized by coniferous, evergreen forests, as well as swamps, bogs, and lakes. The largest of the earth's biomes, the taiga covers much of the northern areas of the North American and **Eurasian** continents, including northern European Russia, most of **Siberia**, and parts of the **Russian Far East**.

The taiga region's **climate** is continental, with winter lasting approximately six months of the year. Due to the poor soil quality, **agriculture** is extremely difficult. The taiga's indigenous populations, including **Sakha**, **Evenks**, **Mansi**, and **Komi**, have traditionally engaged in reindeer herding, hunting, and fur farming, though forestry, **mining**, and petroleum extraction are increasingly becoming sources of employment. Sparsely populated, much of the Eurasian taiga was conquered by **Cossacks** during the 16th and 17th centuries, creating what has been called Russia's "boreal empire."

Ecologists are increasingly concerned about the effects of climate change on Russia's boreal forests. Global warming is resulting in massive discharges of carbons from the area, which in turn further elevates temperatures. Central Siberia, the heart of the Eurasian taiga, has seen a 2°C increase in average temperature since 1970. Forest fires, acid rain, and invasive species have exacerbated the problem in recent decades. Efforts to protect the taiga figured prominently in the international community's attempts to have Russia join the **Kyoto Protocol**. *See also* ENVIRONMENTALISM.

TAJIK CIVIL WAR (1992–1997). In the wake of **Tajikistan**'s independence from the Union of Soviet Socialist Republics (USSR), political rivalry between the dominant clans from the Leninabad (Khujand) and Kulob region and marginalized ethnic and social groups from the Garm and Gorno-Badakhshan regions turned violent. The former comprised groups loyal to the Soviet-era *nomenklatura*, while the latter drew support from **Islamists** and liberal democrats who formed a coalition called the United Tajik Opposition (UTO).

Beginning in 1992, **Boris Yeltsin**'s government and **Uzbekistan** provided support to the country's new president, Emomali Rahmon (also Imamali Rakhmanov), hoping to prevent the spread of influence of Afghan groups with ties to the rebels. The war peaked during 1993, with large-scale offensives and numerous instances of ethnic cleansing. Initially positioned as a neutral force with the goal of **peacekeeping**, Russian **military** personnel, specifically the 201st

Motorized Rifle division, were occasionally drawn into direct combat with opposition forces and Afghan volunteers. Yeltsin defended his actions by suggesting that the Tajikistan-**Afghanistan** border was effectively a Russian "frontier" and would be treated as such. This established a precedent that remains in effect, despite the cessation of hostilities.

On 27 June 1997, President Rahmonov, the UTO leadership, and **United Nations** Special Envoy Gerd Merrem signed the "General Agreement on the Establishment of Peace and National Accord in Tajikistan" in **Moscow**, thus ending the war. More than 100,000 Tajiks perished in the conflict, as well as an unknown number of Afghans and dozens of Russian soldiers. More than a million people were displaced by the fighting.

TAJIKISTAN (RELATIONS WITH). Modern Tajikistan came under Russian control during the last decades of the 19th century, when Russia abolished the Khanate of Qoq and and established a protectorate over the Emirate of Bukhara. After the conclusion of the **Russian Civil War** and the Basmachi Rebellion, **Joseph Stalin** oversaw the region's organization as the Tajik **Autonomous Soviet Socialist Republic** (ASSR) within **Uzbekistan**.

In 1929, Tajikistan gained the status of a full **union republic**, though with only a small amount of the historical territory associated with the Indo-Iranian Tajiks (particularly the predominantly Tajik-speaking cities of Samarkand and Bukhara). Mountainous, lacking in fossil fuels, and economically underdeveloped, Tajikistan faced instant hardships when it gained independence from the Union of Soviet Socialist Republics (USSR) in 1991. Within a year, political rivalries between the late Soviet-era *nomenklatura* and opposition forces plunged the country into the **Tajik Civil War**, which lasted until 1997. Fearful of **Islamist** contagion in Central Asia, **Boris Yeltsin** supported the old guard against its rivals, a loose coalition of Islamists and liberal democratic reformers. Both Russia and Uzbekistan intervened to help the government recapture the capital in the early days of the conflict.

In 1992, Emomali Rahmon became the de facto head of state when the country's first president, Rakhmon Nabiyev, stepped down in the midst of widespread unrest. Fighting intensified in 1993, and soon degenerated into clan-based and interregional warfare in much of the country. In 1994, Rahmon became president in an election that was uncontested by opposition political parties. During the war, the Tajik economy collapsed and the country became dependent on Russian aid. In 1997, Rahmon—disturbed by the Taliban's seizure of the Afghan capital, Kabul—signed a peace agreement with the more moderate members of the United Tajik Opposition (UTO), a coalition of moderate Islamists from the Islamic Renaissance Party (IRP) of Tajikistan as well as secular politicians; the deal was brokered with support from Russia and **Iran**. Upward of 100,000 died in the conflict and more than a million were displaced (particularly Pamiris and Gharmis who fled across the Afghan border).

With the support of **Vladimir Putin**, Rahmon agreed to allow the **United States** access to air bases as part of the 2001 campaign against the Taliban in neighboring **Afghanistan**. In June 2004, Tajikistan signed an agreement with Russia allowing for the establishment of a permanent Russian **military** base in Tajikistan; Dushanbe also wrote off much of its foreign debt by granting ownership of the Okno **space** tracking station at Nurek to Russia. Since that time, Russian influence in the national economy has dramatically increased, particularly in infrastructure, hydroelectric power, and the aluminum industry; remittances from Tajik guest workers in Russia are also a vital sector of the economy.

Tajikistan is a member of a number of Russian-backed international organizations such as the **Commonwealth of Independent States** (CIS), the **Collective Security Treaty Organization**, the **Shanghai Cooperation Organization**, and the **Eurasian Economic Community**. Tajikistan hosts Russia's 201st Motorized Infantry Division, a contingent of several thousand soldiers who patrol the 1,344-kilometer Tajik-Afghan border; the multiethnic force includes Tajik, Uzbek, **Kazakh**, and Kyrgyz soldiers and is part of the CIS Collective Peacekeeping Force. During the civil war, the unit—which had strong antidemocratic and pro-**Eurasianist** sympathies—acted as an independent political force, supplying weapons to the pro-government paramilitary group the Popular Front (now the dominant political party and known as the People's Democratic Party of Tajikistan). Russia's Federal Border Guard Service also has a large presence in the country to interdict **narcotics** traffic and

Islamist insurgents attempting to enter Central Asia from the **Middle East** and Pakistan via Afghanistan. In addition to more than 20,000 soldiers, Russia has numerous advisors in the country attached to the Ministry of Defense of Tajikistan.

In August 2008, the new Russian president, **Dmitry Medvyedev**, paid an official visit to Tajikistan to initiate new agreements on buttressing the Russian military presence at Gissar Airport, expanding cultural links, policing intellectual property rights, and participating in joint agricultural projects and new educational exchanges. The summit, which occurred in the wake of the **South Ossetian War**, demonstrated that Rahmon was backing away from plans to expand his country's relationship with Washington in favor of a closer orbit with Moscow.

TAJUDDIN, TALGAT SAFICH (1948–). Also Talgat Tadzhuddinov or Taj al-Din. Religious leader. Considered by many to be the ultimate leader of the Russian *ummah* (Muslim community), Tajuddin is a Kazan **Tatar**. He studied at the Soviet madrasah of Mir-i-Arab in Bukhara, **Uzbekistan**, and al-Azhar Islamic University in Egypt. In 1980, he became *sheikh ul-Islam*, or the supreme Islamic authority of Russia's Muslims, and grand mufti of Soviet Europe and **Siberia**. After the **dissolution of the Soviet Union**, he warded off challenges to his leadership from more radical muftis, including the leader of **Moscow**'s Muslims, **Ravil Gaynutdin**. In the past decade, his moderate stance, based on the traditional Hanafi school of jurisprudence prevalent among **Eurasian** Muslims, and vociferous denunciations of Saudi-influenced **Wahhabism** (*vakhabizm*) have won him the backing of **Vladimir Putin** and shored up his claim to leadership of all Russian Muslims. Tajuddin's close relationship with the **Russian Orthodox Church** and his assertions that Turkic Tengrism (sky worship) was the original monotheism have been condemned by some conservative Muslims. His controversial statements on the **United States**, **homosexuals**, and Scientology have made international headlines. Tajuddin is the head of the Central Directorate of Russian Muslims.

TAMBOV OBLAST. An administrative region of the Russian Federation. Tambov Oblast sits on the East European Plain, and forms part of

Russia's Central Black Earth **Economic Region** and the Central **Federal District**. The **oblast** covers an area of 34,300 square kilometers and has a population of 1.1 million. Tambov was politically separated from the **Penza** region during the late 1930s; the region also shares borders with **Saratov**, **Voronezh**, **Lipetsk**, and **Ryazan**. The administrative capital is Tambov (pop. 291,000); the city hosts an important **military** airfield. Michurinsk is the region's second city.

Like other regions in Russia's European core, the **economy** is divided between **agriculture** and **industry**. Important crops include grain, sugar beets, sunflowers, potatoes, and livestock; beer and mineral water are also key exports. Regional industries include machine building, fertilizers, and plastics. During the 1990s, the **Communist Party of the Russian Federation** overtook the **Liberal Democratic Party of Russia** as the leading party in the regional parliament. During the **1996 presidential election**, the region overwhelmingly favored the candidacy of **Gennady Zyuganov** over **Boris Yeltsin**, placing the region squarely within Russia's **Red Belt** of regions. However, the party's popularity waned by the end of the decade. Oleg Betin, a former Yeltsin advisor, has governed the region since 1999; he succeeded Aleksandr Ryabov, a staunch Communist whose economic management of the region was widely viewed as a failure.

During the 1999 election, Betin found strong support from **Moscow** mayor **Yury Luzhkov** and his **Fatherland—All Russia** party. With the rise of **Vladimir Putin**, Betin placed himself in the pro-Kremlin camp, which guaranteed reappointment after Putin's reform of the regional gubernatorial system. As governor, Betin has sought to expand small business through a partnership with **Sberbank**. He has also raised the region's international profile by expanding **foreign trade** with Italy, **Serbia**, and other European countries. In 2007, he led a campaign to clearly mark **Estonian** goods sold in the region as part of an effort to boycott products from the Baltic state during the crisis over the bronze soldier and the subsequent **Estonian Cyberwar**. In 2008, Betin drew criticism from activists across Russia for his attack on **homosexuals** in an interview with the newspaper *Komsomolskaya Pravda*. *See also* CHERNOZEM.

TATARS. Ethnic group. The original Tatars were a northeast **Eurasian** ethnos that was subsumed into the Mongol hordes during the conquests of Genghis Khan. Eventually, the ethnonym came to be applied to a number of ethnically heterogeneous, Eurasian, Turkic-speaking peoples from the **Black Sea** to **Siberia**. There are more than 5.5 million Tatars within the Russian Federation; at 4 percent of the total population, they are the largest **national minority** in the country. The largest subgroup is the Volga Tatars; other communities include the Crimean Tatars and Siberian Tatars. The Volga or Kazan Tatars enjoy the status of titular majority in the Republic of **Tatarstan**.

The Kazan variant of the Tatar **language** is a member of the North Kipchak or Volga-Ural subbranch of Turkic languages; unlike most other Turkic tongues, it is heavily influenced by neighboring Finno-Ugric languages. Tatar is spoken by over 90 percent of ethnic Tatars, and it is also the native language of many ethnic **Bashkirs** and some **Mari**. The Tatar language employed a modified Arabic script until the Latin alphabet was adopted in 1928. After 1938, modified Cyrillic became the official orthography. Tatarstan readopted the Latin script in 2000; however, this change was outlawed by the federal government. The Latin alphabet continues to be used in cyberspace and as a vehicle for interlingual communication with other parts of the Turkic world, particularly **Turkey** and **Uzbekistan**, which use the Latin alphabet.

The Tatars adopted **Islam** during the 10th century and were brought under Russian rule in the 16th century. A small number converted to Eastern **Orthodoxy**, but the vast majority remained **Muslims**. While the Tatars gained fluency in the Russian language and the mores of the **Romanov** Empire, they tended to maintain their own language—which had possessed a developed **literature** since the 15th century and vibrant popular press since the end of the 19th century—and cultural identity. This endowed the Tatars with a privileged status as preceptors of Russian influence in the Muslim lands of **Central Asia**: Tatar merchants and missionaries spread Russian influence across modern Uzbekistan, **Kazakhstan**, and Turkey. During the 1917 Russian Revolution, Tatar nationalists—many of whom espoused a progressive form of **Islamism** known as Jadidism—created the Idel-Ural State, a federation of Turkic, Finnic, and Uralic peoples from the **Volga** basin and **Ural Mountains**. The Bolsheviks destroyed the state and divided the territory among the Tatars, Bashkirs, Chuvash, **Mordvins**, and **Udmurts**.

Tatar nationalism quickly expanded from the **intelligentsia** to the masses under **Mikhail Gorbachev**'s tenure. **Glasnost** allowed for a flowering of Tatar culture, while **perestroika** allowed local elites to expand their control over Tatarstan's ample natural resources. As the 1980s came to an end, the nationalist organization the All-Tatar Public Center (Tatar: *Bötentatar İctimağí Üzäge*), or VTOTS, lobbied intensely for an elevation of the Tatar ASSR to the status of a sovereign entity (Tatarstan had long been denied the status of a **union republic**, ostensibly due to its lack of an international border). Soon the organization was joined by more radical groups such as Milli Mejlis and Ittifaq (Unit), the first non-Communist political party registered in Tatarstan, which espoused strident Russophobia and anticolonialism. Ittifaq's founder, Fauzia Bayramova, remains a potent force in current Tatar politics.

With the 1990 declaration of sovereignty, Tatarstan emerged as guarantor of the linguistic and **national identity** of Tatars across the **Russian Soviet Federative Socialist Republic** and, later, the Russian Federation. In 1992, the First Worldwide Congress of Tatars was held in Kazan in 1992 to promote unity among Kazan Tatars and the larger Tatar diaspora; further congresses have been held since. In 2005, **Vladimir Putin** marked the millennium of Kazan by delivering a speech in Tatar, which symbolized the importance of the Tatar community to the identity of contemporary Russia. **Mintimer Shaymiyev**'s policies of multiculturalism within Tatarstan hewed the sharp edges from Tatar nationalism and promoted the incipient development of a new Tatarstani identity based on civic loyalty to the Republic of Tatarstan. Despite this, a majority of ethnic Tatars support **separatism**, the highest of any **ethnic republic**.

In recent years, Tatar identity has been influenced by resurgent **pan-Turkism** as well as **neo-Jadidism**; the popularity of both movements reflects the Tatars' seminal role in shaping the identity of Russophone Muslims for more than a century. There has also been a marked rise in the level of religiosity among ethnic Tatars, with an increasing use of the *hijab*, or headscarves, among women and demands for *halal* food to be served in the **military**. However, most Tatars are resistant to the austere allure of fundamentalist Islam, instead embracing a modified form of "Euro-Islam." The Muslim Board of Tatarstan, under the leadership of Gusman Hazrat Iskhakov, has worked to mitigate radical influences from the **Middle East** and South Asia; his recent efforts include the establishment of a small Islamic university in Tatarstan.

TATARSTAN, REPUBLIC OF. An **ethnic republic** of the Russian Federation. With the exception of **Chechnya**, which gained its current status through two wars, Tatarstan is recognized as the most sovereign of all of Russia's **federal subjects** and the paragon of **Boris Yeltsin**'s **asymmetrical federalism**. In nearly every way, the region functions as a country within a country.

Relations between **Muslim Tatars** and **Orthodox** Russians date back centuries, and though interactions have often been plagued by mutual suspicion, cooperation and cultural exchange have also been evident. Tatarstan, then known as the Khanate of Kazan, was incorporated into Russia during the reign of the first tsar of Russia, Ivan the Terrible (1547–1584). The inclusion of a large non-Christian, Turkic nation into Russia secured the multicultural nature of the **Romanov** Empire for centuries. During the late 19th century, Tatarstan became an important center of **education** in the Muslim world due to the spread of the progressive **Islamist** ideology of Jadidism. Tatars, in turn, became agents of both Islamicization and **Russification** across Russian **Central Asia**. During the Russian Civil War, Tatar nationalists created a short-lived federation of Turkic and Finno-Uralic peoples known as the Idel-Ural State. Once the Bolsheviks consolidated power in the Volga region, Tatarstan was organized into an **Autonomous Soviet Socialist Republic** (ASSR) on 27 May 1920, epitomizing the Leninist slogan of "nationalist in form but socialist in content." The republic failed to include the majority of ethnic Tatars and purposefully created political divisions between the Tatars and their fellow Turkic Muslims in neighboring **Bashkortostan**. However, Tatarstan was unofficially bestowed with the position of *primus inter pares* among Russia's ASSRs.

Modern Tatarstan is part of the Volga **Federal District** and **Economic Region**. The republic covers an area of 68,000 square kilometers, and its mostly flat topography is defined by a mixture of forests and plains. The **Volga River** roughly divides the country along a north-south axis. The republic has a population of 3.7 million, thus ranking it eighth among federal subjects. Tatars represent a majority at 53 percent, while **ethnic Russians** are the largest minority (40 percent); **Chuvash** are the region's other statistically significant **national minority**. Only one-quarter of all Tatars reside in the republic. Kazan (pop. 1.1 million) is the capital of the republic. The city served as capital of the Khanate of Kazan and the Idel-Ural State.

During World War II, a sizable portion of the Soviet **military**-industrial complex was relocated to the city. Today, it is an important scientific, cultural, and educational center in the Volga region. **Vladimir Lenin** studied briefly at Kazan State University, as did Leo Tolstoy. In 2005, a single-line metro was opened in the city, as was Russia's largest mosque, Qolşärif. Other important cities in the region are Nabrezhnye Chelny, Zelenodolsk, and Nizhnekamsk. The Tatarstan **economy** is well developed and diversified between **agriculture**, **industry**, and the export of hydrocarbons. Tatarstan accounts for more than half of Russia's heavy **oil** production and nearly 10 percent of all oil extraction; there are more than 400 oil fields in the region, with reserves of more than 2 billion tons. Despite its oil wealth, the republic must import **natural gas** for heating and industrial purposes.

Industrial sectors include petrochemicals, machine building, aircraft manufacture, and instrument making. The republic is also an international exporter of **arms**. Residential and industrial construction is also a key driver of the local economy. The automotive manufacturer Kamsky Motor Works is a major regional corporation, as are Tatneft, Kazan Helicopters, and Kazanorgsintez. Small businesses, joint stock companies, and other forms of private enterprise are an important part of the republican economy.

Foreign investment is substantial, with injections of cash coming from General Motors, Hyundai, and other companies. The region's "low risk" ratings from international auditors, local **tax** incentives, and special economic zones have proved particularly attractive to foreign capital. On a national level, the largest investors include Luxembourg, Ireland, **Turkey**, **Great Britain**, and the **United States**. Animal husbandry, beekeeping, and **fishing** are key parts of the agrarian economy. Major crops include grains, sugar beets, and potatoes. The region is an important transit zone for the Russian Federation and the **Commonwealth of Independent States** (which collectively account for more than a quarter of the region's $20 billion **foreign trade** turnover) as well as for European-bound petroleum products. The republic also has a robust communications and **media** infrastructure, including the media companies Tatmedia, Novy Vek, and Efir.

Under the leadership of **Mintimer Shaymiyev**, Tatarstan emerged as an early and vocal supporter of asymmetrical federalism during the Yeltsin era. As head of the Tatar ASSR's Supreme Soviet, Shaymiyev declared Tatarstan to be a sovereign republic on 31 August 1990. The republic was the scene of unbridled nationalism during the first year of post-Soviet independence, prompting fear amongst the sizable Slavic population. Along with Chechnya, Tatarstan rejected the new **Federation Treaty** in 1992, opting instead for its own constitution, which was promulgated on 6 November 1992. While federal troops amassed on the border, no invasion of the republic occurred, as the local leadership, unlike in Chechnya, stopped short of declaring outright independence. In February 1994, the republic led the way in establishing bilateral relations with Moscow, which included full ownership of natural resources and much of its industrial base, as well as retention of 50 percent of all value-added tax (VAT), twice as much as its peers. Tatarstan also gained the right to conclude economic, cultural, and scientific-technical relations with foreign powers (to date, such agreements have been signed with **Cuba**, **Poland**, **Germany**, **India**, Turkey, the United States, most countries of the Commonwealth of Independent States, and others).

Shaymiyev's concessions to the Russians—though unpopular with Tatar nationalists—preserved peace within the region and allowed for better relations with the rest of the Russian Federation. During the 1990s, Tatarstan exerted sovereignty over nearly every aspect of its governance except **foreign relations** and external security (Tatar conscripts were even exempted from fighting in conflict zones). Controversially, the republic also introduced the institution of Tatar citizenship, separate from Russian citizenship.

Along with this, came the notion of a Tatartstani or *Tatarstanets*, that is, a nonethnic categorization of residents of the republic similar to that employed in Russia at large and **Kazakhstan**. The "Tatarstan model" became an example for other ethnic republics and even

oblasts to follow in the 1990s. Tatarstan also introduced extensive reforms to rehabilitate the Tatar **language** and culture, including the introduction of Tatar-language education, subsidies for Tatar **media**, elevation of Tatars within the governmental structure of Tatarstan at the expense of Russian cadres, economic support of Tatar cultural initiatives beyond the borders of Tatarstan, and other measures.

With the ascent of **Vladimir Putin**, relations with the center came under new scrutiny. As part of his creation of a **vertical of power**, federal authorities declared dozens of articles of the Tatarstan constitution in violation of federal laws. While Shaymiyev's government was forced to relent on some policies, such as the introduction of the Latin alphabet for the Tatar language in 2000, he was able to preserve much of the republic's "special status" throughout Putin's administration; however, the Kremlin was able to regain control of certain bodies in the region including the **security services**. Fearful of a backlash in a key republic and hoping to stave off international criticism for his abolition of popularly elected governors, Putin nominated Shaymiyev to keep his post in 2005. *See also* NEO-JADIDISM; PAN-TURKISM; RUSSIAN LANGUAGE; TRANSPORTATION.

TAXATION. Since independence, the Russian taxation system has regularly been criticized as one of the country's most pernicious problems. Under **Boris Yeltsin**, it was estimated that barely one-half of all tax revenues were collected. In 1999, a major reform of the system was initiated, focusing on simplification and the elimination of loopholes. Under **Vladimir Putin**, there has also been an attempt to lessen the burden on businesses and individuals. One of the mainstays of the system is a profit tax on corporations; however, firms developed extremely effective mechanisms for avoiding reporting gains. A popular saying in Russia is: "If a company reports a profit, then it has a bad accountant." Other sources of tax revenue for the federal government include a capital gains tax, a 13 percent personal income tax, the Unified Social Tax to support the welfare and **health care** systems, a value-added tax or VAT (18 percent on most goods), customs duties, and federal license fees. Asset taxation is an important source of income for regional governments. Other funds come from taxes on real estate, gambling, and **transportation**, as well as sales taxes and excise taxes on luxury goods, tobacco, and alcohol.

Income taxes on foreign residents are often higher than those on Russian citizens, but profit taxes are lower in order to attract **foreign investment**. Taxes on the **oil** and **natural gas** industries are critical to the government budget. **Mikhail Khodorkovsky**, once Russia's wealthiest person, was arrested in 2004 on fraud and tax evasion charges, though **politics** are thought to have been the driving force behind his detention.

TAYMYRIYA/DOLGAN-NENETS MUNICIPAL DISTRICT. An administrative district of **Krasnoyarsk Krai**. Formerly a **federal subject** of the Russian Federation known as the Taymyr Dolgan-Nenets **Autonomous Okrug** (AOk), the region (along with the Evenk AOk) was merged with Krasnoyarsk Krai on 1 January 2007, following a 2005 referendum. In the poll, 70 percent of registered voters gave their support for the merger, slightly less than in neighboring **Evenkiya**. The last governor of the region was Oleg Budargin, who was formerly mayor of Norilsk. Mostly **tundra**, the region accounts for 40 percent of Krasnoyarsk's territory. The Taymyr Peninsula is washed by the Kara and Laptev seas and includes the Severnaya Zemlya islands; Cape Chelyuskin is the northernmost point on the Eurasian continent. Dudinka (pop. 25,000) was the administrative capital of the region when it was an AOk. The region's two titular groups—the Turkic-speaking Dolgans and Uralic-speaking **Nenets**—make up 14 percent and 8 percent of the population, respectively; **ethnic Russians** form a majority at 57 percent.

TELEVISION. As a technology, television was first made available in the Union of Soviet Socialist Republics (USSR) during the 1930s; however, it did not become a mainstream medium until the late 1960s due to ideological concerns on the part of the **Communist Party of the Soviet Union** leadership. Early broadcasting was confined to **Moscow** and Leningrad (**St. Petersburg**). Stretching across 11 time zones, the USSR's expansive territory posed both broadcasting and programming challenges. The concentration of the population in the European part of the country defined not only the geographical focus of broadcasting, but also its thematic and programming principles. By the end of the 1960s, virtually every household in urban centers had a TV set, and by the mid-1980s, it was extremely rare to find a household without at least one TV set.

Originally, there were four main channels: Channel 1, the main channel that was also used for broadcasting in the **union republics**; the Moscow channel, which targeted the population of the capital and **Moscow Oblast**; and two "All-Union" channels. In many **rural** parts of the USSR, only Channel 1 and one of the All-Union channels were available into the late 1980s. In addition to the national television channels, there were also additional channels in each of the union republics and in most of the **Autonomous Soviet Socialist Republics** (ASSRs) of the **Russian Soviet Federative Socialist Republic**. These channels broadcast in the **language** of the titular nationality as well as in the **Russian language**. The language policy on television would become one of the catalysts of the **ethnic violence** of the 1980s and 1990s. In addition to terrestrial broadcasting, the Soviet Union had its own satellite system that allowed nationwide coverage, as well as simultaneous broadcasting in various time zones. The system was known as Orbita, and throughout the Soviet period it grew to include over 90 satellites that provided programming to 900 main transmitters and over 4,000 relay stations. This enabled the system to broadcast television programs across the territory of the Soviet Union, as well as the **Eastern Bloc** countries.

In the 1980s, Soviet programming became more diverse and included news programs, **films**, documentaries, children's programs, and **educational**, sports, and culture programs; however, content was prerecorded, reflecting the geographical organization of broadcasting, as well as Soviet ideological considerations. News programs normally consisted of items related to international, national, and regional political and economic affairs and presented only one point of view, that of the Communist Party. Soviet-era news programs typically featured news presenters reading page after page of news with few visuals to accompany the text. There was no advertising on Soviet television because of the centralized **economy**. The gaps between program slots were filled with static images of flowers and other scenes of nature. As the majority of programs were prerecorded, few talk shows were available. This approach to broadcasting changed under **perestroika**, when the youth program *12 etazh* ("The 12th Floor") reintroduced live broadcasting.

Soviet entertainment programs included concerts of classical and folk **music** as well as **ballet** and opera performances. Serialized television shows were virtually unknown, with the exception of *Seventeen Moments of Spring* (*Semnadtsat' mgnovenii vesny*), a 1973 television series devoted to the work of Soviet intelligence agencies at the end of World War II. Representations of violence, **sex**, and vulgarity were not permitted, and generally Soviet television presented a series of well-produced but incredibly dull programs. Adaptations of Russian classical **literature** dominated the entertainment sector. Directors often used literary scripts to indirectly criticize the Soviet regime. Programs for children were very creative: *Sleep Well, Babies* (*Spokoinoi nochi, malyshi*) has survived on Soviet and Russian television since the 1960s. Children's and youth programs were invariably didactic in nature and were intended to indoctrinate the contemporary ideological ethos, although this approach began to wane in the 1980s.

Television's role in the period of perestroika and **glasnost** was to present information that revealed the **corruption** and inefficiency of the regime. Along with live broadcasting, which minimized the time gap between events and their televised version, a culture of investigative **journalism** was established. The press attained an elevation of their status as they maintained high levels of authority through gaining access to and distributing information that had been previously unavailable. A few programs of glasnost became particularly prominent: *Vzgliad* ("The Glance") and *Prozhektor perestroiki* ("The Spotlight of Perestroika"). While these programs focused on national events, others attempted to bridge the information gap between the Soviet Union and the West. These "television link-ups" (*telemosty*) included televised debates between Soviet and American youth; a series co-hosted by Russian journalist Vladimir Pozner and American talk show host Phil Donahue became increasingly important. With a set of new talk shows, live interviews, press conferences, and other live broadcasts, Soviet television changed from a static monolith to a diverse and highly dynamic entity. These new characteristics played a critical role in the early 1990s, particularly during the **August Coup** of 1991, which was crushed partly due to the decision of the journalists to broadcast details of the events.

In the 1990s, television emerged as the central arena for political and economic debates. With the rise of **oligarchs**, television became a tool of propaganda and information wars. Business tycoon **Boris Berezovsky** obtained a controlling share in Channel 1, while **Vladimir Gusinsky** established the private **NTV**, and **Yury Luzhkov** gained influence over TVS. The oligarchs used their television channels to influence the government and to distribute "black PR" against one another. Television was central to **Boris Yeltsin**'s 1996 reelection campaign.

During this period, television programs were flooded with poor-quality advertising; still, it was in the 1990s that television finally emerged as a profit-making operation. However, Russian television networks generally lacked sufficient funds to produce their own entertainment programs. As a result, Western exports entered the Russian television market, including soap operas, game shows, and thrillers. As these often low-quality programs came to dominate prime time, Russian audiences assumed a more cynical view of the medium, permanently impacting television's role in Russian culture: once a lever of liberalization and free debate, television ultimately came to be viewed as a tool for commercial interests and as a social evil. To counteract this trend, the channel Kul'tura (Culture) was established in 1997 as a bastion of propriety and taste in a **media** environment plagued by political scandals, repetitive commercials, and mediocre television series.

The ascent of **Vladimir Putin** in 2000 marked a new era, both in Russian **politics** and television culture. In the first wave of Putin's attacks on private media, NTV was handed over to **Gazprom** and the channel's best journalists left to join TV-6. The most outspoken critics of the regime would finally be silenced in another clampdown on television journalists in 2004. The victims of the government's actions were not only overtly political shows, but also entertainment shows that presented the past or the present of the country in an unsanctioned manner. For example, Leonid Parfenov's *Namedni* ("The Other Day"), which explored the cultural legacy of the Soviet Union, and the satirical *Kukly* ("Puppets") both found themselves on the wrong side of the Kremlin.

During the 2000s, the new government's main objective was to consolidate television channels and to ensure propagation of the "official" interpretation of political events and social life. Putin was particularly keen on disseminating a vision of the Russian Federation as a strong, confident, and united country. The nationalistic project was disseminated through a series of newly created programs, as well as special television channels like Zvezda (The Star) dedicated to the Russian **army**, or the Nostal'gia (Nostalgia) channel, which broadcasted Soviet film and television productions. Oppositional voices migrated either to regional media outlets, print publications, or the **Internet**, turning Russian television into a politically neutered forum where entertainment rather than information reigned supreme. While the role of television in relation to Russian **civil society** has diminished, television has continued to play a central role in Russia's cultural revival: it is because of the growing television industry that audiences became interested in Russian-made television series and films, which was a huge boost for the ailing Russian cinema industry.

In 2009, Russia's national television channels included the following: Channel 1 (51 percent of the company's shares belong to the state); Rossiia (previously the second All-Union channel), Kul'tura and Sport, both controlled by the All-Russia State Television and Radio Broadcasting Company; NTV and TNT, both owned by Gazprom; 5th Channel and REN-TV, both owned by the National Media Group; CTC, Domashnii, and DTV, owned by CTC media; and TV-3, 2x2, and MTV-Russia, owned by Prof-Media. Russian major satellite, cable, and Internet television channels include RBK (Russian Business Consulting), Pravo-TV, Ekspert TV, **Russia Today**, NTV-Sport, NTV+, and many others. In addition to national television channels, there are hundreds of regional and local television studios and channels.

TENGRISM. *See* NEO-PAGANISM.

TERRORISM. While the Soviet Union escaped the wave of terror that gripped Europe from the late 1960s until the early 1980s, the Russian Federation has not been so lucky. During the first **Chechen War**, **Chechen** nationalism and radical **Islamism** combined, resulting in a homegrown terrorist threat to Russia, both in the **North Caucasus** and the capital, **Moscow**.

On **Boris Yeltsin**'s watch, the guerilla leader **Shamil Basayev** began a terror campaign that would span more than a decade. In 1995, he took 1,500 hostages at a hospital in Budyonnovsk, **Stavropol Krai**; 166 people died during fighting to free the captives. The following year, 2,000 people were taken captive in Kizylar, **Dagestan**, resulting in the deaths of two dozen civilians. In 1999, a series of **apartment bombings** in Moscow killed roughly 300 people just a few months before **Vladimir Putin** took office as president. Two years later, a bomb blast in Moscow's Byelorusskaya metro station wounded 15 people. In 2002, Victory Day (9 May) celebrations in the Dagestani city of Kaspiisk were marred by a bomb explosion that killed 42 and injured more than 130 people. On 19 October 2002, a bomb killed one person outside a Moscow McDonald's restaurant.

Four days later, 42 heavily armed men under the leadership of the Chechen guerilla leader Movsar Barayev took over the Dubrovka theater where the play *Nord-Ost* was being staged. In the ensuing gas attack on the Moscow theater and raid by Russian Special Forces (*Spetsnaz*), all the terrorists were killed, along with 130 hostages. 2003 was a particularly bloody year; in May, dozens died in bombings in **Chechnya**. On 5 July, 15 people were killed by a bomb attack on a Moscow rock concert by female suicide bombers, an event that was dubbed the "Black Widow" bombings by the Russian press. Later that summer, explosions killed more than 50 people in a **North Ossetiya** hospital and seven people on a train in southern Russia. In December, another train bombing in the south claimed nearly 50 lives and a blast in Moscow killed six. On 6 February 2004, a bomb in the Moscow metro left 41 dead. The bombings of two domestic flights claimed 90 lives on 24 August, and on the last day of the month a suicide bomber killed 10 and injured 30 at a northern Moscow metro station.

The next morning, the **Beslan hostage crisis** began when terrorists stormed School Number One during opening day celebrations; when it was over, 344 civilians were dead, the majority of whom were children. In 2005, Chechen rebels attacked federal buildings and police stations in Nalchik, **Kabardino-Balkariya**; the conflict took the lives of 137, including 92 guerillas. Since 2005, however, Russia's **counterterrorism** efforts, aided by the de facto end to the second Chechen War, have paid off. In recent years, there have been few terrorist attacks, with the exception of several minor bombings in **Sochi**, the site of the 2014 Winter Olympiad.

As president, Putin took dramatic steps to eliminate the terrorist threat, including putting severe restraints on **media** coverage of ongoing terror-related events, increasing federal security personnel in the North Caucasus, and instituting the appointment, rather than election, of regional governors to strengthen the **vertical of power**. Putin also increased security precautions in Moscow, particularly in the metro, tourist sites, and shopping areas, and in the vicinity of government buildings. Despite the deaths of nearly 1,000 Russian citizens from terror attacks during his administration, Putin retained the support of the people due to his tough talk and drastic measures to combat the threat of Islamic radicalism. *See also* ELECTORAL REFORMS OF 2004–2005.

TITOV, KONSTANTIN ALEKSEYEVICH (1944–). Politician. Appointed by **Boris Yeltsin** in 1991, Titov, a centrist reformer, served as head of the **Samara Oblast**'s regional administration in the immediate post-Soviet period. He was popularly elected to the post of governor in 1996. During the late 1990s, he attracted significant **foreign investment** to the region and dismantled certain aspects of Soviet-era social programs. Titov was reelected in 2000, after briefly resigning, and was reappointed by **Vladimir Putin** in 2005; he joined the pro-Kremlin **United Russia** party the same year. A former leader in **Our Home—Russia**, Titov left the party over the selection of **Viktor Chernomyrdin** as its presidential candidate in 2000. In 1999, he formed Russia's Voice (*Golos Rossii*) to give more voice to the regions; he was also associated with the **Union of Right Forces** and **Mikhail Gorbachev**'s recently formed **Social Democratic Party of Russia**. In 2000, he stood in Russia's presidential election, winning over a million votes.

TOMSK OBLAST. An administrative region of the Russian Federation. Tomsk is located within the Western Siberian **Economic Region** and the Siberian **Federal District**. Occupying an area of 316,900 square kilometers, the region's population is slightly more than 1 million. **Ethnic Russians** are the dominant group (88 percent), but there are also minorities of **Ukrainians** (2.6 percent) and

Tatars (2.1 percent). The **oblast** is bounded by **Khantiya-Mansiya** (a constituency of **Tyumen**), **Krasnoyarsk Krai**, **Kemerovo**, **Novosibirsk**, and **Omsk**. The region is crossed by a number of rivers, including the Ob, Chulym, Ket, and Vasyugan.

Tomsk's topography is defined by the **taiga**, but also includes boggy areas and forest **steppe**. The regional capital is Tomsk (pop. 487,000), a city known for its strong scholastic traditions; it was a closed city during Soviet times. The region possesses significant amounts of natural resources, including **oil**, coal, and **natural gas**, which are key drivers of the regional **economy**; various deposits of metal such as titanium, gold, copper, zirconium, and quartz are also found in the area. Engineering, metalworking, and generation of **nuclear energy** further contribute to the region's economic output. Forestry, woodworking, hunting, and **fishing** are significant sources of employment. In terms of **agriculture**, the region is known for its mushrooms, berries, and wild herbs; cattle and dairy farms are also important.

The oblast has been governed by the **Yeltsin** appointee Viktor Kress since 1991, despite the **Communist Party of the Russian Federation** being the most powerful **political party** in the local Duma during the early 1990s. Kress, an ethnic **German**, won reelection in 1995, 1999, and 2003 before being reappointed for another five-year term by **Vladimir Putin** in 2007. He is the chairman of the Siberian Accord Interregional Association and a member of the **Our Home—Russia** movement. An avid writer, he has penned a number of books on improving the situation in Russia through advancing the **education** system. He has established educational exchanges with **Great Britain**, **France**, **Kazakhstan**, and other countries, while building technological and **foreign trade** links with **China** and **Japan**. In 1993, an accident at the Tomsk-7 plutonium separation factory in the Seversk suburb of Tomsk led to the release of uranium and plutonium into the atmosphere, contaminating an area of about 75 square kilometers.

TOURISM. During the pre-1991 era, tourism for Soviet citizens was generally confined to the regions of the Union of Soviet Socialist Republics (USSR) and the **Eastern Bloc**. Due to the quasi-totalitarian nature of Communist rule, most Soviet citizens were prevented from traveling abroad (foreign travel was a privilege of the Soviet *nomenklatura*), and few tourist visas were granted to visitors from Western Europe and North America. Since the **dissolution of the Soviet Union**, this has changed radically, with Russia seeking to attract revenues from tourists from the **European Union**, the **Commonwealth of Independent States** (CIS), and, increasingly, the People's Republic of **China**.

For foreign tourists, the key destinations are **Moscow**, which enjoys such architectural and cultural gems as the Kremlin, Red Square, and the Bolshoi Theater, and the historic capital of **St. Petersburg**, known for the **Hermitage**, neoclassical architecture, canals, and numerous tsarist palaces. Both cities teem with art and history museums. **Transportation**-themed tours, such as river tours, are popular on the **Volga** and the **Trans-Siberian Railway**. Beyond Moscow, the late medieval cities of the Golden Ring attract tourists interested in Russia's **Orthodox** past. Heritage tourism is also popular, particularly among **ethnic Germans** and **Jews**. In recent years, Russia has developed its eco-tourism industry, which caters to environmentally minded visitors; the country's pristine northwestern lake region and surrounding **taiga**, the **Russian Far East**, the Altay Mountains, and **Lake Baykal** are primary destinations.

In terms of domestic tourism, Russian citizens continue to observe Soviet norms, including vacations to the **Black Sea** coast or resorts and health spas across southern Russia (**Abkhazia** and **Crimea** are also popular). **Sochi**, long a mecca for sun worshippers, will host the XXII Winter Olympiad in 2014. Since 2000, a booming **economy** and an increasing standard of living has allowed average Russians to travel abroad, with top destinations being **Turkey**, Egypt, Bulgaria, and China. Many Russians have also purchased property in these countries, often for purposes of retirement.

Difficulties in securing visas to the European Union prevent large-scale Russian tourism to Western Europe, though **France** and **Great Britain** are popular destinations for affluent Russians. Citizens from outside the CIS require visas to visit Russia, an expensive and sometimes arduous process. A substandard tourism infrastructure outside of the two capitals, limited English-**language** proficiency among older staff, and a number of high-profile arrests of tourists on **espionage** and antiquities-smuggling charges also dampen Russia's attraction to foreign visitors. The rapid rise of the **ruble** in 2005 resulted in a significant drop in demand for foreign tourist visas. *See also* ALTAY REPUBLIC; FOREIGN TRADE; KALININGRAD OBLAST.

TRADE. *See* FOREIGN TRADE.

TRADE UNIONS. The history of trade unions and **labor** in Russia is paradoxical. Given that the **Communist Party of the Soviet Union** (CPSU) ruled in the name of the workers, the party did not see a need for independent trade unions in the Soviet Union. As a result, the Soviet trade union system was incorporated into the state apparatus, thus depriving workers of effective bargaining power and giving them little influence over the firms and **industries** in which they were employed, though the trade unions had some say over housing conditions, distribution of welfare benefits, and working conditions.

In 1990, the Federation of Independent Trade Unions of Russia, known by its Russian acronym FNPR, was established to provide an independent voice to workers. Today, the organization has approximately 30 million members, representing nearly half of the country's workforce of 70 million. The FNPR controls disbursement of social insurance payments, protects workers from being dismissed unfairly, and seeks fair wages for its members. Despite the image of independence, the trade unions—including the FNPR—are closely tied to the government, a reflection of the Soviet heritage. Pressure was put on the trade unions to support the idea of "social partnership" with the government to prevent the collapse of the system during the chaotic transition to a market **economy**. During the 1998 **ruble crisis**, the FNPR demanded **Boris Yeltsin**'s resignation in an open letter, throwing its support behind **Yevgeny Primakov** (who was ultimately chosen as prime minister). Other major trade unions include the General Confederation of Trade Unions, the All-Russia Confederation of Labor, and the Confederation of Labor in Russia.

Since coming to power, **Vladimir Putin** has sought to wrest control of distribution of social benefits away from the trade unions, arguing that the state should administer such payouts. The neoliberal Labor Code of 2001 also granted more control to employers on hiring and firings and limited some forms of collective bargaining. Putin has also backed the creation of new, state-sponsored trade unions in the chemical, energy, and **mining** sectors, a move viewed with suspicion by older trade unionists. Putin's clampdown on **civil society** has also weakened the country's 50,000 trade unions. *See also* TRUD.

TRANSNEFT. Operating the largest **oil** pipeline system in the world, the state-owned Transneft is responsible for building, maintaining, and operating more than 50,000 pipelines across **Eurasia**. Established by presidential decree on 17 November 1992, the company wields a near monopoly over Russia's pipelines (transporting more than 90 percent of the country's oil) and has stakes in the national pipeline systems of **Belarus** and **Kazakhstan** as well. Minority shareholders in the company include the government of Kazakhstan, Chevron, and ExxonMobil. The company is currently building a major pipeline from eastern **Siberia** to the Pacific Ocean, with an additional spur running to the interior of **China**, the world's second-largest importer of oil. A new pipeline to the **Baltic Sea** is also in the works. In 2009, the Russian government approved a rate hike to help pay for new pipelines. The company operates nearly 400 pump stations and has reservoir capacity to store more than 15 million cubic meters of petroleum. Headquartered in **Moscow**, Transneft is run by Nikolay Tokarev and recorded revenues of $67.6 billion in 2007. *See also* ROSNEFT.

TRANSNISTRIA/PRIDNESTROVIAN MOLDAVIAN REPUB-LIC. Once an **Autonomous Soviet Socialist Republic** (ASSR) within **Ukraine**, this small strip of land east of the Dnestr River was combined with territory annexed from Romania in 1940 to create the Moldovan Soviet Socialist Republic (SSR). During the late 1980s, a nationalist movement among ethnic Moldovans, Romanians in all ways but their Cyrillic script, prompted fears among Slavs and other Russophones living in the heavily industrialized areas that had once been part of Soviet Ukraine.

In 1990, local politicians proclaimed the Pridnestrovian Moldavian Republic, a move condemned by the leadership in the Moldovan capital of Chişinău. Fierce fighting soon broke out between republican and **separatist** forces, the latter backed by Russian-speaking volunteer militias and **Cossack** regiments. The violence only increased in ferocity after **Moldova** gained independence from the Union of Soviet Socialist Republics (USSR) in 1991. After the arrival of **Aleksandr Lebed** in the summer of 1992 and the intervention of the pro-separatist Russian 14th Army, Moldovan President Mircea Snegur and **Boris Yeltsin** hammered out a cease-fire that stipulated the ultimate withdrawal of Russian troops from Transnistria, which was granted "special status" within Moldova. Domestic concerns over the safety of **ethnic Russians** in the province, however, prevented the **State Duma** from ratifying the agreed troop withdrawals.

While Moscow reaffirmed its commitment to leave Transnistria in 1999 at an Istanbul summit of the **Organization for Security and Co-operation in Europe**, the 2002 deadline was never met. Since the conflict was frozen in 1992, Transnistria has developed into a **mafia**-run statelet under de facto Russian economic control. Like **Belarus**, the republic continues to maintain Soviet-era controls on prices and guarantees wages. Former union organizer Igor Smirnov has ruled the self-proclaimed republic since 1991. A 2006 referendum in Transnistria saw support for unification with the Russian Federation; however, the poll was not recognized by the international community and Moscow does not officially sanction the state's declaration of independence from Moldova.

In 2004, the breakaway republic attracted worldwide attention when authorities closed several schools that were using the Latin alphabet for the Moldovan (Romanian) **language**; continuing controversy over pedagogy has resulted in a steady **Russification** of the **education** system.

TRANSPORTATION. Given Russia's vast size and harsh **climate**, the country's transportation system is integral to the country's economic development and settlement patterns. Shaped both by tsarist and Soviet political considerations, the Russian Federation's network of roads, railways, shipping channels, and air links bears a strong imperial legacy. The Russian **military** continues to maintain a pivotal role in the development of the country's transportation links, which are considered vital to national security. Since the **dissolution of the Soviet Union**, federal subsidization of the transportation network has significantly decreased, resulting in substandard conditions in many parts of the country, particularly the **North Caucasus**, the **Far North**, and the **Russian Far East**.

Because of the harsh climate (especially in the Far North), Russia has far fewer roads per square kilometer than other industrialized countries, even in densely populated areas. Although Russia is much larger than the **United States**, its 1 million kilometers of roads equal less than one-sixth of the U.S.'s, with many being unpaved or dedicated to industrial or military use. This has resulted in critical levels of traffic congestion, particularly in **Moscow**.

Safety is also a major issue. Road deaths average well over 30,000 per year, roughly equal to that of the entire **European Union**, though the Russian Federation has less than one-third of the EU's population; a Russian is 10 times more likely to die in an automobile accident than a citizen of **Germany**. Average Russians' frustration with the situation on the roads has often resulted in social tension, and represents an area where **civil society** has made an impact on the government. The federal government maintains a system of highways across European Russia and the southern periphery of **Siberia** and the Russian Far East; with the exception of the M56 Kolyma Highway, colloquially known as the "Road of Bones," these roads link together Russia's largest cities. Russian suffers from high mortality because of road accidents: in 2009, President **Dmitry Medvyedev** launched a series of government-sponsored programs aimed at improving traffic control in Russia.

Russia's railway network, however, is particularly well developed, though it is in need of maintenance and investment. The Soviet emphasis on heavy **industry** resulted in the building of a complex rail network connecting the country's **agricultural** and industrial regions to its population centers. Proximity to rail lines emerged as a vital factor in determining demographic patterns outside the European core of Russia; the **Trans-Siberian Railway**, in particular, has shaped the development of Asiatic Russia. While cargo is the focus of most rail traffic, trains continue to dominate domestic travel among Russia's citizenry. Overall, the country has more than 150,000 kilometers of rail lines, though less than 100,000 kilometers are for public use. The national railroad monopoly is managed by Russian Railways (*Rossiiskie zheleznye dorogi*).

During the Soviet period, air travel fell under the monopoly of **Aeroflot**. Today, a number of competing companies operate flights between Russia's more than 1,200 regional airports. Certain remote regions in Siberia and northeastern **Eurasia** remain accessible only via air. Since the late 1980s, international flights have increased dramatically, owing to the Kremlin's abandonment of restrictions on overseas travel and increasing openness to foreign **tourists** and business travelers.

Russia has more than 100,000 kilometers of inland waterways, which link the country's many rivers, lakes, and reservoirs to the **Baltic**, **Black**, and **Caspian** seas via an impressive system of man-made canals. Further connecting Russia's shipping industry to the outside world are the important port cities of **St. Petersburg** and Kaliningrad on the Baltic Sea, the **Arctic** port of Murmansk, and the Pacific Rim city of Vladivostok.

Intracity public transportation in Russia depends on the minibus (*marshrutka*), which is relatively cheap and convenient, if sometimes uncomfortable and unsafe. Standard buses and trams fell out of use with the collapse of the public transportation system in the 1990s. Only seven cities have underground metro systems: Moscow, St. Petersburg, Nizhny Novgorod, Yekaterinburg, Novosibirsk, Samara, and Kazan; the newest is Kazan, which opened in 2005. Moscow's metro system is the world's second most traveled on a daily basis. Public transportation remains highly subsidized in the Russian Federation, a lingering aspect of the socialist system. However, **privatization** and economic reform during the 1990s led to a reduction of state control over the sector. *See also* GULAG.

TRANS-SIBERIAN RAILWAY. During the 19th century, the **Romanov** tsars initiated the building of a railway to connect **St. Petersburg** to Russia's Pacific Ocean provinces. The most important section of this transport line was the Trans-Siberian Railway, a 9,289-kilometer line that connects **Moscow** to Vladivostok in the **Primorsky Krai**. The route crosses seven time zones and takes several days to complete. The railway also has connections to Ulan Bator (**Mongolia**), Pyongyang (**North Korea**), and Beijing (**China**). The route determined settlement patterns, particularly among **ethnic Russians**, across southern **Siberia** and the **Russian Far East**. During the Russian Civil War (1918–1922), control of the railway proved vital to both the Bolsheviks and their White adversaries. Due to its historic nature, the railroad is popular among **tourists** and **transportation**

enthusiasts. Much of the line is in disrepair, and the federal government has committed to upgrading the rail network to better facilitate the transportation of goods from East Asia (particularly **Japan** and China) to the **European Union** via Russia. The rise in oceanic piracy has provided further stimulus to improve land-based links between the Pacific Rim and Europe.

***TRUD*. Newspaper.** Translated from the Russian language as "Labor," *Trud* was established in 1921 as the mouthpiece of the Soviet **trade unions**. It published official decrees, and focused on workers' issues and economic analysis. In the late 1980s, the newspaper had the world's largest circulation (21.5 million copies per day). After the **dissolution of the Soviet Union**, *Trud* lost most of its readership, dipping to 1.5 million readers a day. In 2005, it was acquired by a financial group and became the core asset of the Media-3 holding company, which also includes *Argumenty i Fakty*, a popular weekly newspaper. Recently, *Trud* underwent a major rebranding effort: it changed its format from broadsheet to a compact format, with full-color graphics and a classifieds section. Today, the publication (and its online version, www.trud.ru/) focuses on international and national news, as well as lifestyle stories. It particularly appeals to working people aged 20–45 with upwardly mobile career and lifestyle aspirations. *Trud* often employs some degree of sensationalism in the coverage of events. The publication's weekend edition is known as *Trud-7*.

TULA OBLAST. An administrative region of the Russian Federation. Located on the Eastern European Plain, Tula is bordered by the **Moscow**, **Ryazan**, **Lipetsk**, **Orel**, and **Kaluga oblasts**. It is part of the Central **Federal District** and **Economic Region**. The regional capital of Tula (pop. 481,000) is an industrial city on the Upa River less than 200 kilometers from **Moscow**; it was founded in 1146. At 27,500 square kilometers, it is one of Russia's smaller **federal subjects**. The population is 1.6 million, thus making it one of the most densely populated **oblasts** in Russia (second only to **Moscow Oblast**); more than 80 percent of the region's inhabitants live in urban areas.

Natural resources include coal, iron, limestone, clay, and sand. Regional **industries** include engineering, metallurgy, and chemicals.

Historically, the region was the center of Russia's **arms** industry, and remains central to Russia's **military**-industrial complex. **Agricultural** production is focused on animal husbandry and grain cultivation. In terms of **tourism**, Tula boasts Yasnaya Polyana, a large open-air estate and museum that was once the residence of Leo Tolstoy.

In 1993, the region was the scene of political wrangling when the head of the oblast ordered the region's lesser Soviet disbanded in response to its anti-**Yeltsin** rhetoric surrounding the **constitutional crisis**. The **Communist Party of the Russian Federation** came to dominate the new regional administration, making Tula a dependable **Red Belt** constituency. Elected in 1997, Vasily Starodubtsev, one of the nine **August Coup** organizers, remained true to his hardline Communist convictions through 2000, supporting **Gennady Zyuganov** over Yeltsin's heir apparent, **Vladimir Putin**. He was reelected in 2001 with 72 percent of the vote.

Despite his ideological orientations, Starodubtsev sought to expand private enterprise in the region and attracted **foreign investment** from a number of firms including Procter & Gamble. In 2005, Putin nominated Vyacheslav Dudka, a comparatively young technocrat without strong links to local **oligarchs**, to replace Starodubtsev. In 2007, Dudka accused Mormon and Jehovah's Witness missionaries of spying for the **United States**.

TULIP REVOLUTION. *See* KYRGYZSTAN.

TUNDRA. A Russian word of Finno-Ugric origin describing arctic hills, the tundra, which dominated Russia's **Far North**, is the world's northernmost terrestrial biome, abutting the **Arctic Ocean** coast on both the North American and **Eurasian** continents. The tundra is characterized by treeless plains and low hills; the subsoil is permanently frozen (permafrost), resulting in an ecosystem that can only support mosses, lichens, and seasonal flowers. The **climate** is extremely cold, making life difficult for both fauna and human populations. The indigenous peoples of the region include **Nenets**, Nganasan, **Evens**, **Sakha**, and **Chukchi**; historically, they maintained a nomadic lifestyle, herding reindeer and hunting whales, seals, and other Arctic animals. Poor **transportation** links and the harsh climate, combined with the cessation of Soviet-era subsidies, have resulted in a rapid drop in living standards among the peoples of the taiga. **Environmentalists** have undertaken efforts to protect the fragile ecosystem through the Biodiversity Action Plan and other global initiatives. However, Moscow's plans to develop the Arctic's **oil** and **natural gas** potential in the coming decades threaten such measures. Climate change is resulting in increasing amounts of greenhouse gases being released from the region. **Pollution** from aluminum smelting is also a major concern. *See also* INDIGENOUS PEOPLES OF THE NORTH.

TURKEY (RELATIONS WITH). Russo-Turkish relations were forged on mutual hostility and civilizational confrontation. From the 16th century onward, the Ottoman and **Romanov** empires engaged in no less than a dozen wars, including World War I (1914–1918), which ultimately brought an end to both dynasties. Both Mustafa Kemal's Turkish Republic and **Vladimir Lenin**'s Soviet Russia developed radically different systems of governments in the interwar period, but conflicting geopolitical orientations prevented genuine rapprochement though the two powers remained cordial.

Turkey's admission to the **North Atlantic Treaty Organization** (NATO) in 1952 (and subsequent **United States** deployment of **nuclear weapons** on Turkish soil) and its draconian repression of Communists placed the two countries at loggerheads throughout the **Cold War**. Despite the **dissolution of the Soviet Union** in 1991 (and the end of a common border between the states), Russia remained wary of Turkey's role in the Balkans, the **Caucasus**, the Eastern Mediterranean, and **Central Asia**—all zones of historical conflict between the two states. Ankara's promotion of **pan-Turkism** in Russia's **near abroad** and **ethnic republics**, as well as perceived support for **Muslim** insurgencies in **Chechnya** and the former Yugoslavia, weighed heavily on bilateral relations. Conversely, Turkey views Russian support of **Armenia**, Greek-held Cyprus, and Kurdish rebels with intense suspicion.

As a result, relations during the **Yeltsin** administration remained tense. However, Turkey's economic crisis and its diminished nationalism under the **Islamist** AK party, combined with Russia's economic resurgence and geopolitical pragmatism under **Vladimir**

Putin, has had a calming effect on tensions between the two countries. Washington's mediation between the parties has also helped. In 2004, Putin signed the Joint Declaration on Improvement of Friendship and Multidimensional Partnership between the Turkish Republic and the Russian Federation, after a visit to Turkey earlier that year.

Under the leadership of Recep Tayyip Erdoğan, Russo-Turkish economic relations have improved dramatically; in 2009, Russia became Turkey's largest **foreign trade** partner, with annual exchange of approximately $40 billion. Russian **tourism** in Turkey, shuttle commerce, and Turkish construction projects in the Russian Federation are two important drivers of trade. However, Moscow continues to resent the development of the Baku-Tbilisi-Ceyhan (BTC) pipeline, which is viewed as an explicit attempt to bypass Russia's economic, physical, and political hegemony over **oil** and **natural gas** exports from the **Caspian Sea**, though Russia and Turkey agreed on developing their own Blue Stream route. In the wake of the United States' war in Iraq (and the rise of an autonomous Kurdistan in northern Iraq), Turkey has grown more amenable to the emergence of a multipolar world with Russia and the other **BRIC** (Brazil, Russia, India, and China) countries playing a greater role in global affairs; both countries have also played up their common **Eurasianism** as a potential linkage.

Putin has also voiced support for Turkey's admission to the **Shanghai Cooperation Organization**, and both countries have developed common strategies for combating Islamist **terrorism**, including reigning in Chechen and Kurdish groups on their respective territories. Recent movements on the final settlement of the **Nagorno-Karabakh** issue have also demonstrated improved working relations between Ankara and Moscow. Most dramatically, given Ankara's past support for Tbilisi, Turkey's muted response to the **South Ossetian War** demonstrates the predominance of economic questions over political issues. *See also* AZERBAIJAN; BLACK SEA; IRAN; MIDDLE EAST.

TURKMENISTAN (RELATIONS WITH). The territory of modern Turkmenistan was annexed by tsarist Russia in the late 1800s. The incorporation of the region, which was dominated by Turkmen nomads, extended Russia's border with **Iran** and its influence over much of the **Caspian Sea**. Originally part of Soviet Turkestan, the Turkmen Soviet Socialist Republic (SSR) was established as part of the national delimitation of **Central Asia** on 27 October 1924. After the 1991 **August Coup**, the Turkmen population voted overwhelmingly for independence from the Union of Soviet Socialist Republics (USSR). The local **Communist Party of the Soviet Union** leader, Saparmurat Niyazov, despite his support for the coup and desire to maintain the Soviet Union and Turkmenistan's place within it, refashioned himself as a reformer and declared his country's independence on 27 October 1991. In 1992, Niyazov ran unopposed to become the country's first popularly elected president. He also took the grandiloquent title of *Turkmenbashi* or "Leader of All Turkmen." He was declared president for life in 1996 and held the position until his death in late 2006. His rule was characterized by a bizarre cult of personality based on his spiritual and political opus, the *Ruhnama* (Turkmen: "Book of the Soul"). Political dissention was unknown, and the government maintained totalitarian restriction on the press, the **Internet**, and travel.

Unlike other Central Asian states, Turkmenistan adopted a policy of strict neutrality after independence, though the country did join the **Commonwealth of Independent States** (CIS). In 2005, Turkmenistan reduced its affiliation to that of associate member in accordance with **United Nations** rules for international recognition of a state's status of neutrality. Ashgabat eschewed membership in the CIS Collective Security Treaty during the 1990s and has not joined its successor, the **Collective Security Treaty Organization**. Despite the signing of a treaty of friendship and cooperation between the two countries on 31 July 1992, Russo-Turkmen relations declined throughout the decade due to Niyazov's erratic domestic policies, disputes over Caspian **oil** rights, and his intransigent foreign policy.

In 1997, Turkmenistan halted gas exports to Russia in protest over unpaid balances from other post-Soviet republics; shipments were resumed again in 1999. Moscow's concerns for the **ethnic Russian** and Russophone minorities in the country also complicated relations during the late 1990s. In fact, Turkmenistanis could hold dual citizenship with the Russian Federation until 2004, when the provision was abolished in a row precipitated by Niyazov's exaggerated claims that Russia was engaging in a campaign to discredit him. Shortly before the incident, **Vladimir Putin** and Niyazov had signed an oil and **natural gas** deal that heralded a new era in bilateral relations.

Relations with Russia had previously been strained over Niyazov's ire that his enemies had been given refuge in the country after a failed 25 November 2002 assassination attempt (which many outside observers believed to be orchestrated by the president himself); similar complications affected relations with neighboring **Uzbekistan**. Niyazov's governance reached its nadir in 2006 with constant purges, closing of hospitals, and reduction in oil and gas output. His unexpected death on 21 December 2006 opened the door for a revival in relations. After making the hajj to Saudi Arabia, the new president, Kurbanguly Berdymukhamedov, flew to Moscow for meetings with Putin. Shortly after his accession, Berdymukhamedov also signaled he would attenuate his predecessor's restrictive policies on the Internet, as well as improving social programs.

Since **Dmitry Medvyedev** assumed the Russian presidency, relations have remained cordial, with no significant changes. Turkmenistan possesses the world's fifth-largest natural gas reserves and produces approximately 60 billion cubic meters of natural gas per year. Two-thirds of its natural gas exports go to **Gazprom**. In 2006, a long-running dispute on pricing was settled, with the Russian company agreeing to increase its purchase price by more than 50 percent. Much to the Kremlin's dismay, **China** and the **European Union** have both competed aggressively with Russia to develop routes for the export of natural gas. The **United States**–led war in neighboring **Afghanistan** has also accelerated the process of developing a transshipment route to the Indian Ocean. Good relations with Iran have also been used by Ashgabat to offset Russian dominance in the region. *See also* FOREIGN RELATIONS.

TUVA, REPUBLIC OF/TYVA. An ethnic republic of the Russian Federation. Located at the geographic center of the Asian continent, Tuva shares an international frontier with **Mongolia** and internal borders with the **Altay Republic**, **Khakasiya**, **Krasnoyarsk Krai**, **Irkutsk**, and **Buryatiya**. The republic is part of the Siberian **Federal District** and the East Siberian **Economic Region**.

The Yenisei River (known locally as *Ulug-Khem*) cuts through the middle of the country; while the Sayan Mountains dominate the topography of the eastern part of the republic, **steppe** and dry steppe prevail in the western half. More than one-third of the region is forested. Tuva covers an area of 170,500 square kilometers and has a population of 300,000.

The titular majority, **Tuvans**, comprise more than three-quarters of the population, while **ethnic Russians** make up the largest minority at 20 percent. Russians are generally confined to the capital, Kyzyl (pop. 104,000); however, they only account for 17 percent of the city's population. Due to the demographic superiority of the indigenous population, the Tuvan **language** is commonly used across the republic, though the **Russian language** holds equal sway with Tuvan in Kyzyl. Lamaist **Buddhism**, **shamanism**, and Russian **Orthodoxy** are the predominant faiths of the republic; however, a number of Protestant sects have also attracted converts in the region.

Tuva is unique among Russia's **federal subjects** as it was an independent country as recently as 1944. Formerly part of the Qing Empire, Tuva declared its independence from **China** in the wake of that country's 1911 revolution. Tuva quickly became a protectorate of Russia, and ultimately a client state of the Soviet Union. The region had experienced Russian settlement since the 1860s, and a self-governing Russian Bolshevik community resided in the state during the interwar period. In October 1944, the Tuvinian People's Republic was incorporated into the Union of Soviet Socialist Republics (USSR), becoming an autonomous **oblast** of the **Russian Soviet Federative Socialist Republic**.

Unlike the **Baltic States**, which were annexed at the same time, there was little international interest in the case of Tuva, and the event remains shrouded in secrecy. On 10 October 1961, Tuva was elevated to the status of an autonomous republic within Russia. During the Soviet era, Tuva was a closed region, and cultural contacts with Mongolia and China were prohibited. Under **perestroika**, **Mikhail Gorbachev** allowed for cross-border contacts with the Mongolians to be reinitiated. As in other **ethnic republics**, a nationalist movement centered on the use of the indigenous language emerged as the principal platform for political dissent.

In June 1990, protests exploded in the capital, Kyzyl, over the 1944 annexation, prompting Soviet authorities to use force. Sporadic instances of **ethnic violence** directed at Russians continued throughout the year, resulting in the deaths of over 80 people. In the wake of the violence, thousands of ethnic Slavs fled the region. Tuva declared its sovereignty on 11 December 1990, renaming itself the Republic of Tuva in 1991 (the name change to non-Russified "Tyva" occurred in 1993 with the adoption of a new republican constitution).

Sherig-ool Oorzhak governed the republic from 1992 until 2007. He was succeeded by Sholban Kara-ool, a graduate of the Philosophy Department of Urals State University and former parliamentary leader. Fifty years of international isolation and dependence on federal subsidies dampened the desire for full independence upon the **dissolution of the Soviet Union** in 1991, though some nationalists continued to call for a referendum on secession throughout the early 1990s. In 1993, they gained a provision in the republican constitution providing for the ability to secede from the Russian Federation; this measure was negated in a 2001 referendum. Support for separation from Russia still runs high among ethnic Tuvans, with half supporting complete independence.

During the 1990s, a territorial dispute with Mongolia flared, resulting in cross-border raids on livestock herds. Russian border guards continue to treat the area as highly sensitive and prevent **tourists** from visiting much of the frontier. Tuva's regional **economy** is primarily dependent on **agriculture**, particularly animal husbandry, with hunting and forestry also providing local jobs. While the region possesses some light **industry** and natural resources, including gold, coal, and mercury, production and extraction remain limited due in part to the republic's poor **transportation** infrastructure (itself a legacy of the late incorporation into the Soviet Union). Tuva remains one of Russia's worst-performing regions in terms of wage arrears, and remains comparatively underdeveloped in the areas of **education** and medical services. Due to its remote location and unspoiled landscape, the region has proved somewhat attractive to the eco-tourism industry.

TUVANS. Ethnic group. The Tuvans are the titular majority of the Republic of **Tuva**; numbering over 200,000, most live in Tuva, though small diasporas reside in **China** and **Mongolia**. In terms of culture and appearance, Tuvans closely resemble Mongolians; however, they have retained their Turkic tongue, which is part of the South Siberian subgroup of Northeastern Common Turkic **languages**.

The Tuvan language makes extensive use of Mongolian loan words, reflecting a long history of political subordination to Mongolia, which itself was under Chinese hegemony prior to 1911. With Soviet support, a Latin-based orthography was developed for Tuvan in the early 1930s; like other Soviet Turkic languages, the Tuvan alphabet was replaced by a Cyrillic script during World War II.

Historically, Tuvans were shamanistic, practicing a form of sky-worship or Tengrism. The Tos Deer Respubliki Tuvy (Nine Heavens of the Republic of Tuva) was established in the post-Soviet period to provide a national organization for the republic's shamanists. In the 17th century, Lamaist **Buddhism** made inroads into the region, though in most cases, it was practiced alongside **shamanism**. Today, Lamaism is given state support, but shamanism is also a protected form of worship. Recognizing the centrality of Buddhism to the region, the Dalai Lama visited Tuva in 1992. A small number of Tuvans profess Russian **Orthodoxy**.

In the 1980s, a resurgence of Tuvan ethnic identity grew under the policy of **glasnost**. Khostug Tyva (Free Tuva) emerged as the leading voice of Tuvan nationalism, often espousing strident anti-Russian and anti-Christian rhetoric. The organization initially lobbied for elevating Tuva to the status of a **union republic**, and later supported a referendum on independence. However, the movement weakened with the election of its leader Kadyr-ool Bicheldei to federal office in 1990. Tuvans are world-renowned for their unique variety of throat singing, a tradition that was celebrated in the film *Genghis Blues* (1999), which chronicled an American blues singer's journey to the republic to compete in a throat-singing competition.

TVER OBLAST. An administrative region of the Russian Federation. Known as the Kalinin Oblast from 1931 until 1990, Tver Oblast is situated less than 100 kilometers northwest of **Moscow** and 50 kilometers east of **Belarus** on the Eastern European Plain. It borders the **oblasts** of **Novgorod**, **Vologda**, **Yaroslavl**, **Moscow**, **Smolensk**, and **Pskov**. The oblast is located within the Central **Economic Region** and **Federal District**.

Tver has a population of 1.4 million and covers an area of 84,500 square kilometers. It is the source of the **Volga River**, upon which its regional capital Tver (pop. 408,000) sits; more than 7,000 buildings were destroyed in the World War II occupation and liberation of the city. With over 500 lakes (Seliger being the largest), the mountainous Valdai Highlands, and a number of medieval Russian settlements, the region is attractive to **tourists** from Russia and abroad. However, environmental degradation in the region is acute due to industrial **pollution**. The regional **economy** is divided between heavy manufacturing, including railway cars, farm machinery, and excavation equipment; chemicals; and the textile **industry**. Traditional industries of printing, woodworking, and glassmaking also contribute to the local economy. Dairy and cattle farming are also part of the regional economic output. The region possesses important reserves of peat, as well as mineral resources such as limestone and brown coal. It is also an important **transportation** hub, linking Moscow and **St. Petersburg**, and providing a conduit to **Latvia** and thus the **European Union**. The Surgut-Polotsk and other **oil** pipelines also cross the region.

Tver's regional authorities, historically resentful of the capital's hegemony, were highly critical of President **Boris Yeltsin**'s actions during the **constitutional crisis of 1993**. When the Tver Regional Soviet was subsequently disbanded, the **Communist Party of the Russian Federation** (KPRF) won a majority of seats in the new legislative assembly and won the governorship in a contest against a Yeltsin appointee in 1995. The new governor, Vladimir Platov, secured a power-sharing agreement with Moscow. Platov, sensing a changing political environment, allied himself with the pro-**Putin** **Unity** party and defeated a KPRF challenger in the 2000 gubernatorial elections.

Under Platov's rule, Tver became known for its "slothful" economic development and as a major transit zone for illegal **narcotics**. In the next election, Platov placed fourth after criminal proceedings were opened against him; in 2005, Platov began serving a five-year sentence at Moscow's Matrosskaya Tishina prison for abuse of office relating to a scam in which nearly $15 million was misappropriated. The current governor is Dmitry Zelenin; he was elected in 2003 and reappointed by Putin in 2007. In 2008, Zelenin issued an invitation for settlement in Tver to all **ethnic Russian** "compatriots" living in the **near abroad**. In 2009, Zelenin was rebuked by his party, **United Russia**, for allowing the KPRF to win a plurality in the election for the regional legislature.

TYUMEN OBLAST. An administrative region of the Russian Federation. Tyumen stretches nearly 2,000 kilometers, from the Kara Sea in the north to the Kazakh **steppe** in the south. Existing as **autonomous okrugs** (AOks) within Tyumen, the **federal subjects** of **Yamaliya** and **Khantiya-Mansiya** are both constituent parts of the **oblast**. Including its AOks, Tyumen covers more than 1.4 million square kilometers, accounting for more than 8 percent of Russia's land mass.

Tyumen is Russia's third-largest federal subject and its largest oblast. Located on the Western Siberian Plain, Tyumen proper borders **Kazakhstan, Kurgan, Sverdlovsk, Omsk,** and **Tomsk**; Khantiya-Mansiya also borders **Komi** and **Krasnoyarsk Krai**, while Yamaliya shares a border with **Nenetsiya**. Tyumen is part of the Urals **Federal District** and the West Siberian **Economic Region**. Its current population is 3.25 million, of which 71 percent are **ethnic Russians**. Minorities include **Tatars** (7 percent), **Ukrainians** (6.5 percent), **Bashkirs** (1.5 percent), and 30 other statistically significant groups including many **indigenous peoples of the north**. The regional capital, Tyumen (pop. 590,000), is the economic center of this vast region, as most exports pass through the city. Other main cities include Tobolsk, Surgut, and Nadym. Tyumen is crossed by many rivers including the Irtysh, Ishim, Tobol, Ob, Taz, Pur, and Nadym.

Most of the oblast's topography is **taiga**, with bands of **tundra** in the extreme north and forest steppe in the deep south. **Agriculture** is most productive in the southern areas of Tyumen proper, with the key crops being grains, potatoes, and vegetables; in the north, animal husbandry predominates. The regional per capita GDP is several times higher than that in the rest of Russia, owing principally to the exploitation of vast reserves of hydrocarbons in the region. Tyumen controls over half of Russia's **oil** exports (originating in the Samotlor, Kholmogorsk, and Fedorovsk fields) and more than three-quarters of its **natural gas** shipments (centered in the Urengoy, Medvezhye, and Yamburg fields).

Petrochemicals naturally rank as a secondary **industry** in the region, and **mining** of construction materials is likewise a key driver of the **economy**. The privately owned TNK-BP is one of Russia's largest companies and a major employer in the region; **Gazprom, Lukoil,** and Surgutneftegaz are also vital players in the regional economy. Forestry is an important source of local employment, and there is some light manufacturing as well. In the north, traditional occupations such as hunting, reindeer herding, **fishing**, and fur farming predominate.

Due to its economic dynamism, Tyumen enjoys population growth rates higher than nearly all other oblasts, though illegal **immigration** has emerged as a social problem with the influx of migrants from the **near abroad** seeking work in the energy industry. Nearly 100 foreign countries have investment in the region, with the most important trading partners being **Germany**, **Poland**, the Czech Republic, **Belarus**, **Ukraine**, and Hungary. Tyumen accounts for roughly 7 percent of Russia's **foreign trade** and is one of the leading regions in terms of fixed capital investments. Foreign trade turnover in the first six months of 2008 accounted for $482 billion.

In the wake of the **constitutional crisis of 1993**, resentment of the federal government remained high. The **Communist Party of the Russian Federation** performed well in the poll to elect a new legislature in 1994. The first regional governor was Yury Shafranik, who held office from 1991 to 1993; he was quickly promoted to federal office, opening the way for the chairman of the Tyumen Oil Company (TNK), Leonid Roketsky, to take over governance of the region. However, Roketsky ultimately ran afoul of powerful corporate interests within Gazprom and Sibneft and elites in the autonomous oblasts. In 2001, Kremlin loyalist Sergey Sobyanin won election to the governor's office and also subsequently replaced his predecessor Roketsky as chairman of TNK. In 2005, Sobyanin, formerly a presidential representative to the Urals Federal District, was reappointed by **Vladimir Putin**, who shortly thereafter tapped the governor to head up his presidential administration. He was replaced by the mayor of Tyumen, Vladimir Yakushev. *See also* FOREIGN INVESTMENT.

– U –

UDMURTIYA. An **ethnic republic** of the Russian Federation. Situated in the Upper Kama Highlands, Udmurtiya is the ethnic homeland of the **Udmurts**, a Finnic people formerly known as the Votyaks. Originally created by the Soviets as the Votsk **Autonomous Oblast** (AO) in 1920, the region was renamed the Udmurt AO in 1932 before being elevated to the status of an **Autonomous Soviet Socialist Republic** (ASSR) within the **Russian Soviet Federative Socialist Republic** in 1934. The Udmurt Republic declared sovereignty on 21 September 1990.

Udmurtiya covers 42,100 square kilometers of territory, of which approximately half is forested. The Kama River is the main waterway in the region; other rivers include the Cheptsa, Izh, Kilmez, and Siva. The republic is bordered by **Bashkortostan**, **Tatarstan**, **Kirov**, and **Perm**. The population of the republic is 1.5 million; Udmurts are a titular minority, comprising approximately 30 percent of the population. **Ethnic Russians** are a majority at 60 percent; more than 100,000 **Tatars** also reside in the region.

The capital of the republic is Izhevsk (pop. 632,000), home to Mikhail Kalashnikov, inventor of the popular AK-47 assault rifle, which was originally manufactured in the city's armory. Reflecting its long history of weapons production, Udmurtiya remains an important manufacturer of arms within Russia (accounting for 80 percent of hunting and target firearms). Safety issues associated with the disposal of chemical weapons at the Kambarka facility have lately emerged as a controversial issue.

Major **industrial** sectors include **oil** extraction, machine building (including nearly half of all Russian motorcycles), metalworking, glassmaking, forestry, and woodworking. **Agriculture** accounts for about a quarter of the regional **economy**; Udmurts enjoy a reputation as the preeminent farmers of the **Volga** basin as well as fine brewers. Livestock breeding and dairy farming are also part of the local economy. Udmurtiya has a well-developed **banking** sector, and also enjoys a moderate level of **foreign investment**. The republic's **foreign trade** turnover in 2007 was in excess of $1 billion; Udmurtiya's commercial relations with **Germany** and **India** are particularly well developed. Udmurtiya also sells weapons to **Iran** and **Venezuela**. Exports—particularly due to **arms sales**—dramatically outstrip imports. Overall, Udmurtiya's economy is well developed and the republic is a dependable donor region within the Russian Federation.

Unlike most ethnic republics, Udmurtiya has seen little popular support for **separatism**. A republican constitution and new **flag** were promulgated in 1993; however, republican authorities did not see fit to demand the same level of sovereignty that other republics gleaned from **Boris Yeltsin**'s administration. In 2000, a referendum passed creating the office of president, and Aleksandr Volkov was elected to the post the same year on an anti-**corruption** platform. He also promised to maintain ethnic stability and avoid challenges to federal authority.

Volkov had served as chair of the republican legislature, the highest political position, for the five years previous to his appointment to the presidency. He was reelected in 2004 to a second five-year term with the backing of **Vladimir Putin**. In early 2009, more than 1,000 protested in the capital demanding Volkov's dismissal due to rising energy costs and economic mismanagement of the republic. Volkov has also been criticized at home and abroad for his hamhanded domination of Udmurt **media** outlets. *See also* WEAPONS OF MASS DESTRUCTION.

UDMURTS. Ethnic group. Udmurts (Meadow People), formerly known as Votyaks, developed into an identifiable ethnicity in the 6th century. After violently resisting Slavic colonization and Islamicization under the Khanate of Kazan, the Udmurts began accepting **Orthodox Christianity** in the 16th century, though most only nominally embraced the new faith. Certain elements of pre-Christian animism (worship at sacred groves, sacrifices, and other rituals) have persevered among the Udmurts, particularly in southern **Udmurtiya**, to the present day. Since 1994, the **neo-pagan** revival has been led by the national animist organization Vos.

Udmurts remained a predominantly **rural** people well into the 20th century, and supported the formation of a non-Russian Idel-Ural State in the wake of the Bolshevik Revolution. Sovietization of the region and subsequent industrialization combined with the influx of Slavic settlers suppressed Udmurt identity in the second half of the 20th century. The Udmurt **language**, existing in written form since the 18th century, is part of the Finno-Permic subgroup within the Uralic language family; it is most closely related to Komi and Komi-Permyak but possesses links to Finnish, Estonian, and, most distantly, Hungarian. Udmurt enjoys co-official status with **Russian** in Udmurtiya.

Two-thirds of all Udmurts reside in the Udmurt Republic, also known as Udmurtiya; worldwide, the population is in excess of

600,000, making the Udmurts the fourth-largest Finno-Ugric nation. In terms of appearance, Udmurts—like the Irish—are internationally recognized for their red hair, a fact initially recorded by the Greek historian Herodotus when identifying the proto-Udmurts. Due to intense **Russification**, many Udmurts registered as **ethnic Russians** during the Soviet era; however, most reembraced their ethnic identity during **glasnost** as organizations like the Udmurt National Center, Club of Udmurt Culture (later known as Demen), and radical Udmurt Kenesh (Udmurt Council) made identification with the nation socially acceptable.

The Udmurt language served as a key tool for preserving **national identity**. More than three-quarters of all Udmurts use Udmurt as their first language, and many rural Udmurts do not possess proficiency in the Russian language. In 1996, all Udmurts in the republic gained the right to be **educated** in their native language. Udmurt nationalists have emerged as key voices in the pan-Volga (i.e., non-Russian) and transnational Finno-Ugric movements. *See also* FINLAND; KOMI.

UKRAINE (RELATIONS WITH). No foreign country is as important to Russian identity as Ukraine, particularly given that Russia traces its statehood back to 9th-century Kiev, now the capital of Ukraine. In 1654, the Left Bank of Ukraine (east of the Dnieper River) was incorporated into Russia, and during the latter part of the next century, the partition of the Polish-Lithuanian Commonwealth brought the rest of "Little Russia" into the **Romanov** Empire. Russia and Ukraine, along with **Belarus**, were founding members of the Soviet Union in 1922; however, **Joseph Stalin**'s purge of religious and political elites, as well as Soviet economic policies and the ensuing famine in Soviet Ukraine (known as the Holodomor) soured relations between Kiev and Moscow.

Ukraine, like the other **union republics**, saw a dramatic rise in support for independence from the Union of Soviet Socialist Republics (USSR) in 1991, particularly after the failed **August Coup**. On 24 August 1991, the Ukrainian parliament adopted the Act of Independence, declaring Ukraine an independent and democratic state. On 21 December 1991, the former Communist-turned-nationalist Leonid Kravchuk was one of the three signatories of the **Belavezha Accords**, effectively **dissolving the Soviet Union** (later certified by the Alma-Ata Protocol on 21 December); Kravchuk would lead the country until 1994.

Despite concerns about the existence of millions of **ethnic Russians** in Ukraine, the two states gained independence in 1991, with both joining the **Commonwealth of Independent States**. Decommissioning of Ukraine's **nuclear weapons** arsenal and Soviet troops on Ukrainian soil quickly emerged as major issues between Kiev and Moscow. During the early 1990s, Ukraine agreed to and then stalled its commitment to deliver its nuclear arsenal to Russia for destruction. After receiving security assurances, economic assistance, and compensation in the form of nuclear fuel and debt relief, Ukraine delivered its last nuclear warhead to Russia in 1996.

Territorial disputes further complicated bilateral relations. The most immediate issue was the status of **Crimea** in general and the port of **Sevastopol** in particular. **Nikita Khrushchev** transferred the Crimean Peninsula from the **Russian Soviet Federative Socialist Republic** to the Ukrainian Soviet Socialist Republic on the 300th anniversary of the union of the two countries. Reflecting the history of the region, the vast majority of the population in 1991 was Russian or Russophone. The dispute was ultimately settled with Kiev's granting of autonomy to the republic, though Ukraine's sovereignty over Crimea remains a rallying point for ultranationalists in the Russian **State Duma**.

In recent years, Kiev has criticized its neighbor for issuing Russian passports to residents of the region. The stationing of Russia's Black Sea Fleet in the Crimean city of Sevastopol also created bilateral tensions as the Russian Federation initially refused to recognize Ukrainian sovereignty over its **naval** facilities; in 1997, a renewable 20-year lease was signed allowing for joint use of the port city by both Russian and Ukrainian naval forces at the cost of $97.5 million per annum. Recently, Ukraine has signaled that it will not renew the lease in 2017, forcing relocation of the Russian fleet to Novorossiysk.

Under Leonid Kuchma, whose support stemmed from Russophone and pro-Russian eastern Ukraine, Ukraine sought to navigate a careful path between Washington and Moscow. While Kuchma endorsed the idea of Ukraine's ultimate admission to the **North Atlantic Treaty Organization** (NATO) and opted against joining the Russian-backed **Collective Security Treaty Organization** and the "Slavic Union" of

Russia and Belarus, he also signed a Treaty of Friendship, Cooperation, and Partnership with Russia in 1997 (renewed in 2008). Under
both Kravchuk and Kuchma, Ukraine's privatization led to the domination of the economy by **oligarchs**, many of whom were backed by
Russian economic interests.

Foreign trade between the two countries exceeds $30 billion per
year, with Russia being Ukraine's single largest import and export
partner. Kuchma oversaw dramatic improvement in bilateral relations in his last years in power; however, the events surrounding
Ukraine's "Orange Revolution" in 2004–2005 shattered the burgeoning rapprochement. Backed by **Vladimir Putin** and pro-Russian oligarchs from Kuchma's faction, Prime Minister Viktor Yanukovych
ran for president and was declared the winner, before the widely
criticized and likely falsified election results were annulled after two
weeks of protests.

His rival, Viktor Yushchenko, who had reputedly suffered from
dioxin poisoning in September 2004, assumed office and reoriented
Ukraine toward the West; despite the new orientation, Ukraine's
new "orange" leadership stressed the country's return to sovereignty
and its refusal to be taken for granted by either Moscow or Brussels.
Moscow's vocal support for Yanukovych and the implication of a
Russian **FSB** agent in Yushchenko's poisoning immediately chilled
Ukrainian-Russian relations. That summer, Yushchenko's prime
minister, Yulia Tymoshenko, and the president of **Georgia**, **Mikheil
Saakashvili**, signed the Borjomi Declaration, ultimately creating
the **Community of Democratic Choice**, an organization dedicated
to preserving and promoting democracy in the region between the
Black, **Baltic**, and **Caspian** seas. The organization is viewed as a
pro-European counterbalance to Russian hegemony and a successor
to the **GUAM Organization for Democracy and Economic Development**. However, in 2006, Yushchenko appointed Yanukovych as
his new prime minister, suggesting a return to a more pro-Russian
orientation.

While out of office, Tymoshenko penned a damning critique of
Vladimir Putin in the respected American journal *Foreign Affairs*;
however, upon her return to the office of prime minister in 2007,
Tymoshenko struck a more conciliatory note with the Kremlin and
has developed a working relationship with **Dmitry Medvyedev**.

Despite this, major issues between the two countries continue to dog relations.

The most serious dispute relates to **natural gas**; as the primary route for transshipment to southern **Germany**, Italy, Austria, and the Balkans, Ukraine is vital to Gazprom's sale of energy to the **European Union** (EU). Ukraine's illegal siphoning of gas and disputes over pricing, however, led to cessation of shipments in the winters of 2005–2006, 2007–2008, and 2008–2009. **Gazprom** defends its pricing increases in market terms, arguing that Soviet-era subsidies are anachronistic, while Moscow describes the Ukrainian authorities as "criminal"; Ukraine counters by suggesting that the timing of the price disputes is politically motivated in an effort to cow the "orange" leadership. In the most recent dispute, natural gas flows to Bulgaria, Romania, and Hungary were acutely affected, triggering a debate across Europe about energy security and the dependence on Russia and its **near abroad**.

In February 2009, a 10-year deal on transit was signed and included an end to the use of middlemen, a 20 percent discount on market prices for Ukraine, and the implementation of a new dispute resolution system. Russo-Ukrainian relations were also severely impacted by the **South Ossetian War**; Ukraine's president Yushchenko vehemently condemned Russia's actions as neo-imperialist, while Moscow accused Kiev of supplying weapons and military advisors to the Georgian forces. Both Ukraine and Georgia have been actively moving toward NATO admission against the wishes of the Kremlin. Russia's invasion of **South Ossetia** and recognition of **Abkhazia** was viewed as a prologue for potential actions in Crimea by many Ukrainian politicians; protection of Russia's "countrymen" against forced Ukrainianization remains a major political issue in the Duma. Despite their frequently incendiary rhetoric, most Ukrainian political elites continue to seek good relations with both Russia and the West, namely, the EU and the U.S. *See also* COLOR REVOLUTIONS.

UKRAINIANS, ETHNIC. Ethnic group. At nearly 3 million or more than 2 percent of the total population, Ukrainians represent the third-largest nationality within the Russian Federation (in neighboring **Ukraine**, there are 37.5 million Ukrainians). Closely related to both **Russians** and Belarusians, Ukrainians are an East Slavic ethnicity and are predominantly Eastern **Orthodox**, though a minority profess Greek Catholicism. The majority of Ukrainians residing in Russia use the **Russian language** in their daily lives, though many maintain some level of fluency in Ukrainian or Surzhyk, a Russian-Ukrainian patois.

While the **federal subjects** adjacent to Ukraine (particularly **Krasnodar Krai**) and traditional **Cossack** areas (such as **Orenburg**) include significant numbers of ethnic Ukrainians, the diaspora is resident in every part of the Russian Federation, a legacy of both tsarist and Soviet settlement policies that favored Slavic settlement of peripheral areas of the Russian Empire/Union of Soviet Socialist Republics (USSR). In the provinces of **Chukotka**, **Magadan**, and **Khantiya-Mansiya**, Ukrainians make up nearly one-tenth of the population. The political identity of Ukrainians within the Russian Empire, the Soviet Union, and contemporary Russia remains a hotly debated issue. Some estimates suggest that upward of 10 million citizens of the Russian Federation are of Ukrainian origin; however, policies of **Russification** and social pressure against the use of the Ukrainian **language** led to high levels of assimilation during the second half of the 20th century. Since 1991, a number of cultural organizations for the so-called Eastern Diaspora have been established in **St. Petersburg**, **Moscow**, and other large cities, the most prominent of which is the Slavutych Society. *See also* NATIONAL IDENTITY.

ULYANOVSK OBLAST. An administrative region of the Russian Federation. The birthplace of **Vladimir Ilyich Lenin**, born in Ulyanov, after whom it is named, Ulyanovsk is situated in the Volga Highlands. The capital, Ulyanovsk (pop. 635,000), formerly Simbirsk, sits on the bank of the **Volga River** just downstream from the Kuybyshev Reservoir; the region's second city is Dimitrovgrad. The **oblast** borders **Samara**, **Saratov**, **Penza**, and the **ethnic republics** of **Mordoviya**, **Chuvashiya**, and **Tatarstan**. Ulyanovsk covers a territory of 37,300 square kilometers and has a population of more than 1.3 million. While **ethnic Russians** are a majority (72 percent), the region is ethnically diverse, including **Tatars** (12 percent), **Chuvash** (4 percent), **Mordvins** (4 percent), and others. Approximately 15 percent of the population is of **Muslim** origin.

The topography includes large tracts of deciduous forests, and the soil is predominantly **chernozem**. The region is rich in minerals (chalk, limestone, quartz, and glassmaking sand) and has a major mineral water bottling plant. In terms of local **industry**, the leading sectors include aircraft (Avistar) and automotive manufacturing (UAZ), textiles, construction, **food** processing, and woodworking. **Agriculture** and animal husbandry are important to the regional **economy**. A small number of **oil** fields are also under development in the area.

Not surprising given its association with Lenin, the region was a bastion of the **Communist Party of the Russian Federation** (KPRF) during the 1990s. In 1995, the KPRF won more than one-third of the **State Duma** elections in the region and gained the governorship for its candidate, Yury Goryachev, in 1996. Turning the oblast into a "socialist preserve," Goryachev maintained strict **media** controls, railed against foreign economic control of Russia, worked against **privatization**, and maintained food subsidies. After losing to Vladimir Shamanov in the 2000 elections, Goryachev took up a role as leader of the regional opposition and formed a nongovernmental organization dedicated to the less fortunate citizens of Ulyanovsk.

Shamanov, a retired army general who lacked a strong local base of support, suffered withering attacks from *Simbirskiie Izvestiia*, the local **newspaper**, during his first term as he confronted an environment of political nihilism in the region. He was defeated in 2004 by Sergey Morozov, who quickly moved to slash jobs in the regional administration; Morozov was reappointed by **Vladimir Putin** in 2006. The governor made national headlines when he demanded his top officials go back to the classroom to improve their English-language skills in an effort to make the region more attractive to **foreign investment**; he had previously ordered administrators to retake high school–level exams in the **Russian language** to prove their proficiency. Morozov also moved to expand his region's relations with **Azerbaijan**, including the erection of a monument to the late president, Heydar Aliyev. *See* MILITARY.

UNEMPLOYMENT. In the Union of Soviet Socialist Republics (USSR), unemployment, a social "evil" associated with capitalism, was officially declared to be absent in Soviet society, despite clear evidence to the contrary. The right to employment was considered sacrosanct, and failure to work was viewed as a **crime** against the state. However, **perestroika** inevitably turned many Soviet citizens out of work, while others came to suffer from chronic underemployment. After the **dissolution of the Soviet Union**, the problem was exacerbated as the **economy** shrunk dramatically, particularly in heavy **industry** and the public sector. **Boris Yeltsin**'s combination of rapid **privatization** and the elimination of mass subsidies quickly led to a rise in joblessness. In 1997, the official statistics registered a rate of 10 percent; however, actual figures were estimated to be much higher. The state's inability to pay unemployment benefits, combined with wage arrears, proved devastating to the economy; the 1998 **ruble crisis** only worsened the situation.

Under **Vladimir Putin**, the economy improved significantly, mainly thanks to **oil** and **natural gas** exports, but also as a result of hitting rock bottom in 1998, after nearly a decade of industrial rationalization. Upon taking office, Putin inherited a country with a joblessness rate of more than 12 percent; by 2002, this had dropped to 8 percent, where it would remain for the next three years. In 2005, unemployment began another period of steady decline, reaching 6.2 percent in 2008. As a result of the 2008–2009 **global economic crisis**, the rate rose to 8 percent in early 2009. President **Dmitry Medvyedev** responded by announcing a $1.3 million package to create new jobs and fund retraining programs.

UNIFIED ENERGY SYSTEM (UES). Established on 15 August 1992, the Unified Energy System was Russia's electric power holding company, and ran the national power grid until 1 July 2008. UES controlled 70 percent of the country's electricity capacity and transmission lines and nearly the entire high-voltage grid. Headquartered in **Moscow** and employing more than half a million people, UES ranked as one of Russia's most important companies. The government maintained a majority stake in the company, but allowed minority ownership. Beginning in 2006, portions of UES underwent **privatization** to attract investment, creating more than 20 new companies. In 2008, UES was reorganized as the Federal Grid Company of Unified Energy System (UES FGC); federal law requires the state to maintain at least a 75 percent ownership of the new concern. **Anatoly Chubais** was the last chair of UES.

UNION OF RIGHT FORCES (SPS). Political party. Known in Russian as Soiuz Pravykh Sil, the SPS was a center-right reformist party established at the end of the 1990s. The party was co-founded by a group of well-known economic liberals, many from the **Yeltsin** administration, including **Irina Hakamada**, **Boris Nemtsov**, **Anatoly Chubais**, **Yegor Gaydar**, and **Sergey Kiriyenko**. It also brought together a number of small, liberal parties including the Right Cause, the New Force, **Konstantin Titov**'s Voice of Russia, and Russia's Democratic Choice. The party platform was dedicated to fostering liberal values, expanding citizen participation in government, eliminating censorship of the press, and instituting Western-style economic reforms.

During the 1999 legislative elections, the SPS won a respectable 8.6 percent of the vote and gained 32 seats in the **State Duma**. While the SPS supported the candidacy of **Vladimir Putin** in the 2000 presidential election, Nemtsov soon emerged as a vocal critic of the new president's authoritarian policies. In the 2003 parliamentary elections, the SPS narrowly failed to reach the required 5 percent threshold to obtain seats in the Duma. Nemtsov subsequently stepped down, admitting that his dispute with other party members over whether to take a more accommodating line toward the Kremlin had caused the poor showing. The party's next leader was Nikita Belykh, who, after leaving the party, was appointed governor of **Kirov Oblast** by Putin. Belykh was responsible for a 2005 deal with **Grigory Yavlinsky** that allied the SPS and **Yabloko** together in coalition to contest the **Moscow** City Duma elections, where the Yabloko-United Democrats were able to win seats alongside **United Russia** and the **Communist Party of the Russian Federation**.

Though there were discussions of a merger with Yabloko, these collapsed by the end of 2006. The party's last leader was Leonid Goizman. The party was dissolved on 1 October 2008. At its height, the party commanded 35,000 members and had a presence in nearly all of Russia's regions. Many of the party faithful are expected to gravitate to the newly proposed Independent Democratic Party of

Russia under the leadership of **Aleksandr Lebedev** and **Mikhail Gorbachev**.

UNION OF RUSSIA AND BELARUS. Originally known as the Commonwealth of Russia and Belarus, the special relationship between the Russian Federation and **Belarus** dates to 2 April 1996 when Minsk and Moscow expanded on the existing linkage provided by their joint membership in the **Commonwealth of Independent States**. A bicameral parliament, with equal representation from both states, was subsequently convened. The relationship was further expanded under **Boris Yeltsin** and Aleksandr Lukashenko in 1997 through the Treaty on the Union between Belarus and Russia, which gave rise to the current name of the union. Disputes over common **economic** and energy policies stymied meaningful integration in the ensuing years, and enthusiasm for the project waned. Customs controls were resumed in 2001, effectively terminating one of the most important benefits of the original relationship. Despite a resurgence of interest in 2006, the countries' failure to introduce a common currency and Minsk's decision to fix its ruble to the U.S. dollar in 2008 demonstrated the weakness of a common front on financial matters. However, the tenets of the union still govern bilateral relations between the two neighbors. On several occasions, other states have expressed interest in joining the so-called Union State, including **Serbia**, **Kazakhstan**, **Kyrgyzstan**, **Moldova**, and the breakaway republics of **Transnistria**, **Abkhazia**, and **South Ossetia**.

UNION OF SOCIAL-DEMOCRATS. *See* SOCIAL DEMOCRATIC PARTY OF RUSSIA.

UNION OF SOVIET SOCIALIST REPUBLICS (USSR). *See* DISSOLUTION OF THE SOVIET UNION.

UNION REPUBLICS. During the Soviet era, the union republics—also known as the Soviet Socialist Republics (SSRs)—were the constituent parts of the Soviet Union. Since the 1950s, there have been 15 union republics (the **Russian Soviet Federative Socialist Republic**, **Ukraine**, **Belarus**, **Moldova**, **Armenia**, **Azerbaijan**, **Georgia**, **Kazakhstan**, **Kyrgyzstan**, **Uzbekistan**, **Turkmenistan**,

Tajikistan, **Estonia**, **Latvia**, and **Lithuania**), each with a titular nation. Prior to World War II, the last three—collectively known as the **Baltic States**—had been independent countries, and their annexation into the Union of Soviet Socialist Republics (USSR) as union republics was never recognized by many Western governments. Moldova was created on 2 August 1940 through a merger of Ukrainian territory and lands annexed from neighboring Romania. From 1940 to 1956, **Kareliya** was known as the Karelo-Finnish SSR, making it the 16th union republic. Nominally a federation, the USSR permitted the right of secession to each republic. During the summer of 1991, the Baltic States seceded from the union. In early December 1991, Russia, Belarus, and Ukraine de facto exercised this right by signing the **Belavezha Accords**. On 25 December 1991, the Alma-Ata Protocol completed the **dissolution of the Soviet Union**, with the remaining republics gaining their independence. During the late **Gorbachev** era, the parliaments of a number of Russia's **Autonomous Soviet Socialist Republics** (ASSRs), including **Chechnya**, unsuccessfully attempted to elevate their status to that of a union republic.

UNION TREATY (1991). *See* NEW UNION TREATY.

UNITED KINGDOM. *See* GREAT BRITAIN.

UNITED NATIONS (RUSSIAN ROLE IN). As a result of successful negotiations at the February 1945 Yalta Conference, the Union of Soviet Socialist Republics (USSR) agreed to join the United Nations (UN) when the organization was founded on 24 October 1945. **Joseph Stalin**, ever protective of Soviet interests, gained the right of veto and permanent membership on the Security Council for Moscow; the other four principal victors of World War II (**France**, **China**, **Great Britain**, and the **United States**) also enjoy this privilege.

During the first decade of the UN, the USSR issued 79 vetoes compared to almost none by the other permanent members of the Security Council. During the 1960s, the USSR enjoyed significant influence among the swelling membership of the international governmental organization, as newly independent, anti-imperialist states backed many of the Soviet Union's positions, which were directed at the Anglo-American alliance and various members of the **North Atlantic Treaty Organization** (NATO).

Upon the **dissolution of the Soviet Union** in December 1991, the Russian Federation assumed the seat occupied by the USSR since 1945, including its veto power. Earlier that year, the **Baltic States** joined the UN; in 1992, the other non-Slavic former Soviet republics acceded to the organization as independent states (**Belarus** and **Ukraine** had been members in their own right since 1945).

Despite the shift from an ideologically driven state (the USSR) to a nationally motivated entity (the Russian Federation), Russia—often supported by the People's Republic of China—continues to balance the power of the West, particularly the Anglo-American alliance. During the 1990s, the veto was used sparingly; however, **Boris Yeltsin** did shield the Bosnian Serbs from international criticism and used his country's position in the UN to attempt to broker a peace settlement in the Balkans on several occasions, as well as demand a role as a **peacekeeping** force in the area.

Under **Vladimir Putin** and **Dmitry Medvyedev**, Russia has used its veto (or threat of a veto) to prevent what it sees as "meddling" in the internal affairs of sovereign states. In 2003, Russia effectively scuttled American plans to invade Iraq under the writ of the UN; in 2008, Russia vetoed sanctions on Robert Mugabe's regime in Zimbabwe, angering much of the international community. The Kremlin has also used its position to prevent **Kosovo** from joining the UN since its declaration of independence from **Serbia**. In recent years, the United Nations and Russia have disputed the latter's claim to increasingly large areas of the **Arctic Ocean**. *See also* FOREIGN RELATIONS.

UNITED RUSSIA. Political party. Known in Russian as Iedinaia Rossiia, United Russia is currently the country's largest political party. The party was created in 2001 with the merger of **Sergey Shoygu**'s pro-government **Unity** party and **Yury Luzhkov**'s centrist **Fatherland—All Russia**. With the backing of then-President **Vladimir Putin**, United Russia quickly became Russia's "party of power," attracting a large number of regional governors and members of the country's political elite, including **Mintimer Shaymiyev**.

From 2002 until 2008, the party was led by **Boris Gryzlov**, chairman of the **State Duma** and a close ally of Putin. Since its inception, United Russia has been closely associated with Putin, who became chairman in 2008 in a successful bid to become prime minister after two terms as president. The platform is centrist, conservative, and patriotic, and relies on support from the Kremlin and populism to maintain its position. Its stated aim is to raise Russian living standards to European levels, and it argues that such nationwide progress will only come with presidential-parliamentary cooperation. United Russia supports a strong presidency, anti-**corruption** measures, increased **military** spending, improved social welfare, streamlining of government functions, and the elevation of Russia's standing as a world power.

United Russia opposes radicalism on the right and the left, placing it at odds with the **Communist Party of the Russian Federation** (KPRF) as well as **neofascist** groups like the **National Bolsheviks**. It also advocates the idea of Russia as a "sovereign democracy," free to pursue its own political development without interference from other members of the international community. In 2003, in its first appearance in parliamentary elections, the party took 37 percent of the vote and 223 of the **State Duma**'s 450 seats, trouncing the KPRF and other parties. It then threw its full support behind Putin's reelection campaign in 2004, resulting in the incumbent winning 71 percent of the vote. By 2005, United Russia expanded its seats in the Duma to 305 and controlled nearly half of the **Federation Council** as well. Its activities in advance of the 2007 parliamentary elections drew criticism from a number of domestic and international election-monitoring agencies, including GOLOS and the **Organization for Security and Co-operation in Europe**.

Vladimir Putin's decision to place himself at the top of the party's list also guaranteed United Russia's exceptional performance. In the final tally, United Russia won 64 percent of the vote. Due to a new 7 percent minimum threshold, only three other parties—the KPRF, the **Liberal Democratic Party of Russia**, and **Fair Russia**—gained seats in the Duma, resulting in United Russia controlling 315 of the house's 450 seats. The new majority eliminated any barriers to presidential dictation and implementation of new laws in the Russian Federation. In 2008, the party supported **Dmitry Medvyedev**'s candidacy for president, and facilitated the transition of Putin from president to prime minister. Founded in 2005, the Young Guard (*Molodaia gvardiia*) is the party's youth movement. The party commands nearly 1 million members and has a presence in all of Russia's regions. *See also* NASHI; VERTICAL OF POWER.

UNITED STATES (RELATIONS WITH). Romanov Russia and the United States established relations in the 18th century. After a period of rivalry in North America, Russia opted to sell its colony of Alaska to Washington in 1867. During World War I (1914–1918), Russia and the U.S. briefly fought together on the side of the Entente before the Bolshevik Revolution terminated the former's role in the war. Shortly thereafter, U.S. troops invaded Soviet Russia, hoping to quash the new regime. Relations were not formally established with the Union of Soviet Socialist Republics (USSR) until 1933.

After a brief alliance during World War II, Soviet-American relations plummeted, and by 1947, the two nations embarked on an epic geopolitical standoff known as the **Cold War**, with the two countries nearly going to war during the 1962 Cuban Missile Crisis. With the election of **Ronald Reagan** in 1980, U.S.-Soviet relations, which had warmed somewhat under détente, entered into a deep freeze with Reagan engaging in militarist rhetoric, which was returned by the geriatric leadership of the Kremlin. The U.S.'s surreptitious support to the mujahideen in Soviet-occupied **Afghanistan** further hampered relations.

The ascendancy of **Mikhail Gorbachev** in 1985 triggered a new direction. Gorbachev's reforms of **perestroika** and **glasnost**, combined with new agreements on arms reductions, ushered in a period of cordial relations. Reagan's condemnation of the USSR's "evil empire" in the **Eastern Bloc** placed intense pressure on Moscow to loosen its control of the region, culminating in the 1989 issuance of the so-called **Sinatra Doctrine**, which granted autonomy (as well as ultimate responsibility for their actions) to the Communist parties of the Soviet bloc; ultimately, the countries of **Poland**, East **Germany**, Czechoslovakia, and Hungary abandoned the one-party system and their defense relationships with Moscow.

Arms reduction initiatives, including START I, and normalization of relations continued under the new president **George H. W. Bush** (1989–1993), resulting in support from the USSR for the U.S.-led invasion of Moscow's erstwhile ally Iraq in the Persian Gulf War (1990–1991) and the reunification of Germany. During the Bush presidency, independence movements among the **union republics** gathered steam, particularly in the **Baltic States** and **Georgia**. While American popular opinion favored such **separatist** movements, Washington pursued a realpolitik policy of balancing democratic idealism with maintenance of its burgeoning relations with Gorbachev. Bush stood behind both Gorbachev and **Boris Yeltsin** during the failed **August Coup** in 1991, providing key information to the latter about Soviet **military** activity.

In the fall of 1991, as the USSR dissolved, Bush sought to expand his relations with Yeltsin, while simultaneously reaching out to the nationalist leaders of the non-Russian republics. In 1992, the United States committed itself to helping the new Russian Federation and other post-Soviet states to secure "loose" **weapons of mass destruction**, particularly nuclear material, under the Nunn-Lugar Act. The United States and Russia also moved to expand cooperation on **space** exploration and defense, while eliminating Cold War–era impediments to **foreign trade**, communication, and cultural exchange. In 2007, United States and Russia approached parity in imports and exports, with bilateral trade totaling nearly $20 billion.

The U.S. is also an important source of **foreign investment** for Russia, though the figure—at $3.6 billion in 2007—is now on the decline, with offshore and European investors commanding the lion's share. Under President **Bill Clinton** (1993–2000), Washington committed to helping Moscow through its painful transition from a command-and-control **economy**; however, the imposition of **shock therapy**, combined with the U.S.'s failure to fully deliver on its promises of aid to Moscow, resulted in a meltdown of the Russian economy. A subsequent purge of Yeltsin's pro-Western, market-oriented appointees produced a new leadership, personified by the rise of **Yevgeny Primakov**, that was more **Eurasianist** in its orientation and opposed to America's domination of the world system.

With a concomitant rise in poverty and a precipitous drop in their country's international position, many Russians came to view the United States as benefiting from the country's destabilization, particularly during the war in **Chechnya**. Despite this, Clinton and Yeltsin maintained a strong personal relationship throughout their two terms as president. In 1999, however, expansion of the **North Atlantic Treaty Organization** (NATO) into east-central Europe and plans to include the Baltic States, combined with events in Yugoslavia, drove post-Soviet relations to their nadir.

Vladimir Putin and **George W. Bush** were able to improve relations with a June 2001 summit in Slovenia, at which Bush declared he was able to get a "sense of Putin's soul." With the **September 11 attacks**, Putin was the first world leader to call President Bush, vociferously condemning the **terrorist** acts and committing Russian support to the effort to punish the perpetrators, a stance that was unpopular with much of Russia's political elite. This turning point in relations resulted in extensive cooperation on **counterterrorism**, Russian backing of U.S. military installations in **Central Asia**, and Washington's reestimation of the value of the **Shanghai Cooperation Organization** and **Chechen** links to the global **Islamist** jihadi movement. Relations began to sour with Washington's declaration of its intention to invade Iraq in 2002; Moscow organized a group of "old" European states (**France**, Germany, etc.) to block the military adventure, but to no avail.

Buttressed by growing **oil** prices and challenged with a rising terrorist threat, the Kremlin adopted a number of authoritarian measures within the Russian Federation, curtailing press freedom and limiting representative **democracy**, while acting increasingly aggressively toward its former Soviet neighbors, especially **Ukraine** and **Georgia**. Both trends drew pointed criticism from the Bush White House, which angered the Kremlin with its recognition of **Kosovo**'s declaration of independence and new plans for a missile defense shield in Poland and the Czech Republic. With the ascendancy of **Dmitry Medvyedev** and the election of **Barack Obama** in 2008, relations have changed little. Russo-American ties remain frayed after the **South Ossetian War**, which was viewed by Western policymakers as an ominous warning to aspiring NATO members in the Russian periphery. Medvyedev's overt backing of **Kyrgyzstan**'s 2009 decision to oust the U.S. from its base at Manas has further demonstrated that Russia seeks to marginalize U.S. interests in the **near abroad**. *See also* MIDDLE EAST; NUCLEAR WEAPONS; SERBIA; UNITED NATIONS; UZBEKISTAN.

UNITY/INTERREGIONAL MOVEMENT "UNITY." Political party. Known in Russian as Iedinstvo, Unity was a pro-**Yeltsin**

party established in 1999 to combat the growing influence of **Fatherland—All Russia**. The party was colloquially known as Medved'
(The Bear), for the acronym of its longer name (*Mezhregional'noie
Dvizheniie Iedinstvo*). The party's early backers were regional governors who hoped to shape the future direction of Russian politics.
Then Prime Minister **Vladimir Putin** quickly threw his support
behind the group and its leader, Minister of Emergency Situations
Sergey Shoygu. Despite its lack of a cogent political platform, the
party's support for the popular second **Chechen War** and its promotion in pro-Kremlin **media** outlets aided the party's rise to prominence. In the **State Duma** elections of 1999, the party took second
place behind the **Communist Party of the Russian Federation**
with 23 percent of the vote and 84 seats in the lower house; 10 more
members soon joined the faction. In 2000, **Boris Gryzlov** took over
as leader of the party. Also that year, Unity backed Vladimir Putin's
candidacy for president. In 2001, Unity merged with its former rival,
Fatherland—All Russia, to form **United Russia**, which soon became
the dominant **political party** in Russia.

URAL MOUNTAINS. The Ural Mountains extend nearly 2,500 kilometers from the shores of the **Arctic Ocean** to the Kazakh Steppe,
separating European Russia from **Siberia**. The range is one of the
several geographic features dividing Europe from Asia. The highest peak is Mount Narodnaya (1,895 m). Geopolitically, the **federal
subjects** of Russia associated with the Urals include **Bashkortostan**,
Khantiya-Mansiya, **Udmurtiya**, **Yamaliya**, **Tyumen**, **Sverdlovsk**,
Perm Krai, **Orenburg**, **Kurgan**, and **Chelyabinsk**. Most of these
regions also comprise the Urals **Economic Region**. During the 1930s
and especially World War II, a significant portion of European Russia's **industrial** capacity was transferred to the immediate environs
of the Urals, establishing important manufacturing centers including
Magnitogorsk. **Mining** remains an important economic driver in the
area, as the Urals contain significant deposits of gold, platinum, coal,
iron, and other metals, as well as **oil**.

USKORENIIE. Usually translated into English as "acceleration,"
uskoreniie is derived from Russian *skorost'* (speed), and is used to

denote the modernization of the Soviet **economy** with the purpose of achieving higher efficiency and flexibility. **Yury Andropov** originally used the term in 1982 in an effort to summarize his attempts to reverse the Soviet Union's economic stagnation under **Leonid Brezhnev**. However, the concept gained greater usage under **Mikhail Gorbachev** in the mid-1980s. The new premier linked economic reform to the Soviet Union's national security by stressing the need for innovative thinking, a shift away from heavy **industry**, competitiveness in the world market, modernization of economic institutions, and improvement of social conditions. He launched his plan for *uskoreniie* with the 12th Five-Year plan, which covered the period from 1986 to 1990. Gorbachev linked successful acceleration to the human factor (*chelovecheskii faktor*), which he felt was vital to improving the international position of the Soviet Union vis-à-vis the First World; as such, the anti-**alcoholism** campaign was an early salvo in the larger program. In order to further accelerate the economy, Gorbachev introduced a number of other interlinked policies, including **perestroika**, **glasnost**, **informatization**, and **democratization**.

UST-ORDA BURYATIYA. *See* IRKUTSK OBLAST.

UZBEKISTAN (RELATIONS WITH). The historical area of Transoxiana, which comprises modern-day Uzbekistan, was adjoined to the Russian Empire in the late 19th century. Portions of the country were annexed outright, while the Khanate of Khiva and the Emirate of Bukhara remained nominally independent under Russian suzerainty. The Uzbek Soviet Socialist Republic (SSR) was created in 1924 with the dismemberment of Soviet Turkestan; **Tajikistan** remained an autonomous region within the republic until 1929. With the new borders, the republic became the most urban of Central Asia, possessing the Silk Road cities of Samarkand, Bukhara, Kokand, and Khiva, as well as Tashkent.

Soviet rule saw significant industrial development, but an overreliance on the cotton monoculture continued from tsarist times. During the 1980s, Moscow purged much of the republican leadership and renewed its anti-**Islam** campaign, sparking an upsurge in Uzbek **nationalism**. Ethnic tensions between Uzbeks and **ethnic minorities** increased during the period, culminating in mass violence against

Meskhetian Turks in 1989, a crisis that rocked the Union of Soviet Socialist Republics (USSR) to the core. In the incident's wake, First Party Secretary Rafik Nishanov was replaced by Islom Karimov, who would steer the country toward independence and win election as its first president in December 1991.

Karimov's rule became increasingly authoritarian throughout the 1990s, banning the main opposition party, Birlik (Uzbek: "Unity"), and taking a particularly harsh approach toward political **Islamist** groups such as the Islamic Movement of Uzbekistan and Hizb ut-Tahrir. Karimov had a tempestuous relationship with **Boris Yeltsin**, whom he saw as a threat to Uzbekistan's rise as a regional power in **Central Asia**, particularly after 1994. Doubly landlocked, but possessing the region's largest population and significant deposits of **oil** and **natural gas**, Uzbekistan must rely on its neighbors (including the Russian Federation) in order to conduct **foreign trade**. This situation has created a number of problems in the region, which are often compounded by Tashkent's proactive "protection" of its co-nationals in neighboring states.

Although Karimov backed Yeltsin's 1996 bid for reelection as the lesser of two evils, he also sought to undermine Russian influence in the region (particularly on **military** cooperation within the **Commonwealth of Independent States** and in the **Tajik Civil War**) and courted an alliance with the **United States** during the late 1990s after the Turkish economic crisis eviscerated the nascent program of **pan-Turkism** (Uzbekistan joined the **North Atlantic Treaty Organization** [NATO] **Partnership for Peace** program in 1994). Karimov's strident nationalism and rapid Uzbekification of the public sector and military prompted an exodus of some 2 million **ethnic Russians** in the wake of independence, further damaging Russo-Uzbek relations.

In 1999, Uzbekistan left the Russian-led **Collective Security Treaty Organization** (CSTO) and joined the **GUAM Organization for Democracy and Economic Development**, a collection of post-Soviet states wishing to distance themselves from Moscow's embrace. When **Vladimir Putin** took office, **foreign relations** between the two countries were at their nadir. However, Tashkent continued to pursue a multivectored foreign policy that included Russia; the republic joined the Shanghai Five in 2001, causing it to be renamed the **Shanghai Cooperation Organization** (SCO). In the wake of the

September 11 attacks, Tashkent rapidly expanded cooperation with the **United States**, including the creation of an air base at Karshi-Khanabad (K2) for operations in the Afghan War. However, the partnership with Washington quickly created two problems: the need for democratization and a spike in Islamist ire at the Karimov regime.

The U.S.-sanctioned **color revolutions** in **Georgia** (2003) and **Ukraine** (2004) weighed heavily on Karimov, who felt that America might be more of a liability than an asset. On 12 May 2005, a prison break in the Ferghana Valley city of Andijan sparked protests that were brutally repressed by the security forces. The loss of life was roundly condemned by the U.S. and the **European Union**, while the Russian Federation and **China** backed Uzbekistan's actions. At a July meeting of the SCO, the group demanded that a timetable be established for all U.S. soldiers to leave Uzbekistan, which occurred by November.

In the wake of the Andijan crisis, Tashkent rapidly renewed ties with Moscow. Joint ventures flourished, the **Russian language** retuned to Uzbek schools, and **counterterrorism** efforts expanded. On 14 November 2005, the two countries signed a Treaty of Allied Relations providing mutual defense guarantees. In 2006, Uzbekistan rejoined the CTSO and became a member of the **Eurasian Economic Community**.

– V –

VALDAI DISCUSSION CLUB. The group, which meets regularly to discuss Russia's role in international affairs, is comprised of the Russian Information Agency (**RIA Novosti**), the Council for Foreign and Defense Policy, *Russia Profile* and *Russia in Global Affairs* magazines, and *The Moscow News*. Attendees include pro-Kremlin intellectuals, as well as mild critics of the government. The club meets annually with the Russian president, and more recently with the prime minister as well. The organization was launched in 2005, and its meetings are well covered by domestic and international **media**. *See also* FOREIGN RELATIONS.

VEKSELBERG, VIKTOR FELIKSOVICH (1957–). Oligarch.
Viktor Vekselberg is one of the richest men in the world. Like other
Russian oligarchs, he made his fortune in the 1990s through contro-
versial **privatization** deals.

He was born in western **Ukraine** into a **Jewish** family. In his early
life, Vekselberg exemplified the upwardly mobile Soviet technical
intelligentsia, making a research career at institutions affiliated with
heavy industry, such as the Irkutsk Aluminum Plant. He started his
business career in the 1990s, when he created a joint-stock holding
company and began purchasing shares of aluminum plants. In 1996,
he founded a few aluminum consortia that enabled him to capitalize
his assets. In the same year, he began operating on the **oil** market; his
activities resulted in creation of the TNK oil company.

He is particularly notorious for his extravagant art purchases.
In 2004, he bought nine of the Fabergé eggs at a Sotheby's auc-
tion. The collection was transported to Russia and exhibited in the
Kremlin. In 2006, he agreed to pay a million dollars to transport
the Lowell House Bells from Harvard University, Massachusetts,
back to their original location in the Danilov Monastery in **Moscow**.
He also purchased replacement bells. The historic bells returned to
Moscow in 2008.

VENEZUELA (RELATIONS WITH). Historically, bilateral ties
between Moscow and Caracas have been weak to nonexistent; however, beginning in 1999 with the election of Hugo Chavez, a populist,
left-leaning president, the two countries have drawn closer.

Chavez quickly replaced Fidel Castro as the leading voice of
anti-Americanism in Latin America, courting leaders from **Iran** and
Iraq, much to the dismay of Washington. In the wake of the **United
States**–led invasion of Iraq and U.S.-supported **color revolutions**
in Russia's **near abroad**, **Vladimir Putin** began to court closer ties
to the Chavez government, hoping to facilitate the emergence of
multipolarity in world politics as well as to expand Russia's flagging
international **arms sales**. Russian exports to Venezuela, nominal
until 2004, have increased dramatically with the new relationship,
totaling over $1 billion in 2007. The bulk of this trade has been in
arms, particularly submarines, helicopters, late-model Kalashnikovs,

and antiaircraft missile systems; total arms sales now exceed $4.4 billion.

At a presidential summit between **Dmitry Medvyedev** and Chavez in mid-2008, the two countries agreed to coordinate energy policies, particularly with respect to **oil** and **natural gas**; a deal on **nuclear energy** has also been signed. Russian corporations such as **Lukoil** and **Gazprom** have benefited from Chavez's "Bolivarian revolution," which has displaced British and American transnationals from much of his country's economy. The two states have also increased **military** and **naval** cooperation in recent years, which is seen as a signal regarding Russia's intent to increase influence in Latin America at the expense of Washington. On 10 September 2009, Venezuela recognized the independence of **Abkhazia** and **South Ossetia**, a move welcomed in Moscow.

VERTICAL OF POWER. While the notion of a "vertical of power" (*vertikal' vlasti*) within the Russian state dates to 1993, when **Boris Yeltsin** used it to describe an attempt to streamline governance in the Russian Federation, the concept became synonymous with the administration of **Vladimir Putin**. From 2000 to 2005, Putin set about implementing his plans to reduce the power of the **federal subjects** vis-à-vis the central government, especially with the gubernatorial **electoral reforms of 2004–2005**, which allowed him to create a "single chain of command" and expand the power of the executive branch of the government. In addition to the depletion of **asymmetrical federalism**, Putin also sought to reign in the press and eliminate the **oligarchs** as a political force in the country. Through the encouragement of an alliance between the so-called *siloviki* and corporate interests, he was able to create synergy between Russia's **economic** and **political** elites. Putin framed his neo-authoritarian agenda as an attempt to purge Russia of the chaos (*bespredel*) of the 1990s, when **mafia**, **separatists**, and other antistate interests sapped Russia of its power and prestige around the world. The dramatic resurgence of the state under Putin, however, has been viewed as acutely detrimental to the country's fledgling **civil society**. Since assuming the presidency, **Dmitry Medvyedev** has signaled his intent to hew the sharper edges of the vertical of power.

VILLAGE LIFE. *See* RURAL LIFE.

VISUAL ARTS. Russia's ongoing debates about its cultural heritage are especially evident in the realm of visual arts. Starting with **Slavophiles**, all Russian thinkers and artists were forced to place themselves on either the Western or Eastern front of the cultural divide. With the abolition of censorship and deregulation of cultural industries in the 1990s, Russian artists gained access to vast, previously unavailable art traditions of the world, while gaining an opportunity to display their works abroad. Once protected by Soviet cultural policies, artists—who had generally been loyal to the **Communist Party of the Soviet Union**—had to learn to survive in new market conditions.

The 1990s were a transitional period when state art institutions lost their dominance in the field, and Russian artists began searching for their individual, depoliticized voices. The first decade of the new century witnessed a rise of private galleries and institutions, as well as a new generation of Russian artists who were simultaneously cognizant of global art tendencies and attentive to their local cultural milieu.

If the 1980s were about dismantling the canon of socialist realism and staging art provocations, the 2000s have been about an unprecedented artistic diversity and the attempt to conceptualize what makes Russian art. In the same period, some artistic voices gained full power outside Russia. Artists such as Ilia Kabakov and art critics like Boris Groys emerged as leading authorities both in the West and in Russia. Like Russian **film**, Russian visual arts in the 1990s were focused on **Moscow**, though the cultural space outside the Russian capital has been embraced more recently.

Russian visual arts of the period continued and adapted the overly grandiose Soviet tradition: with support of Moscow's mayor, **Yury Luzhkov**, Zurab Tsereteli erected a number of controversial architectural pieces in the capital. Political activists have also found their voice in new works of art: the Blue Noses, a **Siberian** group, has produced a series of satirical anti-Kremlin, anti–global capitalism videos and paintings, and the **St. Petersburg**–based group Protez (Prosthesis) has been involved in political activism through their trash-art shows. Many Russian artists gained international fame and/ or notoriety; for example, Oleg Kulik became world famous thanks to his provocative live performances as a barking dog. Others are known to art specialists and a select group of art enthusiasts (e.g., Andrei Bakhurin's flash animation).

Russia's contemporary art scene has been partially defined by the rediscovery of the artistic tradition (there were major retrospectives in Moscow's central museums) and the revisiting of specific genres and media (in 2007–2009 the Moscow Center for Contemporary Art showed works of Russian video art). As regards classical art, the current period is characterized by the continuing dominance of Russia's major art museums, such as the **Hermitage** and the Tretiakov Gallery. Russian contemporary artists have also obtained new state-supported and private venues, including Moscow's Vinzavod (Wine Factory) gallery, among others.

The Ministry of Culture of the Russian Federation, established in 2005, has supported the resurgence of contemporary art in Russia, particularly through the Moscow Biennale. The ministry also runs an annual national art competition known as Innovatsiia (Innovation), which gives awards in the following categories: Best Work of Visual Art, Best Curatorial Project, Best "New Generation," Best Regional Project, and Art Criticism.

While Moscow remains the center of Russian cultural life, the contemporary art scene is developing in the provinces as well. In fact, a number of art and curatorial projects focused on artists outside the capital. For example, in 2007, the art project called "9000 Kilometers" (referring to the distance between Russia's most western and eastern points) brought together artists and curators from Russian provincial cities along the axis stretching from **Kaliningrad** to **Vladivostok**. The aim of the project was to demonstrate Russia's cultural diversity and to create a sense of national belonging through art practices. In the same year, the art project ironically called "Nemoskva" (Not Moscow) was supposed to travel across Russia in a few train carriages, stopping in Russian provinces and engaging with the local cultural scene. The curators of the project attempted to reveal the tensions between Russia's cultural center and periphery through a number of innovative curatorial and educational strategies.

Christie's and Sotheby's auctions have reported a surge of interest in Russian art since 2000; they have seen record sales of Russian art, often to Russian museums and **oligarchs**. Visual arts have recently emerged as a tool of political and financial speculation. Some Russian oligarchs took part in returning works of Russian art to the nation; others, like **Roman Abramovich**, made art-sales history by purchasing classical works for a Moscow art gallery run by his girlfriend. In 2009, the Russian government decided to change regulations in order to enable Russian banks and investment companies to invest in art. *See also* VEKSELBERG, VIKTOR.

VLADIMIR OBLAST. An administrative region of the Russian Federation. Located 50 kilometers east of **Moscow**, Vladimir Oblast is situated on the Eastern European Plain. The region borders the **oblasts** of **Moscow**, **Ryazan**, **Nizhny Novgorod**, **Ivanovo**, and **Yaroslavl**, and is adjacent to **Tver**. It is part of the Central **Economic Region** and **Federal District**. The regional capital, Vladimir (pop. 315,000), is part of the Golden Ring and one of the oldest cities in Russia. Two of its cathedrals are listed as UNESCO Heritage Sites.

The region covers an area of 29,000 square kilometers and has a population of 1.5 million, 80 percent of whom live in urban areas, making it one of Russia's most densely populated oblasts. Vladimir Oblast comprises much of the historical region of Zalesye, a heavily wooded area that was central to the state-building process of medieval Russia. Today, half of the territory remains forested, and the oblast includes the Meschera National Park. A number of historically important Russian towns are located in the area, including Suzdal, Yuriev-Polsky, Aleksandrov, and Murom. The major rivers in the region are the Dubna and the Oka. Economically, the region is highly developed and ranks among Russia's 20 highest-performing **federal subjects**.

Important **industrial** sectors include electricity generation, engineering, metalworking, **food** processing, glassmaking, forestry, woodworking, construction materials, and petrochemicals. The Vladimir Tractor Plant is the largest employer in the capital. Research and development is also a key sector of the local **economy**. **Agriculture** employs less than 10 percent of the population, focusing mainly on animal husbandry and vegetables.

During the 1990s, no single political bloc dominated the region, though the **Communist Party of the Russian Federation** (KPRF) was the single most popular party. **Boris Yeltsin**, however, won the regional poll in the second round of the **1996 presidential election**. Nikolay Vinogradov, a former cement company engineer and chair of the Central Executive Committee of the KPRF, won the governorship in 1996 by defeating incumbent Yury Vlasov. Vinogradov, though remaining within the Communist Party, ultimately joined the pro-Kremlin **Our Home—Russia** movement. He was reelected by a wide margin in 2000 and was later reappointed by **Vladimir Putin** (2005) and by **Dmitry Medvyedev** (2009). The most recent appointment was seen as a sign of the Communists' newfound power within Russia, a result of the 2008–2009 **global financial crisis**. *See also* TOURISM.

VODKA. *See* ALCOHOLISM.

VOLGA GERMANS. *See* GERMANS.

VOLGA RIVER. Europe's largest river in terms of length, discharge, and watershed, the Volga rises in the Valdai Hills of western Russia and empties into the **Caspian Sea**. The river is more than 3,600 kilometers in length and has a watershed of 1.3 million square kilometers. Sometimes referred to as the national river of Russia, the Volga is often depicted in **literature**, **art**, and **film**. More than half of Russia's largest cities lie on the river or one of its tributaries, which include the Kama, Oka, Sura, and Vetluga. Some of the largest reservoirs in the world can be found along the Volga, and the river is well connected to other waterways via a series of canals and locks constructed during the Soviet period. The Volga basin is home to a number of Russia's **ethnic minorities**, including the **Tatars**, **Mari**, **Mordvins**, and **Chuvash**. *See also* TRANSPORTATION.

VOLGA TATARS. *See* TATARS.

VOLGA-URAL REGION. While lacking administrative legitimacy, the Volga-Ural region is a historical and cultural concept with the Russian Federation. Located at the crossroads of Europe and Asia, the **Volga River** basin and the foothills of the **Ural Mountains** are home to a sizable percentage of Russia's **national minorities**. During the Russian Civil War, a confederation of **Tatars, Bashkirs, Mari, Udmurts, Mordvins**, and **Chuvash** and other non-Russian groups was established known as the Idel-Ural State, using the Tatar name for the Volga. The region is rich in **oil** reserves and possesses a fairly well-developed **industrial** base. In 2001, the Russian **military** consolidated two of its districts to create the Volga-Ural Military District with its command at Yekaterinburg.

VOLGOGRAD OBLAST. An administrative region of the Russian Federation. The Volgograd Oblast is located in southern European Russia on the border with **Kazakhstan**. It shares internal borders with **Astrakhan, Kalmykiya, Rostov, Voronezh**, and **Saratov**. It forms part of the Volga **Economic Region** and the Southern **Federal District**. Naturally, the **Volga River** is the region's most important waterway, but the **oblast** also includes the Volga-Don Canal, portions of the Don River, and much of the Tsimlyansk Reservoir. Volgograd is thus a key part of the Unified Deep Water System of European Russia connecting the **Caspian Sea** to the **Sea of Azov**, and thus the world's oceans.

The oblast covers an area of 113,900 square kilometers, and its topography ranges from **chernozem** in the west to dry **steppe** in the east. The region has a population of 2.9 million; **ethnic Russians** make up 89 percent of the population, and the largest minorities are **Ukrainians** (3 percent), **Kazakhs** (1.7 percent), and **Tatars** (1 percent).

The regional capital is the important **industrial** city and **transportation** hub of Volgograd (pop. 1 million). From 1925 until 1961, it bore the name Stalingrad, and was known as Tsaritsyn prior to the 1920s. While there is strong local support for a restoration of the World War II–era name of both the city and the region among the local populace, **Vladimir Putin** effectively killed the plan with a televised statement in 2002. The city witnessed one of the fiercest battles of World War II, with upward of 2 million casualties; the Soviet victory in 1943 is recognized as the turning point in the campaign against the Axis Powers. The heights outside the city, known as Mamayev Kurgan, host a monument to the defense of Stalingrad.

At 82 meters, "The Motherland Calls" was the world's tallest memorial when it was erected in 1967. Other important urban areas include Volzhsky and Kamyshin.

Given its comparatively warm **climate**, Volgograd is an important producer of a number of **agricultural** products including sunflowers, fruits, and mustard; it produces enough grain to export abroad. The region boasts significant mineral wealth including **oil**, **natural gas**, clay, limestone, and mineral water. The well-developed industrial base is focused on heavy equipment manufacturing (drilling, energy extraction, farm machinery, etc.), defense, shipbuilding, energy production, plastics, construction, and oil refining. Textiles, animal husbandry, forestry, woodworking, and **food** processing are also important. In the mid-1990s, the region ceased to function as a donor region due to an overdependence on heavy **industry**; however, the regional finances are far from bleak.

The old *nomenklatura* maintained a hold on the regional administration during the **Yeltsin** era, resulting in high levels of protectionism and subsidies. The region earned the nickname of the "buckle" of the **Red Belt** for its allegiance to the **Communist Party of the Russian Federation** (KPRF). In 1996, Nikolay Maksyuta, a KPRF candidate, chairman of the Volgograd City Duma, and local son, won the governorship. He worked to develop warm relations with the federal center and regional business interests, resulting in criticism from his own party. Despite this, he was able to hold off a challenge from Volgograd mayor Yury Chekov in the 1999 elections.

In 2000, Maksyuta took a strong stance against **neofascists** in the region when skinheads attacked a group of Indian medical students. He became a staunch supporter of Putin and was reelected in 2004. In recent years, Maksyuta has cut administrative spending in the region and overseen a dramatic increase in **foreign trade** with **Germany**. However, he has been identified as one of the governors most likely to be removed in the future by the new president, **Dmitry Medvyedev**.

VOLOGDA OBLAST. An administrative region of the Russian Federation. Measuring more than 700 kilometers from east to west, Vologda Oblast occupies 145,700 square kilometers of northwestern European Russia. It is part of the Northern **Economic Region** and the Northwestern **Federal District**. The population of the **oblast** is 1.2 million; it borders the **Republic of Kareliya** and the oblasts of **Arkhangelsk**, **Kirov**, **Kostroma**, **Yaroslavl**, **Novgorod**, and **Leningrad**.

The region sits on Lake Onega in the northwest and Rybinskoye Reservoir in the southwest, and includes a number of other large lakes including Ozero Beloye (White Lake) and Ozero Vozhe. The main rivers are the Sukhona, Yug, Sheksna, and Mologa. Accompanying its geographic attributes, the region is rich in historical sites, including the Kirillo-Belozersky monastery and the UNESCO-recognized Ferapontov convent, making the region an important **tourism** destination.

The regional capital, Vologda (pop. 293,000), is not the largest city in the region; instead Cherepovets (pop. 311,000), an important steel- and chemical-producing center within Russia, wields that distinction. Despite its northerly location, Vologda's agribusiness sector is well developed and produces milk, meat, and eggs, as well as world-famous butter. In **industrial** terms, metallurgy is the most important sector. The region excels at producing steel, fertilizers, timber, and linen, and is a leader in terms of industrial goods among Russia's **federal subjects**. OAO Severstal is Russia's largest producer of rolled metal.

Vologda is internationally recognized as one of the most stable regions in Russia for **foreign investment**. Companies from **Finland**, **Germany**, Sweden, Switzerland, and the **United States** are particularly active in the region.

In 1996, Vyacheslav Pozgalev, a former manager at the Severstal, won election to the post of governor; he had been appointed by **Boris Yeltsin** shortly before the election. Pozgalev was reelected with a strong mandate in 1999. In the early 1990s, Pozgalev had been part of **Yegor Gaydar**'s Russia's Choice movement. An economic liberal, his platform was built on economic stability, attraction of foreign capital, and avoidance of scandal and **corruption** (his predecessor, Nikolay Podgornov, was removed for taking bribes). Through **tax** breaks and other incentives, he turned Vologda into an attractive destination for foreign companies. He also supported **women**'s rights and **media** freedom.

In the late 1990s, he joined **Konstantin Titov**'s Russia's Voice (*Golos Rossii*) movement. He was able to hold onto his position throughout both administrations of **Vladimir Putin** (who nominated him for reappointment in 2007), and has a good working relationship with **Dmitry Medvyedev**. Pozgalev is one of the few regional executives who actively support the appointment of governors by the president. In recent years, the region has expanded its relationship with **Belarus**, including building a steel mill and developing a number of joint projects.

VORONEZH OBLAST. An administrative region of the Russian Federation. Situated within the heart of Russia's "Black Earth" (**chernozem**) region, Voronezh Oblast borders the **oblasts** of **Belgorod, Kursk, Lipetsk, Tambov, Saratov,** and **Volgograd**. It also shares an international border with **Ukraine**. It is part of the Central Black Earth **Economic Region** and the Central **Federal District**. The oblast covers a territory of 52,400 square kilometers and has a population of 2.3 million. **Ethnic Russians** make up 94 percent of the population, with **Ukrainians** being the largest minority (3 percent). The regional capital, Voronezh (pop. 848,000), is located on the Voronezh River, some 12 kilometers from where it meets the Don.

The city has been the site of a number of international incidents in recent years, including the killing of a Peruvian student in 2005 and the 2001 **espionage** accusations associated with an American student after his arrest for possession of marijuana. A number of UFO sightings in the late 1980s brought the city global attention. The city is home to Voronezh State University (formerly housed in Tartu, **Estonia**), one of the largest and oldest centers of learning in the country.

Voronezh Oblast's **economy** is diversified between **industry, agriculture,** and **transportation**. The region is an important gateway between Moscow and the **North Caucasus**, as well as parts of the **Commonwealth of Independent States**. The region accounts for nearly half of the agricultural output of the fertile chernozem region; crops include wheat, sunflowers, corn, and other sun-dependent produce. The region is also an important source of Russia's sugar production. The Voronezh Agricultural Machinery Plant (Voronezhselmash) is the country's leading maker of farm equipment. Airline manufacturing, chemicals, communications equipment, and rubber are also important local industries. While the region enjoys certain mineral resources necessary for the construction industry, it is comparatively poor in terms of energy resources and must import **oil** and **natural gas**.

Part of Russia's **Red Belt** during the 1990s, Voronezh was also known for its radical right-wing politics. In 1996, Ivan Shabanov, a Communist-backed critic of **Boris Yeltsin** with ties to extreme nationalists, won the governorship. A year later, members of **Russian National Unity** were patrolling the streets alongside regular police; the region proved to be a major recruiting ground for the ultranationalist organization in the late 1990s. Shabanov's failure to combat **corruption** cost the Communists their dominance in the region and he lost his 2000 reelection bid to an **FSB** officer, Vladimir Kulakov, who also enjoyed the support of **Vladimir Putin**. Despite being selected by the Kremlin to bring stability to the region, Kulakov's governance was unpopular and he failed to effectively manage local interests. His reforms soon resulted in social unrest, particularly over reductions of subsidies. In 2009, **Dmitry Medvyedev** chose not to reappoint him, instead backing Aleksey Goreyev, Russia's minister of agriculture, for the spot. Kulakov's dismissal was the first of four executive dismissals by the new president.

– W –

WAHHABISM. Derived from the name of the 18th-century Arab Islamic reformer Muhammad ibn Abd-al-Wahhab, Wahhabism (*vakhabizm*) is used as a generic term by the Russian government to describe radical **Islamists**. In the wake of the **Soviet-Afghan War**, some returning veterans of **Muslim** descent brought back the radical ideals of the Afghan mujahideen. In the early 1990s, Saudi and Egyptian missionaries further spread an austere interpretation of **Islam** that promotes the use of *sharia* (Islamic law) and is antithetical to **Christianity** and syncretic practices common among Muslims of the **North Caucasus** and the **Volga-Ural region**.

In the wake of the first **Chechen War**, radical Islamism gained ground among impoverished **Chechens**, **Ingush**, and Dagestanis, prompting fears of wider conflict between Russia's **Orthodox** populations and Caucasian Muslims (the doctrine had only limited appeal in **Tatarstan** and **Bashkortostan**). By the late 1990s, **Shamil**

Basayev's increasingly deadly attacks on civilians and his support for the establishment of a caliphate in the North Caucasus made Wahhabism one of the greatest threats to the security and territorial integrity of Russia. In an effort to defuse this threat, Moscow and regional authorities began a crackdown on Muslim organizations that espoused Wahhabism or that were supported from abroad.

Within the Russian *ummah* or Muslim community, Wahhabism is controversial, with some clerics decrying the influence of Saudi, Pakistani, and other foreign religious authorities, while **Moscow**'s chief mufti, **Ravil Gaynutdin**, has expressed more openness toward such interpretations of Islam. In April 2009, Chechen president **Ramzan Kadyrov** declared that both **terrorism** and Wahhabism had been "defeated" in his republic.

WARSAW PACT/WARSAW TREATY ORGANIZATION (WTO). Created in 1955 as a response to West **Germany**'s admission to the **North Atlantic Treaty Organization** (NATO), the Treaty of Friendship, Cooperation and Mutual Assistance—or as it was known in the West, the Warsaw Treaty Organization (WTO) or Warsaw Pact—was a mutual defense arrangement between the Soviet Union and its allies in the **Eastern Bloc**. In addition to the Union of Soviet Socialist Republics (USSR), the original members included **Poland**, East Germany, Czechoslovakia, Hungary, Romania, Bulgaria, and Albania. Despite a pledge of noninterference in the internal affairs of fellow members, the WTO invaded Czechoslovakia in 1968 in response to internal reforms of the Communist Party. As a result of the events of 1989, which saw the end of one-party rule across the Eastern Bloc, the viability of the Warsaw Pact was fundamentally challenged; the reunification of Germany in 1990 only deepened doubts about the WTO's future. On 1 July 1991, the organization was officially dissolved in Prague. In the wake of its dissolution, a number of former members began talks with NATO, resulting in Hungary, Poland, and the Czech Republic joining the **United States**–backed security organization in 1999. Former WTO members Slovakia, Romania, and Bulgaria followed suit five years later. Albania, which left the Warsaw Pact in 1968, joined NATO on 1 April 2009.

WEAPONS OF MASS DESTRUCTION (WMDs). The Russian Federation possesses the world's largest stockpiles of chemical, biological, and **nuclear weapons**. Its nuclear arsenal includes thousands of strategic and tactical weapons, and, reportedly, a number of "suitcase" nuclear weapons. The large quantities of spent nuclear fuel that Russia processes each year have led to fears that **terrorists** might try to use the material to create a radiological or "dirty" bomb.

The Soviet Union officially possessed an active biological weapons program until 1973, though informants suggest weapons development and testing continued until 1992 under Biopreparat, the "civilian" firm (funded by the **Ministry of Internal Affairs**) charged with disease control and biotechnology. Like the **United States** and other countries, Russia maintains samples of highly infectious strains of bacteria and viruses that could potentially be weaponized.

During the Soviet era, the **military** produced thousands of tons of chemical weapons including sarin and other nerve gases, as well as mustard gas and other caustic agents suitable for use in artillery shells and tactical missiles. Russia ratified the Chemical Weapons Convention on 5 November 1997, declaring it possessed an arsenal of 40,000 tons of chemical weapons. Russia is technologically and financially assisted by the U.S. in its chemical weapons destruction program, and has sites in three different locations for this purpose: Kambarka, **Udmurtiya**; Gorny, **Saratov Oblast**; and Maradykovsky, **Kirov Oblast**.

International experts, however, fear that lax security, disgruntled former scientists, and **corruption** could lead to some of these weapons reaching the black market. Reflecting the popular manifestation of such fears, a long list of American blockblusters depicting such scenarios appeared during the 1990s and 2000s, including *The Peacemaker* (1997), *Tomorrow Never Dies* (1997), *The World Is Not Enough* (1999), *XXX* (2002), and *The Sum of All Fears* (2002). Russian **arms exports** and sales of dual-use technologies to **Iran** and **North Korea** also worry the international community. *See also* POLLUTION.

WESTERNIZERS (*ZAPADNIKI*). In 19th-century Russia, Westernizers were predominantly intellectuals who emphasized Russia's common historic and cultural identity with the West, as opposed to **Slavophiles**, who believed that Russia's traditions and destiny were unique. The term derives from the Russian word *zapadnik*, which signifies someone associated with the West. Westernizers maintained that Russia depended upon the adoption of Western European technology and liberal government. The debates between Westernizers and Slavophiles were represented in the Russian 19th-century **literature**, most notably in Ivan Turgenev's novels. In contemporary usage, the term refers to supporters of Western-style economic development, particularly **Boris Yeltsin**'s earliest appointees in the Russian government such as **Yegor Gaydar**. In the 1990s, the Westernizers grew increasingly unpopular among the Russian masses, who gravitated toward ultranationalists like **Vladimir Zhirinovsky**, Soviet nostalgia, or neo-**Eurasianism**, is an ideology that has much in common with Slavophilism. **Vladimir Putin**'s rise to power and subsequent popularity destroyed the Westernizers as a potent force in the country. *See also* ATLANTICISM.

WILDLIFE. With its diverse **climate**, vast **geography**, and low population densities, the Russian Federation—particularly Asiatic Russia—is home to a wide variety of wildlife. In the **Far North**, species such as the Arctic fox, lemmings, polar bears, and harp seals are well suited to the **tundra**. Bowhead whales, gray whales, orcas, and other cetaceans can be found off the **Arctic** and Pacific sea coasts, as can the Greenland shark and Pacific sleeper shark. In the **taiga** and forest zones, which make up more than half of the country's landmass, reindeer, elk, moose, bears, lynx, sable, boar, deer, mink, and marten thrive. A variety of avian species can also be found, including Steller's sea eagle. In the country's various mountain ranges, there are yaks, chamois, badgers, polecats, mountain goats, wild sheep (argali), and gazelles. **Lake Baykal** is home to several unique species, including the Nerpa freshwater seal (*Pusa siberica*). Russia's aquatic wildlife is equally diverse, with many types of salmon, sturgeon, eel, cod, herring, pike, whitefish, and bream. The country is home to a number of critically endangered species including the Beluga sturgeon, Amur leopard, Saiga antelope, and Siberian white crane. *See also* FISHING INDUSTRY.

WOMEN. Considering that it was a woman-led demonstration in 1917 that initiated the February Revolution, and given the strong support of the Bolsheviks for the economic independence of women, it is surprising how poorly most women fared under the Soviet system. After a brief period of upward mobility spearheaded by feminist leader Aleksandra Kollontai, **Joseph Stalin** undermined the women's liberation movement, most notably by banning abortion and abolishing the Soviet Women's Committee (Zhenotdel). In the 1960s, as part of de-Stalinization, the volunteer organization was reincarnated at the Constituent Assembly of Soviet Women (Zhensovet); however, it had little impact on society until the imposition of **perestroika** when the local chapters provided access to a **food** distribution network in a time of growing need brought on by the "shortage **economy**."

By the late Soviet period, symbolic gender equality existed (guaranteed by the 1977 Soviet constitution); however, the position of women in society was characterized by a lack of representation in decision-making positions within **industry** and government (e.g., no woman ever held full membership in the Politburo of the **Communist Party of the Soviet Union**); the feminization of low-paid, low-skilled work within the **economy**; the double burden of working and "traditional" duties (such as housekeeping, child care, shopping); and by specific cultural traditions associated with the **religious** and/or **ethnic minority** group to which women belonged. In a blow to women's rights, **Mikhail Gorbachev** commented on the difficulties of balancing work and family life in 1998 by supporting policies that would "make it possible for women to return to their purely womanly mission." His remarks led to the introduction of the neologism *domostroika* (from the Russian *domostroi* or "domestic order") by Western feminist academics to describe the "masculinization" (*maskulinizatsiia*) of Russian society and the promotion of traditional notions of hearth and family where the woman assumed her "rightful place."

Under **glasnost**, a number of social problems affecting women were pushed into the spotlight including **sexual** harassment and **HIV/AIDS**; however, many subjects, such as lesbianism, remained taboo. By the end of the 1980s, parliamentary quotas for women were reduced, further depleting the power of women in the Union of Soviet

Socialist Republics (USSR), though feminist leaders such as Anastasiya Posadskaya-Vanderbeck played an important role in the political activities that weakened the hold of the Communist Party on society. In 1991 and 1992, feminists held two Independent Women's Forums in Dubna, a university town outside **Moscow**, laying the groundwork for a sociopolitical movement in independent Russia.

Despite modest support for the "Women of Russia" movement and the Women's Union of Russia in the 1990s, political identity based on **gender** faltered among Russian women. Patriarchal traditions returned with a vengeance with the **dissolution of the Soviet Union**, particularly due to the rising power of the **Russian Orthodox Church** and a resurgence of **Islam** in Russia's traditionally **Muslim** regions such as **Chechnya**. The deepening and spread of social problems such as **alcoholism**, poor **health care**, and domestic violence negatively impacted women during this period. Rape, comparatively rare in Soviet times, increased dramatically after 1991. Trafficking in women for sex work in Western Europe also emerged as an acute social problem. The introduction of capitalism in the **Yeltsin** era served to further denigrate the social position of women due to changes in the workforce that favored men, resulting in disproportionately high levels of **unemployment** and poverty among women.

Rather than harmonizing with the more progressive states of northern Europe, post-Soviet Russia witnessed retrogression in terms of gender equality, a trend made worse by the spread of pornography and the increasing objectification of the female body in popular **media**. Yeltsin gave few women positions of power in his cabinet; those he did appoint, such as **Galina Starovoytova** and Ella Pamfilova, enjoyed little influence. Yeltsin's daughter, **Tatyana Dyachenko**, wielded substantial power, though informally and solely based on her familial connections. Under **Vladimir Putin**, the issue of women's rights received almost no attention, though the former president once blithely stated that "women should have one unquestionable privilege: the right to be protected by men." In the 2000s, the most high-profile Russian women were the governor of **St. Petersburg**, Valentina Matviyenko, and the opposition politician **Irina Hakamada**. *See also* ARBATOVA, MARIYA; FEMINISM; HOMOSEXUALITY; KARELOVA, GALINA; MATVIYENKO, VALENTINA; YASINA, IRINA.

– Y –

YABLOKO/RUSSIAN UNITED DEMOCRATIC PARTY "YABLOKO." Political party.

Formed by **Grigory Yavlinsky**, Yury Boldyrev, and Vladimir Lukin in November 1993, Yabloko (Apple) takes its name from the first letters of its founders; its full name in Russian is *Rossiiskaia ob'edinionnaia demokraticheskaia partiia "Iabloko."* The party is the Russian Federation's oldest and most popular liberal party.

Yabloko began as an anti-**Yeltsin** bloc, which, in opposition to its fellow opposition parties, the **Communist Party of the Russian Federation** (KPRF) and the right-wing **Liberal Democratic Party of Russia** (LDPR), stood for liberal pluralism and democratic reform. The party platform is dedicated to creating a European-style socially responsible economic system in Russia, replete with **health care** benefits, a modern **education** system, and a functioning pension system. After allying with ecologist Aleksey Yablokov's Green Russia in 2006, Yabloko added a strong ecological component to its ideology, though the party had been burnishing its **environmentalist** credentials for some time prior.

The party is popular among urban voters and has distinguished itself in Russia's largest cities. The party gained formal status in 2001, but has contested all parliamentary elections in some form since 1993 when it won 7.8 percent of the vote and 25 seats in the **State Duma**. Two years later, the party won 45 seats and placed fourth behind the KPRF, **Our Home—Russia**, and the LDPR. Grigory Yavlinsky, the party's candidate in the **1996 presidential election**, won 7.3 percent of the vote, finishing in fourth place. In the 1999 Duma poll, the party's seats dropped to 20, though it won 6 percent of the vote.

In 2003, the party failed to meet the 5 percent threshold for seats in the Duma based on party affiliation, though it won four seats through individual candidate victories. In 2005, the party joined forces with the **Union of Right Forces** to contest the **Moscow** City Duma elections; a plan to formally merge the two parties, however, failed the following year. In 2007, Yabloko failed to win representation in the Duma. In 2008, Yavlinsky stepped down and was replaced by Sergey Mitrokhin.

YAKUTS. *See* SAKHA.

YAMALIYA/YAMALO-NENETS AUTONOMOUS OKRUG. An administrative district of the Russian Federation. Yamaliya is one of three ethnic homelands of the **Nenets** people, the other two being **Nenetsiya** and **Taymyriya** (both of which share a border with Yamaliya). Yamaliya also neighbors the **Komi Republic, Krasnoyarsk Krai**, and **Khantiya-Mansiya**. The region's northern coast is washed by the Kara Sea, and hems in the Gulf of Ob, which in turn is fed by the Ob River. An **autonomous okrug** (AOk), Yamaliya is a **federal subject** of the Russian Federation but is simultaneously subjugated to **Tyumen Oblast**.

Established by **Cossacks** in 1595, the administrative center is Salekhard (pop. 96,000), one of the world's largest towns located above the Arctic Circle; it was previously known as Obdorsk. Salekhard is connected to Russia proper by a railway constructed in the 1950s with **gulag** labor.

The region has an area of 750,300 square kilometers and a population of 500,000. The titular nation, Nenets, makes up only 5 percent of the population, while **ethnic Russians** account for 59 percent. **Ukrainians, Tatars**, and indigenous peoples of the **Far North** make up the remainder.

Yamaliya is a major center of **natural gas** extraction, and home to Russia's largest independent natural gas company, Novatek. **Gazprom** also has a large presence in the area and signed a major cooperation agreement with the local government to promote environmental protection, investment, relocation of retirees to warmer climes, and new jobs. More than 90 percent of Russia's natural gas is produced in the region. **Transneft**'s Yamal-Europe is a 4,200-kilometer pipeline connecting the region to **Germany**; other routes connect to the southern **Urals** and other parts of Russia.

Oil is also found in abundance in the region, which has attracted the interest of **Rosneft, Lukoil**, and other major companies. Gold, timber, lead, iron ore, copper, and other natural resources also contribute to the local **economy**, as do construction, maritime and riverine shipping, and manufacturing. Fur farming, **fishing**, and animal husbandry remain traditional occupations among the indigenous population, often supplemented by sales of mammoth ivory, which is abundant in the region.

The longtime governor of the region is Yury Neyolov. His tenure has been marked by attempts to preserve Nenets culture and protect the environment, while attracting investment to the region and establishing relations with foreign governments, including **Canada** and Iceland. He has a close relationship with former Prime Minister **Viktor Chernomyrdin**. Yamal Potomkam (Yamal for Our Descendants) is an important Salekhard-based nongovernmental organization that supports **environmentalism** and cultural rights for the native population.

YAROSLAVL OBLAST. An administrative region of the Russian Federation. Yaroslavl Oblast is part of the Central **Economic Region** and **Federal District**. The region is bordered by the **oblasts** of **Tver**, **Vologda**, **Kostroma**, **Ivanovo**, and **Vladimir**, and is adjacent to **Moscow Oblast**. The majority of the Rybinskoye Reservoir is located within the oblast, along with many natural lakes.

The **Volga** is the region's major river; however, there are more than 4,000 smaller rivers, making the region a natural **tourism** destination. Nearly half of the region is forested, allowing for a great diversity of **wildlife** and flora. The oblast has a population of 1.3 million and covers an area of 36,400 square kilometers. The regional capital, Yaroslavl (pop. 613,000), is a major river port, and its old town is recognized as a UNESCO World Heritage Site; it is considered the preeminent member of the Golden Ring of cities northwest of **Moscow**.

Natural resources include peat and materials for construction; the region possesses unexploited reserves of **oil** and, possibly, **natural gas**. Major local **industries** include chemicals and petrochemicals (particularly rubber, tires, and paints), oil refineries, forestry, textiles, engineering, and manufacturing of diesel engines for heavy machinery. **Agriculture** is comparatively underdeveloped, focusing on potatoes, grains, vegetables, and animal husbandry; **fishing** is also important around the Rybinskoye Reservoir. Given the excellent rail, road, and river links of the region, transit is an important source of income.

The city of Yaroslavl has a long tradition of merchant activity, and a number of **banks** and foreign and joint-stock companies are active in the capital, including Komatsu (**Japan**). Given the historical association with free-market enterprise, the region proved to be fairly liberally oriented in its **politics** during the 1990s. Anatoly Lisitsyn, the former mayor of Rybinsk and a **Yeltsin** appointee, won the popular election in 1995; he was easily reelected in 1999 and 2003. Lisitsyn was reappointed in 2006, despite an earlier rebuke from Moscow for overstepping his authority by giving interest-free loans to churches and other organizations. In December 2007, he was removed from office due to the pitiful performance of the pro-Kremlin **United Russia** party in local elections; however, his criticism of federal social reforms also played a role in the dismissal. President **Vladimir Putin** nominated one of his personal envoys, Sergey Vakhrukov, to fill the post. The appointment has provoked a backlash in the region that has been largely directed at the new president, **Dmitry Medvyedev**.

YASINA, IRINA (1964–). Journalist. The daughter of a former economics minister, Irina Yasina graduated from the **Moscow State University** in 1986 and received her PhD in Economics in 1990. As a member of the press, Yasina worked for the news agency Interfax, *The Moscow Times*, *Itogi*, and the radio station Echo of Moscow. In recent years, she has been part of the nongovernmental organization Open Russia, which seeks to build **civil society** in the country.

YAVLINSKY, GRIGORY ALEKSEYEVICH (1952–). Politician. Born into a prosperous **military** family in Lviv, **Ukraine**, Yavlinsky, who is of mixed **Jewish**-Russian origin, became a junior boxing champion before studying economics. He ultimately earned a *kandidat* (PhD) in the field. During the late Soviet period, he gained national fame as the author of the controversial **500 Days Program**, which intended to transition the Union of Soviet Socialist Republics (USSR) from a command-and-control system to a free-market **economy** in rapid fashion.

In order to push through his plans, he was appointed deputy chairman of the Council of Ministers of the **Russian Soviet Federative Socialist Republic** and placed in charge of economic reform; when his program was rejected, he left the post. In the wake of the **constitutional crisis of 1993**, he and two other economic liberals established the **Yabloko** political bloc, which would ultimately emerge as Russia's premier liberal **political party**. Yavlinsky's political goal was to create an anti-**Yeltsin** force that functioned within the established norms of a democratic, pluralist political system. He was a fierce critic of the war in **Chechnya** and an early supporter of **Yevgeny Primakov** as prime minister.

He twice ran for president, in 1996 and 2000, placing fourth and third, respectively. He had a complicated relationship with **Vladimir Putin**, sometimes winning praise from the president, as was the case with his role as a negotiator in the **Nord-Ost theater** crisis, while vociferously opposing his policies at other times, particularly the concentration of power in the executive branch and the arrest of **Mikhail Khodorkovsky**. On 22 June 2008, he stepped down as head of Yabloko after more than a decade at the helm.

YELTSIN, BORIS NIKOLAYEVICH (1931–2007). Born in the village of Butko in **Sverdlovsk Oblast**, Boris Yeltsin was the son of a construction worker and a seamstress. As a youth, he lost the thumb and index finger of his left hand while dismantling a grenade he stole from a weapons depot. After studying construction, he worked as a foreman in Sverdlovsk, climbing the ranks of the **Communist Party of the Soviet Union** (CPSU).

From a humble **apparatchik**, he became First Secretary of the CPSU in the **oblast** in 1976, holding the position for a decade. In that capacity, he ordered the site of the last **Romanovs'** execution, Ipatyev House, to be razed. Yeltsin's move to **Moscow** in 1985 coincided with the appointment of **Mikhail Gorbachev** as general secretary of the CPSU. Yeltsin assumed the position of first secretary of the CPSU Moscow City Committee, effectively becoming mayor of the city. Backed by Gorbachev and **Yegor Ligachev**, Yeltsin assumed the role of reformer, using populism to guarantee his support from the city's residents. However, in 1987, he was stripped of his position in a dispute that began over the role of Gorbachev's wife, Raisa, in Soviet **politics** and ended with Yeltsin's denunciation of the slow pace of reform and the CPSU leadership.

Despite a failed suicide attempt, a lack of funds, and a **media smear** campaign instituted by the CPSU, Yeltsin was able to use his popularity among the masses and the relatively new practice of **television** campaigning to return to public life in 1989. He was elected to the newly formed **Congress of People's Deputies**, where he railed against the gerontocracy's stifling of **perestroika**. Embracing his role as an antiestablishment folk hero, Yeltsin managed to win the position of chairman of the Russian **Supreme Soviet** in May 1990. He quit the Communist Party a few months later, refashioning himself as a nationalist; he also began supporting free-market reforms, following a fateful trip to the **United States** a year earlier.

On 12 June 1991, democratic elections were held for the office of president of the **Russian Soviet Federative Socialist Republic**; Yeltsin won 57 percent of the vote, easily defeating the Gorbachev-backed CPSU candidate Nikolay Ryzhkov. At the time of the **August Coup** against Gorbachev, Yeltsin was visiting **Kazakhstan**. Upon his return to the capital, he rallied the public and segments of the **military**—most dramatically from the turret of a T-72 tank—against the Communist hard-liners, resulting in the putsch's failure. In the wake of the event, he was hailed as a hero at home and abroad.

He quickly eclipsed Gorbachev as the preeminent politician in the Union of Soviet Socialist Republics (USSR), and moved to outlaw the CPSU; he also recognized the independence of the **Baltic States**. In December, he met with the leaders of **Belarus** and **Ukraine** outside Minsk, where he signed the **Belavezha Accords**, effectively terminating Russian membership in the USSR. Later that month, he and the leaders of the remaining **union republics** agreed to the **dissolution of the Soviet Union** and the creation of the **Commonwealth of Independent States**.

As president of the newly independent Russian Federation, Yeltsin moved quickly to eradicate state control of the **economy** based on the radical **shock therapy** model. He introduced neoliberal reforms, slashed price subsidies, stripped the welfare and **health care** systems, and allowed the **ruble** to float. Taking cues from the Western economists Anders Åslund and Jeffrey Sachs, Yeltsin's financial advisor **Yegor Gaydar** oversaw what was to be the first wave of **privatization**, through a vouchers plan (a later wave of state sell-offs of assets would be undertaken through the controversial **loans for shares**

program). The result was hyperinflation, massive **unemployment**, Soviet nostalgia, and ultranationalism.

Resentful of Yeltsin's increasingly powerful executive branch, a number of parliamentarians moved against him in 1993, precipitating the **constitutional crisis**. Yeltsin used force to bring the situation under control. He abolished both the Supreme Soviet and the Congress of People's Deputies in the aftermath, weakening his image as a genuine democrat abroad, though he retained the confidence and support of U.S. President **Bill Clinton**. When the new parliament was seated, the **State Duma** was packed with members of the right-wing **Liberal Democratic Party of Russia** (LDPR) and left-wing **Communist Party of the Russian Federation** (KPRF). Collectively, they represented a rising tide of angst directed at the rapid changes going on inside the country while Yeltsin was trying to keep on the path of reform.

In terms of **foreign relations**, Yeltsin used the early years of independence to solidify and then manage Russia's role as the rightful heir of the USSR. His country assumed the Soviet Union's permanent seat (and thus veto power) on the **United Nations** Security Council, as well as all of the Soviet Union's **nuclear weapons**. He developed ties with historic enemies such as **Turkey**, **Japan**, and South Korea, while forging new relationships with the former Soviet republics. His approach toward the **near abroad**—manifested through the use of **peacekeepers**, economic domination, and geopolitical manipulation—was often described as the **Monroeski Doctrine**, reflecting Russia's notion of the region as its "backyard." In his first term, he also pursued a decidedly **Atlanticist foreign relations** orientation, hoping to bind Russia to the **European Union** and North America. His hopes of turning Russia into a "normal country," however, would be dashed in the later years of his administration, as the rise of nationalism and **Eurasianism** prompted a return to a more traditional orientation vis-à-vis the West.

As he moved toward his reelection campaign, Yeltsin's advisors suggested he embark on a short, popular war to reintegrate the breakaway **Chechen Republic of Ichkeriya** into the federation. The first **Chechen War** proved to be neither short nor popular, and dragged the economy down further. Desperate for cash, Yeltsin auctioned off shares of major state enterprises for loans to his government, redistributing much of the country's mineral wealth and **industry** into the hands of the **oligarchs**.

Going into the **1996 presidential election**, Yeltsin suffered from abysmal popularity ratings and had grown insular, surrounding himself only with trusted advisors, deep-pocketed backers, and relatives who were referred to, both collectively and derisively, as "the Family." However, the skillful use of political technologies, economic and media backing from the oligarchs, and fear that the KPRF would lead the country toward civil unrest and into a new **Cold War** allowed Yeltsin to scrape by in the first round. After co-opting the popular general **Aleksandr Lebed**, he decisively defeated his KPRF challenger **Gennady Zyuganov** in the second poll.

Yeltsin's second term was marred by the 1998 **ruble crisis**, which wiped out many Russians' savings and savaged the already flagging economy. Cognizant of his own weakness, he took the country in a more anti-Western direction, appointing the nationalist **Yevgeny Primakov** as prime minister and pushing back against the U.S. on the enlargement of the **North Atlantic Treaty Organization** (NATO), the war in Yugoslavia, and **Chechnya**.

Plagued by low popularity ratings, poor health, and the looming threat of impeachment and subsequent **corruption** charges, Yeltsin began paving the way for his successor in 1999. He shuffled **Vladimir Putin** from one important post to another, until the former **KGB** agent was prime minister. Assured that Putin's aggressive management of the second Chechen War was sufficient to get him elected, Yeltsin unexpectedly stepped down on 31 December 1999, begging his constituents for their forgiveness. He appointed Putin as acting president of the Russian Federation. Shortly thereafter, Putin issued a decree granting Yeltsin and his family immunity from prosecution for **corruption** or misuse of state funds. In retirement, Yeltsin rarely spoke out against his successor, though he did make known his dissatisfaction with the 2004–2005 **electoral reforms** in the wake of the **Beslan crisis**.

During his administration, Yeltsin struggled with **alcoholism** and a neurological disorder that affected his balance. He began suffering heart pains as early as 1987; he experienced a heart attack during the 1996 election campaign and underwent bypass surgery later that year. His other health ailments included back pain, bouts of pneumonia, debilitating infections, liver problems, and a stomach ulcer. He died of congestive heart failure on 23 April 2007.

He received a Russian **Orthodox** ceremony at Christ the Savior Cathedral, and was laid to rest at Novodevichy Cemetery, near **Nikita Khrushchev** and the writers Boris Pasternak and Mikhail Bulgakov. His funeral was attended by **George H. W. Bush** and **Bill Clinton**, among other foreign dignitaries. He is survived by his wife of more than 50 years, Naina Yeltsina, and their two daughters.

YUGOSLAVIA. *See* SERBIA.

YUGRA. *See* KHANTIYA-MANSIYA.

YUKOS. Once one of the largest independent petroleum companies in the world, Yukos's assets were seized by the state and auctioned off as part of the criminal case against billionaire **Mikhail Khodorkovsky**. Founded in 1993, Yukos was created through a merger of Yuganskneftgas and the Novokuybyshevsk, Kuybyshev, and Syzran petroleum processing plants in **Samara Oblast**.

At its peak, Yukos accounted for 20 percent of Russian **oil** production and 2 percent of world output. Khodorkovsky and other investors gained control of the company during **privatization**. Khodorkovsky—who controlled the Menatep **bank**—bid $350 million during the controversial **loans for shares program**, thus acquiring 88 percent of Yukos stock; higher bids from competing banks were disallowed on technicalities. Within several months, Yukos's value was estimated at over $3 billion. As oil prices rose, Yukos became a major contributor of **tax** revenues to the federal budget, as well as a massive source of philanthropy for Russian **civil society**.

During the early 2000s, Yukos entered into a period of rapid expansion. The company began exploring the development of new pipelines from **Siberia** to **China** and **Murmansk**. It opened new offices in **Moscow** in what was touted as the first "smart" office building in Russia; and in 2003, a proposed merger with Sibneft (now part of **Gazprom**) was initiated. However, the political rivalry between **Vladimir Putin** and Khodorkovsky came to a head that same year. Khodorkovsky had been supporting various **political parties**, purportedly in an attempt to gain benefits for his company. Such engagement in **politics** was viewed as a violation of Putin's 2000 agreement with the **oligarchs**. He was arrested on 25 October 2003; prevented from selling his shares to ExxonMobil as he wished, Khodorkovsky subsequently transferred a controlling stake of Yukos to fellow Yukos executive Leonid Nevzlin, hoping to preserve the company.

In July 2004, the company was charged with evading $7 billion in taxes via illegal tax havens during the 1990s. Yukos claimed that its tax burden—according to the prosecution—represented more than 100 percent of its profit for some of the years in question. After a drawn-out court battle and intense lobbying on the part of Western governments to preserve Yukos, the company filed bankruptcy in a **United States** court on 15 December 2005. Its creditors followed suit seven months later.

In December, Yukos's Yuganskneftgas subsidiary was put on auction and purchased by Baykalfinansgrup for $9.4 billion, approximately half of the value of the assets; Gazprom had also been present at the auction. On 23 December 2004, Baykalfinansgrup was acquired by state-owned **Rosneft**, making it the largest oil company in the country. The chain of events was widely criticized by the international community as a surreptitious nationalization of Yukos.

– Z –

ZABAYKALSKY KRAI/TRANS-BAYKAL KRAI. An administrative province of the Russian Federation. Zabaykalsky Krai is part of the Siberian **Federal District** and the East Siberia **Economic Region**. It covers an area of 431,500 square kilometers, making it the 10th-largest **federal subject** in the Russian Federation. The province shares internal borders with the **ethnic republics** of **Sakha** and **Buryatiya** and the **oblasts** of **Amur** and **Irkutsk**. Zabaykalsky has a long international border with **Mongolia**, as well as with the Mongol Autonomous Region of the People's Republic of **China** (also known as Inner Mongolia).

Formerly known as Chita Oblast, Zabaykalsky Krai was created on 1 March 2008 as a result of the merger of Chita and Aga-Buryatiya, formerly known as the Agin-Buryat **Autonomous Okrug** (AOk).

Aga-Buryatiya, one of three ethnic homelands of the **Buryats**, was downgraded from an autonomous okrug, and thus **federal subject** of the Russian Federation, to an **okrug** of the **krai** following an 11 March 2007 referendum on merging the political entities. In Chita Oblast, 80 percent of the electorate turned out, supporting the measure by a margin of nine to one; in Aga Buryatiya, an equal percentage of voters went to the polls, delivering an even higher margin of support for the change. The transformation of an oblast into a krai is a somewhat unorthodox move, given that the appellation "krai" is traditionally reserved for frontier regions and carries subtle imperial undertones.

The former administrative capital of Aga Buryatiya is Aginskoye. Chita (pop. 308,000) is the current capital of the krai; it is the headquarters of the Siberian Military District and an important stop on the **Trans-Siberian Railway**. As a site of exile for the liberal Decembrists in the 1820s, the scene of worker demonstrations in the 1905 revolution, and the capital of the nominally independent Far Eastern Republic (1920–1922), the city has a reputation for political activism and an independent orientation. The region is also historically notable as the birthplace of the world conqueror Genghis Khan.

Within Aga Buryatiya, ethnic **Buryats** have majority status (63 percent), while **ethnic Russians** represent slightly more than one-third of the total population of 72,000. In the krai as a whole, Russians make up 90 percent of the population, while Buryats are the largest minority at six percent; the total population of the krai is 1.1 million.

Animal husbandry, particularly sheep and reindeer herding, and fur farming are important sources of local employment. Forestry, textiles, metallurgy, power generation, **food** processing, and fuel extraction are primary regional **industries**; manufacturing accounts for one-third of the regional output. A number of rare metals are found in the area around Balei, including gold, uranium, and thorium; the region suffers from a high rate of radiation-related diseases. Lead, titanium, zirconium, copper, silver, and zinc are mined in other parts of the krai.

Shuttle commerce from China, centered in the capital, is a major component of the local **economy**; the SARS outbreak in 2003 led to economic disruption in the region when border crossings were closed. China is a major **foreign investor** in the region, though investments in the region as a whole remain comparatively low. The province is expected to achieve economic self-sufficiency sometime during the 2010s, a dramatic turnaround from its immediate post-Soviet economic position.

During the 1990s, the **Communist Party of the Russian Federation** (KPRF) and the **Liberal Democratic Party of Russia** (LDPR) placed well in regional elections. Since 1996, Ravil Geniatulin, who is of mixed Russian and **Tatar** parentage, has governed the region (Chita Oblast from 1996 to 2008 and all of Zabaykalsky Krai after 1 March 2008). Geniatulin formerly served as mayor of Chita; he was appointed by **Boris Yeltsin** to replace Boris Ivanov before being popularly elected to the post. Geniatulin presided over the region during a difficult period, particularly in terms of energy shortages and worsening **environmental** degradation. He is a member of the **United Russia** movement, and has overseen the transition of regional leadership from its radical "red-brown" bent in the 1990s to a solidly pro-Kremlin orientation, guaranteeing that **Vladimir Putin** would back his candidacy to become governor of the new krai in 2008.

In 2009, Geniatulin pressed **Dmitry Medvyedev** to grant the krai the ability to create a number of special economic zones to improve the financial position of the province. He has also taken a conciliatory position on **Chinese immigration**, dismissing notions of "Chinese expansion" in the region and calling for the opening of a consular mission in Chita.

ZHIRINOVSKY, VLADIMIR VOLFOVICH (1946–). Politician. Born Vladimir Volfovich Eidelshtein in Alma-Ata (now Almaty), **Kazakhstan**, on 25 April 1946 into what he has called a "multi-national family" (his father was a **Jew** of Polish origin), he left for Moscow to study at the Department of Turkish Studies at the Institute of Asian and African Studies of Moscow State University, graduating in 1969. He worked as a translator in **Turkey** for the Soviet Foreign Economic Relations Committee in 1969–1970, before being deported for spreading "Communist propaganda." He then did his **military** service in Tbilisi, **Georgia**. Zhirinovsky later received a law degree and joined the *Mir* publishing house. In the later 1980s, he briefly participated in the activities of the Kremlin-sanctioned Jewish cultural organization Shalom.

In 1990, he formed the first officially registered opposition **political party** in the Soviet Union, the **Liberal Democratic Party of Russia** (LDPR), which had the backing of both the **Communist Party of the Russian Federation** (KPRF) and the **KGB**. A year later, Zhirinovsky, running on his party's ticket, placed third in Russia's presidential elections; while he commanded only 7.8 percent of the vote, his populism, eccentric humor, and promise to reduce the price of vodka garnered him a sizable following among many disaffected Russians. A darling of the Russian press for his outgoing nature and contentious remarks, Zhirinovsky expanded his **political** base in the early years of the **Yeltsin** administration. He courted support from the business community and youth, while attracting Russian nationalists with his grandiose foreign policy statements. He put forth his geopolitical vision in *The Final Push to the South* (1993); in the text, he argued not only for a restoration of all lost Soviet territory to Russia, but also Alaska and lands south of Russia to the Indian Ocean.

Among other outrageous remarks, he famously threatened to turn **Germany** into Chernobyl, invade the **Baltic States**, and to blockade **Japan** into starvation. Rather than espousing the ethnic Russian nationalism that characterized **Pamyat**, Zhirinovsky promotes a radical form of civic nationalism, considering all residents of the former Union of Soviet Socialist Republics (USSR) to be Russians. His bombastic style and jingoistic rhetoric resulted in his party winning 22.8 percent of the vote in the 1993 elections to the **State Duma**, placing first in 64 out of 87 regions (the high level of support was viewed as a protest vote against the other candidate). In 1995, Zhirinovsky's party enjoyed substantially less positive **media** coverage and won only 11.5 percent of the vote.

In the **1996 presidential election**, he competed against incumbent Boris Yeltsin and the leader of the KPRF, **Gennady Zyuganov**, finishing sixth with a disappointing 5.8 percent of the vote despite commanding second place (ahead of Yeltsin) in early opinion polls. Running again in 2000 against **Vladimir Putin**, he earned a paltry 2.7 percent of the vote. He declined to run for president in 2004 (putting forth Oleg Malyshkin in his stead for the LDPR). In the 2008 election, he won nearly 10 percent of the vote; however, both he and his party have seen their popularity sapped by an increasingly anti-Western and nationalistic political establishment. Zhirinovsky was elected deputy chairman of the Duma in January 2000 and was reelected in 2004. Over his career, Zhirinovsky has been barred, expelled, or declared persona non grata by a number of countries, including Georgia, **Ukraine**, **Kazakhstan**, Germany, and Bulgaria. He remains the chairman of the LDPR, a position he has held since 1990.

ZUBKOV, VIKTOR ALEKSEYEVICH (1941–). Politician. A member of the Leningrad **Communist Party of the Soviet Union** (CPSU) leadership in the late 1980s, Viktor Zubkov began working with **Vladimir Putin** in the early 1990s in the **St. Petersburg** mayor's office. He went on to executive positions in the state tax inspection department, first in St. Petersburg and then on the **federal district** level. He ran for governor of **Leningrad Oblast** in 1999, but finished a disappointing fourth. In 2001, he was appointed first deputy finance minister in Putin's government. Based on his loyalty and experience in combating financial **crime**, Putin tapped him to replace **Mikhail Fradkov** as prime minister; he held that position from September 2007 until May 2008, when Putin himself took over the job as head of government. Zubkov subsequently took over as chairman of **Gazprom**, replacing **Dmitry Medvyedev.**

ZYUGANOV, GENNADY ANDREYEVICH (1944–). Politician. Born to schoolteachers in Mymrino in the **Oryol Oblast**, Zyuganov graduated from the Oryol Pedagogical Institute with a degree from the faculty of mathematics and physics in 1969. He worked as a schoolteacher before and after his military service in a chemical intelligence unit in East **Germany**. In the mid-1970s, he assumed a leadership position in the Komsomol youth organization, and developed a sizable political network of fellow **apparatchiks**. He received a doctorate in the **Communist Party of the Soviet Union** (CPSU) Academy of Social Sciences in 1980. Soon thereafter, he took a job in the propaganda department of the Central Committee of the CPSU.

In 1990, he grew highly critical of **Mikhail Gorbachev**'s reforms and broke from the CPSU, helping to establish a competing hardline Communist party for the **Russian Soviet Federative Socialist Republic** (RSFSR). Driven by a conviction that **Boris Yeltsin**'s admiration for the West and radical **economic** reforms were destroying the country, Zyuganov formed a group of right- and left-wing politicians under the ideological influence of Aleksandr Prokhanov in the early 1990s. While supportive of the anti-Yeltsin coalition that precipitated the **constitutional crisis of 1993**, Zyuganov avoided actual participation in the crisis and was absent from **Moscow** during the period of violence. During the **political** chaos that followed, Zyuganov, ever the pragmatist, founded the **Communist Party of the Russian Federation** (KPRF). With the help of the well-known Soviet-era politicians **Anatoly Lukyanov** and **Yegor Ligachev**, he solidified the new party's image as the rightful heir to the CPSU and captured a respectable share of seats in the 1993 **State Duma** elections.

Zyuganov proved to be an effective leader, not only because of his conciliatory style, but also due to his malleable political views. He sits at the nexus between revivalist **Marxism-Leninism**, contemporary social democracy, and Russian nationalism. His views incorporate a number of political trends that unite both the "reds" (Communists, socialists, etc.) and the "browns" (**neofascists**, ultranationalists, etc.), though he is often criticized by both extremes of his constituency for not going far enough. Influenced by **Aleksandr Dugin** and other conservative ideologues, he tacitly supports both **Slavophilism** and **neo-Eurasianism** and espouses **anti-Semitism** and anti-Americanism. He has even made room for the **Russian Orthodox Church** within his party.

Over the next several years, he turned the KPRF into the most popular **political party** in the Russian Federation. In the run-up to the **1996 presidential election**, he quickly emerged as the front-runner. Buoyed by Yeltsin's unpopularity and strong support from Russia's populous **Red Belt**, Zyuganov seemed guaranteed to become the country's second popularly elected president. Yeltsin emerged victorious only after a coalition of **oligarchs** and stakeholders in the new system rallied to brand the Communists as unstable warmongers intent on starting a new **Cold War** with the West and engaging in class warfare at home. Despite losing the presidency, Zyuganov's vituperative anti-Western orientation, which he describes as "technotronic fascism," went down well among a Russian populace concerned about the **North Atlantic Treaty Organization**'s (NATO) expansion, the war in Yugoslavia, and Russia's diminished power in **foreign relations**. His antiglobalization rhetoric also paid dividends during the **ruble crisis** of 1998, when the Russian ruble was hammered by an economic contagion that began in the Pacific Rim.

Zyuganov's political views have continued to develop over time, as he has sought to expand his political base of support and to grow the KPRF into a party of power. He has heaped praise on **Buddhism** and **Islam** as moral compasses that mitigate the crass individualism and consumerism of Western ideologies. He has also avoided the temptation to turn the KPRF into a vehicle for his personal ambitions, making it one of the few genuine political parties in the country. In 2000, he ran against **Vladimir Putin** for the presidency but suffered a disappointing showing in the race. Recognizing the popularity of the former chekist, Zyuganov sat out the 2004 poll, backing an **Agrarian** candidate instead. He returned to presidential politics in 2008 to run against Putin's heir apparent, **Dmitry Medvyedev**, and did surprisingly well considering the support Medvyedev received from the **media** and regional governors.

In the wake of the **global financial crisis** of 2008–2009, it was reported that Prime Minister Putin installed a direct phone line from Zyuganov's office to his own, reflecting a new realpolitik toward the Communist leader. In addition to his role as first secretary of the KPRF, Zyuganov is also a deputy of the State Duma and a member of the Parliamentary Assembly of the Council of Europe, and holds the chairmanship of Russia's Union of Communist Parties.

Appendix A
Heads of State

SOVIET PREMIER

Vladimir Lenin	1922–1924
Joseph Stalin	1924–1953
Nikita Khrushchev	1953–1964
Leonid Brezhnev	1964–1982
Yury Andropov	1982–1984
Konstantin Chernenko	1984–1985
Mikhail Gorbachev	1985–1991

PRESIDENT OF THE RUSSIAN FEDERATION

Boris Yeltsin	1991–1999
Vladimir Putin	2000–2008
Dmitry Medvyedev	2008–present

Appendix B
Prime Ministers of the Russian Federation

Yegor Gaydar (Acting)	15 June 1992–14 December 1992
Viktor Chernomyrdin	14 December 1992–23 March 1998
Sergey Kiriyenko	23 March 1998–23 August 1998
Viktor Chernomyrdin (Acting)	23 August 1998–11 September 1998
Yevgeny Primakov	11 September 1998–12 May 1999
Sergey Stepashin	12 May 1999–9 August 1999
Vladimir Putin	9 August 1999–7 May 2000
Mikhail Kasyanov	7 May 2000–24 February 2004
Viktor Khristenko (Acting)	24 February 2004–5 March 2004
Mikhail Fradkov	5 March 2004–14 September 2007
Viktor Zubkov	14 September 2007–7 May 2008
Vladimir Putin	8 May 2008–present

Bibliography

CONTENTS

INTRODUCTION

The number of books dedicated to the late Union of Soviet Socialist Republics (USSR) and its successor state, the Russian Federation, is virtually incalculable. This surfeit is due to a number of factors: Russia's geographic size and diverse climate, political and military might, traditional and modern culture, and spectacular array of religious and ethnic groups. Adding to this quiddity, there has been—historically speaking—an intense interest among European and North American audiences in what goes on both in the "Russian mind" (manifesting in politically motivated studies of Russian society and culture) and behind the walls of the Kremlin (geopolitics, strategic studies, international relations, etc.).

During much of the 20th century, fear of Russia and the USSR—often mixed with deep misunderstanding—gave birth to a veritable industry of Western government-funded, or at least -encouraged, analysis. This discipline—once known as Sovietology—has been reborn as "Kremlinology." In fact, many practitioners of this specific branch of academic inquiry went on to high-profile careers in the United States government, including Zbigniew Brzezinski (U.S. national security advisor, 1977–1981), Dmitri K. Simes (advisor to the Nixon administration), and Condoleezza Rice (U.S. secretary of state, 2005–2009). While this state of affairs exponentially expanded the literature dedicated to Russia, it also jaundiced it.

Luckily, the end of the Cold War allowed a fuller picture of Russia to evolve and ultimately thrive. This flowering produced a sophisticated and diverse suite of works covering Russian film, visual art, music, media, literature, religion and spirituality, civil society, ethnic and gender relations, and social change. Due to the availability of a vast catalogue of English-language works (many of which are translations of original Russian, French, and German texts), books printed in English will be the focus of this bibliography.

In terms of reference materials on the Russian Federation, a number of helpful resources are available. The best annotated bibliographies include Steve D. Boilard's *Reinterpreting Russia: An Annotated Bibliography of Books on Russia, the Soviet Union, and the Russian Federation* (1997), Helen Sullivan and Robert Burger's *Russia and Eastern Europe: A Bibliographic Guide to English-Language Publications* (2001), and Paul Louis Horecky's *Basic Russian Publications: An Annotated Bibliography on Russia and the Soviet Union* (2003). For those seeking dictionaries and encyclopedias, recommendations include the *Encyclopedia of Contemporary Russian Culture* (2007), *The Cambridge Encyclopedia of Russia and the Former Soviet Union* (1994), *The Dictionary of Russia: 2500 Cultural Terms* (2002), and *A Political and Economic Dictionary of Eastern Europe* (2002), as well as selected texts from Scarecrow Press's *Historical Dictionaries* series, specifically Boris Raymond and Paul Duffy's volume on Russia (1998). As for yearbooks on the Russian Federation and the wider region, Europa Publications's *Eastern Europe, Russia, and Central Asia*, published since 2000, is the premier source, but a more economical option is Minton Goldman's *Global Studies: Russia, the Eurasian Republics and Central/Eastern Europe* (published since 1998).

Anglophone travel literature on contemporary Russia often suffers from the lingering malady of Russophobia, which has characterized the field since British explorers began writing about Russians centuries ago. Despite this, many of these accounts provide a unique understanding of the country, and one that is often absent in more academic writing. Colin Thubron's *Among the Russians* (2000) and *In Siberia* (2000), Andrew Meier's *Black Earth: A Journey through*

Russia after the Fall (2003), and Naomi F. Collins's *Through Dark Days and White Nights: Four Decades Observing a Changing Russia: Impressions and Reflections* (2008) are excellent choices for those seeking to understand how Russia's transition impacts life, both in Russia's cities and its provinces. Daniel Kalder's uniquely conceived travelogue *Lost Cosmonaut: Observations of an Anti-Tourist* (2006) takes the reader to the lesser-known corners of Russia, humorously exploring neo-paganism in Mari El and chess masters in the wastelands of Kalmykiya. For a wonderful visual experience, one should view the Russian segments of Ewan McGregor and Charley Boorman's *Long Way Round* television series, which documents the actors' trip across northern Eurasia on motorbikes.

Not surprising given the country's vast size, varied climate, and topographical diversity, studies on Russian geography are ample. Denis J. B. Shaw's *Russia in the Modern World: A New Geography* (1999) provides a comprehensive and well-structured introduction to the topic, replete with a series of elucidating maps, charts, and diagrams. Maria Shahgedanova's *The Physical Geography of Northern Eurasia* (2003) is a denser read, but will be of interest to specialists in the field. Philip Hanson and Michael J. Bradshaw's *The Territories of the Russian Federation* (2009) is also recommended.

A host of high-quality periodicals covering all aspects of post-Soviet Russia is available to the researcher in both print and electronic formats. The archives of *Demokratizatsiya: The Journal of Post-Soviet Democratization* is the best starting point for any scholar interested in the country's transition from totalitarianism to (managed) democracy. The online publication *Transitions* provides keen insight on contemporary Russia and other post-Soviet states through a network of local journalists. *International Affairs: A Russian Journal of World Politics, Diplomacy and International Relations* and *Russia in Global Affairs* are the best platforms for accessing the opinions of Russian policymakers and for gaining insight into the country's foreign relations. Social scientists should also seek out *Problems of Post-Communism, Russian Social Science Review*, and *Post-Soviet Affairs*. The comparatively new publication *Russia!* and the venerable *Russian Life* provide cultural snapshots of the "new" Russia as well as pictorial essays on this vast country. For those interested in Russian art, literature, and cultural studies, the best journals are *Slavic Review, Kritika, Slavic and East European Journal*, and *Slavonica*; also of interest is the authors' newly founded journal, *Digital Icons: Studies in Russian, Eurasian, and Central European New Media* (formerly known as *The Russian Cyberspace Journal*).

In order to understand contemporary Russian society and the complicated nature of the Russian Federation, it is absolutely necessary to have a firm grounding in the history of the Soviet Union. While a large number of texts attempt to capture the totality of the first Marxist-Leninist state, Ronald Grigor Suny's *The Soviet Experiment: Russia, the USSR, and the Successor States* (1998) is most recommended, both for its breadth and its readability. A perfect companion volume is Suny's *The Structure of Soviet History: Essays and Documents* (2003), which provides valuable primary source materials including laws, speeches, and memoirs. Robert C. Tucker's *Stalin in Power: The Revolution from Above* (1992), Anne Applebaum's *Gulag: A History of the Soviet Camps* (2004), Francine Hirsch's *Empire of Nations: Ethnographic Knowledge and the Making of the Soviet Union* (2005), and William L. Blackwell's *The Industrialization of Russia: A Historical Perspective* (1994) are particularly helpful in understanding key aspects of Joseph Stalin's reign, Soviet totalitarianism, the nationalities issue, and Russia's transition from a rural empire to an industrial powerhouse.

For those researchers interested in the late Soviet period (1985–1991), it can be difficult sifting through the raft of monographs and edited collections. Mikhail Gorbachev's *Perestroika: New Thinking for Our Country and the World* (1987) is the natural starting point for understanding the mind-set of the Soviet leadership during the reform process, while Jim Riordan and Sue Bridger's edited collection *Dear Comrade Editor: Readers' Letters to the Soviet Press under Perestroika* (1992) brings to life the concerns and hopes of the Russian people in the waning days of Soviet rule. Recommended secondary sources on the period include Neil Felshman's *Gorbachev, Yeltsin, and the Last Days of the Soviet Empire* (1992), Seweryn Bialer's *Politics, Society, and Nationality inside Gorbachev's Russia* (1989), and Françoise Thom's *The Gorbachev Phenomenon: A History of Perestroika* (1989).

In order to understand the challenges that Boris Yeltsin faced in governing postindependence Russia, one should peruse at least one of the biographies of Russia's first president; the better options include Timothy Colton's *Boris Yeltsin: A Life* (2008) and Leon Aron's *Yeltsin: A Revolutionary Life* (2000), or one of Yeltsin's own books, *Against the Grain: An Autobiography* (1990), *The Struggle for Russia* (1994), or *Midnight Diaries* (2000). For a scintillating insider's view of the Clinton-Yeltsin relationship, turn to Strobe Talbott's *The Russia Hand: A Memoir of Presidential Diplomacy* (2003).

Lilia Shevtsova's *Putin's Russia* is recognized as the seminal opus on post-Yeltsin Russia, but other options include Peter Baker and Susan Glasser's *Kremlin Rising: Vladimir Putin's Russia and the End of Revolution* (2005) and Andrew Jackson's *Inside Putin's Russia* (2004). Vladimir Putin makes his own case for Russia's highest office with *First Person: An Astonishingly Frank Self-Portrait by Russia's President* (2000).

For an introduction to post-Soviet Russian politics, Thomas Remington's regularly revised *Politics in Russia* (2009) is the best option. Two thin but competent works are also recommended: Joan DeBardeleben's *Russian Politics in Transition* (1997) and Mikk Titma and Nancy Tuma's *Modern Russia* (2000). Deeper analysis can be found in Dmitri Trenin's pathbreaking *The End of Eurasia: Russia on the Border between Geopolitics and Globalization* (2002), Andrew Kutchin's *Russia after the Fall* (2002), and Lilia Shevtsova's *Russia—Lost in Transition: The Yeltsin and Putin Legacies* (2005). For understanding the nascent political party system in Yeltsin's Russia, see Alexander Dallin's *Political Parties in Russia* (1993); however, for more up-to-date analysis of political parties and elections in Russia, pick up Timothy Colton and Michael McFaul's *Popular Choice and Managed Democracy: The Russian Elections of 1999 and 2000* (2003), Grigorii Golosov's *Political Parties in the Regions of Russia: Democracy Unclaimed* (2004), and David White's *The Russian Democratic Party Yabloko: Opposition in a Managed Democracy* (2006).

On the topics of nationalism, national identity, regionalism, and Russia's ethnic minorities, the field of literature is particularly fecund. A few of the best books are *Russian Nationalism since 1856* by Astrid Tuminez (2000), *The Russian Question: Nationalism, Modernization, and Post-Communist Russia* by Wayne Allensworth (1998), *The Finno-Ugric Republics and the Russian State* by Rein Taagepera (1999), *Of Khans and Kremlins: Tatarstan and the Future of Ethno-Federalism in Russia* by Katherine E. Graney (2009), *Nationalism for the Masses: Minority Ethnic Mobilization in the Russian Federation* by Dmitry Gorenburg (2003), and the edited volume *Making and Breaking Democratic Transitions: The Comparative Politics of Russia's Regions* (2005). For those who wish to learn more about Russia's myriad ethnicities, the single best resource is James Minahan's *The Former Soviet Union's Diverse Peoples: A Reference Sourcebook* (2004).

Much ink has been spilled over the Chechen conflict. The most balanced monographs include Anatol Lieven's *Chechnya: Tombstone of Russian Power* (1998), Yo'av Karny's *Highlanders: A Journey into the Caucasus in Search of Memory* (2000), Moshe Gammer's *The Lone Wolf and the Bear: Three Centuries of Chechen Defiance of Russian Rule* (2006), and James Hughes's *Chechnya: From Nationalism to Jihad* (2007).

Moving beyond the Caucasus, the essential reading list on Russian foreign relations includes the works of Stephen Blank, Michael McFaul, Fiona Hill, Taras Kuzio, Robert Levgold, and Alexander J. Motyl. For catholic analyses of the country's foreign policy, the best monographs are Andrei P. Tsygankov's *Russia's Foreign Policy: Change and Continuity in National Identity* (2006), Nicolai Petro and Alvin Rubinstein's *Russian Foreign Policy: From Empire to Nation-State* (1997), and Robert Donaldson and Joseph Nogee's *The Foreign Policy of Russia: Changing Systems, Enduring Interests* (2002). For penetrating studies of the Russian diaspora, which remains one of Russia's most vexing foreign policy issues, see Jeff Chinn and Robert Kaiser's *Russians as the New Minority: Ethnicity and Nationalism in the Soviet Successor States* (1996) and Vladimir Shlapentokh, Munir Sendich, and Emil Payin's *The New Russian Diaspora: Russian Minorities in the Former Soviet Republics* (1994), as well as the relevant works of the Norwegian scholar Pål Kolstø.

On the topic of religion in the Russian Federation, Nathaniel Davis's *A Long Walk to Church: A Contemporary History of Russian Orthodoxy* (2003) and Jane Ellis's *Russian Orthodox Church: Triumphalism and Defensiveness* (2007) are helpful resources on Russian Christianity, while Shireen Hunter's *Islam in Russia: The Politics of Identity and Security* (2004), Gordon M. Hahn's *Russia's Islamic Threat* (2007), and the relevant works of Dmitry Gorenburg are solid explorations of Russia's Muslim population. For a fascinating look at the politics of neo-paganism, French scholar Marlène Laruelle is unsurpassed.

For an overview of Soviet culture, Andrei Sinyavsky's *Soviet Civilization: A Cultural History* (1991) makes a wonderful entry into the subject matter. For more contemporary studies, Vitaly Chernetsky's *Mapping Postcommunist Cultures: Russia and Ukraine in the Context of Globalization* (2007) and Eliot Borenstein's *Overkill: Sex and Violence in Contemporary Russian Popular Culture* (2007) are suggested. Within the larger field of cultural studies, Valerie A. Kivelson and Joan Neuberger's *Picturing Russia: Explorations in Visual Culture* (2008), Mark Lipovetsky's *Russian Postmodernist Fiction: Dialogue with Chaos* (1999), Birgit Beumers's *A History of Russian Cinema* (2009), Nancy Condee's *The Imperial Trace: Recent Russian Cinema* (2009), and Thomas Cushman's *Notes from Underground: Rock Music Counterculture in Russia* (1995) are all paragons. For cogent and timely analyses of the Russian media, review *Media and Power in Post-Soviet Russia* (2002), *Control + Shift: Public and Private Uses of the Russian Internet* (2006), and *The Post-Soviet Russian Media: Conflicting Signals* (2009).

Sociological studies of note include *National Identity and Globalization: Youth, State and Society in Post-Soviet Eurasia* (2007), *Russian Civil Society: A Critical Assessment* (2006), *Darkness at Dawn: The Rise of the Russian Criminal* (2003), and *Migration, Displacement, and Identity in Post-Soviet Russia* (1998). The rapidly expanding literature dedicated to women's issues in post-Soviet Russia includes Sarah Ashwin's *Gender, State, and Society in Soviet and Post-Soviet Russia* (2000) and Helena Goscilo's *Dehexing Sex: Russian Womanhood during and after Glasnost* (1996), as well as the edited volumes *Gender, Generation, and Identity in Contemporary Russia* (1996) and *Women in Contemporary Russia* (1995).

In terms of the military, economic, judicial, agrarian, and industrial infrastructure of post-independence Russia, the following texts can provide the researcher with an introduction to discrete topics: *Owning Russia: The Struggle over Factories, Farms, and Power* (2006); *Russian Military Reform, 1992–2002* (2003); *Rural Reform in Post-Soviet Russia* (2002); *Russia's Agricultural in Transition* (2007); *Ruling Russia: Law, Crime, and Justice in a Changing Society* (2005); and *The Russian Economy: From Lenin to Putin* (2007). Alena Ledeneva's *How Russia Really Works: The Informal Practices That Shaped Post-Soviet Politics and Business* (2006) is especially helpful in decoding the post-Soviet business world.

Last, there is a wide range of valuable Internet resources for scholars working on the Russian Federation. Important government portals include President Dmitry Medvyedev's website (http://eng.kremlin.ru/) and Prime Minister Putin's website (www.premier.gov.ru/). One can find a copy of the Russian constitution at www.russianembassy.org/russia/constit/. For breaking news and video on the country in English, *Russia Today* (http://russiatoday.com/) is the best option. For localized coverage the websites of the *St. Petersburg Times* (www.sptimes.ru/) and the *Moscow Times* (www.themoscowtimes.com/) are good choices as well.

GENERAL

Bibliographies and Bibliographic Essays

Boilard, Steve D. *Reinterpreting Russia: An Annotated Bibliography of Books on Russia, the Soviet Union, and the Russian Federation, 1991–1996.* Lanham, Md.: Scarecrow Press, 1997.

Horecky, Paul Louis. *Basic Russian Publications: An Annotated Bibliography on Russia and the Soviet Union.* Chicago: Chicago University Press, 2003.

Muckle, James Y. *Education in Russia Past and Present: An Introductory Study Guide and Select Bibliography.* Nottingham: Bramcote Press, 1993.

Ruthchild, Rochelle Goldberg. *Women in Russia and the Soviet Union: An Annotated Bibliography.* New York: G. K. Hall, 1993.

Schaffner, Bradley L. *Bibliography of the Soviet Union, Its Predecessors and Successors.* Metuchen, N.J.: Scarecrow Press, 1995.

Sullivan, Helen, and Robert Burger. *Russia and Eastern Europe: A Bibliographic Guide to English-Language Publications, 1992–1999.* Santa Barbara, Calif.: Libraries Unlimited, 2001.

Dictionaries and Encyclopedias

Branover, Herman. *The Encyclopedia of Russian Jewry.* Northvale, N.J.: Jason Aronson, 1998.

Day, Alan John, Roger East, and Richard Thomas, eds. *A Political and Economic Dictionary of Eastern Europe*. London: Routledge, 2002.

Dixon-Kennedy, Mike. *Encyclopedia of Russian and Slavic Myth and Legend*. Santa Barbara, Calif.: ABC-CLIO, 1998.

Kabakchi, V. V. *The Dictionary of Russia: 2500 Cultural Terms*. Moscow: Soyuz, 2002.

Millar, James R. *Encyclopedia of Russian History*. New York: Macmillan Reference, 2004.

Noonan, Norma Corigliano, and Carol Nechemias, eds. *Encyclopedia of Russian Women's Movements*. Westport, Conn.: Greenwood, 2001.

Olson, James Stuart, Lee Brigance Pappas, and Nicholas Charles Pappas, eds. *An Ethnohistorical Dictionary of the Russian and Soviet Empires*. Westport, Conn.: Greenwood, 1994.

Pribylovskii, Vladimir, Dauphine Sloan, amd Sarah Helmstadter, eds. *Dictionary of Political Parties and Organizations in Russia*. Ann Arbor: University of Michigan, 2008.

Pringle, Robert W. *Historical Dictionary of Russian and Soviet Intelligence*. Lanham, Md.: Scarecrow Press, 2006.

Raymond, Boris, and Paul Duffy. *Historical Dictionary of Russia*. Lanham, Md.: Scarecrow Press, 1998.

Saul, Norman E. *Historical Dictionary of United States–Russian/Soviet Relations*. Lanham, Md.: Scarecrow Press, 2008.

Senelick, Laurence. *Historical Dictionary of Russian Theatre*. Lanham, Md.: Scarecrow Press, 2007.

Smith, Gerald Stanton, Archie Brown, and Michael Kaser, eds. *The Cambridge Encyclopedia of Russia and the Former Soviet Union*. Cambridge: Cambridge University Press, 1994.

Smorodinskaya, Tatiana, Karen Evans-Romaine, and Helena Goscilo, eds. *Encyclopedia of Contemporary Russian Culture*. London: Routledge, 2007.

Statistical Abstracts and Yearbooks

Batalden, Stephen K., and Sandra L. Batalden. *The Newly Independent States of Eurasia: Handbook of Former Soviet Republics*, 2nd ed. Westport, Conn.: Greenwood, 1997.

Brassey's Eurasian and East European Security Yearbook. Washington, D.C.: Brassey's, 2000–present (annual).

The Demographic Yearbook of Russia. Moscow: Goskomstat, 1995–present (annual).

Eastern Europe, Russia, and Central Asia. London: Europa Publications, 2000–present (annual).

Goldman, Minton. *Global Studies: Russia, the Eurasian Republics and Central/Eastern Europe.* Columbus, OH: McGraw-Hill, 1998–present (annual).

Political Risk Yearbook: Russia Country Forecast. East Syracuse, N.Y.: PRS Group, 2003–present (annual).

Russia and the Commonwealth of Independent States. London: Europa Publications, 1999.

The Russian Social History Yearbook. Moscow: International Institute of Social History, 1997–present (annual).

Travel and Description

Braden, Kathleen, and Natalya Prudnikova. "The Challenge of Ecotourism Development in the Altay Region of Russia." *Tourism Geographies* 10, no. 1 (February 2008): 1–21.

Charlton, Angela. *Frommer's Moscow & St. Petersburg.* Hoboken, N.J.: Frommer's, 2008.

Collins, Naomi F. *Through Dark Days and White Nights: Four Decades Observing a Changing Russia: Impressions and Reflections.* Washington, D.C.: Scarith, 2008.

Dabars, Zita, and Lilia Vokhmina. *The Russian Way: Aspects of Behavior, Attitudes, and Customs of the Russians.* 2nd ed. Columbus: McGraw-Hill, 2002.

Ely, Christopher. "The Origins of Russian Scenery: Volga River Tourism and Russian Landscape Aesthetics." S*lavic Review: Interdisciplinary Quarterly of Russian, Eurasian, & East European Studies* 62, no. 4 (Winter 2003): 666–82.

Frank, Ben G. *A Travel Guide to Jewish Russia & Ukraine.* Gretna, La.: Pelican, 1999.

Gusachenko, Andrey. "Ryazan Gateway to the Russian Heartland." *Russian Life* 51, no. 2 (March/April 2008): 30–35.

Kalder, Daniel, *Lost Cosmonaut: Observations of an Anti-Tourist.* New York: Scribner, 2006.

Koenker, Diane P. "Travel to Work, Travel to Play: On Russian Tourism, Travel, and Leisure." *Slavic Review: Interdisciplinary Quarterly of Russian, Eurasian, & East European Studies* 62, no. 4 (Winter 2003): 657–65.

Kolesnikova, Maria. "Exploring Donland." *Russian Life* 49, no. 4 (July/August 2006): 28–29.

McGregor, Ewan, Charley Boorman, David Alexanian, and Russ Malkin. *Long Way Round.* DVD. Elixir Productions/Image Wizard Media, 2004.

Meier, Andrew. *Black Earth: A Journey through Russia after the Fall.* London: W. W. Norton, 2003.

Mitchneck, Beth. "The Heritage Industry Russian Style." *Urban Affairs Review* 34, no. 1 (September 1998): 28–51.

Murrell Berton, Kathleen. *Discovering the Moscow Countryside: A Travel Guide to the Heart of Russia.* London: I. B. Tauris, 2001.

Ovcharov, Anton. "The Russian Tourist Industry: Trends and Risks." *Social Sciences* 39, no. 3 (2008): 4–15.

Perreault, Laura-Julie. "Tatarstan." *Russian Life* 46, no. 2 (March 2003): 54–59.

Richmond, Simon, Mark Elliott, Patrick Horton, Steve Kokker, John Noble, Robert Reid, and Mara Vorhees. *Russia & Belarus*, 4th ed. Footscray, Australia: Lonely Planet, 2006.

Richmond, Simon. *Russia (Country Guide).* Footscray, Australia: Lonely Planet, 2009.

Shmyrov, Victor. "The Gulag Museum." *Museum International* 53, no. 1 (January 2001): 25–27.

Tayler, Jeffrey. "Escape to Old Russia." *Atlantic Monthly* 298, no. 3 (October 2006): 129–33.

——. "White Nights in Siberia." *Atlantic Monthly* 286, no. 6 (December 2000): 36–40.

Thubron, Colin. *Among the Russians.* New York: Harper Perennial, 2000.

——. *In Siberia.* New York: Harper Perennial, 2000.

Williams, Laura. "The Wonders of Kamchatka." *Russian Life* 49, no. 4 (July/August 2006): 42–49.

Zhelvis, Vladimir. *The Xenophobe's Guide to the Russians.* London: Oval Books, 2001.

Geography

Bradshaw, Michael J. *Geography and Transition in the Post-Soviet Republics.* Chichester, UK: John Wiley & Sons, 1997.

Demko, George J., Grigory Ioffe, Zhanna Zayonchkovskaya. *Population under Duress: The Geodemography of Post-Soviet Russia.* Boulder, Colo.: Westview Press, 1999.

Garmaeva, Tatiana. "Lake Baikal: Model for Sustainable Development of the Territory." *Lakes & Reservoirs: Research and Management* 6, no. 3 (September 2001): 253–57.

Gilbert, Martin. *The Routledge Atlas of Russian History*, 4th ed. London: Routledge, 2007.

Hanson, Philip, and Michael J. Bradshaw, eds. *The Territories of the Russian Federation 2009.* London: Routledge, 2009.

PKO Kartografiya. *Atlas, Russia and the Post Soviet Republics.* Moscow: Atkar-PKO Kartografiya, 1994.

Ruble, Blair A. *Money Sings: The Changing Politics of Urban Space in Post-Soviet Yaroslavl.* Washington, D.C.: Woodrow Wilson Center Press, 1995.

Shahgedanova, Maria. *The Physical Geography of Northern Eurasia.* Oxford: Oxford University Press, 2003.

Shaw, Denis J. B. *Russia in the Modern World: A New Geography.* Oxford: Blackwell Publishers, 1999.

——, ed. *The Post-Soviet Republics: A Systematic Geography.* Harlow, UK: Longman Scientific & Technical, 1994.

Surkov, Feodor A. "Southern Russia's Three Seas: The ABCs of Sustainable Development." *Problems of Post-Communism* 54, no. 2 (March/April 2007): 26–37.

Periodicals

Ab Imperio: Studies of New Imperial History and Nationalism in the Post-Soviet Space. Kazan, Russia: Kazan State University, 2000–present (quarterly).

Chtenia: Fine Readings from Russia. Montpelier, Vt.: RIS, 2008–present (quarterly).

Communist and Post-Communist Studies. Amsterdam: Elsevier, 1968–present (quarterly).

Demokratizatsiya: The Journal of Post-Soviet Democratization. Washington, D.C.: Helen Dwight Reid Educational Foundation, 1992–present (quarterly).

Digital Icons: Studies in Russian, Eurasian, and Central European New Media. London, 2008–present (semiannual).

East European Politics and Societies. Thousand Oaks, Calif.: Sage Publications, 1986–present (quarterly).

Eastern European Quarterly. Boulder: University of Colorado, 1967–present (quarterly).

Eurasian Geography and Economics. Columbia, Md.: Bellwether Publishing, 1960–present (bimonthly).

Europe-Asia Studies. Glasgow: University of Glasgow, 1992–present (bimonthly).

International Affairs: A Russian Journal of World Politics, Diplomacy and International Relations. Minneapolis, Minn.: East View Press, 1996–present (bimonthly).

Journal of Communist Studies and Transition Politics. London: Routledge, 1985–present (quarterly).

Kritika. Bloomington, Ind.: Slavica Publishers, 2000–present (quarterly).

Nationalities Papers. London: Taylor & Francis, 1972–present (bimonthly).

Post-Soviet Affairs. Columbia, Md.: Bellwether Publishing, 1985–present (bimonthly).

Problems of Post-Communism. Armonk, N.Y.: M. E. Sharpe. 1992–present (bimonthly).

Russia in Global Affairs. Moscow: ANO RID Globus, 2002–present (quarterly).

Russia! New York: Press Release Group, 2007–present (quarterly).

Russian Life. Montpelier, Vt.: RIS, 1956–present (bimonthly).

Russian Politics and Law. Armonk, N.Y.: M. E. Sharpe, 1962–present (bimonthly).

Russian Social Science Review. Armonk, N.Y.: M. E. Sharpe, 1960–present (bimonthly).

Slavic Review. Urbana-Champaign, Ill.: American Association for the Advancement of Slavic Studies, 1941–present (quarterly).

Slavonica. Leeds, UK: Maney Publishing, 1994–present (semiannual).

The Russian Review. Lawrence, Kan.: University of Kansas, 1941–present (quarterly).

The Soviet and Post-Soviet Review. Leiden, Netherlands: Brill, 1974–present (annual).

Transitions Online. Prague: Transitions Online 1999–present.

HISTORICAL

General Russian/Soviet History

Applebaum, Anne. *Gulag: A History of the Soviet Camps.* London: Penguin, 2004.

Black, Joseph Laurence. *The Russian Federation.* Gulf Breeze, Fla.: Academic International, 2001.

Bressler, Michael L. *Understanding Contemporary Russia.* Boulder, Colo.: Lynne Rienner, 2008.

Brzezinski, Zbigniew, and Paige Sullivan. *Russia and the Commonwealth of Independent States: Documents, Data, and Analysis.* Armonk, N.Y.: M. E. Sharpe, 1997.

Chubarov, Alexander. *Russia's Bitter Path to Modernity: A History of the Soviet and Post-Soviet Eras.* New York: Continuum, 2001.

Conquest, Robert. *The Nation Killers: The Soviet Deportation of Nationalities.* London: Macmillan, 1970.

Curtis, Glenn E., ed. *Russia: A Country Study.* Washington: GPO for the Library of Congress, 1996.

Duncan, Peter J. S. *Russian Messianism: Third Rome, Holy Revolution, Communism and After.* London: Routledge, 2000.

Fritz, Verena. *State-Building: A Comparative Study of Ukraine, Lithuania, Belarus, and Russia.* Budapest: Central European University Press, 2007.

Galeotti, Mark. *Afghanistan: The Soviet Union's Last War.* London: Frank Cass, 1995.

Garcelon, Marc. *Revolutionary Passage: From Soviet to Post-Soviet Russia, 1985–2000.* Philadelphia: Temple University Press, 2005.

Gladman, Imogen. *Europe, Russia and Central Asia.* 6th ed. London: Routledge, 2006.

Higham, Robin, and Frederick W. Kagan, eds. *The Military History of the Soviet Union.* York, UK: Palgrave, 2002.

Hirsch, Francine. *Empire of Nations: Ethnographic Knowledge and the Making of the Soviet Union.* Ithaca, N.Y.: Cornell University Press, 2005.

Holden, Gerard. *Russia after the Cold War: History and the Nation in Post-Soviet Security Politics.* Frankfurt am Main: Campus Verlag, 1994.

Isakova, Irina. *Russian Governance in the Twenty-first Century: Geo-Strategy, Geopolitics, and Governance.* New York: Frank Cass, 2005.

Isham, Heyward. *Remaking Russia: Voices from Within.* Armonk, N.Y.: M. E. Sharpe, 1995.

Kenez, Peter. *A History of the Soviet Union from the Beginning to the End.* Cambridge: Cambridge University Press, 2006.

Kochan, L., and Keep, J. *The Making of Modern Russia.* Harmondsworth, UK: Penguin, 1997.

Lester, Jeremy. *Modern Tsars and Princes: The Struggle for Hegemony in Russia.* London: Verso, 1995.

Nahaylo, Bohdan, and Victor Swoboda. *Soviet Disunion: A History of the Nationalities Problem in the USSR.* London: Hamish Hamilton, 1990.

Nekrich, Alexander M. *The Punished People: The Deportation and Fate of Soviet Minorities at the End of the Second World War.* New York: W. W. Norton, 1978.

Nove, Alec. *An Economic History of the USSR: 1917–1991.* London: Penguin, 1992.

Perrie, Maureen, ed. *The Cambridge History of Russia.* Cambridge: Cambridge University Press, 2006.

Schleifman, Nurit. *Russia at a Crossroads: History, Memory and Political Practice.* London: Routledge, 1998.

Sherlock, Thomas D. *Historical Narratives in the Soviet Union and Post-Soviet Russia: Destroying the Settled Past, Creating an Uncertain Future.* New York: Palgrave Macmillan, 2007.

Suny, Ronald G. *Making Workers Soviet: Power, Culture, and Identity.* Ithaca, N.Y.: Cornell University Press, 1994.

——. *The Revenge of the Past: Nationalism, Revolution, and the Collapse of the Soviet Union.* Stanford, Calif.: Stanford University Press, 1993.

——. *The Soviet Experiment: Russia, the USSR, and the Successor States.* Oxford: Oxford University Press, 1998.

——. *A State of Nations: Empire and Nation-Making in the Age of Lenin and Stalin.* Oxford: Oxford University Press, 2001.

——. *The Structure of Soviet History: Essays and Documents.* Oxford: Oxford University Press, 2003.

Toker, Leona. *Return from the Archipelago: Narratives of Gulag Survivors.* Bloomington: Indiana University Press, 2000.

Trepanier, Lee. *Political Symbols in Russian History.* Lanham, Md.: Rowman & Littlefield, 2007.

Truscott, Peter. *Russia First: Breaking with the West.* New York: I. B. Tauris, 1997.

Tucker, Robert C. *Stalin in Power: The Revolution from Above, 1928–1941.* New York: W. W. Norton, 1992.

Usitalo, Steven A., and William Benton Whisenhunt. *Russian and Soviet History: From the Time of Troubles to the Collapse of the Soviet Union.* Lanham, Md.: Rowman & Littlefield, 2008.

The Gorbachev Era (1985–1991)

Aganbegian, Abel Gezevich, and Michael Barratt Brown, eds. *The Economic Challenge of Perestroika.* Translated by Pauline M. Tiffen. Bloomington: Indiana University Press, 1988.

Bialer, Seweryn, ed. *Politics, Society, and Nationality inside Gorbachev's Russia.* Boulder, Colo.: Westview Press, 1989.

Brown, Archie. "Change in the Soviet Union." *Foreign Affairs* 64, no. 5 (Summer 1986): 1048–65.

Brutents, Karen. "Origins of the New Thinking." *Russian Social Science Review* 47, no. 1 (January/February 2006): 73–102.

Conquest, Robert. "Reflections on the Revolution." *National Review* 43, no. 17 (1991): 24–26.

D'Agostino, Anthony. *Gorbachev's Revolution.* New York: New York University Press, 1998.

Davidow, Mike. *Perestroika: Its Rise and Fall.* New York: International Publishers, 1993.

DeLuca, Anthony R. *Politics, Diplomacy, and the Media: Gorbachev's Legacy in the West.* Westport, Conn.: Praeger, 1998.

Despard, Lucy Edwards, and Robert Legvold. "The August Coup: The Truth and the Lessons." *Foreign Affairs* 71, no. 2 (Spring 1992): 205.

Evanier, David. "Will the Soviet Union Survive Until 1994?" *National Review* 41, no. 6 (1989): 24–30.

Felshman, Neil. *Gorbachev, Yeltsin, and the Last Days of the Soviet Empire.* New York: St. Martin's Press, 1992.

Gati, Charles. "Gorbachev and Eastern Europe." *Foreign Affairs* 65, no. 5 (Summer 1987): 958–75.

Goldman, Marshall I. "Gorbachev and Economic Reform." *Foreign Affairs* 64, no. 1 (Fall 1985): 56–73.

Gorbachev, Mikhail Sergeyevich. *Perestroika: New Thinking for Our Country and the World.* New York: Harper & Row, 1987.

Gorshkov, M. K. "Perestroika through the Eyes of Russians: Twenty Years Later." *Sociological Research* 44, no. 6 (November/December 2005): 8–76.

Hill, Ronald J., and Jan Åke Dellenbrant. *Gorbachev and Perestroika: Towards a New Socialism?* Aldershot, UK: E. Elgar, 1989.

Hough, Jerry F. "Gorbachev's Strategy." *Foreign Affairs* 64, no. 1 (Fall 1985): 33–55.

Huber, Robert T., and Donald R. Kelley, eds. *Perestroika-Era Politics: The New Soviet Legislature and Gorbachev's Political Reforms.* Armonk, N.Y.: M. E. Sharpe, 1991.

Kaiser, Robert G. "Gorbachev: Triumph and Failure." *Foreign Affairs* 70, no. 2 (Spring 1991): 160–74.

Knight, A. "The Coup That Never Was: Gorbachev and the Forces of Reaction." *Problems of Communism* 40, no. 6 (November/December 1991): 36–43.

Laibman, David. "The Soviet Demise: Revisionist Betrayal, Structural Defect, or Authoritarian Distortion?" *Science & Society* 69, no. 4 (October 2005): 594–606.

Odom, W. E. "Alternative Perspectives on the August Coup." *Problems of Communism* 40, no. 6 (November/December 1991): 13–19.

Riordan, Jim, and Sue Bridger, eds. *Dear Comrade Editor: Readers' Letters to the Soviet Press under Perestroika.* Bloomington: Indiana University Press, 1992.

Robinson, Neil. "Gorbachev and the Place of the Party in Soviet Reform." *Soviet Studies* 44, no. 3 (1992): 423–43.

———. "What Was Soviet Ideology? A Comment on Joseph Schull and an Alternative." *Political Studies* 43, no. 2 (June 1995): 325–32.

Sheinis, Viktor Leonidovich. "August 1991: A Pyrrhic Victory." *Russian Social Science Review* 49, no. 1 (2008): 4–23.

Sondhi, Manohar L., ed. *Beyond Perestroika: Choices and Challenges Facing Gorbachev*. New Delhi: Abhinav Publications, 1989.

Strayer, Robert W. *Why Did the Soviet Union Collapse? Understanding Historical Change*. Armonk, N.Y.: M. E. Sharpe, 1998.

Tatu, Michel. *Mikhail Gorbachev: The Origins of Perestroika*. Translated by A. P. M. Bradley. Boulder, Colo.: East European Monographs, 1991.

Thom, Françoise. *The Gorbachev Phenomenon: A History of Perestroika*. Translated by Jenny Marshall. London: Pinter Publishers, 1989.

Walker, Rachel. *Six Years That Shook the World: Perestroika—the Impossible Project*. Manchester: Manchester University Press, 1993.

The Yeltsin Era (1992–1999)

Aron, Leon Rabinovich. *Yeltsin: A Revolutionary Life*. New York: St. Martin's Press, 2000.

Brown, Archie. "The Russian Transition in Comparative and Russian Perspective." *Social Research* 63, no. 2 (Summer 1996): 403–15.

Cohen, Ariel. "The 'Primakov Doctrine': Russia's Zero-Sum Game with the United States," FYI No. 167 (December 15). Washington, D.C.: Heritage Foundation, 1997.

Colton, Timothy J. *Boris Yeltsin: A Life*. New York: Basic Books, 2008.

Columbus, Frank H., ed. *Who Lost Russia? (Or Was It Lost?)*. Huntington, N.Y.: Nova Science Publishers, 2001.

Ellison, Herbert J. *Boris Yeltsin and Russia's Democratic Transformation*. Seattle: University of Washington Press, 2006.

Felkay, Andrew. *Yeltsin's Russia and the West*. Westport, Conn.: Praeger, 2002.

Kozyrev, Andrei. "The Lagging Partnership." *Foreign Affairs* 73, no. 3 (May/June 1994): 59–71.

Larrabee, F. Stephen. *Foreign and Security Policy Decisionmaking under Yeltsin*. Santa Monica, Calif.: Rand, 1997.

McFaul, Michael. *Russia's 1996 Presidential Election: The End of Polarized Politics*. Stanford, Calif.: Hoover, 1997.

Medvedev, Roy Aleksandrovich. *Post-Soviet Russia: A Journey through the Yeltsin Era*. Translated by George Shriver. New York: Columbia University Press, 2000.

Morrison, John. *Boris Yeltsin: From Bolshevik to Democrat*. New York: Dutton, 1991.

Quinn-Judge, Paul, and James L. Graff. "Russia's New Icon." *Time* 152, no. 19 (9 November 1998): 74–76.

Rubinstein, Alvin Z. "The Geopolitical Pull on Russia." *Orbis* 38, no. 4 (Fall 1994): 567–83.

Sestanovich, Stephen. "Andrei the Giant." *New Republic* 210, no. 15 (11 April 1994): 24–27.

Smith, Gordon B., ed. *State-Building in Russia: the Yeltsin Legacy and the Challenge of the Future.* Armonk, N.Y.: M. E. Sharpe, 1999.

Smith, Kathleen E. *Mythmaking in the New Russia: Politics and Memory in the Yeltsin Era.* Ithaca, N.Y.: Cornell University Press, 2002.

Solovyov, Vladimir. *Boris Yeltsin: A Political Biography.* Translated by David Gurevich. New York: Putnam, 1992.

Steele, Jonathan. *Eternal Russia: Yeltsin, Gorbachev, and the Mirage of Democracy.* Cambridge, Mass.: Harvard University Press, 1994.

Straus, Ira. "Russia's Potential Futures in the Euro-Atlantic-OECD World." *Demokratizatsiya* 9 no. 4 (Fall 2001): 485–97.

Talbott, Strobe. *The Russia Hand: A Memoir of Presidential Diplomacy.* New York: Random House, 2003.

Waller, J. Michael. "Yeltsin Keeps It All in 'the Family' — Boris Yeltsin's Selection of Vladimir Putin as Russian Prime Minister." *Insight on the News* (6 September 1999).

Yeltsin, Boris Nikolayevich. *Against the Grain: An Autobiography.* Translated by Michael Glenny. London: J. Cape, 1990.

———. *Midnight Diaries.* Translated by Catherine A. Fitzpatrick. New York: Public Affairs, 2000.

———. *The Struggle for Russia.* Translated by Catherine A. Fitzpatrick. New York: Times Books, 1994.

The Putin Era and Beyond (2000–present)

Baker, Peter, and Susan Glasser. *Kremlin Rising: Vladimir Putin's Russia and the End of Revolution.* New York: Scribner, 2005.

Black, Joseph Laurence. *Vladimir Putin and the New World Order: Looking East, Looking West?* Lanham, Md.: Rowman & Littlefield, 2004.

Blank, Stephen J. "Putin's Twelve-Step Program." *The Washington Quarterly,* 25, no. 1 (2002): 147–60.

Bragin, M. "Vladimir Putin-George Bush: 'Playing the Same Game.'" *International Affairs: A Russian Journal of World Politics, Diplomacy and International Relations* 53, no. 5 (2007): 1–11.

Bremmer, Ian, and Alexander Zaslavsky. "Bush and Putin's Tentative Embrace." *World Policy Journal* 18, no. 4 (Winter 2001/2002): 11–17.

Chebankova, Elena. "The Unintended Consequences of Gubernatorial Appointments in Russia, 2005–6." *Journal of Communist Studies and Transition Politics* 22, no. 4 (December 2006): 457–84.

Goldgeier, James M. "The United States and Russia: Keeping Expectations Realistic." *Policy Review* 109 (2001): 47–56.

Goode, J. Paul. "The Puzzle of Putin's Gubernatorial Appointments." *Europe-Asia Studies* 59, no. 3 (May 2007): 365–99.

Herspring, Dale R., ed. *Putin's Russia: Past Imperfect, Future Uncertain,* 3rd ed. Lanham, Md.: Rowman & Littlefield, 2006.

Homan, Kees. "Putin Is Testing Western Resolve." *Helsinki Monitor* 18, no. 3 (July 2007): 177–79.

Jack, Andrew. *Inside Putin's Russia.* Oxford: Oxford University Press, 2004.

Kagarlitsky, Boris. *Russia under Yeltsin and Putin: Neo-liberal Autocracy.* London: Pluto Press, 2002.

LeVine, Steve. *Putin's Labyrinth: Spies, Murder, and the Dark Heart of the New Russia.* New York: Random House, 2008.

Politkovskaya, Anna. *A Russian Diary: A Journalist's Final Account of Life, Corruption, and Death in Putin's Russia.* Translated by Arch Tait. New York: Random House, 2007.

———. *Putin's Russia: Life in a Failing Democracy.* Translated by Arch Tait. New York: Metropolitan Books, 2005.

Pravda, Alex, ed. *Leading Russia—Putin in Perspective: Essays in Honour of Archie Brown.* Oxford: Oxford University Press, 2005.

Putin, Vladimir Vladimirovich. *First Person: An Astonishingly Frank Self-Portrait by Russia's President.* Translated by Catherine A. Fitzpatrick. New York: Public Affairs, 2000.

Ross, Cameron, ed. *Russian Politics under Putin: Normality, Normalcy or Normalisation.* Manchester: Manchester University Press, 2004.

Sakwa, Richard. *Putin: Russia's Choice*, 2nd ed. London: Routledge, 2008.

Schmidt, Matthew. "Is Putin Pursuing a Policy of Eurasianism?" *Demokratizatsiya* 13, no. 1 (Winter 2005): 87–99.

Shevtsova, Lilia. *Putin's Russia.* Translated by Antonina W. Bouis. Washington, D.C.: Carnegie Endowment for International Peace, 2005.

Shlapentokh, Dmitry. "Trends in Putin's Russia." *Society* 41, no. 1 (2003): 72–80.

Tikhomirov, Vladimir, ed. *Russia after Yeltsin.* Aldershot, UK: Ashgate, 2001.

POLITICAL

Domestic Affairs

Russian Politics

Applebaum, Anne. "The Fate of Individual Liberty in Post-Communist Europe." *American Spectator* 41, no. 3 (April 2008): 30–38.

Barany, Zoltan, and Robert G. Moser. *Russian Politics: Challenges of Democratization.* Cambridge: Cambridge University Press, 2001.

Beichelt, Timm. "Autocracy and Democracy in Belarus, Russia and Ukraine." *Democratization* 11, no. 5 (December 2004): 113–32.

Bonnell, Victoria E., and George W. Breslauer, eds. *Russia in the New Century: Stability or Disorder?* Boulder, Colo.: Westview Press, 2001.

Breslauer, George. *Gorbachev and Yeltsin as Leaders.* Cambridge: Cambridge University Press, 2002.

———, ed. *Russia: Political and Economical Development.* Claremont, Calif.: Keck Center for International and Strategic Studies, Claremont McKenna College, 1995.

Brown, Archie, and Lilia Shevstova, eds. *Gorbachev, Yeltsin, and Putin: Political Leadership in Russia's Transition.* Washington, D.C.: Carnegie Endowment for International Peace, 2001.

Brzezinski, Zbigniew. *The Grand Chessboard: American Primacy and Its Geostrategic Imperatives.* New York: Basic Books, 1997.

Bukkvoll, Tor. *Ukraine and European Security.* London: Continuum International Publishing Group, 1997.

Carnaghan, Ellen. *Out of Order: Russian Political Values in an Imperfect World.* College Park: Pennsylvania State Press, 2007.

Cockerham, William C., Brian P. Hinote, Pamela Abbott, and Geoffrey B. Cockerham. "Health Lifestyles and Political Ideology in Belarus, Russia, and Ukraine." *Social Science and Medicine* 62, no. 7 (April 2006): 1799–1809.

Colton, Timothy J., and Robert C. Tucker, ed. *Patterns in Post-Soviet Leadership.* Boulder, Colo.: Westview Press, 1995.

Danks, Catherine. *Russian Politics and Society: An Introduction.* Harlow, UK: Longman, 2002.

DeBardeleben, Joan. *Russian Politics in Transition.* 2nd ed. Boston: Houghton Mifflin, 1997.

Desai, Padma. *Conversations on Russia: Reform from Yeltsin to Putin.* Oxford: Oxford University Press, 2006.

Dryzek, John S., and Leslie Holmes. *Post-Communist Democratization: Political Discourses across Thirteen Countries.* Cambridge: Cambridge University Press, 2002.

Eckstein, Harry, ed. *Can Democracy Take Root in Post-Soviet Russia? Explorations in State-Society Relations.* Lanham, Md.: Rowman & Littlefield, 1998.

Friedgut, Theodore H., and Jeffrey W. Hahn. *Local Power and Post-Soviet Politics.* Armonk, N.Y.: M. E. Sharpe, 1994.

Gaman-Golutvina, Oxana. "Political Elites in the Commonwealth of Independent States: Recruitment and Rotation Tendencies." *Comparative Sociology* 6, nos. 1–2 (February 2007): 136–57.

Gill, Graeme J. *Russia's Stillborn Democracy? From Gorbachev to Yeltsin*. Oxford: Oxford University Press, 2000.

Goldfarb, Alexander. *Death of a Dissident: The Poisoning of Alexander Litvinenko and the Return of the KGB*. New York: Free Press, 2007.

Hahn, Jeffrey W. *Regional Russia in Transition: Studies from Yaroslavl'*. Washington, D.C.: Woodrow Wilson Center Press, 2001.

Herman, Arthur. "Putin and the Polite Pundits." *Commentary* 126, no. 3 (October 2008): 11–17.

Huskey, Eugene. *Presidential Power in Russia*. Armonk, N.Y.: M. E. Sharpe, 1999.

Kagarlitsky, Boris. *Russia under Yeltsin and Putin: Neo-liberal Autocracy*. London: Pluto Press, 2002.

Kamiński, Bartłomiej. *Economic Transition in Russia and the New States of Eurasia*. Armonk, N.Y.: M. E. Sharpe, 1996.

Kempton, Daniel R., and Terry D. Clark, eds. *Unity or Separation: Center-Periphery Relations in the Former Soviet Union*. Westport, Conn.: Praeger, 2002.

Korosteleva, Julia, and Stephen White. "'Feeling European': The View from Belarus, Russia and Ukraine." *Contemporary Politics* 12, no. 2 (June 2006): 193–205.

Kubicek, Paul. "Delegative Democracy in Russia and Ukraine." *Communist and Post-Communist Studies* 27, no. 4 (December 1994): 423–41.

Kutchins, Andrew C., ed. *Russia after the Fall*. Washington, D.C.: Carnegie Endowment for International Peace, 2002.

Lankina, Tomila. *Governing the Locals: Local Self-Government and Ethnic Mobilization in Russia*. Lanham, Md.: Rowman & Littlefield, 2004.

Lebed, Alexander. *General Alexander Lebed: My Life and My Country*. Washington, D.C.: Regnery Publishing, 1997.

Legvold, Robert. "National Identity and Foreign Policy: Nationalism and Leadership in Poland, Russia, and Ukraine." *Foreign Affairs* 78, no. 3 (May/June 1999): 145–46.

March, Luke. "Power and Opposition in the Former Soviet Union." *Party Politics* 12, no. 3 (May 2006): 341–65.

——. "The Contemporary Russian Left after Communism: Into the Dustbin of History?" *Journal of Communist Studies and Transition Politics* 22, no. 4 (December 2006): 431–56.

McAuley, Mary. *Russia's Politics of Uncertainty*. Cambridge: Cambridge University Press, 1997.

McFaul, Michael. *Russia's Unfinished Revolution: Political Change from Gorbachev to Putin*. Ithaca, N.Y.: Cornell University Press, 2001.

Meleshevich, Andrey. "Geographical Patterns of Party Support in the Baltic States, Russia, and Ukraine." *European Urban and Regional Studies* 13, no. 2 (April 2006): 113–29.

Miller, Arthur H., and Vicki L. Hesli. "Comparing Citizen and Elite Belief Systems in Post-Soviet Russia and Ukraine." *Public Opinion Quarterly* 59, no. 1 (Spring 1995): 1–40.

Miller, Arthur H., William M. Reisinger, and Vicki L. Hesli. *Public Opinion and Regime Change: The New Politics of Post-Soviet Societies.* Boulder, Colo.: Westview Press, 1993.

Molchanov, Mikhail A. "Russia and Globalization." *Perspectives on Global Development and Technology* 4, nos. 3–4 (2005): 397–429.

Mommen, André. "Russia's Response to Globalization." *International Journal of Political Economy* 31, no. 4 (Winter 2001): 53–78.

Myagkov, Mikhail, Peter C. Ordeshook, and Dimitry Shakin. "Fraud or Fairy-tales: Russia and Ukraine's Electoral Experience." *Post-Soviet Affairs* 21, no 2 (April–June 2005): 91–131.

Orenstein, Mitchell. "The Left Transformed in Post-Communist Societies: The Cases of East-Central Europe, Russia, and Ukraine." *Slavic Review: Inter-disciplinary Quarterly of Russian, Eurasian, and East European Studies* 63, no. 4 (Winter 2004): 853–54.

Ozbay, Fatih, and Bulent Aras. "Polish-Russian Relations: History, Geography and Geopolitics." *East European Quarterly* 42, no. 1 (Spring 2008): 27–42.

Porter, Anna. "Between the Devil and the EU." *Maclean's* 121, no. 22 (9 June 2008): 40–42.

Prizel, Ilya. "Populism as a Political Force in Postcommunist Russia and Ukraine." *East European Politics and Societies* 15, no. 1 (Spring 2001): 54–63.

Protsyk, Oleh. "Domestic Political Institutions in Ukraine and Russia and Their Responses to EU Enlargement." *Communist and Post-Communist Studies* 36, no. 4 (December 2003): 427–42.

———. "Ruling with Decrees: Presidential Decree Making in Russia and Ukraine." *Europe-Asia Studies* 56, no. 5 (July 2004): 637–60.

Protsyk, Oleh, and Andrew Wilson. "Centre Politics in Russia and Ukraine: Patronage, Power and Virtuality." *Party Politics* 9, no 6 (November 2003): 703–27.

Ra'anan, Uri, ed. *Flawed Succession: Russia's Power Transfer Crises.* Lan-ham, Md.: Lexington Books, 2006.

Remington, Thomas. *Politics in Russia*, 9th ed. Harlow, UK: Longman, 2009.

Robinson, Neil. *Russia: A State of Uncertainty.* London: Routledge, 2002.

Rogerson, Ken. "The Role of the Media in Transitions from Authoritarian Political Systems: Russia and Poland." *East European Quarterly* 31, no. 3 (1997): 329–53.

Rosefielde, Steven, and Romana Hlouskova. "Why Russia Is Not a Democracy." *Comparative Strategy* 26, no. 3 (May 2007): 215–29.

Ruffin, M. Holt, ed. *The Post-Soviet Handbook: A Guide to Grassroots Organizations and Internet Resources*. Seattle, Wash.: Center for Civil Society International, 1999.

Saunders, Paul J. "Why 'Globalization' Didn't Rescue Russia." *Policy Review* 105 (February/March 2001): 27–39.

Sedov, Leonid. "Russia: A Glimpse from Poland and Back." *Russian Politics and Law* 41, no. 3 (May/June 2003): 84–95.

Shevchenko, Iulia. *The Central Government of Russia: From Gorbachev to Putin*. Aldershot, UK: Ashgate, 2004.

Shevtsova, Lilia. *Russia—Lost in Transition: The Yeltsin and Putin Legacies*. Translated by Arch Tait. Washington, D.C.: Carnegie Endowment for International Peace, 2007.

Shlapentokh, Vladimir. *Contemporary Russia as a Feudal Society: A New Perspective on the Post-Soviet Era*. New York: Palgrave Macmillan, 2007.

Snyder, Timothy. *The Reconstruction of Nations: Poland, Ukraine, Lithuania, Belarus, 1569–1999*. New Haven, Conn.: Yale University Press, 2003.

Spohr Readman, Kristina, and Hans-Dietrich Genscher. *Germany and the Baltic Problem after the Cold War: The Development of a New Ostpolitik, 1989–2000*. New York: Routledge, 2004.

Srivastava, Vinayak N. *The Separation of the Party and the State: Political Leadership in Soviet and Post-Soviet Phases*. Aldershot, UK: Ashgate, 1999.

Steen, Anton, and Vladimir Gelman, eds. *Elites and Democratic Development in Russia*. London: Routledge, 2003.

Stoner-Weiss, Kathryn. *Resisting the State: Reform and Retrenchment in Post-Soviet Russia*. Cambridge: Cambridge University Press, 2006.

Szporluk, Roman. "After Empire: What?" *Daedalus* 123, no. 3 (Summer 1994): 21–39.

Thatcher, Ian D. *Regime and Society in Twentieth-Century Russia: Selected Papers from the Fifth World Congress of Central and East European Studies, Warsaw, 1995*. New York: St. Martin's Press, 1999.

Titma, Mikk, and Nancy Tuma. *Modern Russia*. Columbus: McGraw-Hill, 2000.

Trenin, Dmitri. *The End of Eurasia: Russia on the Border between Geopolitics and Globalization*. Washington, D.C.: Carnegie Endowment for International Peace, 2002.

Tucker, Joshua Aaron. *Regional Economic Voting: Russia, Poland, Hungary, Slovakia, and the Czech Republic, 1990–1999.* Cambridge: Cambridge University Press, 2006.

Turovskii, R. F. "A Comparative Analysis of Trends in Regional Development in Russia and Ukraine." *Sociological Research* 40, no. 5 (September/October 2001): 52–75.

Warren, Frank A. *Liberals and Communism: The "Red Decade" Revisited.* New York: Columbia University Press, 1993.

White, Stephen, Alex Pravda, and Zvi Gitelman, eds. *Developments in Russian Politics*, 5th ed. Durham, N.C.: Duke University Press, 2001.

Wilson, Andrew. *Virtual Politics: Faking Democracy in the Post-Soviet World.* New Haven, Conn.: Yale University Press, 2005.

Yakushko, Oksana. "The Impact of Social and Political Changes on Survivors of Political Persecutions in Rural Russia and Ukraine." *Political Psychology* 29, no. 1 (February 2008): 119–30.

Zarycki, Tomasz. "Uses of Russia: The Role of Russia of the Modern Polish National Identity." *East European Politics and Societies* 18, no 4 (Fall 2004): 595–627.

Zyuganov, Gennady. *My Russia: The Political Autobiography of Gennady Zyuganov.* Armonk, N.Y.: M. E. Sharpe, 1997.

Political Parties

Dallin, Alexander. *Political Parties in Russia.* Berkeley: University of California Press, 1993.

Flikke, Geir. "Patriotic Left-Centrism: The Zigzags of the Communist Party of the Russian Federation." *Europe-Asia Studies* 51, no. 2 (March 1999): 275–99.

Gelman, Vladimir. "From 'Feckless Pluralism' to 'Dominant Power Politics'? The Transformation of Russia's Party System." *Democratization* 13, no. 4 (August 2006): 545–61.

———. "Party Politics in Russia: From Competition to Hierarchy." *Europe-Asia Studies* 60, no. 6 (August 2008): 913–30.

———. "Political Opposition in Russia." *Russian Social Science Review* 46, no. 4 (July/August 2005): 5–30.

Gerber, Theodore R. "Membership Benefits or Selection Effects? Why Former Communist Party Members Do Better in Post-Soviet Russia." *Social Science Research* 29, no. 1 (March 2000): 25–50.

Golosov, Grigorii V. "Political Parties, Electoral Systems and Women's Representation in the Regional Legislative Assemblies of Russia, 1995–1998." *Party Politics* 7, no. 1 (January 2001): 45–68.

———. *Political Parties in the Regions of Russia: Democracy Unclaimed.* Boulder, Colo.: Lynne Rienner, 2004.

Hale, Henry E. "The Origins of United Russia and the Putin Presidency: The Role of Contingency in Party-System Development." *Demokratizatsiya* 12, no. 2 (Spring 2004): 169–94.

Hashim, Syed Mohsin. "KPRF Ideology and Its Implications for Democratization in Russia." *Communist and Post-Communist Studies* 32, no. 1 (March 1999): 77–89.

Hutcheson, Derek Stanford. *Political Parties in the Russian Regions.* London: Routledge, 2003.

Kertman, Grigorii. "The Status of the Party in Russian Political Culture." *Russian Social Science Review* 49, no. 4 (July/August 2008): 24–39.

Kiewiet, D. Roderick, and Mikhail G. Myagkov. "Are the Communists Dying Out in Russia?" *Communist and Post-Communist Studies* 35, no. 1 (March 2002): 39–51.

Kulik, Anatoly, and Susanna Pshizova. *Political Parties in Post-Soviet Space: Russia, Belarus, Ukraine, Moldova, and the Baltics.* Westport, Conn.: Praeger, 2005.

Kurilla, Ivan. "Civil Activism without NGOs: The Communist Party as a Civil Society Substitute." *Demokratizatsiya* 10, no. 3 (Summer 2002): 392–400.

Laverty, Nicklaus. "Limited Choices: Russian Opposition Parties and the 2007 Duma Election." *Demokratizatsiya* 16, no. 4 (Fall 2008): 363–82.

Lester, Jeremy. "Overdosing on Nationalism: Gennadii Zyuganov and the Communist Party of the Russian Federation." *New Left Review* 221 (1997): 3–33.

March, Luke. "For Victory? The Crises and Dilemmas of the Communist Party of the Russian Federation." *Europe-Asia Studies* 53, no. 2 (March 2001): 263–90.

———. *The Communist Party in Post-Soviet Russia.* Manchester: Manchester University Press, 2002.

Mote, Victor L., and William Trout. "Political Territoriality and the End of the USSR." *Space and Polity* 7, no. 1 (April 2003): 21–43.

Ogushi, Atsushi. "Money, Property and the Demise of the CPSU." *Journal of Communist Studies and Transition Politics* 21, no. 2 (June 2005): 268–95.

———. "Why Did CPSU Reform Fail? The 28th Party Congress Reconsidered." *Europe-Asia Studies* 59, no. 5 (July 2007): 709–33.

Otto, Robert C. "Gennadii Ziuganov." *Problems of Post-Communism* 46, no. 4 (1999): 37–47.

Oversloot, Hans, and Ruben Verheul. "Managing Democracy: Political Parties and the State in Russia." *Journal of Communist Studies and Transition Politics* 22, no. 3 (2006): 383–405.

Pasynkova, Veronika. "The Communist Party in Contemporary Russia: Problems of Transformation." *Perspectives on European Politics and Society* 6, no. 2 (August 2005): 237–47.

Rabotyazhev, Nikolay, and Eduard Solovyov. "Metamorphoses of the Geopolitical Views of the Communist Party of the Russian Federation." *Social Sciences* 38, no. 4 (2007): 97–109.

Riggs, Jonathan W., and Peter J. Schraeder. "Russia's Political Party System as a (Continued) Impediment to Democratization: The 2003 Duma and 2004 Presidential Elections in Perspective." *Demokratizatsiya* 13, no. 1 (Winter 2005): 141–51.

Rose, Richard. "Ex-Communists in Post-Communist Societies." *Political Quarterly* 67, no. 1 (January/March 1996): 14–25.

Stoner-Weiss, Kathyrn. "The Limited Reach of Russia's Party System: Underinstitutionalization in Dual Transitions." *Politics and Society* 29, no. 3 (September 2001): 385–404.

Wegren, Stephen K. "The Communist Party of Russia." *Party Politics* 10, no. 5 (September 2004): 565–82.

White, David. *The Russian Democratic Party Yabloko: Opposition in a Managed Democracy.* Burlington, VT: Ashgate, 2006.

Wilson, Kenneth. "Party Finance in Russia: Has the 2001 Law 'On Political Parties' Made a Difference?" *Europe-Asia Studies* 59, no. 7 (2007): 1089–1113.

Elections

Åslund, Anders. "The December 2003 and March 2004 Elections in Russia: A Framing Comment." *Eurasian Geography and Economics* 45, no. 4 (June 2004): 280–84.

Clark, William A. "Communist Devolution: The Electoral Decline of the KPRF." *Problems of Post-Communism* 53, no. 1 (2006): 15–25.

Colton, Timothy J., and Jerry F. Hough, eds. *Growing Pains: Russian Democracy and the Election of 1993.* Washington, D.C.: Brookings Institution Press, 1998.

Colton, Timothy J., and Michael McFaul. *Popular Choice and Managed Democracy: The Russian Elections of 1999 and 2000.* Washington, D.C.: Brookings Institution Press, 2003.

Emmons, Terence. *The Formation of Political Parties and the First National Elections in Russia.* Bloomington, Ind.: Iuniverse, 1999.

Gelman, Vladimir, and Grigorii Golosov. *Elections in Russia, 1993–1996: Analyses, Documents and Data.* Berlin: Edition Sigma, 1999.

Herron, Erik S. "Political Actors, Preferences and Election Rule Re-design in Russia and Ukraine." *Democratization* 11, no. 2 (April 2004): 41–59.

Hesli, Vicki L., and William Mark Reisinger. *The 1999–2000 Elections in Russia: Their Impact and Legacy*. Cambridge: Cambridge University Press, 2003.

Kagarlitsky, Boris. "Russia Chooses—and Loses." *Current History* 95, no. 603 (October 1996): 305–15.

Konitzer, Andrew. *Voting for Russia's Governors: Regional Elections and Accountability under Yeltsin and Putin*. Washington, D.C.: Woodrow Wilson Center Press, 2005.

Lentini, Peter. *Elections and Political Order in Russia: The Implications of the 1993 Elections to the Federal Assembly*. Budapest: Central European University Press, 1995.

March, Luke. "Elections by Design: Parties and Patronage in Russia's Regions." *Slavonic and East European Review* 86, no. 3 (July 2008): 587–89.

McFaul, Michael. *Russia between Elections: What the December 1995 Results Really Mean*. Moscow: Carnegie Center, 1996.

Mitchell, R. Judson. *Getting to the Top in the USSR: Cyclical Patterns in the Leadership Succession Process*. Stanford, Calif.: Hoover Press, 1990.

Moraski, Bryon J., and William M. Reisinger. "Eroding Democracy: Federal Intervention in Russia's Gubernatorial Elections." *Democratization* 14, no. 4 (August 2007): 603–21.

Moser, Robert G. *Unexpected Outcomes: Electoral Systems, Political Parties, and Representation in Russia*. Pittsburgh, Pa.: University of Pittsburgh Press, 2001.

Oates, Sarah. *Television, Democracy and Elections in Russia*. London: Taylor & Francis, 2008.

Quinn-Judge, Paul. "Party Spoilers." *New Republic* 203, no. 4 (1990): 11–13.

Rose, Richard, and Neil Munro. *Elections without Order: Russia's Challenge to Vladimir Putin*. Cambridge: Cambridge University Press, 2002.

Smyth, Regina. *Candidate Strategies and Electoral Competition in the Russian Federation: Democracy without Foundation*. Cambridge: Cambridge University Press, 2006.

Wegren, Stephen K. and Andrew Konitzer. "The 2003 Russian Duma Election and the Decline in Rural Support for the Communist Party." *Electoral Studies* 25, no. 4 (December 2006): 677–95.

Wilson, Gary N. "The 1999–2000 Elections in Russia: Their Impact and Legacy." *Canadian Journal of Political Science* 28, no. 3 (September 2005): 794–95.

Ultranationalism

Allensworth, Wayne. *The Russian Question: Nationalism, Modernization, and Post-Communist Russia*. Lanham, Md.: Rowman & Littlefield, 1998.

Andreev, Vasily. "The Seeds of Fascism in Russia." *Prism* 2, no. 7 (5 April 1996).

Dunlop, John B. "Alexander Barkashov and the Rise of National Socialism in Russia." *Demokratizatsiya* 4 (Fall 1996): 519–30.

Eatwell, Roger. "The Rebirth of Right-Wing Charisma? The Cases of Jean-Marie Le Pen and Vladimir Zhirinovsky." *Totalitarian Movements and Political Religions* 3, no. 3 (Winter 2002): 1–22.

Korey, William. *Russian Antisemitism, Pamyat, and the Demonology of Zionism.* Jerusalem: Hebrew University of Jerusalem, 1995.

Laruelle, Marlène. "Aleksandr Dugin: A Russian Version of the European Radical Right?" Kennan Institute Occasional Papers Series #294. Washington, D.C.: Woodrow Wilson International Center for Scholars (2006): 1–32.

———. "The Two Faces of Contemporary Eurasianism: An Imperial Version of Russian Nationalism." *Nationalities Papers* 32, no. 1 (March 2004): 115–36.

Rangsimaporn, Paradorn. "Interpretations of Eurasianism: Justifying Russia's Role in East Asia." *Europe-Asia Studies* 58, no. 3 (May 2006): 371–89.

Romov, Roman. "Russian National Unity and the 'Nation of Slaves.'" *Russian Politics and Law* 39, no. 3 (May/June 2001): 66–77.

Rossman, Vadim Joseph. *Russian Intellectual Antisemitism in the Post-Communist Era.* Lincoln: University of Nebraska Press, 2005.

Shenfield, Stephen D. *Russian Fascism: Traditions, Tendencies, Movements.* Armonk, N.Y.: M. E. Sharpe, 2001.

Shnirelman, Victor A. "Russian Neo-Pagan Myths and Antisemitism." *ACTA— Analysis of Current Trends in Antisemitism.* Jerusalem: Hebrew University of Jerusalem, 1998.

Solovyov, Vladimir, and Elena Klepikova. *Zhirinovsky: The Paradoxes of Russian Fascism.* New York: Viking, 1995.

Yoffe, Mark. "Vladimir Zhirinovsky, the Unholy Fool." *Current History* 93, no. 585 (October 1994): 324–26.

Ethnicity and National Identity

Austin, Paul M. "Soviet Karelian: The Language that Failed." *Slavic Review* 51, no. 1 (Spring 1992): 16–35.

Beskhlebnaya, Natasha. "Sleeping on Graveyards: Traveling through 300 Years of Khakass History." *Russian Life* 50, no. 3 (May/June 2007): 52–58.

Brodsky, Peter. "Are Russian Jews in Danger?" *Commentary* 95, no. 5 (May 1993): 37–40.

Cruikshank, Julie. "Reinscribing Meaning: Memory and Indigenous Identity in Sakha Republic (Yakutia)." *Arctic Anthropology* 37, no. 1 (2000): 96–199.

Derluguian, Georgi M., and Serge Cipko. "The Politics of Identity in a Russian Borderland Province: The Kuban Neo-Cossack Movement, 1989–1996." *Europe-Asia Studies* 49, no. 8 (December 1997): 1485–1500.

Duncan, Peter J. S. "Contemporary Russian Identity between East and West." *Historical Journal* 48, no. 1 (March 2005): 277–94.

"The Dying Fish Swims in Water." *Economist* 377, no. 8458 (24 December 2005): 73–74.

European Commission against Racism and Intolerance. *Report on the Russian Federation.* Strasbourg, France: Council of Europe, 1999.

Faller, Helen M. "Repossessing Kazan as a Form of Nation-Building in Tatarstan, Russia." *Journal of Muslim Minority Affairs* 22, no. 1 (April 2002): 81–90.

Golovnev, Andrei V., and Gail Osherenko. *Siberian Survival: The Nenets and Their Story.* Ithaca, N.Y.: Cornell University Press, 1999.

Gorenburg, Dmitry. "Identity Change in Bashkortostan: Tatars into Bashkirs and Back." *Ethnic and Racial Studies* 22, no. 3 (May 1999): 554–80.

——. *Nationalism for the Masses: Minority Ethnic Mobilization in the Russian Federation.* Cambridge: Cambridge University Press, 2003.

——. "Nationalism for the Masses: Popular Support for Nationalism in Russia's Ethnic Republics." *Europe-Asia Studies* 53, no. 1 (January 2001): 73–104.

Gray, Patty A. *The Predicament of Chukotka's Indigenous Movement: Post-Soviet Activism in the Russian Far North.* Cambridge: Cambridge University Press, 2005.

Gudkov, Lev D. *Negativnaya Identichnost* [Negative identity]. Moscow: Novoe Literaturnoe Obozrenie, 2004.

Hanbury-Tenison, Robin. "Native Peoples of Russia's Far East." *Asian Affairs* 25, no. 2 (June 1994): 131–37.

Iskhakov, Damir M. "The Tatar Ethnic Community."*Anthropology and Archeology of Eurasia* 43, no. 2 (Fall 2004): 8–28.

Iurchenkov, Valerii. "The Mordvins: Dilemmas of Mobilization in a Biethnic Community." *Nationalities Papers* 29, no. 2 (March 2001): 85–95.

Jacobson, Jessica. "Descendants of the Swan." *Russian Life* 46, no. 6 (November/December 2003): 56–62.

Jordan, Peter. "Ethnic Survival and the Siberian Khanty: On-Going Transformations in Seasonal Mobility and Traditional Culture." *Nomadic Peoples* 8, no. 1 (2004): 17–42.

Khakimov, R. S. "The Tatars." *Anthropology and Archeology of Eurasia* 43, no. 3 (Winter 2004/2005): 45–61.

Khazanov, Anatoly. *After the USSR: Ethnicity, Nationalism and Politics in the Commonwealth of Independent States.* Madison: University of Wisconsin Press, 1995.

Korostelina, Karina V. "Identity, Autonomy and Conflict in Republics of Russia and Ukraine." *Communist and Post-Communist Studies* 41, no. 1 (March 2008): 79–91.

Korotayev, Andrey, Alexander Kazankov, Svetlana Borinskaya, Daria Khaltourina, and Dmitri Bondarenko. "Ethnographic Atlas XXX: Peoples of Siberia." *Ethnology* 43, no. 1 (Winter 2004): 83–92.

Kuzio, Taras. "Russian National Identity and Foreign Policy toward the 'Near Abroad.'" *Prism* 8, no. 4 (30 April 2002).

Mandelstam Balzer, Majorie. "Hot and Cold: Interethnic Relations in Siberia." In *At the Risk of Being Heard: Identity, Indigenous Rights, and Postcolonial States*, edited by Bartholomew Dean and Jerome M. Levi. University of Michigan Press, 2003.

Marushiakova, Elena, and Vesselin Popov. "Ethnic Identities and Economic Strategies of the Gypsies in the Countries of the Former USSR." In *Nomaden und Sesshafte—Fragen, Methoden, Ergebnisse*. Edited by Thomas Herzog and Wolfgang Holzwarth, 289–310. Halle, Germany: Orientwissenschaftliches Zentrum, 2003.

Matveeva, A., and C. McCartney. "Policy Responses to an Ethnic Community Division: Lezgins in Azerbaijan." *International Journal on Minority and Group Rights* 5, no. 3 (1997): 213–51.

Minahan, James. *The Former Soviet Union's Diverse Peoples: A Reference Sourcebook.* Santa Barbara, Calif.: ABC-CLIO, 2004.

Molchanov, Mikhail A. *Political Culture and National Identity in Russian-Ukrainian Relations.* College Station: Texas A&M University Press, 2002.

Panfilov, Oleg. "Rebirth of Russian Nationalism." *Index on Censorship* 35, no. 1 (2006): 142–48.

Pika, Alexander, Jens Dahl, and Inge Larsen, eds. *Anxious North: Indigenous Peoples in Soviet and Post-Soviet Russia, Selected Documents, Letters, and Articles.* Copenhagen: IWGIA, 1996.

Popov, Anton, and Igor Kuznetsov. "Ethnic Discrimination and the Discourse of 'Indigenization': The Regional Regime, 'Indigenous Majority' and Ethnic Minorities in Krasnodar Krai in Russia." *Nationalities Papers* 36, no. 2 (May 2008): 223–52.

Resler, Tamara J. "Dilemmas of Democratisation: Safeguarding Minorities in Russia, Ukraine and Lithuania." *Europe-Asia Studies* 49, no. 1 (January 1997): 89–116.

Robbek, Vasili. "Language Situation in the Sakha Republic (Yakutia)." *Bicultural Education in the North: Ways of Preserving and Enhancing Indigenous Peoples' Languages and Traditional Knowledge.* Edited by Erich Kasten, 113–22. Munster: Waxmann Verlag.

Ryvkina, Rozalina V., and Murray Yanowitch. "Jews in Present-Day Russia." *Russian Social Science Review* 39, no. 3 (May/June 1998): 52–68.

Schindler, Debra L. "Redefining Tradition and Renegotiating Ethnicity in Native Russia." *Arctic Anthropology* 34, no. 1 (1997): 193–211.

Shabaev, I. P. "The Territorial Community and Ethnic Views of the Population of Komi." *Sociological Research* 46, no. 2 (March/April 2007): 62–76.

Shlapentokh, Dmitry. "'Red-to-Brown' Jews and Russian Liberal Reform." *Washington Quarterly* 21, no. 4 (Autumn 1998): 107–26.

Skinner, Barbara. "Identity Formation in the Russian Cossack Revival." *Europe-Asia Studies* 46, no. 6 (October 1994): 1017–37.

Stricker, Gerd. "Ethnic Germans in Russia and the Former Soviet Union." In *Ethnic Identity and Cultural Belonging*, edited by Stefan Wolff. London: Berghahn, 2001.

Tishkov, Valery. "Ethnic Conflicts in the Former USSR: The Use and Misuse of Typologies and Data." *Journal of Peace Research* 36, no. 5 (September 1999): 571–91.

——. "Forget the Nation: Post-nationalist Understanding of Nationalism," *Ethnic and Racial Studies* 23, no. 4 (2000): 625–50.

Toje, Hege. "Cossack Identity in the New Russia: Kuban Cossack Revival and Local Politics." *Europe-Asia Studies* 58, no. 7 (November 2006): 1057–77.

Tolts, Mark. "The Post-Soviet Jewish Population in Russia and the World." *Jews in Russia and Eastern Europe* 1, no. 52 (2004): 37–63.

Tolz, Vera. 1998. "Forging the Nation: National Identity and Nation Building in Post-Communist Russia." *Europe-Asia Studies* 50, no. 6 (September): 993–1022.

Tsypanov, Evgenii. "Language and Ethnic Mobilization among the Komi in the Post-Soviet Period." *Nationalities Papers* 29, no. 2 (March 2001): 109–28.

Tuminez, Astrid S. *Russian Nationalism since 1856: Ideology and the Making of Foreign Policy*. Lanham, Md.: Rowman & Littlefield, 2000.

Veinguer, Aurora Alvarez, and Howard H. Davis. "Building a Tatar Elite." *Ethnicities* 7, no. 2 (June 2007): 186–207.

Vitebsky, Piers. *The Reindeer People: Living with Animals and Spirits in Siberia*. Chicago: Houghton Mifflin Harcourt, 2006.

Wiget, Andrew, and Olga Balalaeva. "Khanty Communal Reindeer Sacrifice: Belief, Subsistence and Cultural Persistence in Contemporary Siberia." *Arctic Anthropology* 38, no. 1 (2001): 82–99.

Williams, Brian Glyn. *The Crimean Tatars: The Diaspora Experience and the Forging of a Nation*. Leiden, Netherlands: Brill, 2001.

Ethnic Republics and Regionalism

Aidinov, Iurii. "The 'Red Belt.'" *Russian Social Science Review* 38, no. 4 (July/August 1997): 46–51.

Akhmetov, Rashid. "Presidential Elections in Chuvashia: Martial Arts, Eastern-Style." *Prism* 4, no. 4 (20 February 1998).

Alatalu, Toomas. "Tuva—A State Reawakens." *Soviet Studies* 44, no. 5 (1992): 881–94.

Alexander, James, and Jorn Gravingholt. "Evaluating Democratic Progress inside Russia: The Komi Republic and the Republic of Bashkortostan." *Democratization* 9, no. 4 (Winter 2003): 77–105.

Alexseev, Mikhail A. *Center-Periphery Conflict in Post-Soviet Russia: A Federation Imperiled.* New York: Macmillan, 1999.

Alexseev, Mikhail A., and Vladimir Vagin. "Russian Regions in Expanding Europe: The Pskov Connection." *Europe-Asia Studies* 51, no. 1 (January 1999): 43–64.

Argounova-Low, Tatiana. "Diamonds: A Contested Symbol of the Republic of Sakha (Yakutia)." In *Properties of Culture—Culture as Property*, edited by Erich Kasten, 257–65. Berlin: Fietrich Reimer Verlag.

Balzer, Marjorie. "The Tension between Might and Rights: Siberians and Energy Developers in Post-Socialist Binds." *Europe-Asia Studies* 58, no. 4 (June 2006): 567–88.

Balzer, Marjorie Mandel, and Uliana Vinokurova. "Nationalism, Interethnic Relations and Federalism: The Case of the Sakha Republic (Yakutia)." *Europe-Asia Studies* 48, no. 1 (January 1996): 101–19.

Birch, Julian. "Ossetiya—Land of Uncertain Frontiers and Manipulative Elites." *Central Asian Survey* 18, no. 4 (December 1999): 501–34.

Boiko, Ivan, Iuri Markov, and Valentina Kharitonova "The Chuvash Republic." *Anthropology and Archeology of Eurasia* 44, no. 2 (Fall 2005): 41–60.

Borisov, Sergei V. "The Actual Political Regime in Nizhnii Novgorod Oblast." *Sociological Research* 40, no. 2 (2001): 18–43.

Brooke, James. "Birobidzhan Journal: A Promised Land in Siberia?" *New York Times* (11 July 1996): 4.

Browning, Christopher S., and Pertti Joenniemi. "Contending Discourses of Marginality: The Case of Kaliningrad." *Geopolitics* 9, no. 3 (Autumn 2004): 699–730.

Brumfield, William C. "Perm Gateway to Eurasia." *Russian Life* 43, no. 1 (January/February 2000): 44–54.

Brushtein, Il'ia. "The Island of Kalmykia." *Russian Politics and Law* 45, no. 6 (November/December 2007): 6–52.

Bukharaev, Ravil. *Tatarstan: A "Can Do" Culture—President Mintimer Shaimiev and the Power of Common Sense.* Folkstone, UK: Global Oriental, 2007.

———. *The Model of Tatarstan: Under President Mintimer Shaimiev.* New York: Macmillan, 1999.

Bychkova Jordan, Bella, and Terry G. Jordan-Bychkov. *Siberian Village: Land and Life in the Sakha Republic*. Minneapolis: University of Minnesota Press, 2001.

Cashaback, David. "Assessing Asymmetrical Federal Design in the Russian Federation: A Case Study of Language Policy in Tatarstan." *Europe-Asia Studies* 60, no. 2 (March 2008): 249–75.

Černy, Karel. "From the Land of a Chess Despot." *New Presence: The Prague Journal of Central European Affairs* 8, no. 1 (Spring 2006): 22–23.

Clogg, Rachel. "The Politics of Identity in Post-Soviet Abkhazia: Managing Diversity and Unresolved Conflict." *Nationalities Papers* 36, no. 2 (May 2008): 305–29.

Cornell, Svante E. "Conflicts in the North Caucasus." *Central Asian Survey* 17, no. 3 (1998): 409–41.

Crosston, Matthew. *Shadow Separatism: Implications for Democratic Consolidation*. Surrey, UK: Ashgate, 2004.

Domorin, Alexander N. "Russian Federation." In *A Global Dialogue on Federalism*. Vol. 3, edited by Katy Le Roy and Cheryl Saunders. Montreal: McGill-Queen's University Press, 2006.

Drobizheva, Leokadiya. "Comparison of Elite Groups in Tatarstan, Sakha, Magadan and Orenburg." *Post-Soviet Affairs* 15, no. 4 (1999): 387–406.

"Earth to Kalmykia, Come in Please." *Economist* 345, no. 8048 (20 December 1997–2 January 1998): 39–40.

Ferguson, Rob. "Will Democracy Strike Back? Workers and Politics in Kuzbass." *Europe-Asia Studies* 50, no. 3 (May 1998): 445–67.

Filatov, Sergei, and Lawrence Uzzell. "Religious Life in Siberia: The Case of Khakasia." *Religion, State and Society* 28, no. 1 (March 2000): 105–15.

Fondahl, Gail, and Olga Lazebnik. "Aboriginal Territorial Rights and Sovereignty of the Sakha Republic." *Post-Soviet Geography and Economics* 41, no. 6 (September 2000): 401–16.

Fuller, Liz. "Russia: Balkars Launch New Campaign for Own Republic." *Radio Free Europe/Radio Liberty* (31 May 2005).

Gelman, Vladimir, Sergei Ryzhenkov, Michael Brie, Boris Ovchinnikov, and Igor Semenov, eds. *Making and Breaking Democratic Transitions: The Comparative Politics of Russia's Regions*. Lanham, Md.: Rowman & Littlefield, 2005.

Giulliano, Elise. "Secessionism from the Bottom Up." *World Politics* 58, no. 2 (January 2006): 276–310.

Glatter, Pete. "Continuity and Change in the Tyumen' Regional Elite 1991–2001." *Europe-Asia Studies* 55, no. 3 (May 2003): 401–35.

Golosov, Grigorii V. "From Adygeya to Yaroslavl: Factors of Party Development in the Regions of Russia, 1995–1998." *Europe-Asia Studies* 51, no. 8 (December 1999): 1333–65.

Graney, Katherine E. "Education Reform in Tatarstan and Bashkortostan: Sovereignty Projects in Post-Soviet Russia." *Europe-Asia Studies* 51, no. 4 (1999): 611–30.

———. *Of Khans and Kremlins: Tatarstan and the Future of Ethno-Federalism in Russia.* Lanham, Md.: Lexington Books, 2009.

Grin, François. "Kalmykia, Victim of Stalinist Genocide: From Oblivion to Reassertion." *Journal of Genocide Research* 3, no. 1 (March 2001): 97–116.

Guchinova, Elza-Bair. *The Kalmyks.* Translated by David C. Lewis. London: RoutledgeCurzon, 2006.

Hagendoorn, Louk, Edwin Poppe, and Anca Minescu. "Support for Separatism in Ethnic Republics of the Russian Federation." *Europe-Asia Studies* 60, no. 3 (May 2008): 353–73.

Halemba, Agnieszka. "Contemporary Religious Life in the Republic of Altai: The Interaction of Buddhism and Shamanism." *Sibirica* 3, no. 3 (October 2003): 165–82.

Herd, Graeme P., and Anne Aldis, eds. *Russian Regions and Regionalism: Strength through Weakness.* London: RoutledgeCurzon, 2003.

Hughes, James. "Regionalism in Russia: The Rise and Fall of Siberian Agreement." *Europe-Asia Studies* 47, no. 7 (1994): 1133–61.

Hutcheson, Derek S. "The Dynamics of Russian Politics: Putin's Reform of Federal-Regional Relations." *Slavic Review: Interdisciplinary Quarterly of Russian, Eurasian, and East European Studies* 64, no. 1 (Spring 2005): 209–10.

Ilishev, Ildus G. "Nation-Building and Minority Rights in Post-Soviet Russia: The Case of Bashkortostan." In *Democracy and Pluralism in Muslim Eurasia*, edited by Yaacov Ro'i, 307–28. London: Frank Cass, 2004.

Kahn, Jeff. "The Parade of Sovereignties: Establishing the Vocabulary of the New Russian Federalism." *Post-Soviet Affairs* 16, no. 1 (2000): 58–89.

Kaloudis, Stergos. "The Institutional Design of Russian Federalism: A Comparative Study of Three Republics; Tatarstan, Dagestan, and Chechnya." *Demokratizatsiya* 15, no. 1 (Winter 2007): 139–51.

Kempton, Daniel R., and Terry D. Clark, eds. *Unity or Separation: Center-Periphery Relations in the Former Soviet Union.* Westport, Conn.: Greenwood Publishing Group, 2002.

Kirkow, Peter. "Regional Politics and Market Reform in Russia: The Case of the Altai." *Europe-Asia Studies* 46, no. 7 (1994): 1163–87.

Kolbin, Boris. "Republic of Bashkortostan: International and Foreign Economic Relations." *International Affairs: A Russian Journal of World Politics, Diplomacy and International Relations* 51, no. 1 (2005): 135–43.

Kondrashov, Sergei. *Nationalism and the Drive for Sovereignty in Tatarstan, 1988–92: Origins and Development*. New York: St. Martin's Press, 2000.

Kontorovich, Alexei, Vladimir Kashirtsev, Andrei Korzhubaev, and Alexander Safronov. "The General Plan for a Gas and Oil Complex in East Siberia and the Republic of Sakha (Yakutia) and Its Significance for Russia's Socioeconomic Development and Energy Security." *Far Eastern Affairs* 35, no. 1 (2007): 74–81.

Laine, Antti. "Where East Meets West: The Last Stand of Finns and Karelians in Contemporary Karelia?" *Nationalities Papers* 29, no. 1 (March 2001): 53–67.

Lallemand, Jean-Charles. "Who Rules Smolensk Oblast?" EWI Russian Regional Report 3, no. 40 (8 October 1998): 1–5.

Lallukka, Seppo, and Liudmila Nikitina. "Continuing with Perm', Turning to Syktyvkar, or Standing on One's Own? The Debate about the Status of the Komi-Permiak Autonomous Okrug." *Nationalities Papers* 29, no. 1 (March 2001): 129–51.

Leisse, Olaf, and Utta-Kristin Leisse. "A Siberian Challenge: Dealing with Multiethnicity in the Republic of Buryatia." *Nationalities Papers* 35, no. 4 (September 2007): 773–88.

Luehrmann, Sonja. "Recycling Cultural Construction: Desecularisation in Postsoviet Mari El." *Religion, State and Society* 33, no. 1 (March 2005): 35–56.

Malashenko, Alexei. "Moscow Keeps Wary Eye on Daghestan." *Le monde diplomatique* (October 1999).

Marples, David R. "Environmental and Health Problems in the Sakha Republic." *Post-Soviet Geography and Economics*, 40, no. 1 (January/February 1999): 62–77.

Martianov, Viktor. "The Decline of Public Politics in Russia: From Public Politics to Political Administration: The Depoliticization of the Regions." *Russian Politics and Law* 45, no. 5 (September/October 2007): 67–82.

Matsuzato, Kimitaka. "Authoritarian Transformations of the Mid-Volga National Republics: An Attempt at Macro-Regionology." *Journal of Communist Studies and Transition Politics* 20, no. 2 (June 2004): 98–123.

McCann, Leo. *Economic Development in Tatarstan: Global Markets and a Russian Region*. London: Routledge, 2005.

Misiunas, Romuald J. "Rootless Russia: Kaliningrad—Status and Identity. *Diplomacy and Statecraft* 15, no. 2 (June 2004): 385–411.

Moses, Joel C. "Political-Economic Elites and Russian Regional Elections 1999–2000: Democratic Tendencies in Kaliningrad, Perm and Volgograd." *Europe-Asia Studies* 54, no. 6 (September 2002): 905–31.

Mote, Victor L. *Siberia—Worlds Apart*. Boulder, Colo.: Westview Press, 1998.

680 • BIBLIOGRAPHY

Nunn, Sam, and Adam N. Stulberg. "The Many Faces of Modern Russia." *Foreign Affairs* 79, no. 2 (March/April 2000): 45–62.

Nyman, Ann-Sofie. "The Human Rights Situation of the Mari Minority of the Republic of Mari El: A Study of the Titular Nationality of One of Russia's Ethnic Regions." Vienna: International Helsinki Federation for Human Rights, 2006.

Oversloot, Hans, and Ger P. van de Berg. "Politics and the Ethnic Divide: Is Dagestan Changing from Complex to Simple Oligarchy?" *Journal of Communist Studies and Transition Politics* 21, no. 3 (September 2005): 307–31.

Pallot, Judith, and Moran, Dominique. "Surviving the Margins in Post-Soviet Russia: Forestry Villages in Northern Perm' Oblast." *Post-Soviet Geography and Economics* 41, no. 5 (July 2000): 341–62.

Perovic, Jeronim. "Regionalisation Trends in Russia: Between the Soviet Legacy and the Forces of Globalisation." *Geopolitics* 9, no. 2 (Summer 2004): 342–77.

Petro, Nicolai N. "A Tale of Two Regions: Novgorod and Pskov as Models of Symbolic Development." *Journal of Socio-Economics* 35, no. 6 (December 2006): 946–58.

Ponarin, Eduard. "Changing Federalism and the Islamic Challenge in Tatarstan." *Demokratizatsiya* 16, no. 3 (Summer 2008): 265–76.

Pustilnik, Marina. "Karachaevo-Cherkessia: Caucasian Stresses." *Transitions* 1, no. 3 (15 March 1995).

Richardson, Curtis. "Stalinist Terror and the Kalmyks' National Revival: A Cultural and Historical Perspective." *Journal of Genocide Research* 4, no. 3 (September 2002): 441–51.

Ross, Cameron. *Federalism and Democratisation in Russia.* Manchester: Manchester University Press, 2002.

——, ed. *Regional Politics in Russia.* Manchester: Manchester University Press, 2002.

Round, John. "Rescaling Russia's Geography: The Challenges of Depopulating the Northern Periphery." *Europe-Asia Studies* 57, no. 5 (July 2005): 705–27.

Ruttkay-Miklián, Eszter. "Revival and Survival in Iugra." *Nationalities Papers* 29, no. 1 (March 2001): 153–70.

Schrad, Mark Lawrence. "Rag Doll Nations and the Politics of Differentiation on Arbitrary Borders: Karelia and Moldova." *Nationalities Papers* 32, no. 2 (June 2004): 457–96.

Sharafutdinova, Gulnaz. "Chechnya versus Tatarstan." *Problems of Post-Communism* 47, no. 2 (March/April 2000): 13–22.

——. "Paradiplomacy in the Russian Regions: Tatarstan's Search for Statehood." *Europe-Asia Studies* 55, no. 4 (June 2003): 613–29.

Skvortsova, Galina. "Karelia, Where the Northern Rivers Run." *Russian Life* 42, no. 5 (August/September 1999): 18–29.

Slocum, John W. "A Sovereign State within Russia? The External Relations of the Republic of Tatarstan." *Global Society: Journal of Interdisciplinary International Relations* 13, no. 1 (January 1999): 49–75.

Specter, Michael. "Planet Kirsan." *New Yorker* 82, no. 10 (24 April 2006): 112–22.

Starobin, Paul. "Send Me to Siberia." *National Geographic* 213, no. 6 (June 2008): 60–85.

Stavrakis, Peter J., Joan DeBardeleben, and Larry Black, eds. *Beyond the Monolith: The Emergence of Regionalism in Post-Soviet Russia.* Washington, D.C.: Woodrow Wilson Center Press, 1997.

Stepanov, Valery. "Ethnic Tensions and Separatism in Russia." *Journal of Ethnic and Migration Studies* 26, no. 2 (April 2000): 305–32.

Sullivan, Stefan. "Interethnic Relations in Post-Soviet Tuva." *Ethnic and Racial Studies* 18, no. 1 (January 1995): 64–88.

Taagepera, Rein. *The Finno-Ugric Republics and the Russian State.* New York: Routledge, 1999.

Thornton, Judith, and Charles E. Ziegler, eds. *Russia's Far East: A Region at Risk.* Seattle: University of Washington Press, 2002.

Tichotsky, John. *Russia's Diamond Colony: The Republic of Sakha.* London: Routledge, 2000.

Troyakova, Tamara. "The Russian Far East: Isolation or Integration?" *Problems of Post-Communism* 54, no. 2 (March/April 2007): 61–71.

"Understanding Russian Regionalism." *Problems of Post-Communism* 54, no. 2 (March/April 2007): 72–74.

Vesilind, Priit J., and Dennis Chamberlin. "Kaliningrad." *National Geographic* 191, no. 3 (March 1997): 110–23.

Vovina, Olessia P. "Building the Road to the Temple: Religion and National Revival in the Chuvash Republic." *Nationalities Papers* 28, no. 4 (December 2000): 695–706.

Ware, Robert Bruce, and Enver Kisriev. "After Chechnya: At Risk in Dagestan." *Politics* 18, no. 1 (February 1998): 39–47.

———. "Political Stability in Dagestan." *Problems of Post-Communism* 47, no. 2 (March/April 2000): 23–33.

Ware, Robert Bruce, Enver Kisriev, Werner Patzelt, and Ute Roericht. "Dagestani Perspectives on Russia and Chechnya." *Post-Soviet Affairs* 18, no. 4 (December 2002): 306–331.

———. "Stability in the Caucasus." *Problems of Post-Communism* 50, no. 2 (March/April 2003): 12–23.

Williams, Brad. "Federal–Regional Relations in Russia and the Northern Territories Dispute: The Rise and Demise of the 'Sakhalin Factor.'" *Pacific Review* 19, no. 3 (September 2006): 263–85.

———. *Resolving the Russo-Japanese Territorial Dispute: Hokkaido-Sakhalin Relations.* London: Routledge, 2007.

Yemelianova, Galina M. "Islam and Nation Building in Tatarstan and Dagestan of the Russian Federation." *Nationalities Papers* 27, no. 4 (December 1999): 605–29.

———. "Shaimiev's 'Khanate' on the Volga and Its Russian Subjects." *Asian Ethnicity* 1, no. 1 (March 2000): 37–52.

Yorke, Andrew. "Business and Politics in Krasnoyarsk Krai." *Europe-Asia Studies* 55, no. 2 (March 2003): 241–62.

Zhukovskaia, N. L. "The Republic of Kalmykia." *Russian Social Science Review* 34, no. 5 (September/October 1993): 80–96.

Ziker, John P. "Assigned Territories, Family/Clan/Communal Holdings, and Common-Pool Resources in the Taimyr Autonomous Region, Northern Russia." *Human Ecology: An Interdisciplinary Journal* 31, no. 3 (September 2003): 331–68.

Zimine, Dmitri A., and Michael J. Bradshaw. "Regional Adaptation to Economic Crisis in Russia: The Case of Novgorod Oblast." *Post-Soviet Geography and Economics* 40, no. 5 (July/August 1999): 335–353.

Chechen Conflict

Anonymous. "What Life Is Like in Chechnya under the Russian Occupation—the Realities of Today's Chechnya." *Central Asian Survey* 22, no. 4 (December 2003): 459–64.

Bowker, Mike. "Russia and Chechnya: The Issue of Secession." *Nations and Nationalism* 10, no. 4 (October 2004): 461–78.

Boykewich, Stephen. "Russia after Beslan." *Virginia Quarterly Review* 81, no. 1 (Winter 2005): 156–88.

Campana, Aurélie. "The Effects of War on the Chechen National Identity Construction." *National Identities* 8, no. 2 (June 2006): 129–48.

Colarusso, John. "Chechnya: The War without Winners." *Current History* 94, no. 594 (October 1995): 329–36.

de Waal, Thomas. "A Journalist Reflects on the Two Wars in Chechnya." *Central Asian Survey* 22, no. 4 (December 2003): 465–68.

Evangelista, Matthew. *The Chechen Wars: Will Russia Go the Way of the Soviet Union?* Washington, D.C.: Brookings Institution Press, 2002.

Finch, Raymond C., III. "A Face of Future Battle: Chechen Fighter Shamil Basayev." *Military Review* 77, no. 3 (May/June 1997): 34–42.

Gall, Carlotta, and Thomas de Waal. *Chechnya: Calamity in the Caucasus.* New York: New York University Press, 1998.

Gammer, Moshe. *The Lone Wolf and the Bear: Three Centuries of Chechen Defiance of Russian Rule.* Pittsburgh, Pa.: University of Pittsburgh Press, 2006.

German, Tracey C. *Russia's Chechen War.* London: RoutledgeCurzon, 2003.

Goltz, Thomas. *Chechnya Diary: A War Correspondent's Story of Surviving the War in Chechnya.* New York: St. Martin's Press, 2003.

Greene, Stanley. *Open Wound: Chechnya 1994 to 2003.* London: Trolley, 2003.

Groskop, Viv. "Chechnya's Deadly 'Black Widows.'" *New Statesman* 133, no. 4704 (6 September 2004): 32–33.

Hahn, Gordon M. "The Jihadi Insurgency and the Russian Counterinsurgency in the North Caucasus." *Post-Soviet Affairs* 24, no. 1 (January–March 2008): 1–39.

Hertog, Katrien. "A Self-Fulfilling Prophecy: The Seeds of Islamic Radicalisation in Chechnya." *Religion, State and Society* 33, no. 3 (September 2005): 239–52.

Hughes, James. *Chechnya: From Nationalism to Jihad.* Philadelphia: University of Pennsylvania Press, 2007.

——. "The Chechnya Conflict: Freedom Fighters or Terrorists?" *Demokratizatsiya* 15, no. 3 (Summer 2007): 293–311.

Jean, Francois. "Chechnya: Moscow's Revenge." *Harvard International Review* 22, no. 3 (Fall 2000): 16–21.

Karny, Yo'av. *Highlanders: A Journey into the Caucasus in Search of Memory.* New York: Macmillan, 2000.

Lieven, Anatol. *Chechnya: Tombstone of Russian Power.* New Haven, Conn.: Yale University Press, 1998.

Nichols, Johanna. "The Chechen Refugees." *Berkeley Journal of International Law* 18, no. 2 (2000): 241–59.

Politkovskaya, Anna. *A Small Corner of Hell: Dispatches from Chechnya.* Translated by Alexander Burry and Tatiana Tulchinsky. Chicago: University of Chicago Press, 2003.

Russell, John. "Terrorists, Bandits, Spooks and Thieves: Russian Demonisation of the Chechens before and since 9/11." *Third World Quarterly* 26, no. 1 (2005): 101–16.

——. "The Geopolitics of Terrorism: Russia's Conflict with Islamic Extremism." *Eurasian Geography and Economics* 50, no. 2 (March/April 2009): 184–96.

Sagramoso, Domitilla. "Violence and Conflict in the Russian North Caucasus." *International Affairs* 83, no. 4 (July 2007): 681–705.

Sakwa, Richard. *Chechnya: From Past to Future*. New York: Anthem Press, 2005.

Shlapentokh, Vladimir. "The Terrorist Basayev as a Major Political Actor in Russia." *World Affairs* 167, no. 4 (Spring 2005): 139–45.

Sokirianskaia, Ekaterina. "Families and Clans in Ingushetia and Chechnya. A Fieldwork Report." *Central Asian Survey* 24, no. 4 (December 2005): 453–67.

Soldatova, G. U. "The Former Checheno-Ingushetia." *Russian Social Science Review* 34, no. 6 (November/December 1993): 52–72.

Tishkov, Valery. *Chechnya: Life in a War-Torn Society*. Berkeley: University of California Press, 2004.

Trenin, Dmitri V., Aleksei Vsevolodovich Malashenko, and Anatol Lieven. *Russia's Restless Frontier: The Chechnya Factor in Post-Soviet Russia*. Washington, D.C.: Carnegie Endowment for International Peace, 2004.

Trenin, Dmitri, Aleksei V. Malashenko, and Anatol Lieven, eds. *Russia's Restless Frontier: The Chechnya Factor in Post-Soviet Russia*. Washington, D.C: Carnegie Endowment for International Peace, 2004.

Wood, Tony. *Chechnya: The Case for Independence*. London: Verso, 2007.

Foreign Policy and International Relations

Adams, Jan S. "The U.S.-Russian Face-off in the Caspian Basin." *Problems of Post-Communism* 47, no. 1 (2000): 49–58.

Akerman, Ella. "September 11: Implications for Russia's Central Asian Policy and Strategic Realignment." *Review of International Affairs* 1, no. 3 (Spring 2002): 1–16.

Allison, Roy, and Lena Jonson. *Central Asian Security: The New International Context*. Washington, D.C.: Brookings Institution Press, 2001.

Allison, Roy, Margot Light, and Stephen White, eds. *Putin's Russia and the Enlarged Europe*. Malden, Mass.: Blackwell, 2006.

Ambrosio, Thomas. *Challenging America's Global Preeminence: Russia's Quest for Multipolarity*. Aldershot, UK: Ashgate, 2005.

———. "The Political Success of Russia-Belarus Relations: Insulating Minsk from a Color Revolution." *Demokratizatsiya* 14, no. 3 (Summer 2006): 407–34.

Ananieva, Elena. "Great Britain: Summit in Chequers." *International Affairs: A Russian Journal of World Politics, Diplomacy and International Relations* 48, no. 2 (2002): 54–62.

Åslund, Anders. "Putin's Lurch toward Tsarism and Neoimperialism: Why the United States Should Care." *Demokratizatsiya* 16, no. 1 (Winter 2008): 17–25.

Asmolov, Konstantin. "Russian and South Korean Scholars on Today's Problems of North Korea and Interkorean Relations." *Far Eastern Affairs* 34, no. 4 (2006): 133–43.

Azizian, Rouben, and Peter Vasilieff. "Russia and Pakistan: The Difficult Path to Rapprochement." *Asian Affairs: An American Review* 30, no. 1 (Spring 2003): 36–55.

Bacik, Gökhan. "The Blue Stream Project, Energy Co-operation and Conflicting Interests." *Turkish Studies* 2, no. 2 (Autumn 2001): 85–93.

———. "Turkey and Russia: Whither Modernization?" *Journal of Economic and Social Research* 3, no. 2 (2001): 51–72.

Bain, Mervyn J. *Cuban Russian Relations since 1992: Continuing Camaraderie in a Post-Soviet World*. Lanham, Md.: Rowman & Littlefield, 2008.

Baranovsky, Vladimir. *Russia and Europe: The Emerging Security Agenda*. Oxford: Oxford University Press, 1997.

Batbayar, Tsedendamba. "Mongolian-Russian Relations in the Past Decade." *Asian Survey* 43, no. 6 (November/December 2003): 951–70.

Bazhanov, Eugene, and Natasha Bazhanov. "The Evolution of Russian-Korean Relations: External and Internal Factors." *Asian Survey* 34, no. 9 (September 1994): 789–98.

Beloff, Max. *Beyond the Soviet Union: The Fragmentation of Power*. Aldershot, UK: Ashgate, 1997.

Bishku, Michael B. "Turkey, Ethnicity, and Oil in the Caucasus." *Journal of Third World Studies* 18, no. 2 (Fall 2001): 13–23.

Blank, Stephen. "Russian Energy and the Korean Peninsula." *East Asia: An International Quarterly* 25, no. 1 (April 2008): 7–33.

———. "Russian Policy and the Changing Korean Question." *Asian Survey* 35, no. 8 (August 1995): 711–25.

Blank, Stephen, and Alvin Z. Rubinstein, eds. *Imperial Decline: Russia's Changing Role in Asia*. Durham, N.C.: Duke University Press, 1997.

Bregadze, Aleksandr. "Russia-France: Old Friends are Best." *International Affairs: A Russian Journal of World Politics, Diplomacy and International Relations* 49, no. 1 (2003): 64–73.

Brovkin, Vladimir. "Who Is with Whom: The United States, the European Union, and Russia on the Eve of War in Iraq." *Demokratizatsiya* 11, no. 2 (Spring 2003): 212–22.

Bunce, Valerie. "Peaceful versus Violent State Dismemberment: A Comparison of the Soviet Union, Yugoslavia, and Czechoslovakia." *Politics and Society* 27, no. 2 (June 1999): 217–37.

———. "Subversive Institutions: The End of the Soviet State in Comparative Perspective." *Post-Soviet Affairs* 14, no. 4 (October–December 1998): 323–54.

Buszynski, Leszek. "Oil and Territory in Putin's Relations with China and Japan." *Pacific Review* 19, no. 3 (September 2006): 287–303.

Chang, Gordon G. "How China and Russia Threaten the World." *Commentary* 123, no. 6 (June 2007): 24–29.

Chufrin, Gennadii I. *The Security of the Caspian Sea Region.* Oxford: Oxford University Press, 2001.

Cichock, Mark A. "The Soviet Union and Yugoslavia in the 1980s: A Relationship in Flux." *Political Science Quarterly* 105, no. 1 (Spring 1990): 53–74.

Coleman, Fred. "The Kaliningrad Scenario." *World Policy Journal* 14, no. 3 (Fall 1997): 71–75.

Cordovez, Diego, and Selig S. Harrison. *Out of Afghanistan: The Inside Story of the Soviet Withdrawal.* Oxford: Oxford University Press, 1995.

Cotton, James. "Whither the Six-Party Process on North Korea?" *Australian Journal of International Affairs* 59, no. 3 (September 2005): 275–82.

Darst, Robert G. *Smokestack Diplomacy: Cooperation and Conflict in East-West Environmental Politics.* Cambridge, Mass.: MIT Press, 2001.

Donaldson, Robert H., and Joseph L. Nogee. *The Foreign Policy of Russia: Changing Systems, Enduring Interests.* Armonk, N.Y.: M. E. Sharpe, 2002.

Epstein, Alek D. "Russia and Israel: A Romance Aborted?" *Russia in Global Affairs* 5, no. 4 (October–December 2007): 180–90.

Ferdinand, Peter. "Russia and China: Converging Responses to Globalization." *International Affairs: A Russian Journal of World Politics, Diplomacy and International Relations* 83, no. 4 (July 2007): 655–80.

Fomenko, A. "Geopolitical Antiquities: Russian-American Confrontation in the Presence of China." *International Affairs: A Russian Journal of World Politics, Diplomacy and International Relations* 54, no. 1 (2008): 54–66.

Ginsburgs, George, Alvin Z. Rubinstein, and Oles M. Smolansky. *Russia and America: From Rivalry to Reconciliation.* Armonk, N.Y.: M. E. Sharpe, 1993.

Gladkyy, Oleksandr. "American Foreign Policy and U.S. Relations with Russia and China after 11 September." *World Affairs* 166, no. 1 (Summer 2003): 3–22.

Goldgeier, James M. "The United States and Russia: Keeping Expectations Realistic." *Policy Review* 109 (October/November 2001): 47–56.

Goldgeier, James, and Michael McFaul. "George W. Bush and Russia." *Current History* 101, no. 657 (October 2002): 313–24.

———. "What to Do about Russia." *Policy Review* 133 (October/November 2005): 45–62.

Goldman, Marshall I. "Russia and the West: Mutually Assured Distrust." *Current History* 106, no. 702 (October 2007): 314–20.

Goldsmith, Benjamin E. *Imitation in International Relations: Observational Learning, Analogies, and Foreign Policy in Russia and Ukraine.* New York: Palgrave Macmillan, 2005.

Gomart, Thomas. "France's Russia Policy: Balancing Interests and Values." *Washington Quarterly* 30, no. 2 (Spring 2007): 147–55.

Gorodetsky, Gabriel, ed. *Russia between East and West: Russian Foreign Policy on the Threshold of the Twenty-first Century.* London: Frank Cass, 2003.

Gratcheva, Ekaterina. "The New Russia: Friend or Foe?" *Kennedy School Review* 8 (2008): 25–33.

Gresh, Alain. "Russia's Return to the Middle East." Journal of Palestine Studies 28, no. 1 (Autumn 1998): 67–77.

Gromyko, Alexei. "Civilizational Guidelines in the Relationship of Russia, the European Union, and the United States." *Russian Politics and Law* 46, no. 6 (2008): 7–18.

Herd, Graeme P., and Jennifer D. P. Moroney. *Security Dynamics in the Former Soviet Bloc.* London: Routledge, 2003.

Hill, Fiona. "Seismic Shifts in Eurasia: The Changing Relationship between Turkey and Russia and Its Implications for the South Caucasus." *Journal of Southeast European and Black Sea Studies* 3, no. 3 (September 2003): 55–75.

Hill, William. "Making Istanbul a Reality: Moldova, Russia, and Withdrawal from Transdniestria." *Helsinki Monitor* 13, no. 2 (April 2002): 129–45.

Horowitz, Shale. *From Ethnic Conflict to Stillborn Reform: The Former Soviet Union and Yugoslavia.* Bryan: Texas A&M University Press, 2005.

———. "War after Communism: Effects on Political and Economic Reform in the Former Soviet Union and Yugoslavia." *Journal of Peace Research* 40, no. 1 (January 2003): 25–48.

Hunter, Robert E., and Sergey M. Rogov. *Engaging Russia as Partner and Participant: The Next Stage of NATO-Russia Relations.* Santa Monica, Calif.: Rand, 2004.

Inozemtsev, Vladislav. "The Scale of the Postcommunist Disaster Is Not Understood outside Russia." *Russian Politics and Law* 43, no. 4 (2005): 69–83.

Iourine, Alexandre. "The 'Blame Russia First' Syndrome in the U.S." *International Affairs: A Russian Journal of World Politics, Diplomacy and International Relations* 52, no. 3 (2006): 33–39.

Isakova, Irina. *Russian Governance in the Twenty-first Century: Geo-Strategy, Geopolitics and Governance.* London: Frank Cass, 2005.

Ivanov, Vladimir I., and Karla S. Smith, eds. *Japan and Russia in Northeast Asia: Partners in the 21st Century.* Westport, Conn.: Praeger, 1999.

Jalali, Ali A. "The Strategic Partnership of Russia and Iran." *Parameters: U.S. Army War College* 31, no. 4 (Winter 2001/2002): 98–111.

Jonson, Lena. *Vladimir Putin and Central Asia: The Shaping of Russian Foreign Policy.* London: I. B. Tauris, 2004.

Josephson, Paul R. "Decommissioning Russia's Nuclear Subs." *Science* 302, no. 5652 (12 December 2003): 1893–93.

Kalugin, Oleg D. "Window of Opportunity: Russia's Role in the Coalition against Terror." *Harvard International Review* 25, no. 3 (2002): 56–60.

Kanet, Roger E., ed. *The New Security Environment: The Impact on Russia, Central and Eastern Europe.* Aldershot, UK: Ashgate, 2005.

Katz, Mark. "Comparing Putin's and Brezhnev's Policies toward the Middle East." *Society* 45, no. 2 (March/April 2008): 177–80.

———. "The Putin-Chavez Partnership." *Problems of Post-Communism* 53, no. 4 (July/August 2006): 3–9.

Khripunov, Igor. "How Safe Is Russia? Public Risk Perception and Nuclear Security." *Problems of Post-Communism* 54, no. 5 (September 2007): 19–29.

Kim, Yu-nam, Tanguk Taehakkyo, and Mi-So Yonguso, eds. *Soviet Russia, North Korea, and South Korea in the 1990s: Nuclear Issues and Arms Control in and around the Korean Peninsula.* Seoul: Dankook University Press, 1992.

Kimura, Hiroshi. *Japanese-Russian Relations under Gorbachev and Yeltsin.* Armonk, N.Y.: M. E. Sharpe, 2000.

Kiniklioğlu, Suat, and Valeriy Morkva. "An Anatomy of Turkish-Russian Relations." *Journal of Southeast European and Black Sea Studies* 7, no. 4 (December 2007): 533–53.

Kirby, David. *The Baltic World, 1772–1993: Europe's Northern Periphery in an Age of Change.* London: Longman, 1995.

Kohn, Marek. "The Arctic Killers." *New Statesman* 137, no. 4857 (13 August 2007): 24–26.

Kozin, Vladimir. "UK: The State Visit by the Russian President." *International Affairs: A Russian Journal of World Politics, Diplomacy and International Relations* 49, no. 5 (2003): 60–70.

Kuvaldin, V. "The Quest for Russia's Foreign Policy." *International Affairs: A Russian Journal of World Politics, Diplomacy and International Relations* 53, no. 4 (2007): 64–73.

Kvalvik, Ingrid. "Assessing the Delimitation Negotiations between Norway and the Soviet Union." *Acta Borealia* 21, no. 1 (June 2004) 55–78.

Labarre, Frederic. "NATO-Russia Relations and NATO Enlargement in the Baltic Sea Region." *Baltic Defence Review* 6, no. 2 (June 2001): 46–69.

Legvold, Robert. "Eastern Europe and Former Soviet Republics." *Foreign Affairs* 81, no. 6 (November–December 2002): 197–99.

———, ed. *Russian Foreign Policy in the Twenty-first Century and the Shadow of the Past.* New York: Columbia University Press, 2007.

Lieven, Anatol. "Ham-Fisted Hegemon: The Clinton Administration and Russia." *Current History* 98, no. 630 (October 1999): 307–16.

———. "The Secret Policemen's Ball: The United States, Russia and the International Order after 11 September." *International Affairs* 78, no. 2 (April 2002): 245–59.

Lo, Bobo. *Axis of Convenience: Moscow, Beijing, and the New Geopolitics.* London: Chatham House, 2008.

———. *Vladimir Putin and the Evolution of Russian Foreign Policy.* Oxford: Blackwell, 2003.

Losiukov, Aleksandr. "Russia–Australia: 65 Years of Diplomatic Relations." *International Affairs: A Russian Journal of World Politics, Diplomacy and International Relations* 53, no. 6 (2007): 105–12.

Lucas, Edward. *The New Cold War: The Future of Russia and the Threat to the West.* New York: Palgrave Macmillan, 2008.

Lukacs, John. "Finland Vindicated." *Foreign Affairs* 71, no. 4 (Fall 1992): 50–63.

Lynch, Allen C., and Kenneth W. Thompson. *Soviet and Post-Soviet Russia in a World in Change.* Lanham, Md.: UPA, 1994.

Malik, Hafeez. *Russian-American Relations: Islamic and Turkic Dimensions in the Volga-Ural Basin.* New York: Macmillan, 2000.

Maloney, Sean M. "A Cold War in Cold Waters." *Maclean's* 121, no. 2 (21 January 2008): 34–35.

Mankoff, Jeffrey. "Russian Foreign Policy and the United States after Putin." *Problems of Post-Communism* 55, no. 4 (2008): 42–51.

Matlock, Jack F., Jr. "Dealing with a Russia in Turmoil." *Foreign Affairs* 75, no. 3 (May/June 1996): 38–51.

McFaul, Michael. "Getting Russia Right." *Foreign Policy* 117 (Winter 1999/2000): 58–72.

———. "Political Transitions." *Harvard International Review* 28, no. 1 (Spring 2006): 40–45.

———. "Russia and the West: A Dangerous Drift." *Current History* 104, no. 684 (October 2005): 307–12.

McNeill, Terry. "Humanitarian Intervention and Peacekeeping in the Former Soviet Union and Eastern Europe." *International Political Science Review* 18, no. 1 (January 1997): 95–113.

Merkushev, Vitaly. "Relations between Russia and the EU: The View from across the Atlantic." *Perspectives on European Politics and Society* 6, no. 2 (August 2005): 353–71.

Meshchaninov, Maxim. "Trans-Border Cooperation between Russia and Mongolia." *Far Eastern Affairs* 31, no. 2 (2003): 68–78.

Milani, Abbas. "Russia and Iran: An Anti-Western Alliance?" *Current History* 106, no. 702 (October 2007): 328–32.

Moltz, James Clay. "U.S.-Russian Relations and the North Korean Crisis." *Asian Survey* 45, no. 5 (September/October 2005): 722–35.

Motyl, Alexander J., Blair A. Ruble, and Lilia Shevtsova, eds. *Russia's Engagement with the West: Transformation and Integration in the Twenty-first Century.* Armonk, N.Y.: M. E. Sharpe, 2005.

Narochnitskaia, Natalia. "Russia in the New Geopolitical Context." *International Affairs: A Russian Journal of World Politics, Diplomacy and International Relations* 50, no. 1 (2004): 60–73.

Nichols, Thomas M. "Russia's Turn West." *World Policy Journal* 19, no. 4 (Winter 2002/2003): 13–22.

Nikolaev, M. "New Northern Dimension." *International Affairs: A Russian Journal of World Politics, Diplomacy and International Relations* 53, no. 3 (2007): 81–89.

Nimmo, William F. *Japan and Russia: A Revaluation in the Post-Soviet Era.* Westport, Conn.: Greenwood Press, 1994.

Nizameddin, Talal. *Russia and the Middle East: Towards a New Foreign Policy.* New York: St. Martin's Press, 1999.

Nordsletten, Oyvind. "Norway and Russia: Development of Cooperation." *Military Thought* 10, no. 6 (2001): 64–69.

Olson, Robert. *Turkey's Relations with Iran, Syria, Israel, and Russia, 1991–2000.* Costa Mesa, Calif.: Mazda, 2001.

———. "Turkish and Russian Foreign Policies, 1991–1997: The Kurdish and Chechnya Questions." *Journal of Muslim Minority Affairs* 18, no. 2 (October 1998): 209–27.

Oude Elferink, Alex G. *The Law of Maritime Boundary Delimitation: A Case Study of the Russian Federation.* Leiden, Netherlands: Martinus Nijhoff Publishers, 1994.

Oznobishchev, Sergey. "Russia and the United States: Is 'Cold Peace' Possible?" *International Affairs: A Russian Journal of World Politics, Diplomacy and International Relations* 50, no. 4 (2004): 53–60.

Peimani, Hooman. *Failed Transition, Bleak Future? War and Instability in Central Asia and the Caucasus.* Westport, Conn.: Greenwood Press, 2002.

———. *Regional Security and the Future of Central Asia: The Competition of Iran, Turkey, and Russia.* Westport, Conn.: Greenwood Press, 1998.

Petro, Nicolai, and Alvin Rubinstein. *Russian Foreign Policy: From Empire to Nation-State.* Harlow, UK: Longman, 1997.

Petrov, S. "Russia and Canada: Close Neighbors and Natural Partners." *International Affairs: A Russian Journal of World Politics, Diplomacy and International Relations* 54, no. 3 (2008): 149–55.

Postol, Theodore A. "The Target Is Russia." *Bulletin of the Atomic Scientists* 56, no. 2 (March/April 2000): 30–35.

Rogov, Sergei. "Russia and the United States at the Threshold of the Twenty-first Century." *Russian Social Science Review* 40, no. 3 (May/June 1999): 12–33.

Rozman, Gilbert, Mikhail G. Nosov, and Koji Watanabe, eds. *Russia and East Asia: The 21st Century Security Environment.* Armonk, N.Y.: M. E. Sharpe, 1999.

Rubin, Barnett R., and Jack Snyder. *Post-Soviet Political Order: Conflict and State Building.* London: Routledge, 1998.

Ruseckas, Laurent. "Turkey and Eurasia." *Journal of International Affairs* 54, no. 1 (Fall 2000): 217–36.

Rywkin, Michael. "Russia's Place in the World." *American Foreign Policy Interests* 30, no. 5 (2008): 310–14.

Saunders, Paul J. "The U.S. and Russia after Iraq." *Policy Review* 119 (June/July 2003): 27–44.

Schneider, Mark. "The Nuclear Forces and Doctrine of the Russian Federation." *Comparative Strategy* 27, no. 5 (October–December 2008): 397–425.

Schram Stokke, Olav. *Beauty and the Beast? Norway, Russia and the Northern Environment.* Polhøgda, Norway: Fridtjof Nansens Institutt, 1994.

Sestanovich, Stephen. "What Has Moscow Done?" *Foreign Affairs* 87, no. 6 (November/December 2008): 12–28.

Shapiro, Isaac. "To Russia with Love: A Plea for Normalcy." *World Policy Journal* 25, no. 4 (Winter 2008): 63–73.

Shiraev, Eric, and Vladislav Zubok. *Anti-Americanism in Russia: From Stalin to Putin.* Houndsmills, UK: Palgrave, 2000.

Shuja, Sharif. "China, Iran and Central Asia: The Dawning of a New Partnership." *Contemporary Review* 287, no. 1676 (September 2005): 145–51.

Simes, Dmitri K. "Losing Russia." *Foreign Affairs* 86, no. 6 (November/December 2007): 36–52.

Simic, Predrag. "Russia and the Conflicts in the Former Yugoslavia." *Journal of Southeast European and Black Sea Studies* 1, no. 3 (September 2001): 95–114.

Simon, Sheldon W., ed. *East Asian Security in the Post-Cold War Era.* Armonk, N.Y.: M. E. Sharpe, 1993.

Soni, Sharad K. *Mongolia-Russia Relations: Kiakhta to Vladivostok.* New Delhi, Shipra Publishers, 2002.

Stent, Angela, and Lilia Shevtsova. "America, Russia and Europe: a Realignment?" *Survival* 44, no. 4 (Winter 2002): 121–33.

Thaden, Edward. "State and People in the History of Northern Norwegians and White Sea and Kola Russians." *East European Quarterly* 35, no. 2 (Summer 2001): 129–60.

Tiryakian, Edward A. "Secession, Autonomy and Modernity." *Society* 35, no. 5 (July–August 1998): 49–58.

Toloraia, Georgii. "Korean Peninsula and Russia." *International Affairs: A Russian Journal of World Politics, Diplomacy and International Relations* 49, no. 1 (2003): 24–34.

Trenin, Dmitri. *Getting Russia Right.* Washington, D.C.: Carnegie Endowment for International Peace, 2007.

———. "Where U.S. and Russian Interests Overlap." *Current History* 107, no. 709 (May 2008): 219–24.

Tsygankov, Andrei P. *Russia's Foreign Policy: Change and Continuity in National Identity.* Lanham, Md.: Rowman & Littlefield, 2006.

Vorontsov, Alexander. "Current Russia-North Korea Relations: Challenges and Achievements." Washington, D.C.: The Brookings Institution, 2007.

Voskressenski, Alexei, Boris Porfiriev, and Frank Columbus, eds. *Russia on the Brink of the Millennium: International Policy and National Security Issues.* Commack, N.Y.: Nova Science Publishers, 1998.

Wallander, Celeste. "Silk Road, Great Game or Soft Underbelly? The New U.S.-Russia Relationship and Implications in Eurasia." *Journal of Southeast European and Black Sea Studies* 3, no. 3 (September 2003): 92–104.

Warhola, James W., and William A. Mitchell. "The Warming of Turkish-Russian Relations: Motives and Implications." *Demokratizatsiya* 14, no. 1 (Winter 2006): 127–43.

Withington, Thomas. "The Other Allies: Russia, India, and Afghanistan's United Front." *Current History* 101, no. 651 (January 2002): 40–44.

Yanik, Lerna K. "Allies or Partners? An Appraisal of Turkey's Ties to Russia, 1991–2007." *East European Quarterly* 41, no. 3 (Fall 2007): 349–70.

Yükseker, Deniz. "Shuttling Goods, Weaving Consumer Tastes: Informal Trade between Turkey and Russia." *International Journal of Urban and Regional Research* 31, no. 1 (March 2007): 60–72.

Zlobin, Nikolai V. "The United States, Russia, and the New Challenges." *Demokratizatsiya* 11, no. 1 (Winter 2003): 44–50.

Russia and the Near Abroad

Abbott, Pamela, and Roger Sapsford. "Life-Satisfaction in Post-Soviet Russia and Ukraine." *Journal of Happiness Studies* 7, no. 2 (June 2006): 251–87.

Allison, Roy. "Strategic Reassertion in Russia's Central Asia Policy." *International Affairs* 80, no. 2 (March 2004): 277–93.

Arbatov, Aleksei G., Abram Chayes, Antonia Handler Chayes, and Lara Olson, eds. *Managing Conflict in the Former Soviet Union: Russian and American Perspectives*. Cambridge, Mass.: MIT Press, 1997.

Åslund, Anders. *How Ukraine Became a Market Economy and Democracy*. Washington, D.C.: Peterson Institute, 2009.

Baker, John C. *Non-Proliferation Incentives for Russia and Ukraine*. Oxford: Oxford University Press, 1997.

Balmaceda, Margarita Mercedes. "Gas, Oil and the Linkages between Domestic and Foreign Policies: The Case of Ukraine." *Europe-Asia Studies* 50, no. 2 (March 1998): 257–86.

Bertsch, Gary K., and William C. Potter. *Dangerous Weapons, Desperate States: Russia, Belarus, Kazakhstan, and Ukraine*. London: Routledge, 1999.

Bildt, Carl. "The Baltic Litmus Test." *Foreign Affairs* 73, no. 5 (September/October 1994): 72–85.

Bilinsky, Yaroslav. "Ukraine, Russia, and the West." *Problems of Post-Communism* 44, no. 1 (January/February 1997): 27–34.

Blank, Stephen. "Russia and the Baltics in the Age of NATO Enlargement." *Parameters: U.S. Army War College* 28, no. 3 (Autumn 1998): 50–68.

———. "The Strategic Importance of Central Asia: An American View." *Parameters: U.S. Army War College* 38, no. 1 (Spring 2008): 73–87.

———. "What Comes after the Russo-Georgian War? What's at Stake in the CIS." *American Foreign Policy Interests* 30, no. 6 (November 2008): 379–91.

Bodie, William C. *Moscow's "Near Abroad": Security Policy in Post-Soviet Europe*. Washington, D.C.: Institute for National Strategic Studies, National Defense University, 1993.

Bugajski, Janusz. *Cold Peace: Russia's New Imperialism*. Westport, Conn.: Praeger, 2004.

Bukkvoll, Tor. "Off the Cuff Politics—Explaining Russia's Lack of a Ukraine Strategy." *Europe-Asia Studies* 53, no. 8 (December 2001): 1141–57.

———. *Ukraine and European Security*. London: Continuum International Publishing Group, 1997.

Butler, William Elliott. *The Law of Treaties in Russia and the Commonwealth of Independent States: Text and Commentary*. Cambridge: Cambridge University Press, 2002.

Ciscel, Matthew H. *The Language of the Moldovans: Romania, Russia, and Identity in an Ex-Soviet Republic*. Lanham, Md.: Lexington Books, 2007.

Ciziunas, Pranas. "Russia and the Baltic States: Is Russian Imperialism Dead?" *Comparative Strategy* 27, no. 3 (May/June 2008): 287–307.

Coppieters, Bruno, Alexei Zverev, and Dmitri Trenin. *Commonwealth and Independence in Post-Soviet Eurasia*. London: F. Cass, 1998.

Crowther, William. "Moldova, Transnistria and the PCRM's Turn to the West." *East European Quarterly* 41, no. 3 (Fall 2007): 273–304.

D'Anieri, Paul. "Dilemmas of Interdependence." *Problems of Post-Communism* 44, no. 1 (January/February 1997): 16–26.

Danilovich, Alex. *Russian-Belarusian Integration: Playing Games behind the Kremlin Walls*. Aldershot, UK: Ashgate, 2006.

Dekmejian, R. Hrair, and Hovann H. Simonia. *Troubled Waters: The Geopolitics of the Caspian Region*. New York: I. B.Tauris, 2003.

Dergachev, Alexander. "Ukrainian-Russian Relations—European and Eurasian Contexts." *Russian Politics and Law* 39, no. 6 (November/December 2001): 57–73.

De Waal, Thomas. *Black Garden: Armenia and Azerbaijan through Peace and War*. New York: NYU Press, 2003.

Deyermond, Ruth. *Security and Sovereignty in the Former Soviet Union*. Boulder, Colo.: Lynne Rienner Publishers, 2008.

Dressler, Wanda. "Between Empires and Europe: The Tragic Fate of Moldova." *Diogenes* 53, no. 2 (2006): 29–49.

Godin, Iurii. "Will Ukraine Join the Slavic Union?" *Russian Politics and Law* 40, no. 4 (July/August 2002): 44–55.

Goltz, Thomas. *Georgia Diary: A Chronicle of War and Political Chaos in the Post-Soviet Caucasus*. Armonk, N.Y.: M. E. Sharpe, 2006.

Greene, Robert H. "Letters from Heaven: Popular Religion in Russia and Ukraine." *Canadian Journal of History* 42, no. 2 (Autumn 2007): 293–95.

Haerpfer, Christian W. "Support for Democracy and Autocracy in Russia and the Commonwealth of Independent States, 1992–2002." *International Political Science Review* 29, no. 4 (September 2008): 411–32.

Hamilton, Daniel S. "The Baltics: Still Punching above Their Weight." *Current History* 107, no. 707 (March 2008): 119–25.

Herron, Erik S. "Mixed Electoral Rules and Party Strategies: Responses to Incentives by Ukraine's Rukh and Russia's Yabloko." *Party Politics* 8, no. 6 (November 2002): 719–33.

Jackson, Nicole J. *Russian Foreign Policy and the CIS: Theories, Debates and Actions*. London: Routledge, 2003.

Janmaat, Jan Germen. "The Ethnic 'Other' in Ukrainian History Textbooks: The Case of Russia and the Russians." *Compare: A Journal of Comparative Education* 37, no. 3 (June 2007): 307–24.

Janmaat, Jan Germen, and Nelli Piattoeva. "Citizenship Education in Ukraine and Russia: Reconciling Nation-Building and Active Citizenship." *Comparative Education* 43, no. 4 (November 2007): 527–52.

Kincade, William H., and Cynthia M. Nolan. "Troubled Triangle: Russia, Ukraine and the United States." *Journal of Strategic Studies* 24, no. 1 (March 2001): 104–42.

King, Charles. "The Five-Day War." *Foreign Affairs* 87, no. 6 (November/December 2008): 2–11.

———. *The Moldovans: Romania, Russia, and the Politics of Culture.* Stanford: Hoover Press, 1999.

Korostelina, Karina V. "Identity, Autonomy and Conflict in Republics of Russia and Ukraine." *Communist and Post-Communist Studies* 41, no. 1 (March 2008): 79–91.

Kramer, Mark. "Russian Policy toward the Commonwealth of Independent States: Recent Trends and Future Prospects." *Problems of Post-Communism* 55, no. 6 (November/December 2008): 3–19.

Kubicek, Paul. "End of the Line for the Commonwealth of Independent States." *Problems of Post-Communism* 46, no. 2 (March/April 1999): 15–24.

Kuzio, Taras. "Identity and Nation-Building in Ukraine: Defining the 'Other.'" *Ethnicities* 1, no. 3 (December 2001): 343–65.

———. "National Identities and Virtual Foreign Policies among the Eastern Slavs." *Nationalities Papers* 31, no. 4 (December 2003): 431–52.

———. "Russian Policy toward Ukraine during Elections." *Demokratizatsiya* 13, no. 4 (Fall 2005): 491–517.

Lieven, Anatol. "Restraining NATO: Ukraine, Russia, and the West." *Washington Quarterly* 20, no. 4 (Fall 1997): 55–77.

———. *Ukraine and Russia: A Fraternal Rivalry.* Washington, D.C.: United States Institute of Peace Press, 1999.

Lynch, Dov. *Engaging Eurasia's Separatist States: Unresolved Conflicts and De Facto States.* Washington, D.C.: United States Institute of Peace Press, 2004.

Mackinlay, John, and Peter Cross, eds. *Regional Peacekeepers: The Paradox of Russian Peacekeeping.* Tokyo: United Nations University Press, 2003.

Miller, Eric A. "The Changing Face of Eurasia: Russian and Ukrainian Foreign Policy in Transition." *Comparative Strategy* 22, no. 4 (October/November 2003): 373–90.

Mitrasca, Marcel. *Moldova: A Romanian Province under Russian Rule: Diplomatic History from the Archives of the Great Powers.* New York: Algora Publishing, 2002.

Molchanov, Mikhail A. "Borders of Identity: Ukraine's Political and Cultural Significance for Russia." *Canadian Slavonic Papers* 38, nos. 1–2 (March–June 1996): 178–94.

Morozov, Viatcheslav. "Russia in the Baltic Sea Region: Desecuritization or Deregionalization?" *Cooperation and Conflict* 39, no. 3 (September 2004): 317–31.

Motyl, Alexander J. *Dilemmas of Independence: Ukraine after Totalitarianism.* New York: Council on Foreign Relations, 1993.

Muižnieks, Nils, ed. *Latvian-Russian Relations: Domestic and International Dimensions.* Riga, Latvia: LU Akadēmiskais Apgāds, 2006.

Neukirch, Claus. "Transdniestria and Moldova: Cold Peace at the Dniestr." *Helsinki Monitor* 12, no. 2 (April 2001): 122–35.

Nichol, James P. *Diplomacy in the Former Soviet Republics.* Westport, Conn.: Greenwood Publishing Group, 1995.

Nygren, Bertil. "Putin's Use of Natural Gas to Reintegrate the CIS Region." *Problems of Post-Communism* 55, no 4 (July/August 2008): 3–15.

Ortmann, Stefanie. "Diffusion as Discourse of Danger: Russian Self-Representations and the Framing of the Tulip Revolution." *Central Asian Survey* 27, nos. 3–4 (September–December 2008): 363–78.

Pastukhov, Vladimir B. "Ukraine Is Not with Russia." *Russian Politics and Law* 44, no. 2 (March/April 2006): 39–54.

Pourchot, Georgeta. *Eurasia Rising: Democracy and Independence in the Post-Soviet Space.* Westport, Conn.: Praeger, 2008.

Puglisi, Rosaria. "Clashing Agendas? Economic Interests, Elite Coalitions and Prospects for Co-operation between Russia and Ukraine." *Europe-Asia Studies* 55, no. 6 (September 2003): 827–45.

Quester, George H. *The Nuclear Challenge in Russia and the New States of Eurasia.* Armonk, N.Y.: M. E. Sharpe, 1995.

Quinlan, Paul D. "Back to the Future: An Overview of Moldova under Voronin." *Demokratizatsiya* 12, no. 4 (Fall 2004): 485–504.

Rumer, Eugene B. "Eurasia Letter: Will Ukraine Return to Russia?" *Foreign Policy* 96 (Fall 1994): 129–44.

Rushailo, V. "CIS: Today and Tomorrow." *International Affairs: A Russian Journal of World Politics, Diplomacy and International Relations* 53, no. 6 (2007): 71–79.

Sabonis-Helf, Theresa. "Catching Air? Climate Change Policy in Russia, Ukraine and Kazakhstan." *Climate Policy* 3, no. 2 (June 2003): 159–71.

Sanders, Deborah. *Security Co-operation between Russia and Ukraine in the Post-Soviet Era.* Houndmills, UK: Palgrave, 2001.

Schipani-Adúriz, Andrés. "Through an Orange-Colored Lens: Western Media, Constructed Imagery, and Color Revolutions." *Demokratizatsiya* 15, no. 1 (Winter 2007): 87–115.

Shapiro Zacek, Jane, and Ilpyong J. Kim, eds. *The Legacy of the Soviet Bloc.* Gainesville: University Press of Florida, 1997.

Sherr, James. "Russia-Ukraine Rapprochement? The Black Sea Fleet Accords." *Survival* 39, no. 3 (Autumn 1997): 33–50.

Simon, Gerhard. "Russia and Ukraine Ten Years after the Fall of the Communist Regimes." *Russian Politics and Law* 39, no. 6 (November/December 2001): 74–79.

Smith, David James, Artis Pabriks, Aldis Purs, and Thomas Lane. *The Baltic States: Estonia, Latvia and Lithuania.* London: Routledge, 2002.

Solchanyk, Roman. *Ukraine and Russia: The Post-Soviet Transition.* Lanham, Md.: Rowman & Littlefield, 2001.

———. "Ukraine, the (Former) Center, Russia, and 'Russia.'" *Studies in Comparative Communism* 25, no. 1 (March 1992): 31–45.

Szporluk, Roman. "Ukraine: From an Imperial Periphery to a Sovereign State." *Daedalus* 126, no. 3 (Summer 1997): 85–119.

Titarenko, Larissa. "On the Shifting Nature of Religion during the Ongoing Post-Communist Transformation in Russia, Belarus and Ukraine." *Social Compass* 55, no. 2 (June 2008): 237–54.

Topalova, Viktoriya. "In Search of Heroes: Cultural Politics and Political Mobilization of Youths in Contemporary Russia and Ukraine." *Demokratizatsiya* 14, no. 1 (Winter 2006): 23–41.

Torbakov, Igor. "Apart from Russia or a Part of Russia: A Sad Sign of Ukrainian-Russian Relations." *Review of International Affairs* 1, no. 1 (Autumn 2001): 70–84.

Tuathail, Gearóid Ó. "Russia's Kosovo: A Critical Geopolitics of the August 2008 War over South Ossetia." *Eurasian Geography and Economics* 49, no. 6 (November/December 2008): 670–705.

Vozzhenikov, A. V., and S. M. Alkhlayev. "The Evolution of CIS Military-Political Cooperation." *Military Thought* 16, no. 1 (2007): 136–45.

Wallander, Celeste A. "Silk Road, Great Game or Soft Underbelly? The New U.S.-Russia Relationship and Implications in Eurasia." *Journal of Southeast European and Black Sea Studies* 3, no. 3 (September 2003): 92–104.

Wilson, Andrew. "The Donbas between Ukraine and Russia: The Use of History in Political Disputes." *Journal of Contemporary History* 30, no. 2 (April 1995): 265–89.

Wright, Sue, ed. *Language Policy and Language Issues in the Successor States of the Former USSR.* Clevedon, UK: Multilingual Matters, 1999.

Wydra, Doris. "The Crimea Conundrum: The Tug of War between Russia and Ukraine on the Questions of Autonomy and Self-Determination." *International Journal on Minority and Group Rights* 10, no. 2 (2003): 111–30.

The Russian Diaspora

Arel, Dominique, and Blair A. Ruble. *Rebounding Identities: The Politics of Identity in Russia and Ukraine.* Washington, D.C.: Woodrow Wilson Center Press, 2006.

Braun, Aurel. "All Quiet on the Russian Front?" In *The New European Diasporas: National Minorities and Conflict in Eastern Europe*, edited by Michael Mandelbaum, 81–158. New York: Council on Foreign Relations Press, 2000.

Chinn, Jeff, and Robert Kaiser. *Russians as the New Minority: Ethnicity and Nationalism in the Soviet Successor States*. Boulder, Colo.: Westview Press, 1996.

Kolstø, Pål, ed. *Nation-Building and Ethnic Integration in Post-Soviet Societies: An Investigation of Latvia and Kazakstan*. Boulder, Colo.: Westview Press, 1999.

———. "Territorialising Diasporas: The Case of the Russians in the Former Soviet Republics." *Millennium: Journal of International Studies* 28, no. 3 (December 1999): 607–31.

———. "The New Russian Diaspora—An Identity of Its Own?" *Ethnic and Racial Studies* 19, no. 3 (July 1996): 609–39.

Laitin, David D. *Identity in Formation: The Russian-Speaking Populations in the Near Abroad*. Ithaca, N.Y.: Cornell University Press, 1998.

Melvin, Neil. *Russians beyond Russia: The Politics of National Identity*. London: Continuum, 1995.

Payin, Emil. "The Disintegration of the Empire and the Fate of the 'Imperial Minority.'" In *The New Russian Diaspora: Russian Minorities in the Former Soviet Republics*, edited by Vladimir Shlapentokh, Munir Sendich, and Emil Payin, 21–36. Armonk, N.Y.: M. E. Sharpe, 1994.

Sasse, Gwendolyn. *The Crimea Question: Identity, Transition, and Conflict*. Cambridge, Mass.: Harvard University Press, 2007.

Saunders, Robert A. "A Marooned Diaspora: Ethnic Russians in the Near Abroad and Their Impact on Russia's Foreign Policy and Domestic Politics." In *International Migration and the Globalization of Domestic Politics*, edited by Rey Koslowski, 173–94. London: Routledge, 2005.

Shlapentokh, Vladimir, Munir Sendich, and Emil Payin, eds. *The New Russian Diaspora: Russian Minorities in the Former Soviet Republics*. Armonk, N.Y.: M. E. Sharpe.

Smith, Graham. *The Nationalities Question in the Post-Soviet States*. London: Longman, 1996.

Waller, Michael, Bruno Coppieters, and Alexei Malashenko. *Conflicting Loyalties and the State in Post-Soviet Russia and Eurasia*. London: F. Cass, 1998.

Williams, Christopher, and Thanasis D. Sfikas, eds. *Ethnicity and Nationalism in Russia, the CIS and the Baltic States*. Aldershot, UK: Ashgate, 1999.

Ziegler, Charles E. "The Russian Diaspora in Central Asia: Russian Compatriots and Moscow's Foreign Policy." *Demokratizatsiya* 14, no. 1 (Winter 2006): 103–26.

SOCIAL STRUCTURES

Religion

Russian Orthodoxy

Agadjanian, Alexander. "Breakthrough to Modernity, Apologia for Traditionalism: the Russian Orthodox View of Society and Culture in Comparative Perspective." *Religion, State and Society* 31, no. 4 (December 2003): 327–46.

Basil, John. "Church-State Relations in Russia: Orthodoxy and Federation Law, 1990–2004." *Religion, State and Society* 33, no. 2 (June 2005): 151–63.

Borowik, Irena. "Between Orthodoxy and Eclecticism: On the Religious Transformations of Russia, Belarus and Ukraine." *Social Compass* 49, no. 4 (December 2002): 497–508.

———. "Orthodoxy Confronting the Collapse of Communism in Post-Soviet Countries." *Social Compass* 53, no. 2 (June 2006): 267–78.

Curanovic, Alicja. "The Attitude of the Moscow Patriarchate towards Other Orthodox Churches." *Religion, State and Society* 35, no. 4 (December 2007): 301–18.

Davis, Nathaniel. *A Long Walk to Church: A Contemporary History of Russian Orthodoxy*. Boulder, Colo.: Westview Press, 2003.

Ellis, Jane. *Russian Orthodox Church: Triumphalism and Defensiveness*. New York: Palgrave Macmillan, 2007.

Evans, Andrew. "Forced Miracles: The Russian Orthodox Church and Post-Soviet International Relations." *Religion, State and Society* 30, no. 1 (March 2002): 33–43.

Husband, William B. "Looking Backward, Looking Forward: The Study of Religion in Russia after the Fall." *Journal of Religious History* 31, no. 2 (June 2007): 195–202.

Knox, Zoe. *Russian Society and the Orthodox Church: Religion in Russia after Communism*. London: Routledge, 2004.

Lewis, David C. *After Atheism: Religion and Ethnicity in Russia and Central Asia*. New York: Palgrave Macmillan, 2000.

Marsh, Christopher. "Russian Orthodox Christians and Their Orientation toward Church and State." *Journal of Church and State* 47, no. 3 (Summer 2005): 545–61.

Mayorov, M. "The Russian Orthodox Church: Healing the Rift." *International Affairs: A Russian Journal of World Politics, Diplomacy and International Relations* 53, no. 4 (2007): 107–20.

Orlov, Boris, and Sophia Kotzer. "The Russian Orthodox Church in a Changing Society." In *Russia at a Crossroads: History, Memory and Political Practice*, edited by Nurit Schleifman, 147–72. London: Routledge, 1998.

Papkova, Irina. "The Russian Orthodox Church and Political Party Platforms." *Journal of Church and State* 49, no. 1 (Winter 2007): 117–34.

Shubin, Daniel H. *A History of Russian Christianity: Tsar Nicholas II to Gorbachev's Edict on the Freedom of Conscience.* New York: Algora Publishing, 2006.

Tataryn, Myroslaw. "Russia and Ukraine: Two Models of Religious Liberty and Two Models for Orthodoxy." *Religion, State and Society* 29, no. 3 (September 2001): 155–72.

van den Bercken, Wil. "Theological Education for Laypeople in Russia, Belarus and Ukraine: A Survey of Orthodox and Catholic Institutions." *Religion, State and Society* 32, no. 3 (September 2004): 299–311.

Walters, Philip. "Turning Outwards or Turning Inwards? The Russian Orthodox Church Challenged by Fundamentalism." *Nationalities Papers* 35, no. 5 (November 2007): 853–79.

Wasyliw, Zenon V. "Orthodox Church Divisions in Newly Independent Ukraine, 1991–1995." *East European Quarterly* 41, no. 3 (Fall 2007): 305–22.

Willems, Joachim. "The Religio-Political Strategies of the Russian Orthodox Church as a 'Politics of Discourse.'" *Religion, State and Society* 34, no. 3 (September 2006): 287–98.

Islam and Islamism

Belenkaya, Marianna. "The History of Russia's Muslims." *Organization of Asia-Pacific News Agencies* (3 November 2005).

Bilz-Leonhardt, Marlies. "Islam as a Secular Discourse: the Case of Tatarstan." *Religion, State and Society* 35, no. 3 (September 2007): 231–44.

Bowers, Stephen R., Yavus Akhmadov, and Ashley Ann Derrick. "Islam in Ingushetia and Chechnya." *Journal of Social, Political and Economic Studies* 29, no. 4 (Winter 2004): 395–407.

Boykewich, Stephen. "Russia after Beslan." *Virginia Quarterly Review* 81, no. 1 (Winter 2005): 156–88.

Forest, Benjamin, Juliet Johnson, and Mariėtta Tigranovna Stepaniants, eds. *Religion and Identity in Modern Russia: The Revival of Orthodoxy and Islam.* Aldershot, UK: Ashgate, 2005.

Giuliano, Elise. "Islamic Identity and Political Mobilization in Russia: Chechnya and Dagestan Compared." *Nationalism and Ethnic Politics* 11, no. 2 (Summer 2005): 195–220.

Gorenburg, Dmitry. "Russia Confronts Radical Islam." *Current History* 105, no. 693 (October 2006): 334–40.

Hahn, Gordon M. *Russia's Islamic Threat.* New Haven, Conn.: Yale University Press, 2007.

———. "The Rise of Islamist Extremism in Kabardino-Balkariya." *Demokratizatsiya* 13, no. 4 (Fall 2005): 543–94.

Heleniak, Timothy. "Regional Distribution of the Muslim Population of Russia." *Eurasian Geography and Economics* 47, no. 4 (July 2006): 426–48.

Hunter, Shireen. *Islam in Russia: The Politics of Identity and Security.* Armonk, N.Y.: M. E. Sharpe, 2004.

Kutschera, Chris. "The Muslims of Saratov." *Middle East* 369 (July 2006): 60–62.

———. "The Rebirth of Islam in Russia." *Middle East* 324 (June 2002): 42–45.

Lyagusheva, Svetlana. "Islam and the Traditional Moral Code of Adyghes." *Iran and the Caucasus* 9, no. 1 (2005): 29–35.

Matsuzato, Kimitaka. "Muslim Leaders in Russia's Volga-Urals: Self-Perceptions and Relationship with Regional Authorities." *Europe-Asia Studies* 59, no. 5 (July 2007): 779–805.

Pilkington, Hilary, and Galina Yemelianova. *Islam in Post-Soviet Russia: Public and Private Faces.* New York: RoutledgeCurzon, 2003.

Shlapentokh, Dmitry. "Islam and Orthodox Russia: From Eurasianism to Islamism." *Communist and Post-Communist Studies* 41, no. 1 (March 2008): 27–46.

Other Religions

Abaeva, L. L. "Lamaism in Buryatia." *Anthropology and Archeology of Eurasia* 39, no. 4 (Spring 2001): 20–22.

Balzer, Marjorie Mandelstam. "Beyond Belief? Social, Political, and Shamanic Power in Siberia." *Social Analysis* 52, no. 1 (March 2008): 95–110.

———. "Whose Steeple Is Higher? Religious Competition in Siberia." *Religion, State and Society* 33, no. 1 (March 2005): 57–69.

Bourdeaux, Michael. "In Sacred Groves." *Christian Century* 117, no. 28 (18 October 2000): 1036–37.

Chervyakov, Valeriy, Zvi Gitelman, and Vladimir Shapiro. "Religion and Ethnicity: Judaism in the Ethnic Consciousness of Contemporary Russian Jews." *Ethnic and Racial Studies* 20, no. 2 (April 1997): 280–305.

Fagan, Geraldine. "Buddhism in Post-Soviet Russia: Revival or Degeneration?" *Religion, State and Society* 29, no. 1 (March 2001): 9–21.

Filatov, Sergei. "Yakutia (Sakha) Faces a Religious Choice: Shamanism or Christianity." *Religion, State and Society* 28, no. 1 (March 2000): 113–22.

Gitelman, Zvi, Musya Glants, and Marshall I. Goldman. *Jewish Life after the USSR*. Bloomington: Indiana University Press, 2003.

Kosmin, V. K. "Mongolian Buddhism's Influence on the Formation and Development of Burkhanism in Altai." *Anthropology and Archeology of Eurasia* 45, no. 3 (Winter 2006): 43–72.

Laruelle, Marlène. "Alternative Identity, Alternative Religion? Neo-Paganism and the Aryan Myth in Contemporary Russia." *Nations and Nationalism* 14, no. 2 (April 2008): 283–301.

———. "Religious Revival, Nationalism, and the 'Invention of Tradition': Political Tengrism in Central Asia and Tatarstan." *Central Asia Survey* 26, no. 2 (June 2007): 203–16.

Lunkin, Roman, and Sergei Filatov. "The Rerikh Movement: A Homegrown Russian 'New Religious Movement.'" *Religion, State and Society* 28, no. 1 (March 2000): 135–48.

Walters, Philip. "Religion in Tuva: Restoration or Innovation?" *Religion, State and Society* 29, no. 1 (March 2001): 23–38.

Zhukovskaia, N. L. "Buddhists of Russia at the Turn of the Twenty-first Century." *Anthropology and Archeology of Eurasia* 39, no. 4 (Spring 2001): 15–19.

———. "The Revival of Buddhism in Buryatia." *Anthropology and Archeology of Eurasia* 39, no. 4 (Spring 2001): 23–48.

Culture

Alexeyeva, Ludmila, and Paul Goldberg. *The Thaw Generation: Coming of Age in the Post-Stalininist Era*. Pittsburgh, Pa.: University of Pittsburgh Press, 1993.

Baker, Adele Marie, ed. *Consuming Russia: Popular Culture, Sex, and Society since Gorbachev*. Durham, N.C.: Duke University Press, 1999.

Berlin, Isaiah. *The Soviet Mind: Russian Culture under Communism*. Washington, D.C.: Brookings Institution Press, 2004.

Berry, Ellen E., and Anesa Miller-Pogacar. *Re-entering the Sign: Articulating New Russian Culture*. Ann Arbor: University of Michigan Press, 1995.

Borenstein, Eliot. *Overkill: Sex and Violence in Contemporary Russian Popular Culture*. Ithaca, N.Y.: Cornell University Press, 2007.

Boym, Svetlana. *Common Places: Mythologies of Everyday Life in Russia*. Cambridge, Mass.: Harvard University Press. 1994.

Chernetsky, Vitaly. *Mapping Postcommunist Cultures: Russia and Ukraine in the Context of Globalization*. Montreal: McGill-Queen's University Press, 2007.

Epstein, Mikhail, Alexander Genis, and Slobodanka Vladiv-Glover, eds. *Russian Postmodernism: New Perspectives on Post-Soviet Culture*. Translated by Slobodanka Vladiv-Glover. Oxford: Berghahn Books, 1999.

Figes, O. *Natasha's Dance: A Cultural History of Russia.* New York: Penguin, 2002.

Kelly, Catriona, and David Shepherd. *Russian Cultural Studies: An Introduction.* Oxford: Oxford University Press, 1998.

Sinyavsky, Andrei. *Soviet Civilization: A Cultural History.* New York: Arcade, 1991.

Wageman, Patty, ed. *Russian Legends, Folk Tales and Fairy Tales.* London: Art Data, 2007.

Art

Arkhipov, Vladimir. *Home-Made: Contemporary Russian Folk Artifacts.* London: Fuel Publishing, 2006.

Baigell, Renee, and Matthew Baigell. *Peeling Potatoes, Painting Pictures: Women Artists in Post-Soviet Russia, Estonia, and Latvia: The First Decade.* New Brunswick, N.J.: Rutgers University Press, 2001.

Blakesley, Rosalind P., and Susan E. Reid, eds. *Russian Art and the West: A Century of Dialogue in Painting, Architecture, and the Decorative Arts.* DeKalb: Northern Illinois University Press, 2006.

Coster, Annie, ed. *Russian Book Art, 1904–2005.* Brussels: Fonds Mercator, 2005.

Goscilo, Helena, and Stephen M. Norris, eds. *Preserving Petersburg: History, Memory, Nostalgia.* Bloomington: Indiana University Press, 2008.

Herman, Nicholas, ed. *Russian Art in Translation.* Brooklyn, N.Y.: ANTE, 2007.

Jackson, David, and Patty Wageman. *Russian Landscape.* London: National Gallery, 2003.

Kivelson, Valerie A., and Joan Neuberger, eds. *Picturing Russia: Explorations in Visual Culture.* New Haven, Conn.: Yale University Press, 2008.

Ristolainen, Mari. *Preferred Realities: Soviet and Post-Soviet Amateur Art in Novorzhev.* Helsinki: Kikimora, 2008.

Siben, Isabel, ed. *Ilya & Emilia Kabakov: Installation & Theater.* Munich: Prestel, 2006.

Sporton, Gregory. "Power as Nostalgia: The Bolshoi Ballet in the New Russia." *New Theatre Quarterly* 22, no. 4 (November 2006): 379–86.

Tetsuo, Mochizuki, ed. *Beyond of the Empire: Images of Russia in the Eurasian Cultural Context.* Sapporo, Japan: Slavic Research Center, Hokkaido University, 2008.

Thiemann, Barbara M., ed. *(Non)conform: Russian and Soviet Artists 1958–1995.* Munich: Prestel, 2007.

Tupitsyn, Viktor. *The Museological Unconscious: Communal (Post)Modernism in Russia.* Cambridge, Mass.: MIT Press, 2009.

Literature

Balina, Marina, Nancy Condee, and Evgeny Dobrenko, eds. *Endquote: Sots-art Literature and Soviet Grand Style.* Evanston, Ill.: Northwestern University Press, 1999.

Clark, Katerina. *The Soviet Novel: History as Ritual.* Chicago: Chicago University Press, 1981.

Hutchings, Stephen C., ed. *Russian Literary Culture in the Camera Age: The Word as Image.* London: Routledge, 2004.

Levitt, Marcus C., and Tatyana Novikov, eds. *Times of Trouble: Violence in Russian Literature and Culture.* Madison: University of Wisconsin Press, 2007.

Lipovetsky, Mark, and Eliot Borenstein, eds. *Russian Postmodernist Fiction: Dialogue with Chaos.* New York: M. E. Sharpe, 1999.

Lovell, Stephen, and Birgit Menzel, eds. *Reading for Entertainment in Contemporary Russia: Post-Soviet Popular Literature in Historical Perspective.* Munich: Sagner, 2005.

McMillin, Arnold, ed. *Reconstructing the Canon: Russian Writing in the 1980s.* Amsterdam: Harwood Academic Publishers, 2000.

Porter, Robert. *Russia's Alternative Prose.* Oxford: Berg, 1994.

Shneidman. N. N. *Russian Literature, 1995–2002: On the Threshold of the New Millennium.* Toronto: University of Toronto Press, 2004.

Sutcliffe, Benjamin M. *The Prose of Life: Russian Women Writers from Khrushchev to Putin.* Madison: University of Wisconsin Press, 2009.

Film

Beumers, Birgit. *A History of Russian Cinema.* Oxford: Berg, 2009.

———, ed. *Russia on Reels: the Russian Idea in Post-Soviet Cinema.* London: I.B. Tauris, 1999.

Brashinsky, Michael, and Andrew Horton, eds. *Russian Critics on the Cinema of Glasnost.* Cambridge: Cambridge University Press, 1994.

Condee, Nancy. *The Imperial Trace: Recent Russian Cinema.* Oxford: Oxford University Press, 2009.

Hashamova, Yana. *Pride and Panic: Russian Imagination of the West in Post-Soviet Film.* Bristol, UK: Intellect, 2007.

Hutchings, Stephen. *Russia and Its Other(s) on Film: Screening Intercultural Dialogue.* Basingstoke, UK: Palgrave Macmillan, 2008.

Hutchings, Stephen, and Anat Vernitski, eds. *Russian and Soviet Film Adaptations of Literature, 1917–2001: Screening the Word.* London: Routledge-Curzon, 2004.

Leyda, Jay. *Kino: A History of the Russian and Soviet Film.* London: Allen & Unwin, 1983.

Rollberg, Peter. *Historical Dictionary of Russian and Soviet Cinema.* Lanham, Md.: Plymouth, UK: Scarecrow Press, 2009.

Taylor, Richard, ed. *The BFI Companion to Eastern European and Russian Cinema.* London: British Film Institute, 2000.

Taylor, Richard, and Christie Ian, eds. *Inside the Film Factory: New Approaches to Russian and Soviet Cinema.* London: Routledge, 1991.

Youngblood, Denise J. *Russian War Films: On the Cinema Front, 1914–2005.* Lawrence: University Press of Kansas, 2007.

Music

Cushman, Thomas. *Notes from Underground: Rock Music Counterculture in Russia.* Albany: State University of New York Press, 1995.

Korabelnikov, Ludmila Zinovevna. "The Study of the Music of Expatriate Russians." *Fontes Artis Musicae* 53, no. 3 (July–September 2006): 207–13.

Levin, Theodore C., and Michael E. Edgerton. "The Throat Singers of Tuva." *Scientific American* 281, no. 3 (September 1999): 80–87.

Levin, Theodore C., and Valentina Süzükei. *Where Rivers and Mountains Sing: Sound, Music, and Nomadism in Tuva and Beyond.* Bloomington: Indiana University Press, 2006.

MacFadyen, David. *Èstrada?! Grand Narratives and the Philosophy of the Russian Popular Song 1982–2000.* Montreal: McGill-Queen's University Press, 2001.

———. *Red Stars: Personality and the Soviet Popular Song after 1955.* Montreal: McGill-Queen's University Press, 2001.

Ryback, Timothy W. *Rock around the Bloc: A History of Rock Music in Eastern Europe and the Soviet Union.* New York: Oxford: Oxford University Press, 1990.

Urban, M. "Getting by on the Blues: Music, Culture, and Community in a Transitional Russia." *Russian Review* 61, no. 3 (July 2002): 409–35.

Media

Becker, Jonathan. "Lessons from Russia: A Neo-Authoritarian Media System." *European Journal of Communication* 19, no. 2 (2004): 139–63.

Beumers, Birgit, Stephen Hutchings, and Natalia Rulyova. *The Post-Soviet Russian Media: Conflicting Signals.* London: Routledge, 2009.

Ekecrantz, Jan, and Kerstin Olofsson. *Russian Reports: Studies in Post-Communist Transformation of Media and Journalism.* Stockholm: Almqvist & Wiksell International, 2000.

Ellis, Frank. *From Glasnost to the Internet: Russia's New Infosphere*, Basingstoke, UK: Macmillan, 1998.

Glanley, Gladys D. *Unglued Empire: The Soviet Experience with Communications Technologies.* Norwood, N.J.: Ablex Publishing, 1996.

Lipman, Masha. "Constrained or Irrelevant: The Media in Putin's Russia." *Current History* 104 (2005): 319–24.

Lovell, Stephen. *The Russian Reading Revolution: Print Culture in the Soviet and Post-Soviet Eras.* Houndmills, UK: Macmillan, 2000.

Mickiewicz, Ellen. "The Election News Story on Russian Television: A World Apart from Viewers." *Slavic Review* 65, no. 1 (2006): 1–23.

Oates, Sarah. *Introduction to Media and Politics.* London: Sage, 2008.

Pietiläinen, Jukka. "Media Use in Putin's Russia." *Journal of Communist Studies and Transition Politics* 24, no. 3 (September 2008): 365–85.

———. *The Regional Newspaper in Post-Soviet Russia: Society, Press and Journalism in the Republic of Karelia 1985–2001.* Tampere, Finland: Tampere University Press, 2002.

Rantanen, Tehri. "The Old and the New: Communications Technology and Globalization in Russia." *New Media and Society,* 3, no. 1 (2001): 85–105.

Rantanen, Terhi, and Elena Vartanova. "Empire and Communications: Centrifugal and Centripetal Media in Contemporary Russia." In *Contesting Media Power: Alternative Media in a Networked World*, edited by Nick Couldry and James Curran, 147–60. Lanham, Md.: Rowman & Littlefield, 2003.

Saunders, Robert A. "Denationalized Digerati in the Virtual Near Abroad: The Paradoxical Impact of the Internet on National Identity among Minority Russians." *Global Media and Communication* 2, no. 1 (April 2006): 43–69.

Schmidt, Henrike, Katy Teubener, and Natalja Konradova. *Control + Shift: Public and Private Uses of the Russian Internet.* Norderstedt, Germany: Books on Demand, 2006.

Shkliaev, Aleksandr, and Eva Toulouze. "The Mass Media and the National Question in Udmurtia in the 1990s." *Nationalities Papers* 29, no. 1 (March 2001): 97–108.

Zassoursky, Ivan. *Media and Power in Post-Soviet Russia.* Armonk, N.Y.: M. E. Sharpe, 2002.

Society

Axenov, Konstantin. *The Transformation of Urban Space in Post-Soviet Russia.* London: Routledge, 2006.

Beliaeva, L. A. "Social Stratification and Poverty in the Regions of Russia." *Sociological Research* 47, no. 1 (January/February 2008): 19–40.

Bloch, Alexia. *Red Ties and Residential Schools: Indigenous Siberians in a Post-Soviet State.* Philadelphia: University of Pennsylvania Press, 2004.

Blum, Douglas W. *National Identity and Globalization: Youth, State and Society in Post-Soviet Eurasia.* New York: Cambridge University Press, 2007.

Dawson, Jane I. *Eco-Nationalism: Anti-nuclear Activism and National Identity in Russia, Lithuania, and Ukraine.* Durham, N.C.: Duke University Press, 1996.

Eklof, Ben, Larry E. Holmes, and Vera Kaplan. *Educational Reform in Post-Soviet Russia: Legacies and Prospects.* London: Frank Cass, 2005.

Field, Mark G., and Judyth L. Twigg, eds. *Russia's Torn Safety Nets: Health and Social Welfare during the Transition.* New York: St. Martin's Press, 2000.

Glad, Betty, and Eric Shiraev. *The Russian Transformation: Political, Sociological, and Psychological Aspects.* New York: St. Martin's Press, 1999.

Ioffe, Grigory, Tatyana Nefedova, and Ilya Zaslavsky. *The End of Peasantry: The Disintegration of Rural Russia.* Pittsburgh, Pa.: University of Pittsburgh Press, 2006.

Jones, Anthony. *Education and Society in the New Russia.* Armonk, N.Y.: M. E. Sharpe, 1994.

Lane, David Stuart, ed. *Soviet Society under Perestroika.* Boston: Unwin Hyman, 1990.

Manning, Nick, and Nataliya Tikhonova, eds. *Health and Health Care in the New Russia.* Aldershot, UK: Ashgate, 2008.

Mendelson, Sarah H., and Theodore P. Gerber. "Failing the Stalin Test." *Foreign Affairs* 85, no. 1 (2006): 2–8.

Morton, Henry W. "The Soviet Union in the 1980s: Housing in the Soviet Union." *Proceedings of the Academy of Political Science* 35, no. 3 (1984): 69–80.

O'Loughlin, John, Alexander Panin, and Frank Witmer. "Population Change and Migration in Stavropol' Kray: The Effects of Regional Conflicts and Economic Restructuring." *Eurasian Geography and Economics* 48, no. 2 (March 2007): 249–67.

Parfitt, Tom. "Russia's Population Crisis." *Lancet* 365, no. 9461 (2005): 743–44.

Patico, Jennifer. *Consumption and Social Change in a Post-Soviet Middle Class.* Washington, D.C.: Woodrow Wilson Center Press, 2008.

Petro, Nicolai N. "The Putin Generation." *Harvard International Review* 30, no. 2 (Summer 2008): 22–26.

Service, Robert. *Russia: Experiment with a People.* Cambridge, Mass.: Harvard University Press, 2003.

Stephenson, Svetlana. *Crossing the Line: Vagrancy, Homelessness, and Social Displacement in Russia.* Aldershot, UK: Ashgate, 2006.
Twigg, Judyth, and Kate Schecter, eds. *Social Capital and Social Cohesion in Post-Soviet Russia.* Armonk, N.Y.: M. E. Sharpe, 2003.
Weiler, Jonathan. *Human Rights in Russia: A Darker Side of Reform.* Boulder, Colo.: Lynne Rienner, 2004.

Civic Organizations

Daniel, Wallace L. *The Orthodox Church and Civil Society in Russia.* College Station: Texas A&M University Press, 2006.
Elkner, Julie. "Dedovshchina and the Committee of Soldiers' Mothers under Gorbachev." *The Journal of Power Institutions in Post-Soviet Societies* 1 (2004). Available at www.pipss.org/.
Evans, Alfred B., Jr., Laura A. Henry, and Lisa McIntosh Sundstrom, eds. *Russian Civil Society: A Critical Assessment.* Armonk, N.Y.: M. E. Sharpe, 2006.
Howard, Marc Morjé. *The Weakness of Civil Society in Post-Communist Europe.* Cambridge: Cambridge University Press, 2003.
Marsh, Christopher, and Nikolas K. Gvosdev. *Civil Society and the Search for Justice in Russia.* Lanham, Md.: Lexington Books, 2002.
Reilley, Brigg, Dave Burrows, Vitalec Melnikov, Tatiana Andreeva, Murdo Bijl, and Hans Veeken. "Injecting Drug Use and HIV in Moscow: Results of a Survey." *Journal of Drug Issues* 30, no. 2 (Spring 2000): 305–21.
Sundstrom, Lisa McIntosh. *Funding Civil Society: Foreign Assistance and NGO Development in Russia.* Stanford, Calif.: Stanford University Press, 2006.
Sutton, Jonathan. "Civil Society, Religion and the Nation: Reflections on the Russian Case." In *Civil Society, Religion, and the Nation: Modernization in Intercultural Context: Russia, Japan, Turkey,* edited by Gerrit Steunebrink, Evert van der Zweerde, and Wout Cornelissen. Amsterdam: Rodopi, 2004.
Tismăneanu, Vladimir. *Political Culture and Civil Society in Russia and the New States of Eurasia.* Armonk, N.Y.: M. E. Sharpe, 1995.
White, Anne. *Democratization in Russia under Gorbachev, 1985–91: The Birth of a Voluntary Sector.* Houndmills, UK: Macmillan, 1999.

Crime

Firestone, Thomas. "What Russia Must Do to Fight Organized Crime." *Demokratizatsiya* 14, no. 1 (Winter 2006): 59–65.

Galeotti, Mark. *Russian and Post-Soviet Organised Crime*. Aldershot, UK: Ashgate, 2002.

Gerber, Jurg. "On the Relationship between Organized and White-Collar Crime: Government, Business and Criminal Enterprise in Post-Communist Russia." *European Journal of Crime, Criminal Law and Criminal Justice* 8, no. 4 (2000): 327–42.

Gilinskiy, Yakov. "Police and the Community in Russia." *Police Practice and Research* 6, no. 4 (September 2005): 331–46.

Goldman, Marshall I. *The Piratization of Russia: Russian Reform Goes Awry*. London: Routledge, 2003.

Handelman, Stephen. *Comrade Criminal: The New Russian Mafiya*. New Haven, Conn.: Yale University Press, 1995.

Holmes, Leslie. "Corruption and Organised Crime in Putin's Russia." *Europe-Asia Studies* 60, no. 6 (August 2008): 1011–31.

Huskey, Eugene. "Ruling Russia: Law, Crime, and Justice in a Changing Society." *Demokratizatsiya* 14, no. 3 (Summer 2006): 461–62.

Ledeneva, Alena V., and Marina Kurkchiyan. *Economic Crime in Russia*. Amsterdam: Kluwer Law International, 2000.

McAuley, Mary, and Kenneth I. MacDonald. "Russia and Youth Crime." *British Journal of Criminology* 47, no. 1 (January 2007): 2–22.

Paoli, Letizia. "Drug Trafficking in Russia: A Form of Organized Crime?" *Journal of Drug Issues* 31, no. 4 (Fall 2001): 1007–37.

Sanford, Tawnia. "The Creation of Criminal Russia." *Canadian Slavonic Papers* 41, nos. 3–4 (1999): 391–412.

Satter, David. *Darkness at Dawn: The Rise of the Russian Criminal*. New Haven, Conn.: Yale University Press, 2003.

Sergeyev, Victor M. *The Wild East: Crime and Lawlessness in Post-Communist Russia*. Armonk, N.Y.: M. E. Sharpe, 1998.

Shcherbakova, E. M. "The Narcotics Invasion in Russia." *Sociological Research* 44, no. 5 (September/October 2005): 53–63.

Stenvoll, Dag. "From Russia with Love? Newspaper Coverage of Cross-Border Prostitution in Northern Norway, 1990–2001." *European Journal of Women's Studies* 9, no. 2 (May 2002): 143–62.

Varese, Federico. *The Russian Mafia: Private Protection in a New Market Economy*. Oxford: Oxford University Press, 2001.

Williams, Phil, ed. *Russian Organized Crime: The New Threat?* London: Routledge, 1989.

Migration

Alexseev, Mikhail. "Russia as a Declining Migration State." *NewsNet: News of the American Association for the Advancement of Slavic Studies* 49, no. 2 (March 2009): 1–8.

Alexseev, Mikhail A., and C. Richard Hofstetter. "Russia, China, and the Immigration Security Dilemma." *Political Science Quarterly* 121, no. 1 (Spring 2006): 1–32.

Balzer, Harley. "Demography and Democracy in Russia: Human Capital Challenges to Democratic Consolidation." *Demokratizatsiya* 11, no. 1 (Winter 2003): 95–109.

Gavrilova, Irina. "Migration Policy in Modern Russia: To Be or Not to Be." *Perspectives on European Politics and Society* 2, no. 2 (August 2001): 261–87.

Hareven, Gail. "From Russia with Luggage: Absorbing the Exodus." *Tikkun* 6, no. 2 (March/April 1991): 39–90.

Munz, Rainer. *Diasporas and Ethnic Migrants: Germany, Israel and Russia in Comparative Perspective*. London: Routledge, 2003.

Naumova, T. V., and Anthony Jones. "Russia's 'Brain Drain.'" *Russian Social Science Review* 39, no. 2 (1998): 49–57.

Nazarova, E. A. "Characteristics of Migration Processes in the Southern Regions of Russia." *Sociological Research* 46, no. 4 (July 2007): 78–89.

Oussatcheva, Marina. "Institutions in Diaspora: The Case of Armenian Community in Russia." Working Paper WPTC-01-09, 1–23. Oxford: Transnational Communities Programme, 2001.

Pilkington, Hilary. *Migration, Displacement, and Identity in Post-Soviet Russia*. London: Routledge, 1998.

Portyakov, Vladimir. "New Aspects of the Immigration Policy of Russia." *Far Eastern Affairs* 336, no. 2 (2008): 113–18.

Rybakovskii, L. L. "The Demographic Future of Russia and Processes of Migration." *Russian Social Science Review* 48, no. 1 (January/February 2007): 29–47.

Saul, Norman. "Documenting Non-Russian Immigrants from Russia." *Slavic and East European Information Resources* 7, nos. 2–3 (2006): 139–51.

White, Anne. "Internal Migration Trends in Soviet and Post-Soviet European Russia." *Europe-Asia Studies* 56, no. 6 (September 2007): 887–911.

Yudina, Tatiana Nikolaevna. "Labour Migration into Russia: The Response of State and Society." *Current Sociology* 53, no. 4 (July 2005): 583–606.

Women and Gender Issues

Adlam, Carol. *Women in Russian Literature after Glasnost: Female Alternatives*. London: Legenda, 2005.

Ashwin, Sarah. *Gender, State, and Society in Soviet and Post-Soviet Russia*. London: Routledge, 2000.

Baigell, Renée, and Matthew Baigell. *Peeling Potatoes, Painting Pictures: Women Artists in Post-Soviet Russia, Estonia, and Latvia: The First Decade.* New Brunswick, N.J.: Rutgers University Press, 2001.

Barrett, Jennifer B., and Cynthia Buckley. "Gender and Perceived Control in the Russian Federation." *Europe-Asia Studies* 61, no. 1 (January 2009): 29–49.

Barta, Peter I., ed. *Gender and Sexuality in Russian Civilisation.* London: Routledge, 2001.

Buckley, Mary. *Post-Soviet Women: From the Baltic to Central Asia.* Cambridge: Cambridge University Press, 1997.

Costlow, Jane T., Stephanie Sandler, and Judith Vowles, eds. *Sexuality and the Body in Russian Culture.* Stanford, Calif.: Stanford University Press, 1993.

Edmondson, Linda Harriet, ed. *Women and Society in Russia and the Soviet Union.* Cambridge: Cambridge University Press, 1992.

Golosov, Grigorii V. "Political Parties, Electoral Systems and Women's Representation in the Regional Legislative Assemblies of Russia, 1995–1998." *Party Politics* 7, no. 1 (January 2001): 45–69.

Goscilo, Helena. *Dehexing Sex: Russian Womanhood during and after Glasnost.* Ann Arbor: University of Michigan Press, 1996.

Goscilo, Helena, and Andrea Lanoux, eds. *Gender and National Identity in Twentieth Century Russia.* DeKalb: Northern Illinois University Press, 2006.

Harden, Jeni. "'Mother Russia' at Work." *European Journal of Women's Studies* 8, no. 2 (May 2001): 181–99.

Hemment, Julie. *Empowering Women in Russia: Activism, Aid, and NGOs.* Bloomington: Indiana University Press, 2007.

Johnson, Janet Elise. "Privatizing Pain: The Problem of Woman Battery in Russia." *NWSA Journal* 13, no. 3 (Fall 2001): 153–68.

Johnson, Janet Elise, and Jean C. Robinson, eds. *Living Gender after Communism.* Bloomington: Indiana University Press, 2007.

Kay, Rebecca. *Russian Women and Their Organizations: Gender, Discrimination and Grassroots Women's Organizations, 1991–96.* Houndmills, UK: Macmillan, 2000.

Kelly, Catriona. *Refining Russia: Advice Literature, Polite Culture, and Gender from Catherine to Yeltsin.* Oxford: Oxford University Press, 2001.

Kon, Igor, and James Riordan, eds. *Sex and Russian Society.* Bloomington: Indiana University Press, 1993.

Koval, Vitalina, ed. *Women in Contemporary Russia.* Oxford: Berghahn Books, 1995.

Kuehnast, Kathleen, and Carol Nechemias. *Post-Soviet Women Encountering Transition: Nation Building, Economic Survival, and Civic Activism.* Washington, D.C.: Woodrow Wilson Center Press, 2004.

Mamonova, Tatyana, and Chandra Niles Folsom. *Women's Glasnost vs. Naglost: Stopping Russian Backlash.* Westport, Conn.: Bergin & Garvey, 1994.

Marsh, Rosalind J. *Women in Russia and Ukraine.* Cambridge: Cambridge University Press, 1996.

Pilkington, Hilary, ed. *Gender, Generation and Identity in Contemporary Russia.* London: Routledge, 1996.

Posadskaya-Vanderbeck, Anastasia, ed. *Women in Russia: A New Era in Russian Feminism.* Translated by Kate Clarke. New York: Verso, 1994.

Racioppi, Linda, and Katherine O'Sullivan. *Women's Activism in Contemporary Russia.* Philadelphia: Temple University Press, 1997.

Rivkin-Fish, Michele R. *Women's Health in Post-Soviet Russia: The Politics of Intervention.* Bloomington: Indiana University Press, 2005.

Rosenberg, Chanie. *Women and Perestroika.* London: Bookmarks, 1989.

Rubchak, Marian J. "In Search of a Model Evolution of a Feminist Consciousness in Ukraine and Russia." *European Journal of Women's Studies* 8, no. 2 (May 2001): 149–60.

Rule, Wilma, and Norma C. Noonan. *Russian Women in Politics and Society.* Westport, Conn.: Greenwood, 1996.

Rzhanitsyna, L. "Working Women in Russia at the End of the 1990s." *Russian Social Science Review* 42, no. 4 (July/August 2001): 52–63.

Salmenniemi, Suvi. *Democratisation and Gender in Contemporary Russia.* New York: Routledge, 2008.

Shlapentokh, Vladimir, and Tatiana Marchenko. "Family Values on the Rise While Women Fall in Russia." *Feminist Issues* 12, no. 2 (Fall 1992): 43–46.

Sperling, Valerie. *Organizing Women in Contemporary Russia: Engendering Transition.* Cambridge: Cambridge University Press, 1999.

Štulhofer, Aleksandar, and Theo Sandfort, eds. *Sexuality and Gender in Postcommunist Eastern Europe and Russia.* New York: Haworth Press, 2005.

White, Anne. "Gender Roles in Contemporary Russia: Attitudes and Expectations among Women Students." *Europe-Asia Studies* 57, no. 3 (May 2005): 429–55.

INFRASTRUCTURE

Military and Security Services

Aldis, Anne, and Roger N. McDermott. *Russian Military Reform, 1992–2002.* London: Routledge, 2003.

Austin, Greg, and Alexey D. Muraviev. *The Armed Forces of Russia in Asia.* London: I. B.Tauris, 2000.

Bordiuzha, Nikolai. "Collective Security Treaty Organization." *International Affairs: A Russian Journal of World Politics, Diplomacy and International Relations* 52, no. 2 (2005): 34–41.

Bordyuzha, Nikolai Nikolaievich. "CSTO: Counteraction Tool against New Threats." *International Affairs: A Russian Journal of World Politics, Diplomacy and International Relations* 53, no. 2 (2007): 54–59.

Cowell, Alan S. *The Terminal Spy: A True Story of Espionage, Betrayal and Murder.* New York: Random House, 2008.

de Haas, Marcel. "Putin's Security Policy in the Past, Present and Future." *Baltic Defence Review* 12, no. 2 (June 2004): 39–59.

Earley, Pete. *Comrade J: The Untold Secrets of Russia's Master Spy in America after the End of the Cold War.* New York: G. P. Putnam's Sons, 2008.

Gleason, Gregory, and Marat E. Shaihutdinov. "Collective Security and Non-State Actors in Eurasia." *International Studies Perspectives* 6, no. 2 (May 2005): 274–84.

Haas, Marcel. *Russian Security and Air Power, 1992–2002: The Development of Russian Security Thinking under Yeltsin and Putin and Its Consequences for the Air Forces.* London: Routledge, 2004.

Herspring, Dale R. *The Kremlin and the High Command: Presidential Impact on the Russian Military from Gorbachev to Putin.* Lawrence: University Press of Kansas, 2006.

Kainikara, Sanu. *Red Air: Politics in Russian Air Power.* Boca Raton, Fla.: Universal-Publishers, 2007.

Moran, John P. *From Garrison State to Nation-State: Political Power and the Russian Military under Gorbachev and Yeltsin.* Westport, Conn.: Praeger, 2002.

Muraviev, Alexey D. "Russia's Long-Range Aviation: An Airborne Spear of the Nation." *Defense Analysis* 17, no. 1 (April 2001): 89–98.

Omelicheva, Mariya. "Russia's Counterterrorism Policy: Variations on an Imperial Theme." Paper presented at the annual meeting of the ISA's 49th Annual Convention, San Francisco, March 26, 2008.

———. "Russia's Counterterrorism Policy: Variations on an Imperial Theme." *Perspectives on Terrorism* 3, no. 1 (April 2009): 3–10.

Pyrkovsky, V. F., and A. R. Korabelniko. "New Approaches to Air Defense of the Russian Federation." *Military Thought* 16, no. 1 (2007): 72–77.

Rekuta, A. L. "The Collective Security Treaty Organization: Averting Security Threats in Central Asia." *Military Thought* 15, no. 4 (2006): 1–9.

Suib, Stella. *Inside Russia's SVR: The Foreign Intelligence Service.* New York: Rosen Publishing Group, 2002.

Webber, Stephen L., and Jennifer G. Mathers, eds. *Military and Society in Post-Soviet Russia*. Manchester: Manchester University Press, 2006.
Woolf, Amy F. "Nuclear Weapons in Russia: Safety, Security, and Control Issues." CRS Issue Brief for Congress, Foreign Affairs, Defense, and Trade Division. Washington, D.C.: Congressional Research Service, 15 August 2003.

Transportation

Davies, R. E. G., and Mike Machat. *Aeroflot, an Airline and Its Aircraft: An Illustrated History of the World's Largest Airline*. McLean, Va.: Paladwr Press, 1992.
Holt, Jane. *Transport Strategies for the Russian Federation*. Washington, D.C.: World Bank, 1993.
Kirichenko, A. V. "Logistics of Military Transportation: Transport Systems and Its Substantiation." *Military Thought* 17, no. 4 (2008): 124–32.
Kolesnichenko, Alesandr. "Russia's Deadly Roads." *Time* (May 29, 2008).
Manley, Deborah. *Trans-Siberian Railway*. New York: Random House, 1999.
Ryzhikov, Maj. Gen. B. A. "Issues in Preparing the National Transportation System for Defense." *Military Thought* 10, no. 1 (2001): 19–25.
Sokolov, G. G. "Military Transport Communications Agencies: Their Role in Reforming the Russian Federation's Transport System." *Military Thought* 13, no. 3 (2004): 128–31.

Science and Industry

Ahrend, Rudiger. "Can Russia Break the 'Resource Curse'?" *Eurasian Geography and Economics* 46, no. 8 (December 2005): 584–609.
Barnes, Andrew Scott. *Owning Russia: The Struggle over Factories, Farms, and Power*. Ithaca, N.Y.: Cornell University Press, 2006.
Campbell, Robert Wellington. *Soviet and Post-Soviet Telecommunications: An Industry under Reform*. Boulder, Colo.: Westview Press, 1995.
Crotty, Jo. "Economic Transition and Pollution Control in the Russian Federation: Beyond Pollution Intensification?" *Europe-Asia Studies* 54, no. 2 (March 2002): 299–316.
Cusumano, Michael A. "Where Does Russia Fit into the Global Software Industry?" *Communications of the ACM* 49, no. 2 (February 2006): 31–34.
Earle, John S., and Ivan Komarov. "Measuring Defense Conversion in Russian Industry." *Defence and Peace Economics* 12, no. 2 (2001): 103–44.
Feakins, Melanie. Offshoring in the Core: Russian Software Firms Onshoring in the USA." *Global Networks* 9, no. 1 (January 2009): 1–19.

Filtzer, Donald A. *Soviet Workers and the Collapse of Perestroika: The Soviet Labour Process and Gorbachev's Reforms, 1985–1991.* Cambridge: Cambridge University Press, 1994.

Hønneland, Geir. "Enforcement Co-operation between Norway and Russia in the Barents Sea Fisheries." *Ocean Development and International Law* 31, no. 3 (July/September 2000): 249–67.

Ivanov, Vladimir I. "Russia's Energy Future and Northeast Asia." *Asia-Pacific Review* 13, no. 2 (November 2006): 46–59.

Josephson, Paul R. *Red Atom: Russia's Nuclear Power Program from Stalin to Today.* Pittsburgh, Pa.: University of Pittsburgh Press, 2005.

Kuboniwa, Masaaki, Shinichiro Tabata, and Nataliya Ustinova. "How Large Is the Oil and Gas Sector of Russia? A Research Report." *Eurasian Geography and Economics* 46, no. 1 (February 2005): 68–76.

Sagers, Matthew J. "Developments in Russian Gas Production since 1998: Russia's Evolving Gas Supply Strategy." *Eurasian Geography and Economics* 48, no. 6 (November/December 2007): 651–98.

Salnikov, V. A., and D. I. Galimov. "The Competitiveness of Russian Industries: Current State and Outlook." *Studies on Russian Economic Development* 17, no. 2 (2006): 149–68.

Sanchez-Andres, Antonio. "Restructuring the Defence Industry and Arms Production in Russia." *Europe-Asia Studies* 52, no. 5 (July 2000): 897–914.

Uskova, T. V. "The Vologda Oblast Industrial Sector: Growth Problems and Trends." *Studies on Russian Economic Development* 19, no. 5 (2008): 501–6.

Vann, Elizabeth F. "Domesticating Consumer Goods in the Global Economy: Examples from Vietnam and Russia." *Ethnos: Journal of Anthropology* 70, no. 4 (December 2005): 465–88.

Agriculture

Balanova, Yevgeniya, Alexandr Bedny, and Alexandr Grudzinsky, "Property Concentration as a Means of Creating Efficient Enterprises in Agriculture." *Social Sciences* 36, no. 4 (2005): 53–65.

Bonanno, Alessandro, and Katherine L. Lyman. "The Introduction of Capitalism in Russian Agriculture: Popular Response to Neo-Liberal Reforms." *Rural Sociology* 64, no. 1 (1999): 113–32.

Csaki, Csaba, John Nash, Vera Matusevic, and Holger Kray, eds. *Food and Agricultural Policy in Russia.* Technical Paper No. 523. Washington, D.C.: World Bank, 2002.

Infanger, Craig L. "Reforming Russia's Agriculture: A Slow Path from Plan to Market." *Choices: The Magazine of Food, Farm and Resource Issues* 10, no. 2 (1995): 40–42.

Ioffe, Grigory. "The Downsizing of Russian Agriculture." *Europe-Asia Studies* 57, no. 2 (March 2005): 179–208.

Ioffe, Grigory, and Tatyana Nefedova. "Marginal Farmland in European Russia." *Eurasian Geography and Economics* 45, no. 1 (February 2004): 45–59.

———. "Russian Agriculture and Food Processing: Vertical Cooperation and Spatial Dynamics." *Europe-Asia Studies* 53, no. 3 (May 2001): 389–418.

Ioffe, Grigory, Tatyana Nefedova, and Ilya Zaslavsky. "From Spatial Continuity to Fragmentation: The Case of Russian Farming." *Annals of the Association of American Geographers* (December 2004): 913–43.

Lerman, Zvi. *Russia's Agricultural in Transition.* Lanham, Md.: Rowman & Littlefield, 2007.

O'Brien, David J., and Stephen K. Wegren, eds. *Rural Reform in Post-Soviet Russia.* Washington, D.C.: Woodrow Wilson Center Press, 2002.

Southworth, Caleb. "The Dacha Debate: Household Agriculture and Labor Markets in Post-Socialist Russia." *Rural Sociology* 71, no. 3 (2006): 451–78.

Wegren, Stephen K. *Agriculture and the State in Soviet and Post-Soviet Russia.* Pittsburgh, Pa.: University of Pittsburgh Press, 1998.

———. "Russian Agriculture and the WTO." *Problems of Post-Communism* 54, no. 4 (July/August 2007): 46–59.

———. "Socioeconomic Transformation in Russia: Where Is the Rural Elite?" *Europe-Asia Studies* 52, no. 2 (March 2000): 237–71.

Legal System

Hahn, Jeffrey W., ed. *Democratization in Russia: The Development of Legislative Institutions.* Armonk, N.Y.: M. E. Sharpe, 1996.

Jordan, Pamela A. *Defending Rights in Russia: Lawyers, the State, and Legal Reform in the Post-Soviet Era.* Vancouver: UBC Press, 2005.

Marsh, Christopher, and Nikolas K. Gvosdev. *Civil Society and the Search for Justice in Russia.* Lanham, Md.: Lexington Books, 2002.

Pridemore, William Alex, ed. *Ruling Russia: Law, Crime, and Justice in a Changing Society.* Lanham, Md.: Rowman & Littlefield, 2005.

Economy

Aalto, Pami. *The EU-Russian Energy Dialogue: Europe's Future Energy Security.* Aldershot, UK: Ashgate, 2008.

Ahrend, Rudiger. "Russia's Post-Crisis Growth: Its Sources and Prospects for Continuation." *Europe-Asia Studies* 58, no. 1 (January 2006): 1–24.

Ashwin, Sarah, and Simon Clarke. *Russian Trade Unions and Industrial Relations in Transition*. Houndmills, UK: Palgrave Macmillan, 2003.

Åslund, Anders. *How Russia Became a Market Economy*. Washington, D.C.: Brookings Institution Press, 1995.

———. *The Post-Soviet Economy: Soviet and Western Perspectives*. New York: St. Martin's Press, 1992.

Berglöf, Erik, ed. *The New Political Economy of Russia*. Cambridge, Mass.: MIT Press, 2003.

Blasi, Joseph R., Maya Kroumova, and Douglas Kruse. *Kremlin Capitalism: The Privatization of the Russian Economy*. Ithaca, N.Y.: ILR Press, 1997.

Brown, J. David, and John S. Earle. *Economic Reforms and Productivity-Enhancing Reallocation in the Post-Soviet Transition*. Kalamazoo, Mich.: W. E. Upjohn Institute for Employment Research, 2004.

Clark, Terry D. *Changing Attitudes toward Economic Reform during the Yeltsin Era*. Westport, Conn.: Praeger, 2003.

Davis, Sue. *Trade Unions in Russia and Ukraine, 1985–95*. Houndmills, UK: Palgrave, 2001.

Fortescue, Stephen. *Russia's Oil Barons and Metal Magnates: Oligarchs and the State in Transition*. Basingstoke, UK: Palgrave Macmillan, 2006.

Gregory, Paul R., and Robert C. Stuart. *Russian and Soviet Economic Performance and Structure*. Reading, Mass.: Addison-Wesley, 1998.

Gustafson, Than. *Capitalism Russian-Style*. Cambridge: Cambridge University Press, 1999.

Hanson, Philip. "Putin and Russia's Economic Transformation." *Eurasian Geography and Economics* 45, no. 6 (September 2004): 421–28.

Hoffman, David E. *The Oligarchs: Wealth and Power in the New Russia*. New York: Public Affairs, 2002.

Humphrey, Caroline. *The Unmaking of Soviet Life: Everyday Economies after Socialism*. Ithaca, N.Y.: Cornell University Press, 2002.

Klebnikov, Paul. *Godfather of the Kremlin: The Decline of Russia in the Age of Gangster Capitalism*. San Diego: Harcourt, 2001.

Lane, David Stuart, ed. *Russian Banking: Evolution, Problems and Prospects*. New York: E. Elgar Publishing, 2002.

Ledeneva, Alena V. *How Russia Really Works: The Informal Practices That Shaped Post-Soviet Politics and Business*. Ithaca, N.Y.: Cornell University Press, 2006.

———. *Russia's Economy of Favours: Blat, Networking, and Informal Exchange*. Cambridge: Cambridge University Press, 1998.

Lovell, Stephen, Alena Ledeneva, and Andrei Rogachevskii, eds. *Bribery and Blat in Russia: Negotiating Reciprocity from the Middle Ages to the 1990s*. Houndmills, UK: Macmillan, 2000.

Reddaway, Peter. *The Tragedy of Russia's Reforms: Market Bolshevism against Democracy.* Washington, D.C.: United States Institute of Peace Press, 2001.

Robinson, Neil. *Reforging the Weakest Link: Global Political Economy and Post-Soviet Change in Russia, Ukraine, and Belarus.* Aldershot, UK: Ashgate, 2004.

Rosefielde, Steven. *Efficiency and Russia's Economic Recovery Potential to the Year 2000 and Beyond.* Aldershot, UK: Ashgate, 1998.

———. *The Russian Economy: From Lenin to Putin.* Malden, Mass.: Blackwell, 2007.

Samorodov, Alexander T. "Transition, Poverty and Inequality in Russia." *International Labor Review* 131, no. 3 (1992): 335–53.

Satre Ahlander, Ann-Mari. 2001. "Women's and Men's Work in Transitional Russia: Legacies of the Soviet System." *Post-Soviet Affairs* 17, no. 1 (2001): 55–80.

Seabright, Paul. *The Vanishing Rouble: Barter Networks and Non-Monetary Transactions in Post-Soviet Societies.* Cambridge: Cambridge University Press, 2000.

Shankina, Alina. "The Middle Class in Russia." *Russian Politics and Law* 41, no. 6 (November/December 2003): 5–20.

Standing, Guy. *Russian Unemployment and Enterprise Restructuring: Reviving Dead Souls.* Geneva: ILO, 1999.

Surovell, Jeffrey. *Capitalist Russia and the West.* Aldershot, UK: Ashgate, 2000.

Van Atta, Don. *The "Farmer Threat": The Political Economy of Agrarian Reform in Post-Soviet Russia.* Boulder, Colo.: Westview Press, 1993.

Worth, Owen. *Hegemony, International Political Economy and Post-Communist Russia.* Aldershot, UK: Ashgate, 2005.

Yergin, Daniel, and Thane Gustafson. *Russia 2010: And What It Means for the World.* New York: Vintage Books, 1995.

INTERNET RESOURCES

General Information

www.allrussias.com/ (general information about history, institutions, leaders)
www.state.gov/r/pa/ei/bgn/3183.htm/ (general information about the U.S. State Department)
www.mail.ru/; www.rambler.ru/; www.yandex.com/ (popular Russian web portals providing search engines, e-mail services, etc.)

www.rbp.ru/regions/ (information about Russian regions)
www.rusflag.ru/ (site about Russian state symbols)

Political

General

www.polit.ru/; www.vz.ru/; www.expert.ru/ (analysis of Russian politics)
http://eng.kremlin.ru/ (president of Russia's website)
www.premier.gov.ru/ (prime minister of Russia's website)
www.indem.ru/ (information on oppositional political activism)
www.russianembassy.org/RUSSIA/CONSTIT/ (copy of 1993 Russian Constitution)

Domestic Issues

www.edinros.ru/ (United Russia political party)
www.politnauka.org/library/russia/ (analysis of Russian political parties and politics)
www.chechnya.ru/ (comprehensive information on Chechen issues)
www.pravoslavie.ru/ (information on the Russian Orthodox Church)
www.muslim.ru/ (information on Russian Muslim communities)
http://rcnc.ru/ (site of the National Association of the Peoples of the Caucasus)
http://armyrus.ru/ (site dedicated to the Russian army)
http://pripyat.com (history of Chernobyl)

News and Analysis

http://english.pravda.ru/ (*Pravda*'s English-language website)
www.kommersant.ru/ (*Kommersant* online)
http://izvestia.com/ (*Izvestiya* online)
www.sptimes.ru/ (*St. Petersburg Times* online)
www.moscowtimes.com/index.php (*Moscow Times* online)
http://russiatoday.com/ (*Russia Today* online)
http://en.rian.ru/russia/ (*RIA Novosti* online)
www.bbc.co.uk/russian/ (the Russian service of the BBC)
www.guardian.co.uk/world/russia/ (*Guardian* [UK], Russian news and events)
http://topics.edition.cnn.com/topics/russia (CNN online, Russian news and events)

www.yakutiatoday.com/ (regional news from Sakha)
www.udmurt.ru/ (regional news from Udmurtiya)
http://vladivostoktimes.com/ (regional news from Vladivostok)

SOCIETAL

http://wciom.ru/ (site of the Russian Society Polling Agency)
www.cityvision.ru/en/index.php/ (information on Russian cities)
www.euroeducation.net/prof/russco.htm (information on Russian educational system)
http://echo.msk.ru/ (radio station site providing exhaustive information about Russian society)
www.ruj.ru/ (site of the Russian Union of Journalists)
www.anti-corr.ru/awbreport/indextxt.asp?filename=rutxt/01.xml (analysis on corruption in Russia)

Cultural

http://eng.rusathletics.com/ (information on Russian sports)
www.kinotavr.ru/ru (site of the Russian film festival in Sochi)
www.museum.ru/ (information on Russian museums)
www.russianmuseum.spb.ru/ (information on museums in St. Petersburg)
www.tvkultura.ru/ (portal of the Kul'tura television channel providing information about Russian culture)
www.kinokultura.com/index.html/ (reviews of Russian, Central Asian, and Eastern European films and animation)
www.moscow.ucla.edu/ (samples and reviews of contemporary Russian music)
http://xz.gif.ru/ (website of the Moscow Art Journal)
http://lib.ru/ ("The Moshkov Library"; displays Russian classics and contemporary Russian literature)
www.nlobooks.ru/ (Russia's most prominent literary studies journal)
www.afisha.ru/ (news about Russian culture)
http://sochi2014.com/sochi_russian (site of the 2014 Olympic Games in Sochi)
http://fashiony.ru/ (information and news on Russian fashion)
www.lookatme.ru/ (information on Russian glamour and society)

Economy

www.rbc.ru/ (comprehensive analysis of Russian business, finance, and enterprise) www.cbr.ru/ENG/ (site of the Bank of Russia)

www.economy.gov.ru/wps/wcm/myconnect/economylib/mert/welcome/main/ (site of the Russian Ministry for Economic Development)

www.gazprom.ru/ (site of Gazprom)

www.ngfr.ru/ (main portal of Russian oil and gas industries)

www.world-nuclear.org/info/inf45.html/ (information on Russia's nuclear power)

www.rusref.nm.ru/indexoop.htm (analysis of Russian economy)

www.polit.ru/institutes/2009/08/13/rubli.html (news on Russian economy)

www.iet.ru/index.php?lang=ru (analysis of Russian economy)

www.rzd.ru/ (site of the Russian national rail company)

www.nalog.ru/ (site of the national tax and revenue agency)

About the Authors

Robert A. Saunders studied Eastern European and Russian History at the University of Florida (BA, 1994) and Stony Brook University (MA, 1997). From 1998 until 2002, he worked as a management consultant in the telecommunications and Internet industries. In 2005, he received a PhD in Global Affairs from Rutgers, The State University of New Jersey. His dissertation explored the impact of the Internet and new media on national identity among ethnic Russians in the former Soviet republics of Latvia and Kazakhstan. Currently, he is an assistant professor in the Department of History, Economics and Politics at the State University of New York, Farmingdale, where he teaches courses on Russian politics, Central Asia, and global history. Dr. Saunders is the author of *The Many Faces of Sacha Baron Cohen: Politics, Parody, and the Battle over Borat* (2008) and *The Web of Identity: Minority Nationalism and Ethnopolitics in Cyberspace* (in press). He is one of the founding editors of *Digital Icons: Studies in Russian, Eurasian and Central European New Media* (formerly known as *The Russian Cyberspace Journal*).

Vlad Strukov studied in Russia (Voronezh and Moscow universities), Scotland (Edinburgh University), and Belgium (Catholic University of Leuven). He received his PhD in Postmodern Philosophy and Cultural Studies in 1998. Currently, he is an assistant professor in the Department of Russian and Slavonic Studies and the Centre for World Cinemas at the University of Leeds (United Kingdom). He is a founding editor of *Static*, an international journal supported by the Tate and The Institute of Contemporary Arts, London, and *Digital Icons: Studies in Russian, Eurasian and Central European New Media*. He also works independently as a new media and animation curator. He is currently completing a co-authored volume entitled *Celebrity and Glamour in*

Contemporary Russian Culture (scheduled to appear in 2010). Dr. Strukov's research on film, animation, mass media, and national identity has appeared in the *Slavic and East European Journal*, *Animation: An Interdisciplinary Journal*, and other publications, and he is the author and editor of a number of books published in Russia.